GUI Bloopers

Don'ts and Do's for Software Developers and Web Designers

The Morgan Kaufmann Series in Interactive Technologies

Series Editors:

- Stuart Card, Xerox PARC
- Jonathan Grudin, Microsoft
- Jakob Nielsen, Nielsen Norman Group
- Tim Skelly, Design Happy

GUI Bloopers

Don'ts and Do's for Software Developers and Web Designers

Jeff Johnson
UI Wizards, Inc.

MORGAN KAUFMANN PUBLISHERS

An Imprint of Elsevier

Amsterdam   Boston   Heidelberg   London   New York   Oxford   Paris   San Diego
San Francisco   Singapore   Sydney   Tokyo

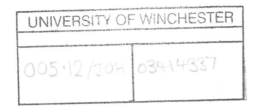
Senior Editor	Diane D. Cerra
Director of Production & Manufacturing	Yonie Overton
Senior Production Editor	Edward Wade
Editorial Coordinator	Belinda Breyer
Cover Design	Ross Carron Design
Text Design & Composition	Rebecca Evans & Associates
Editorial, Technical, & Spot Illustration	Cherie Plumlee
Copyeditor	Ken DellaPenta
Proofreader	Carol Leyba
Indexer	Steve Rath
Printer	Maple Vail

Designations used by companies to distinguish their products are often claimed as
trademarks or registered trademarks. In all instances in which Morgan Kaufmann
Publishers is aware of a claim, the product names appear in initial capital or all
capital letters. Readers, however, should contact the appropriate companies for more
complete information regarding trademarks and registration.

Morgan Kaufmann Publishers
An Imprint of Elsevier
340 Pine Street, Sixth Floor
San Francisco, CA 94104-3205
www.mkp.com

Library of Congress Cataloging-in-Publication Data
Johnson, Jeff, Ph.D.
    GUI bloopers: don'ts and do's for software developers and Web designers/Jeff Johnson.
      p.   cm.
    Includes bibliographical references and index.
    ISBN 1-55860-582-7
    1.   Graphical user interfaces (Computer systems) I. Title
QA76.9.U83 J63 2000
005.4'37-dc21

Contents

Chapter 1   **First Principles**

Chapter 2   GUI Component Bloopers

Acknowledgments

I could not have written this book without the help and support of many other people.

First of all, I would like to thank my wife and friend, Karen Ande, for giving me her love and support while I was writing this book, and for putting up with significant reductions in our ability to travel and socialize together.

I thank my mother-in-law, Dorothy Hadley, for always asking, whenever she called in late 1998 and 1999: "How's the book going?" I thank my father, Ben Johnson, for helping me to develop an analytic and critical mind and an ability to express myself in writing.

I am grateful for the willingness of several software developers to usability-test earlier versions of this book and give me their frank feedback. The ways in which their feedback helped improve this book are described in the Appendix: How This Book Was Usability Tested. The programmer-testers are Pat Caruthers, Brent Emerson, Stuart Ferguson, Mairé Howard, and Sandi Spires.

The book was greatly improved by the comments and suggestions from several reviewers: Stuart Card, Tom Dayton, Jonathan Grudin, Deborah Mayhew, Bonnie Nardi, Jakob Nielsen, Terry Roberts, and Terry Winograd.

The book also was helped immeasurably by the care, oversight, excellent lunches, layout and organization advice, legal advice, excellent lunches, logistical support, nurturing, and excellent lunches provided by the staff at Morgan Kaufmann Publishers, especially Diane Cerra, Belinda Breyer, Edward Wade, and Marilyn Alan, and copyeditor Ken DellaPenta, and illustrator Cherie Plumlee. And did I mention those excellent lunches?

Many of the ideas in Chapter 7, Responsiveness Bloopers, had their origins in a conference paper and presentation that I co-authored with Dave Duis [Duis and Johnson, 1990], while I was a researcher at Hewlett-Packard Laboratories and he was a student intern. I am grateful for the ideas and prototyping work Dave contributed at that time. Dave Duis's MIT Master's thesis [1990] was also based on the same paper and presentation, and so shares some ideas with Chapter 7. Another source of insights and ideas for that section came from conversations with Stuart Card of Xerox Palo Alto Research Center. I am grateful for his willingness to chat about the issue of responsiveness.

Regarding the *Fork in the Tale* war story (Chapter 10): I am grateful for the opportunity to work with the creative designers and developers at Advance Reality, especially film director and game designer Rob Lay and lead programmer Ken Carson. Thanks also to the graphic artists at 415 Productions and McMacken Graphics, to staff members at AnyRiver who contributed ideas to the user interface, especially Chuck Clanton and Stewart Bonn, and to several anonymous people who reviewed the version of the story I presented at the ACM CHI'98 conference.

Finally, I would like to thank my clients and former employers. Without them, this book would not have been possible...or necessary.

. Introduction

Why is this book needed?

Throughout the software industry, software engineers develop user interfaces with little—sometimes no—support and guidance from professional user interface designers. For example, some software is developed by individual freelance programmers who lack training in designing user interfaces or access to people who have such training, and then is sold to a company that markets it. Even when software is developed by sizable organizations, there may be no developers who have user interface expertise. Some companies do have user interface professionals, but not enough of them to cover all the development projects needing user interface design skills.

The marketplace of software products, software-controlled appliances, and online services is therefore full of programs designed entirely by people who, though they are professional programmers, are user interface amateurs. Such software is a drag on the success of the entire industry.

As a user interface consultant, I am often called in late in the development process to review or test software that was developed by people who have little user interface design experience. Such software is typically full of design errors. Many of these errors are extremely common, occurring over and over in projects across companies and even within companies.

A programmer at a client company once told me, "You're our *lint* for UIs," referring to a Unix utility program that checks C-programs for common programmer errors. To a large exent, that's a pretty fair description of how many client companies want to use me: as a filter against user interface design errors.

To reduce the incidence of common errors and my need to police my clients' user interfaces, I have tried advising programmers to read one or more books on designing and evaluating user interfaces that have come out of the Human-Computer Interaction (HCI) community, such as Shneiderman [1987], Nielsen [1993], Weinshenk et al. [1997], and Bickford [1997]. Such advice usually goes unheeded because most such books are (1) too academic for programmers, or (2) written for experienced user interface professionals.

Even the few programmers who read the recommended books and understand the general design guidelines continue to make many of the same common design errors. It seems that the problem is that the guidelines in these books are too abstract. It is too easy for a programmer to rationalize violations of abstract guidelines: "Yeah, I understand the rule, but this situation is different. It's a special case that isn't covered in the rules." Or they might say: "I may be bending the rule, but it's for a good reason."

Another problem is that, as one GUI programmer I know said: "Most programmers believe they are UI experts." After all, programmers use computers more than most people do, and so are exposed to more user interfaces. They assume that that, coupled with the fact that they may have designed some user interfaces, makes them user interface designers.

Because of these two problems, I have found, when working with developers while consulting for client companies, that it helps to point out the *errors* they have made and explain why the errors are errors. Similarly, when training developers in an attempt to reduce the likelihood of future design errors, I have found that it helps to focus on common design *errors* and work from those to design rules. In other words, show GUI developers the mistakes they often make, and provide rules for avoiding those mistakes. It is also important to provide some of the principles underlying the design *rules,* so that developers can generalize beyond specific examples.

This experience suggested that a book focused on design errors and how to avoid them might be more effective than many previous user interface design books have been, or at least would be a useful complement to such books. Accordingly, this book is structured as design guidelines in reverse: here's a common error; here's how to avoid it.

Not all of the errors that hurt the usability of products and services are made by programmers implementing user interfaces. Many software development organizations commit errors at the *management* level that negatively affect the user interfaces of the products and services they develop. Furthermore, these management errors are in many ways more important than specific GUI design errors because they affect more projects and are harder to diagnose and correct. I therefore wanted to describe those sorts of errors as well and warn developers away from them. That is the reason for Chapter 8, Management Bloopers.

The main goal of this book is to help GUI developers and designers become better at catching their own design mistakes and—even better—at avoiding them altogether.

I sometimes think it would be wonderful if the real world had error dialog boxes. They would pop up out of thin air in front of your face whenever you made a mistake. Real-world error dialog boxes would be a great way to train software developers and development managers to recognize when they have committed, or are about to commit, a blooper. (Some software developers and managers I know would get a lot of them!)

Since there are no error dialog boxes in the real world, we need to program them into developers' heads. Hopefully, this book will help with some of that programming.

What is a GUI blooper?

This book describes "bloopers" (that is, mistakes) that software developers frequently make when designing graphical user interfaces (also known as GUIs). The bloopers in this book do not cover all of the mistakes GUI designers could make, or even all of the mistakes I have seen. Believe me, in over two decades of working as a user interface professional, I've seen some design mistakes that were simply *amazing*— true "howlers," as some of my colleagues call them.

To get into this book, it wasn't enough for a design mistake to be a howler. It also had to be common. There is little value in warning software developers away from very rare or application-specific mistakes, no matter how horrible the errors may be. On the other hand, there is great value in warning developers away from errors that they—at least statistically speaking—are likely to make.

Furthermore, I selected most of the bloopers long before finding examples of them. What I am referring to as "bloopers" are not just specific examples of design errors I have seen in software. The bloopers are mistakes that developers make over and over and over again. The examples only serve to illustrate the bloopers—to make them more concrete.

Therefore, this book is not simply a collection of user interface "outtakes"— embarrassing mistakes software developers have made. My purpose is *not* to provide a parade of user interface howlers that embarrass the perpetrators and cause readers to laugh, shake their heads, and wonder how any designer could be so stupid. My purpose is to help GUI designers and developers learn to produce better GUIs.

The bloopers in this book are described verbally and, where possible, illustrated using screen images captured from real products and online services, made-up screen images, and anecdotes from my experience. With each blooper is the design rule that developers should follow to avoid the blooper. As with the bloopers, each design rule is illustrated, where possible, with examples, both real and made-up.

To show clearly whether a screen image is an example of a design error or a correct design, I have marked most of them with symbols for "bad example" and "good example." Bad examples—examples of bloopers—are marked using a "thumbs down" hand symbol. Good examples—examples of correct design— are marked using a "thumbs up" hand symbol (see symbols shown in the margin to the left of this paragraph). Screen images that are neutral are unmarked.

The bloopers in this book are classified into seven categories: GUI component, layout and appearance, textual, interaction, Web, responsiveness, and management. GUI component bloopers correspond to erroneous decisions about how to use components provided in a user interface toolkit. Layout and appearance bloopers are errors in arranging and presenting GUI components. Textual bloopers are mistakes in how text is used in user interfaces, not graphical problems involving text, such as poor choice of fonts, but problems in what the text says. Interaction bloopers are violations of general user interface design principles, independent of which user interface toolkit is used. Web bloopers are problems that are specific to Web sites and Web-based applications. Responsiveness bloopers are aspects of a product's or service's design that interfere with user work pace. Management bloopers are management-level problems that affect the usability and usefulness of software and electronic appliances.

How were the bloopers compiled?

The bloopers in this book represent a sampling from over two decades of personal experience designing, critiquing, and testing user interfaces for software products, especially my experience since 1996, when I began working as a user interface consultant. They were compiled mainly from user interface critiques, usability test reports, design guidelines documents, and talks I have prepared for employers and consulting clients. A few were suggested to me by colleagues.

The examples of bloopers come from a variety of sources. Very few of the examples that actually identify a product or a software company come from my consulting clients. In most cases, I worked for clients under nondisclosure agreements that prevent me from revealing details of what was developed, even for software that never made it to the market. Therefore, in most of the anecdotal stories in this book, the names of companies and specific products are altered or withheld. For the same reason, the screen images exemplifying bloopers come mainly from commercially available software and online services developed by companies other than my consulting clients, that is, from software and Web sites I have used. On the other hand, I did obtain permission in a few cases to use real names and screen images when discussing client software.

A few examples of bloopers in this book are from the Interface Hall of Shame *(www.iarchitect.com/mshame.htm)*, a large collection of GUI design errors compiled by Brian Hayes of Isys Information Architects, Inc., a user interface consulting firm. The site presents examples—found by Mr. Hayes or by visitors to the site—of poor user interface design in commercially available products and services.[1] Some of the examples on exhibit at the Interface Hall of Shame provided good illustrations for bloopers I wanted to discuss, so, with Isys Information Architects' kind permission, I have included them.

Finally, some of the screen images that illustrate bloopers in this book were made up—created specifically for this book in order to depict certain bloopers clearly.

Although they were not sources of bloopers or examples of bloopers in this book, three other impressive catalogues of design errors deserve mention:

- *Designing Visual Interfaces,* a book on software graphic design by Kevin Mullet and Darrell Sano [1995]. For each of the design issues covered in their book (for example, "elegance and simplicitiy," "scale, contrast, and proportion," "organization and visual structure"), Mullet and Sano present not only principles and examples of good design, but also common design errors.

- *UseIt.com,* a Web site created and maintained by Jakob Nielsen, a Web design expert and commentator on Web trends. Useit.com lists Nielsen's top ten Web design errors in addition to providing other useful Web design advice. Nielsen has recently written a book on the same topic [Nielsen, 1999d].

- *WebPagesThatSuck.com,* a Web site compiled by Web designer Vincent Flanders that uses examples of bad Web site design to teach good Web site design. Corresponding to the Web site (or at least to a snapshot of it at one point in time) is an excellent book, *Web Pages That Suck,* by Flanders and Willis [1998].

The main impact of these error collections on this book was to convince me that their authors had already covered their respective territory pretty thoroughly and well. Mullet and Sano didn't leave much that needed to be said about

---

1 I encourage readers who have not visited the Interface Hall of Shame to do so. Some readers may even have favorite design howlers to contribute to the Hall of Shame.

graphic design bloopers. Similarly, Web design bloopers had already been well covered by Nielsen and by Flanders and Willis. Therefore, I steered clear of topics they had discussed, and focused on design problems I had seen that they, to my knowledge, had not covered.

Chapter 8, Management Bloopers, was influenced by three books about management-level problems that contribute to poor usability in computer-based products and services:

- *The Trouble with Computers*, by Tom Landauer [1995]
- *The Invisible Computer*, by Don Norman [1999]
- *The Inmates Are Running the Asylum*, by Alan Cooper [1999]

These three books are not systematic collections of bloopers. Their main purpose is to offer in-depth analysis of the reasons for the software industry's tendency to turn out products and services that mystify and annoy people and hamper productivity. However, these books do include examples of the types of user-hostile design that can result from software development organizations and processes that are focused on technology rather than on user requirements.

Who should read *GUI Bloopers*?

The main intended audience for this book is working programmers who develop software or Web sites with little or no guidance and feedback from user interface professionals. For such programmers, this book is intended to serve both as a tool for self-education and as a reference. It is intended to supplement—not replace—user interface design guidelines for specific GUI platforms.

A second target audience is managers of software development teams. It is primarily for their benefit that the book includes a chapter on management bloopers.

A third target audience is user interface designers, especially those who are just entering the profession. For them, this book supplements the standard references and textbooks on user interface design and evaluation by warning against common design errors and by providing practical examples.

How is this book organized?

This book has 10 chapters: First Principles, GUI Component Bloopers, Layout and Appearance Bloopers, Textual Bloopers, Interaction Bloopers, Web Bloopers, Responsiveness Bloopers, Management Bloopers, Software Reviews, and War Stories.

Chapter 1, First Principles, provides a basis for understanding both the bloopers and the design rules for how to avoid bloopers.

The seven bloopers chapters describe and illustrate the common mistakes software developers and their managers make, when designing software and Web sites, that result in user-hostile software, online services, and electronic appliances.

Chapter 9, Software Reviews, reviews two software products in detail, describing the bloopers they contain as well as other, less common design errors. It also provides suggestions for how the bloopers could have been avoided.

The last chapter, War Stories of a User Interface Consultant, describes in detail some experiences that I have had as a consultant that provide insight into (1) why software developers commit user interface design bloopers and (2) how to overcome bloopers.

How should you use this book?

As stated above, this book is intended for three categories of readers—GUI programmers, software development managers, and new user interface professionals. These three different types of readers will be able to get different information out of this book.

GUI programmers will probably want to jump right into the very specific bloopers: GUI component, layout and appearance, textual, and Web. They can either start with Chapter 1, First Principles, before reading about the bloopers, or they can go back and read the principles as they arise in the design rules for avoiding bloopers. After those chapters, I would recommend that programmers read the chapters on interaction and responsiveness bloopers, and then the software reviews. Programmers can consider the management bloopers, war stories, and appendix to be "extracurricular"—to be read if they have time or interest.

For software managers, the chapter on management bloopers is obviously the most important. Following that in order of importance for managers are textual bloopers, responsiveness bloopers, war stories, software reviews, and interaction bloopers. Chapter 1, First Principles, may be of interest to managers who have a background or interest in user interface design and human-computer interaction. Development managers can probably skip the chapters on GUI component, appearance and layout, and Web bloopers completely. They can just tell their programmers and designers to "read those sections and do what Johnson says." :-)

Budding user interface professionals should definitely start by reading Chapter 1, First Principles. I suggest they then skim the chapters on GUI component, layout and appearance, and textual bloopers mainly to familiarize themselves with what is in them; they can revisit specific bloopers in these chapters later on an as-needed basis. On the other hand, the chapters on inter-action, responsiveness, and management bloopers are highly recommended for new user interface professionals. For people who will be designing Web sites or Web applications, the chapter on Web bloopers is important, but others can skip it. The final two chapters, Software Reviews and War Stories, will provide newcomers to the user interface field with a glimpse of what experienced professionals do. Finally, some user interface professionals may be interested in reading the Appendix to see how this book was improved through usability testing.

Table I.1 summarizes these recommendations.

Table I.1   Recommended reading by type of reader

GUI programmers	New UI professionals	Development managers
(First Principles)	First Principles	Management Bloopers
GUI Component Bloopers	GUI Component Bloopers (skim)	Textual Bloopers
Layout and Appearance Bloopers	Layout and Appearance Bloopers (skim)	Responsiveness Bloopers
Textual Bloopers	Textual Bloopers (skim)	Software Reviews
(Web Bloopers)	Interaction Bloopers	War Stories
Interaction Bloopers	Responsiveness Bloopers	Interaction Bloopers
Responsiveness Bloopers	Management Bloopers	(First Principles)
Software Reviews	(Web Bloopers)	
(Management Bloopers)	Software Reviews	
(War Stories)	War Stories	
(Appendix)	(Appendix)	

First Principles

Introduction

The main purpose of this book is to describe user interface bloopers that are often made by developers of computer-based products and services, and to provide design rules and guidelines for avoiding each blooper. First, however, it is useful to ground the discussion of the bloopers by laying out the principles that underlie the design of effective, user-friendly user interfaces. That is the purpose of this chapter.

The principles given in this chapter are *not* specific design rules for graphical user interfaces (GUIs). There is nothing in this chapter about the right or wrong way to design dialog boxes, menus, toolbars, Web links, and so on. Specific design rules about such issues are provided in later chapters of the book, in the design rules for avoiding each blooper.

Specific user interface design rules are also given in "official" style guides for specific industry-standard GUI platforms, such as the *Java Look and Feel Design Guildelines* [Sun, 1999], the *Windows Interface Guidelines for Software Design* [Microsoft, 1995], the *OSF/Motif Style Guide: Rev 1.2* [OSF, 1993], and the *Macintosh Human Interface Guidelines* [Apple, 1993]. Specific GUI guidelines are also provided by many "unofficial" but nonetheless good books, such as Bickford [1997], Fowler [1998], Mandel [1997], McFarland and Dayton [1995], Mullet and Sano [1995], Nielsen [1999d], Shneiderman [1987], Tufte [1983], Weinshenk et al. [1997].

Rather than providing specific GUI design rules, the principles given in this chapter provide the basis for GUI design rules. They are based on the cumulative wisdom of many people, compiled over several decades of experience in designing interactive systems for people. They are also based on a century of research on human learning, cognition, reading, and perception. Later chapters of this book refer to these principles as rationale for why certain designs or development practices are bloopers, and why the recommended remedies are improvements.

1.1 Principle 1: Focus on the users and their tasks, not the technology

This is Principle Numero Uno, the Main Principle, the mother of all principles, the principle from which all other user interface design principles are derived:

Focus on the users and their tasks, not the technology.

Now that I've stated it, and you've read it, we're done, right? You now know how to design all your future products and services, and I needn't say anything more.

I wish! Alas, many others have stated this principle before me, and it doesn't seem to have done much good. And no wonder: it is too vague, too open to interpretation, too difficult to follow, and too easily ignored when schedules and resources become tight. Therefore, more detailed principles, design rules, and examples of bloopers are required, as well as suggestions for *how* to focus on users, their tasks, and their data. Not to mention that this would be a very thin book if I stopped here.

Before proceeding to those more detailed principles, design rules, and bloopers, I'll devote a few pages to explaining what I mean by "focus on the users and their tasks."

Focusing on users and their tasks means starting a development project by answering the following questions:

- For whom is this product or service being designed? Who are the intended customers? Who are the intended users? Are the customers and the users the same people?[1]
- What is the product or service for? What activity is it intended to support? What problems will it help users solve? What value will it provide?
- What problems do the intended users have now? What do they like and dislike about the way they work now?
- What are the skills and knowledge of the intended users? Are they motivated to learn? How?
- How do users conceptualize and work with the data in their task domain?
- What are the intended users' preferred ways of working? How will the product or service fit into those ways? How will it change them?

It would be nice if the answers to these questions would fall out of the sky into developers' laps at the beginning of each project. But, of course, they won't. The only way to answer these questions is for the development organization to make an explicit, serious effort to do so. Making a serious effort to answer these questions takes time and costs money. But it is crucial, because the cost of not answering these questions before beginning to design is much, much higher.

1.1.1 Understand the users

Several of the questions listed above that developers should answer before starting to design are questions about the intended users of the product: Who are they? What do they like and dislike? What are their skills, knowledge, vocabulary, and motivation? Are they going to be the ones who make the decision to buy the software, or will someone else do that? These questions are best

---

1. Hint: The customer is the person who makes the buying decisions, while the user is the person who . . . well . . . uses the software. These different roles may imply different criteria and needs.

"Darn these hooves! I hit the wrong switch again! Who designs these instrument panels, raccoons?"

answered using a process that is part business decision, part empirical investigation, and part collaboration.

Decide who the intended users are

To a certain extent, the development organization needs to decide who it is developing the product or service for. It is tempting to decide that the intended user base is "everyone"; most development organizations want the broadest possible market. However, that temptation must be strongly resisted: a product or service designed for everyone is likely to satisfy no one. Developers should choose a specific primary target population as the intended user base in order to focus their design and development efforts, even if they suspect that the software might also have other types of users.

In reaching this important decision, the designers should seek input from other parts of the organization in order to assure that the target user base of the product or service is in line with strategic goals. In particular, developers should seek input from the Marketing and Sales departments because it is they who are usually responsible for identifying and categorizing customers. However, it is important to keep in mind that Marketing and Sales focus—as their job responsibilities dictate—on future *customers* of the product or service, whereas the designers need to understand the future *users*. A product's customers and its users are not necessarily the same people, or even the same type of people, so Marketing and Sales' ideas about who the product is aimed at may have to be filtered or augmented in order to be useful to designers.

Investigate characteristics of the intended users

As described above, understanding the users also requires empirical investigation. Empirical investigation means making an effort to learn the relevant characteristics of potential users. This investigation, first of all, provides information to guide the above-described decision: going out and surveying potential users helps developers discover specific populations of users whose requirements and demographics make them attractive as a target user base. Second, once the above-described decision has been made and the primary target user population has been identified, developers should use empirical methods to learn as much as possible about that target population.

How do developers gather information about the intended users? By going and talking with them. By talking to their management. By inviting groups of them—and possibly their management—to participate in focus groups. By reading market analyses and magazines about their business. Perhaps even by socializing with them.

Collaborate with the intended users to learn about them

Finally, understanding the users is best accomplished by working with them as collaborators. Don't treat users merely as objects to be studied. Bring some of them onto the development team. Treat them as experts, albeit a different kind of expert than the developers. They understand their job roles, experience, management structure, likes and dislikes, and motivation. They probably don't understand programming and user interface design, but that's fine—that's what the rest of the team is there for. A useful slogan to keep in mind when designing software is

*Software should be designed neither **for** users nor **by** them, but rather **with** them.*

Bringing it all together

The goal of this three-part process—part decision, part investigation, part collaboration—is to produce a profile that describes the typical intended user of the planned product or service, or perhaps a range of intended users. The profile should include information such as job description, job seniority, education, salary, hourly versus salaried, how their performance is rated, age, computer skill level, and relevant physical or social characteristics, if any. With such a profile in hand, developers know what they are aiming at. Without it, they are, as Bickford [1997] says, "target shooting in a darkened room."

Some designers even go beyond constructing profiles for the intended users of a software product or service. Cooper [1999] advocates making user profiles concrete by instantiating them as fully elaborated *personas:* characters with names, vocations, backgrounds, families, hobbies, skills, and lifestyles. This is similar to the practice among novelists and script writers of writing "backstories" for every significant character in a book or movie. A character's backstory helps ground discussions about the sorts of things that character would and would not do. Similarly, the personas in Cooper's design methodology help ground discussions of the sorts of designs a particular target user type would find easy, difficult, annoying, fun, useful, useless, and so on.

The trick, of course, is to build profiles and personas from real data obtained from prospective users. If software developers just make up target user profiles and personas based on armchair speculation, they might as well not have them.

1.1.2   Understand the tasks

Some of the questions listed above pertain to the intended function of the product or service, that is, the "task domain" it is intended to support. As with understanding the users, understanding the task domain is best accomplished by a three-part process: part business decision, part empirical investigation, and part collaboration.

Decide what the intended task domain is

Understanding the intended task domain is partly a business decision because a software development organization is never completely open-minded about what products or services to develop. No software development organization is going to pick a group of potential customers purely at random, figure out what they need, and design a product to fill that need. Instead, decisions about what products and services to offer are strongly influenced—one might even say "predetermined"—by

- the organization's strategic goals, reflecting the interests of its founders, top management, and shareholders
- the expertise of its employees
- its past history
- its assets, processes, and infrastructure
- its perception of market opportunities and niches
- new technologies that have been developed by its researchers

cathy®   **by Cathy Guisewite**

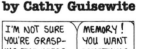

As a concrete example, a company that had been founded to develop music instruction software would be unlikely to decide to develop air traffic control systems unless it underwent such a radical change of management and employees that it was really a different company that happened to have the same name.

The last item in the previous list, "new technologies that have been developed by its researchers," is an especially important one. In the computer and software industries, decisions about what products or services to bring to market are often more strongly influenced by technological "push" than by other factors [Johnson, 1996b]. Whether this is good or bad is a subject of frequent debate. Norman [1999] argues that it is often good for emerging markets, but usually bad for mature ones. In my opinion, it is more often bad than good.

Regardless of which of the above factors are responsible, most development organizations decide in advance what general product or service area to target, such as document creation and management, information retrieval, banking, music, home finance, presentation slide-making. This decision combines with the decision about the primary target user base to yield a fairly specific product category, such as document-editing software for technical writers, or banking software for bank tellers.

As with identifying the target users, designers should seek input from other parts of their organization in order to assure that the target task domain of the product or service is in line with strategic goals. Again, developers should seek input from the Marketing and Sales departments because it is they who are usually responsible for identifying market opportunities, and because they often have at least a secondhand understanding of the work the target users do.

Investigate the intended task domain

Once a product category has been decided, the empirical investigation part of "understanding the tasks" comes into play. Before starting to design or implement anything, developers need to learn as much as they can about exactly how the intended users do the tasks that the software is supposed to support. This is called conducting a "task analysis." The goal of a task analysis is to develop a thorough understanding of the activities the product or service is intended to support.

The best way to conduct a task analysis is for members of the development team to arrange to talk with and observe people who either will eventually be users or whose demographics match the profiles of the intended users. Since the product or service will not have been developed yet, these interviews and observation sessions are concerned with understanding the work as it is done *before* the new product or service is introduced. Users can be interviewed or observed individually and in groups, face-to-face or by telephone or email, while they work or apart from their work.

It is important to both interview users and observe them working; the two techniques are complementary. Interviews and focus groups provide explanations, rationales, goals, and other information that cannot be directly observed. However, interviews may also provide *mis*-information, such as how a process is *supposed* to (but doesn't) work, or what the user thinks the interviewer wants to hear. Observation, on the other hand, lets developers see what actually happens, but leaves it to the observers to interpret what they see. Since the observers are, by definition, naive about the task domain—otherwise they wouldn't need to learn about it—their ability to interpret correctly what they observe is severely limited.

It is possible to combine interviewing with observing users: developers can interview prospective users at their workplaces, encouraging them to answer questions not only verbally, but also by demonstrating what they normally do. When gathering task information in this way, developers should ask users to talk while they work in order to explain what they are demonstrating; otherwise many users fall into their common habit of working silently or mumbling under their breath.

Developers can supplement interviews and observation of users by interviewing the users' managers. This provides another perspective on the same tasks, which is always useful. However, even more than interviews of users, interviews of users' managers must be interpreted carefully; managers are highly likely to talk in terms of how the work is *supposed* to be rather than how it really is.

Collaborate with users to learn about the task domain

Collaborating with users is even more important for understanding the task domain than it is for understanding the users themselves. The limitations of both straight interviews and straight observation are too great for developers to rely upon conclusions obtained purely by those methods. These limitations can be overcome by introducing two-way feedback into the task discovery and analysis process. Designers should not simply collect data from users; they should provide preliminary analyses and conclusions to users and seek their reactions. In such a process, the designers are not the only ones who learn; the users also gain a greater awareness of how they themselves work and about what sorts of technology might help them work better. In return for the effort required to establish a collaborative working relationship, the designers get more reliable data from the users.

Further information about involving users in analyzing a target task domain is provided in an article by Dayton et al. [1998] and a book by Greenbaum and Kyng [1991].

Bringing it all together

Fortunately, analyzing the task domain involves much the same activity as investigating the users. Although the two investigations were discussed separately here in order to better explain each one, developers usually conduct them at the same time, in the same interview and collaboration sessions. This synergy is helpful because access to prospective users is likely to be quite limited.

This principle began with a list of questions developers should answer before designing a product or service. Those questions were fairly broad. A well-done task analysis answers some fairly detailed questions:

- What tasks does the person do that are relevant to the application's target task area?
- Which tasks are common, and which ones are rare?
- Which tasks are most important, and which ones are least important?
- What are the steps of each task?
- What is the product of each task?
- Where does the information for each task come from, and how is the information that results from each task used?
- Which people do which tasks?
- What tools are used to do each task?
- What problems, if any, do people have performing each task? What sorts of mistakes are common? What causes these problems and mistakes?
- What terminology do people who do these tasks use?
- How are different tasks related?
- What communication with other people is required to do the tasks?

Example task analysis questions

In 1994, as part of a research project on the benefits of task-specific versus generic application software [Johnson and Nardi, 1996], a colleague and I investigated how people prepare presentation slides. Our investigation amounted to a task analysis. We interviewed people in their offices, encouraging them to both talk about and demonstrate how they work. The questions covered in the interviews are listed below. The interviewer allowed the conversation to flow naturally rather than strictly following the list of questions, but made sure answers to all of the questions had been captured on tape before ending the interview.

1. What is your role in producing presentation slides?
   1.1 Do you produce slides yourself or do you supervise others who do it?
      1.1.1 What sort of training or experience is required to do the job you do?
      1.1.2 [If supervises others] What is the skill level of your employees?
   1.2 How much of your total job involves producing presentation slides?
   1.3 For whom do you produce these presentation slides?
      1.3.1 Who is the customer (i.e., who approves the slides)?
      1.3.2 Who is the audience for the presentations?

1.4   What sort of quality level is required for the slides?

    1.4.1   How important are elaborate special effects (e.g., animation, dissolve)?

    1.4.2   Who decides on appearance and quality, you or the customer?

    1.4.3   Are there different kinds of presentations with different quality requirements?

1.5   Do you (your department) follow slide formatting standards?

    1.5.1   How do you assure that slides adhere to those standards?

    1.5.2   Does your slide-making software help with standardization of presentations?

2. What software do you use to create presentation slides?

  2.1   Who decides what software you use for this?

  2.2   Do you use one program or a collection of them?

    2.2.1   [If many] What are the different programs used for?

  2.3   Do you use general-purpose drawing software or slide-making software?

    2.3.1   Why?

  2.4   What do you like about each of the programs you use?

  2.5   What do you dislike about each one? What would you like to see changed?

    2.5.1   Describe some of the things you do to "work around" limitations of the software.

  2.6   How easy is the software for new users to learn?

    2.6.1   How do they learn the software (classes, manuals, using, asking)?

    2.6.2   How did you learn it?

  2.7   What other software have you used, tried, or considered for making slides, either here or in previous jobs?

    2.7.1   Why don't you use it now?

3. What is involved in making slides?

  3.1   Describe the complete process of producing a presentation, from when you take the assignment to when you deliver it to the customer.

    3.1.1   How much revision is usually required before a presentation is considered done?

  3.2   Do you usually create new presentation slides?

    3.2.1   What is hard and what is easy about creating new material (i.e., what goes quickly and what takes time and work)?

  3.3   Do you reuse old slides in new presentations?

    3.3.1   What is hard and what is easy about reusing old material (i.e., what goes quickly and what takes time and work)?

  3.4   How do you (your department) organize and keep track of slides and presentations?

    3.4.1   Is each slide a separate file, or are all the slides in a presentation together in one file?

    3.4.2   Do you use directories (folders) and subdirectories (subfolders) to organize your material?

3.4.3 How do you name your slide (or presentation) files?

3.4.4 Do you ever fail to find a slide you know you have?

3.4.5 How does your software hinder you in reusing material?

3.4.6 How easily can you include a single slide in several different presentations?

3.5 What kinds of revisions are often required in the process of preparing a presentation?

3.5.1 Which are easy and which are hard?

3.5.2 Are the same revisions easy and hard for each of the slide-making programs you use?

3.5.3 Some specific cases we'd like to know about:

3.5.3.1 A slide used in multiple presentations is changed.

3.5.3.2 A company logo or standard border must be added to every slide in a presentation.

3.5.3.3 The order of slides in a presentation must be changed.

3.5.3.4 The round bullets throughout a presentation must be changed to square bullets.

3.5.3.5 The font used throughout a presentation must be changed.

3.5.3.6 Each of the points on a particular slide must be expanded into a separate slide.

1.1.3 Interactive products and services function in a broad context

When engineers design computer hardware, software, online services, and electronic appliances, they often regard what they are designing as if it were the center of the universe, or even the only thing in the universe. They fail to consider the broad context in which the technology will be used, and what the users' total experience will be in using the technology in that context.

Sometimes even people who purchase technology fall prey to technocentric tunnel vision. They have a problem they want to solve and are hoping that, by simply acquiring and using some technology, they can fix it. Wishful thinking often predisposes technology buyers to perceive the problem as being simpler than it really is, that is, easily correctable by available technology. It also often predisposes them to believe the often inflated claims of technology manufacturers and vendors.

The fact that engineers and technology buyers often manifest technocentric tunnel vision does not mean that they are stupid or overly gullible, just that they are human. People focus on their own goals and desires or those of their organization, and often fail to take into account that there are other things in the environment that influence the outcome of applying technology to a problem.

Consider a person who designs a car alarm or the person who buys one for his or her automobile. The designer is focused on the goal of designing an appliance that can signal when a car is being burglarized or vandalized. The

Wishful thinking and military computer applications

The following are cases in which both developers and potential buyers of computer-based military technology were seduced by technocentric wishful thinking into overlooking important contextual factors.

SDI: In the 1980s, then-President Ronald Reagan proposed that the United States build a defensive "shield" against nuclear attack. Out of that proposal grew a research program called the Strategic Defense Initiative (SDI), often referred to in the popular press as "Star Wars." An important part of the SDI "shield" would be satellites for detecting and shooting at enemy missiles. A major problem with SDI was that these orbiting detectors and battlestations could easily be tracked and shot down by an enemy. Thus, crucial components of SDI would only remain operational if the enemy were nice enough not to shoot at them. SDI proponents were seduced by the appeal of a highly desirable goal—a shield against nuclear attack—to overlook critical facts about the world in which the system would have to operate.

Remote-controlled vehicle: An article in the *Wall Street Journal* on November 28, 1990, described a prototype of an autonomous vehicle that U.S. soldiers might someday use to explore enemy territory without risking their own lives. The vehicle was being designed so that it could be driven "like an ordinary car" to the edge of an enemy-occupied area, then driven into the area using remote controls and a "virtual reality" helmet that allowed a soldier to see the vehicle's surroundings as if he were still physically in the vehicle. The designers of the vehicle overlooked two important contextual factors: (1) the possibility that people and dogs might notice the vehicle as it clanked around, and (2) that soldiers in or near a combat zone might hesitate to put on a helmet that obscured their view of their immediate surroundings.

Range-finding guns: An article in the *Christian Science Monitor* on April 6, 1998, described a prototopye of a new gun that would allow soldiers to "shoot around corners." The gun would shoot shells that would explode at a specified distance and rain shrapnel onto enemy soldiers hiding behind walls, rocks, vehicles, and so on. To gauge the distance to the target, the gun had a laser-based range finder. However, like an autofocus camera, the gun's range finder would have to be pointed at some object. The gun's designer failed to consider that when an enemy is hiding around a corner, there is no real target at which to aim the range finder. Thus, soldiers trying to use the gun in combat would probably have to aim at objects *near* the corner, shoot, and manually adjust the distance estimate—perhaps several times—before finding the correct distance.

buyer is thinking solely of how to protect the car. Neither one stops to consider that the alarm must function in an environment in which many other people have similar car alarms, and in which many events besides break-ins can trigger the alarm. When an alarm goes off in the neighborhood, it will be difficult to tell whose car it is and whether it signals an actual attempt at theft or vandalism. It usually will not. An otherwise sound idea and resulting product fails to provide value, not because of a flaw in the idea itself, but because the designer and buyer didn't consider the larger picture.

Applying technological tunnel vision to an office containing a desktop computer, one would see the office as a darkened room with a spotlight on the computer. One would see people (users) come into the spotlight, use the computer, and leave, disappearing back into the darkness (see Figure 1.1). The things the people do with the computer would be seen as disconnected, and those they do without it would be seen as unimportant. Using the computer, the people word process, they create graphics, they perform calculations, they enter and retrieve data. Where does the input come from? Unimportant. What is the output used for? Irrelevant. This perspective induces engineers to ask questions like "What should this product do?"

In fact, the office computer would be embedded in a work context. The proper way to view the office is as a large collection of paths of light flowing into, through, and out of the office. In each light path is a person. Some of the light paths intersect the computer; others don't (see Figure 1.2). The paths represent the flow of information, communication, and work; they show where it comes from and where it goes. This contextual view of the office induces designers to ask rather different questions. Instead of asking, "What should this product do?", designers would ask, "What does this *office* do?", "How does it do it?", and "What kind of computer software would support doing that (better)?"

To produce an effective product or service, developers must understand the context in which it will be used. When designers of a software application don't consider the context in which the application will be used, a common result is

Figure 1.1

Figure 1.2

that the application's users find themselves typing data into it that just came out of another computer program they use. The application's designers didn't think about where the data would come from, and so didn't design their application to take input directly from the other program.

To understand the context in which a planned product or service will be used, developers must study that context. Studying the context means talking to prospective or representative users, observing them, and analyzing the data thus collected. Representative users can even be recruited as fellow analyzers. Good advice on how to do these things is provided by two books: Greenbaum and Kyng [1991] and Beyer and Holtzblatt [1998].

1.2 Principle 2: Consider function first, presentation later

When given an assignment to develop a computer-based product or service, many GUI developers—even many user interface designers—immediately begin trying to decide how it will look. Some people sketch designs using paper and pencil or computer drawing tools. Some use interactive GUI or Web site construction tools to lay out the product's displays and controls. Some begin hacking actual implementation code.

Starting by worrying about appearances is putting the cart before the horse. It is tempting, but it is almost always a mistake. Yielding to this temptation results in products and services that lack important functionality, that contain many components and functions that are irrelevant to the work users have to do, and that seem ad hoc and arbitrary to users and so are difficult to learn and to use.

1.2.1 What "consider function first" does not mean

There is a danger that some readers will misinterpret Principle 2, so I will take a moment to explain what it does not mean. It does not mean "Get the functionality designed and implemented first, and worry about the user interface later." This misinterpretation matches the approach many software developers and development managers use to develop software. I want to state clearly that that approach will not produce successful software. The user interface is not something that can successfully be "worried about" or tacked on at the end of a development project.

The assumption underlying Principle 2 is that the user interface of a software product or service is not only—not even mainly—about the software's presentation. User interfaces are like human skin. Human skin isn't just the surface layer that we can see. It has aspects besides the superficial ones such as color, smoothness, and amount of hair. It has depth. It has structure: the epidermis, the endodermis, capillaries, nerve endings, hair follicles, pores, and so on. Most importantly, it has a function, or rather many functions, such as protection, transfer of moisture, and tactile sensation. Furthermore, we have different kinds of skin, each serving different functions in addition to the basic ones. The skin on the back of our hand looks and feels different from that on our palm, or from that on our lips, or on our knees, or on our scalp because it serves different purposes. Finally, the structure and function of our skin is related to our overall structure and function.

Similarly, there is more to user interfaces than meets the eye (or the mouse). They have depth, structure, and function. They also have variety: they vary according to their function, within an application as well as between applications. And, like human skin, user interfaces are related to the overall structure and function of the software they serve.

1.2.2 What "consider function first" does mean

Principle 2 states that software developers should consider the purpose, structure, and function of the user interface—and of the software as a whole—before considering the presentation—the surface appearance—of the user interface. The word "function" here does not mean "implementation"—how does it work? It means "role"—what does it do?

Before sketching displays, laying out controls, cutting foam prototypes, or hacking code, developers should focus their efforts on answering first the questions given under Principle 1, and then the following questions:

- *What concepts will the product or service expose to users?* Are they concepts that users will recognize from the task domain, or are they new concepts? If new, can they be presented as extensions of familiar concepts, or are they completely foreign concepts from the domain of computer science or electrical engineering?

- *What data will users create, view, or manipulate with the software?* What information will users extract from the data? How? What steps will they use? Where will data that users bring into the product or service come from, and where will data produced in the product or service be used?

- *What options, choices, settings, and controls will the application provide?* This is not a question about how to *represent* controls (e.g., as radiobuttons, type-in fields, menus, sliders); it is about their *function, purpose,* and *role* in the product or service (e.g., day of the week, dollar amount, email address, volume level). It is about what options the software provides and what the possible values of those options are.

1.2.3   Develop a conceptual model

Determining the answers to the above questions is often referred to as developing a "conceptual model" for the product or service.

What is a conceptual model and what is it not?

A conceptual model is, in a nutshell, the model of a product or service that the designers want users to understand. By using the software and reading its documentation, users build a model in their minds of how it works. Hopefully, the model that users build in their minds is close to the one the designers intended. This hope has a better chance of being realized if the designers have explicitly designed a clear conceptual model beforehand.

Developing a conceptual model before designing a user interface is often difficult; it is tempting for developers to jump right into discussing user interface concepts, such as control panels, menus, and data displays. The temptation is exacerbated by the tendency of Sales and Marketing personnel to state functional requirements in terms of window layout and mouse clicks. When marketing requirements are stated in such terms, developers should gracefully decline them, and ask instead for requirements stated in terms of the task domain: the problems users face and the goals they wish to achieve.

A conceptual model is not a user interface. It is not expressed in terms of keystrokes, mouse actions, dialog boxes, controls, or screen graphics. It is expressed in terms of the concepts of the intended users' task domain: the data that users manipulate, the manner in which that data is divided into chunks, and the nature of the manipulations that users perform on the data. It explains, abstractly, the function of the software and what concepts people need to be aware of in order to use it. The idea is that by carefully crafting an explicit conceptual model, then designing a user interface from that, the resulting software will be cleaner, simpler, and easier to understand.

Keep it as simple as possible, but no simpler

One goal, when developing a conceptual model for a planned software product or service, is to keep it as simple as possible, that is, with as few concepts as are needed to provide the required functionality. In the design of computer-based products and services, as in many things, the following slogan is a helpful design guide:

Less is more.

A related goal is to keep the conceptual model as focused on the task domain as possible, that is, with few or no concepts for users to master that are not found in the task domain.

However, the overriding goal of a conceptual model is to capture the way the software's intended users think about the target task domain. If, in trying to minimize complexity, developers omit important concepts from the conceptual model, or merge concepts that users regard as separate, the usability and usefulness of the resulting software will suffer just as it will if extraneous concepts are included.

 A case of oversimplification

Consider the Unix operating system. In its raw forms, Unix does not provide a function for renaming files. The designers of Unix did not consider an explicit *rename* command necessary because files can be renamed using the *move* (mv) command. To rename a file, users just move it to a file that has a different name.

For example, the command "mv MyInfo JeffsInfo" moves the content of the file *MyInfo* into a new file named *JeffsInfo* and then deletes *MyInfo*. Effectively, *MyInfo* has been renamed "JeffsInfo".

The problem is that when most Unix users need to rename a file, they will look for some kind of *rename* command, not a *move* command. Thus, many Unix users had trouble figuring out or remembering how to rename files. Some such users created command aliases on their computers so that they could have an explicit *rename* command.

The moral of this story is that Unix's conceptual model was oversimplified: it merged two concepts that users regarded as distinct.

Perform an objects/actions analysis

The most important component of a conceptual model is an objects/actions analysis. An objects/actions analysis is a listing of all the objects that the planned product or service will expose to users, and the actions that users can perform on each of those objects.

The software's implementation may include objects and associated operations other than those listed in the conceptual model, but those are not supposed to be visible to users. In particular, purely implementation objects and their associated actions—such as a text buffer, a hash table, or a database record—have no place in a conceptual model. Furthermore, the conceptual model and the implementation model may differ radically from each other. The implementation may not even be object oriented. For example, the application might be written in Visual Basic on top of an old database.

For the benefit of the developers of a planned software application, the objects in the conceptual model can be organized into a type hierarchy, with subtypes inheriting actions and attributes from their parent types. This makes commonalties and relationships between objects clearer to the developers.

It should be kept in mind, however, that organizing the objects in a class hierarchy is purely a way of facilitating the implementation of the software. Subclasses and inheritance are not concepts that will make sense to users (unless the software's target task domain is programming). Therefore, if the conceptual model is to be presented to users (e.g., in participatory design sessions or in software documentation), great care should be taken to express computer science concepts such as class hierarchies in terms that make sense to users. For example, most people can understand the relationship "is one type of," as in "A checking account is one type of bank account."

Depending on the application, objects may also be organized into a containment hierarchy, in which some objects contain other objects. For example, an email folder may contain email messages and other email folders.

Laying out a conceptual model's objects and actions according to these two hierarchies—type and containment—greatly facilitates the design and development of a coherent, clear user interface.

An example of a conceptual model

If the software to be developed was an application to help people manage their checking accounts, the conceptual model should include objects like checks, accounts, and amounts of money, and actions like depositing, withdrawing, voiding, and balancing. The conceptual model should exclude non-task-related objects like buffers, dialog boxes, modes, databases, tables, and strings, and non-task-related actions like clicking on buttons, backing up databases, editing table rows, and flushing buffers.

Because computer-based checkbook software sometimes includes capabilities not found in paper checking account registers, some additional concepts not found in the conventional (i.e., noncomputer) task domain may creep into the conceptual model, for example, objects like transaction templates and actions like defining templates. But it is important to realize that each such additional concept comes at a high cost, for two reasons:

- It adds a concept that users who know the task domain will not recognize and therefore must learn.
- It increases the complexity of the application exponentially because each added concept interacts with many of the other concepts in the application.

Therefore, additional concepts should be strongly resisted, and admitted into the design only when they provide high benefit and their cost can be minimized through good user interface design.

 An extraneous concept: Save

> One concept that developers often add to software conceptual models despite the fact that it doesn't exist in most actual task domains is an explicit action for saving the results of the user's work. When a person writes or draws on a physical piece of paper, there is no need for the person to do anything to save his or her work. Computer software has been adding Save actions to software conceptual models for so long that frequent computer users now consider it to be natural to most task domains. It isn't.
>
> Software developers add Save actions to conceptual models partly because doing so gives users a way to back out of changes they have made since the last Save. However, the ability to back out of changes could also be provided in other ways, such as (1) making all changes reversible, or (2) automatically creating backup versions of users' data. This is in fact how most computer file managers operate: when users move data files and folders from place to place, they do not have to save their changes. Users back out of changes by simply reversing the operations. Why are file managers designed differently than, say, most document editors? Tradition and habit, nothing more. ⊕

Develop a lexicon

A second component of a conceptual model is a *lexicon* of terminology to be used in the product or service and its documentation. Once the team agrees what each user-visible concept in the software is, the team should also agree on what to call that concept. The lexicon is best managed by the team's head technical writer. As the software is developed and the corresponding documentation written, it is the lexicon manager's role to make sure the terminology that appears in the documentation and in the software is consistent. For example:

"Hey, Bill. We called this thing a 'widget' in this dialog box, but we call it a 'gadget' in this other dialog box. Our official name for them is 'widgets,' so we need to correct that inconsistency."[2]

The goal is to avoid referring to objects or actions with different names in different places in the software or documentation, and also to avoid having distinct objects or actions being referred to with the same name. It is also the lexicon manager's role to be on the lookout for user-visible concepts in the software or documentation that aren't in the lexicon, and to resist them. For example:

"Hey, Sue, I see that this window refers to a 'hyper-connector.' That isn't in our conceptual model or lexicon. Is it just the wrong name for something we already have in our conceptual model, or is it something new? And if it's something new, can we get rid of it, or do we really, *really* need it?"

Write task scenarios

Once a conceptual model has been crafted, it should be possible to write scenarios depicting people using the application, using only terminology from the task domain. In the case of the checkbook application, for example, it should be possible to write scenarios such as "John uses the program to check his checking account balance. He then deposits a check into the account and transfers funds into the checking account from his savings account." Note that this scenario refers to task domain objects and actions only, not to specifics of any user interface.[3]

The *user interface design* translates the abstract concepts of the conceptual model into concrete presentations and user actions. Scenarios can then be rewritten at the level of the user interface design. For example: "John double-clicks on the icon for his checking account to open it. The account is displayed, showing the current balance. He then clicks in the blank entry field below the last recorded entry and enters the name and amount of a check he recently received...."

Extra benefit: implementation guide

A side benefit of developing a conceptual model is that the model can help guide the implementation because it indicates the most natural hierarchy of implementation objects and the methods each must provide. A conceptual

---

2. In an ideal development organization, Bill the programmer would have little to do with reconciling labels. All labels would be in a separate file, which the writer would translate to proper terminology. However, in many development organizations, messages are often still embedded in source code.

3. It is also possible to begin writing task scenarios as soon as developers have performed a task analysis (i.e., before devising a conceptual model), then translate them to the conceptual model lexicon when it is ready.

model can also simplify the application's command structure by allowing designers to see what actions are common to multiple objects and so can be designed as generic actions (see Section 1.3.4).

For example, imagine a software application in which users can create both Thingamajigs and Doohickeys. If Thingamajigs and Doohickeys are related, similar if not identical user interfaces can be used to create them. Thus, after learning how to create one of them, users will already know how to create the other. Similarly, copying, moving, deleting, editing, printing, and other functions might have similar UIs for both Thingamajigs and Doohickeys.

This, in turn, makes the command structure easier for users to learn because instead of a large number of object-specific commands, a smaller number of generic commands apply to many kinds of objects.

Summary: Benefits of developing a conceptual model

Starting a design by devising a conceptual model has several benefits:

- By laying out the objects and actions of the task domain, it allows designers to notice actions that are shared by many objects. Designers can then use the same user interface for operations across a variety of objects. This, in turn, makes for a user interface that is simpler and more coherent, and thus more easily mastered.

- Even ignoring the simplification that can result from noticing shared actions, devising a conceptual model forces designers to consider the relative importance of concepts, the relevance of concepts to the task domain (as opposed to the computer domain), the type hierarchy of objects, and the containment hierarchy of objects. When these issues have been thought through before the user interface is designed, the user interface will be "cleaner"—simpler and more coherent.

- A conceptual model provides a product lexicon—a dictionary of terms that will be used to identify each of the objects and actions embodied in the software. This fosters consistency of terminology, not only in the software, but also in the accompanying documentation. Software developed without such a lexicon often suffers from (1) a variety of terms for a given concept, and (2) using the same term for distinct concepts. For examples, see Blooper 33: Inconsistent terminology (Section 4.1.1).

- A conceptual model allows the development team to write, at a level of description that matches the target task domain, imaginary scenarios of the product in use. Those scenarios are useful in checking the soundness of the design. They can be used in product documentation, in product functional reviews, and as scripts for usability tests. They also provide the basis for more detailed scenarios written at the level of detail of the eventual user interface design.

- Finally, developing a conceptual model provides a first cut at the object model (at least for the objects that users will be aware of), which developers can then use in implementing the software. This is especially true if the developers are coding the software in an object-oriented language.

For more detail on how to construct a conceptual model, see Dayton et al. [1998]. Most of the industry standard style guides for specific GUI platforms also provide advice on devising conceptual models before designing a GUI for a planned product or service.

1.3 Principle 3: Conform to the users' view of the task

Computer software and appliances should be designed from the users' point of view. Obviously, developers cannot do that if they don't know what the users' point of view is. The best way to discover the users' point of view is to talk with representative users, observe their work, and collaborate with them to perform a task analysis and develop a conceptual model, as described in Principles 1 and 2.

Conforming to the users' point of view has several subprinciples, which I'll discuss in turn.

1.3.1 Strive for naturalness

One important benefit of performing a task analysis before beginning to design is that it provides an understanding of what activities belong "naturally" to the target task domain and what activities are extraneous, artificial, "unnatural." Stated simply, the goal is to avoid forcing users to commit "unnatural acts."

Don't make users commit unnatural acts

"Unnatural acts" is my term for steps users have to perform to get what they want that have no obvious connection to their goal. Software that requires users to commit unnatural acts seems arbitrary, nonintuitive, and amateurish to users because unnatural acts are difficult to learn, easy to forget, time-consuming, and annoying. Unfortunately, many computer-based products, services, and appliances force users to commit unnatural acts.

An example: Playing chess

As an example of how performing a task analysis can help clarify what actions are natural, consider the game of chess. An important action in playing chess is

making a move, that is, moving a chess piece to a new board position. In order to move a piece, what must be specified? Think about this for a few seconds. Answer the question in your own mind first, then read on.

Moving a piece in a chess game requires indicating (1) which piece is to be moved, and (2) where it is to be moved. I'm not talking about the user interface of a chess program. I'm talking about the task of playing chess, whether it is played on a computer, across a table on a wooden chess board, by mail, or by fax. Wherever, whenever, and however chess is played, moving a piece requires specifying the piece to be moved and where it is to be moved.

Now, let's consider a computer chess program. If a chess program requires users to specify *anything* other than the piece to be moved and the destination square, it is requiring unnatural acts. What sorts of unnatural acts might a computer chess program require? Here are some:

- *Switching to command mode in order to be able to give the Move command.* The software might have a mode for specifying moves and a mode for typing messages to the other player. If the software is always in one or other of these modes, it is a safe bet that users will often forget to switch modes, and either type Move commands when in message mode, or type messages when in command mode. For more on modes, see Blooper 51: Unnecessary or poorly marked modes (Section 5.3.2).
- *Stating the reason for the move.* Perhaps the software requires users to record their reasoning for each move, to provide a record that can be used in later postmortem analyses of the outcome.

- *Assigning a name to this move.* Perhaps the software requires users to give each move a name so that there is a way to refer back to that move later, or to allow the move to be saved for reuse.

- *Specifying which of several ongoing chess games this move is for.* Perhaps the software allows users to play several different games with different opponents at once, but provides only one place on the screen for specifying moves. The user must therefore identify the game in addition to the piece and the destination.

The bottom line is that moving a piece in a chess game should be a simple operation, but software can easily make it more complicated by adding extra, "unnatural" steps. Similar analyses can be performed for the other operations provided by a chess program. The ideal is for *all* operations in the program to be as free as possible of actions that are foreign to playing chess.

Other examples

Software developers should perform this sort of analysis on every operation of every product or service they develop. Here, for example, are some operations for widely used products and services that might benefit from an analysis of what actions the user must specify to complete each listed action:

- *Automatic teller machine:* withdraw money, deposit money, transfer money, check balance

- *Checkbook accounting software:* record check, record deposit, record transfer, reconcile with bank statement

- *Document editor:* create new document, open existing document, find text in document, print document

- *Email program:* retrieve new messages, view received message, save message, print message, compose message, add attachment to message

- *Web shopping service:* open account, close account, find product, order product, download product, submit comment or complaint

- *Airline reservation system:* find flights on required dates, check availability of seats on flights, check ticket price, check restrictions, make reservation

Imposing arbitrary restrictions

Another way in which computer-based products and services can violate users' sense of naturalness and intuitiveness is by imposing arbitrary or seemingly arbitrary restrictions on users. Examples of such restrictions include

- limiting person names to 16 characters
- allowing table rows to be sorted by at most three columns

- providing Undo for only the last three actions
- forcing all address book entries to specify a fax number even though some people don't have fax machines

Arbitrary restrictions, like unnatural acts, are hard for users to learn, easy for them to forget, and annoying. A product with many arbitrary restrictions won't have many satisfied users. Obviously, size and length restrictions are more bothersome the more users bump into them. If a limit is so large that users never encounter it, it isn't really a problem. For examples of bloopers involving arbitrary restrictions, see Blooper 43: Exposing the implementation to users, Variation B (Section 5.1.1).

1.3.2 Use the users' vocabulary, not your own

Computer-based products and services are infamous for being full of techno-babble—jargon that computer engineers understand but most users do not. Even when words in computer software come from the users' standard vocabulary, they are often redefined to have specific technical meanings; users don't understand this either. An overabundance of technobabble is one of the enduring shames of the industry. Figure 1.3 shows some examples of the techno-babble that computer users are exposed to. For more examples, see Blooper 35: Speaking Geek (Section 4.1.3).

When writing text for the software or its documentation, avoid computer jargon. Developing a conceptual model for the product or service produces, among other things, a project lexicon. The lexicon should name each and every concept (object or action) that will be seen by users. The terms in the lexicon should match those used in the task domain. Once the lexicon has been developed, text in the software or in the documentation should adhere strictly to it.

Figure 1.3

1.3.3 Keep program internals inside the program

Software users are not interested in how the software works. They just want to get their work done. Details of the software's internal workings should therefore remain internal—out of sight and out of mind of the users.

The user interface of a computer-based product or service should represent the concepts (objects and actions) of the users' target task domain, and *only* those concepts. All other concepts, especially concepts from the implementation that are not in the target task domain, are extraneous. General computer technology concepts are also extraneous, since they are almost certainly not part of the target task domain (unless the software is a programming tool).

Principle 2: Consider function first, presentation later (Section 1.2), recommends developing a conceptual model before designing a user interface. Part of developing a conceptual model is analyzing the objects and actions of the target task domain. The result of such an analysis is an outline listing all objects in the task domain, the relationships between objects, the attributes of objects, and all actions on those objects. This outline provides an excellent filter for deciding which concepts to expose to users; if a concept isn't listed in the conceptual model, it shouldn't be in the user interface.

1.3.4 Find the correct point on the power/complexity trade-off

There is usually a trade-off between power and usability. For every feature, function, or capability in a computer-based product or service, there must be a way for users to invoke or control it. Unfortunately, in the computer industry, there is too much of an emphasis on lengthy feature lists, and not enough recognition of the price that one pays for power.

Computer programmers tend to believe "the more options, the more controls, the more power, the better." In contrast, most people who use computer products and services want just enough power or functionality to do their work—no more, no less. Most users learn to use only a small portion of the features of any given software product or service, and ignore many—if not most—of the software's other features. Sometimes users ignore a software feature because they regard it as too complicated to be worth learning. Sometimes the problem isn't the complexity of the feature itself, but rather a matter of sheer quantity of stuff to learn. The user sees the feature as "just one more thing to learn" and is not sufficiently motivated to do so. The mere presence of less important features can make more important ones harder to find and use, causing common and simpler tasks to become harder.

The problem for software designers is finding the optimal point on the trade-off between power and complexity, or devising the software so that users can set that point themselves. Clearly, in order to do that, developers must talk

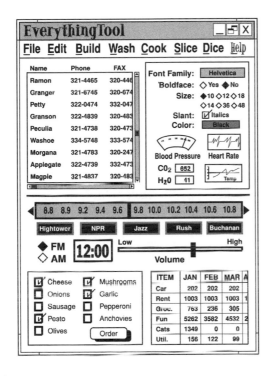

with and observe representative users, maybe even bring some onto the design team. Otherwise, developers are just guessing.

Once developers have learned how much functionality users need, they can also use one or more of these important design techniques for reducing complexity.

- *Sensible defaults:* Make sure that every setting in an application has a default value. Users should be able to leave all or most of the settings at their default values and still get a reasonable result. This allows users to ignore most of the settings for most of what they do with the application.

- *Templates or canned solutions:* Instead of making users start every task from scratch, provide partially or fully completed solutions for users to choose from and then modify to satisfy their specific goals. This approach, like sensible defaults, allows users to simply bypass most of the software's functionality. Users can get useful results without even knowing how to produce results from scratch.

- *Progressive disclosure:* Hide detail and complexity until the user needs it. One way to do this is to deactivate controls and not display menubar menus until they are relevant. A second way is to hide seldom-used settings, or controls requiring advanced knowledge of the software, under auxiliary panels labeled "Details" or "Advanced." A third way to hide detail—and hence to provide progressive disclosure—is to assign names to *combinations* of settings, allowing users to work with the named combinations instead of all the individual settings. For example, Macintosh users would face an overwhelming selection of operating system "extensions," except that the MacOS Extension Manager lets users name different combinations of extensions (e.g., "Basic Mac Extensions," "My Normal Extensions") and turn entire named combinations on or off at once. Progressive disclosure is discussed more fully under Blooper 46: Overwhelming users with decisions and detail (Section 5.2.1).

- *Generic commands:* Use a small set of commands to manipulate all types of data objects. A carefully chosen set of generic commands, mapped onto all of the types of data objects in an application, can provide most of the required functionality while giving users the perception that there isn't much to learn. Generic commands that have been used successfully are Create, Open, Move, Copy, Save, Delete, Print, Show Properties, and Follow Link.

Almost anything people do with computers can be expressed in terms of these nine commands. Some products have even simplified the set further. For example, the Xerox Star didn't have a Print command; files were printed by Copying them to a printer icon. The alternative to generic commands is a separate set of commands for each type of data object that users can manipulate using the software, greatly increasing the amount that users have to learn in order to use the software productively. As described under Principle 2 (Section 1.2), starting the design process by developing a conceptual model of the application can show designers which actions are common to multiple objects and so are candidates for generic commands.

- *Task-specific design:* Support a very limited range of tasks very well. Instead of offering users big feature-rich programs that attempt to support a wide range of tasks, offer them a collection of small specialized programs, each of which supports one task extremely well. For example, instead of developing a single document editor that can be used for creating everything from song lyrics and to-do lists to corporate financial reports and presentation slides, develop many small, simple editors, such as a song lyric editor, a to-do list editor, a corporate financial reports editor, and a presentation slide editor. This approach has been used successfully for household tools and appliances, including information appliances. It is even more successful when task-specific appliances and software can transfer information to and from each other. For a more complete discussion of the advantages and disadvantages of task-specific software applications, see the articles by Nardi and Johnson [1994] and Johnson and Nardi [1996].

1.4 Principle 4: Don't complicate the users' task

An important design principle is that the users' task—whatever it is that the user is trying to do—is complicated enough; the computer shouldn't complicate matters further. This principle is best explained as two separate subprinciples.

1.4.1 Common tasks should be easy

In any task domain, users will have goals ranging from common to rare. Computer software should be designed to recognize this range. If a user's goal is predictable and common, the user shouldn't have to do or specify much in order to get it. On the other hand, it is OK if unusual goals require more effort and specification to achieve.

Here is a more formal way of stating this design principle: The amount users should have to specify in order to get a desired result should not be proportional to the absolute complexity of the desired result. It should be proportional to how much the desired result *deviates* from a standard, predefined result.

To understand this principle, consider the following: If a man goes into a restaurant every day for dinner and always orders the same thing, he can just say, "I'll have the usual." Perhaps he usually has a hamburger. Perhaps he usually has a wilted spinach and belgian endive salad topped with organic walnuts and curried free-range chicken and a basil-artichoke mustard dressing. Whether his usual dinner is simple or complicated, he can just order "the usual." Furthermore, if on a particular day he wants a little change from his usual meal, he can specify it as a change, for example, "I'll have the usual with the mustard on the side." However, if he ever decides to eat something out of the ordinary, he's got to tell the waiter what menu item he wants and specify all of that menu choice's options.

Returning now to computer software, if someone is preparing a presentation and wants simple, mostly word slides with a few business graphics, all conforming to the company's standard format, the slide preparation program should make that a snap—just plug in the content and the slides are done. However, it may take significant work—including help from graphics experts—to prepare a presentation that includes fancy dissolves, animations, or other visual effects, or that doesn't conform to the standard format.

There are several ways to make common tasks easy. Two of them were already mentioned under Principle 3 (Section 1.3) as ways of reducing user interface complexity: providing sensible defaults, and providing catalogues of templates or "canned" solutions. Both approaches allow users to get a lot by specifying only a little. Two additional important techniques for making common tasks easy are

- *Support customization:* Allow users—or developers local to the users' organization acting on behalf of users—to set their own defaults, define macros, create templates, and otherwise customize the software for their specific requirements.

- *Provide wizards:* Give users the option of doing tasks using multipage dialog boxes that guide users step by step through otherwise complicated processes, with copious instructions and choices specified mainly through menus instead of type-in fields.

The bottom line is that users should be able to get a lot without specifying much. Do a little; get a lot. That's what users want.

1.4.2 Don't give users extra problems to solve

The human mind is amazingly good at multitasking. It allows us to handle many different tasks at once, for example, carrying on a phone conversation while beating an egg while keeping watch on our child while planning a pending vacation, all while tapping a foot to a song we heard on the radio this morning.

However, our ability to multitask is pretty much limited to activities that are well learned or based on perceptual and motor skills. One way to categorize activities that we can multitask is "stuff we already know how to do." In contrast, working out solutions to novel problems is one activity that human minds cannot multitask effectively. Problem solving—which can be regarded as "stuff we don't already know how to do"—requires concentration and focused attention. We're pretty much limited to solving one novel problem at a time.

People have plenty of their own problems to solve and goals to achieve in the domain of their work, their hobbies, and their personal lives. That is why they use computer products and services: to solve those problems and achieve those goals. They don't need or want to be distracted from those problems and goals by extra ones imposed by computer products and services. Unfortunately, computers often require users to stop thinking about their real problems and goals, and think instead about some computer-related problem. For example:

- A student wants to put a picture on his Web site, but the picture is in TIFF format rather than the required GIF or JPEG graphics format. His graphics software won't convert images from TIFF to GIF or JPEG; it will only convert from BMP format to GIF. He checks around the dorm to see if anyone else has a graphics program that will perform the desired conversion, or at least convert from TIFF to BMP.

- A manager has installed a new program on her computer, but it won't work. The installation instructions say that the program may be incompatible with software accessories already on the computer. She begins turning off the accessories one by one in an attempt to figure out which one is conflicting with her new software.

- An author is using his computer to type a chapter of a book. While he is typing, a message suddenly appears on the screen saying, "Out of memory. Try closing some other applications before continuing." No other applications are open. He stares at the computer screen, trying to figure out what to do.

- A stockbroker is using her computer to check the status of a client's stock order. To search for the order, the investment-tracking software wants her to specify an "Instrument ID." She thinks this is probably the same thing as the "Stock Symbol" she specified when she first recorded the order, but she isn't sure. She asks a coworker.

Computer-based products and services should be designed to let users focus their attention on their own problems and goals, whatever they may be: analyzing financial data, looking up job prospects on the Web, keeping track of relatives' birthdays, and so on. Software should be designed so as to support activity—including problem solving—in the software's target task domain, but it should minimize or eliminate the need for users to spend time problem solving in the domain of computer technology.

Minimizing the need for problem solving in the domain of computer technology includes not requiring users to figure out how software works by a process of elimination. Users should not have to go through thought processes such as the following:

- "I want page numbers in this document to start at 23 instead of 1, but I don't see a command to do that. I've tried the 'Page Setup' settings, the 'Document Layout' settings and the 'View Header and Footer' commands, but it isn't there. All that's left is this 'Insert Page Numbers' command. But I don't want to *insert* page numbers; the document already has page numbers. I just want to change the number they start at. Oh well, I'll try 'Insert Page Numbers' because that's the only one I haven't tried."
- "Hmmm. This checkbox is labeled 'Align icons horizontally.' I wonder what happens if I uncheck it. Will my icons be aligned vertically, or will they simply not be aligned?"
- "This online banking service is asking me for a 'PIN number.' But the card they sent me has a 'password.' I wonder if that's it? It must be, because they haven't sent me anything called a 'PIN number.'"

The function of controls, commands, and settings in a user interface should be clear and obvious. Operating computer software should not require deductive reasoning. To the extent that it does, it distracts users from their own tasks and goals.

1.5 Principle 5: Promote learning

A frequent complaint about computer-based products and services is that they are too difficult to learn. Learning takes time; the more a user has to learn in order to use a product or service, the longer it will be before that user can be productive. Time is money. Furthermore, if a user is not *required* to learn how to use a particular product or service (e.g., because of his or her job), the user may simply decide not to bother; there are plenty of other products (or services) to choose from.

The user interface of a software product or service can promote learning in several different ways, described in each of the following subprinciples.

1.5.1 Think "outside-in," not "inside-out"

Developers of computer-based products often design as if they assume that the users will automatically know what the developers intended. I call this thinking "inside-out" instead of "outside-in." When a software developer has designed software, he or she knows how it works, what information is displayed in what place and at what time, what everything on the screen means, and how information displayed by the software is related. Most designers think inside-out: they use their own knowledge of the software to judge whether the displays and controls make sense. They assume that users perceive and understand everything the way the designer intended it to be perceived and understood.

The problem is, users *don't* know what the designer knows about the software. When people first start using a software product, they know very little about how it works or what all that stuff on the screen is supposed to mean. They are not privy to the designer's intentions. All they have to base their understanding on is what they see on the screen and, in some cases, what they read in the software's documentation.

Examples: *Textual ambiguity*

Thinking inside-out is a problem that is not limited to software developers. Newspaper headline writers sometimes commit the same error when they fail to notice that a headline they've written has interpretations other than the one they intended. Some examples:

> Crowds Rushing to See Pope Trample 6 to Death
> Drunk Gets Nine Months in Violin Case
> Vineland Couple to Take on Missionary Position
> Teacher Strikes Idle Kids
> British Left Waffles on Falkland Islands
> Iraqi Head Seeks Arms
> New Vaccine May Contain Rabies
> Two Soviet Ships Collide, One Dies
> Farmer Bill Dies in House

Examples: *Typographical ambiguity*

Figure 1.4

A famous example of textual ambiguity in a computer system—and thus inside-out thinking by the designers—is a LISP workstation, circa 1985, that had a key on its keyboard labeled "DoIt", as in "do it". The key was labeled in a sans serif font, in which lowercase *L* and uppercase *I* characters looked alike. The key is shown in Figure 1.4. The designers of this keyboard apparently assumed that users would read the label as intended, but predictably, some users read it as "Dolt"—D-O-L-T—and wondered why anyone would press that key.

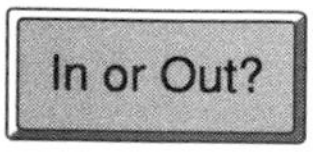

Examples: *Graphical ambiguity*

Figure 1.5

Ambiguity need not be textual. It can also be graphical. For example, is the button shown in Figure 1.5 poked out or pressed in?

It turns out that whether you see it as poked out or pressed in depends on your assumption about where the light source is. If you assume that the light is coming from the upper left, the button looks poked out. If you assume that the light is coming from the lower right, the button looks pressed in. In fact, you can make the button flip back and forth between poked out and pressed in by mentally switching the light source from upper left to lower right.

Window-based operating systems often use shading effects to create an illusion of three-dimensional controls on the screen of a computer. However, for users to perceive such images in the proper orientation—or even in 3D at all—they must imagine that the light is shining from a particular direction. In GUIs, the standard location of the imaginary light source is somewhere to the upper left of the screen.

People don't automatically perceive these simulated 3D displays as the designers intended; they have to *learn* to do that. People who have never encountered such a display before may either perceive no 3D effects or may perceive them in the "wrong" orientation. However, many designers of simulated 3D displays have known for so long that the imaginary light in GUIs comes from the upper left that they have forgotten that they had to learn that. They believe everyone else will just automatically know where the light is coming from and see the 3D controls as the designers intended. They are thinking inside-out, and they are wrong.

Similarly, graphic designers are thinking inside-out if they assume that an icon they've drawn will "naturally" convey the intended meaning to users. Designers at one of my client companies were surprised when usability testing showed that most test participants thought an antenna symbol for a Transmit function was a martini glass with a swizzle stick in it (see Figure 1.6).

Similarly, a colleague told me: "There is an icon in Lotus Notes that everyone at my company refers to as 'the lollipop.'" Further examples of graphic designers thinking inside-out are given in Section 10.1.

Figure 1.6

The right way to design: Think outside-in

Thinking outside-in requires assessing the meaning of the displays and controls based on what a *user* can be assumed to know at that point. It is a part of what it means to design from the user's point of view. It does not mean assuming that users are stupid. The users, in fact, probably know much more about the tasks that the software is intended to support than the developers do. What users don't know is the software. They don't know the meaning of the various sections of the display. They don't know what is dependent on what.

The bottom line is that if the user interface of the software that you develop is ambiguous—textually or graphically—and users misinterpret it, they aren't the real losers; you are. If your intended users misperceive or misunderstand your design, they may have an immediate problem, but you will have the more serious and longer-term problem: unsatisfied users, resulting in diminished sales.

1.5.2 Consistency, consistency, consistency, but don't be naive about it

Computer-based software should foster the development of habits. When using interactive software and electronic appliances, users want to fall into unconscious habits as quickly as possible. They want to be able to ignore the software or device and focus on their work. The more consistent the software is, the easier it is for users to do that.

Consistency avoids "gotchas"

Software that is full of inconsistencies, even minor ones, forces users to keep thinking about it, thereby detracting from the attention they can devote to the task at hand. I characterize this sort of software as being full of "gotchas": it's constantly saying to the user "Aha! Gotcha! Stay on your toes, buster, or I'll getcha again." Designers should try to minimize the number of "gotchas" in their software by striving for a high degree of user interface consistency.

When beginning a design, develop a conceptual model and perform an object/action analysis to expose operations that are common to many different types of objects. This allows the design to make use of generic commands (see Principle 3, Section 1.3.4), or at least to use highly similar user interfaces for similar but distinct functions. When adding new features to a product or service, reuse user interfaces from other parts of the software instead of inventing new user interfaces for the specific new feature.

The alternative is to provide a bewildering array of different ways of doing more or less the same thing in different contexts. For example, Figure 1.7 illustrates the large number of different ways found in computer-based products for deleting items; the method of deletion depends on the type of item to be deleted.

Dangers of trying to be consistent

Exhorting software developers to make their user interfaces "consistent" is somewhat risky; it could do more harm than good. Why? Because consistency is a more complex concept than many people think it is. In particular, it is

- *Difficult to define:* Many experts have tried without success.
- *Multidimensional:* Items that are consistent on one dimension (e.g., function) may be inconsistent on another (e.g., location).
- *Subject to interpretation:* What seems consistent to one person may seem inconsistent to another.

Many designers have naive notions of consistency, and either are unaware that users might see things differently or arrogantly believe that they can define con-

Figure 1.7

sistency for users. Some astonishingly bad designs have been produced in the name of consistency. Examples include software applications in which everything is controlled by forms or by hierarchies of menus even though forms or menus may not be appropriate for controlling certain functions. Grudin [1989] even goes as far as to suggest that consistency is such an ill-defined concept that it should be abandoned as a user interface design principle.

Why I advocate consistency anyway

While there are indeed dangers in advocating consistency in user interfaces, I don't advocate abandoning the concept. Just because theorists haven't yet found a formal definition of consistency doesn't mean that the concept is useless. It clearly has value to users, even though their ideas of what is and is not consistent may not match those of user interface designers. Users search for consistency along the dimensions that are relevant to them. They are so anxious to disengage their conscious mind from the task of controlling the computer—so they can apply it to their own problems—that they make up consistency even when it is absent.

For example, programmers argue: "Yes, most items on this computer are opened by double-click, but this application is different because items can only be opened, not selected, so a single-click should open them." So they design it that way, and users of the new application double-click to open items anyway and are annoyed when items often open accidentally. Similarly, the designers of the Apple Macintosh decided that it made sense for dragging a file within a disk to be a Move operation, whereas dragging it between disks is a Copy operation, and—surprise—Mac users complain about not knowing when their files will be moved versus copied.

Users gladly expend physical effort in controlling the computer to reserve mental effort for working on their own tasks. For example, while being observed using a software application developed at a company where I once worked, a user said:

I was in a hurry so I did it the long way.

Making consistency user-centered

Instead of abandoning consistency as a user interface design goal, we need to refine it to make it more user-centered. Therefore, when interviewing or observing users to understand them, the target tasks, and the work environment, software designers should try to determine how the users perceive consistency. What aspects of the users' current tools seem consistent and inconsistent to them?

When sketches or other prototypes of the new software are available, they should be tested on representative users, and developers should be on the lookout for aspects of the user interface that the users perceive as inconsistent. The bottom line is that the consistency of a user interface should be evaluated based not on how "logical" it seems to designers and developers, but rather on how predictable it is to users.

off the mark   by Mark Parisi

www.offthemark.com   ATLANTIC FEATURE © 1994 MARK PARISI

1.5.3 Provide a low-risk environment

An important fact to consider when designing an interactive product or service is that people make mistakes. A product or service that is risky to use is one that makes it too easy for users to make mistakes, does not allow users to correct their mistakes, or makes it costly or time-consuming to correct mistakes. People won't be very productive in using it; they will be wasting too much time correcting mistakes. Such a product or service will not be popular.

Even more important than the impact on time is the impact on users' learning. A high-risk situation discourages exploration; people will tend to stick to familiar, safe paths. When exploration is discouraged, learning is severely hampered. A low-risk situation, in which people don't have to worry about mistakes—either because they are hard to make or are easy to correct—encourages exploration and hence greatly fosters learning. In such situations, users aren't hesitant to try unfamiliar paths: "Hmmm, I wonder what *that* does."

1.6 Principle 6: Deliver information, not just data

A common saying about computers is that they promise a fountain of information, but mainly deliver a glut of data ... most of it useless. Data is not necessarily information. In particular, the information in data is what the recipient learns from examining it.

If I want to know whether my colleague Bill is in his office or not, all I want is one bit of information: yes or no, true or false, 1 or 0. But I can get the answer to my question by a variety of methods, involving the transfer of widely different amounts of data. For example, I can

- knock on the wall separating our offices and listen to hear whether Bill knocks back (one bit)
- send him email and wait to see if he sends a reply (several hundred bytes, including the mail headers)
- call him on the intranet phone and listen to see if he answers (several kilobytes)
- visit his Web site and download an image of him that is updated once a minute from the video camera in his office (several megabytes)

Regardless of the method I use and the amount of *data* transferred, I receive only one bit of *information,* assuming that all I care about is the answer to my question.

Historically, computer-based products and services have had an unfortunate tendency to treat data as if it were the same thing as information: they put it all in your face and make you find the information in it.

Software designers need to counter this tendency by designing interactive software so that it focuses users' attention on the important information and does not distract them from it. That is what this principle and its various subprinciples are about.

1.6.1 Design displays carefully; get professional help

Principle 2 (Section 1.2) says, "Consider function first, presentation later." There comes a time, however, in every software development effort when it is necessary to consider presentation. I am talking about the presentation of the software's data, of the data's properties and relationships, and of the software's controls and status. When the time comes to consider presentation, designers should consider it very seriously and carefully. That means trying to achieve the following:

- *Visual order and user focus:* One important feature of a successful presentation is that it doesn't simply present. It *directs* users' attention toward the important information. For example, find the selected text in each of the computer screens shown Figure 1.8. The large amount of contrast present on the screens of many window-based computer systems (shown in the left screen) makes it difficult for users to focus on the relevant information. On the computer screen, the current selection should be the users' main focus;

Figure 1.8

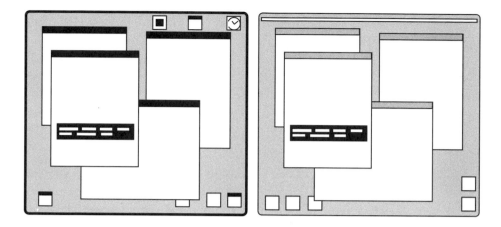

it is the object of the next operation. The screen on the right illustrates how the displays of the Xerox Star and the Apple Macintosh minimize the presence of contrast on the screen in order to focus attention on the current selection.

- *Match the medium:* One mark of a poorly designed user interface is a failure to match the design to the limitations of the medium in which it is presented. The software marketplace has plenty of examples of mismatches: window systems presented on character displays or on two-inch screens, visual metaphors presented aurally through a telephone, point-and-click GUIs on computers that have no pointing device other than arrow keys, using subtle colors or gray shades on a display that cannot render them well. Well-designed user interfaces match the medium in which they will be presented.

- *Attention to detail:* It is often said that success is in the details. Nowhere is this more true than in the design of effective information displays. Hiring user interface and graphic designers for a software development project may seem expensive, but they bring an eye for detail that few other members of the team can provide, and thus easily repay their cost, especially considering the alternative. A lack of attention to detail yields incoherent displays, design inconsistencies, horrendous installation experiences, indecipherable symbols, and a generally cheesy appearance. In short, it yields many of the bloopers described elsewhere in this book. These bloopers can hamper the success of the product or service by giving prospective customers an impression of a shoddy product and also by decreasing the product's usability.

In order to assure that all of the important issues are considered in designing presentations, software developers should make sure they have the right people for the job. You would not hire a plumber—even a skilled one—to repair your car. Yet many software development teams assign GUI programming to student interns and new hires, or expect GUI programmers to design as well as implement the GUIs, or use icons created by programmers or managers. This sort of corner-cutting is misguided and counterproductive.

Don't assume that just anyone can design information displays well. The people with the necessary skills are user interface designers (sometimes called "interaction designers") and graphic designers: user interface designers for gross characteristics of the display, and graphic designers for the exact details.

Programmers, even GUI programmers, lack the required experience and skills. Though they are professional programmers, they are amateurs in the area of presentation and graphic design. Products and services that rely on graphics drawn or designed by programmers will be perceived by users (and customers) as amateurish, and rightly so. For further discussion of the difference between user interface designers, graphic designers, and GUI programmers, see Blooper 76: Misunderstanding what user interface professionals do (Section 8.1.1) and Blooper 77: Treating user interface as low priority (Section 8.1.2).

1.6.2 The screen belongs to the user

This design principle was recognized as far back as the mid-1970s by researchers at Xerox Palo Alto Research Center (PARC). At the time, personal computers with bit-mapped displays, mouse pointers, and windows were still new, and the GUI as we know it today hadn't yet settled down; researchers at PARC were still trying all sorts of different design ideas. Some worked better than others.

Fairly quickly, PARC researchers realized that one thing that did *not* work very well was for the computer—or more accurately, its software—to unilaterally move objects around on the screen. Some researchers had initially assumed that it would be helpful to users and more efficient for software to sometimes move or "warp" the mouse pointer automatically to new positions. Similarly, some researchers tried having their software automatically reposition, stretch, and shrink windows "when appropriate." Although well-meaning, these attempts to be helpful and efficient disoriented and frustrated users more than they helped them. In a well-meaning attempt to help users, the designers had interfered with users' perception of the screen as being under their control.

This is especially true for the screen pointer. Moving the screen pointer is a hand-eye coordination task. After a user has gotten used to using a pointing device such as a mouse, moving the pointer becomes a reflex—an action controlled more by "muscle memory" than by conscious awareness. The users' conscious mind is freed to think about other things besides moving the pointer, such as the task he or she is trying to accomplish. Automatic, unilateral movement of the pointer by the software disrupts the coordination, causing disorientation and yanking the user's conscious mind back to the task of moving the pointer. Users aren't sure which pointer movements are the result of their actions versus those of the computer.

At Xerox PARC, years of experience and observation of users eventually gave rise to the important GUI principle "The screen belongs to the user." Graphical user interfaces are supposed to be based on direct manipulation of data by users, and that is what users expect. When software changes too much on its own initiative, users become disoriented and annoyed.

The principle can be generalized beyond screen pointers and windows to include desktop icons, lists of email messages, and many other sorts of data objects that people manipulate using software. It suggests that, in general, software should avoid trying to "help" users by rearranging their data displays for them. It should let users arrange and manage their data themselves, as they wish.

To assist users in arranging and formatting their data, software can provide "rearrange" or "reformat" commands that users have to invoke explicitly. Examples of such commands are the MacOS Clean-up Desktop command, the Balance or Align functions of some graphics editors, and Microsoft Word's AutoFormat command.

1.6.3 Preserve display inertia

Closely related to the principle that "the screen belongs to the user" is the principle of "display inertia."

When software changes a graphical display to show the effect of a user's actions, it should try to minimize what it changes. Small, localized changes to the data should produce only small, localized changes on the display. Another way of stating the principle is that when a user changes something on the screen, as much of the display as possible should remain unchanged.

Failing to localize changes in the display to what has actually changed can be quite disorienting to users. For example, if someone were editing the name of a file displayed in a folder, it would be very disorienting and annoying if the file constantly jumped around to different alphabetical positions as the name was being edited. Therefore, most file managers—wisely—leave the file temporarily where it is until users indicate that they are done by pressing RETURN or moving the selection elsewhere.

When large or nonlocal changes in the display are necessary (such as re-paginating a document, or swapping the positions of branches of a family tree diagram), they should not be instantaneous. Rather, they should be announced clearly, and they should be carried out in ways that

- foster users' recognition and comprehension of the changes that are occurring

- minimize disruption to users' ability to continue working

1.7 Principle 7: Design for responsiveness

To design software that satisfies its users, designers must of course ask, What do the users want?

Considerable evidence has been amassed over the past four decades of computer use that responsiveness—the software's ability to keep up with users and not make them wait—is the most important factor in determining user satisfaction with computer-based products and services. Study after study has found this [Miller, 1968; Thadhani, 1981; Barber and Lucas, 1983; Lambert, 1984; Shneiderman, 1984; Carroll and Rosson, 1984; Rushinek and Rushinek, 1986]. The findings of all these studies are well summarized by Peter Bickford in his book *Interface Design* [1997]:

> Many surveys have tried to determine what it is about a computer that makes its users happy. Time and time again, it turns out that the biggest factor in user satisfaction is not the computer's reliability, its compatibility with other platforms, the type of user interface it has, or even its price. What customers seem to want most is speed. When it comes to computers, users hate waiting more than they like anything else.

Bickford goes on to explain that by "speed," he means *perceived* speed, not actual speed:

> Computers actually have two kinds of speed: ... real (machine) speed and ... perceived speed. Of these two, the one that really matters is perceived speed. For instance, a 3-D rendering program that saves a few moments by not displaying the results until the image is complete will inevitably be seen as slower than a program that lets the user watch the image as it develops. The reason is that while the latter program's users are watching an image form, the first program's users are staring impatiently at the clock, noticing every long second tick by. Users will say that the first program ran slow simply because the wait was more painful.

Research also suggests that improving the responsiveness of software, in addition to increasing user satisfaction, actually improves the productivity of its users [Brady, 1986].

1.7.1 Defining responsiveness and the lack thereof

Responsive software keeps up with users even if it can't fulfill every request immediately. It prioritizes feedback based on *human* perceptual, motor, and cognitive requirements. It provides enough feedback for users to see what they are doing. It lets users know when it is busy and when it isn't. It gives users ways to judge how much time operations will require. Finally, it does its best to let users set their own desired work pace.

In contrast, when software is said to exhibit poor responsiveness, it means that the software does not keep up with users. It doesn't provide timely feedback about user actions, so users are often unsure of what they have done or are doing. It makes users wait at unpredictable times or for unpredictable periods. It limits—moderately or severely—users' work pace.

Examples of poor responsiveness include

- delayed or nonexistent feedback for user actions
- time-consuming operations that block other activity and cannot be aborted
- providing no clue how long lengthy operations will take
- periodically ignoring user input while performing internal "housekeeping" tasks

When software manifests these problems, it not only impedes users' productivity, it frustrates and annoys them as well. Unfortunately, a lot of software manifests these problems. Despite all the research showing that responsiveness is very important to user satisfaction and productivity, much of the software in today's marketplace exhibits poor responsiveness.

1.7.2 Responsiveness on the Web: A big deal

Responsiveness is an especially important issue on the Web. One reason is that the Web is completely user-driven. A user of a traditional desktop computer application is somewhat "captive" because of the work required to install the application and the additional work that would be required to replace it. On the Web, users are in no way captive. If they don't like a Web site for any reason, they can go elsewhere with a few simple clicks. There is no shortage of sites out there to choose from. If a user gets frustrated with how long it is taking for a Web site to display the desired information, he or she simply hits the Back key and moves on to the next site.

Responsiveness is also important on the Web for a technical reason: the huge difference in the time it takes to execute operations that can be performed entirely on the client side (e.g., displaying pop-up menus in forms or executing Java/Javascript functions) versus operations that require communicating with a Web server (e.g., loading a page). This difference places strong constraints on the design of Web user interfaces. For example, forms on the Web can't check the validity of users' input as frequently as do forms in conventional desktop applications, thereby limiting the immediacy of error feedback.

1.7.3 Summary of responsiveness design principles

In addition to describing the many ways software can be designed so as to be unresponsive to its users, Chapter 7, Responsiveness Bloopers, provides design principles and techniques for designing software that is highly responsive. For present purposes, it will suffice to summarize the seven responsiveness design principles that are described fully in Chapter 7. They are:

- *Responsiveness is not the same thing as performance:* Software can be responsive even if its performance—that is, speed of execution—is low; conversely, improving performance does not necessarily improve responsiveness

- *Processing resources are always limited:* Computer users probably have older computers than developers have, and when users do get faster computers, they just load them down with more software

- *The user interface is a real-time interface:* It has time constraints and deadlines that are just as important as the time constraints on software that interfaces with real-time devices

- *All delays are not equal:* Software can and should prioritize its responses to users

- *The software need not do tasks in the order in which they were requested:* Tasks can be reordered based on priority or to improve the efficiency with which the entire set of tasks can be completed

- *The software need not do everything it was asked to do:* Some requested tasks are unnecessary and can simply be ignored, freeing time for the software to perform necessary tasks

- *Human users are not computer programs:* People do not interact with computer software in the same way as other software does, and should not be forced to do so

For examples of design bloopers developers make that contribute to poor responsiveness, and techniques that can help designers avoid responsiveness bloopers, see Chapter 7, Responsiveness Bloopers.

1.8 Principle 8: Try it out on users, then fix it!

Most people in the computer industry have heard the saying "Test early and often." Although there are many different kinds of testing to which computer software and hardware can be subjected, the kind that is relevant to this book is "usability testing"—trying a product or service out on prospective users to see what problems they have in learning and using it. Such testing is extremely important for determining whether a design is successful, that is, whether it helps users more than it hinders them.

1.8.1 Test results can surprise even experienced designers

Developers can learn surprising things from usability tests. Sometimes the results can surprise even user interface experts.

I usually review the user interface of software products or services before testing them on representative users. Reviewing the user interface beforehand gives me an idea of how to design the test, what sorts of problems to look for in it, and how to interpret the problems I observe users having. However, conducting the test almost always exposes usability problems I hadn't anticipated.

For example, one of my client companies was developing software for analyzing and predicting the performance of database servers. One feature of the software was the ability to plot the expected performance of one or more servers for a varying number of simultaneous users. To do this, users had to specify not only the characteristics of the database servers they wanted analyzed, but also the type of plot they wanted. The software provided radiobuttons for choosing a plot type. The radiobutton choices were labeled textually, but next to the radiobutton setting was an image panel showing a small thumbnail example of the currently chosen type of plot. What surprised both the developers and me was that the usability tests showed that many users thought the small thumbnail images were the actual data plots for the specified servers! The moral of this story is that it is always useful to test; you never know what you will learn, but you *will* learn something that will help you improve your software.

1.8.2 Schedule time to correct problems found by tests

Of course, it isn't enough just to test the usability of a product or service. Developers must also provide enough time in the development schedule to correct problems uncovered by testing. Otherwise, what is the point of testing?

1.8.3 Testing has two goals: Informational and social

Usability testing has two important but different goals: one informational, the other social.

Informational goal

The informational goal of usability testing is the one most people are familiar with: find aspects of the user interface that cause users difficulty, and use the

exact nature of the problems to suggest improvements. This goal can be accomplished by a wide variety of testing and data collection methods, some expensive and time-consuming, some cheap and quick (see Section 1.8.4).

Social goal

The social goal of usability testing is at least as important as the informational goal. It is to convince developers that there are problems in the design that need to be corrected. Most developers naturally are resistant to suggestions for change, partly because of the time and effort required and partly because of the perception that the need to change a design reflects poorly on the original design and hence on the designer. To achieve the social goal of usability testing, I have found it most effective to either have developers present as passive observers during testing, or to videotape the test sessions and show the tapes—or excerpts from them—to developers. When developers observe tests in person, it is important to stress that they remain *passive* observers because, in my experience, programmers can become quite agitated while watching a user who is having trouble with the programmers' software.

I have found that emphasizing the importance of the social goal of usability testing has benefits beyond convincing developers to make the indicated changes. It also makes them much more accepting of the notion that usability testing is an essential development tool rather than a way to evaluate developers. Some programmers who initially resisted usability testing became "converts" after witnessing a few tests; in later development efforts, they actively sought opportunities to test their designs in order to get feedback.

1.8.4 There are tests for every time and purpose

Many people in the computer industry have the mistaken impression that usability testing is always conducted when a software product or appliance is nearly ready to ship, using elaborate testing facilities and equipment. In fact, a wide variety of different sorts of tests can be considered "usability testing," each having its benefits and drawbacks. I find it useful to categorize usability testing along two independent dimensions: (1) the point in the development process when testing occurs, and (2) the formality of the testing method.

Implementation stage of testing

First let's consider the point in development when testing is done. I find it helpful to divide this dimension into three categories:

- *Before development.* Before anything has been implemented, developers can test a design using mock-ups. Mock-ups can be storyboards—hand-drawn sketches of the design on paper that are shown to users in approximately the order they would see them in the running product. They can be screen images created using interactive GUI building tools, printed out onto paper, and placed in front of users with a person acting as "the computer" as the user "clicks" the controls shown on the screens. They can be "cardboard computers" with rear projection screens that show slides simulating the display (see the chapter "Cardboard Computers" in the book by Greenbaum and Kyng [1991]). Finally, they can be "Wizard of Oz" systems in which the display on the computer screen is controlled by a person in another room who watches what the user does and changes the user's screen accordingly.

- *During development.* A development team can use prototyping software (e.g., Macromedia Director, Hypercard, Toolbook) to create working software mock-ups of an application. GUIs prototyped with such tools would be only prototypes; their underlying code would not be used in the eventual implementation. Alternatively, some GUI building tools allow user interfaces to be partially wired together and "run." This allows the early versions of the user interface to be tested even before any back-end code has been written. Another way to test during development is to test parts of the planned application in isolation, to resolve design issues. For example, you could test a table widget used in an application long before any of the rest of the application was ready.

- *After development.* Many usability tests are conducted when most or all of the product has been implemented and it is being prepared for release. At this late stage, it is rare for the results of usability tests to have much of an impact on the pending release because the development organization is usually anxious to ship it. The main reason for conducting usability tests at this stage is to provide guidance for a preshipping cleanup of minor usability problems. Nonetheless, such testing can also uncover "showstopper" problems that are deemed important enough to delay the release. Another

DILBERT reprinted by permission of United Feature Syndicate, Inc.

reason for testing "completed" software is to get feedback on how to improve the user interface for *future* releases. This sort of testing can be conducted after a release, when the schedule is not so frantic and the team is beginning to think about the next release.

Formality of testing

The second dimension along which usability testing can be categorized is the formality of the testing method. Usability test formality has to do with the degree of control the tester exerts over what people do in the test session, and whether the measurements are qualitative or quantitative. Again, I find it helpful to divide this dimension into three categories:

- *Informal testing.* This type of testing includes situations where users are interviewed about the software, for example, how they use it, what they use it for, how they like it. Sometimes this is done in front of a computer with the software running so the user can show what he or she is talking about, and sometimes it isn't. Informal testing also includes situations in which users are observed while they do their real work or while they explore the software in an unguided fashion. The observers note the users' expressed likes and dislikes, and record any problems they notice users having. The session may be videotaped or audiotaped. The observations are qualitative.

- *Quasi-formal testing.* In this type of testing, users are asked to do tasks that have been predetermined by the testers, who also prepared the necessary materials and data files and set up the software as required. In other words, users aren't just exploring the software or doing their own work; they are doing what the tester asks them to do. However, as in informal testing, the measurements are mainly observational. The testers record (and count) any errors users make, as well as situations in which users need help (either from online help documents or from the testers). The testers also record the time required to complete each of the tasks. The session may be videotaped.

It is best to start each test session with simple tasks and give the test participant progressively harder tasks over the course of the session.

- *Formal testing.* This is the type of usability testing that is most similar to the psychology experiments many people remember from their college days. They are true "controlled experiments," conducted to compare alternative designs (e.g., control layouts A versus B) or to determine an optimal value of a design parameter (e.g., number of cascading menu levels). The tasks that test participants are asked to perform are highly prescribed, and their relation to real-world tasks often seems tenuous (e.g., use the mouse to hit a sequence of randomly positioned targets on the screen; find a file using this file browser). In fact, the materials or software used for the test often are devised purely for the test itself, rather than being part of a pending product. The data collected are mainly quantitative (e.g., user reaction or completion time, number of errors) and are analyzed statistically. Often, the data are collected automatically, by the same computer that is running the test software. In addition, such sessions are usually videotaped.

Each level of formality has its place in product development. The important thing to realize, however, is that the formality level of the test is independent of the point in development when the test is conducted. One can find or devise examples of usability tests at any level of formality at any stage of development.

For examples from my consulting files of usability tests conducted at a variety of development stages and formality levels, see the design rule for Blooper 78: Discounting the value of testing and iterative design (Section 8.1.3).

Further reading

Methodologies for understanding users and tasks

Beyer, H., and Holtzblatt, K. 1998. *Contextual Design: Defining Customer-Centered Systems.* San Francisco: Morgan Kaufmann Publishers.

Dayton, T., McFarland, A., and Kramer, J. 1998. "Bridging User Needs to Object Oriented GUI Prototypes via Task Object Design." In L. Wood, ed., *User Interface Design: Bridging the Gap from Requirements to Design*, pp. 15–56. Boca Raton, FL: CRC Press.

Greenbaum, J., and Kyng, M. 1991. *Design at Work: Cooperative Design of Computer Systems.* Hillsdale, NJ: Lawrence Erlbaum Associates.

Official platform-specific GUI style guides

Apple Computer, Inc. 1993. *Macintosh Human Interface Guidelines.* Reading, MA: Addison-Wesley.

Microsoft. 1995. *The Windows Interface Guidelines for Software Design: An Application Design Guide.* Redmond, WA: Microsoft Press.

Microsoft. 1999. *Microsoft Windows User Experience*. Redmond, WA: Microsoft Press.

Open Software Foundation. 1993. *OSF/Motif Style Guide: Rev 1.2*. Englewood Cliffs, NJ: Prentice Hall.

Sun Microsystems. 1999. *Java Look and Feel Design Guidelines*. Reading, MA: Addison-Wesley.

Platform-independent design guidelines

Bickford, P. 1997. *Interface Design: The Art of Developing Easy-to-Use Software*. Chestnut Hill, MA: Academic Press.

Fowler, S. 1998. *GUI Design Handbook*. New York: McGraw-Hill.

Mandel, T. 1997. *The Elements of User Interface Design*. New York: John Wiley and Sons.

McFarland, A., and Dayton, T. 1995. *Design Guide for Multiplatform Graphical User Interfaces*. Issue 3, LPR13. Piscataway, NJ: Bellcore.

Nielsen, J., 1999d. *Designing Web Usability: The Practice of Simplicity*. Indianapolis, IN: New Riders Publishing.

Shneiderman, B. 1987. *Designing the User Interface: Strategies for Effective Human-Computer Interaction*. Reading, MA: Addison-Wesley.

Weinshenk, S., Jamar, P., and Yeo, S. 1997. *GUI Design Essentials*. New York: John Wiley and Sons.

Graphic design guidelines

Mullet, K., and Sano, D. 1995. *Designing Visual Interfaces*. Mountain View, CA: SunSoft Press.

Tufte, E. R. 1983. *The Visual Display of Quantitative Information*. Cheshire, MA: Graphics Press.

GUI Component Bloopers

Introduction

Most software applications these days are built using graphical user interface (GUI) development tools. Such tools provide a set of controls—also known as "widgets"—out of which user interfaces can be composed. The controls include such interactive devices as editable text fields, number fields, checkboxes, radiobuttons, sliders, scrollbars, buttons, knobs, dials, meters, and various sorts of menus.

Some GUI tools are referred to as "toolkits"; they are essentially libraries of user interface components. Other GUI tools are called user "interface management systems" (UIMSs); they are prebuilt application infrastructures that provide not only user interface components, but also runtime support for communication between user interface components and application semantic modules. Some GUI toolkits and UIMSs provide "builder" programs that allow designers to create user interfaces interactively and visually, by dragging the desired components into position using a pointing device. Others require developers to describe the desired user interface (i.e., the components of which it is to be composed) using a programming language. (For more details, see Zarmer and Johnson [1990].)

The distinction between UIMSs and GUI toolkits is not relevant to this book. Also irrelevant here is the distinction between interactive and programmatic specification of user interfaces. Throughout this book the terms "GUI tool" and "GUI toolkit" are used generically, to refer to all component-based user interface development tools and building blocks.

GUI tools are supposed to ease the task of developing graphical user interfaces and thereby make programmers more productive. However, most existing GUI toolkits fail to fulfill this promise because they are too primitive. The following are manifestations of this primitiveness:

- *The components are too low level.* Constructing applications from them is like constructing a wooden house out of wood blocks instead of panels, boards, or logs; it can be done, but it's going to take a long time and a lot of work. Sometimes toolkit components are low level in a misguided attempt to allow maximum flexibility in the user interfaces that can be built. However, unguided and unprincipled flexibility is more often a curse than a blessing (see next list item). Sometimes toolkits are low level for less purposeful reasons: for example, the toolkit developers ran out of time, or were not motivated or skilled enough to design high-level building blocks that would cover the desired range of user interfaces.

- *The tools are too unguided.* All GUI toolkits that I know of allow programmers to create user interfaces that violate guidelines for usability, and give programmers little or no guidance for creating good designs. Most toolkits claim to support one or more graphical user interface standards—such as Windows, MacOS, CDE/Motif—but in fact make it just as easy to violate the target standard as adhere to it. They allow designers to make poor choices, like using the wrong control for a setting. The control may look snazzy, but that's a minor detail if it's the wrong control or behaves unexpectedly, such as a checkbox used for a non-ON/OFF setting (see Blooper 10: Using a checkbox for a non-ON/OFF setting, Section 2.3.3).

■ *The tools are too focused on appearance.* Most GUI tools require application designers to spend too much time fiddling with the appearance and layout of their user interfaces. Are the labels for these settings aligned properly? Should this number be presented as a digital readout or a position on a dial? Should this choice be presented as a set of radiobuttons or as a menu? What font family and size should be used in this text field? These are mere presentation issues—the "low-order" bits of GUI design. The important issues are about the *semantics* of the user interface, such as whether a setting is a *date*, a *filename*, a *volume level*, or a choice between *fonts*. Decisions about presentation are likely to change from day to day or even hour to hour as the design evolves, and so should not require recoding. For example, changing the presentation of a discrete choice from radiobuttons to an option menu should require only an attribute change, not ripping out the radiobutton setup code and replacing it with the very different option menu setup code. Time spent fiddling with presentation would be better spent conducting user studies, analyzing the task and work context, and planning the software's functionality.

The low level of the building blocks provided by GUI toolkits is a problem because of the unfortunate truth that many GUIs are not carefully designed by user interface professionals. Rather, they are quickly assembled on tight deadlines by programmers who lack the user interface expertise that would be needed to make up for the lack of guidance provided by the toolkits.

The result is that user interfaces constructed from GUI tools are typically full of design errors. Some of these errors are semantic in nature and can be detected only by people who have some understanding of the application's intended task domain and users. However, many GUI design errors are ones that would be immediately obvious to most user interface professionals, even those who lack an understanding of the application's task domain. I categorize such errors as "GUI component" bloopers. GUI component bloopers have one of two causes:

1. Misuse of the GUI toolkit by programmers
2. Attempting to build an application's user interface using a GUI toolkit that is inadequate for the job

GUI component bloopers give users and customers an impression of a shoddy, unprofessional product, especially when a design contains many of them. More importantly, they make the software harder to use.

Fortunately, GUI component bloopers are fairly easy to detect in user interface reviews (assuming the reviewers aren't the designers). They are also concrete and relatively easy to explain. Finally, they are usually easy to correct unless they are caused by limitations of the GUI tools that were used to build the software.

This section describes the most common GUI component errors, along with design rules for avoiding them. Because the various GUI toolkits in common use are so similar to each other (at least in the components they provide), it is not necessary to distinguish between them when describing the errors.

2.1 Complicating access to functionality

The following four bloopers are cases in which the user interface of a software product or service makes it difficult for users to access the software's functionality.

2.1.1 Blooper 1: Dynamic menus

Most GUI-based applications provide a menubar, which displays most or all of the application's commands, organized by category, for example, File, Edit, View, . . . , . . . , Tools, Window, Help. In MacOS, the menubar for the currently selected application is displayed on the top of the screen. In Windows and most Unix-based window systems (e.g., CDE/Motif), each application's menubar is at the top of its main window.

A common mistake made by GUI developers is to try to reduce the size and complexity of the menubar menus by adding and removing items based on the state of the application. Commands shown in the menus at any given moment are only those that are applicable to whatever data object in the application is selected at that moment. Figure 2.1 shows an example of this: the commands in the Edit menu depend on the users' current activity.

This may seem like a good idea, but it isn't. It confuses users: if they scan the menus at different times, they will find different menu items. If users haven't learned the software very well yet and don't know what depends on what else, they may not understand why some commands are present at some times and not at others. They may not initially even realize that the menus change.

Users faced with software applications that commit this error are often heard complaining as they search in vain through the menus: "Where the heck *is* that Edit Formula command? I *know* I saw it here somewhere." I've uttered similar words myself.

For example, a usability test I conducted of a client's application yielded the following observation and recommendation, which the development team followed:

Figure 2.1

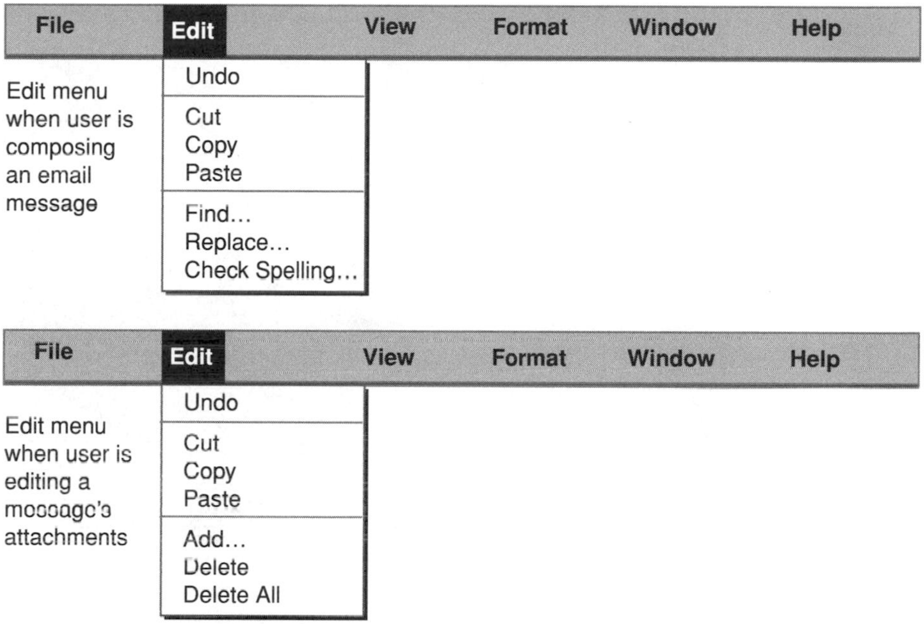

File	**Edit**		View	Format	Window	Help

Edit menu
when user is
composing
an email
message

> Undo
> ___
> Cut
> Copy
> Paste
> ___
> Find…
> Replace…
> Check Spelling…

File	**Edit**		View	Format	Window	Help

Edit menu
when user is
editing a
message's
attachments

> Undo
> ___
> Cut
> Copy
> Paste
> ___
> Add…
> Delete
> Delete All

Observation: Some test participants were disoriented by the fact that results-view choices disappear from the View menu when no Project is open. Similarly, there is a top-level menu label that appears and disappears depending on what view is selected.

Recommendation: Leave view choices in View menu at all times, but deactivate them when no Project open. Leaving items on menus, but graying them out, helps keep users oriented, and also clues them that there are conditions (which they may not yet understand) that determine when each item is active.

An example of a released product that commits this blooper is Sybase's PowerBuilder 5.0, an interactive GUI-building tool. As can be seen in Figure 2.2, the content of the File menu varies greatly depending on whether or not a GUI is under construction.

Dynamic menus are a specific manifestation of a more general error that many software developers make: thinking *inside-out* instead of *outside-in*. Thinking inside-out is using one's own knowledge of the software to judge whether the displays and controls make sense. Thinking outside-in requires assessing the meaning of the displays and controls based on what a *user* can be assumed to know at that point. The difference is explained more fully in Section 1.5.1.

Designers who make the menus of an application dynamic (i.e., change content depending on what the user is doing) are thinking inside-out. They are assuming that users start with or quickly gain an understanding of how and why menu items appear and disappear. They are wrong.

Figure 2.2

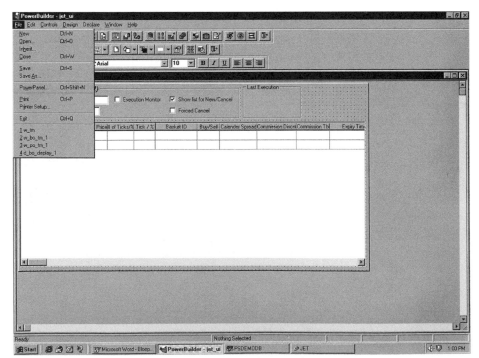

Software applications that have dynamic menus can be grouped into two main categories: those that support plug-in applications or compound documents, and those that do not.

Applications that do not support plug-in applications or compound documents basically have no good excuse for having dynamic menubar menus. These are commonly applications that either

- have modes of operation, with different menubar commands being available in different modes, or
- support several different built-in datatypes, with different commands being available depending on which of the built-in datatypes is currently selected.

Developers of such applications no doubt mean well: they are trying to help users by restricting what commands are available in different situations. The problem is that adding and removing menu commands is unfriendly to users. In particular, it is much less friendly than is activating and deactivating menu items, that is, graying out menu items that are not currently applicable.

Applications that support plug-ins or compound documents—for example, Web browsers or software that supports the ActiveX, OpenDoc, or CORBA protocols—have a more plausible excuse for adding and removing items from menubar menus as the software runs: their developers don't know in advance what all the datatypes and associated operations will be. Applications that support plug-ins and compound documents allow users to view and edit types of data that cannot be viewed or edited by the basic application. If developers don't know in advance all the commands that will be available through the application, they obviously cannot design them all into its menus. Therefore, dynamic menubar menus are common in applications that support plug-ins or compound documents.

However, there is an alternative. Applications can provide for unknown future commands without adding and removing them from menubar menus. Instead, applications can add and remove entire menubar *menus* depending on the current selection. That way, users can actually see menus appearing and disappearing as the selection changes. In contrast, when items change inside menus, users don't see the changes as the occur, and so learn the dependencies much more slowly, if at all. Because there is an alternative, dynamic menus are considered a blooper even for applications that support plug-ins or compound documents.

Avoiding Blooper 1: *The design rule*

The content of an application's menubar menus should be stable. Users get their bearings in new applications by scanning the menubar menus, seeing what's where and how many commands there are. Therefore, commands in menubar menus should not be present or absent depending on the applica-

Figure 2.3

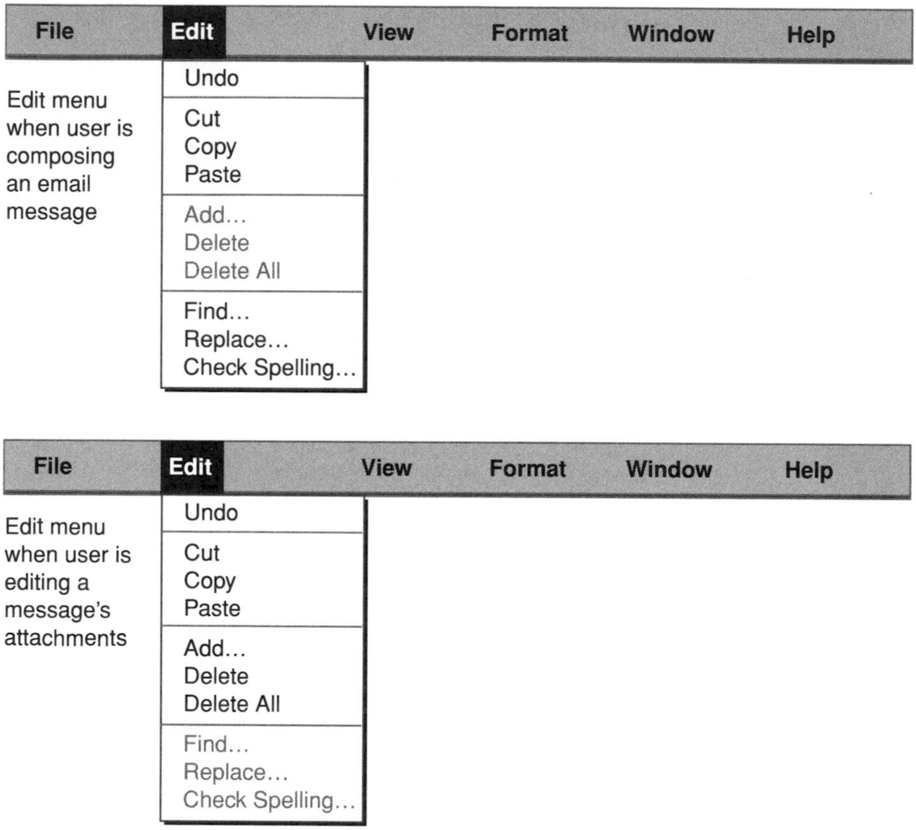

File	**Edit**	View	Format	Window	Help

Edit menu when user is composing an email message

Undo

Cut
Copy
Paste

Add...
Delete
Delete All

Find...
Replace...
Check Spelling...

File	**Edit**	View	Format	Window	Help

Edit menu when user is editing a message's attachments

Undo

Cut
Copy
Paste

Add...
Delete
Delete All

Find...
Replace...
Check Spelling...

tion's state. To reduce menu complexity, deactivate (i.e., gray out) inapplicable commands, rather than removing them (see Figure 2.3).

It is also OK for an application to add and remove entire menubar menus as the user moves from one context to another. For example, if a user opens a specific function window, perhaps that window has commands that are not needed anywhere else. When that window opens, it can add its own menus of commands to the menubar. As described above, this is the approach that should be used in applications that support plug-ins or compound documents.

One problem with adding and removing only entire menus at a time is that it requires designers to think harder about what goes into what menu. The menus must be chosen and designed very carefully to avoid anomalies such as multiple similarly named menus, or menus with only one item in them.

One way to avoid the need to add and remove menus is for plug-ins and implementations for "foreign" datatypes in compound documents to rely on generic commands. This allows commands already in the application's regular menus (such as Create, Move, Copy, Delete) to be applicable to the currently selected object. A variation is for the precise meaning of a command in a particular menu to change depending on the selection. For example, when the selection is changed from one datatype to another, a Delete command on a menu could be changed to point to the new datatype's Delete method, rather than the old one's. From the users' point of view, the menu is stable, but from the software's point of view, one type-specific command has been replaced by another.[1]

The foregoing does *not* mean that applications cannot add *any* items to menubar menus as the program runs. Many GUI applications include in their menus lists providing quick access to recently edited files, currently opened but possibly obscured windows, and bookmarked documents. Such lists are by definition dynamic: they change over time. As long as the changes in the menubar menus are restricted to these data lists, the designer has not violated the design rule.

The likelihood of making this and many other sorts of design errors is greatly reduced by a commitment to design from the users' point of view—to think outside-in. When designers think outside-in and then check their designs by testing them, they do not make this mistake.

2.1.2 Blooper 2: Duplicate menu items

Sometimes GUI designers put a command into more than one menubar menu. Figure 2.4 shows a menubar containing duplicated commands.

Sometimes the reason is that the developers couldn't decide which menu to put a particular command into, so they put it into multiple menus. Alternatively, a developer who does this may believe that having a command in multiple menus increases the chance that users will find it. While the latter justification contains a grain of truth, putting a command in multiple menus also has an adverse side effect: users see the duplicated commands and either wonder if they are different or—worse—assume that they are.

Figure 2.4

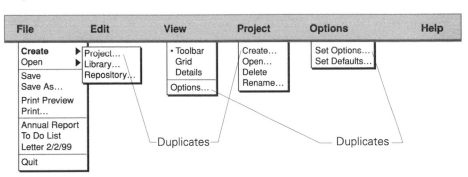

---

1. Some object-oriented systems have compile-time method binding, so the application actually has to remove one Delete command from the menu and replace it with another Delete command (or at least replace the method associated with the command). Other object-oriented systems have run-time method binding, so the application can leave the Delete command alone, and the command, when invoked, will send a "delete" message to the current object, which does the right thing with it.

Corresponding Web design problem

Although Web sites and Web applications rarely make use of menubar menus, they often exhibit an analogous blooper: many links to the same place, all labeled differently. It is very common to see Web pages containing three, four, or more links to the same other page: a link from a part of an image, a link from a navigation bar, a plain-text link at the bottom of the page, a link on a word in a text paragraph, and so on.

Sometimes Web developers do this out of a sincere belief that providing more links to a page will help users find the page and the information it provides. Perhaps they weren't sure where the link would be most noticeable, so they put it in several places. Perhaps they thought that different users would have different expectations about where to find links. They may believe, wrongly, that users pay close attention to the link destination indicator at the bottom of the browser window.

However, users judge the complexity of a Web site by how many links are on each page. They start with the sensible assumption that each link goes to a different page. Providing many different links to the same pages—especially if the links are labeled differently—needlessly inflates the site's apparent size and complexity, which is the opposite of what a designer should be trying to do. A designer's goal should be for users to consider the Web site to be simple and easy to find one's way around in. Why make the site seem larger or more complicated than it is?

The only nonharmful use of duplicate links is to provide textual versions of all important links on the page so that people who use text-only browsers can use the Web site. Providing such links is a widespread, strong convention on the Web and is now recognized by most Web users—even those who use graphical browsers. Even the position and format of textual links—the bottom or top edge of each page, centered—is fairly standard and well known, as can be seen in the three sets of textual links in Figure 2.5, from the Web sites *www.ACM.org/SIGCHI,* *www.eStats.com,* and *www.Stanford.edu,* respectively, which were displayed at the bottom of their respective Web pages. Therefore, when users see arrays of textual links at the bottom or top of a Web page, they don't assume they point to unique pages; they know they are duplicates of other links on the page.

Figure 2.5

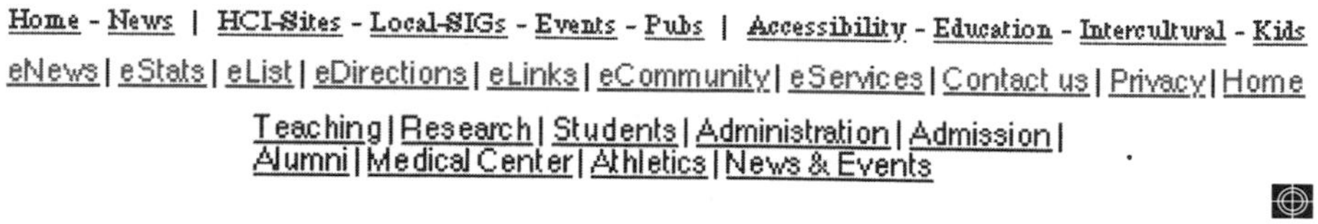

Home - News | HCI-Sites - Local-SIGs - Events - Pubs | Accessibility - Education - Intercultural - Kids

eNews | eStats | eList | eDirections | eLinks | eCommunity | eServices | Contact us | Privacy | Home

Teaching | Research | Students | Administration | Admission |
Alumni | Medical Center | Athletics | News & Events

An even more blatant mistake is when designers put the same command onto different menus, but label it differently. For example, an application might have a Create Project command on the File menu and a Create command on the Project menu.

I once reviewed a software product in which many commands were duplicated, with different names, on the Action, Edit, View, and Tools menus. In the list shown below, each duplicated menu item is identified by a menu name, a colon (:), and the command name.

```
Action: Shrink View            = View: Shrink
Action: Enlarge View           = View: Enlarge
Edit: Tables                   = Action: Table Properties
Edit: Models                   = Action: Properties (if selection is model)
Edit: Tasks                    = Action: Task Edit
Tools: Save Fields Definition  = Action: Save Table Fields
```

Another software application I reviewed contained the following duplicate pairs of menu items:

```
File: New                      = Tool: Create
File: Open Library             = Tool: Library
```

Duplicate menubar menu items is a pretty common blooper. It's fairly serious because users almost always assume that differently labeled commands invoke different functions.

Another problem with putting the same command on multiple menus is that it misleads users into believing that the application is more complex than it really is. Users who are new to a GUI application almost always scan the menus quickly to see what is in them, thereby getting a general impression of what the software can do, without paying close attention to details. They gauge the complexity of the application from the number of menus and commands in them. Duplicating commands adds to the software's apparent "bulk."

Avoiding Blooper 2: The design rule

Each command provided by a software application should appear only once in its menubar menus. The only duplication should be between the menubar menus, a toolbar, and right-button popup menus; frequently needed menu commands can be put onto a toolbar or a right-button popup menu for easy access.

During development, fine, but get rid of duplicates before shipping

During design and development, it is OK—perhaps even recommended—to try out different locations for menu commands. For example, suppose it is unclear whether the menu item that allows users to edit an application's Option settings should be in:

DILBERT reprinted by permission of United Feature Syndicate, Inc.

- the Edit menu, since users edit the options,
- the View menu, since the options often pertain to controlling what information the application displays, or
- the Tools menu.

Designers who aren't sure where to put it should first consult the industry standard guideline for their target platform (discussed next). If the correct location for the command is still unclear, they should try—that is, test on representative users—all three locations, maybe in successive prerelease versions, or maybe all at once. But, before shipping the software, designers should decide on *one* location for each menu command.

Follow industry standards

Some commands are unique enough that placing them in the menubar menus might be tricky. However, most commands can be placed fairly easily if the designers clearly understand their function and follow industry standards for command placement.

For example, the leftmost menu in a window's menubar should be either File or the type of object to which the window corresponds. In that menu are the Load, Save, Save As ..., Import, Export, and Print commands. If the window is an application's main window, the last command in the leftmost menu is Exit, which terminates the application. If the window is not the application's main window, there should be no Exit command, but rather a Close command, which closes the window but does not terminate the application.

For details on industry standards for menubars and the placement of commands in them, see the following industry standard style guides:

- *The Windows Interface Guidelines for Software Design* [Microsoft, 1995], pages 65–66, 187, 219, and 220.
- *DSF/Motif Style Guide: Rev 1.2* [OSF, 1993], page 173.

- *Design Guide for Multiplatform Graphical User Interfaces* [McFarland and Dayton, 1995], pages 3-25–3-38.

2.1.3 Blooper 3: Hidden functions

Developers sometimes make the mistake of designing interactive software—including GUI software—such that some of the functions of the application are accessible only through key combinations, gestures, or context-sensitive pop-up menus. In other words, the application provides functions that are not displayed explicitly anywhere in the application, such as in a menu or on a button. To use such "hidden" functions, users must first know that they exist and how to invoke them. But users cannot learn that by using the software; they have to read it in a user manual or hear about it from other people who have used the software. Since self-guided exploration—"Hmmm...I wonder what *this* does"—is a common means of learning to use computer software, committing this blooper hinders learning by depriving users of an important way in which they learn.

For example, a design might

- allow users to drag and drop items between two scrolling lists, but not provide a visible button for transferring selected items between lists (see Figure 2.6)
- require users to delete selected data items by typing COMMAND-D or CTRL-X, without providing a visible Delete button or recognizing the keyboard's DELETE key

Figure 2.6

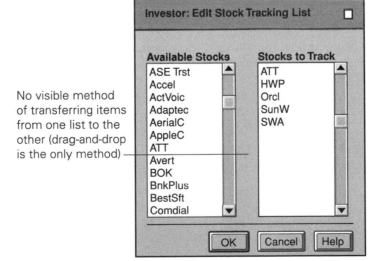

No visible method of transferring items from one list to the other (drag-and-drop is the only method)

- provide an Add Item command on a menu that appears when the user clicks the right mouse button, but fail to provide equivalent commands in the application's menubar menus

One reason that programmers sometimes hide functionality is that they design software to resemble software that they know and use. For example, *emacs* and *vi* are two popular text editors—designed by programmers for programmers—that have user interfaces that are controlled by combinations of keyboard keys. However, *emacs, vi,* and many other programming tools are vestiges of bygone days—the B.G. (Before Graphics) era of interactive computing. The style of user interface they represent was necessary when computer screens were limited to text characters. Now that almost every PC, terminal, workstation, and appliance display is capable of displaying high-resolution graphics, user interfaces based only on key combinations and other hidden command invocation methods are unnecessarily cryptic.

Another common excuse for hiding functionality is a lack of space. Obviously, visible methods of invoking functionality take up screen space. Hidden methods—invoked via key combinations, right mouse button menus, and the like—do not take up screen space. On the other hand, hidden controls must be explicitly taught and then remembered, whereas visible controls notify and constantly remind users of their existence. Design usually involves trade-offs. In this case, the trade-off is between saved screen space and ease of learning and retention. In my opinion, software developers too often sacrifice ease of learning and retention for too little savings in screen space. It would take a *very large* savings in screen space to sway me toward making the control of a particular software function totally invisible.

A third reason for hiding functionality is a belief that hidden methods of invoking functions, such as right-click popup menus, key combinations, and drag-and-drop, are faster to operate than on-screen buttons or commands on pulldown menus. That belief may be true in some cases, or it may not be, but in any case, it is irrelevant. Invisible user interfaces per se are not a problem for users. In fact, providing certain kinds of invisible user interfaces, such as keyboard accelerators for menu commands, is highly recommended (see Blooper 4: No keyboard equivalents, Section 2.1.4). What *does* cause problems for users is when a software program provides some of its functionality *only* through invisible user interfaces.

Avoiding Blooper 3: The design rule

An important principle of GUI design is that application functionality should be accessible by seeing and pointing, rather than by remembering and typing [Johnson et al., 1989]. Good GUI design requires that a visible means should be provided to invoke all commands. In Figure 2.7, Add and Delete buttons provide a visible means of adding items to and deleting items from the list on the right, even though drag-and-drop might also work.

Figure 2.7

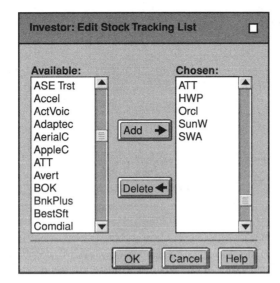

Hidden UIs are OK...as long as they aren't the only way

This is not to say that one shouldn't put functionality in context-sensitive right mouse button popup menus, function key combinations, drag-and-drop, and other hidden user interfaces, just that that should not be the *only* way in which a function can be invoked. Users should be able to figure out an application or a Web site purely by inspection and trial and error. If by reading the manual or talking with colleagues they can learn other, perhaps faster, ways of operating the application, fine, but the application should not be designed so as to depend on that.

Less visible methods of operating an application—such as keyboard accelerators, right mouse button popup menus, and drag-and-drop—can be provided, but they should always be secondary methods, with more visible methods (e.g., menubar menus, buttons, option menus) being primary. Furthermore, if they are used, nonvisible user interfaces should be used very consistently within a software application, so users will be able to predict where they will be. Inconsistent use of nonvisible user interfaces makes a software application unpredictable, arbitrary, and difficult to learn and remember.

Making UIs visible versus providing progressive disclosure: A contradiction?

Requiring that software always provide visible UIs for functionality may initially seem to contradict another GUI design technique recommended in this book: progressive disclosure (see Blooper 46: Overwhelming users with decisions and detail, Section 5.2.1). Providing progressive disclosure means hiding less important functionality or detail until it is needed, such as hiding extra controls behind a panel.

In fact, there is no contradiction. If progressive disclosure is done correctly, the *access route* to the "hidden" functionality is visible. For example, although a menubar command is not visible until the user displays the menu, the route to the command is clearly visible: the name of the menu containing the command.

2.1.4 Blooper 4: No keyboard equivalents

Graphical user interfaces are designed to be operated primarily by pointing at, clicking on, and dragging objects on the screen using a pointing device such as a mouse, trackball, or touchpad. However, most GUI-based applications require the use of the keyboard for text or data entry, which means that most users switch back and forth between the keyboard and the pointing device. For a variety of reasons, some people prefer to keep their hands on the keyboard and not use a pointing device. Some such reasons are

- *To avoid switching.* Some people simply find switching between the keyboard and the pointing device to be disruptive and too much of a bother.

- *Still use pre-GUI software.* Some users still use older tools that were designed for pre-GUI text character displays. Many programmers, for example, still use the text editors *emacs* and *vi* to write program code, even though these text editors were written in the 1970s for use on character terminals connected to time-shared computers and still reflect their origins.

- *To save time.* In the time it takes to remove a hand from the keyboard, grasp the mouse, move the mouse to an on-screen control component (e.g., a menu or a button), and return to the keyboard, most users can execute several commands from the keyboard if they can remember the required keys. Sometime situations favor keyboard methods over pointing methods (e.g., several successive commands are to be executed on the selected data object).

- *Can't operate a mouse.* Some users cannot use a mouse or other pointing device. Maybe they have to work in a vehicle that bounces and shakes so much they can't be accurate with a pointing device. Perhaps they have a temporary injury—such as wrist tendonitis—or a permanent physical disability. In addition, there are people who, while not physically disabled in any obvious sense, are unable to coordinate the movement of a mouse (or trackball or touchpad) on the desk with the movement of the pointer on the screen, and thus simply cannot use a pointing device effectively.

- *Don't have a mouse.* Most personal computers sold since the late 1980s have a pointing device. However, sometimes pointing devices break. Sometimes the software that translates the movements of the pointing device into

Figure 2.8

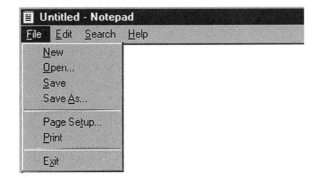

pointer movements on the screen is missing or not set up correctly. Users should still be able to operate their computers in such situations.

- *Can't see.* Using a pointing device is a hand-eye coordination task, so point ing devices—and graphical user interfaces in general—are useless to blind people.

Despite all of the above quite legitimate reasons for not using a pointing device, many software applications cannot be operated without one. In some software, menubar commands or controls in dialog boxes don't have keyboard equivalents. In other software, control panels don't allow users to switch between controls by "tabbing," that is, by pressing the TAB key to shift the input focus from one control to another.

For instance, the partial screen image in Figure 2.8 is from Microsoft's Notepad accessory. Notice that the commands in Notepad's File menu don't have the usual keyboard equivalents. In most applications and accessories for the Windows platform (including most Microsoft products), commands in the File menu have the following keyboard equivalents: New = CTRL N, Open = CTRL-O, Save = CTRL-S, and Print = CTRL-P.

Such omissions may occur because the programmers had to develop the software quickly and didn't have time to arrange for keyboard control or to decide how to assign keys to functions. Alternatively, a lack of time may not have been the issue: perhaps the developers simply didn't consider keyboard equivalents to be required. Whatever the reason for omitting keyboard equivalents, doing so is a design blooper because it severely reduces usability for many people.

Avoiding Blooper 4: *The design rule*

GUIs should provide keyboard equivalent means of invoking or controlling all functions. This accommodates users who prefer to do everything from the keyboard. It also allows users to operate the application even if the mouse is broken or if the user cannot operate a pointing device because of an injury, handicap, or a bouncy work environment.[2]

There are two types of keyboard equivalents: keyboard *mnemonics* and keyboard *accelerators* (*access* keys and *shortcut* keys in Microsoft Windows terminology). Every menu and every menu command should have a keyboard mnemonic—a way to invoke it from the keyboard. Keyboard accelerators are fast ways to invoke frequently used functions. They need not be provided for all functions.

Keyboard mnemonics

For keyboard mnemonics, there are well-established industry conventions. Here are some of them:

- Every menubar menu and menu item should have an assigned mnemonic—a letter key on the keyboard that triggers that menu item. On Windows, controls in dialog boxes (buttons, checkboxes, text and number fields) should also have mnemonics (i.e., access keys).
- Mnemonics are indicated by underlining the character.
- Mnemonics for menu names and for right mouse button menu items should be unique across the entire application. Mnemonics for menu items (except right button menu items) and dialog boxes must be unique within their immediate context, for example, in the menu or the dialog box.
- *The Windows Interface Guidelines for Software Design* defines a set of preferred mnemonics (access keys) for about 100 standard controls. Those should be used for Windows applications whenever possible [Microsoft, 1995].
- If the mnemonic for a particular control is not predefined, use the following guidelines, in order of preference:
  1. The first character of the item's label.
  2. The first character of another word in the item's label.
  3. A clearly pronounced consonant in the command (don't use silent letters, and consonants at the beginning of the command name are better than those near the end).
  4. Start from the beginning of the item's label, examine each character in succession, and use the first character that is unique from all other items in this item's context.
- If a function is available in multiple places in an application, the mnemonic used to invoke it should be the same everywhere.
- If a menu item or property label changes depending on the state of the control (e.g., a button that alternates between "Hide Details" and "Show

---

2. Due to equal access laws and regulations, provision of keyboard equivalent means to operate software is sometimes a contractual or legal requirement.

The 5th Wave   **By Rich Tennant**

"...AND TO ACCESS THE PROGRAMS 'HOT KEY', YOU JUST DEPRESS THESE ELEVEN KEYS SIMULTANEOUSLY. HERB OVER THERE HAS A KNACK FOR DOING THIS THAT I THINK YOU'LL ENJOY— HERB! GOT A MINUTE?"

© The 5th Wave by Rich Tennant, Rockport, MA. Email: the5wave@tiac.net.

Details"), use the same mnemonic for both items, so the user doesn't have to know what state the control is in before selecting an access key (in this case, *D* would be best).

- Mnemonics are case insensitive: the same mnemonic should be recognized whether a user types *d* or *D*.

Keyboard accelerators

Keyboard accelerators are not yet as standardized as are keyboard mnemonics. However, some conventions have emerged. For example, the following assignments of keys to functions are pretty standard (on the Macintosh, substitute COMMAND for CTRL):

- CTRL-X: Cut
- CTRL-C: Copy
- CTRL-V: Paste
- CTRL-S: Save
- CTRL-A: Select all
- CTRL-W: Close
- CTRL-F: Find
- CTRL-Z: Undo

For a summary of the conventions for several industry standard GUI platforms, see the *Design Guide for Multiplatform Graphical User Interfaces* [McFarland and Dayton, 1995], pages 5-78–5-84. When guidelines for keyboard accelerators are lacking, the guidelines for keyboard mnemonics (see above) can be applied, coupled with common sense as interpreted by a trained user interface designer. And, of course, when in doubt, test it on users.

2.2 Unconventional application windows

Next we have three bloopers that result from developers not knowing the conventions for application windows.

2.2.1 Blooper 5: Confusing primary windows with dialog boxes

Most GUI-based software applications consist of a main window, possibly some other primary windows, and several dialog boxes. A common blooper is GUI programs that blur the distinction between primary windows and dialog boxes.

Primary windows and dialog boxes have distinct functions and different appearances. Mixing up the two types of windows confuses users and impedes their learning of the software. Software developers tend to confuse primary windows and dialog boxes in three different ways.

Variation A: Main window is a dialog box. The most common mistake is to design an application window that looks like a dialog box: no menubar, controls in the body, control buttons at the bottom, as in Figure 2.9.

Figure 2.9

Figure 2.10

Variation B: Hybrid windows. The next most common mistake is to design a window that has aspects of both, such as a menubar at the top and control buttons at the bottom, an example of which is shown in Figure 2.10.

Variation C: Dialog boxes that are minimizable. A third way to confuse primary windows and dialog boxes is for an application to include dialog boxes that can be "minimized" or reduced to desktop icons or taskbar buttons. Desktop icons and taskbar buttons are supposed to represent either user data files or software applications. Primary windows usually represent one or the other of these (and sometimes both), but dialog boxes represent neither. Therefore, a dialog box that can be minimized to the taskbar or a desktop icon is an error.

Avoiding Blooper 5: *The design rule*

Primary windows and dialog boxes have different roles. Primary windows represent either software applications (for example, Netscape Navigator) or specific user data objects viewed using an associated application (for example, my checking account viewed using Quicken). They tend to remain displayed for relatively long periods of time. In contrast, dialog boxes are almost always transient information displays or control panels. They can represent messages that the software wants the user to see (for example, "Printer Tiger3 is out of paper"). They can represent a function that needs to collect additional data before it can operate (for example, "Save As ..."). Finally, they can represent the properties of a particular (selected) object (for example, the paragraph properties of the currently selected paragraph).

Because primary windows and dialog boxes are each designed to serve their respective roles, it is a mistake to use either type of window for the other type's role. For example, it is wrong to use a primary window for a transient information display such as an error message. Likewise, it is wrong to use a dialog box to represent an application.

A primary window

- can be minimized to a desktop icon or taskbar button
- remains displayed unless explicitly closed or minimized
- is likely to remain displayed for an extended time (to do multiple operations or to keep program data in view)
- is never modal; that is, it does not block input to other windows, whether in this application or another
- has a menubar containing the application's commands, categorized
- has a Help menu as the rightmost menu on the menubar
- optionally has a toolbar containing buttons representing a subset of the commands from the menubar menus—either those that are frequently used or ones the user has placed there
- has a full set of window decorations, including minimize, maximize, and resize
- has a Close command (if it is not the application's main window) or an Exit command (if it is the main window) at the bottom of the leftmost menu
- has no window control buttons along the bottom or right edge

In contrast, a dialog box

- is never minimizable to a desktop icon or taskbar button
- disappears when its parent window is closed or minimized, and reappears when its parent window is unminimized
- is usually displayed only temporarily, for example, to set arguments of a pending command or to view or alter properties of an object
- can be modal, although this should be fairly rare
- is usually temporary; that is, it is displayed only to support a specific operation and is dismissed thereafter
- is often not resizable, although it can be if it contains a scrolling list or other component with a resizable viewport
- has a row of window control buttons along the bottom, or, less commonly, along the right edge

Table 2.1   Primary windows versus dialog boxes

Window feature	Primary window	Dialog box
Display duration	Usually long	Usually short
Modal	No	If needed
Menubar	Yes	No
Toolbar	If needed	No
Help provided	Rightmost menubar menu	Help button (optional)
Window control buttons	No	Bottom or right edge
Resizable	Yes	Usually not
Minimizable	Yes	No
Maximizable (to full screen)	Yes	No
Window close function	If main: Exit cmd in File menu	OK (or function specific), Close, Cancel buttons
	If not main: Close cmd in leftmost menu	
Titlebar	App: function - data	App: function

- has a Close or Cancel button as one of the action buttons
- if it offers online help, does so via a Help button that is the rightmost action button
- has no menubar or button toolbar

Table 2.1 summarizes the differences between primary windows and dialog boxes. Figure 2.11 illustrates their proper use. For more details on the differences between primary windows and dialog boxes (which many GUI guidelines refer to as "secondary windows"), see the industry standard style guides for the various GUI platforms: Windows [Microsoft, 1995], MacOS [Apple, 1993], CDE/Motif [OSF, 1993], and Java [Sun, 1999]. All the style guides say pretty much the same thing about the different types of windows an application can display.

Here is what *Java Look and Feel Guidelines* [Sun, 1999, p. 93] says:

> A *primary* window is a window in which users' main interaction with the data or document takes place. An application can use any number of primary windows, which can be opened, closed, minimized, or resized independently.
>
> A *secondary* window [aka dialog box] is a supportive window that is dependent on a primary window (or on another secondary window). In the secondary window, users can view and provide additional information about actions or objects in a primary window.

Figure 2.11

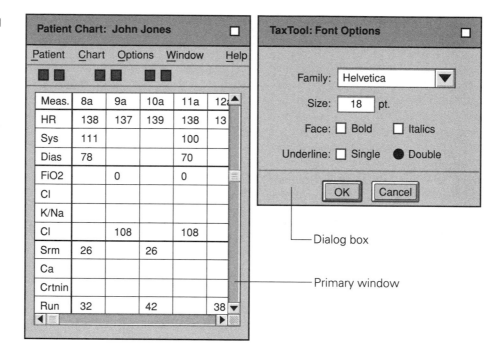

Dialog box

Primary window

A *utility* window is a window whose contents affect an active primary window. Unlike secondary windows, utility windows remain open when primary windows are closed or minimized. An example of a utility window is a tool palette that is used to select a graphic tool.

A *plain* window is a window with no title bar or window controls, typically used for splash screens.

2.2.2 Blooper 6: Commands are only on toolbar buttons

An application's main window and function-specific primary windows normally each include a menubar containing most of the application's commands, and an optional toolbar containing buttons representing the application's most frequently used commands.

A frequent mistake made by software developers lacking in user interface design experience is to provide some or all of an application's commands only as buttons on a toolbar. Three different variations of this blooper can be found among GUI-based software applications:

- The menubar menus contain only a subset of the commands that are on the toolbar, rather than the other way around.

- The menubar and toolbar contain different sets of commands, perhaps overlapping, perhaps not.

Figure 2.12

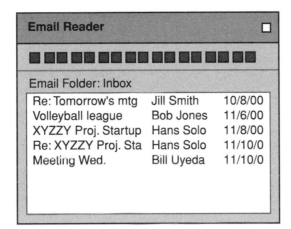

- The application has no menubar at all—only a toolbar, as shown in Figure 2.12.
- All three variations are examples of misusing toolbars and misunderstanding the proper relationship between toolbars and menubar menus. Such designs violate users' expectations and thereby impede learning.

A menubar makes the organization of—and relationships between—an application's commands much clearer than a toolbar can because it is an explicit hierarchy in which each top-level menu represents a category of related commands. In contrast, a toolbar is a relatively flat collection of buttons, at best physically spaced to show related groups of functions, but without labels for the categories.

Also, menubar menus can show the keyboard-based methods of invoking each command, thereby providing a natural way for users to learn them. Toolbar buttons provide no information about keyboard equivalents for commands.

Finally, some users simply prefer menus to toolbars. For them, commands that are provided only on the toolbar are *less*—not more—available.

Another possible negative consequence of committing this blooper is that the buttons on the toolbar are a mix of frequently used and infrequently used ones. Such designs overburden the toolbar, filling it so full of function buttons that its value in providing quick access to application functions becomes questionable (see Blooper 7: All menubar commands are on toolbar, Section 2.2.3).

Avoiding Blooper 6: The design rule

Primary windows should always include a menubar. The menubar should contain all of the application's top-level commands, organized into categories. Each menubar command should also provide a keyboard-only method of invoking it.

Figure 2.13

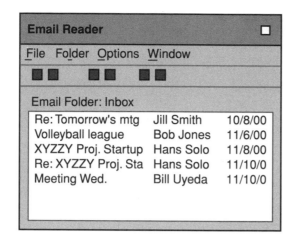

A toolbar is optional. If provided, a toolbar contains commands that users will use frequently, as is shown in Figure 2.13. In most cases, the designers predict (or learn from prerelease user testing) which commands will be used most frequently and place those on the toolbar. Ideally, users should be able to customize the toolbar to add or remove commands as their work dictates. For more details, see the design rules for Blooper 5: Confusing primary windows with dialog boxes (Section 2.2.1) and Blooper 7: All menubar commands are on toolbar (Section 2.2.3).

2.2.3 Blooper 7: All menubar commands are on toolbar

As explained in the discussion of Blooper 6: Commands are only on toolbar buttons (Section 2.2.2), main windows and primary windows of GUI applications normally include menubars containing all of the top-level commands and may also include a toolbar containing buttons representing frequently used commands.

Sometimes programmers make the mistake of duplicating on the toolbar *every* command that is in the application's menubar menus, as shown in Figure 2.14. Most applications have dozens of commands or more, so committing this blooper often results in a toolbar that is packed with buttons. This has two strong negative consequences:

1. It makes it difficult for users to distinguish command buttons from each other, especially since buttonbar buttons are normally labeled graphically. It places a heavy burden on the application's graphic designer to design button icons that are easy to distinguish from each other, but it is very difficult to achieve this goal because graphical button labels are usually limited to a size of only 16 × 16 pixels.

Figure 2.14

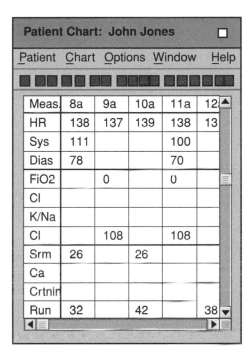

Meas.	8a	9a	10a	11a	12
HR	138	137	139	138	13
Sys	111			100	
Dias	78			70	
FiO2		0		0	
Cl					
K/Na					
Cl		108		108	
Srm	26		26		
Ca					
Crtnir					
Run	32		42		38

Patient Chart: John Jones

Patient   Chart   Options   Window   Help

2. A tightly packed toolbar requires that users move more carefully—and hence more slowly—when reaching for a button, to make sure they hit the right one.

Avoiding Blooper 7: The design rule

If an application has a toolbar, it should contain only those commands that users will use frequently. As shown in Figure 2.15, the toolbar will be much less crowded, which makes the heavily used functions that are on it easier to access.

In most cases, the designers predict (or learn from prerelease user testing) which commands will be used most frequently and place those on the toolbar. Ideally, users should be able to customize the toolbar to add or remove commands as their work dictates.

Two commands that should never be included on the toolbar are Exit (terminate the application) and Close (close this window of the application). Why? First, because neither function is invoked many times during the period that the corresponding primary window is open. In fact, by definition, they are invoked only once. Second, because putting them on the toolbar would be redundant; quick access to Exit or Close is—or should be—already provided on the window titlebar provided by the window manager (e.g., MacOS, Windows, Unix Common Desktop Environment).

Figure 2.15

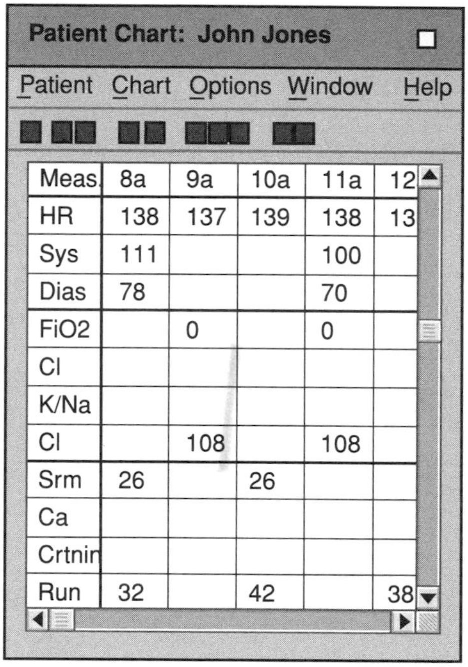

Meas.	8a	9a	10a	11a	12
HR	138	137	139	138	13
Sys	111			100	
Dias	78			70	
FiO2		0		0	
Cl					
K/Na					
Cl		108		108	
Srm	26		26		
Ca					
Crtnin					
Run	32		42		38

Patient Chart: John Jones

Patient Chart Options Window Help

2.3 Misusing choice controls and tabs

The next six bloopers are misuses of controls that present choices to users, such as radiobuttons and tabbed panels.

2.3.1 Blooper 8: Confusing checkboxes and radiobuttons

All GUI toolkits provide controls for choosing one value from a set of *N* possible values, for example, *Text Font:* {*Times, Helvetica, Courier, New York*}. One type of one-from-*N* control is called "radiobuttons." Radiobuttons display the possible values of the setting as an array of buttons. Users choose a value by clicking on one of the buttons. The chosen value is highlighted. The set of radiobuttons is connected such that only one can be selected at a time. This type of control is called "radiobuttons" because it behaves similarly to the buttons on automobile radios that allow riders to set the radio to one of a preselected set of favorite stations. Interestingly, radiobuttons in GUI toolkits are seldom designed to look like automobile radiobuttons.[3] They usually consist of a set of round dots, each

---

3. In the Xerox Star, the first commercially available GUI-based software system, radiobuttons actually did look like radiobuttons in automobile radios.

Figure 2.16

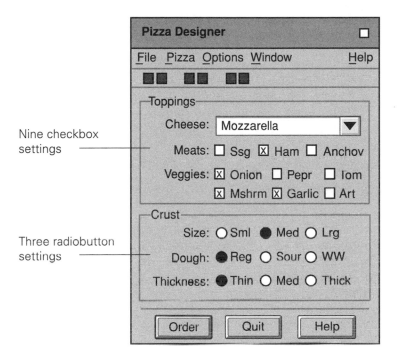

Nine checkbox settings ——

Three radiobutton settings ——

with a label indicating that button's value, and one of which is marked as the setting's current value. A typical application primary window containing both checkboxes and radiobuttons is illustrated in Figure 2.16.

Most GUI toolkits treat each individual radiobutton in a one-from-*N* setting as a separate component, requiring programmers to "wire" radiobuttons together so that they highlight in a mutually exclusive manner. A few GUI toolkits treat the entire control (i.e., entire set of radiobuttons) as one component, prewired to be mutually exclusive.

GUI toolkits also provide controls for simple ON/OFF, TRUE/FALSE, or YES/NO settings, for example, *Automatic spell-checking:* {*OFF, ON*}. One such control is called a *checkbox* because that is what it looks like: a box that is empty when OFF and contains a check mark or *X* when ON. Each checkbox is a separate component. Related checkboxes may be placed near each other, but each checkbox can be set ON or OFF independent of the others.

A common blooper in graphical user interfaces is to confuse radiobuttons and checkboxes. Often this is due to the unfortunate fact that some GUI toolkits implement radiobuttons and checkboxes as variants of a single component type—*togglebutton*—based on their somewhat similar appearance. The generic togglebutton component is specialized to be a radiobutton or a checkbox by setting its attributes. Not surprisingly, many GUI programmers either fail to set the attribute or set it incorrectly, and so end up with the wrong type of control. However, the fault does not lie completely with GUI toolkits; programmers

Figure 2.17

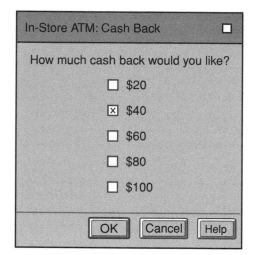

often confuse radiobuttons and checkboxes even when they are using toolkits that treat the two as distinct types. Whatever the reasons, confusion between radiobuttons and checkboxes manifests itself in several different ways.

Variation A: Mutually exclusive checkboxes. One variation of this blooper is to "wire" a group of checkboxes together so that only one can be ON at a time, that is, to make them mutually exclusive. This is misusing checkboxes as if they were radiobuttons. Figure 2.17 shows an example of this variation of the blooper.

Sometimes this error occurs because the GUI toolkit treats radiobuttons and checkboxes as variants of a generic togglebutton component type, the default appearance of which is usually a checkbox. With such a toolkit, a programmer could easily forget to set the relevant attribute to make the togglebuttons appear as radiobuttons, or vice versa.

Sometimes this error occurs because the programmer took a group of formerly independent ON/OFF settings and made them mutually exclusive to accommodate a change in the software's functional requirements, but for some reason (e.g., lack of time, ignorance, carelessness) neglected to change the checkbox components into radiobuttons. Note that this second reason is more likely if the GUI toolkit treats radiobuttons and checkboxes as distinct component types; the programmer has to replace the components rather than just changing their attributes.

A programmer might also commit this error for more "semantic" reasons. He or she may think of the choices as independent ON/OFF settings, but an implementation limitation requires that only one of the settings be ON at once. For example, a display of a patient's medical chart might be capable of showing several different categories of data, but the display can only fit one category at a

Figure 2.18

```
┌Effects──────────────────────────┐
│ □ Strikethrough   □ Hidden      │
│ □ Superscript     □ Small Caps  │
│ □ Subscript       □ All Caps    │
│ □ Shadow          □ Outline     │
└─────────────────────────────────┘
```

time. The programmer therefore assumes that the best way to present this choice is as checkboxes—one for each of category of data—that are wired together so that turning one ON turns others OFF. With a bigger display, it might be feasible to disconnect the checkboxes from each other.

Microsoft Word 6.0 contains an example of checkboxes that should be radiobuttons. In Figure 2.18, excerpted from Word's Font dialog box, some of the checkboxes function properly, while others function like radiobuttons. The Superscript and Subscript checkboxes are really a single setting: only one of them can be checked at a time; checking one unchecks the other. The same is true of the Small Caps and All Caps pair of checkboxes.

Without talking with the designers of this panel, we can only speculate on why they designed it so as to violate standard checkbox behavior. I see two possible reasons:

1. The Superscript/Subscript setting really has three values: superscript, subscript, and neither. Such a setting cannot be represented by a pair of radiobuttons because in a radiobutton setting, one radiobutton must always be ON (see Blooper 9: One-from-*N* settings with no initial value, Section 2.3.2). Therefore, *three* radiobuttons would be required to represent the three possible values accurately. The designers may therefore have used checkboxes to avoid having to use three radiobuttons. The same applies to the Small Caps/All Caps setting. The problem with this reasoning is that a pair of checkboxes doesn't accurately represent three possible values either. Since checkboxes are expected to be independent of each other, a pair of checkboxes is seen by users as representing *four* possible values. In the case of the Superscript/Subscript setting, the four values would be superscript, subscript, neither, and both. Using checkboxes to avoid an awkward set of radiobuttons is simply replacing one design problem with another.

2. The designers placed more importance on visual appearance than on functional correctness. It simply *looked* better for all the Effects settings to be checkboxes than it did if the group box contained a mixture of radiobuttons and checkboxes. This is what we might expect if the designers were graphic designers who tend to worry more about appearance than function, rather than user interface designers, who tend to worry more about function.

Whatever the reason for "wiring" checkboxes together into mutually exclusive groups, it is a design error.

Figure 2.19

Color: O Red

Variation B: One radiobutton. A second variation of this blooper is for a control to consist of a single radiobutton (see Figure 2.19). This is misusing radio-buttons as if they were checkboxes.

It may seem unlikely that anyone would make this error, but I have seen it enough times that I classify it as common. For example, an email program offered by a major computer company I used to work for exhibited this error for years, despite my repeated reminders that it should be corrected.

This error can occur if the GUI toolkit provides a generic togglebutton and the programmer sets its attributes incorrectly. However, the default appearance of generic togglebuttons is usually a checkbox, so it is unlikely that the error would occur for this reason. On the other hand, if a particular GUI toolkit provides a generic togglebutton and its default appearance is a radiobutton, programs built using it would be more likely to contain lone radiobuttons.

More commonly, this error occurs because a programmer simply does not understand the difference between radiobuttons and checkboxes and so uses the wrong component.

Finally, this error can occur if some of the possible values of a set of radio-buttons are eliminated due to a change in functional requirements for the software. Suppose only one value remains, but no one on the development team notices.

Whatever the reason, a single radiobutton is a design error, plain and simple.

Variation C: Radiobuttons and checkboxes in menus look the same. A third variation of this error is for ON/OFF and one-from-N settings to be visually indistinguishable when placed in menus (see Figure 2.20).

Usually, this error in a software application is due to a deficiency in the GUI toolkit from which it was constructed. Many GUI toolkits allow programmers to place radiobuttons and checkboxes into pulldown menus (i.e., the menus that are available on the menubar). In a menu, checkboxes and radiobuttons look like menu items, as one would expect. Unfortunately, some GUI toolkits do not

Figure 2.20

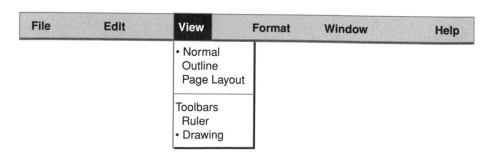

distinguish between radiobuttons and checkboxes that are placed in menus: they all appear as generic toggling menu items. This forces users to actually try the menu items to determine whether they are mutually exclusive or independent. That is poor design.

Avoiding Blooper 8: The design rule

I'll describe first the rule for using radiobuttons, then the rule for using checkboxes.

Radiobuttons

Radiobuttons are for one-from-N settings. They are best suited when two conditions hold:

1. The number of possible values is fixed and small, for example, between two and eight.
2. Sufficient space is available on the enclosing control panel to constantly display all of the setting's values.

Radiobuttons always occur in sets of at least two; a single radiobutton would not be a valid control. See Blooper 10: Using a checkbox for a non-ON/OFF setting (Section 2.3.3) for details on when to use a checkbox.

Other choice controls

Most GUI toolkits provide additional controls for presenting one-from-N settings. The situations for which each is best suited depend on the number of possible values in a setting and the space available for displaying the values. Radiobuttons require a lot of space because all of the values are constantly on display. Other controls for presenting one-from-N settings require less space.

- *Option menus*: These are also sometimes called "dropdown" menus. They display their current value and present a menu of possible values when released (see Figure 2.21). Option menus are distinct from "pulldown" menus, which are menus consisting mainly of commands (and occasionally some setting values) that are accessed from a menubar at the top of a screen or the top of a primary window (see Blooper 3: Hidden functions, Section 2.1.3).
- *Cycle buttons*: These are also known as "spin boxes." They display their current value and switch to their next available value when clicked on (see Figure 2.22). Cycle buttons are best suited for presenting one-from-N choices when space is at a premium and the number of possible values is small.
- *Scrolling listboxes*. These display a list of items and allow users to select one or more of them (see Figure 2.23). ⊕

Figure 2.21

Figure 2.22

Figure 2.23

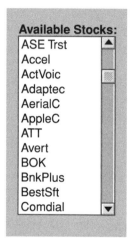

Checkboxes

Checkboxes can represent a single ON/OFF setting (Figure 2.24). The values of checkboxes should be independent of each other.

Checkboxes can be grouped to present a related set of independent ON/OFF settings (Figure 2.25).

Occasionally checkboxes are used in groups to present controls that allow users to select a limited subset of the available options (Figure 2.26). Such cases present a dilemma: values of checkboxes are supposed to be independent, yet the group of checkboxes should enforce a limit on how many of its items are checked. The solution to this should not be to turn OFF an already-checked item when a user turns ON an item that would exceed the maximum because that would violate the independence of the check-box items (in addition to seeming arbitrary: "Why did it turn that one OFF instead of another one?").

Instead, either of the following solutions are acceptable:

- Refuse to turn items ON that would exceed the maximum and notify users, for example, by beeping

- Allow users to turn any number of items ON, and inform the user at some later point that he or she has chosen more than the allowed number of

Figure 2.24

☒ Bold

Figure 2.25

Choose pizza toppings: ☐ Anchovies

☒ Mushrooms

☒ Onions

☒ Garlic

Figure 2.26

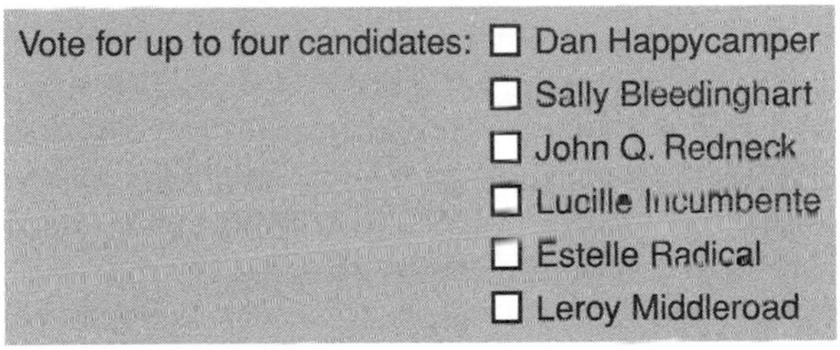

Vote for up to four candidates: ☐ Dan Happycamper

☐ Sally Bleedinghart

☐ John Q. Redneck

☐ Lucille Incumbente

☐ Estelle Radical

☐ Leroy Middleroad

items, for example, when the user clicks OK or Apply on the enclosing dialog box.

Radiobuttons and checkboxes in menus

When checkbox and radiobutton items appear in menus, they should be visibly different so users can tell by inspection (not just by trying them) whether a group of items in a menu comprise a single one-from-N setting or are independent ON/OFF settings. For example, checkbox items could be marked by check marks, while radiobutton items could be marked with bullets.

Groups of radiobutton items can also be separated from other items by separator menu items.

A comment about GUI toolkits

GUI toolkits that treat checkboxes and radiobuttons as variants of the same type of widget (e.g., togglebutton) are not as user friendly as those that treat them as distinct. By "user friendly," I mean both the programmer-users of the toolkit and the eventual users of applications programmers build using the toolkit. Such toolkits make it easy for programmers to display the wrong control in their applications, which, in turn, detracts from the usability of the application.

Furthermore, GUI toolkits that force programmers to construct one-from-N settings out of N radiobutton components should be considered inferior to those that treat mutually exclusive groups of radiobuttons as a single component. Finally, GUI toolkits in which different one-from-N choice components

have different application program interfaces (APIs) and therefore force programmers to choose between different components based on their appearance
should be considered inferior to those that regard a one-from-*N* setting as a single type of component that has several possible presentations [Johnson, 1992].
See Blooper 79: Using poor tools and building blocks (Section 8.2.1) for further
discussion of the value of using a flexible and versatile GUI toolkit to construct
applications.

2.3.2 Blooper 9: One-from-*N* settings with no initial value

A common blooper that I often see in GUIs designed by people who lack user
interface design experience is one-from-*N* choice settings with no initial value.

For example, I often see radiobutton settings that initially have none of the
radiobuttons selected, as shown in Figure 2.27. Often, this error is simply a bug:
the result of incorrect logic in the code that connects the radiobuttons and makes
them mutually exclusive. (Never mind that application programmers should
not have to write such code. Sets of radiobuttons are common enough that the
necessary logic to make the buttons mutually exclusive should be built in.)

However, sometimes programmers design radiobuttons like this intentionally; they think it is a good way to allow users not to specify a value. Alternatively, they prefer not to pick a setting for the user.

Unfortunately, radiobutton settings that start out with no value aren't a good
idea. It violates users' expectations about how a radiobutton choice should
operate. It also violates the logical type of a radiobutton set: a one-from-*N*
choice, not a zero-or-one-from-*N* choice.

Another manifestation of the blooper is option menus with no initial value,
as shown in Figure 2.28. Like radiobuttons, option menus are for representing
one-from-*N* choices. Starting them with a blank value is starting them with an
invalid value, unless one of the values available in the menu for users to choose
is blank.

Avoiding Blooper 9: *The design rule*

A connected set of radiobuttons is, from the users' point of view, a single setting that presents a one-from-*N* choice. Even more clearly, an option menu rep-

Figure 2.27

Cheese: ○ Mozzarella   ○ Jack   ○ Swiss

Figure 2.28

Format: [_____ ▼]

Figure 2.29

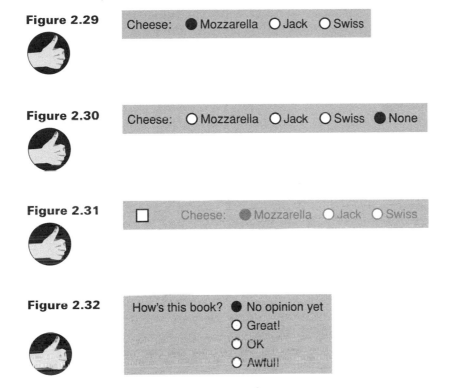

Cheese: ● Mozzarella ○ Jack ○ Swiss

Figure 2.30

Cheese: ○ Mozzarella ○ Jack ○ Swiss ● None

Figure 2.31

☐   Cheese: ● Mozzarella ○ Jack ○ Swiss

Figure 2.32

How's this book?   ● No opinion yet
                  ○ Great!
                  ○ OK
                  ○ Awful!

resents a one-from-N choice. Logically, such a setting represents a discrete variable that has N possible values. It should never be in a state of having no value. Some GUI toolkits embody this principle and therefore prevent such errors, always starting with an initial value as in Figure 2.29. Unfortunately, many GUI toolkits do not, especially those in which radiobutton settings are constructed of individual radiobutton components.

Following the previous example, if an application needs to allow users to indicate that they don't want any cheese on their pizza, then the radiobutton set should include a fourth explicit value: "None," as is shown in Figure 2.30.

Alternatively, the entire setting could have an associated checkbox that, when unchecked, deactivates the radiobutton choice (i.e., causes it to be displayed with a grayed-out appearance and not be responsive) and, when checked, activates it (see Figure 2.31). This design alternative would only be recommended in cases where this method of indicating "set" versus "not set" was used consistently throughout an application or suite of applications, so that users would learn what it meant.

Similarly, if a designer of an online questionnaire doesn't want to bias users' answers by picking one of the possible answers to each question as a default value, the designer should add an explicit "no opinion" value to each setting and make those the defaults, as shown in Figure 2.32.

2.3.3   Blooper 10: Using a checkbox for a non-ON/OFF setting

Sometimes you see software in which a programmer has inappropriately used a checkbox for a setting that is really a one-from-*N* choice where *N* just happens to be two. In Figure 2.33, the color setting has two possible values: red and green. The programmer used a checkbox because he or she thought that it would be an easy, space-saving way to implement a two-valued choice. The problem is that users can't tell from looking at the setting what *unchecking* the box would mean.

A more subtle example of this blooper was committed by a programmer at one of my client companies. The program he was developing gave users the option of having the program display its toolbar horizontally under the main window's menubar or vertically along the left side of the window. He presented the choice to users using the checkbox setting shown in Figure 2.34. By default, the program displayed a horizontal toolbar, so the checkbox was checked. The programmer assumed that users would realize that unchecking it would mean that the toolbar should be displayed vertically. Unlikely.

A programmer at another client company committed a similar blooper. The application he was developing could sort data either in ascending or descending order, as the user chose. The programmer presented the choice as a checkbox, as shown in Figure 2.35. This is a borderline case. Most users could probably figure out that unchecking the checkbox would mean that the data would be sorted in descending order, but as explained in Chapter 1, Principle 4 (Section 1.4), users should not have to deduce how software works by a process of elimination; it should be clear from the start.

More or less the same blooper can be seen in the screen image in Figure 2.36 from Sybase's PowerBuilder 5.0, an interactive GUI-building tool. Ironically,

Figure 2.33

Color: ☒ Red

Figure 2.34

☒ Horizontal Toolbar

Figure 2.35

Sort Order: ☒ Ascending

Figure 2.36

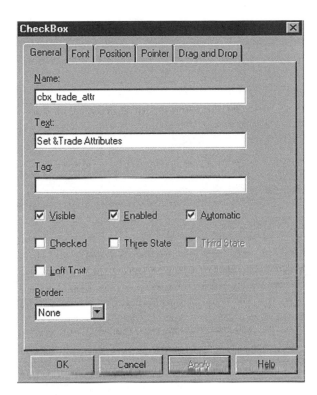

Figure 2.37

Type-in Mode: ☒ Insert vs. Overstrike

PowerBuilder's misuse of a checkbox occurs in a dialog box for setting the properties of checkbox GUI components.

Most of the checkboxes in this dialog box are fine. For example, it is clear what the opposite of "Visible" is, for the case in which the user turns that checkbox off. However, the one labeled "Left Text" is a misuse of a checkbox because it is not obvious what the opposite of "Left Text" is. This setting controls the position of the label on the currently selected checkbox in the GUI being constructed. If "Left Text" is checked, the label will be displayed on the left side of the checkbox. But where will the label be displayed if "Left Text" is left unchecked (the default)? In fact, the label will be on the right side, but in order to know that, a user has to first know that PowerBuilder allows checkbox labels to be positioned either on the left or right of the checkbox, not, say, above or below them.

Figure 2.37 shows another example, from my consulting files, of a misused checkbox. In this case, the programmer, in an attempt to be helpful, named both possible values in the label. Now users can't tell which value is chosen when they uncheck *or* check the box.

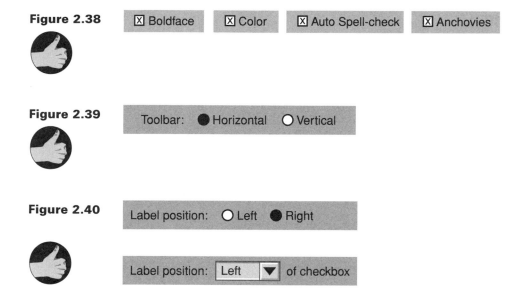

Figure 2.38

☒ Boldface   ☒ Color   ☒ Auto Spell-check   ☒ Anchovies

Figure 2.39

Toolbar: ● Horizontal   ○ Vertical

Figure 2.40

Label position: ○ Left   ● Right

Label position: | Left   ▼ | of checkbox

Avoiding Blooper 10: *The design rule*

Checkboxes are not supposed to be used for settings that just happen to have two values. They should be used only for two-valued settings for which the two values are natural, obvious opposites, such as ON/OFF, true/false, color/b&w, or present/absent. In such settings, one value label serves three functions simultaneously: it labels the entire setting, it labels one value, and it makes clear what the opposite value is.

Examples

Some examples of valid uses of checkboxes are shown in Figure 2.38. If a two-valued setting does not fit the requirements for being presented as a checkbox, it should be presented in a way that makes both values explicit, such as radio-buttons or an option menu. For example, the toolbar position option setting that one of my clients developed should have been presented as a pair of radio-buttons, as shown in Figure 2.39. That is in fact what I suggested to the client.

PowerBuilder's bogus "Left Text" checkbox

PowerBuilder's erroneous "Left Text" checkbox is a case in which an option menu (as is used in this dialog box for the Border setting) or a pair of radio-buttons would have been more appropriate. See Figure 2.40 for two examples of how PowerBuilder's designers could have made the setting less confusing than they did.

2.3.4 Blooper 11: Using command buttons as toggles

One GUI toolkit component that is often misused is the command button. Most GUI toolkits provide a command button component, which, when clicked, triggers the execution of some code. This code is supposed to invoke an action or trigger an event. An alternate name for command buttons is "pushbuttons." Here, I will use the name "command button."

One sometimes sees command buttons used to control ON/OFF settings. Clicking the button once switches something ON; pushing it again switches it OFF.[4] The problem in such cases is that the software developer used a *command* button, rather than another component better suited to presenting ON/OFF settings.

For example, in a review of a client's Web search service, I noted the following problem:

> All of the Search Option buttons look alike, yet four behave as toggles and two behave as command buttons (Reset and Hide Form). Users can't tell by looking at them how they'll behave; they have to try them. If a user had the intention of turning all the options ON, he or she might sometimes also click the Reset button without thinking, since it is right next to the togglebuttons. That would turn OFF all the options the user had just turned ON.

In Figure 2.41, the leftmost button is a valid use of a command button; the other two buttons are not.

In many cases, command buttons misused as toggle controls provide no indication of their current state. Perhaps the programmer decided that was OK because the state is clear from other aspects of the application's display. For example, perhaps the button is labeled "Show Medical History" and the medical history is either visible or it is not.

An example of this from an actual software product is shown in Figure 2.42, which is a toolbar from the main window of the music accompaniment program Band in a Box Pro 6.0 for Macintosh. The Not'n button switches the program between displaying a tune as a chord chart or in music notation. Normally, the program displays tunes as a chord chart. Clicking once on the Not'n button changes the display to show the tune in music notation. Clicking

Figure 2.41

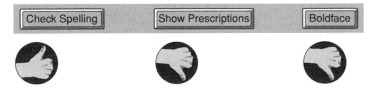

---

4. I am referring here to command buttons. Some GUI toolkits provide a form of ON/OFF control that looks similar to a command button, but operates as a toggle: push-on, push-off buttons. These are discussed more fully in the design rule.

Figure 2.42

`Play` `Stop` `Replay` `Hold` `From` `Rec` `Lyrics` `Not'n`
`Open` `Save` `.MID` `.STY` `Set.` `Pref.` `Copy` `Print`

Figure 2.43

`Print...` `Next Page` `Prev Page` `Two Page` `Zoom In` `Zoom Out` `Close`

it again changes the display back to the chord chart. The button label does not change. All of the other buttons on this toolbar either initiate commands or display auxiliary windows.

In other cases, the programmer changes the command button label after each press to indicate what the effect of clicking it again will be; for example, a button label "Show Data" might change to "Hide Data." Such label changes are better than no indication, but not much better; they can easily be overlooked.

Toggling the label of a command button can also confuse users: if users cannot determine which of the two states is in effect without referring to the button label, they won't be sure whether the button label indicates the *current* state or the state that pressing the button will switch to. For example, if a button label reads "Flaps Down," does that mean that the flaps *are* down, or that clicking the button *will put* the flaps down? It is best not to confuse users about such matters.

Figure 2.43 is an image from Kodak's Picture Disk software (reviewed more fully in Chapter 9). The image shows buttons from the Print Preview window. Most of the buttons invoke commands, but the "Two Page" button is a command button being misused as a toggle control. It toggles the display back and forth between showing a single page of a slide show and showing two pages side by side. The button label changes between "Two Page" and "One Page" to indicate what mode it will change to when clicked. That is, when the program is showing one page, the button is labeled "Two Page"; when the program is showing two pages, the button is labeled "One Page."

In this case, users are unlikely to be confused about whether the button label indicates the current mode or the mode that results from clicking on the button because the data area of the window clearly shows either one or two pages. However, the simple fact that this command button acts like a checkbox—and is the only one here that does—may confuse some users, at least initially. A pair of radiobuttons would make the setting much clearer.

Toggling the label of a command button can be even more confusing when its two alternate states aren't clear opposites like "Show X" versus "Hide X," but rather a more arbitrary two-valued contrast. For example, users seeing a button labeled "Show Music Notation" would not immediately guess its other state even if they knew the button was a toggle; it could be "*Hide* Music Nota-

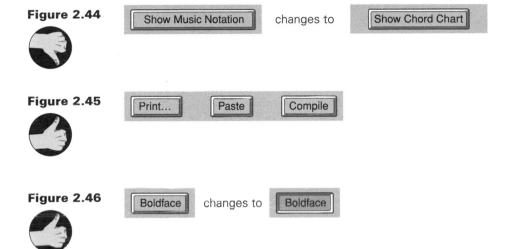

Figure 2.44

Show Music Notation   changes to   Show Chord Chart

Figure 2.45

Print...   Paste   Compile

Figure 2.46

Boldface   changes to   Boldface

tion," "Show Music *Tablature,*" or a variety of other contrasting values. "Show Chord Chart," as in Figure 2.44, would not be the first thing most users would think of.

The more primitive the GUI toolkit being used, the more limited the selection of built-in control types. This puts more pressure on programmers to use the command button for all types of controls, which, in turn, makes misusing them more likely.

Avoiding Blooper 11: The design rule

Command button components in GUI toolkits are for invoking commands or initiating events. They appear pressed while the command is executing, but revert to an unpressed appearance thereafter. They have no persistent state. Figure 2.45 shows examples.

ON/OFF settings should be presented using checkboxes or other types of toggle controls. Some GUI toolkits provide click ON, click-OFF togglebuttons as an alternative to checkboxes. These usually look similar to command buttons, but behave differently from both the users' and the software's point of view: they remain depressed while in the ON state, thereby providing an indication of their state other than an easily overlooked label change (see Figure 2.46). Because these components are not command buttons, but rather a distinct type of control, using them does not constitute misusing command buttons as toggle controls. Nonetheless, I recommend that they only be used where it is clear from the label or the context that they are toggles rather than command buttons.

Some GUI toolkits provide other types of togglebuttons for specialized situations (see Figure 2.47), for example, expand/contract switches for opening and closing auxiliary data panels, and rocker switches (which look like light switches from the physical world). Some GUI toolkits allow programmers to

Figure 2.47

define variants of built-in components that retain the behavior of the component upon which they are based but have a different appearance. This extension mechanism can be used to create togglebuttons for specialized uses.

2.3.5 Blooper 12: Using tabs as radiobuttons

For cases in which a user interface provides more settings or data displays than can be shown at once, many GUI toolkits provide a tabbed-panel component. Alternative names for such components include "tabbed pane" and "notebook." I'll call them "tabbed panels." An example of a typical correct use of tabbed panels is shown in Figure 2.48, from the Keyboard Properties dialog box of Microsoft Windows.

Tabbed panels are an on-screen simulation of tabbed cards such as those in a recipe box. They consist of superimposed panels, only one of which is displayed at a time, with labeled tabs along one edge corresponding to the panels. When a user clicks on a tab, the application brings the corresponding panel to the "front" of the stack of panels, displaying the information and controls on it. Tabbed panels provide a way of organizing a lot of information and controls into a relatively compact space. They also provide many opportunities for misuse.

A common misuse of tabs is to use them as if they were radiobuttons, that is, as a way to present choices that affect what the application will do, rather than just which controls are displayed.

For example, suppose a developer were designing a dialog box for a document editor's Save As... function (see Figure 2.49). The Save As... function displays a dialog box to get the destination filename and other instructions from the user and, when the user clicks OK, saves the document. Suppose this Save As N... function, like many, allowed users to choose one of several formats for saving the document: the document editor's own format, HTML, Rich Text Format (RTF), and plain text. A developer might design the Save As... dialog box to contain a set of tabbed panels—one for each available data format. Users would be expected to click the tab for the desired format, set that panel's format-specific settings, and then click the OK button at the bottom of the dialog box.

Figure 2.48

Figure 2.49

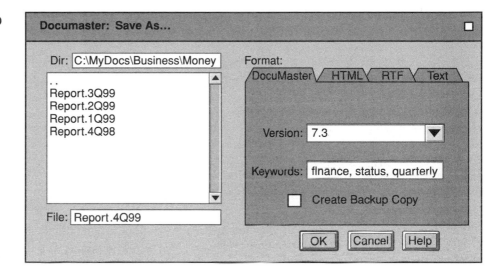

The problem with this design is that it violates users' perception of tabbed panels as being purely a control for navigating between different panels. The format used to save the document depends on whichever tab panel happens to be "in front" when the user clicks the OK button. It is a safe bet that many users would be confused and annoyed by this. With this design, it is certain that some users would click on a tab, look at the settings there and perhaps set some, then click on another tab, look at the settings there, decide not to do anything on that tab panel, then click OK, and be dismayed when the program does the "wrong" thing, that is, uses the file format corresponding to the last tab panel viewed. Users would also be annoyed that data they entered on one of the tab panels was ignored and may be lost simply because that panel was not in front when OK was clicked.

A common lame excuse. Software developers sometimes defend this use of tabs by noting that other one-from-N choice controls, such as radiobuttons and option menus, have historically been used for both navigation and application data settings. They are referring to cases where changing a radiobutton or option menu's value causes other settings to appear or disappear. According to this argument, tabs are, in the abstract, just another type of one-from-N setting and are a more "natural" control for such cases than are radiobuttons or menus.

It is true that radiobuttons and option menus have historically been used to control the presence or absence of other settings. It is also true that tabs are, in a formal sense, just another type of one-from-N setting. However, it is an unwarranted leap of logic to assume that because radiobuttons and menus can be used successfully in navigatory or quasi-navigatory roles as well as nonnavigatory ones, tabs make sense in nonnavigatory roles.

Figure 2.50

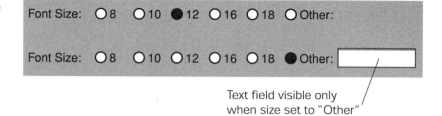

Text field visible only
when size set to "Other"

The important point of view is the users'. First, what is important is what makes
sense to *users*, not what makes sense to software designers and developers.
Years of conducting usability tests and informally observing users has convinced me that people intuitively regard tabbed panels as being purely for navigation. Users don't like it when just changing from one tabbed panel to another
affects the application. For example, they don't like it when the application
treats the tab itself as a setting as in the previous example, or when the settings
on one tab panel automatically go into effect when the user switches to another
panel (see Blooper 55: Cancel button doesn't cancel, Section 5.4.3). Users are
more flexible in their expectations about radiobuttons and menus than they are
in their expectations about tabbed panels.

Navigation versus progressive disclosure. Second, radiobuttons or menus that
affect the visibility of other settings are not primarily navigatory in nature. They
are instances of the well-established user interface design principle of "progressive disclosure"—hiding detail until it is relevant or needed (see Principle
3, Section 1.3.4).

   For example, consider a dialog box for setting text font properties, as in Figure 2.50. Such a dialog box might provide radiobuttons or an option menu for
choosing the font size. The choices might include "Other," to allow users to
specify a nonstandard, unlisted font size. The dialog box would need a number
field to allow users to type unlisted sizes, but that field needn't be displayed
unless the font setting were set to "Other." In this case, the radiobutton or
menu setting is not for navigation; it is an application setting that specifies the
font size. It has the *side effect* of changing the visibility of the text field.

Avoiding Blooper 12: *The design rule*

Tabs are purely *navigation* controls. They affect where the user is in the application, that is, the availability of other settings. They are not supposed to *be* settings. A user's choice of which panel out of a set of tabbed panels to display
should not affect the application's data or have consequences for the software's
subsequent behavior. Figure 2.51 shows a typical well-designed use of tabbed
panels.

   The hypothetical "Save As ..." dialog box described earlier would make
more sense to users if the tabbed panels were replaced by an option menu or

Figure 2.51

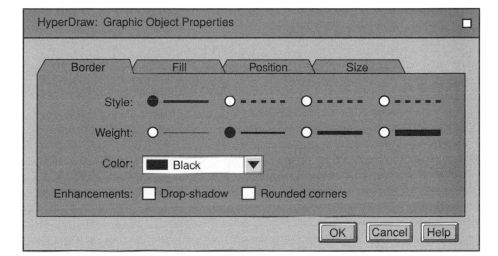

Figure 2.52

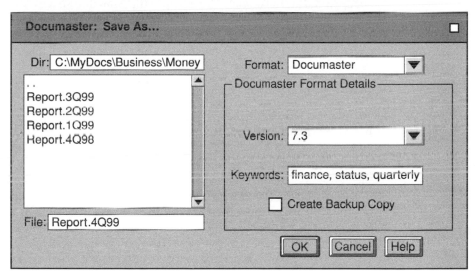

radiobuttons, with a labeled group box to display the format-specific settings (see Figure 2.52). Users would be much more likely to interpret the Format choice as an application setting that determines how the file is saved.

Conventions are evolving

As described above, radiobuttons and option menus can by convention be used either as application data settings or as navigation controls. However, conventions evolve. Tabbed panels were introduced in GUIs after radiobuttons and option menus were and may eventually replace them in cases where the primary function is navigation.

However, sometimes tabbed panels aren't practical. If the number of choices is large or the labels of some choices are long, it may not be possible to fit all the required tabs onto the display. It is also poor design to embed one set of tabbed panels within another because users lose track of where they are. Therefore, sometimes radiobuttons and menus are indispensable as navigation controls.

2.3.6 Blooper 13: Too many tabs

An important purpose of tabbed panels is to save space by overlaying different control or information panels so they share the same screen real estate. Tabbed panels provide a user interface for doing this that capitalizes on users' familiarity with tabbed sheets, notebooks, and folders in the physical world.

Ironically, the labeled tabs, which show users what panels are available and provide a means of choosing which panel to display next, take up significant space. It doesn't take many tabs before the available space along one edge (usually the top) of an overlaid stack of panels has been filled.

The trouble starts—and the blooper count rises—when software developers try to "scale" tabs beyond that limit. There simply is no good way to do it—not that some creative application and GUI toolkit developers haven't tried. Their attempts give rise to some interesting variations of this blooper.

Variation A: Wagging the dog. One obvious way to work around the limit imposed by the size (usually width) of the panel is to widen the panel, thereby adding space for another tab or two. But each panel in the tabbed "stack" presumably has only a certain amount of settings or data to display, so widening the shared panel space can easily result in a lot of wasted blank space on many of the panels in the set (see Figure 2.53). In such a case, the developer has crossed the line from using tabs in order to save space (their true purpose), to wasting space in order to use tabs. The tail is wagging the dog.

Variation B: Tabs to the left of us! Tabs to the right of us! Tabs all around us! A second, somewhat less obvious way to provide more tabs than will fit along one edge of the panel is to use more than one edge, that is, extend the tabs "around the corner" and down the left or right side of the panel. And why stop there? Why not run 'em across the bottom too (see Figure 2.54)! Of course, people never see this in the physical world. But who cares? This is a computer screen; we can do whatever we want, right?

The main problem with this workaround is that users will be unsure whether the tabs along different edges constitute independent choice dimensions or are just more choices on a single choice dimension. In other words, some users will interpret such a display as offering several tabs down the side (or across the bottom) for each tab across the top, or vice versa. They will. Try it. On top of that usability problem, displaying tabs on several edges of the panel looks terrible.

Figure 2.53

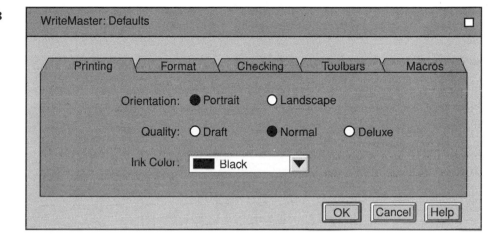

Figure 2.54

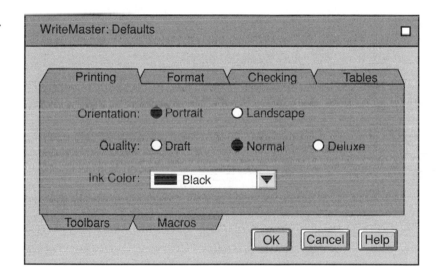

Variation C: Shrt lbls. Some designers are so desperate to have all the tabs fit that they devise ways to decrease the width of each tab. The most common approach is to abbreviate the tab labels, for example, using "PS" instead of "PostScript" (see Figure 2.55). This of course sacrifices clarity to achieve narrower tabs, and so is another case of the tail wagging the dog.

Another way to narrow the tabs is to break their labels into two lines, as is shown in Figure 2.56. This is not a bad approach, but some GUI toolkits don't allow it; they support only one-line tab labels. This approach also only works well when labels contain more than one word; breaking single words into two lines makes them hard to read. Finally, it looks bad when some tabs have two-line labels while others have one-line labels.

Figure 2.55

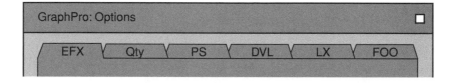

Figure 2.56

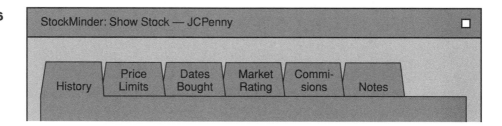

Variation D: Dancing tabs. The least obvious—but unfortunately most popu-lar—"solution" to running out of space for tabs is to display multiple rows of tabs. Instead of one row of tabs across an edge (usually the top) of the shared panel, there are two...or three...or four rows. It's supposed to be as if the user were looking down at a file drawer full of tabbed manila folders, seeing the tabbed tops of all the folders from the front to the back of the drawer. A nice idea, but it has a serious flaw.

In all tabbed panels, whether single-row or multirow, when a tab is selected, its panel is displayed as if it had moved to the front of the "stack." That is as it should be. However, when tabs are presented in multiple rows, selecting a tab from any row other than the first row not only displays the selected tab's panel but also shifts the tab's row so it is now the *first* row of tabs. For example, if you click on a tab in the second row, that row instantly moves—right out from under your pointer—to the first row and displays the corresponding panel. Meanwhile, the row of tabs that used to be first either swaps with the row you clicked on or shifts to the back row.

The pair of screen images in Figure 2.57 from a real product illustrate this. They are images of the Print Setup/Options dialog box for a printer control tool by Hewlett-Packard, FontSmart version 1.64. The image on the left shows the dialog box as it first appears—with the Watermarks tab panel displayed. Note the second row of tabs. The image on the right shows what happens if a user then clicks on the Graphics tab, which started out in the second row: the Graph-ics panel is displayed and the two rows of tabs switch places.

This is very disorienting to users. They click on a tab and it seems to vanish. It didn't vanish; it just moved to a new position, but it takes users a few con-fused seconds to find it again. Furthermore, contrary to what computer engi-neers might expect, users do not quickly get over the disorientation caused by shifting tab rows; their previous and continuing experience with single rows of tabs (as well as with tabs in the physical world) perpetuates their expectation

Figure 2.57

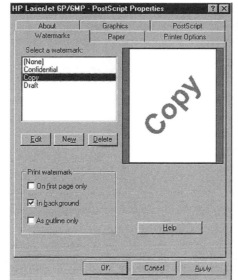
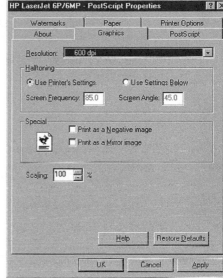

that tabs stay put when selected. There is no question: users *do not like* multiple rows of tabs.

Why shift rows of tabs around if it disorients users so? Why not just display a tab's corresponding panel and leave the tab where it is? Because selecting a tab from the second, third, or other row requires connecting that tab to the displayed panel to show which panel is being displayed. If tabs did not move to the first row when selected, connecting them with the displayed panel would hide tabs in rows in front of the selected tab's row, making it impossible to select them. So shifting is unavoidable if tabs are in multiple rows.

Avoiding Blooper 13: *The design rule*

You can avoid this blooper by following these rules of thumb.

Avoid large numbers of tabs

Clearly, the most straightforward way to avoid the various problems associated with having too many tabs is not to have too many tabs. If the number of data or control panels is so large that their tabs will not fit across a reasonably wide shared panel in a single row, perhaps the real problem is that the information and controls are not grouped in the best way. It might pay to consider reorganizing them onto fewer panels, requiring fewer tabs.

The Amazon.com Web site uses tabbed panels. As Figure 2.58 shows, the large amount of information available at the site has been organized into a very reasonable number of tabbed panels.

Figure 2.58

Use another control instead of tabs

Another way to avoid too many tabs is not to use tabs. Use other user interface components for switching between alternative displayed panels. GUI components that are sometimes used in this way are radiobuttons, option menus, and scrolling lists.

For example, a client of mine developed an application that included a Defaults dialog box to allow users to customize the defaults for settings throughout the application. The defaults were grouped according to which window of the application they applied to. Since this application had several dozen windows, tabbed panels were clearly not a reasonable way to allow users to switch between groups of default settings. Instead, the developers used a scrolling list (see Figure 2.59); selecting an item in the list on the left side of the dialog box displayed the corresponding group of settings on a panel on the right side.

Widen panel (slightly) or make tab labels narrower

If a set of tabs is close to fitting in one row across the available space, but is just a little too wide, a designer can use two approaches mentioned earlier. The designer can widen the entire panel, at the cost of wasting some of the space that using tabs is intended to save. As stated previously, widening the panel too much just to make the tabs fit is a case of the tail wagging the dog and should be avoided.

Alternatively, the designer can narrow the tab labels by breaking them into two lines. However, this only works if (1) the GUI toolkit supports two-line tab labels, and (2) the desired labels each contain two or more words. Narrowing tab labels by abbreviating them should be avoided unless the abbreviations are so common that all users would know what they mean (e.g., "Info" for "Information"). Furthermore, even if the developers are sure that users will understand the abbreviations, the assumption should be tested before shipping the product.

Never use dancing tabs

Multiple rows of tabs, with their unavoidable shifting tab rows, are simply wrong and should never be used. They violate two separate long-standing GUI design

Figure 2.59

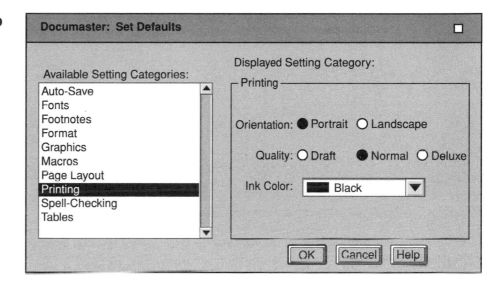

principles: (1) the screen belongs to the *user*, and (2) preserve screen inertia. For more about these two principles, see Principle 6 (Section 1.6) and also Blooper 48: Unexpected rearrangement of display (Section 5.2.3).

2.4 Providing faulty feedback

The next three bloopers are about providing users with inadequate feedback, making it difficult for them to keep track of what they have done and what the computer is doing.

2.4.1 Blooper 14: Buttons that trigger on "mouse down"

A blooper sometimes seen in software developed without the oversight of an experienced user interface designer is buttons that trigger on "mouse down." Stated in detail, such buttons trigger their assigned (i.e., labeled) action when a user moves the mouse pointer over them and presses the "select" (left) mouse button down (Figure 2.60). By convention, most on-screen buttons do not trigger their assigned action until the mouse button is released over the button (see "Avoiding Blooper 14," below).

Triggering a button's function on mouse down is not just a violation of convention and hence users' expectations. It is also poor user interface design because it doesn't give users a chance to back out of invoking the button's func-

Figure 2.60

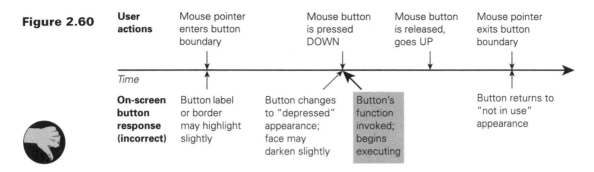

User actions	Mouse pointer enters button boundary	Mouse button is pressed DOWN	Mouse button is released, goes UP	Mouse pointer exits button boundary
Time				
On-screen button response (incorrect)	Button label or border may highlight slightly	Button changes to "depressed" appearance; face may darken slightly	Button's function invoked; begins executing	Button returns to "not in use" appearance

tion. That is why the convention is to wait until the mouse button is released to trigger the button's function.

This error is especially common when programmers who are inexperienced in user interface design write their own code for determining what happens when the user interacts with a button. They may not know how buttons are supposed to behave, or they may not consider it worth the trouble to code the correct behavior, so they code the incorrect behavior. The following are examples of situations in which this is likely:

- The GUI toolkit from which the user interface is built is exceedingly primitive, or the user interface was developed from scratch, that is, without any GUI toolkit at all. In this case, the programmer creates each button from very low-level components and graphics primitives, and must code all the button's event-handling logic.

- The GUI toolkit itself was developed by programmers who were inexperienced in user interface and therefore ignorant of GUI design principles. In this case, the button components have the incorrect behavior built into them, so the blooper is not the application programmer's fault. In a sense, it is a "bug" in the toolkit. Application programmers who recognize the bug can sometimes work around it by extending the toolkit with their own buttons or by modifying the behavior of the button components. However, the programmers might not know how to extend or modify the toolkit, or the toolkit might simply not be extensible or modifiable.

- The GUI toolkit is designed to be extremely flexible and so allows programmers to provide procedures or methods for every conceivable user event, including "button down." In this case, the programmer, who may not know how buttons are supposed to behave, specifies a procedure or method for the "button down" event that triggers the button's function.

Avoiding Blooper 14: *The design rule*

On-screen "soft" buttons should provide feedback that they have been pressed on "mouse button down," but should not invoke their corresponding action

Figure 2.61

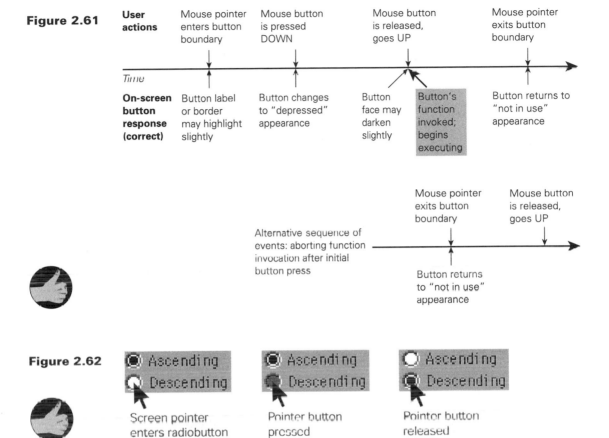

User actions	Mouse pointer enters button boundary	Mouse button is pressed DOWN	Mouse button is released, goes UP	Mouse pointer exits button boundary

Time

On-screen button response (correct)	Button label or border may highlight slightly	Button changes to "depressed" appearance	Button face may darken slightly	Button's function invoked; begins executing	Button returns to "not in use" appearance

		Mouse pointer exits button boundary	Mouse button is released, goes UP

Alternative sequence of events: aborting function invocation after initial button press

Button returns to "not in use" appearance

Figure 2.62

Screen pointer enters radiobutton

Pointer button pressed

Pointer button released

until "mouse button up" (see Figure 2.61). Furthermore, they should provide users a way to abort a button press: move the mouse pointer off the button before releasing the mouse button. If the pointer moves off an on-screen button while the user is holding the pointer button down, the on-screen button should revert to its normal "not in use" appearance. When the user subsequently releases the pointer button, the button's associated function should not be invoked.

The above-described behavior should be exhibited by *all* types of buttons, not just command buttons. For example, a radiobutton setting should operate as follows:

- "Pointer button down" over one of the radiobuttons changes that button to an appearance that signifies "pressed but not the current value," while the button corresponding to the current value remains fully highlighted (see Figure 2.62).

- "Pointer button up" while the pointer is still over the button leaves the new value highlighted and turns off the radiobutton corresponding to the old value.

- Dragging the mouse pointer over the radiobutton's different values while the mouse button is held down highlights them as long as the pointer remains over them, but the original value remains highlighted regardless of where the pointer moves.

- Dragging the mouse pointer completely off the radiobutton set while the pointer button is still down leaves only the button corresponding to the original value highlighted.

2.4.2 Blooper 15: Ambiguous selections

Some GUI-based tools display several different types of application data or content. Different types of content are usually displayed in different container controls on a window, in panes of a window, or in different windows. For example, Microsoft's file Explorer consists of two scrollable panes: one that displays the file hierarchy and one that lists the files in a directory (Figure 2.63).

Many applications make the mistake of displaying selections in several different controls or data containers at once, such as an item in a scrolled list and some text in an unrelated text field. The problem in such cases is not that the

Figure 2.63

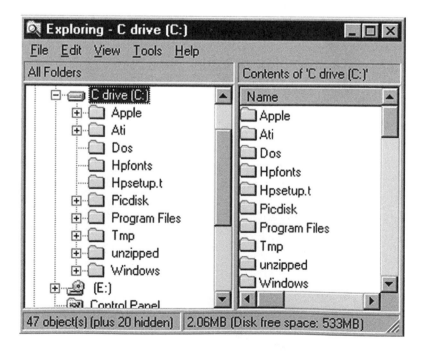

Figure 2.64

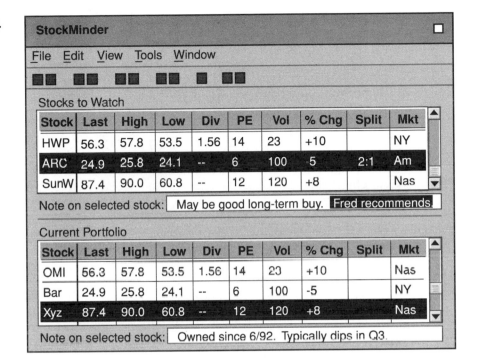

selection contains multiple items. Selections that include several items in the same data container or control are perfectly normal and acceptable. The technical term for these is "multiple selections." Multiple selections are fine. With a multiple selection, it is clear—or at least it should be—that the next selection-based operation will affect *all* of the objects in the selection, or at least all that are relevant.

The problem is that some applications display several distinct selections simultaneously—selections that are in different controls, of different types. This creates ambiguity in the user interface because users cannot predict which selection will be affected by the next keyboard, menubar, or toolbar command, for example, "Delete" or "Underline."

For example, in the hypothetical stock investment software tool in Figure 2.64, the user currently has selections in three different container components (two tables and a text field). It is not clear which container currently has the input focus, that is, which selection is "active." If the user pressed the keyboard's DELETE key, what would be deleted? The stock ARC from the "Stocks to Watch" table, the stock Xyz from the "Current Portfolio" table, or the words "Fred recommends" from the text field under the upper table? Users might understand the application well enough to know that stocks can't be deleted from the "Current Portfolio" table except by explicitly selling them, and then again, they might not. However, even if they understand that, that still leaves two quite plausible targets for the DELETE key. Other commands in this application that operate on a current selection might be similarly ambiguous, for example, View:Details.

Avoiding Blooper 15: *The design rule*

Commands and keyboard keys in GUI-based applications often operate on the current selection, so it should always be obvious what is currently selected. GUI environments usually mark selections by highlighting them. The purpose of highlighting the selection is to draw the users' attention to it. If several different objects in different areas of the screen were marked as selected at the same time, the system would in effect be trying to draw the users' attention to several areas at once. Needless to say, that isn't good design. Therefore, even though there may be multiple selections on the screen at any given time, only one of them should stand out as "the selection."

Display only one primary selection, possibly many secondary selections

For this reason, most GUI environments distinguish between the *primary* selection, of which there is only one on the screen at a time, and *secondary* selections, of which there may be any number. The primary selection is the one that is marked so as to grab the users' attention. It is usually marked by inverting the colors of the selected object. Secondary selections may be marked or not, depending on the application in which they reside. A common way to mark secondary selections is to underline them or surround them with a thin gray or dotted line.

Be a good GUI citizen: Cooperate with the Selection Manager

In GUI environments, each component that can contain application data manages and displays selections inside of itself. However, the various selections on the screen need to be coordinated to avoid confusing users with multiple visible selections. To do this, most GUI-based operating systems provide a global Selection Manager, which presides over the entire computer display, keeping track of the current primary selection and coordinating the various components in which users can select data. One of the Selection Manager's duties is to make sure there is only one primary selection on the screen at a time, even though several different controls or windows may have selections.

However, in order for the Selection Manager to be able to do its job properly, GUI components on the screen that can contain selections (such as windows, scrolling lists, tables, and text fields) must cooperate with the Selection Manager. They first must register their presence with it. Then they must follow its protocol: dehighlight their selection when they lose the input focus and keep track of their selection even though it may not be highlighted. Depending on

Figure 2.65

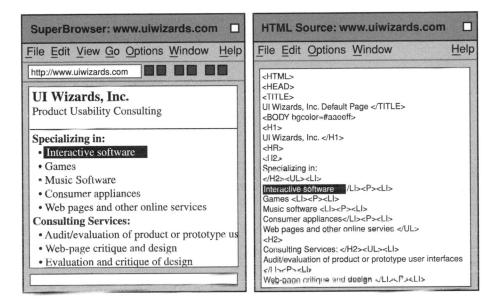

the Selection Manager's protocol, components that contain selections might have to notify the Selection Manager when they get the input focus.

If a GUI application (or the components of which it is constructed) does not cooperate with the Selection Manager, the result will often be multiple selections simultaneously marked as primary, much to the consternation of users.

Exception: Multiple views of the same data

Besides so-called multiple selection, which as I said above is not really multiple distinct selections, there are situations where it is useful to show more than one primary selection at once. This is when software simultaneously shows different views of the *same* data. Two examples are

- A Web page editor that simultaneously shows the Web page currently being edited and the HTML code that defines it (see Figure 2.65). If the user selects some text in the browser view, the Web page editor may also highlight that text in the HTML view, especially if the text can be edited in either view.

- A text editor may allow users to split its window, allowing them to view and edit different parts of the document at the same time in different, independently scrollable window panes. If the panes are ever scrolled such that the same text is visible in both panes, and that text is selected, the selection should be reflected in both panes of the split window (see Figure 2.66).

When multiple views of the same data are displayed and the user selects all or part of that data, it is important to show the selection in all visible views of

Figure 2.66

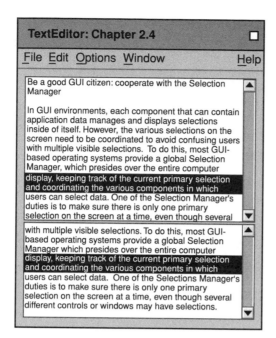

the data object. This makes it clear that the views are of the same object, rather than mere copies. In such cases, *not* highlighting all the views of the selected object is a blooper.

2.4.3 Blooper 16: Not showing busy cursor

Ever since the Xerox Star and the Apple Macintosh, most GUI-based software has displayed a "busy cursor" to indicate that it is busy computing something and therefore temporarily unavailable for other activities. Some people use the term "wait cursor" instead of "busy cursor." Displaying a busy cursor involves changing the screen pointer from the usual arrow to a symbol that suggests waiting. On most GUI platforms, the busy cursor is an hourglass (see Figure 2.67, left). On the Macintosh, it is a clockface (see Figure 2.67, right). Changing the cursor—the more accurate name for which is "screen pointer"—is a great way to show users the status of a GUI because the pointer is almost always where users will be looking.

However, it is not automatic that a busy cursor will be displayed when an application is busy. The operating system cannot be responsible for doing that

Figure 2.67

because it has no way to know when an application is or is not busy. The busy cursor must be displayed by application software when it begins executing a function that will take a noticeable (by users) amount of time and blocks other user activity. Therefore, it is the responsibility of application programmers to recognize which functions should display a busy cursor and to include the necessary code to do that.

Unfortunately, many GUI-based programs do not display a busy cursor in situations where they should. In many cases, this is because the programmer was unaware of the need, either in general or for the execution of a particular function.

An excuse I often hear is that the function is supposed to execute quickly and so doesn't need to display a busy cursor. But how quickly is "quickly"? What if the function sometimes doesn't execute quickly? What if the user has a slower computer than the developer (see Blooper 82: Giving programmers the fastest computers, Section 8.2.4)? What if the function tries to access data that is temporarily locked by another function or application? What if the function accesses network services and the network is hung or overloaded?

In some cases, an application's failure to display a busy cursor is not entirely the application programmer's fault. One GUI programmer told me:

> I'm trying *really hard* to display a busy cursor, but something out of my control keeps switching it back to a normal cursor. There's probably a way around it if I programmed hard enough.

This lament mentions two problems: (1) something out of her control was changing the cursor, and (2) she didn't have time to diagnose and fix the problem. I have heard other GUI programmers mention these problems as well. The "something out of their control" is usually one of three things:

- *Pointer movement*: In a GUI environment, no single application has complete control over the display. Users are free to move the cursor out of the application's window(s) onto the desktop or into windows displayed by other applications. As the cursor moves into areas controlled by other programs, those programs assume control of the cursor's appearance and can change it as they require. The first application regains control of the cursor only when the cursor returns to one of the application's windows. If the application is still busy when it regains the cursor, it must change the cursor back to a busy cursor.

- *Multitasking:* Most modern GUI platforms are multitasking environments, and many applications are multithreaded. Therefore, while an application program is executing a function, other processes and threads can be running as well. If any of them alters the cursor, they may undermine the efforts of the application program to control it.

- *Exceptions:* Many modern programs handle unexpected situations by "throwing exceptions." Exceptions add a degree of complexity to program logic that makes it extremely difficult for programmers to assure that global state—which the cursor display is—is always correctly managed. In less technical terms: exceptions, despite their many advantages, make it easy for software to contain bugs that cause the cursor to get out of synch with what the programmers intended.

Whether the complicating factor is the window manager, other processes and threads competing for control of the cursor, or faulty exception handling causing the cursor to get out of synch, correcting the problem can be devilishly time-consuming and require great programming skill. The GUI programmer mentioned earlier alluded to this when she said: "There's probably a way around it if I programmed hard enough." This programmer could afford to be optimistic because she had enough experience to allow her to wade into the morass of processes, threads, and exception handlers and find and correct the problem, and enough seniority to allow her to adjust the development schedule as necessary. However, many GUI programmers lack such experience and scheduling clout (see Blooper 77: Treating user interface as low priority, Section 8.1.2). As a result, the blooper is common.

A blooper is a blooper. Whatever the reason for not showing a busy cursor at the appropriate times, the effect on users is the same. It leaves users clueless as to what is happening, and so is a blooper.

Avoiding Blooper 16: The design rule

In general, interactive applications should be highly responsive to users. This means keeping up with users' actions, and keeping users informed of program status. Applications should be designed so as to recognize that there are performance limitations, and therefore to take other measures to ensure responsiveness, rather than to simply assume that performance will (or should) be fast. To be responsive, applications should do the following:

- Display busy cursors for any function that blocks further use of the application while the function is executing, even if the function normally executes instantaneously. The rule is that any function that could *ever* take longer than 0.1 second to complete should display a busy cursor.
- Display "working" indicators somewhere on the application's main window. One common practice is to include a graphic on an application's main window that doubles as the application's logo and as its "working" indicator (e.g., Microsoft Internet Explorer, Netscape Navigator).
- Display progress indicators (e.g., progress bars) for functions that will take more than a second.

- Spawn threads whenever possible to free the user interface so users can work on other things while waiting for the function to complete.
- Work ahead where possible (on the most likely next task) while waiting for user input.

For more guidelines on when to show busy cursors and related issues, see Section 7.2.

A good rule: Show busy cursors for any function

Any function that could *ever*—even if rarely—take longer than a small fraction of a second should display a busy cursor. If the function usually executes so quickly that users don't get a chance to see the busy cursor, fine, but the busy cursor should be displayed for the times when the function executes slowly or gets stuck.

GUI platform developers take note: Your help is needed

The programmer's lament above about struggling against forces "beyond her control" merely shows that a complete, reliable solution may require improvements in GUI platforms, tools, and building blocks as well as greater effort from application developers and their management.

2.5 Abusing text fields

Our last three GUI component bloopers involve various ways of misusing text entry fields.

2.5.1 Blooper 17: Using text fields for read-only data

Every toolkit for building GUIs includes a component intended mainly for allowing users to type textual (including numeric) values. Such components go by a variety of names, depending on the GUI toolkit and the platform for which it is designed. The most common name for such components is probably *text field* and is the name I will use. Other common names for this type of component are "data entry field," "type-in field," and "text box."

A blooper I often find when I review GUI software for clients is text fields that cannot be edited. I am not referring to text fields that are temporarily not editable because they are inactive; I mean text fields that are *never* editable

Figure 2.68

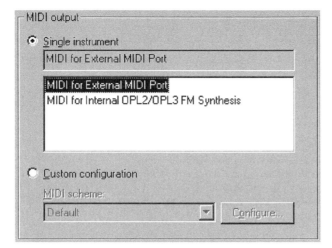

Figure 2.69

● Single instrument: MIDI for External MIDI Port.

because they are only data displays. Also, I do not mean that users cannot change the displayed value; I mean only that the value cannot be changed by editing the text field itself.

An example of the blooper is shown in Figure 2.68, in the Multimedia control panel for Microsoft Windows. The text field below the "Single instrument" radiobutton simply shows which instrument is selected in the list immediately below it. Selecting a different item from the list changes the value shown in the noneditable text field.

The text field has a gray background to show that it is not editable, but that isn't good enough. Many users will misinterpret the gray background to mean that the text field is only temporarily deactivated (especially since applications in Windows are not consistent about how they display inactive components; see Blooper 32: Inactive controls insufficiently grayed out, Section 3.4.3).

Instead of appearing in a text field, the current instrument should be displayed in this control panel using a simple text label component, as shown in Figure 2.69.

GUI developers typically commit this blooper for one of four different reasons.

Variation A: A text field requires programmers to set appearance separately from editability. In most GUI toolkits, text fields have an attribute that controls whether or not they are editable. If the toolkit is well designed, setting a text field to noneditable will automatically change its appearance to look very different from an editable field: the border becomes invisible and the interior background color becomes the same as the surrounding panel.

Unfortunately, many GUI toolkits do not link appearance with editability; when set to noneditable, they retain their normal (editable) appearance. To make them look different, a programmer must separately set appearance attributes, such as the border visibility or the interior background color. Predictably, many programmers simply set the control to noneditable and don't set any appearance attributes, either because they forget to or don't know they should. The result is Blooper 17.

Sometimes the programmer understands that noneditable text fields are supposed to look different from editable ones, but believes that setting the background color to gray is sufficient. It isn't. Such a text field looks to users as if it is temporarily not editable but will become editable at some point, such as when the state of the application changes.

This variation of Blooper 17 is a classic case of a GUI toolkit that, in the interest of flexibility, is so low level that it allows programmers to create components and GUIs that violate well-established user interface design guidelines. Since many programmers don't know the guidelines (because they have never seen any), they assume that if the toolkit they are using allows something, it must be OK to do it. Bad assumption!

Variation B: Confusion between active/inactive and editability settings. Most GUI toolkits allow controls to be made *inactive*, meaning that they don't respond to user actions until they are once again made *active*. Inactive controls have a distinctive, grayed-out appearance. (See Blooper 32: Inactive controls insufficiently grayed out, Section 3.4.3, for more details.)

Some GUI toolkits don't distinguish between active/inactive and editability for controls; they provide only one attribute on controls, often misnamed "editable." Some programmers see that attribute and assume that they can set it to OFF when they want to use a text field to display read-only data. Even if setting the "editable" attribute automatically changes the appearance of the text field, the appearance won't be correct for a truly noneditable value. Instead, it will be the right appearance for a temporarily *inactive* value, giving rise to the blooper. And if setting the "editable" attribute doesn't automatically change the appearance of the text field, we are back to Variation A.

When GUI toolkits do provide both an active/inactive attribute and an editability attribute on text fields, some programmers don't know which one to use. If they use active/inactive when they are trying to create a read-only data display, they are committing the blooper.

Variation C: Programmer won't use a "label" component for anything but a setting label. The third variation of Blooper 17 is due to misleading names of components in GUI toolkits. Most GUI toolkits provide a component for simply displaying noneditable text on a panel. The idea is that editable and noneditable text are presented using different types of components, rather than by one type of component with different attribute settings.

Unfortunately, many toolkits call noneditable text components "labels." This is a poor choice of a name because it suggests to some GUI programmers that the "label" component is meant to be used only for text in the user interface that actually serves as a label for something. That, in turn, suggests that text that doesn't function as a label, such as read-only data values, should be displayed using some other component. Which component? The only other plausible component for displaying text is a text field. Hence, the blooper.

In some GUI toolkits, the name for noneditable text components is not so misleading. Instead of "label," such components are sometimes called "text item," "static text," or just plain "text."

Variation D: Programmer wants data to look like an editable version displayed elsewhere. The final variation of Blooper 17 occurs when an application displays a text value in more than one window, but the value is editable in only *some* of the windows. In such cases, programmers sometimes display all of the values as text fields in the name of consistency. In such cases, the noneditable fields usually are given gray backgrounds to show that they are not editable. As described above, that isn't enough of a difference because users will regard such text fields as temporarily noneditable.

This is a misapplication of the consistency principle. It is consistency from a programmer's point of view. It doesn't seem consistent to users because it means they can't tell from the appearance of a data value whether it is editable, temporarily noneditable, or permanently noneditable.

Avoiding Blooper 17: *The design rule*

The standard appearance for editable text fields on all modern GUI platforms is a rectangular box with a visible border (Figure 2.70). The border may have a three-dimensional inset appearance or it may just be a black line, but it is clearly visible. The background of an editable text field is almost always white.

Inactive is not the same as read-only

As described previously and in Blooper 32: Inactive controls insufficiently grayed out (Section 3.4.3), when a text field is inactive, every part of it should be grayed out (Figure 2.71). That includes its background, its border, its text content, and maybe even its label.

Figure 2.70

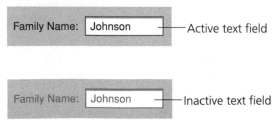

Active text field

Figure 2.71

Inactive text field

Figure 2.72

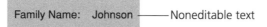

Family Name: Johnson ———— Noneditable text

Figure 2.73

Application: NCSA Telnet [Choose...]

In contrast, textual values that are not editable should not be enclosed in a visible border and should have the same background color as the surrounding panel (Figure 2.72).

For an example of a correctly displayed noneditable textual value, see the "Application" value in Figure 2.73, from the Preferences settings in Netscape Communicator 4.5. This preference setting shows the application that will be used to open a specified type of data file. To associate a different application with a datatype, users click on the Choose button, select an application from their computer's hard disk, and click OK. Compare this setting with the "Single instrument" setting in Microsoft Window's Multimedia control panel (Figure 2.68).

Summary

To summarize, textual data on a computer display should either be

- editable and active, in which case it is enclosed in a black box with a white background
- normally editable but inactive, in which case it looks like an editable field but is entirely grayed out
- noneditable, in which case it should not be enclosed in a black box and should look the same as a label

These are the only three choices for displaying textual data. Software should never—repeat: *never*—display noneditable textual data in something that looks even remotely like a text field.

Exactly how a programmer constructs a display for noneditable text data depends on the details of the GUI toolkit upon which an application is based. In most GUI toolkits, the text field component doesn't have an editability setting that achieves the correct "noneditable" appearance. Therefore, with most GUI toolkits, programmers should not use text fields for permanently noneditable textual data. They should use the "noneditable text" components instead, even if they happen to be called "labels."

The only case in which a text field component should be used to display a noneditable value is when the text field component has an editability setting that automatically produces the correct (label-like) appearance. However, GUI toolkits that do this are rare to nonexistent.

2.5.2   Blooper 18: Overusing text fields

Without question, the text field is the most heavily used interactive component in graphical user interfaces. In my opinion, it is heavily overused. The software marketplace and the Web are full of software that uses text fields for specifying structured or constrained data values such as times of day, volume levels, dates, telephone numbers, postal codes, money amounts, and numbers of dependent children (see Figure 2.74).

The problem is that text fields are too unstructured and unconstrained for such data. They give users little or no advance guidance about what values are acceptable. The feedback they do provide about the validity of values is after the fact. At some point after a user types a structured or restricted value into a text field, the software checks the validity of what the user entered, and if the value was invalid, displays an error message. Such post hoc error messages would not be necessary if the user interface were designed such that users

Figure 2.74

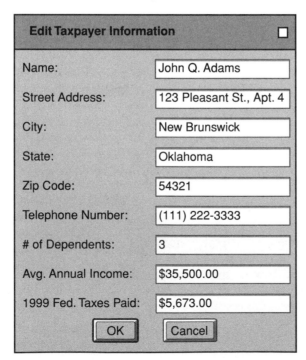

could not supply invalid values in the first place, using controls and settings that were more specialized for the type of data to be entered.

I often hear the excuse that using text fields is easier for programmers than is using or building datatype-specific controls. Of course, ease of programming is supposed to be a lower priority than ease of use. But even ignoring that concern, the excuse is poor because it is false.

Using a text field for a structured datatype requires that the programmer find or write a parser for the field to check that entered values are valid. In some cases, programmers try to help users by writing very flexible parsers that allow users to type the data in a variety of formats. However, if the control were more specialized for the type of input that users will supply, the work of finding or writing a parser—whether flexible or inflexible—and wiring it to the text field would be avoided because no parser would be needed.

I believe that many programmers are biased toward immediately thinking of any data input problem in terms of a text field and a parser. The source of this bias is that most programmers learn their craft in school by writing text-processing programs—not GUI programs—as class assignments.

Overuse of text fields is especially common in GUI-based software that was converted from older, pre-GUI software, that is, software that had a user interface based on command-line arguments and on textual prompts and typed responses. For further discussion of this reason for overusing text fields, see Blooper 45: TTY GUIs (Section 5.1.3).

Avoiding Blooper 18: The design rule

Text fields should be used only for data that really is unstructured, free-form text. Examples of such text are names of people, user-defined passwords, comments, and transaction reasons. Examples of textlike data that is not completely free-form are telephone numbers, social security numbers, dates, state, city, font family, and zip codes.

Alternatives to text fields

There are several alternatives to ordinary text fields, all of them better for specifying highly structured data values.

One simple alternative to an ordinary text field is a text field specialized for a particular type of input. Bank automatic teller machines (ATMs) in the United States require users to specify dollar amounts when making withdrawals, deposits, or transfers. Most do so by displaying a data field and prompting users to type a dollar amount using the ATM's keypad. However, ATM users who want to deposit $35.75 do not have to type "$35.75" or even "35.75". They just type "3575" and the machine places the digits in their correct positions relative to the decimal point. Users cannot enter arbitrary text into ATM dollar amount fields because alphabetic characters are just an alternate interpretation of the

Figure 2.75

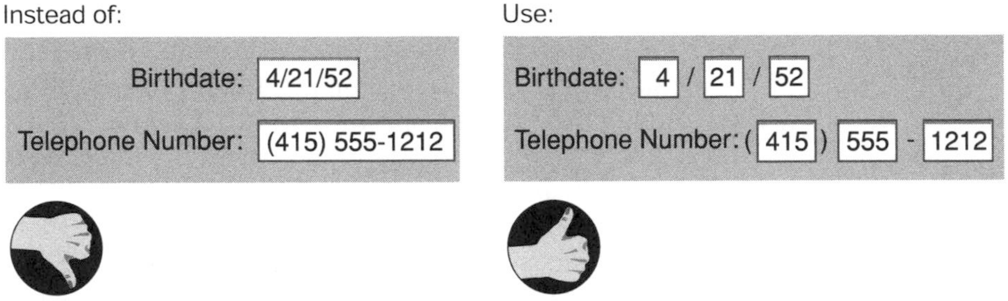

Instead of:

Birthdate: 4/21/52

Telephone Number: (415) 555-1212

Use:

Birthdate: 4 / 21 / 52

Telephone Number: (415) 555 - 1212

Figure 2.76

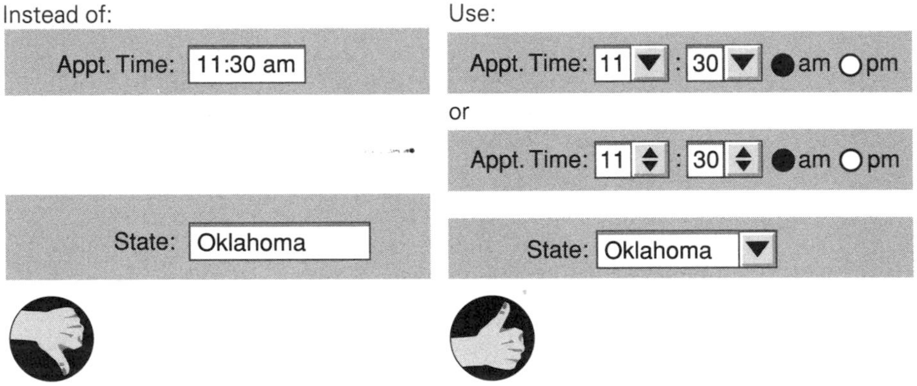

Instead of:

Appt. Time: 11:30 am

State: Oklahoma

Use:

Appt. Time: 11 ▼ : 30 ▼ ●am ○pm

or

Appt. Time: 11 ⬍ : 30 ⬍ ●am ○pm

State: Oklahoma ▼

same keys as the digits 0–9, and the dollar amount field interprets the keys as numbers.

A second relatively simple alternative to using an unstructured text field is simply to use multiple text fields, corresponding to the parts of the data. This eliminates the need for users to include punctuation characters in the typed data and reduces the likelihood of syntax errors. For example, data fields intended for telephone numbers can be broken up into several fields: country code, area code, exchange, and final digits. Similarly, dates can be broken up into day, month, and year. Labels can be used between the separate text fields to provide "built-in" punctuation (see Figure 2.75). Of course, to avoid requiring users to use the mouse (or trackball) to move the insertion point from one text field to the next, it must be possible to do that using the TAB key. Even better, digits beyond the number expected for each field could automatically flow into the next field.

A more sophisticated, but preferable, alternative to text fields is to use datatype-specific controls that match the data's structure and constrain the input to valid values. For example, you can use a slider for a numerical value between 1 and 100, a digital clock for a time, radiobuttons for a small integer value like number of dependents, or a scrolling menu of states for a State data field (see Figure 2.76). After all, the goal is presumably to design a *GUI*, in which the *G* stands for "graphical," not "textual."

2.5.3   Blooper 19: Type-in fields that behave abnormally

One of the worst design mistakes a GUI developer can make is to provide a familiar-looking control that behaves abnormally, such that users cannot operate it in the usual, industry standard way. In reviewing software for client companies, I have seen a wide variety of quirky controls. Many are mentioned elsewhere in this book, such as

- checkboxes that operate like radiobuttons, that is, turning on one checkbox turns another off (see Blooper 8: Confusing checkboxes and radiobuttons, Section 2.3.1)

- command buttons that function as checkboxes, that is, that toggle between two values (see Blooper 11: Using command buttons as toggles, Section 2.3.4)

- tabs that specify a data value rather than being merely navigational (see Blooper 12: Using tabs as radiobuttons, Section 2.3.5)

- buttons of any type (command, radio) that take action on "button down" instead of waiting for "button up" (see Blooper 14: Buttons that trigger on "mouse down," Section 2.4.1)

- cancel buttons that don't cancel (see Blooper 55: Cancel button doesn't cancel, Section 5.4.3)

- option menus that require users to click and release to display the menu, then click again to choose a value, rather than displaying on "button down" and allowing users to choose an item on "button up" (see Blooper 79: Using poor tools and building blocks, Section 8.2.1)

At the moment, however, I wish to focus on one type of component—text and number type-in fields—and some of the creative ways developers devise to make them behave abnormally. Fortunately, application software developers are usually content to use the text field controls supplied by a GUI toolkit, which in most cases means that the text fields will behave correctly. However, there are still cases in which GUI software is developed without a GUI toolkit (see Section 10.2). And even when a GUI toolkit is used, situations arise in which the "canned" text fields aren't quite suitable and need to be altered—at least in the minds of the developers. I've found two sorts of abnormal text field behavior to be the most common.

Variation A: Allowing only replacement, not editing, of text. An especially annoying sort of "rogue" text field allows users to replace its content completely, but not to edit its content. For example, if such a text field contained "123 Pleasant St., Apt. A" and a user wanted to change "Apt. A" to "Apt. B," he or she would have to retype the entire address or copy and paste the whole line from somewhere else on the computer screen.

Figure 2.77

Text can be fully
edited only here ——

Text here can only
be replaced ——

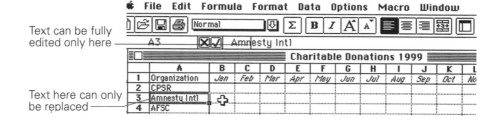

I have most often encountered this flaw when textual and numerical values are presented as cells in a table. For example, many GUI applications use property lists—two-column tables in which each row contains a variable and its value. Some value cells in property lists contain textual or numeric values. Clicking on such a cell "opens" it to allow users to change the value. Unfortunately, a significant number of textual value cells in property lists do not allow users to set the text insertion point within the text of the cell or use normal text-editing operations there. Instead, all users can do is type new text, which completely replaces what was in the cell. Grrrrr!

Microsoft Excel provides another example of a tabular presentation of data that does not allow normal text-editing operations. If a user clicks on a cell containing the number 123456, the user might expect—based on her experience editing text in other applications—to be able to set the insertion point between the 4 and the 5 and insert the digit 7. However, Excel does not allow that. If the user wants to interact directly with the cell contents, she must either retype the entire number with the new digit, or, alternatively, use an indirect method to alter the value in the cell: When a user clicks on a cell, Excel displays the cell's value on a "command line" above the spreadsheet table. That command line supports the expected editing operations (see Figure 2.77). However, interacting with Excel through the command line harkens back to the days before GUIs. This seems odd for a product that when first released was targeted largely at the Apple Macintosh.

Variation B: Requiring ENTER *or* RETURN *to "set" value.* Another annoying abnormality one sometimes encounters in text fields is a requirement that users press the ENTER or RETURN key after typing the desired text in order to "set" or "confirm" it. Such text fields are a serious throwback to the bad old days of command-line user interfaces.

Users of GUI-based applications expect to be able to click in a text field, type a value there, and then click somewhere else, press the TAB key, or simply close the window. Text fields that wait for ENTER or RETURN to signal "done entering new value" violate that expectation. When users encounter this type of text field, they often neglect to press ENTER or RETURN, so the value they typed never really gets entered. When they return to the same display later, the text field still contains its previous value—the value they thought they had replaced.

Figure 2.78

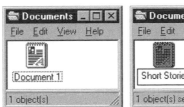

This variant of the blooper seems to show up most commonly in database software, especially software that was ported to a GUI style of user interface from either the IBM 3270 full-screen forms style or the glass-teletype prompt-response style. The prevalence of this design error in database software is somewhat odd, given that the text fields used in database software come from the same GUI toolkits as those used in any other GUI-based software. Perhaps the problem is that programmers who develop GUIs for database software are used to—and therefore try their best to replicate—the older styles of user interfaces.

One especially prominent example of text fields requiring "confirmation" that is not from database software is the mechanism for renaming files in Microsoft Windows. To rename a file in Windows, the user clicks on the filename once to select the file, then again to open the filename for editing.[5] The usual text-editing operations can then be used to type or edit the filename. The new name is not officially "entered" until the user either selects another file or presses RETURN. After editing the name of a file that is in a folder, if the user closes the folder without first pressing RETURN or selecting another file, the new name will be lost. When the user next opens the folder, the file will still have its old name.

This problem is illustrated in the screen images from Windows shown in Figure 2.78. The leftmost image shows a folder containing a document called "Document 1." In the middle image, the user has opened the file's name for editing, and has changed it to "Short Stories." The filename is still open for editing because the user has not yet pressed RETURN or selected another file. The user then closed the folder, either by invoking File:Close or by clicking on the Close [×] control on the titlebar. The rightmost image shows the contents of the folder after the user reopened it: the file has its original name. The name "Short Stories" has vanished into cyberspace.

I consider this a fairly serious problem because users will often not realize that they did not succeed in renaming the file until much later, when something they are trying to do fails because the required file is not found. It is worth noting that Apple's MacOS does not have this problem: closing a folder terminates the name-editing operation, as does pressing RETURN or selecting another file.

---

5. Apple's MacOS does not require the second click. The first click over the filename opens the name for editing.

Avoiding Blooper 19: The design rule

Editing text is one of the most common things people do while using a computer. Because computer users spend so much time editing text for one reason or another, it is important that the knowledge of how to do it be almost unconscious—buried in habits and muscle memory. For that to be possible, the editing of text has to be consistent—totally consistent—from one text-editing situation to another. If there are even minor differences in how text is edited across different situations, users will not be able to fall into unconscious habits. Instead, they will be forced to continually think about the software, about where they are *now* and how text is edited in *this* situation, rather than about what they are writing.

Don't require RETURN to confirm changes

When some text input fields allow editing while others allow only replacement, or when some text fields require users to terminate the editing by pressing RETURN, consistency is destroyed. The immediate victims of a lack of consistency are the software users, but in a commercial marketplace, user dissatisfaction eventually manifests itself as diminished sales. The ultimate victim of text-editing inconsistencies is therefore the company that developed and marketed the software, which, of course, is the same company that committed the design blooper. You would think that this feedback loop would motivate software companies to maximize user interface consistency between their products and with industry standards. However, organizational dysfunction often prevents that (see Section 8.2).

Text editing should be the same everywhere

The best way to achieve total consistency is to treat text editing as a unified service that can be called upon wherever it is needed, rather than as separate applications and GUI components that each implement some kind of text-editing functionality. In other words, all areas into which users can type text, whether single-line text fields, text-valued table cells, names on file icons, text-valued properties in property lists, and multipage text documents, should be served by the same text-editing software.

Further reading

Official platform-specific GUI style guides

Apple Computer, Inc. 1993. *Macintosh Human Interface Guidelines.* Reading, MA: Addison-Wesley.
Microsoft. 1995. *The Windows Interface Guidelines for Software Design: An Application Design Guide.* Redmond, WA: Microsoft Press.

Microsoft. 1999. *Microsoft Windows User Experience.* Redmond, WA: Microsoft Press.

Open Software Foundation. 1993. *OSF/Motif Style Guide: Rev 1.2.* Englewood Cliffs, NJ: Prentice Hall.

Sun Microsystems. 1999. *Java Look and Feel Design Guidelines.* Reading, MA: Addison-Wesley.

Platform-independent GUI guidelines

McFarland, A., and Dayton, T. 1995. *Design Guide for Multiplatform Graphical User Interfaces.* Issue 3, LPR13. Piscataway, NJ: Bellcore.

Mullet, K., and Sano, D. 1995. *Designing Visual Interfaces: Communications Oriented Techniques.* Mountain View, CA: SunSoft Press.

Weinshenk, S., Jamar, P., and Yeo, S. 1997. *GUI Design Essentials.* New York: John Wiley and Sons.

Layout and Appearance Bloopers

135

Introduction

The GUI component bloopers described in Chapter 2 consist of using incorrect or faulty interactive controls in a GUI. Another type of highly visible error has to do with the details of how user interface elements appear and where they are placed relative to each other. I call such errors "layout and appearance" bloopers. Like GUI component bloopers, layout and appearance bloopers can be readily spotted by someone who knows what to look for when reviewing or testing the user interface of a software product or service.

Admittedly, layout and appearance bloopers are usually less important than the other bloopers mentioned in this book. However, I include them anyway because they are extremely numerous in most user interfaces I review or test. Even minor errors can, in sufficient quantity, detract significantly from the usability of a software product or service, and also from its quality as perceived by users and potential customers.

As I point out in Blooper 80: Anarchic development (Section 8.2.2), software developers are not yet accustomed to thinking of themselves as publishers. They come from the world of engineering, and most think they are still in that world. It hasn't yet dawned on most of them how similar their business has become to that of companies that create magazines, newspapers, books, TV shows, and movies. The bulk of software developers have therefore not yet learned to develop and follow strict standards for layout and appearance, and to give the degree of attention to detail that traditional publishers and media production studios give.

In fact, when I point out layout and appearance bloopers to clients, the usual reaction from developers is "Who cares? It looks fine to me. I have more important things to worry about." While it may be optimistic to expect such attitudes to change in the near future, perhaps this section will at least help developers learn to spot and avoid the most common layout and appearance bloopers. In the long run, the attitudes must change or the customers will disappear.

3.1 Poor layout and arrangement of windows and dialog boxes

The first category of layout and appearance bloopers consists of those in which software windows are either laid out or positioned poorly.

3.1.1 Blooper 20: Mixing dialog box control buttons with content control buttons

A very common design error seen in dialog boxes is to mix buttons that control specific data or settings in the dialog box with the standard dialog box control buttons, for example, OK, Apply, Close, Cancel, Help. For example, in a dialog

Figure 3.1

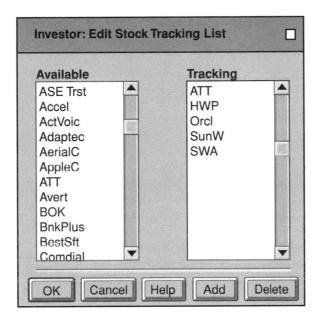

box containing a scrolling list of "Available" items and another scrolling list of "Tracking" items, a programmer might put Add and Delete buttons (which allow users to populate the "Tracking" list from the "Available" list and manage the contents of the "Tracking" list) at the bottom of the dialog box, next to the OK, Cancel, and Help buttons (see Figure 3.1). The programmer probably does this because the bottom row of buttons is a convenient place to put the Add and Delete buttons. Otherwise, he or she would have to figure out where else to put them. Alternatively, the reason could be to use space in the window efficiently.

Figure 3.2 shows the same blooper in an actual product: Microsoft Windows 98 control panels. This is a design error for two reasons:

1. Placing setting-specific buttons not adjacent to the data they control makes it difficult for users to see the relationship between the button and the data.

2. No visual distinction is made between buttons that pertain to the dialog box as a whole (e.g., the standard dialog box control buttons) and those that pertain to specific settings in it.

Avoiding Blooper 20: The design rule

Buttons that affect the entire dialog box should be distinguished from those that control specific data or settings in it. In particular, the standard dialog box control buttons—OK, Apply, Close, Cancel, Help—should be separated from all other buttons in the dialog box.

Figure 3.2

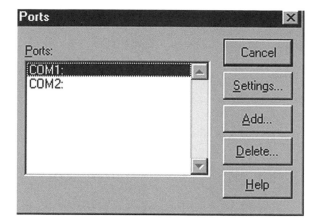

Figure 3.3

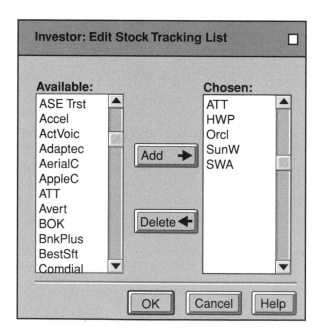

In the dialog box shown in Figure 3.3, the Add and Delete buttons are positioned between the two scrolling lists that they affect, making their function much clearer as well as reserving the bottom row of the dialog box for window control buttons.

Figure 3.4 is an example of correct layout in Microsoft Outlook's Select Names dialog box. I also recommend using a separator (i.e., a line) to separate content control buttons and settings from the dialog box control buttons, as is shown in the Outlook dialog box. However, this is not necessary.

Figure 3.4

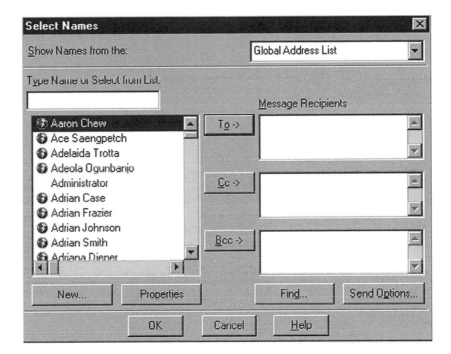

3.1.2 Blooper 21: Layout that doesn't reflect usual or natural order of settings

For obvious reasons, the more complex and feature-loaded a software product or service is, the more likely it is that its developers will feel the need to bring in a user interface consultant. Thus, it makes sense that the GUI software I review or test for clients tends to be on the complex side: lots of data, lots of windows, lots of controls.

Random layout. One problem I often see in complex software is what I call "random" layout of controls, settings, and data fields. By this, I don't mean "random" in a graphic design sense—controls that are poorly aligned or badly spaced. I mean "random" in a logical sense—the layout order is, or at least feels, arbitrary. It doesn't reflect the order in which people expect to be able to work through forms and control panels, it doesn't reflect the relative importance or frequency of use of the various controls, and it doesn't reflect how the controls are related to each other. Instead, it seems as if the GUI programmer, after determining what settings and controls were needed, just tossed them all

Figure 3.5

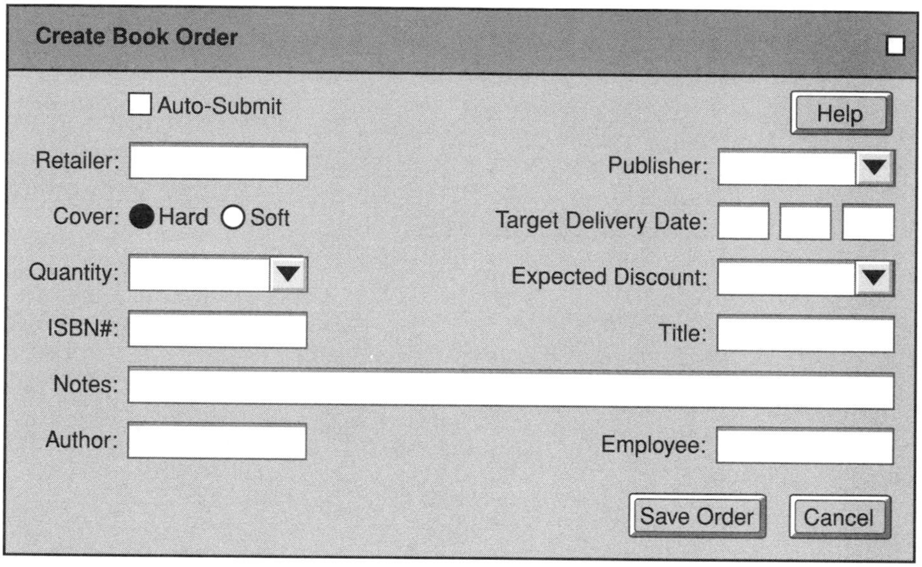

into a grid on the panel more or less at random. Even if the arrangement looks nice, it may still be frustrating.

Figure 3.5 provides a parody of such a control panel: a dialog box for book-store employees to use in ordering books. Users would probably expect to be able start by specifying the book's title, author, and publisher, and the quantity desired. They would want to leave many of the settings—such as Notes, Target Delivery Date, and Expected Discount—at the default values most of the time. However, the ordering of settings on this dialog box is annoyingly arbitrary, requiring users either to enter the data out of order or to bounce back and forth in it from top to bottom and left to right. In order to do anything involving such a panel, users have to hunt through all of the controls to determine which ones need to be set in this case; for example, they set one on the upper left, one over on the lower right, one scrolled down the page on the left side, one in another panel, and so on.

Although this example is a made-up parody, truth, as they say, is often stranger than fiction. Take a look at the Print Options dialog box in Figure 3.6, from Band in a Box 6.0, a music accompaniment program. The dialog box contains everything a user might want to set when printing music for a song or tune. It's all there, if you can find it!

The following passages are excerpts from user interface reviews I prepared for two client companies:

Company 1: The user interface is marred by haphazard logical layout of settings in dialog boxes and control panels. The layout of controls should reflect the usual order in which users set the settings (i.e., fill in the fields), and the frequency with which the settings will be changed (e.g., often vs. rarely). It isn't

Figure 3.6

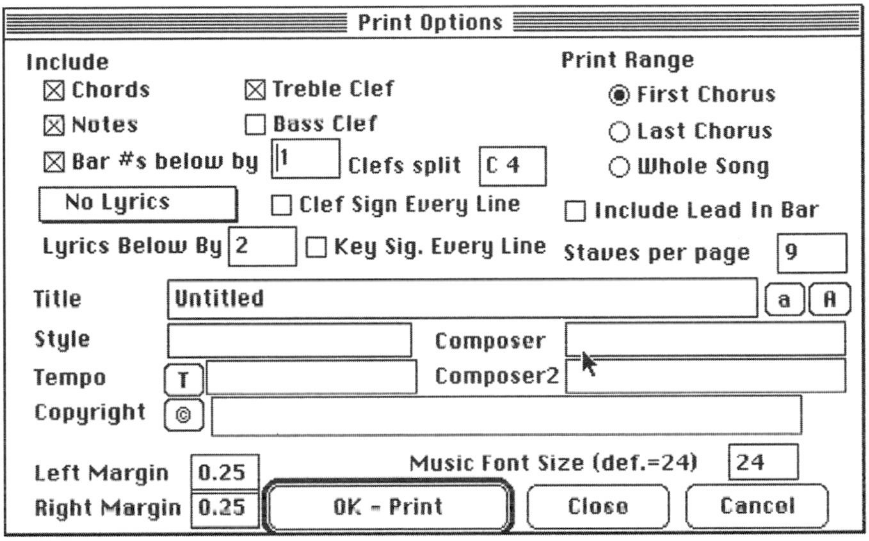

```
┌══════════════════════════ Print Options ══════════════════════════┐
│                                                                    │
│  Include                              Print Range                  │
│     ☒ Chords      ☒ Treble Clef          ◉ First Chorus            │
│     ☒ Notes       ☐ Bass Clef            ○ Last Chorus             │
│     ☒ Bar #s below by [1]   Clefs split [C 4]   ○ Whole Song       │
│     [  No Lyrics  ]    ☐ Clef Sign Every Line                      │
│     Lyrics Below By [2]   ☐ Key Sig. Every Line  Staves per page [9]│
│                                          ☐ Include Lead In Bar     │
│  Title      [Untitled                              ]    [a] [A]     │
│  Style      [                    ]  Composer  [                 ]   │
│  Tempo   [T] [              ]       Composer2 [                 ]   │
│  Copyright [©] [                                  ]                 │
│                                                                    │
│  Left Margin  [0.25]      Music Font Size (def.=24)  [24]           │
│  Right Margin [0.25]  [  OK - Print  ]  [  Close  ]  [  Cancel  ]   │
└────────────────────────────────────────────────────────────────────┘
```

sufficient to simply put all the relevant settings and buttons somewhere on the panel and assume that users will know when to use each one and how they are related to each other. Much more care needs to be given to laying out these control panels and dialog boxes, since there are so many settings. The UI should make more use of progressive disclosure: making frequently used controls easily accessible, hiding rarely used controls behind covers or switches, and using sensible defaults for settings users don't usually care about.

Company 2: The Trade Status display checkbox is too far from what it controls. Recommendation: It should be at the bottom, near the area it expands.

In my experience, "random" layout occurs for three different reasons: no time, no knowledge, and no excuse.

No time. A common cause of "random" layout of controls and data fields in windows and dialog boxes is that the programmer simply didn't have time to do any better. With today's hyperaggressive, "Internet time" development schedules, programmers are often under tremendous pressure to churn out code in absurdly short amounts of time. To cope, many GUI programmers just focus on providing the required functionality in time to meet their deadline, and assume that they or someone else will have time to worry about "prettying it up" later.

The problem arises when, as is common in software development, "later" never arrives. Often, neither the programmer nor anyone else on the team ever gets around to improving the layout order of controls. Perhaps everyone is so busy fighting fires that the tasks on their to-do lists remain neglected. Perhaps they consider improving the control layout less important than adding all those last-minute extra features Marketing keeps demanding.

Perhaps they just keep putting off worrying about it because they view control layout as just a "surface" issue—something easily corrected at the last minute, like changing the text of a message. Of course, making a change may be easy once you know what change you want to make, but what is difficult and time-consuming is figuring out what change you want to make—in this case, figuring out what the layout order should be. Thus, even if someone does eventually decide to do the layout task, it suddenly appears more time-consuming than expected, so it gets pushed to the bottom of the list.

Whatever the reason, a common scenario is that no one on the team ever gets back to the issue of fixing the "random" layout. The development deadline arrives, and, voilà: a product hits the market with a "random," user-hostile layout.

No knowledge. Another common cause of "random" layouts is that the developers know little or nothing about the target users and their tasks, and so don't really know what layout order would make sense to users. Rather than going out and collecting that information, they do one of two things:

- They guess. Maybe it's an educated guess, maybe it's a wild guess, but it's a guess just the same.
- They put on their "user" hats, try to imagine themselves in the users' seats, and design a layout order that makes sense to them.

It isn't clear which one of these methods is worse. They may even be the same thing. In any case, the result is usually just plain wrong. Unless the intended product is a programming environment for software developers, it is never a good idea for software developers to assume that they know what users want.

No excuse. Sometimes I see GUI control panels that are laid out not according to function and not "randomly," but rather according to the physical appearance of the controls. Controls are segregated by type (in the GUI toolkit sense): command buttons are in one place, radiobuttons are in another place, and checkboxes are in yet another. Sliders, text fields, scrolling lists, and so on—each has its designated area on the panel. The layout does not reflect functional relationships between controls. For example: a button at the bottom of the panel deletes an item from a scrolling list in the middle, or a checkbox at the top exposes or hides a scrolling table near the bottom.

Laying out panels based on physical control type rather than function is something engineers have been doing for decades. The problem is not restricted to computers. It was common in early nuclear power plant control panels, airplane cockpits, telephone switchboards, and steam-engine train cabs. It has always been bad for usability. However, at least in physical panels, there was a plausible excuse for it—physical constraints that made it difficult or more costly to do otherwise, such as length of wires and levers, number of gears or pulleys, connections between pipes, layout of underlying circuitry, and so on. Engineers often knowingly sacrificed usability to maximize reliability or minimize cost.

GUI control panels have no such constraints or trade-offs. Therefore, there is no plausible excuse for laying out GUI controls according to their physical appearance.

Avoiding Blooper 21: *The design rule*

The layout order of controls, settings, and data fields in GUI control panels and windows should be based on four criteria:

- *Dominant reading order:* The layout should, first of all, reflect the order in which people typically read documents and fill out paper forms. In North, Central, and South America and most of Europe, the prevailing reading order is left to right, top to bottom. Control panels in GUIs intended for English-speaking users should therefore be laid out based on the expectation that users will encounter the controls at the top left of the window first, then will move to the right, and will zigzag down the panel. In other cultures—for example, Japanese and Middle Eastern—the dominant reading order is different, so software intended for people in those cultures should be laid out accordingly.

- *Frequency of use:* Controls that designers expect users to set or scrutinize frequently should be laid out prominently and placed where users will encounter them early. Conversely, controls that designers expect users to set rarely should be tucked off in a corner somewhere. For related design principles and rules, see Principle 3 (Section 1.3.4) and also Blooper 46: Overwhelming users with decisions and detail (Section 5.2.1).

- *Relationship to other controls:* Controls should be placed near any other controls or data displays they affect. Buttons that affect the content of scrolling lists should be immediately adjacent to those lists. Togglebuttons that open and close auxiliary panels or displays should be next to those panels or displays—not, for example, at the top of the window. This design rule is related to the one described in Blooper 20: Mixing dialog box control buttons with content control buttons (Section 3.1.1).

- *User expectation:* The most important criterion for determining layout order is "whatever users want." This criterion sometimes even contradicts the previous three. Of course, applying this criterion requires that developers find out what users want.

Obviously, the more controls there are on a panel, the more important it is to lay the controls out well. If a control panel, window, or Web page has only two controls, layout order isn't very important. If it has a dozen controls, layout order is more important. If it has several dozen or more, layout order is crucial.

When user expectations beat other considerations

A couple of years ago, a company hired me to review and help improve the user interface of an application they had developed. The application was designed for stockbrokers to use in buying and selling stock for their clients. The first release of the software had been in use for almost a year. The motivation for improving the application's user interface was that users—stockbrokers—had been complaining that the software was difficult to learn and to use.

On reviewing the software, I found that one of its more important windows—the one for creating and specifying a new stock order—had a layout of settings that seemed quite questionable. In particular, it was laid out such that the most frequently used settings were scattered throughout the form, rather than being positioned so that users would encounter them first and could ignore the less frequently used fields.

The majority of stock orders are simple: the client wants to buy or sell a certain number of shares of a specified stock at the market price. There are many extra requirements that a client can place on a stock order, including (among others) wait for a specific price, wait for a specific percentage change in price from the current price, wait for a specified time before submitting order, withdraw order by a specified date if not filled, and accept a specific lower number of shares if the entire order cannot be filled. In practice, the extra requirements are usually absent, so stockbrokers usually leave the corresponding settings on the order specification form at their default value, which for most of the settings is "unspecified."

As the settings were laid out in the Create Order window, stockbrokers had to scan across the entire window to find the settings needed for the most common types of orders. I therefore initially recommended that the settings be reordered based on expected frequency of use. However, discussions with users revealed that reordering the settings was undesirable because the layout of the software's form was based on the layout of paper forms that stockbrokers had been using for decades. The brokers were used to the layout as it was and didn't want it changed.

The users' wish was our command. The layout order remained unchanged.

3.1.3 Blooper 22: Poor initial window location

Most GUI-based computer applications consist of a main window and a number of other windows. One issue that arises is, Where on the computer screen should an application's windows be located? Clearly, once a window has appeared, users should be able to move it anywhere on the screen they want, but the issue I want to address right now is, Where should an application's windows *first* appear?

Figure 3.7

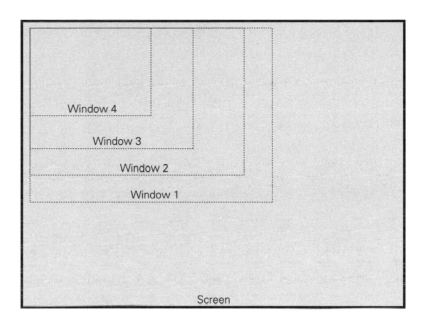

A common blooper is for software to display windows in a location that is more for the convenience of the programmer than for the convenience of users. This blooper has several variations.

Variation A: Displaying all windows at the same coordinate. One surprisingly common form of the blooper is for an application to display all or most of its windows at the same screen position. Since the position of a window on the screen is specified by the screen coordinate of its upper-left corner, positioning windows at the "same location" means that their upper-left corners will coincide. This is certainly easy for programmers: they don't have to consider or calculate where each window should go. However, displaying all of an application's windows at the same screen location forces users to move windows to uncover other ones or to prevent windows from being covered by the next-displayed window.

A special case of Variation A is when GUI programs open all new windows in screen position (0, 0), the upper-left corner of the screen (see Figure 3.7). That is usually the window manager's default location if no location is specified. Taking the default is easy from a programming standpoint, but it stacks all the windows on top of each other, and gives users an impression of a shoddy implementation as well.

A common excuse for bringing up all windows at the same coordinate is that it is difficult for a programmer to decide what initial location would be most suitable for each window that an application can display. But excuses don't help users when dozens of application windows all appear in more or less the same place, obscuring each other, requiring users to move them off each other.

Variation B: Displaying subordinate windows in the middle of the parent. Another common window-positioning strategy is to center each subordinate window over its parent window. The parent window is the window from which the subordinate window is invoked. Since window locations are specified in terms of the position of their upper-left corner, centering one window over another requires a little more calculation than does simply placing two windows at the same screen coordinate. The formulae for calculating the coordinates of the window-to-be-centered (NewWindow) are

```
NewWindow.x = ParentWindow.x + (ParentWindow.width - NewWindow.width) / 2

NewWindow.y = ParentWindow.y + (ParentWindow.height - NewWindow.height) / 2
```

If there is only one "parent" window over which all of an application's subordinate windows appear, obviously this approach has the same problems as Variation A: all the windows appear on top of each other. However, most applications consist of a hierarchy of windows, and so have many different windows serving as parents to other windows. For example, many different windows in an application may contain commands that display dialog boxes.

Spreading the initial locations of subordinate windows out across all the different parent windows alleviates the "all on top of each other" problem somewhat. But the following problems remain:

- All the subordinate windows of a particular parent window still appear over each other. If a given parent window has many subordinate windows, we're back to the "all on top of each other" problem.

- Sometimes subordinate windows are larger than their parent windows. In such a case, the parent is completely obscured when the subordinate window appears.

- In Microsoft Windows and some other windowing systems, applications can display subordinate windows either as "external" windows, which are outside of the parent and can be moved independently of it, or as "internal" windows, which are inside the body of their parent window and move with it. When a subordinate window appears centered directly over its parent and is smaller than its parent, users may not be able to see immediately whether it is external or internal to the parent. To find out which it is, users have to try to move the subordinate window outside of the boundaries of the parent. If its edges are clipped by the parent, it's internal; otherwise, it's external.

Because of these problems, I consider software applications that display all subordinate windows centered over their parents to be a variation of this blooper.

Variation C: Displaying subordinate windows off-screen. Obviously, the most user-hostile variation of the blooper of "poor initial window location" would be to place windows off-screen, so users won't even know they are there. As unbelievable as it sounds, I have seen software that does this.

One of my clients had a Windows application that always displayed a certain subordinate window immediately adjacent to the main window, above it. Thus, if the main window happened to be positioned such that its top edge was at the top of the computer screen—as would be true if the user had simply maximized the main window—the subordinate window would "appear" just off the top of the screen. When I was learning to use the application, I first reported this as a bug: "The 'Trade Monitor Summary' function doesn't seem to be displaying its window," but the programmers pulled the main window down to show me that the Trade Monitor Summary window had indeed appeared...off-screen. How useful! Furthermore, this software had been in customers' hands for over a year. Not many customers, however.

Another client had a released product that sometimes displayed windows partially off-screen, as is shown by this excerpt from my user interface review of the product:

> When function windows appear as a result of choosing a function from the Main Window, the windows appear with their upper left corner centered on the Main Window. Since the Main Window is small, if it is at the extreme right of the screen, large function windows appear mostly off screen. Recommendation: Windows should appear entirely on screen. Continue to center the function windows on the Main Window, but choose which corner of the function window to center there depending on the position of the Main Window.

Variation D: Displaying subordinate windows far away from the parent. Sometimes GUI software brings up new windows too far from the parent window. If a user's computer has more than one display, bringing up subordinate windows far from their parent can cause the subordinate window to appear on a different display from the parent. Worse, the subordinate window might be split across displays.

Avoiding Blooper 22: *The design rule*

The following guidelines will help you avoid stacking windows on top of each other.

Decide where each window should appear

It is the job of the software developers—especially the user interface designer if there is one—to decide where each new window should appear initially. Software developers should not abdicate this responsibility by adopting overly simplistic methods of determining window placement, such as opening all windows at screen coordinate (0, 0).

Optimal position may depend on the type of window

Most software applications display many different types of windows: application main windows, subordinate primary windows, object property dialog boxes, command dialog boxes, error dialog boxes, warning dialog boxes, confirmation dialog boxes, and so on. Although there are heuristics for good window placement that are independent of a window's type (discussed next), the best initial position of a window depends at least partly on what type of window it is.

Error, warning, and confirmation dialog boxes should appear in prominent locations, to capture the users' attention. The best position for that is to center the window at the current mouse pointer position. Almost as good is displaying the dialog box near the command the user just invoked that gave rise to the error, warning, or confirmation (if there was one). Another possible prominent position for error, warning, and confirmation dialog boxes is the center of the computer screen, although I wouldn't recommend placing all such dialog boxes there.

Object property dialog boxes should appear adjacent to the object whose properties they are displaying.

Application main windows and subordinate primary windows can appear just about anywhere on the screen initially, as long as they don't all appear in the same place. However, if a user moves a window to a new location, the software should remember that location and display the same window in the same place next time. Note: This does not apply to error, warning, and confirmation dialog boxes, which should always appear in approximately the same location.

Some general heuristics

Over and above the rules that depend on the type of window, there are heuristic rules that apply to all windows:

- Windows should always appear entirely on-screen. Window positions that are relative to the location of other objects, such as the mouse pointer or the corresponding command or data, should be adjusted as necessary to make sure the new window appears entirely on-screen.

- Staggered placement—each new window appearing a little further rightward and downward from the last one—can be used in conjunction with other placement rules. For example, windows of a certain type may appear in a certain approximate location, but successive windows of that same type may be staggered.

- In Microsoft Windows, an external subordinate window should not appear above a main window's content area, so users can see that it isn't internal to the parent.

- Don't cover important information, especially information in a previous window that the user will need to respond to the new window. Although it is difficult to know what information users still need, it is not impossible. For example, Microsoft Word does a good job, when a user invokes its Find or Replace function, of bringing the dialog box up in a location that leaves some of the document text still visible.

When nothing else is possible, just try to avoid displaying all windows on top of each other. Even random window placement is better than always using location (0, 0), as long as the random positions are generated with the restriction that all windows appear fully on-screen.

3.2 Goofs with group boxes and separators

The second category of layout and appearance bloopers consists of misuses of various graphical means for grouping and separating GUI components.

3.2.1 Blooper 23: Misusing group boxes

Most user interface toolkits provide a type of component for placing a visible border around other components. Its purpose is to indicate meaningful groups of settings. Such components typically have a slot for a label, usually on the top edge near the left side. The actual name for this type of component varies from toolkit to toolkit. Commonly used names are "group box," "border," and "frame."[1] In this book, we will use the term "group box."

Variation A: Group box around one setting. A common GUI layout blooper is to place a group box around a single setting. The usual excuse for doing this is that the designer is using the group box's built-in label to label the setting. For example, one of my client companies had a programmer who, until I reviewed his software, regularly put group boxes around scrolling text areas and tabbed panels in order to label them. Figure 3.8 shows group boxes being used as label holders.

Using group boxes merely as holders for labels is misusing them because it undermines their meaning as a grouping construct, and it clutters the display needlessly. It also often results in redundant borders, since many GUI components—such as tables, scrolling lists, option menus, and text fields—have their own built-in borders.

Examples of this blooper in released software are provided by the Font option dialog box from the file compression tool WinZip 6.3 for Windows (Figure 3.9) and the Text Flow tab panel of the Paragraph dialog box from Microsoft

---

1. The term "frame" has a very different meaning in Web pages. It refers to a mechanism for splitting a browser window to allow multiple Web pages to be viewed at once.

Figure 3.8

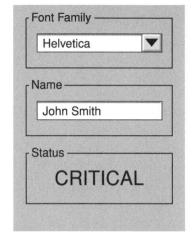

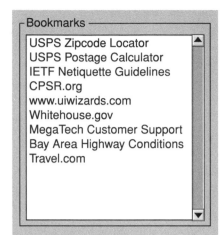

Figure 3.9

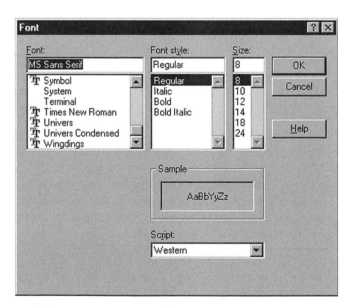

Word 6.0.1 for Macintosh (Figure 3.10). The blooper is in the labeling of the "Sample" and "Preview" areas, which both preview how the chosen settings will look. The group box around them is purely a place to put the label. In both cases, the group box is unnecessary: the label could have simply been placed above the corresponding area.

To misuse group boxes in this way is to be unclear on the purpose of group boxes. They are called *group* boxes for a reason. Items can be labeled without cluttering the display with extra group boxes.

Figure 3.10

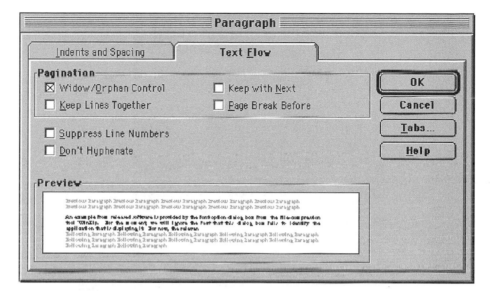

Figure 3.11

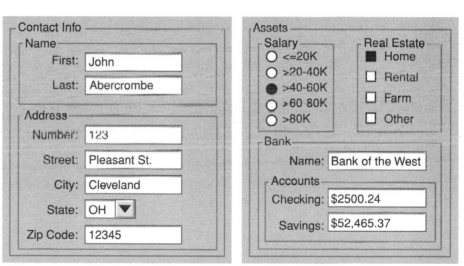

Variation B: Group boxes within group boxes. Another form of this blooper is to nest group boxes within group boxes. This makes for a needlessly cluttered display, as Figures 3.11 and 3.12 show.

Variation C: One group box in a window. A third misuse of group boxes is to put one group box around everything inside a dialog box. The box may group multiple settings, but it doesn't separate those settings from any others. Thus, the group box is unnecessary.

The outer group box in Figure 3.13 (labeled "Edit Stock Tracking List") is unnecessary. The programmer may have included it to hold the name of the

Figure 3.12

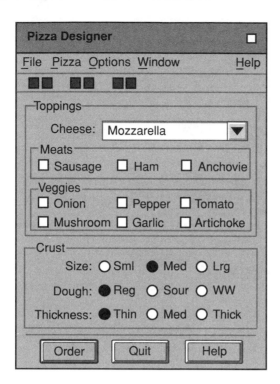

function. However, the function name would be more visible if it were in the window titlebar: for example, "Investor: Edit Stock Tracking List." Alternatively, the programmer's intent might have been to separate the bottom row of control buttons from everything else. However, there are better ways to do that, such as using a separator.

The screen image in Figure 3.14 is a dialog box from SoundBlaster 16 Wave Studio. Ignore (for now) its ambiguously worded window title: Is it for recording settings or is it settings for making recordings? Instead, notice the unnecessary group box around the entire window content and the group boxes around each radiobutton setting. It commits variations B and C of this blooper. This dialog box is more cluttered than it needs to be.

Avoiding Blooper 23: *The design rule*

Group boxes are for grouping settings on a panel, to indicate that those settings are more closely related to each other than they are to other settings on the panel. Complex items such as tables, scrolling lists, and editable text fields provide their own built-in borders and shouldn't require additional borders. Furthermore, their borders should appear different than the borders of group boxes.

A single item should be labeled without putting a group box around it, using the toolkit's Label or Static Text component. Labels should be above or to the left of the item, whichever is better for overall display layout.

Figure 3.13

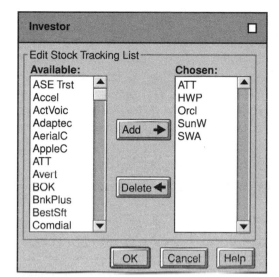

Figure 3.14

Group boxes should be used sparingly. Unnecessary group boxes should be avoided. Placing group boxes within group boxes can clutter the display badly. Careful spacing and labeling can go a long way toward clarifying the organization of a control panel while minimizing the use of group boxes. Compare the

Figure 3.15

Figure 3.16

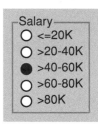

Figure 3.17

Pizza Designer in Figure 3.15 with the one in Figure 3.12 to see how nested group boxes can be avoided. When spacing alone isn't sufficient, vertical and horizontal separators can be used to provide visual order.

A borderline case is a setting consisting of several radiobuttons. Is such a setting a single component or multiple components? Is it OK to put a group box around a set of radiobuttons comprising a single setting (Figure 3.16)?

In some GUI toolkits, a set of radiobuttons is treated as a single component, while in others it is multiple components, but this variation in implementation is not actually relevant to this discussion. We are concerned only with how *users* regard sets of radiobuttons. A set of radiobuttons is a single control or setting because it sets only one value. Therefore, putting a group box around a set of radiobuttons that comprise one setting would be a violation of the above-described group box rule. Accordingly, I usually recommend against doing that. Instead, I recommend that the radiobuttons be laid out and labeled some other way (see Figure 3.17). However, there are rare situations in which a control panel layout is clarified by enclosing a radiobutton setting in a labeled group box. Therefore, I will refrain from saying that you should never do so. But I will caution developers who see a "need" to do this to consult an experienced user interface designer first.

3.2.2   Blooper 24: Inconsistent group box style

Group boxes in most GUI toolkits can be set to display a variety of different border styles, such as simple black line, 3D inset, 3D outset, etched in, etched out, and drop shadow. The group box's border can also be set to a range of widths. The two most common border styles for group boxes are etched in or etched out, probably because most GUI toolkits have one of these as the default setting for newly created group boxes.

Variation A: Mixing etched-in and etched-out group boxes. Since most group boxes use either etched-in or etched-out borders, the most common form of this blooper is to have some group boxes in an application (or collection of related applications) etched in and others etched out. This usually occurs because different programmers develop different parts of the application, with no design guidelines, no communication, and no management oversight (see Blooper 80: Anarchic development, Section 8.2.2). In Figure 3.18, the group box in the dialog box on the left is etched in, while the one in the dialog box on the right is etched out.

Variation B: Inconsistent border styles. Another variation of this blooper is to use entirely different styles of group boxes in different windows in an applica-

Figure 3.18

Figure 3.19

Pizza Designer: Select Toppings □
┌─Toppings─────────────────────┐
Cheese: [Mozzarella ▼]
Meats: ☐ Ssg ☐ Ham ☐ Anchov
Veggies: ☐ Onion ☐ Pepr ☐ Tom
☐ Mshrm ☐ Garlic ☐ Art
[Order] [Quit] [Help]

Pizza Designer: Select Crust □
┌─Crust───────────────────────┐
Size: ○ Sml ● Med ○ Lrg
Dough: ● Reg ○ Sour ○ WW
Thickness: ● Thin ○ Med ○ Thick
[Order] [Quit] [Help]

Figure 3.20

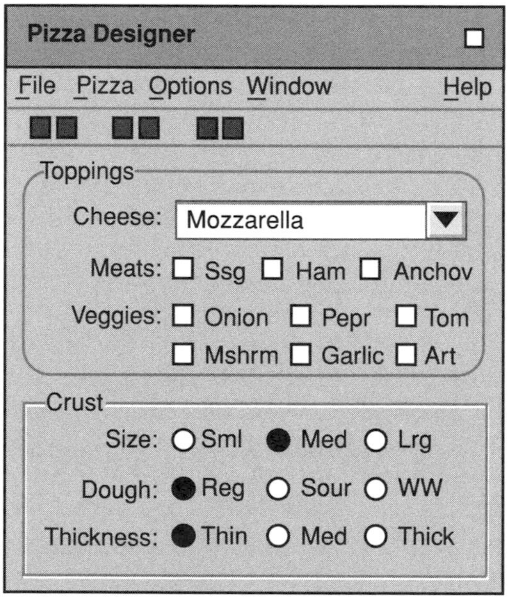

Pizza Designer □
File Pizza Options Window   Help
▪▪ ▪▪ ▪▪
┌─Toppings───────────────────────┐
Cheese: [Mozzarella ▼]
Meats: ☐ Ssg ☐ Ham ☐ Anchov
Veggies: ☐ Onion ☐ Pepr ☐ Tom
☐ Mshrm ☐ Garlic ☐ Art
┌─Crust──────────────────────────┐
Size: ○ Sml ● Med ○ Lrg
Dough: ● Reg ○ Sour ○ WW
Thickness: ● Thin ○ Med ○ Thick

tion, with no systematic difference in meaning for the different styles. Again, this is usually due to a lack of communication and coordination between programmers.

Notice the difference in style of the group boxes in the two dialog boxes in Figure 3.19. I've even seen software that had completely different group box border styles on the same panel! As bizarre as this seems, it happens. An example is shown in Figure 3.20.

How can this happen? Easy. One programmer constructs a panel of controls, encloses the controls in a group box, and encapsulates the panel as a reusable component. Then another programmer incorporates the group component into a control panel where there is another group box that has a different border style, but the second programmer doesn't notice the difference or doesn't consider it worth reconciling.

Avoiding Blooper 24: The design rule

Group boxes in an application or family of applications should all have the same border style.

By far the most common border style for group boxes is etched (in or out), so I recommend following that tradition. I prefer group boxes to have etched-out borders to distinguish them from separators, for which the convention is etched in (see Blooper 25: Inconsistent separator style, Section 3.2.3). However, most designers use etched-in borders on group boxes. Either is OK, as long as you are consistent throughout the application or family of applications.

The best way to make sure you do the "right thing" is to simply follow the style guide of the GUI platform on which your software will be running.

3.2.3   Blooper 25: Inconsistent separator style

Most user interface toolkits provide a type of component for placing a visible line between other components. Its purpose is to separate meaningful groups of settings. Lines can be positioned either vertically or horizontally. The actual name for this type of component varies from toolkit to toolkit. Commonly used names are "separator" and "rule." In this book, we will use the term "separator."

Separators in most GUI toolkits can be set to display a variety of different line styles: for example, simple line, dotted line, etched-in line, and etched-out line. The line can also be set to a range of widths. The most common settings for separators are "simple line" and "etched-in line," probably because most GUI toolkits have one of these as the default setting for newly created separators.

Some primitive toolkits provide no component specifically intended for separating other components. They just provide a simple solid line—with no line style options—that can be oriented horizontally, vertically, or at arbitrary angles. Such line segments can be used as a rudimentary separator. They can also be used to construct fancier separators, for example, by placing a thin dark gray line and a thin white line right next to each other over a gray background to create an etched appearance. Figure 3.21 shows a dialog box containing separators in three different styles.

GUI developers often make one of the same mistakes with separators that they make with group boxes: assigning different styles to separators in different parts of the application. The most common error is to have some separators in an application (or collection of related applications) etched in and others etched out. A less common variation is to use different separator widths, with no systematic difference in meaning for the different thicknesses.

Figure 3.21

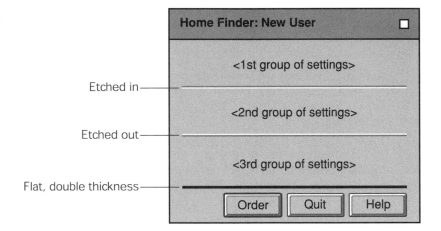

Avoiding Blooper 25: *The design rule*

Separators in an application or family of applications should all have the same line style. By far the most common line style for separators is etched in, and I recommend following that tradition. I also recommend using the thinnest possible line width, to keep the separators looking light and unobtrusive. Whatever separator line style you choose, it is important to use it consistently throughout the application or family of applications.

As with group boxes, the best way to make sure you do the "right thing" is to simply follow the style guide of the GUI platform on which your software will be running.

If the GUI toolkit you are using doesn't have etched separators and the style guide for the target platform requires them, you will need to construct them using adjacent simple lines. Ideally, separators should *not* consist of one black line and one white line. Rather, they should consist of one line that is a darker variation of the *background color* (whatever that is) and one white line. This makes for a separator that looks more like an etched-in (or etched-out) feature of the background surface. Since most backgrounds in a product line or family of applications are the same color (e.g., gray or beige), optimizing separators for the background is not difficult.

3.3 Shoddy labeling and spacing

The third category of layout and appearance bloopers consists of ways to screw up the labeling and spacing of software controls and settings.

3.3.1 Blooper 26: Radiobuttons spaced too far apart

One sometimes sees radiobutton settings in which the individual radiobuttons are so far apart that they don't look like they belong to a single setting (see Figure 3.22). The problem is exacerbated if several radiobutton settings appear next to each other because users might not be able to tell how the radiobuttons are grouped into settings. A common form of this blooper is to arrange radiobutton settings one above the other, such that individual choices in each setting are closer to choices in *other* settings than they are to choices in their *own* setting, as shown in Figure 3.23.

In this example, the settings are defined by rows of radiobuttons, yet the choices in each column are closer together than those in each row. In this case, users would probably be able to figure out how the choices are grouped because of the meaning of the setting and value labels, but we could imagine a case in which that was more difficult. For example, see Figure 3.24 or 3.25.

Figure 3.22

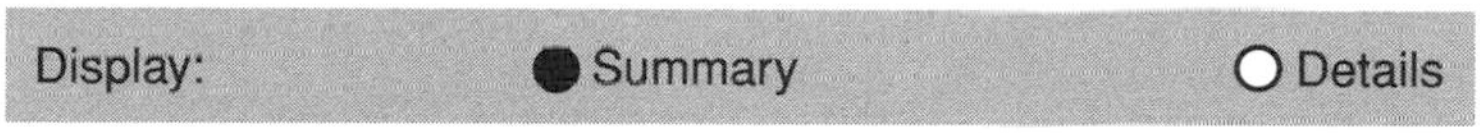

Figure 3.23

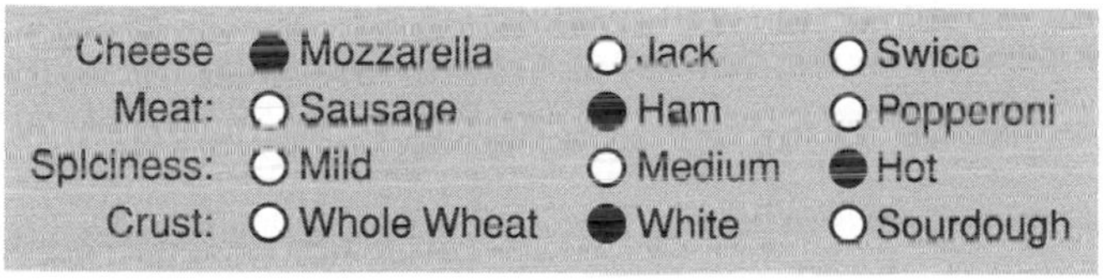

Figure 3.24

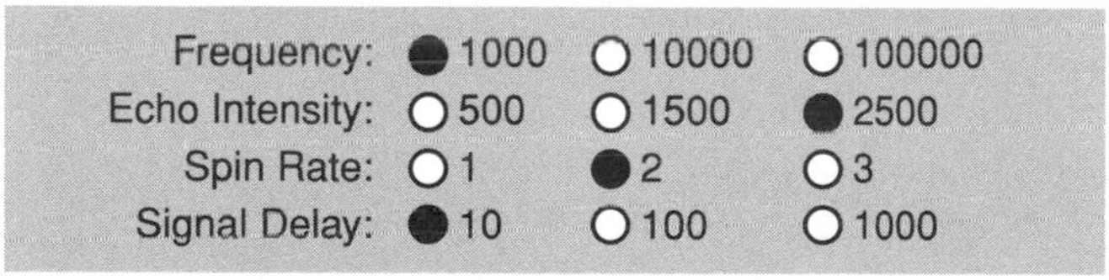

Figure 3.25

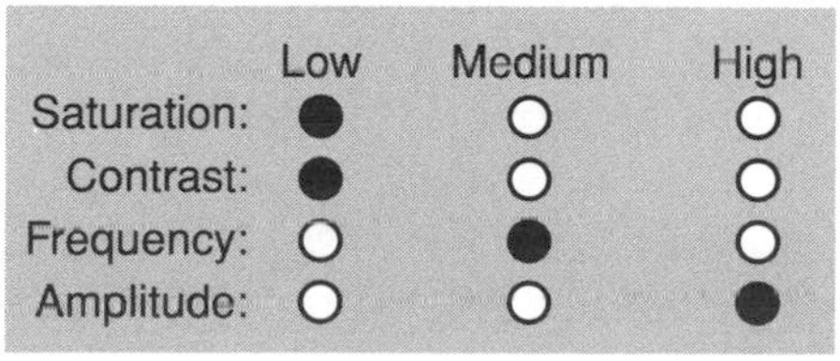

Avoiding Blooper 26: *The design rule*

Radiobutton settings should be laid out so that users can see at a glance which choices go together, that is, comprise a single setting. One way to achieve this is to space the radiobuttons so that the distance between the choices in one setting is less than the distance between choices that are in different settings. It isn't necessary for the actual individual radiobuttons in each setting to be closer together than they are to individual radiobuttons in other settings. As Figure 3.26 shows, if the space between settings is greater than that between the values within each setting (including their labels), people will perceive the intended groupings.

In Figure 3.26, every setting has three choices, and all the choices are arranged in a neat matrix. If the number of choices varies from setting to setting or if labels of choices in different settings vary greatly in length, it is better to space each setting tightly, even though doing so destroys the neat matrix arrangement (see Figure 3.27). I realize that such an irregular layout may bother some graphic designers and software engineers, but we are not trying to avoid bothering them. We are trying to avoid bothering or confusing users.

Irregular layout (as contrasted with regular, matrixlike layout) has the additional benefit of allowing users to use gross visual texture and shape cues to more easily distinguish and recognize different sets of settings. Of course, this should not be used as an excuse for sloppy layout. To be helpful in letting users recognize quickly where they are and what they are looking at, irregular layout must be done in a controlled, purposeful way.

If showing the intended grouping of radiobutton choices through spacing is impractical, then separators or group boxes can be used to achieve the necessary visual separation (see Figure 3.28). My own preference is to use separators for this, rather than group boxes. Users consider each group of radiobuttons

Figure 3.26

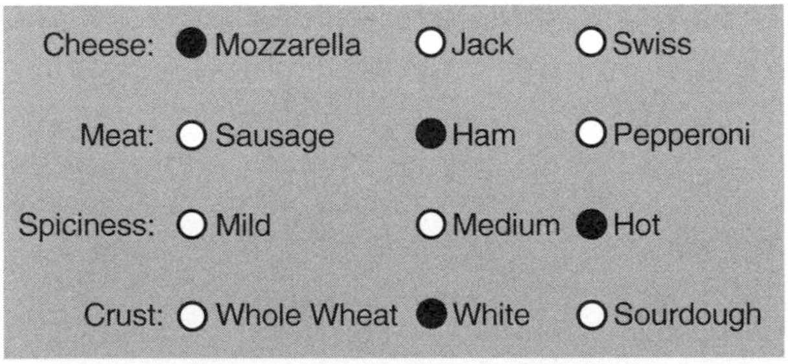

Cheese: ● Mozzarella   ○ Jack   ○ Swiss

Meat: ○ Sausage   ● Ham   ○ Pepperoni

Spiciness: ○ Mild   ○ Medium ● Hot

Crust: ○ Whole Wheat ● White   ○ Sourdough

Figure 3.27

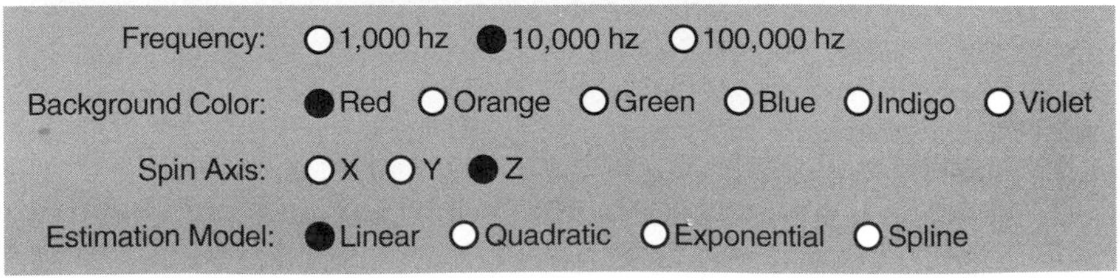

Frequency: ○ 1,000 hz   ● 10,000 hz   ○ 100,000 hz

Background Color: ● Red   ○ Orange   ○ Green   ○ Blue   ○ Indigo   ○ Violet

Spin Axis: ○ X   ○ Y   ● Z

Estimation Model: ● Linear   ○ Quadratic   ○ Exponential   ○ Spline

Figure 3.28

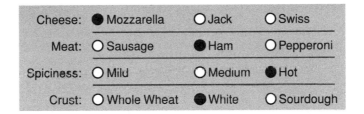

comprising a setting to be a single component (even if the GUI toolkit doesn't). Therefore putting a group box around a setting that is comprised of radiobuttons is technically a case of Variation A of Blooper 23: Group box around one setting (Section 3.2.1). Therefore, I avoid doing that when other means of indicating the radiobutton groupings are practical. However, as explained in the design rule section of Blooper 23, there are occasionally situations in which a control panel layout is clarified by enclosing a radiobutton setting in a labeled group box.

3.3.2 Blooper 27: Inconsistent property label alignment

Most settings in GUIs consist of a label and a value. Setting *values* are always left-aligned, but designers have the choice of left-aligning or right-aligning the setting *labels*. An extremely common blooper is to align the labels of user-settable properties differently in different panels.

Notice in the pair of dialog boxes shown in Figure 3.29 that the setting labels (Name, Soc. Sec. #, Gender, and Address) are left-aligned in the Taxpayer Info dialog box on the left, while the ones in the Font Options dialog box on the right (Family, Size, Face, and Underline) are right-aligned.

Figure 3.29

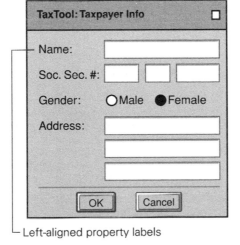

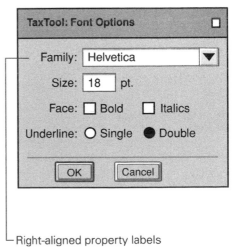

└ Left-aligned property labels   └Right-aligned property labels

Figure 3.30

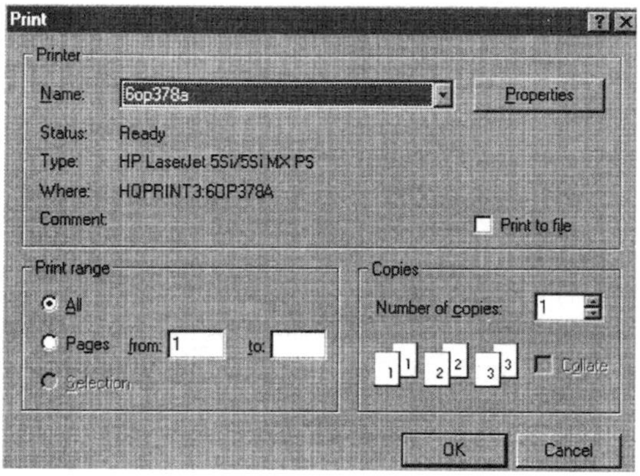

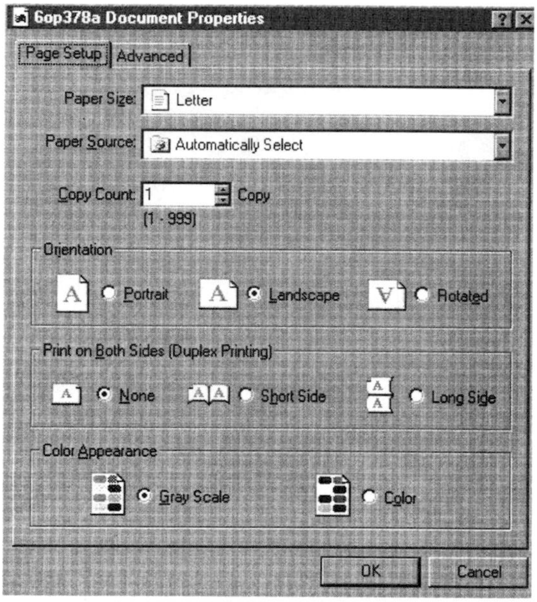

Figure 3.31

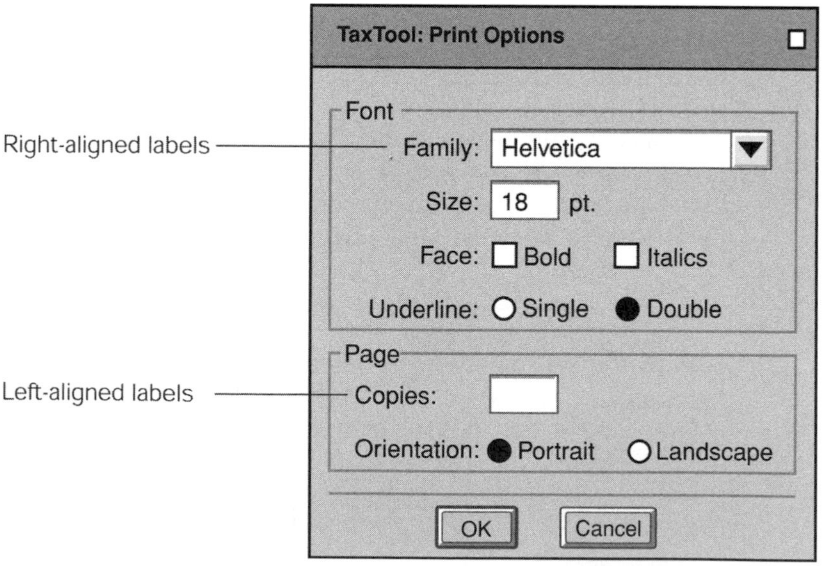

Right-aligned labels ————

Left-aligned labels ————

The same inconsistency can be seen in the pair of dialog boxes from Netscape Communicator 4.04 in Figure 3.30: the labels in the Print dialog box on the left (Name, Status, Type, Where, and Comment) are left-aligned, while the

Figure 3.32

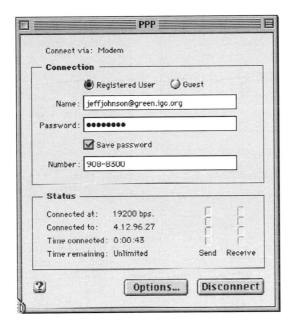

ones in the Document Properties dialog box on the right (Paper Size, Paper Source, and Copy Count) are right-aligned.

I have even seen setting labels aligned differently within a single panel! The example in Figure 3.31 is made up, but Figure 3.32 is a real example: the control panel for Apple Computer's PPP online connection software. In the Connection (upper) group box, the connection setting labels are right-aligned. In the Status (lower) group box, the labels on the displayed data values are left-aligned. While it is true that the upper group box contains editable settings while the lower one contains display-only data values, that by itself would not justify the difference in property label alignment. Most likely, the settings and the status display were developed by different programmers, who did not coordinate their labeling alignment.

Avoiding Blooper 27: The design rule

Within an application or a suite of related applications, alignment of setting labels should be consistent.

Right or left alignment: How's a GUI programmer to choose?

For most GUI platforms, conventions for label alignment either were explicitly developed or have emerged over time as common practice. In the earliest commercially available GUI platform, the Xerox Star, all property labels were left-

Figure 3.33

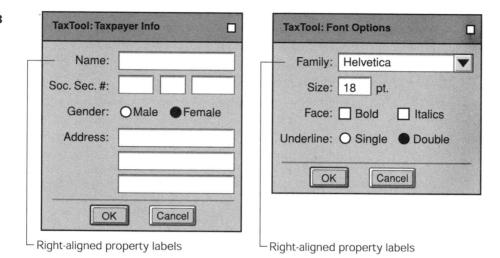

Right-aligned property labels   Right-aligned property labels

aligned, but in Star's immediate successor, Xerox ViewPoint, labels were right-aligned. In the Apple Macintosh, most setting labels are left-aligned, but some Macintosh applications (e.g., Macromedia Director) use right alignment. In the Common Desktop Environment (CDE/Motif) window system for Unix workstations (e.g., Sun Solaris and HP/UX), the convention is to right-align property labels. In Microsoft Windows, left alignment seems to be more common than right alignment, but many applications use right alignment. On the World Wide Web, there is as yet no discernible common practice, and there may never be.

I personally prefer right alignment because it puts the labels closer to the settings and thus makes the correspondence between the label and the setting easier to see (Figure 3.33). However, the GUI guidelines book *GUI Design Essentials* by Weinshenk et al. [1997] recommends left-aligned labels, on the grounds that right-aligned ones create a ragged left margin that makes the settings "difficult to scan."

In fact, it is not important whom you agree with. It is more important that you pick a convention—preferably the dominant practice for your target platform—and use it consistently throughout your application, suite of applications, or product line.

Problem cases: Very, very, very, very, very, very, very long labels

With either left or right alignment of setting labels, developers sometimes encounter pathological cases. These are usually panels or dialog boxes in which one of the settings has a very long label. Aligning *all* the labels and their settings to the long label and its setting wastes a lot of space, as is shown in Figure 3.34. In the case of left alignment, it also puts most of the labels too far away from their settings.

Figure 3.34

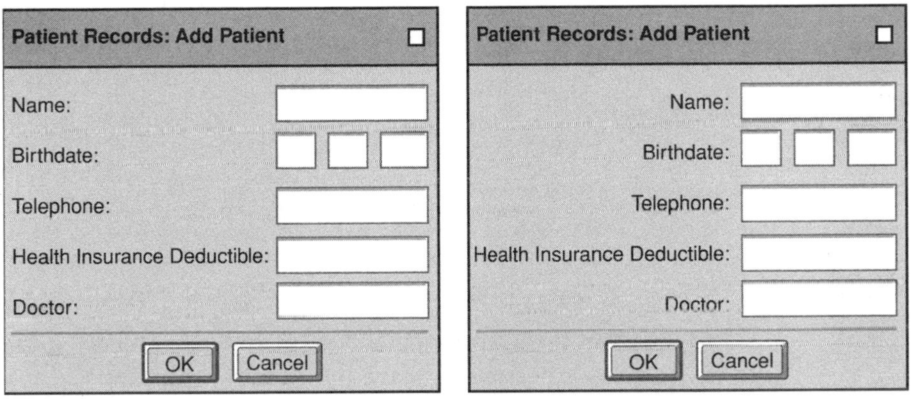

Figure 3.35

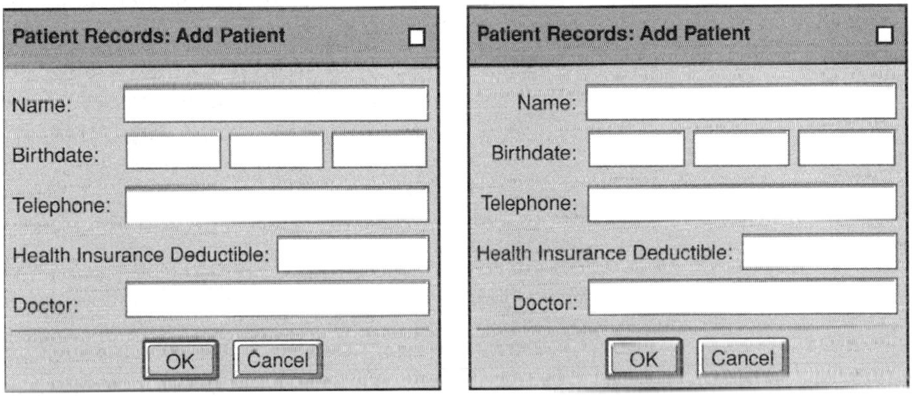

If the long label cannot be abbreviated or broken into two lines in a way that makes sense to users, then one solution is simply to ignore it when aligning the other labels and settings, as is shown in Figure 3.35.

3.3.3 Blooper 28: Poor label placement

In addition to the issues of whether labels should be right- or left-aligned and whether they should end with colons or not, GUI programmers often pay insufficient attention to the relative positioning of controls and their labels. This creates GUIs that look sloppy and amateurish.

Often, programmers fail to pay attention to exact placement because they are under tremendous time pressure to produce a user interface. Therefore, they toss in the widgets as fast as they can without worrying about their exact placement, and assume that the placement can be adjusted sometime in the future when there is more time. Unfortunately, the mythical "sometime in the

Figure 3.36

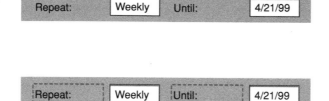

Figure 3.37

future when there is more time" never comes, and even if it did, the programmer does not necessarily have the right skills to notice, let alone correct, the problem.

Of course, GUI development tools are of little help when it comes to providing guidance. In one development project for which I served as a consultant, the GUI development tool used by the programmers provided a "snap grid" to help align GUI components, but the programmers never used the grid. Their reason was that the grid usually was "in their way" so they usually wanted it OFF, and there was no easy way to turn it ON for the few times they did need it. So they always left the snap grid turned OFF and aligned GUI components purely by eye. Needless to say, the GUIs they designed contained many small but noticeable misalignments.

There are two main variations of this blooper.

Variation A: Label too far from setting. The most common error is for property labels to be closer to another property than to the one they are intended to label (see Figure 3.36). Proximity is a powerful determiner of perceived association, so haphazard label placement is not just an aesthetic issue; it can diminish the usability of a tool.

Why do programmers position labels as in Figure 3.36 when it is so easy to position them correctly? For one thing, they may be unaware of how much of an effect label placement has on the speed and ease with which users can comprehend a panel full of settings. In addition, programmers often have to work under tight deadlines.

But a third reason is that programmers may not even regard the labels as being positioned far from the text fields. In Figure 3.37, I've made the actual boundaries of the label components visible.

Assume that the programmer is working under great time pressure. She creates two labels and two text fields. She initially makes each label component plenty wide enough to hold the text of its label and doesn't bother to shrink it to fit the actual text of the label. Maybe she doesn't consider shrinking the label component to fit the label text to be worth the time, or maybe she wants the label components to fit the German translations of the labels also. She specifies that these four components are to be positioned one after another in a line, and just uses the GUI toolkit's default "adjacent" positioning. Voilà! Poor label placement. From her point of view, the labels are next to their settings; from the users' point of view, they aren't. The label placement is poor because the point of view that matters is that of the users.

Variation B: Misaligned text baselines. The other common error is for components within a setting line to be misaligned, as in Figure 3.38.

A real case of misaligned text baselines in a released software product can be seen in Figures 3.39 and 3.40. Figure 3.39 is part of the Attributes dialog box from the Windows Paint Accessory; Figure 3.40 is from the Preference settings of Netscape Communicator 4.5.

An even more blatant example of misaligned text baselines, as well as poorly aligned settings, is provided by the Print Options dialog box of Band in a Box 6.0, a music accompaniment program. A portion of the dialog box is shown in Figure 3.41.

Misalignment of settings and setting labels occurs for one of two reasons. First, as above, the programmer may be in a rush to get something working and doesn't want to take the time to align the components exactly. He just places them manually (with no snap grid to help align them) and makes a mental note to improve the alignment later, when he has more time, which is often never.

Alternatively, the programmer may want to align the components, but simply does not know what sort of alignment is best. Several sorts of alignment are

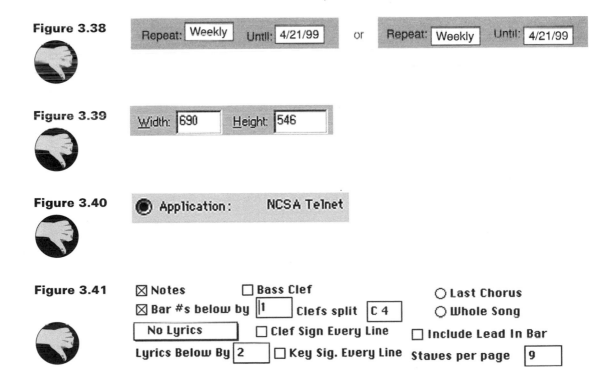

Figure 3.38

Figure 3.39

Figure 3.40

Figure 3.41

Figure 3.42

possible. The example on the right in Figure 3.38 has the tops of the labels aligned with the tops of the text fields. The vertical middles of the labels could also be aligned with the vertical middles of the text fields, or the bottoms of the labels could be aligned with the bottoms of the text fields. However, the correct way to align these components is none of the above as we will see shortly.

Avoiding Blooper 28: *The design rule*

Here are the rules for proper label placement.

Setting labels should be closer to their setting than to other settings

When several labeled setting components (e.g., text fields, menus, sliders) are positioned horizontally, proximity should clearly show the correct pairing of labels with settings. In our example, the spacing between the labels and their associated text fields must be closer than the spacing between the first text field and the second label. If this requires fitting the label components to the actual text—even at run time—so be it.

Align baselines of labels with baselines of text in settings

For correct vertical alignment, all text in a "line" of settings should be positioned so that the baselines (bottoms of letters, ignoring descenders as in *p* and *y*) are aligned. This includes the text *inside* the settings (text fields, menus, etc.). For example, see Figure 3.42.

Note that aligning the baseline of a label with the baseline of the text inside a text field is not the same as aligning the vertical *center* of the label with the vertical center of the text field (which is sometimes called "center" alignment). Depending on the height of the labeled component, center alignment of labels may not result in aligned text baselines. Aligned text baselines is preferred.

3.3.4 Blooper 29: Unlabeled scrolling container components

In addition to buttons, text fields, sliders, and other simple controls, graphical user interfaces often include larger components that display larger quantities of data. These are the lists, tables, multiline text areas, graphs, and other container components. Such components usually allow their content to scroll in case its length or height exceeds that of the container.

Although GUI programmers usually label the smaller components, it is fairly common for them to leave larger scrolling components unlabeled. Per-

Figure 3.43

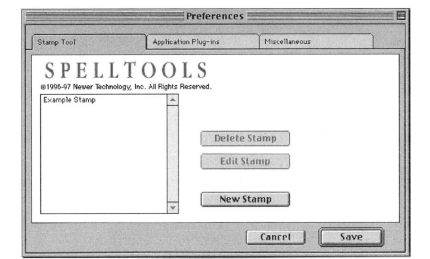

Figure 3.44

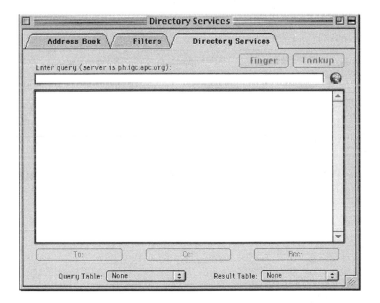

haps they believe that the component's content explains its purpose. This is almost always wrong. What if the component happens to be empty when the user sees it? What if the user doesn't understand what is in the component?

In the dialog box in Figure 3.43, from Newer Technology's SpellTools software, the scrolling list on the left is not labeled. Users just have to know what "stamps" are, and that the Stamp Tool is for managing them. Then they have to deduce that this list must be showing the stamps that have been defined. The default content of the list isn't very helpful in figuring all this out.

An even more problematic example of an unlabeled scrolling area can be seen in the three-panel dialog box from Eudora Pro 4.0 shown in Figure 3.44. The Directory Services panel contains a large scrolling area whose purpose is not entirely clear, even to me, a longtime Eudora user. From the other items on this panel, a fairly computer-savvy user might guess that the scrolling area is for showing the results of querying the directory service, whatever that is. (A computer novice would probably not even realize that.) That would mean that the scrolling area is for output, rather than an area for the user to type data. But with nothing in it—its normal state—even a computer expert can't tell whether this is a scrolling list, a scrolling text area, or an area for displaying a (currently empty) results table. As it turns out, it's a scrolling list of email addresses matching the specified query.

Avoiding Blooper 29: *The design rule*

GUI designers and developers should never assume that the function or purpose of a scrolling list, text area, or table is self-evident. Such components should always be labeled. Even if the meaning of a scrolling component can be deduced from the context in which it appears, a label should be provided. Users don't want to have to analyze a user interface to figure out how it works; they want it to show them how it works.

Some examples

Had I designed the two dialog boxes shown earlier, I would have labeled the scrolling list in SpellTool's Stamp Tool panel something like "Defined Stamps" or "Available Stamps." In Eudora Pro's Directory Services, I would have labeled the scrolling area "Addresses Matching Query" or at least "Query Results."

Figure 3.45, from the Styles dialog box of Microsoft Word 6.0, shows a correctly labeled scrolling list.

Figure 3.45

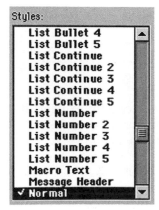

3.4 Troublesome typography and graphic design

The final category of layout and appearance bloopers consists of errors in graphic design, especially in choosing text fonts.

3.4.1 Blooper 30: Inconsistent text *fonts*

An old saying states: "Only two things in life are certain: death and taxes." I'll add another certainty: if a medium allows a variety of text fonts, people will abuse them. We saw this back in the mid-1980s as more people began to use Apple Macintoshes as word processors. Many of my colleagues started sending holiday letters that looked like ransom notes. For example:

Dear **Jeff**,

I just got my new Macintosh last week, just in time to write our annual **Holiday letter**. Boy, is it fun! I'm having a great time using all the wonderful text fonts in everything I write. They let me be so much more e x p r e s s i v e, don't you think?

Well, onto family news. Megan was chosen as MOST VALUABLE PLAYER on her soccer team this year, and boy are we *proud*! She also got straight As (well, a B in home-ec, but who cares about that?) and won the school *piano* competition, but she **always** does that so it's her **soccer** achievements we're crowing about.

People eventually get over the novelty of being able to switch fonts in the middle of sentences and words. Productivity becomes more important. They settle into using a single font most of the time, enhancing it occasionally with boldface, italics, and underlining for emphasis, and increasing the size in headings and titles. All the other fonts in the computer are hardly used, unless one is creating a wedding announcement, party invitation, or the like. But there are new computer users every day, and many of them still go wild with fonts at first.

With GUIs, the situation is similar to that with word processors. Most people who have experience developing GUIs have learned that fonts should be used conservatively and carefully. Newcomers to GUI development haven't. Unfortunately, due to the availability of interactive GUI-development tools, and even more due to the rise of the World Wide Web and Web site-building tools, the number of newcomers to GUI development is huge ... and growing daily! Not surprisingly, the software marketplace and the Web are turning into font jungles.

Figure 3.46

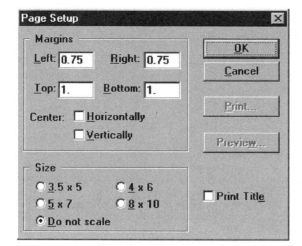

This is even more of a problem in GUIs than it is in printed documents because users try to assign meaning to the various fonts they encounter in an application. When developers use fonts willy-nilly with no underlying rhyme or reason, they *at best* waste the time and mental energy of users who try to figure out what the fonts mean, and *at worst* mislead users who reach false conclusions about the meanings of the fonts.

The font situation on the World Wide Web is utter chaos. On the Web, the font in which text is displayed is, in principle at least, supposed to be determined by the browser (and the browser user), rather than by the Web site designer. Unfortunately, many Web site designers are control freaks. They aren't satisfied with providing useful or entertaining information to site visitors; they want to control the exact fonts in which text is presented on the site. To do this, they specify the font face (e.g., boldface or italics) or the relative font size (on a 1–7 scale), or both. Some Web site developers want even more control over fonts than that, so they embed the text displayed by their site in images rather than encoding it as text.

An example of inconsistent font use can be seen in Figures 3.46 and 3.47, which are both screen images of dialog boxes from Kodak's Picture Disk software. Most of the windows displayed by Picture Disk use the bold font shown in the Page Setup dialog box, but the Print Setup dialog box uses a nonbold font. Granted, the difference between boldface and plain in the same font family and font size isn't a very serious inconsistency. However, it does demonstrate that font inconsistencies can occur in released software. In software I've reviewed for clients, I've seen much grosser inconsistencies.

The main reason fonts get abused is that few development teams establish standards or guidelines for using them. If a variety of fonts is available and pro-

Figure 3.47

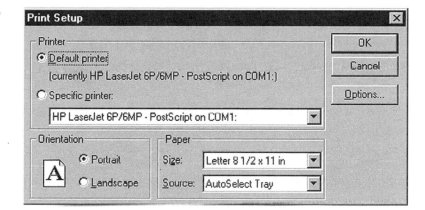

grammers simply use whichever ones strike their fancy, they'll create font pot-pourri.

The chances of ending up with font potpourri are greatly increased when the GUI development tools either don't provide a default text font, or provide one that the developers don't like without providing a way to set a new default. Without a suitable default font, developers must explicitly choose one each time they add any text (or a control into which users type text) to a GUI. If programmers have to choose a font each time, their choices will be somewhat random, unless they make an effort to be more systematic, for example, by putting a yellow sticky note on their computer to remind them what font to use for what purpose.

The chances of font potpourri increase still further when the coding of a product or Web site is divided up between several programmers because communication and agreement between the programmers, as well as management supervision of them, are often insufficient (see Blooper 80: Anarchic development, Section 8.2.2).

Here are some common scenarios that result in inconsistent use of fonts:

- One programmer codes application windows A, B, and C, and chooses Helvetica as the font for setting labels and Times Roman as the font for text entered by users. Another programmer codes windows D, E, F, and G, and chooses New York as the font for setting labels and Helvetica Bold as the font for user-entered text. No one oversees their work.

- A programmer uses 10-point Helvetica for most dialog boxes, but uses 8-point Geneva in a particular dialog box to save space.

- Partway through a development project, a programmer changes her mind about which font to use for error messages, but neglects (or doesn't have time) to go back and change all the error messages she's already coded.

Avoiding Blooper 30: *The design rule*

Using fonts consistently in software and in Web sites is not really very difficult. It mostly requires an awareness that inconsistent use of fonts looks shoddy and amateurish, accompanied by the will to avoid producing a shoddy and amateurish product or service. When a product or service is being developed by a team of programmers, assuring consistency in the use of fonts also requires a bit of management oversight.

The good news: GUI tools have default fonts

Luckily, most development tools and application platforms provide default fonts that are quite satisfactory for most text that an application needs to display. For example, most GUI development tools for the Microsoft Windows platform use the Microsoft font MS Sans Serif (which looks more or less like this) for components that contain text, unless a developer specifies otherwise.

As described above, the trouble begins when developers feel the need—whether for good reason or not—to diverge from the default font. Therefore, one way to avoid trouble is to stick with the default fonts unless you have a strong justification why you shouldn't and a user interface designer who backs you up.

The Web: Relax and let the browser determine the font

Web site designers should spend less time worrying about the exact fonts in which text will be displayed and more time worrying about more important issues, such as navigability, legibility, and responsiveness, not to mention providing value to site visitors. They should encode text as text and let visitors' browsers choose the font.

If Web site designers truly feel that they must control the fonts in which visitors read text, they should establish simple rules and stick to them.

Develop and follow guidelines for font usage

Whether one is developing a software product, an online service, or an electronic appliance that has a display, a little planning can go a long way toward improving the consistency of text font usage. Developers should decide—long before starting to code—what fonts to use for each of the many roles that text can play in a GUI: setting labels, setting values, menu items, group headings, instructions, warnings, popup tooltips, user-entered text, page titles, function names, and so on. Fonts can be standardized for a specific product or service, for a family of products or services, or for an entire development organization. In other words, software development organizations can, if desired, develop local guidelines to augment the platform-specific industry standard design guides.

When developers devise rules governing the use of fonts in their products or services, they should take into account guidelines for font usage that have been developed over centuries of experience in the print media. One such guideline is, Don't mix **serif** and **sans-serif** fonts. In any single product or service, use either all serif fonts or all sans serif fonts. Another guideline is, In a given publication, don't use the same font face (e.g., italics) for two different meanings (e.g., emphasis and book title); restrict each font face to a single role to keep interpretation by readers simple. For more guidelines on using fonts correctly, see Mullet and Sano [1995].

Once developers have established rules for font usage, they should take steps to assure that the rules are followed. For example, as suggested above, programmers can improve their consistency of font usage by simply keeping a yellow sticky note next to their computer listing the names of fonts to use for various situations. Managers, product architects, user interface designers, graphic designers, and technical writers on the project can review the software and point out any discrepancies they spot.

Establishing and following standards for using fonts in software does not mean that there can never be exceptions. The purpose of font standards is just to avoid confusing or annoying users with font potpourri. Sometimes situations will arise where none of the standard fonts seem suitable, possibly because the text that is to be displayed is playing a role not previously encountered or anticipated. In such cases, a user interface or graphic designer should be consulted (ideally, both) to determine what font to use for the special situation without introducing problems or detracting from the application's appearance.

3.4.2 Blooper 31: Tiny fonts

Many software products, online services, and consumer appliances display text in text fonts that are too small. Obviously, the main problem with text displayed using fonts that are too small is that people who have impaired vision can't read it. What may be less obvious is that "people who have impaired vision" includes most people over the age of 45.

Think of startup companies full of twenty-something skateboarders churning out stock investment Web sites that will be used mainly by people who are at or approaching retirement age, and you'll begin to understand the problem. Figure 3.48 shows a fictional stock investment Web site that uses fonts that may be too small for some site visitors to read.

A real example. The Web site in Figure 3.48 is fictional. Of course, truth often surpasses fiction. The image in Figure 3.49 is from the Web site of The Learning Company (*www.learningco.com*), which creates and distributes educational and productivity software for child and adult consumers. The page shown is the main page for the "TLC SuperShop," The Learning Company's online store.

Of course, the Web page shown in the figure has been shrunk to fit into this book, so the font size problem is exaggerated. Nonetheless, most of the text on the page is in an 8-point font, which puts it right on the edge of legibility for me,

Figure 3.48

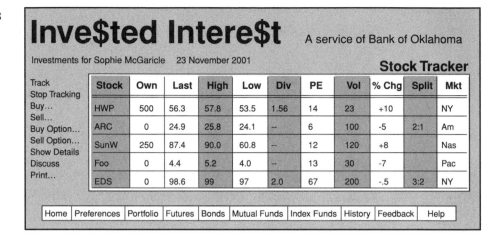

Figure 3.49

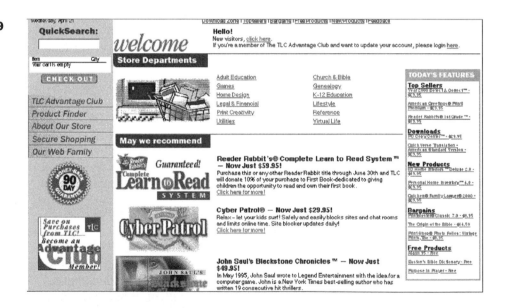

and my vision is not even particularly poor for a 47 year old. Worse, the content items in the "Today's Features" column (on the right) are in an even smaller font—probably 6 point—which I simply cannot read. In fact, that font is so small the browser even has trouble rendering it clearly, so my vision is not the only thing limiting its legibility. The "Today's Features" information might as well not be there, for all the good it does me. Worst of all, none of the fonts on this Web page respond to the font size controls of the browser; the sizes were fixed by the page's designer. Bzzzt. Blooper!

Catching the blooper in client software. The following are comments from reviews I have performed of clients' software and Web sites. They all pertain to fonts that are too small. This collection of comments shows that this blooper is found in a wide variety of products and services, and is committed for a variety of reasons.

- Many of the pages in the Web site use text fonts that are too small for many users to read comfortably, and much of the text is not in fonts that allow users to adjust the size. Because fonts on a computer screen appear smaller and blurrier than their printed equivalents, many users, especially those over 45 years of age, will have trouble with fonts smaller than 12 point.
- The font for chart labels is too small. Many users won't be able to read it.
- The navigation buttons on the left edge of the window are difficult to read because of their orientation and small font size. Since they are bitmaps, the font size doesn't adjust based on the browser Options/font size setting. Some users, especially older ones, will have trouble reading them.
- Most of the text fonts in the new version are too small and not adjustable (even smaller than those in the current product, which were already bordering on being too small). I realize you made the fonts smaller to be able to fit more in, but fitting more in isn't useful if people cannot read the text.
- The default text fonts are in general too small for users over 45 years old to be able to read comfortably. Consider changing to a larger default font, and definitely make it easy for users to increase the font size.
- The labels on the keys of the number pad are too small. Many users will not be able to read these labels comfortably. There is plenty of room on the keys for larger labels.
- The text fonts labeling the symbols in the results graph are too small for many users to read.

Common excuses for tiny fonts. As is clear from the above review comments, developers have many excuses for using fonts that are too small. Here is a sampling of excuses I have heard.

- *"I can read it. What's the problem?"* The stereotype of programmers as nearsighted nerds with thick glasses is outdated. Maybe in the 1950s through the 1970s, programmers tended to be the same people who were called "bookworms" (but even then, the stereotype was an exaggeration). Nowadays, however, most programmers are definitely not the bookish, nearsighted type. Combine that with the fact that programmers tend to be young—under 35 years of age—and self-focused, and you've got a recipe for products full of tiny fonts.
- *"Hey, we gotta fit all this info in somehow."* A developer may feel strongly that users of the product or service need access to many controls or to a

large amount of information. If that programmer lacks the design expertise to employ detail-hiding techniques such as progressive disclosure (see Blooper 46: Overwhelming users with decisions and detail, Section 5.2.1), he or she will often shrink the fonts to try to cram everything in.

■ *"I just used the toolkit's default font size."* The GUI toolkit or interactive GUI builder the programmer is using probably assigns a default font size to all text in components that the programmer adds to the design. If the default font size of a tool is too small (e.g., 8 point), GUIs made with that tool will tend to have fonts that are too small because programmers (for whatever reason) didn't change the font size from its default value.

■ *"It's not my fault. The text is in the image."* Sometimes a programmer just includes images that other people have created. If those images contain embedded text, and the font size of the text is too small, there is little the programmer can do about it other than send the image back to whomever created it and request a new image with larger fonts. Unfortunately, many don't do that, either because they don't notice a problem or they don't consider it important enough to do anything about it.

■ *"It's big enough in low res."* Most GUI platforms allow users to set the screen resolution. For example, MacOS provides a choice of three screen resolutions: 640 × 480, 832 × 624, and 1024 × 768. Windows offers more or less the same three resolutions. At a higher screen resolution, a given font size will appear smaller than it does at a lower resolution. The fonts displayed by an application or a Web site may be large enough when viewed in low resolution, but too small when viewed in high resolution.

 Memo from the Big Boss

Memo

From: The Big Boss

To: All employees

Subject: Font sizes

Date: 1 April 2001

Effective immediately, all employees are asked to use the smallest text fonts available in all documents. The MIS department has informed me that our disk servers are getting full. They asked me to allocate funds to purchase more disk drives, but the request comes at a time when we need to conserve expenses. It occurred to me that by using smaller fonts, we could save a lot of disk space, thereby forestalling the date when we need to purchase additional drives.

With all of your cooperation, we will have a successful 2nd Quarter.

Thanks.

Avoiding Blooper 31: The design rule

Let's face it: You want your software's users to be able to read the text that's on the screen. The following guidelines will help you achieve that goal.

Minimum font point size: 10, but 12 is better

The rule for avoiding this blooper is quite simple: Never use a screen font smaller than 10 point. Ever. Ten points should be the minimum default text size. In fact, I consider even 10-point fonts to be borderline for a computer screen. At high screen resolutions, 10 point will be too small. In designing software and Web sites, in the software I use, and in my Web browser, I almost always set fonts so that the smallest one is 12 point. Even in the highest screen resolutions, 12-point fonts will be legible for most users.

Design for high-res displays

If designers make the fonts in their application or Web site large enough to be legible by the intended users when at the highest screen resolution, there will be no problem at lower resolutions.

Let users adjust font size

Furthermore, font sizes should be adjustable by users. This applies both to application content text (such as an email message, or data in the cells of a spreadsheet) and to text that is part of the user interface (such as button and setting labels, or messages). Of course, providing adjustable font sizes for the text displayed by an application usually requires significant effort. Nonetheless, the only valid excuse for not making font sizes adjustable is when the text in question is a title or heading that the designer knows is big enough for anyone who is not legally blind to see, that is, at least 24 point.

Font control on the Web: Just don't do it

User-adjustable text fonts is one user interface feature that is much easier to accomplish on the Web than in traditional desktop GUI software applications. In Web sites and Web applications, all developers have to do to provide user-adjustable font sizes is to *not* specify a font size. Web developers actually have to do *more* work to commit the blooper than to do the right thing. On the Web, there is no excuse for nonadjustable fonts. In the book *Web Pages That Suck* [Flanders and Willis, 1998], co-author Vincent Flanders makes a strong argument for Web designers to leave the font unspecified and hence adjustable by users in their Web browsers (pages 125–126):

> There are a lot of things I don't understand: atomic theory, Existentialism,... and why Web designers use the < FONT > tag and FACE argument to create unreadable pages.... Granted, I'm 49 years old and have bad eyesight, but still

folks…if the text is too hard for the average person to read, they're going to hit the Back button faster than Larry King gets married.

Test it on users

Finally, whether you're developing software for the Web, PC applications, or consumer appliances, test your text fonts! On real users, not just on other twenty-something programmers. Preferably *before* you release the software or Web site.

3.4.3 Blooper 32: Inactive controls insufficiently grayed out

In most GUI toolkits, controls that represent settings can be made "active" or "inactive." When a control is active, users may interact with it. When it is inactive, users can't interact with it; it won't respond. Controls become active when they are applicable, and inactive when they are not applicable. Whether a particular control is relevant at the moment depends on what the user has done or is doing, and on how other controls are set.

Cases of deactivating controls. The following are examples of typical situations in which software designers activate and deactivate GUI controls:

- Commands in a document editor's menubar menus for cutting and pasting document content are irrelevant—and therefore inactive—until the user creates or loads a document.

- Commands for manipulating the contents of a certain window are not applicable—and are therefore inactive—until the user opens that window.

- Commands to operate on graphic images in a document are inaccessible—and therefore inactive—until a user selects a graphic image.

- Setting a Show Page Numbers checkbox to OFF in a document editor may change a neighboring Page Number Position setting to inactive because the latter setting is irrelevant when no page numbers are being shown.

Grayed out = deactivated. Ever since the first commercial GUI-based computers—the Xerox Star and the Apple Lisa and Macintosh—became available, inactive controls have had a fairly standard appearance. The details vary slightly from one GUI platform to another, but "grayed out" pretty much captures the look. This appearance is so common that many user interface professionals—and even some users—say "grayed out" and "not grayed out" when they really mean "inactive" and "active".

However, exactly *how* controls are "grayed out" is important in determining whether users actually perceive them as active or inactive. Unfortunately, the details are often gotten wrong.

Figure 3.50

The typical GUI control is composed of several parts, including a label, a current-value indicator, and other parts. Some GUI toolkits don't gray out enough of the parts of inactive controls.

The image in Figure 3.50 is from a printer control panel for a Hewlett-Packard LaserJet printer. The Screen Frequency and Screen Angle settings are inactive in this image because they aren't relevant until the Halftoning radiobuttons are set to "Use Settings Below." For present purposes, I will ignore the other problems of these two text settings.[2] The important problem for this discussion is that in these two text settings, the only thing that is grayed out is the text inside the text fields. That isn't enough. Many users will simply not notice that the settings are not editable until they try to edit their values. Furthermore, if either or both of these text fields were blank (which can be easily achieved by changing the radiobutton setting, editing the text fields, and then changing the radiobutton back), they would provide no visual clue that they were inactive.

Other examples. In reviewing software for clients, I've also seen another variation of this problem: text fields are marked as inactive by simply changing the interior background from white to gray and leaving all else as it was. That isn't enough either.

Text and number fields aren't the only types of controls that are often poorly marked as inactive. Other GUI components that are often insufficiently grayed out include

- *Radiobuttons:* Often, only the actual radiobuttons are grayed out. The value labels remain fully saturated. Even worse, sometimes only the *interiors* of the radiobuttons are grayed out, in which case only the one button in each radiobutton setting that is ON indicates whether the setting is active or inactive. In either case, the radiobuttons are so small, users can easily not notice that they are grayed out. This is especially bad in products where active radiobuttons allow users to click on the labels as well as on the togglebutton

2. Other problems with the Screen Frequency and Angle settings: (1) They should be positioned more toward the right side of the containing group box so it would be clearer that they are subordinate to, rather than peers of, the radiobutton setting; (2) the text fields are unnecessarily tall; (3) text fields may not be the best way for users to specify these values, since they provide no indication of what is or is not a valid value (see Blooper 18: Overusing text fields, Section 2.5.2); sliders might be more appropriate. On the other hand, the designers of this panel at least got one detail right: they positioned the text fields so the baselines of the text inside the fields and the labels are aligned (see Blooper 28: Poor label placement, Section 3.3.3).

Figure 3.51

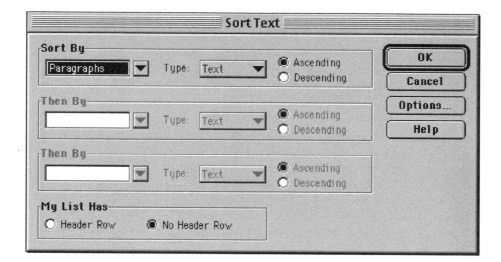

in order to choose a value. Sometimes, as in Microsoft Word 6.0's Sort Text dialog box (Figure 3.51), inactive buttons retain their "active" appearance, but their labels are grayed out. This is better than the converse, but still not quite correct.

■ *Checkboxes:* The same problems that plague radiobuttons (see previous list-item) are also commonly seen in checkboxes.

■ *Sliders:* Sometimes, only the handle of inactive sliders is grayed out. Most users just aren't going to notice this.

■ *Command buttons:* Sometimes, only the button border is grayed out, leaving the label fully saturated. Other times, only the label is grayed out, leaving the button border fully saturated. While the second approach is a clearer indication that a control is inactive than the first approach, neither approach is really enough.

A related problem: Inconsistent graying. Some applications are inconsistent in how they mark inactive command buttons. Figure 3.52 shows two command buttons from two different dialog boxes displayed by Microsoft Word 6.0 for Macintosh. The button group on the left is from Word's Spellcheck dialog box. Notice that in the inactive button (Suggest), only the label is grayed out. Although this is clearer than graying out only the border and leaving the label displayed normally, it is still incorrect. On the right are buttons from the file chooser dialog box displayed by the Open command. Notice that in the inactive button (Eject), the button border as well as the label is grayed out. This is how a disabled button is supposed to look. The reason for the difference is probably that the file chooser dialog box is supplied by MacOS, rather than by Word.

The Windows standard: Close, but no cigar. The Microsoft Windows standard appearance for inactive command buttons is that the button itself appears nor-

Figure 3.52

Figure 3.53

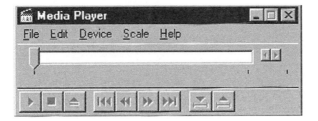

mal, but the button label is grayed out. As indicated above, while this approach is better than the opposite approach, it is still problematic. Consider, for example, the main window of the Windows Media Player accessory (see Figure 3.53). When the program is initially displayed, all of its control buttons are inactive because no media has been loaded for them to act upon. However, as is shown below, users may not recognize them as inactive, especially if they don't know what the labels normally look like; those labels might be the regular "active" ones. These buttons would be more clearly inactive if their borders were also grayed.

In contrast to the above-listed types of controls, command items on menubar menus rarely commit the blooper of being inadequately marked. When I review software for clients, I find that menubar menu items are usually correctly grayed out when they are inactive. Of course, menu items are not always *deactivated* when they should be, but that's a different problem.

Avoiding Blooper 32: *The design rule*

There should be no uncertainty in users' minds as to whether a control is active or inactive. Inactive controls should be heavily grayed out. If controls have multiple parts—and most do—most, if not all, of the parts should be grayed out. Here are recommendations for the most commonly used controls:

- *Command buttons:* Figure 3.54 shows an inactive command button displayed by the Apple MacOS 8.0 File Sharing control panel. Compare it to the inactive command buttons displayed by Microsoft Word (see Figure 3.52). Even viewed in isolation, there is no doubt that it is inactive.
- *Text fields:* Text fields, like other controls, have several aspects that can be grayed out to help indicate that they are inactive: text content, border, background color, and label. Graying only one of these aspects isn't enough.

Figure 3.54

Figure 3.55

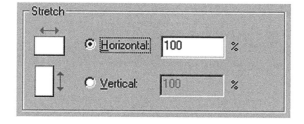

Figure 3.56

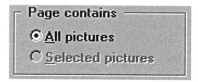

Graying any two is probably sufficient. Graying three eliminates all possible doubt that the control is inactive. Thus, an inactive text field should not have only a gray background, or only gray content text, or only a gray border, or only a gray label. In the Windows environment, the standard is to gray the background and the content text. I think it would be better if the border or label were also grayed, but that's just to be certain no one misinterprets the control. The image in Figure 3.55, from the Windows Paint Accessory, shows two text fields, of which only the one corresponding to the chosen stretch direction (Horizontal versus Vertical) is active. This is an example of an adequately marked inactive text field. Compare it to the ones from the HP Laser Printer control panel (Figure 3.50).

- *Radiobuttons:* The four aspects of a radiobutton that can be grayed are button inside background color, button border, button content "ON" marker, and label. Figure 3.56, from Kodak's Picture Disk software, shows the Windows standard appearance for an inactive radiobutton. In this case, the software makes certain values of the radiobutton inactive or active, depending on what the user has done. It is more common for all the radiobuttons in a setting to be activated or deactivated together, since a linked set of mutually exclusive radiobuttons comprises a single setting.

- *Checkboxes:* The correct appearance for inactive checkboxes is similar to that for inactive radiobuttons. Figure 3.57 is an image from Sybase Power-Builder 5.0 showing the Windows standard for inactive checkboxes. Figure

Figure 3.57

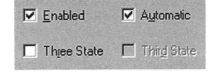

Figure 3.58

☑ **QuickTime Music Synthesizer**
☐ **General MIDI On Modem Port**
☐ **General MIDI On Printer Port**

Figure 3.59

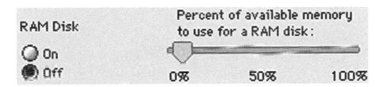

3.58 is an image from the MacOS QuickTime control panel showing the Macintosh standard.

- *Sliders:* When a slider is deactivated, the scale as well as the "handle" should be grayed. This is shown for the MacOS environment by the image in Figure 3.59, from the MacOS Memory control panel.

Grayed-out text should still be legible

When text is grayed out, it is important that it still be legible. In the days before color and gray-scale displays, the only way to gray something was by removing half of its pixels. With many screen fonts, grayed-out text became unreadable. During the design of Apple's Lisa computer, it became apparent that this problem had to be solved. To solve it, Apple designed a special font—Chicago—that was bold enough so that it remained legible when half its pixels were removed. Now that color and gray-scale displays are the rule and graying is done with actual gray pixels rather than by mixing black and white pixels, it is less critical exactly what font is used to display labels that will be grayed out.

Be consistent

Finally, it is crucial that the inactive appearance of each type of control is consistent through all the software that runs on a particular GUI platform (e.g., Windows, MacOS, CDE/Motif).

Further reading

Official platform-specific GUI style guides

Apple Computer, Inc. 1993. *Macintosh Human Interface Guidelines.* Reading, MA: Addison-Wesley.

Microsoft. 1995. *The Windows Interface Guidelines for Software Design: An Application Design Guide.* Redmond, WA: Microsoft Press.

Microsoft. 1999. *Microsoft Windows User Experience.* Redmond, WA: Microsoft Press.

Open Software Foundation. 1993. *OSF/Motif style guide: Rev 1.2.* Englewood Cliffs, NJ: Prentice Hall.

Sun Microsystems. 1999. *Java Look and Feel Design Guidelines.* Reading, MA: Addison-Wesley.

Platform Independent GUI guidelines

McFarland, A., and Dayton, T. 1995. *Design Guide for Multiplatform Graphical User Interfaces.* Issue 3, LPR13. Piscataway, NJ: Bellcore.

Mullet, K., and Sano, D. 1995. *Designing Visual Interfaces: Communications Oriented Techniques.* Mountain View, CA: SunSoft Press.

Weinshenk, S., Jamar, P., and Yeo, S. 1997. *GUI Design Essentials.* New York: John Wiley and Sons.

Textual Bloopers

Introduction

In considering what makes a user interface good or bad, it is important not to underestimate the importance of text. One of the great ironies of graphical user interfaces is that they aren't usually very graphical. The typical GUI consists mainly of textual settings displayed on panels. Most of the values of the settings are textual (even though they may be set via menus or radiobuttons). Most of the setting labels are also textual. Error and warning messages are mainly textual (perhaps augmented by a color and a graphical symbol to indicate the importance of the message). Graphical components such as sliders and gauges aren't really used very much.

Computer-based products and services use text in a variety of ways: in status, error, and warning messages displayed by software for the users' benefit; in labels for settings; in labels for the possible values of settings; in names of commands in menus and on buttons; in brief instructions intended to guide users through important steps; and, of course, in the names users assign to data files and other data objects. Though software designers sometimes express a desire to minimize or avoid the use of text in the products and services they design, the truth is that many concepts simply could not be expressed without using text. The old saying "A picture is worth a thousand words," while true in some ways, is an oversimplification: sometimes a few words are worth more than any number of pictures.

 Graphics or text?

A colleague with whom I worked at Xerox in the mid-1980s recently recalled an interesting exchange she had with a graphic artist back in those days. My colleague was in her office, writing code for ViewPoint, the successor to Xerox's Star workstation software. The graphic artist came into the office carrying a batch of pictures. She wanted feedback on which ones best suggested "move" and "copy," which were operations provided by ViewPoint. My colleague suggested that the words "move" and "copy" seemed pretty clear. The graphic artist was taken aback. She exclaimed: "Oh, but graphics convey more!"

For an example of a case where it proved impossible to do without text, see Section 10.1.

Even in the most graphical of user interfaces, for all but the simplest of products and services, text usually plays a role. Consider the control panel shown in Figure 4.1, for Creative Software's Mixer application, which is part of their SoundBlaster suite. Even though this is nominally a Windows application, it is much more graphical than the typical Windows application. Nonetheless, it makes use of text: the company logo, the application title, the numbers in the volume meter, and the tooltips on every control on the panel.

Figure 4.1

One of the nice things about textual usability problems is that they are usually cheap and easy to correct. However, textual usability problems often have a root cause in the development process or even in the development organization. Correcting systemic problems in either of those areas is, of course, anything but cheap and easy.

Because text plays an important role in the user interfaces of almost all computer-based products and services—whether they are desktop computer applications, Web sites, electronic appliances, or scientific instruments—there are many ways to get it wrong. I refer to such errors as "textual bloopers." This chapter describes several such bloopers, explains why developers sometimes make them, and provides advice on how to avoid them.

4.1 Unprofessional writing

Our first four textual bloopers are about poor writing in the text displayed by software. They are the result of giving the job of writing text to the wrong people: programmers.

4.1.1 Blooper 33: Inconsistent terminology

One of the most damaging text-related mistakes you can make when developing a computer-based product is to be haphazard and inconsistent about what terms are used for what concepts. Unfortunately, this mistake is also one of the most common. Many development organizations aren't even aware that this is a potential problem, so they make no effort whatsoever to assure that their product terminology is consistent and clear. What begins as a flaw in their development *process* turns into a flaw in their *products:* a many-to-one and one-to-many mapping between terms and product concepts.

When I review software products for clients, I often construct a table showing the various terms that are used in the program and in the documentation for each user-visible concept. The results are often eye-opening to development managers: "I had no idea! No wonder users are having trouble learning to use our product!" Unfortunately, the usual reaction from programmers is "So what? We have more important problems to worry about than whether we use the exact same term from one window to the next."

It turns out that there are two different ways to be inconsistent in referring to product concepts, and product developers often stumble across at least one of those ways.

Variation A: Different terms for the same concept. It is surprising how many software products use multiple terms for a single concept. For example, a program might refer to "results" in one window and "output" in another, even though the same thing is meant in both cases.

The following is an excerpt from a user interface review I performed of a client's software product that was being prepared for release:

> Certain terms are used inconsistently in BizAnalyzer [not the product's real name]. For example, the Categorization Assistant uses the term "source table", while dialog boxes throughout the program refer to the same thing as "Discovery table". In one menu, the table properties are invoked via "Tables ..."; in another menu, the same properties are invoked via "Table Properties". Other examples of multiple terms for the same concept: "Specify Goal" vs. "Define Goal", "Goal" vs. "Output Field" vs. "Statistics Task", "Task" vs. "Step".

In reviewing software for clients, I have found the terms in each of the following sets being used interchangeably for a single concept.

- properties, attributes, parameters, settings, resources
- Welcome Window, Introduction Window
- version, revision
- FAQ (Frequently Asked Questions), QNA (Questions aNd Answers)
- find, search, query, inquiry
- Back to results, Back to search results
- arguments, args
- server, service
- Exit, Quit
- Order Size, Order Quantity, Qty
- Stock Symbol, Instrument ID, Instrument, Instr Id

Often, inconsistent terminology results from name changes during development that were not corrected everywhere in the software or documentation. Sometimes it results from a failure to develop a product lexicon during the conceptual design phase of development (see "Avoiding Blooper 33," later in this section), or a means of ensuring compliance with the lexicon after it is developed. Sometimes there simply was no conceptual design phase of development (see Principle 2, Section 1.2). Sometimes it is due to a lack of agreement or a lack of communication between programmers. In some cases programmers may not have considered it important enough, given the time pressure they were under, to make sure that concepts were referred to consistently throughout the software. All of these causes are related to Blooper 80: Anarchic development (Section 8.2.2).

When different words are used in different contexts to describe the same thing, users may not realize that the same thing is being described. Users are thinking mainly about their work—the problem in their own task domain that they are trying to solve (for example, personal finance, letter writing, hotel reservations, information retrieval). They pay close attention to the data they are creating and manipulating, but they devote very little attention to figuring out what *other* things they see on the screen—controls, instructions, messages—mean. Tiny changes in wording can result in failure to recognize a previously encountered concept.

Inconsistent terminology forces users to keep thinking about the software—trying to decide whether two words mean the same thing or not—when they would rather think about their work. Well-designed software, in contrast, recedes into the background by letting users fall into use habits and unconscious activity, thereby allowing them to focus their conscious minds on their work.

Variation B: The same term for different concepts. Almost as common as using more than one term for a single concept is the opposite error: using a single term for more than one concept. For example, here is another excerpt from the previously mentioned user interface review I performed of a client's product:

> Certain terms have different meanings in different places in the program, potentially causing confusion. For example, the word "view" is used to refer to
>
> - the data display windows, e.g., Understanding View, Evaluation View, Fields Ranking View
> - different ways of filtering the Understanding View, e.g., Required View, Specific View
> - actions that affect the data flow diagram, e.g., Shrink View, Enlarge View
> - the View menu, which controls display of the Assistant, Data Flow, Toolbar, and Status bar
>
> Furthermore, the View menu contains some items that assume that "View" is a verb (e.g., "View:Results") and other items that assume "View" is a noun (e.g., "View:Enlarge").

Using the same term to mean different things is usually not intentional; it happens because developers simply don't think about it. After all, when people converse informally with each other, they often use words that have multiple meanings, and listeners can usually determine the intended meaning of a term

Figure 4.2

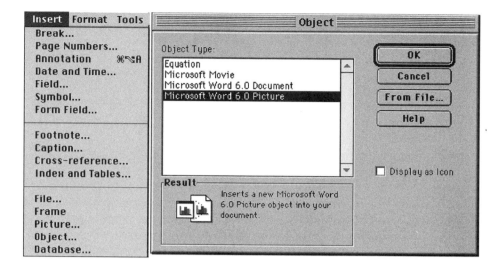

either from the context in which it is used or by asking the speaker to clarify. However, human-computer communication is less forgiving of ambiguity. It does not provide conversational context that is as rich as the context provided by human-human communication—for example, a context that contains redundant cues about the meaning of terms. It does not allow the human participant to ask the computer to clarify what it meant by a particular term.[1] Therefore, sloppy terminology is much less acceptable in software than it is in communication between people.

Microsoft Word exhibits such sloppy terminology in its Insert menu. This menu provides both an "Insert Picture ..." command and an "Insert Object ..." command (see Figure 4.2). The Insert Object command allows users to insert any of several different types of objects, including Equations, Excel charts, Excel worksheets, Word documents, and Word pictures. Users might expect "Insert Picture" to do the same thing as "Insert Object" with "Word picture" as the specified object type for the latter command. However, if they thought that, they'd be wrong. The Insert Picture command is for importing externally created graphic files. It displays a file chooser dialog box that lets users specify the image file to be imported and the file's format (e.g., BMP, TIFF, PICT). In contrast, inserting a Word picture using the Insert Object command does not import a graphics file; it displays a structured graphics editor that allows a user to draw a graphic, which, when completed, is inserted into the document.

An especially common form of using the same term for different concepts is to use the same name both for an object and for a part of the object. For example, an email program might sometimes use the word "message" broadly, to refer to the entire data file it received from another user, including headers, message body, and attachments. Other times, it might use the word narrowly, to

---

1. Although computer software can ask such questions of its users.

Figure 4.3

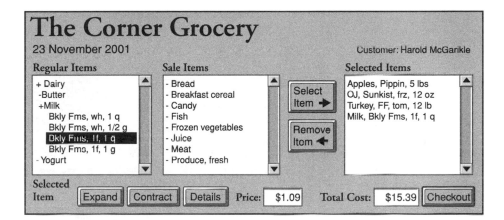

refer just to the textual content of email. A program that did that would confuse new users, impeding their learning. Such an error is the result of a faulty conceptual model, or the lack of one.

A very specific common form of this blooper is using "select" in one place to mean clicking on an object (highlighting it) to make it the operand of the next operation, and in another place to mean choosing an object from a collection to add to a list. Consider, for example, the page from a hypothetical grocery shopping Web site shown in Figure 4.3. The buttons below the two lists of available groceries on the left act on the currently selected item in those two lists, as the label on their left indicates. However, in this Web site, "select" also means adding an item to the list on the right. The list on the right is even labeled "Selected Items," which is very similar to, but has a different meaning than the label "Selected Item" in the lower-left corner. Needless to say, users of this Web site would find this confusing. Although this example is fictional, I have found in reviewing software and Web sites for clients that a great many use the term "select" in multiple, conflicting ways.

An example of misusing the term "select" in commercially available software is provided by the two images in Figure 4.4 from the graphics program Paint Shop Pro. The image on the left shows that the user has invoked the program's Fill function to specify a color or pattern to fill in an enclosed area of the drawing. After setting the menus as desired, the user clicks the Options button to see and possibly set additional attributes. However, no options are available for this choice of Fill Style, so the program displays the error dialog box shown on the right. It misuses the word "selection" to refer to the current Fill Style setting, rather than to a selected part of the users' drawing.

When programmers or technical writers assign nonstandard meanings to "select," they also open the door to highly confusing instructions such as

Figure 4.4

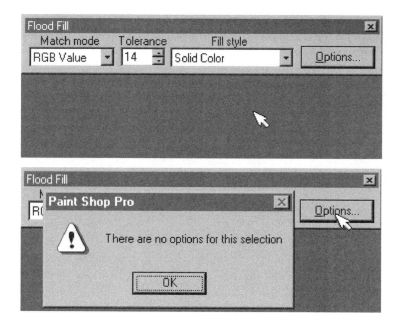

> To select the toppings you want on your pizza, first select them in the Available Toppings list and click the Add button, which adds them to the Selected Toppings list.

In the above sentence, the word "select" has two different meanings. I have seen similar instructions in software products and Web sites I have reviewed for clients.

Another commonly misused term is "refresh," which is often used to mean both "fetch updated data from database (or from network host)" and "repaint the display." Three interrelated terms that are often confused in software and documentation are "cursor," "text insertion point," and "mouse pointer." Before GUIs, there was no such thing as a mouse pointer, and the text insertion point and the cursor were the same thing. With GUIs, these all became distinct concepts. However, one sees the term "cursor" sometimes used to mean the text insertion point and sometimes used to mean the mouse pointer.

Avoiding Blooper 33: The design rule

In general, the terminology used in a software application to describe objects or actions should be *radically* consistent—consistent beyond any ordinary notion of consistency. To maximize learnability and usability, terms used in software should map strictly 1:1 to concepts in the software. Even if a term has more than one meaning in the external world (since the use of ambiguous terms in software is sometimes unavoidable), it should mean one and only one thing in the software. Otherwise, users often have to stop and think about which of the possible meanings is intended in the current situation.

Use radically consistent terminology

Software designers should take a hint from people who design signage for major airports. People who pass through such airports and rely on such signs speak a variety of languages. In particular, many do not speak the primary language of the country in which the airport is located. Some international airports post signs in multiple languages, but of course they cannot post signs in the native language of everyone who uses the airport. Therefore, whatever language or languages the signs are written in, the terminology used on them is very simple and highly consistent. For example, one sees the term "Duty-free shoppers" in American and British airports even where it doesn't make grammatical sense because people from Japan, Finland, or Saudi Arabia who are trying to find a duty-free store will be looking for those exact words. Using any other words, such as "Tax-free store," would send them scurrying the wrong way, as would changing the word order, such as "Shopping: Duty-Free!"

Computer users, almost by definition, are trying to find their way in an environment in which they don't speak the language. They don't know that John, the programmer of windows A, B, and C, calls indicating what one is looking for in the database "making a query" while Sally, the programmer of windows D, E, and F, calls it "specifying an inquiry." They don't know that, as far as the software is concerned, an "employee" and a "record" are the same thing. They don't even know that "record" is a noun.

Not only do computer users not know these things, they don't *want* to know them. The vast majority of computer users these days are interested in getting their work done. They are not interested in the computer and its software per se. They don't care how developers view the software. They want the computer and its software to help them develop habits, and then they want to forget the computer and software and concentrate on their work. In fact, they are often so focused on their work that if they are looking for a Search function but the application window they are using spells it "Find," they may overlook it. For this reason, developers should design user interfaces as if the prospective users were autistic—people who abhor any difference or variation in their routine.

Devise a product lexicon to help achieve consistent terminology

How can a development organization achieve such a high degree of terminological consistency in its products? Here's how:

Very early in the product design process, a development team should specify clearly what concepts the software will expose to users, and what each concept will be called. This is called developing a "conceptual model" (see Principle 2, Section 1.2.3). The result of this exercise is a product "vocabulary" or "lexicon." It lists the names and definitions for each and every concept that will be visible to users in the product and its documentation. It should map terms

1:1 onto concepts that the software exposes to users. It should not assign different terms to a single concept. It also should not assign a single term to different concepts. Preparing the product lexicon is part of understanding the task domain that the application is targeting, and so is part of producing a conceptual design.

In order to assure that a product lexicon is devised and followed, someone on the development team should "own" it, probably the head technical writer assigned to the project. Once the product lexicon has been developed, it should be followed consistently throughout the software and its documentation and marketing literature. The lexicon owner is responsible for reminding the team to either stick to the agreed-upon term for a concept or to explicitly change it. Until the software is released, the lexicon should be regarded as a living document; it will change as the team's understanding of the product's intended functionality and target task domain changes.

Test the lexicon on users

As the lexicon is being devised, it should be tested on people who are representative of the software's intended users. The purpose of such testing is to determine whether the software's lexicon matches the users' vocabulary. If not, the lexicon needs to be changed because what matters is what makes sense to *users,* not to the developers.

Terminology can be tested long before the software is implemented or even designed. It can be tested in a variety of inexpensive ways. Users can be shown terms and asked to explain what each term means to them; the developers would then compare the test participants' descriptions with the intended meanings of the terms. Users can also be asked to match terms with descriptions by arranging 3 × 5 cards or by drawing lines between terms and descriptions printed on paper. Finally, the effectiveness of the product terminology can be assessed during usability testing of the software, or prototypes of it.

Use industry standard terms for common concepts

When developing a product lexicon, a development team should keep in mind that certain concepts in graphical user interfaces have standard names. The names are the GUI equivalents of "reserved words" in programming languages. Designers, developers, and technical writers who rename such concepts, or who assign new meanings to the standard names, run a high risk of confusing users. Standard terms and their definitions are included in the various industry standard style guides, such as the ones for Windows [Microsoft, 1995], Macintosh [Apple, 1993] and CDE/Motif [Open Software Foundation, 1993]. Software designers should familiarize themselves with the industry standard GUI vocabulary for their target platform(s) before inventing their own terminologies.

One such reserved word is "select." It means clicking on an object to highlight it, thereby designating it as the object for subsequent actions. The word

Figure 4.5

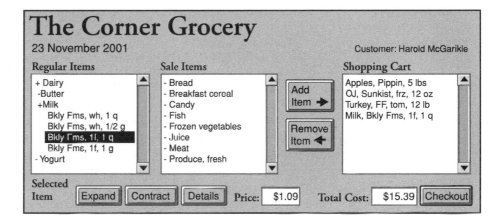

"select" should not be used for any other purpose in a GUI. In particular, it should not be used to mean adding an item to a list or a collection. Thus, the previous example of a grocery shopping Web site could avoid the blooper by using the word "Add" or "Choose" instead of misusing the word "select" (see Figure 4.5).

Use message files; don't embed labels and messages in the code

Both variations of this blooper—different terms for the same concept, and the same term for different concepts—are sometimes the result of developers simply failing to spot the conflicting use of terms. If the only way for a person to review a program's messages, labels, and instructions is by operating the program or by searching through its source code, such oversights are likely.

On the other hand, if the text displayed by a program were all together in one file, reviewing it and checking it for conflicts and inconsistencies would be greatly facilitated. That is exactly what I recommend to all my clients: use message files.

When different parts of the software need to refer to the same concept or present the same message, they simply refer to the same text string in the message file.[2] That reduces the chances of committing Variation A of the blooper—different terms for the same concept.

Message files also make it easier to avoid Variation B of the blooper—the same term for different concepts. A team member—probably the technical writer who is in charge of the product lexicon—should be assigned to "own," review, and maintain the message file. That person should check the message file for duplicate text strings. Any duplicate text strings in the message file constitute one of two cases:

---

2. Ideally, if two different messages in a message file contain the same term, each message should include that term by *referring* to its correct spelling in the message file rather than by containing its own copy of the term. However, most message files in use today are not this sophisticated; they simply contain text strings.

1. *Redundant text strings that should be one.* These are errors. Leaving them separate makes it possible that someone will change one and neglect to change the other, causing the software to manifest Variation A of the blooper. All but one of the duplicates should be deleted, and all references in the program code to the deleted duplicates should be changed to point to the single remaining text string.

2. *Text strings for different situations that are the same.* These are probably errors, giving rise to Variation B of the blooper. They should be reworded so that they differ (while staying true to the product lexicon). However, a few such duplications might be legitimate homonyms. For example, a program might use both the verb "refuse," meaning "decline," and the noun "refuse," meaning "garbage." In such a situation, I would strongly consider changing one of the terms, for example, using the word "garbage" instead of the noun "refuse." However, if the homonyms were natural to the task domain and usability testing showed that users were not confused by their use in the software, it would be OK to leave the nominal "duplication" in the message file. When translated to other languages, the homonyms would probably be translated to different words anyway; for example, in German, the verb "refuse" translates to "ablehnen," whereas the noun "refuse" translates to "Abfall."

Using message files not only enhances textual consistency, it also provides a single locale for technical writers to check and facilitates translation to foreign languages.

Summary

In summary, developers can avoid inconsistent terminology in their computer-based products by taking explicit steps at two different points during development. At the start of development, it is important to develop a product lexicon—following industry standard terminology given in the appropriate platform style guides—and convince everyone to abide by it. Near the end of development, it is important to provide for comprehensive review of the software's text by someone other than the programmers, for example, by technical writers. Using message files greatly facilitates management and review of the text displayed by a program. Finally, it is crucial to test the terminology on representative users, both as it is being devised and as the software approaches completion.

4.1.2 Blooper 34: Unclear terminology

Sometimes terms are used consistently within a software product, but are still unclear in the sense that users can easily misinterpret them. I've found three different ways in which this can happen.

Variation A: Terms for different concepts are too similar. Suppose a software product provides two quite different functions, but the names of the functions are very similar. Users would be likely to confuse them, no? Yes.

An intranet Web search facility I reviewed for a client provided two different functions to allow users to find information related to that returned by their last search. One function was called "Related Concepts"; the other was called "Related Terms." Their effect was quite different. I warned the client that many users would have no idea what the difference between these two functions was and would either avoid them or choose randomly between them.

Another client had developed a Web site for prospective home buyers to use to look for a suitable home...anywhere in the United States. The Web site required users to subscribe to the service and to login when they used it. Requiring users to login allowed the system to provide places for users to store information they had collected while looking for a home for possible future use. One type of information users could store between sessions was information about *them* that would help indicate what type of home they were looking for: financial status, family size, and so on. Another type of information users could store was notes about *houses* they had found so far. These two different types of personalized information were stored and managed by separate facilities provided by the service. Unfortunately, the two facilities had similar names: the facility for storing information about oneself and one's home-buying goals was called the "Personal Planner" and the facility for keeping notes about homes one had found was called the "Personal Journal." Not surprisingly, testing found that users often confused these two facilities.

This variation of the blooper is related to Blooper 35, Variation E: Assigning arbitrary meanings to short, nondescriptive terms (Section 4.1.3).

Variation B: Concepts too similar. In Variation A, it is actually difficult to say whether the problem in the two examples was that the *terms* were too similar, that the *concepts* were too similar, or perhaps both. Sometimes, the problem is clearly that the concepts are so similar that they are easily confused.

The same home-buying Web site described earlier provided two different methods to begin looking for a home. One method was to name the state, county, or town where one wanted to find a home. The other was to point to a location on a map. Users had to choose which of these methods they wanted to use. Users were given the choice of whether to find a home "by Location" or "by Map." A colleague and I conducted a usability test of this Web site. We wrote the following in our test report:

> Many participants did not distinguish between finding a home "by map" vs. "by location." Both are really by location; they differ only in how the location is specified.

The problem was that the designers of this Web site had created an artificial distinction—one that didn't match the real world—and expected users to accept and understand it immediately. Unfortunately for the designers, the users didn't cooperate. See Variation E of Blooper 35 (Section 4.1.3) for a discussion of a related textual problem.

A customer support Web site I reviewed exhibited a similar problem. It provided four concepts that the developers regarded as very different:

- *Membership*: a customer company signs up and pays for the customer support service

- *Subscription*: a customer company subscribes to an online customer support newsletter

- *Access*: users in a customer company have privileges to access certain restricted information and functionality in the customer support Web site

- *Entitlements*: services are provided for each membership level

In my review report, I warned the developers that these four concepts were very similar and would probably be confused by many users. I recommended that they consider merging them into one concept, or at least fewer than four.

Variation C: Ambiguous terms. When reviewing or usability-testing software for clients, I often find terms in it that are confusing because they are ambiguous. I don't mean they have multiple meanings within the software; that's a different problem that I discussed earlier in Variation B of Blooper 33. I'm referring to terms that, although they may have only one meaning in the software, have other meanings outside of it that make as much sense in the software as does the intended meaning. New users are likely to misinterpret such terms. Designers are so focused on their own intended meaning of a term that they often fail to even realize that the term might have other meanings that are equally plausible in the given context. This is a form of thinking inside-out rather than outside-in (see Principle 5, Section 1.5.1). This problem is not restricted to software; newspapers are infamous for printing headlines that meant one thing to the writer, but something else to the reader, such as "Teacher Strikes Idle Kids," or "Miners Refuse to Work after Death," or "Red Tape Holds Up New Bridge."

A common oversight in software is to use words that can be either nouns or verbs, such as "object," "file," "load," "refuse," "train." Consider how difficult it is to read the following newspaper headline: "Bank Funds Swamp Firm."

Textual ambiguity can be further exacerbated when verbs are used as nouns. For example, a software company for which I once worked developed an application development tool for C++ programmers. The menubar in the tool's main window included a command "Build Window." The developers intended this to be a noun phrase: the window for building—programmer jargon for compiling and linking together—a program. Get it? The *Build* Window. Unfortunately, users—yes, even hard-core C++ programmers—persisted in reading the command as a verb phrase: Build *Window*. This alternative interpretation—building a window—made at least as much sense in the application development tool as

cathy®   **by Cathy Guisewite**

Cathy © 1985 Cathy Guisewite. Reprinted by permission of Universal Press Syndicate.

the intended interpretation did. Nonetheless, it was a surprise to the software developers that anyone would interpret the command that way.

The problem caused by turning verbs into nouns is discussed more fully in Variation C of Blooper 35: Speaking Geek (Section 4.1.3).

Some words have a fixed grammatical type, but many meanings. For example, "enter" is often used in computer software to refer to the (users') act of typing data into the computer. However, "enter" also has another meaning in standard English: "to go into." In computer software and especially in Web sites, that meaning of "enter" may make just as much sense to users as the "type data" meaning.

For example, the "Welcome" window of an application I reviewed included a graphically labeled button that supplied the following tooltip text to explain its function:

```
Click here to enter application.
```

Clicking on the button closed the "Welcome" window and displayed the application's main window. However, novice users might easily interpret the label as saying that clicking that button would prompt them to type the name of a software application.

Avoiding Blooper 34: *The design rule*

When developing a conceptual model and lexicon for a product (see Principle 2, Section 1.2; see also Avoiding Blooper 33, Section 4.1.1), developers should follow the rules below.

Avoid similar terms

Try to have the terms assigned to the product's various concepts be clearly distinguishable from each other. Of course, the lexicon should largely reflect the natural terminology of the task domain, so developers are not completely free to assign terms to concepts. However, the natural terminology of most task domains typically won't have highly confusable terms, because if it did, it would foster miscommunication between people. Therefore, software developers mainly need to make sure that they don't add any new terms that can be confused with existing terms or other new ones. When in doubt, test the terminology: show the terms to representatives of the intended users and ask them to explain what the terms mean, or have them match terms with meanings.

Avoid subtly different concepts

Think carefully about the conceptual model. Are the concepts in it clearly distinct, or are users likely to mix them up? If, as in one of the previous examples, there is both a concept of membership in a service and a concept of subscribing to an email newsletter, perhaps the two should be combined into a single concept, thereby simplifying the product's conceptual model. Simpler is usually better.

Avoid ambiguous terms

Try to avoid using terms in the software that are ambiguous in the real world, or that have real-world meaning that could possibly be confused with their meanings in the software. Don't assume that just because you've defined a word to have a certain meaning in the software, users will assign it the same meaning. When assigning terms to concepts and functions in a product, think outside-in, not inside-out; consider how users will interpret the words you've chosen. Test your terminology on representative users and be prepared to change it if necessary. For discussion of related design rules, see Principle 5 (Section 1.5); see also Variations C and E of Blooper 35: Speaking Geek (Section 4.1.3).

Test the terminology on users

I have sometimes heard software developers say: "That term isn't confusing. It's obvious what it means!" However, whether a term is confusing is not for software developers to judge on their own; it must be determined by observing and asking users. Therefore, it is not enough for software developers to produce a conceptual model and product lexicon. The lexicon must be tested, on people who are representative of the software's target users. This can of course be done as part of the usability testing of the software, but it can also be done much earlier, through simple word-matching tests. However the lexicon is tested, if users are confused by the terminology, it should be changed.

The bottom line is that if users misinterpret the terminology used in your software, it's not their problem; it's *your* problem. They'll just go get a different product or service that doesn't mislead or confuse them, or at least that misleads or confuses them less, and your sales will suffer. Therefore, it behooves you to try very hard to find terminology that does not mislead or confuse your users.

4.1.3 Blooper 35: Speaking Geek

In some computer-based products, the terminology is consistent and not prone to misinterpretation...but incomprehensible. Users have no idea what the computer is talking about. Suppose you installed some new software on your computer, but when you tried to use it, you discovered that you had somehow obtained a foreign-language version of the software, and that all of the text displayed by the program was in a language you didn't speak, such as Tibetan, or Amharic, or Greek. You'd probably have difficulty learning and using the software. In fact, you'd probably discard it and try to get the version that was in your own language.

As the number of people who use computer-based products increases to a larger share of the population, more and more people are finding themselves in a similar situation, except that the "foreign" language their software displays is not Greek, but rather Geek. However, users faced with software that uses incomprehensible Geek are actually worse off than those who mistakenly have software that uses Greek because they can't get replacement copies in a language they understand.

As with many of the other bloopers in this book, there are several different ways to speak Geek.

Variation A: Using programmer jargon. Most professional fields and even many hobbies have their own jargon—a specialized vocabulary that allows practitioners of the field or hobby to communicate more precisely and efficiently. Some jargons even include specialized idiomatic expressions. There are jargons for air traffic controllers, stamp collectors, carpenters, model boat builders, lawyers, fishermen, surfers, airplane pilots, you name it.

My wife is a physical therapist. When she converses with other PTs or even with other medical professionals (such as doctors and nurses), I often have no idea what she is talking about. But that's fine; she isn't talking to me. What matters is that the people she is talking to do understand her. However, when she tells me about her workday, she uses standard English rather than the specialized PT jargon. She does that because she wants me to understand what she is saying. Similarly, when I talk to her about my work, I avoid using computer or user interface jargon.

From the looks of many software products and services on the market, many software developers don't switch off their use of jargon when writing software for nonprogrammers. This can happen for a variety of reasons:

© 1998 Randy Glasbergen.
www.glasbergen.com

GLASBERGEN

"We're looking for someone who's bilingual. Do you speak Technobabble?"

- A lack of awareness that there is anything to switch off: they don't realize they use a highly specialized jargon that others don't know and don't want to know.

- An inability to switch the jargon off even though they are aware that they use it, just as some people are unable to switch off their local dialect when they converse with people from other regions.

- A belief that if people want to use a computer, they need to learn to understand computer jargon.

- A tight deadline and insufficient writer support, inducing programmers to simply use the terminology they know and hope that someone will improve the wording later.

- An implementation that exposes to users technical concepts that have no counterpart in the target task domain (see Blooper 43: Exposing the implementation to users, Section 5.1.1).

For the above reasons, and perhaps others as well, much of the computer software on the market and on the Internet today is full of acronyms such as "ROM" and "grep," pure computerese such as "device drivers" and "macro" and "download" and "dot com," words that are rarely used in standard English such as "mode" and "buffer," phrases that turn verbs into nouns such as "do a compare" and "finish an edit," terms that reflect the developer's point of view rather than the user's such as "user defaults." Regardless of the reason, the effect on users is the same: lack of understanding and slowed learning.

 Mismatched terminology

> The Interface Hall of Shame reports an incident in which a secretary called the Compuserve customer support hotline to say that even though she did what the software told her to do, it didn't seem to work. Compuserve's software had displayed an error dialog box containing the message:
>
> Type mismatch.
>
> The secretary said that when she saw this message, she typed "mismatch" several times, but it didn't help.)   ⊕

The image on the top in Figure 4.6 is an error message displayed by the Eudora Pro software, from Qualcomm. What do you suppose the message is trying to say? It is telling the user that the email password the user typed (to download new mail from the mail server) is incorrect. Rather than just saying that, the programmer of this dialog box considered it necessary to explain the entire communications protocol between the Eudora Pro program and the

Figure 4.6

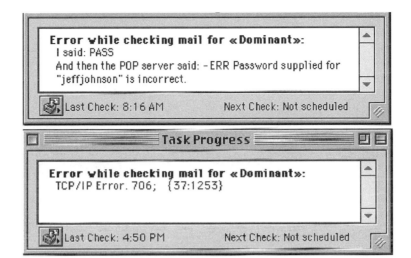

email server. Not only that, the programmer had Eudora refer to itself as "I," as if it were a person. Bzzzt. Blooper! Maybe the developers of Eudora care about this interprocess communication stuff and maybe some system administrators want to see it, but normal users of Eudora do not.

The image on the bottom in Figure 4.6 is an even more geeky error message from Eudora Pro. In this case, an attempt to fetch new mail failed because the email server did not respond. Clear, eh? It is difficult for me to believe that Eudora's designers expect users to understand these messages.

I once conducted a usability test for a company that had developed a business application. The application displayed the structure of the application's data using a Windows-style tree control. The problem was that the application referred to the tree control using those exact words, even though "tree control" is hard-core GUI toolkit jargon. Not surprisingly, user testing showed that many users didn't know what the term meant. Some probably wondered what the software had to do with trees.

 Examples of software speaking Geek

Example 1. An example of a computer product that spoke Geek is provided by a Web-based application developed by one of my clients. Like many Web-based applications, this one required users to login so that it could show them their own data and let them manipulate it. The problem was that the application referred to logging in as "authenticating." The login page was labeled "User Authentication." This is bad in two respects: (1) users don't know what "authentication" means, and (2) the word "user" is software developer jargon; users don't identify with that term.

To make matters worse, if a user did nothing for a long period of time, the application's back-end servers might log the user off automatically, but the application in the user's Web browser would continue to appear as the user had left it. Thus, users who had interrupted their use of the application to do something else (e.g., take a phone call, go to the restroom, chat with a coworker) would sometimes return to the application, find it as they expected, try to do something, and—inexplicably from their point of view—suddenly see the following message:

```
Your session has expired.
Please reauthenticate.
        [OK]
```

When users acknowledged the message by clicking OK, they would be returned to the "User Authentication" page. I advised the developers to get rid of the word "user," change all uses of the term "authenticate" to "login," and increase the automatic logoff timeout of the servers (since they didn't want to eliminate it altogether).

Example 2. Another client was developing an e-commerce application for networked PCs. The application allowed users to create and save templates for common transactions. It gave users the option of saving templates either on their own PC's hard disk or on a server out on the network. Templates stored on the server were accessible by other users; templates stored on the users' PC's hard disk were private. The problem was that the software referred to the two storage options as "database" and "local." The developers used the term "database" to refer to templates saved on the server because the server used a database to organize the templates. They used the word "local" for templates stored on the users' own hard disk because that's what "local" meant to them.

Complicating matters further, the term "database" was also used elsewhere in the application as one option for where the software would get prices for items users could order. The developers used the term "database" for that option because the prices were stored on the same server, using the same database, as the users' templates. In other words, they used the word "database" for any data stored in the database, regardless of the data's function in the application.

My recommendations to this client were as follows:

- For storing templates, use the term "shared" or "public" instead of "database," and the term "private" instead of "local."

- For specifying the source of prices, use the term "price list" instead of "database." ⊕

An especially common form of speaking Geek is when application software uses the word "New" as a name for commands that create new data objects, such as "Message:New" or "Appointment:New." This term derives from the operation in many programming languages—especially object-oriented ones—for allocating and initializing data objects, which is usually called "New." The problem with carrying this term over into the user interface and using it as a command name is that (1) it isn't a verb, and command names should be verbs,

Figure 4.7

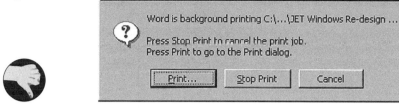

and (2) users of most software applications haven't encountered this use of the term before and will have to learn what it means.

Variation B: Turning common words into programmer jargon. A special case of using programmer jargon is the distinct programmer tendency to redefine common words to have specific meanings in software. The Unix operating system is infamous for command names such as "cat" and "man," which in Unix mean "concatenate a file" and "display the online manual," respectively, rather than "feline mammal" and "male person." When developers of computer-based products and services redefine common words and expect the users to adapt to them, they are not being considerate of users. They are committing a design blooper.

One common term that is often assigned a special jargon meaning is the word "resources." A lot of GUI-based software in today's market misuses this word for what are really attributes or properties. This is especially true of software based on X Windows, a popular basis for Unix window managers (e.g., the Common Desktop Environment GUI platform used in Sun's Solaris and Hewlett-Packard's HP/UX). The word "resource" has a meaning in English: something useful that one has a certain amount of. My Webster's dictionary defines it as "a new or reserve source of supply or support; available means." Managers in companies may refer to their personnel as "resources," and they may also use the term for various business supplies and/or funds, but stretching the term to cover what are essentially parameter settings is, in my opinion, stretching it too far. If programmers want to use this word this way inside their code, fine, but this usage of the term should *never* appear in the user interface.

Another example of an often-seen redefined word is "dialog." When reviewing software for clients, as well as when using software in my work, I often find references in the user interface to "dialog" (as in the dialog box from Microsoft Word shown in Figure 4.7). Although the word means "a conversation" in standard English, it is often used in GUI-based software as shorthand for the term "dialog box." In short, "dialog" is GUI toolkit jargon for a dialog box. For example, one client's software had a button labeled "Close this dialog." Programmers and even user interface designers use this term so often that they forget that it is a redefinition of a standard English word. They also forget that even in GUI toolkit jargon, it's an abbreviation. Given the recent rapid expansion of the

Calvin and Hobbes

by Bill Watterson

Calvin and Hobbes © 1992 Watterson. Reprinted by permission of Universal Press Syndicate.

personal computer market into the mainstream of society, many of today's PC users have never heard of the GUI toolkit definition of "dialog" or "dialog box." They assume the word has its normal meaning—a conversation—and are confused because that meaning doesn't make sense in the context where the term appears.

Other examples of words that are often redefined in computer-based products and services are "string," "object," and "client." A Web application developed by one of my clients displayed a login page titled (in large, prominent letters) "Thin-Client Login." Some of the users who logged into this application were probably surprised and pleased that it offered them the login page for *thin* clients instead of the alternative.

Variation C: Turning verbs into nouns. Another sort of jargon often seen in computer software is verbs used as nouns. This tendency is not restricted to computer software; you can see it in the specialized vocabulary of just about any field. For example: stockbrokers use "buys" and "sells" as nouns when discussing stock transactions, airplane pilots refer to "takeoffs," fishermen talk about the day's "catch," and book reviewers sometimes describe books they like as "a worthwhile read."

Software engineers often use phrases such as "the compile failed," "start the build," "do a compare," "finish an edit." For communication between software engineers, such expressions are fine. However, they become a problem when they are used to communicate with users who are not software engineers, and so might misinterpret the jargon.

As an example, one of my client companies was developing software for finding relationships in business data (sometimes called "data mining"). One function of the software was called "Explore data." The programmers called using that function "doing an Explore." The software included an auxiliary function that predicted the time and resources required to "do an Explore." That auxiliary function was named "Explore Prediction," a noun phrase, not a verb phrase. Got that? There's more: The same software had another function, for comparing two data files. Naturally, using that function was called "doing a Compare." Users could define comparisons that could be run repeatedly on different data files. The function for defining a comparison was called—you guessed it—"Compare Definition," another noun phrase.

Turning verbs into nouns

The following are examples in which verbs were used as nouns in command names and setting labels, creating the strong possibility that users might misinterpret them.

Example 1. A client developed software that provided a "wizard" (i.e., a multistep dialog box) for creating various types of data objects. The button that invoked this wizard for creating objects was labeled "Create Object Wizard." The developers meant for this label to be a noun phrase—the "(Create Object) Wizard." However, users tended to read it as a verb phrase—"Create (Object Wizard)," and wondered what an "Object Wizard" was and why they would want to create one.

Example 2. A client was developing an application for stockbrokers to use to record, submit, and track their clients' stock orders. Stockbrokers could define and name templates that controlled how the application displayed tables of stock orders. By applying different templates to a table of stock orders, the information displayed for each of the stocks in the table could be changed radically. The templates were called "Presets" (a noun), even though "presets" is a verb in standard English. The use of "Presets" as a noun led to property names such as "Preset Title," which is the title of a Preset, rather than a command to preset a title.

Variation D: Exposing terms from the code. A fourth way to speak Geek to users is to lift terms right out of the code and include them in the user interface.

A very common way of exposing users to terms from the code is to include the GUI toolkit name of a component, control, or datatype in its name or label. I see this form of the blooper often in software I review for clients. Figure 4.8 shows a dialog box that includes the word "Dialog" in its title, a "Name" setting that tells users that the program stores the value as a "string," and a menu that has "Menu" in its label.

Figure 4.8

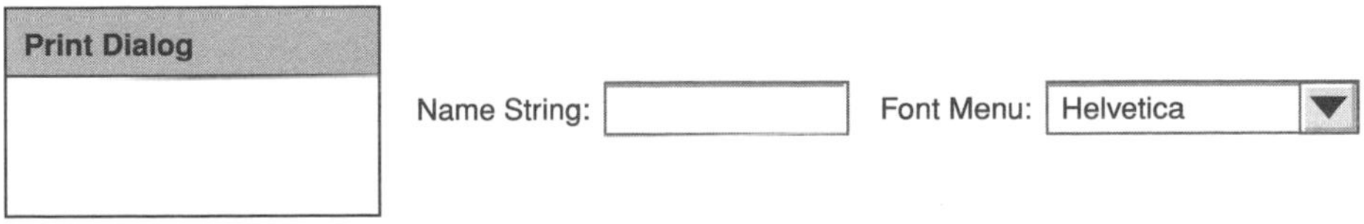

Print Dialog

Name String: [   ]   Font Menu: [Helvetica   ▼]

Example of a message that exposes terms from the code

In a Web application I recently reviewed for a client, I found an error message that exposed terms from the software code. Note that this one message exemplifies several problems in addition to containing code excerpts.

```
Login Failed. Please re-enter your login information and try again.
Error Message: PWDException when invoking constructor
'Session(String name, String pword, String server, String url)'
```

Here are the problems in this message I reported to my client:

a) The first sentence is too unspecific: it just refers to "login information." Users won't know what information (login name, password, server) was incorrect. (Ignore the fact that the invalid field—in this case the password—is identified in the second part of the message, "PWDException," because users won't understand this part at all and will simply ignore it.)

b) Overly technical: The part of the message identifying the type of exception and the method call where the error occurred will be meaningless to users and simply should not be there.

c) Implementation-centric: The second sentence is labeled "Error Message," although from the users' point of view, the error message includes both sentences. What is labeled as the "Error Message" is really error identification information passed from the low-level code that detected the error to the higher-level code that displayed the message. Users don't care what messages are passed between different parts of the application.

d) Redundant: "… re-enter info and try again …" Re-entering the information *is* trying again.

e) Incorrect capitalization: "Login Failed." Why is "Failed" capitalized?

Problems b and c are the ones that involve speaking Geek. Here is how I recommended that the client correct the message:

Recommendation: Have a technical writer rewrite this error message. The invalid field should be identified in the message, so either you'll need multiple messages or you'll have to parameterize the message so you can supply the field name at runtime. Possible revision:

```
The password you entered is not valid.
Please enter a valid password and click again on Login.
```

Lifting words and phrases straight out of the code is also common in error messages. I consider it a serious indictment of the computer industry that most computer users—whether technically oriented or not—have seen error messages like the following:

```
Uncaught Exception: array_index_out_of_range. Execution terminating.
```

```
Bad inode. File not saved.
```

```
ParseObject: Error 347: Unknown data-type.
```

In the first of the above messages, the symbol identifying the exception was provided not only to the error-handling code, which presumably needs the information, but to users as well. Users most emphatically do not need that information. The second example is from the Unix operating system, infamous for forcing users to speak Geek. An "inode" is an implementation term for the data that tells the operating system what it needs to know about a file stored on a disk. In the third message, the user is told that the procedure ParseObject encountered a unknown data type it doesn't recognize, a situation that apparently is classified as error number 347. Do 99 percent of users care about any of this? Is a bear Catholic?

One sometimes sees error messages in released software that mix code excerpts with information users can understand. The code excerpts may have been useful to programmers while the software was still being debugged, but for some reason were not removed before the software was released. Such a message was displayed by software developed and marketed by one of my clients. The message (with minor details changed to mask the client's identity) was

```
OrgSoft.JavaWizard.lib.GUI.NotAcceptingException:
JW.Frame("Names").member("Java.awt.last").select(2, "zoe");
List entry not found.
```

The only part of this message that would make sense to users would be "List entry not found," which was the translated meaning of the preceding Java exception. I advised the client to remove the Java exception from the message and display only the user-friendly translation.

Sometimes users of software applications are exposed to implementation concepts and terms through no direct fault of the application, but rather because the software platform on which the application is based displays error messages on its own instead of passing them to the application. For a more complete discussion of such situations, see Blooper 37: Clueless error messages (Section 4.2.1).

Variation E: Assigning arbitrary meanings to short, nondescriptive terms. Back in prehistoric times, when dinosaurs—that is, command-line user interfaces and glass-teletype terminals—ruled the earth, programmers did everything they could to minimize the amount of typing users would have to do.

One common practice was to refer to each user-visible command, attribute, and data object in a software product using a single-word name. Multiple-word phrases—for example, "delete paragraph"—to refer to commands and other concepts were avoided because they required too much typing. Usually, the assigned names came from the target user language, for example, English. They were selected because their normal meaning fit the software concepts reasonably well. If no suitable single words existed in the language, single-word names were made up (rather than using multiple-word names).

While this naming practice did minimize the amount of typing users had to do, it maximized the amount of learning, remembering, and task-time problem solving they had to do. Some specific problems were

- When two similar software concepts had to be represented, programmers would often use synonyms from English to represent them: for example, "delete" for deleting text and "remove" for deleting files. Users had to learn which synonym meant what.

- Command names that had precise meanings to the program might be ambiguous or vague in the real world. For example, "edit" might mean a specific type of data-changing operation in the software, even though it can refer to many different types of changes in standard English. Users had to learn what the word meant *in the software.*

- Natural language words were assigned to software concepts even though the concepts didn't really fit. Thus, words like "resources" were assigned entirely new meanings inside certain software. This is just another thing users have to learn.

- When names were made up (e.g., "grep," "cat," "awk"), users were forced to add words—usually non-task-relevant words—to their vocabulary to be able to use the software.

However, point-and-click graphical user interfaces remove the motivation for short single-word names. Users don't type command names any more, so brevity is much less important, especially when it comes at the expense of clarity. In modern GUIs, short, cryptic command names are an anachronism of a bygone design era.

Of course, it is well known that people tend to carry over unnecessary concepts, artifacts, and design habits from previous technologies into later ones [Norman, 1988]. For example, early cars looked like and were called "horseless carriages." Thus, we would expect early GUI designers to continue to assign short, cryptic command names for a while. We can therefore perhaps excuse the designers of the Apple Macintosh for using the word "Copy" for copying document content while using the essentially synonymous word "Duplicate" for copying documents, forcing users to learn this arbitrary distinction. Old habits die hard.

However, we would have expected the tendency of programmers to assign cryptic, single-word names to commands to diminish over time, as point-and-click graphical user interfaces became the dominant style. Unfortunately, this has not happened, even as we enter the third decade of the graphical user inter-

Figure 4.9

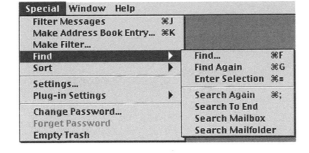

face (as well as a new millennium). This is illustrated by Figure 4.9, a menubar menu from Eudora Pro 4.0 for the Macintosh, an email program released in 1998 by Qualcomm.

The "Special" menu (a vague, grab bag name if there ever was one) contains a "Find" pull-right menu containing various commands for searching stored email messages for specified text or other features. The Find pull-right menu contains the two commands "Find Again" and "Search Again," which are different even though that isn't clear from their names. The "Find Again" command simply reexecutes the last "Find ..." command; it will find exactly what that command last found (if the archived messages haven't changed). The "Search Again" command does much the same thing, but starts its search *after* the item that was previously found; it finds the next text location that matches the description. Even though Eudora Pro has a modern GUI that lets users recognize and choose commands rather than learning, remembering, and typing them, it still requires users to learn and remember which command does what. Forcing users to learn arbitrary distinctions is not user friendly.

As another example of single-word, nondescriptive command naming in a present-day GUI application, see Figure 4.10, a screen image from Macromedia Director, a popular animation, prototyping, and Web development tool. In Director's "Modify" menu, we find a command name that the developers of Director probably thought was cute: "Tweak." This name is extremely vague. It tells users virtually nothing about what sort of modification it performs on an image, since just about anything one could do to an image could be considered "tweaking" it. Although I'm a reasonably experienced user of Director, I have no idea what this command does. Each such command in an application's user interface makes the application a little bit less intuitive—a little harder to learn—and gives users more to remember while they are using it.

It's so unnecessary! In the same "Modify" menu of Director, we see the "Arrange" command. While "arrange" is normally a relatively generic English word, Director's designers made it clearer in this menu by making it a pull-right menu item, effectively giving two-word names to the different ways to "Arrange" graphical items. This example shows clearly how GUIs remove the need to worry about the length of command names; users point at functions rather than typing their names, so the length of the names is much less important.

Figure 4.10

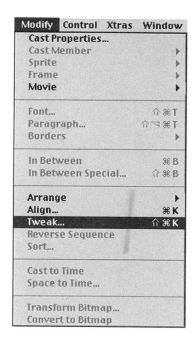

Avoiding Blooper 35: *The design rule*

For computer-based products and services to become as universal as telephones and automobiles are in the industrialized world, the Geek-speak has to go.

Consider the history of automobiles. When commercial automobiles were first introduced and for about 40 years afterward, operating one required mastering a lot of automotive technical jargon: choke, RPMs, oil pressure, alternator voltage. Now, the need for car drivers to master most of that jargon is gone. Now consider computer-based products and services for consumers, which began to appear in the late 1970s. Twenty years have passed since then. In 20 more years, will people who are using computer-based products and services still have to be aware of modems, startup files, device drivers, RAM,...even computers? Hopefully not. Let's not wait 20 more years; let's start moving toward that goal now.

How can developers avoid lapsing into speaking Geek? By following these steps when designing and developing computer-based products and services.

Know thy users

First, learn about the intended users. Visit them, observe them, interview them, invite them to focus groups. Ask them to describe how they work, what they like and don't like about their current tools, and what their most serious problems are. Get their ideas about how their work might be improved. Compile a list of all the concepts the intended users mentioned in their descriptions of their work. Pay special attention to the objects (nouns), actions on objects (verbs), and attributes of objects (adjectives) they mention.

Develop a product lexicon based on the task domain

Use the information gathered from intended users to develop a conceptual model for the planned software product or service. For a more complete discussion of conceptual models, see Principle 2 (Section 1.2.3). The conceptual model of the application will include an object/action analysis and a lexicon. The lexicon should list all the concepts (objects, actions, attributes) that the software exposes to users and indicate the name that will be used for each concept. When possible, industry standard names for concepts should be used.

The goal is that the user interface and documentation will use a vocabulary that is consistent, both internally to the software and with industry standards for the platform, and also grounded firmly in the task domains and vocabulary of the intended users (see Principle 3, Section 1.3). Toward that end, the documentation staff should be charged with developing and maintaining the product lexicon, and with enforcing adherence to it. All labels and messages displayed in the software should be written by, or with the assistance of, the documentation staff. Ideally, labels and messages will be stored in message files, separated from the program code, to facilitate review by the documentation staff (as well as internationalization). When text displayed by the application (and text in the documentation) is reviewed, the review should be carried out with a strong anti-Geek filter.

Some programmers I have spoken with have argued that it is best if the user interface and the terminology it uses match the implementation, so that the user interface does not mislead users about how the application works. Perhaps, but I would argue that the right way to accomplish that kind of correspondence is to design the user interface first and then match the implementation (that is, the structure, concepts, and terminology it is based upon) to that.

Leave GUI component names out of the GUI

Don't include the GUI toolkit name of components in the title or label for a component. Figure 4.11 shows corrected titles and labels for the examples given in Figure 4.8. Not only do these labels eliminate the Geek-speak, they eliminate needless redundancy as well.

Use "Create," not "New"

Earlier, I mentioned the word "New" as a common form of speaking Geek. In my opinion, the word "New" as a command for creating things should be like the word "Object": it should be banned from all applications except software tools for object-oriented programming. When I encounter the command "New" while reviewing or testing end user applications, I advise the client to use "Create" or "Add" instead.

Figure 4.11

Print	

Name: [   ]   Font: [Helvetica   ▼]

4.1.4 Blooper 36: Careless writing

Even if the text displayed by a software product or service uses terms consistently, doesn't redefine common words, and avoids programmer jargon, code terms, and ambiguous words, the writing can still be inadequate for a commercial product or service. It can be inconsistent, varying in style from one message or setting label to another. It can exhibit poor spelling and grammar. It can be misleading. It can be incorrectly capitalized. In short, it can be careless writing.

This section discusses several types of careless writing commonly found in computer-based products and services.

Variation A: Inconsistent writing style. Many applications exhibit stylistic inconsistencies in the text of built-in instructions, command names (in menus and on buttons), setting labels, window titles, and so on. Common inconsistencies include

- naming some commands after actions (verbs) but others after objects (nouns), for example, "Show Details" versus "Properties"
- using terse, "telegraphic" language for some setting labels or messages (e.g., "Enter Send date:") but wordy language for others (e.g., "Please specify the date on which the message is to be sent")
- using title capitalization (e.g., Database Security) for some headings but sentence capitalization (e.g., Database security) for others
- ending some but not all sentences (e.g., in instructions or error messages) with periods

For example, the following is an excerpt from a review I performed of a client's product:

The verbal style used in the program is inconsistent. Two examples:
- In the startup dialog box, two of the choices are "Create New Study" and "Open An Existing Study." The first of these uses telegraphic English, omitting the article before the noun; the second uses standard English, including the article "An."
- Some fields that require a user to type a name are labeled "X Name" while others are labeled "X," e.g., "Table Name:" vs. "File:." Either both should include the word "Name" or neither should.

Figure 4.12

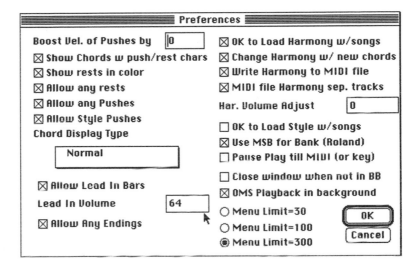

In another client's software, a Graph menu on the menubar contained the inconsistently capitalized commands: "Add Meter ...," "Print meter ...," "Add Graph ...," and "Print graph....." My guess is that one programmer implemented the Add functions and a different programmer implemented the Print functions.

The dialog box shown in Figure 4.12, from Band in a Box 6.0, a music accompaniment program from PG Software, has labels that are capitalized many different ways. Maybe Band in a Box's developers assume that its customers won't notice such inconsistencies. While it is true that most Band in a Box users won't say, "Hey! That dialog box mixes title capitalization and sentence capitalization!," they might well say, "You know, Band in a Box strikes me as kind of amateurish. It just doesn't seem like a polished product."

Variation B: Poor grammar, spelling, and punctuation. Many GUI-based applications suffer from poor spelling and writing in on-screen instructions, warnings, error messages, setting labels, and button labels. Although user documentation is usually written by technical writers, text that appears in the software is usually written by programmers. Programmers are rarely well-trained writers, and it shows in the quality of the writing in many programs.

In the days before GUIs, I worked for a Silicon Valley computer company that had developed an operating system for its computers. The operating system was written mostly by one programmer. He had the responsibility of naming the commands that users would type in order to manipulate files. One of the commands set file attributes to determine who had permission to access each file. The name the programmer assigned to the command was supposed to be an abbreviation of "attributes." Unfortunately, the programmer was a poor speller and spelled the command abbreviation "atrib" instead of "attrib." This error was not discovered before the operating system, including the misspelled

DILBERT reprinted by permission of United Feature Syndicate, Inc.

command, had been shipped to thousands of customers. Needless to say, users had trouble remembering this command because they persisted in trying to spell it correctly. Although the misspelled command had to be left in the operating system so that shell scripts that used it would continue to work, we eventually convinced the programmer to add a correctly spelled alias for the command. Amazingly, he initially resisted adding the alias, arguing that it didn't matter that the command was misspelled because computer command names are arbitrary anyway, and users can just learn them.

A colleague told me about a bank she once worked for that was converting its old text-display-based software to the new windows-and-mouse style of user interface. To save money, the bank hired programmers from Israel and brought them to the United States for the duration of the software conversion project. According to my colleague, the Israelis had a whole floor of the bank's administrative building to themselves. Partly because they were working under a tight deadline, and partly because many of them didn't speak English, the Israeli programmers kept pretty much to themselves. Perhaps this contributed to a lack of supervision, because when the conversion was nearly done, management discovered that (1) the software's messages and labels were written in English heavily influenced by Hebrew syntax, and (2) the controls, data displays, and labels were laid out right to left, as is normal for software that displays text in Hebrew. The bank had to extend the project to reverse the layout of all the windows.

Two recent—and costly—examples of poor writing in software are provided by a couple of medium-sized Silicon Valley companies that were consulting clients of mine. Each had a team developing a large desktop software application for the Microsoft Windows operating system. On both development projects, the engineers were responsible for all text displayed by the software, and none of that text was reviewed by technical writers. In fact, one of the two teams didn't even have any technical writers. As we saw from the "atrib" example earlier, this by itself would probably have been enough to yield products riddled with vague or misspelled command names, inconsistently worded control labels, confusing instructions, and cryptic error messages.

Examples of poor writing in software

Example 1. I once reviewed a computer company's customer support Web site. Although the company had a large number of technical writers on staff, all the text in the Web site had been written by programmers. The following are examples of the text it displayed. The company and service names have been changed.

- On the site's Home page was a link labeled "Information before Getting Started," which displayed odd capitalization as well as poor grammar.

- Also on the Home page was a note inviting visitors to register: "CompanyX welcomes you to become a ServiceX Online member." This is poor grammar: "welcomes you to become." I suggested that they change it to "invites you to become."

- Elsewhere in the site was the note "Connect is your contact to CompanyX technical support." This is totally unintelligible unless one knows that "Connect" is the name of a service. Thus, one problem is that most readers will interpret "connect" as a verb, not a name. There is also the problem that "contact to" is ungrammatical.

- Once visitors to the site logged in as a technical support subscriber, they saw the message "This is a list of serial numbers for which you are a system contact person in our database or you have added." Say what?

- On the page of the site that listed the software patches that were available for downloading, the following warning appeared: "We strongly recommend you to install the patch set as a set." Clearly, this was not written by someone with a great mastery of English.

Example 2. A stock investing application I reviewed for a client contained dialog boxes displaying the messages listed below, reproduced exactly as displayed by the software. Notice the odd capitalization, punctuation, and grammar in all of them. Especially noteworthy was that this was not a prereleased product; the application had been released over a year before my review.

```
Orders have been created Successfully
Do you wish to Submit Order?

Order Size is greater than remainder
.Increase Overall Size?

One or more Summary window(s) are open, cannot close this window.
```

Example 3. A few years ago, I reviewed an application that monitored the load on a remote server. When the application failed to connect to a specified server, it displayed the following message:

```
Can not connect with host server exitting.
```

In this message, "can not" should be one word, a period is needed after "server," "exitting" is misspelled and should be capitalized, and the message fails to identify the server with which it could not connect.

Figure 4.13

> Your virus definitions are more that 30 days old. You should download the latest definitions file from McAfee.

However, the situation at both companies was even worse than that. Although the software was intended for English-speaking customers, none of the developers on either team were native speakers of English. Both of these companies had the practice of hiring most of their programmers from overseas, mainly India, Taiwan, and Russia. While the engineers on both teams were quite competent at programming, their attempts at devising command names, setting labels, error messages, and instructions bordered on amusing. However, potential customers were not amused. Management at each of these two companies probably thought that their hiring practices provided skilled programmers at a discount, but they failed to anticipate that those practices would also either add reviewing and rewriting costs or reduce the sales of the product.

Not all examples of poor writing are serious enough to impair understanding. Sometimes they are just simple typographical errors that were not caught. Nonetheless, software that contains typographical errors in the text it displays is likely to give users an impression of careless workmanship and amateurishness, which isn't an impression that most product development organizations wish to convey. An example of such an error in a long-released software product can be seen in VirusScan 3.0.1 for Macintosh, from McAfee, a subsidiary of Network Associates, Inc. If a user's virus definition files are old, the program displays, in its main window, the message shown in Figure 4.13. The typographical error in this message is a common one. Can you spot it? It should have been caught by technical writers before the product was released.

Variation C: Misleading text. Jakob Nielsen has often pointed out in his critiques of Web sites (see *www.UseIt.com*) that people often write labels, headings, descriptions, and instructions for software without considering how users might interpret the text in the context where it appears. I agree completely.

An example of misleading writing is provided by a customer support Web site I reviewed for a client. The site included a page listing software patches that could be downloaded and installed to correct known bugs in the company's software. A section of the Patch page was set aside for the patches that the company was currently recommending that its customers install. That section was labeled:

Recommended Patches

```
These patches have been tested and will keep your CompanyX workstation
running smoothly.
```

I pointed out in my review of the Web site that this might suggest to some customers that the other patches had *not* been tested. The person who wrote the

Figure 4.14

section label had considered only how the label fit its own section, not what it implied about the rest of the page in which it appeared.

Variation D: Enter Id, Ok?. This variation of the "poor writing" blooper will strike some as trivial and unimportant, but it drives me crazy. Furthermore it is, for reasons I cannot fathom, extremely common. I almost devoted a separate blooper to it.

GUI-based applications contain many dialog boxes. Most dialog boxes have a control button labeled "OK," right? Well, sort of. A great many dialog boxes have a button labeled "Ok," with a lowercase *k*. This is just plain wrong: "OK" is spelled with two capital letters. This minor but annoying error is shown in the dialog box buttons in Figure 4.14, from the Which Chorus dialog box of Band in a Box 6.0 Pro for Macintosh.

Similarly, the term "ID," an abbreviation for "identification," is a common term in application software. Like "OK," it is often misspelled with a lowercase second letter, as "Id," especially by programmers who are not native speakers of English. Misspelled in that way, it can be mistaken for "id," a Latin word that has entered the English language as a term used by psychoanalysts to refer to the part of the human psyche that, according to the American Heritage dictionary, is "the source of instinctual impulses." "Please enter your Id: _____."
Hmmm.

Avoiding Blooper 36: The design rule

By following these rules, software developers can ensure that the text displayed by their software conveys an impression of professionalism and care.

Use writers

If software developers want their products and services to be "professional," they need to get the right professionals for *all* of the jobs that are part of software development. Programmers are professionals at writing code. They are not professionals at writing prose. Programmers should not write the text that appears in software. Technical writers are the right professionals for that job.

Ideally, skilled technical writers should be as involved in the writing of text for the software as they are in the writing of text for the manuals. This includes on-screen instructions, warnings, error messages, setting labels, button labels—all text displayed by the software. At the very least, all text in the software should be reviewed by technical editors or writers. Not only does this improve the quality of labels and messages displayed by software, it also improves their consistency with the software's documentation.

Spell-check all text

All text appearing in an application should be spell-checked. Ideally, the first pass at spell-checking would be done using spell-checking software. However, ingenuity may be required to get such software to check software source code message files. Whether or not the program text is spell-checked by spell-checking software, it should also be checked by human technical editors or writers because human checkers can catch errors that software checkers miss.

Think outside-in

When writing text for a software product or service, consider how users will interpret it. Also, don't simply consider each piece of text in isolation. Consider how well it conveys its intended meaning in the context where it will appear. When in doubt, test it on real users.

ID, OK?

"ID" and "id" are very different words in English. Don't confuse them. Capitalize both letters in "ID." The same goes for "OK." "Ok" is not OK. OK?

4.2 Unfriendly messages and labels

The next four textual bloopers pertain to the quality of error messages and setting labels displayed by software.

4.2.1 Blooper 37: Clueless error messages

As described in the previous blooper, one way that software often speaks Geek is by displaying error messages that are expressed in implementation terms, rather than in terms that are meaningful to users. A related blooper is displaying error messages that announce some generic error condition rather than giving users helpful information about what happened. This happens for three different reasons, giving rise to three variations of this blooper.

Variation A: Message determined by low-level code. This variation occurs when an error is detected by a low-level service function, which either displays an error dialog box directly, or passes the error up the call stack, where it is displayed without translation by a higher-level function. The function that the user explicitly invoked could, in theory, express errors in task-relevant terms, but the lower-level service functions it calls "know" nothing about user tasks and goals and so can only express errors in technical or generic terms. Consider the following hypothetical examples:

Example of an error message displayed by low-level code

At a company where I worked many years ago, a programmer was hired who had emigrated to the United States from the former Yugoslavia. He was a top-notch programmer, but his spelling abilities in English were limited. This was not usually a problem because most of his assignments were to develop deep-down device driver code that had no user interface. At one point he was given the assignment of writing the display driver for a terminal the company was developing. Although his device driver was going to be placed into read-only memory (ROM) on the terminal, making it difficult to correct problems, no one checked his work because the driver was supposed to be completely invisible to users. And it was…almost. Later, it was discovered that a certain unforeseen sequence of events could cause the display driver to go into an infinite recursion, which would eventually hit a memory limit and display the following message in the middle of the screen:

```
Nesting level too dip.
```

This little error message would have been funny except that it had already been burned onto ROM and shipped with tens of thousands of terminals worldwide. The problem with the error message, of course, was not the misspelled word, but rather that people using the computer terminal could be exposed to a message displayed by the terminal's firmware. They would have no idea what the message was about, what caused it, or what to do about it.

- A user tries to follow a link in a Web site. The Web browser prepares to download the indicated data files, but finds that it is out of space in its cache of recently loaded pages. It attempts to delete some of the pages currently in the cache. For some reason, one such page is locked and cannot be deleted. The code that tried to delete the cached page detects this error and displays a dialog box containing the message "Cannot delete cached page. Page locked." From the user's point of view, this error message comes out of nowhere; she clicked on a link and up popped this seemingly unrelated message. The user's response would probably be "Huh? What does *that* have to do with what I was doing?"

- A user receives an email message, reads it, and decides to save it in one of his mail folders. Attempting to pick the Sensor Project folder from a menu of mail folders, the user inadvertently selects the next folder in the list: Sent Messages. The Sent Messages folder does not allow users to save messages into it. The email application implements mail folders and messages as directories and files, respectively. To save the user's message, the application calls an operating system service-function File.Create() with the Sent Messages folder as the destination directory. The Sent Messages folder does not allow the creation of the new file, so File.Create() fails. It displays an error dialog box reading: "File.Create() failed." The user doesn't know (1) that he missed the intended folder in the menu, (2) what File.Create() is, or even (3) that messages are stored in files, so this error message would be triply mysterious.

When this variation of Blooper 37 occurs in an application, it may be difficult to correct. The low-level code that detects the error and displays an unhelpful error message may not be in the application itself. Instead, that code may be in the platform on which the application is running. If an application calls an operating system utility function and the function sometimes displays a poor error message, the application's programmers probably won't be able to fix the message because it is not in their code. Nonetheless, most users will perceive the message as coming from the application. If the message is seriously misleading, the application developers may have no choice other than changing their code so that it does not use the troublesome operating system utility function.

A similar situation can arise with Web-based applications: the Web browser may display cryptic, unhelpful, or misleading error messages in certain situations, but there may be little the application developer can do about it. As an example, users of a Web application developed by a client of mine would occasionally see the following error message:

```
Error 500 HTTP Web Server
GraphicsNotFoundException
```

It turned out that this message was being displayed by the Web browser, so there was little the application developer could do about it, short of recommending that users use a different browser.

Variation B: Reason for error not passed up to higher-level code. Sometimes software displays clueless error messages because the reasons for the errors are not properly passed from lower-level utility functions that detect the errors to the higher-level functions that the user invoked. For example, a client of mine had an application that displayed the following error message when a user tried to load a nonexistent data file:

```
Error parsing datafile. Data not parsed.
```

Although the message was true—no data was parsed—it was highly misleading. The real problem was that the specified data file was not found. After attempting to load the file, the code apparently did not check whether the load operation had succeeded, but rather simply passed an empty data buffer to the data parsing procedure, which duly reported that it couldn't parse the data. Fortunately, this bogus error message was caught before the software was released.

Variation C: Generic message components. Another common way in which software displays unhelpful error messages is by using generic, one-size-fits-all error message texts and dialog boxes even though the software has more specific information that it could provide. After a user edits some settings in a dialog box and clicks OK, the software might display an error message indicating that one of the settings in the dialog box is invalid, but doesn't identify the invalid setting. I see a lot of this sort of message in software I review for my clients.

For example, consider a stock investment application a client of mine had developed. The application allowed users to specify how much of a particular stock they wanted to buy or sell. New users of the application often encountered the following error message when they tried to submit orders:

```
Order size not multiple of trading unit.
```

It turns out that users of this application are not allowed to buy or sell just any old number of shares. The number of shares in a transaction must be a multiple of the "trading unit." The trading unit is (potentially) different for each stock. But the error message does not say what the trading unit for the stock is. The trading unit is also not shown anywhere on the ordering screen. Users just have to know, or guess, what the trading unit is for the stock they want to buy or sell.

Predictably, users of this application who hadn't already memorized the trading units of various stocks wasted a lot of time adjusting the transaction size and resubmitting orders until they chanced on a number of shares that was a multiple of that stock's trading unit. Because of this blooper and a myriad of others in the same application, I sometimes wondered if this client was really interested in selling software.

Figure 4.15 shows a message sometimes displayed by Microsoft Word 6.0 when a user attempts to open a document that contains graphic images. The message tells the user that one of two problems has occurred. If the two possible problems were similar, this might be acceptable, but in this case, the two problems are quite dissimilar; in particular, they have totally different remedies. If Word doesn't have the appropriate graphics filter for the image, the user has to figure out what kind of image it is, and try to find and install the appropriate filter. If Word simply ran out of memory when trying to load the filter, then shutting down some other applications will probably suffice unless there are none to shut down, in which case the user needs to add memory to the com-

Figure 4.15

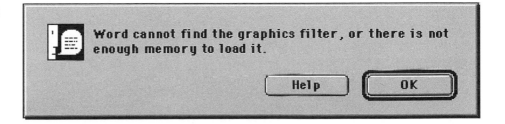

Examples of generic error messages

The following are stories, from my consulting files, of software that displayed generic, uninformative error messages. The stories are suitably anonymized to protect the guilty.

Example 1. An error message displayed when a user tried to give a data object a name containing characters that weren't allowed in names:

```
Name contains invalid characters.
```

Wonderful. Pray tell, which characters might those be? But alas, the software won't tell, even though it knows. How coy!

Example 2. An error message sometimes displayed by a client's application when the user tried to import a data file:

```
File missing or you don't have access.
```

This message is unnecessarily vague: it doesn't say which of two (from the user's point of view) quite different problems has occurred. To be fair, this wasn't entirely the application programmer's fault: the operating system's ReadFile() function returned an error code that lumped the two cases together. However, by writing a bit more code, the programmer could have distinguished between the two situations. But the programmer didn't consider doing so to be worth the effort, so he or she used one message to cover both situations. A second fault of this error message is that it didn't name the file it is talking about, even though it could have.

Example 3. A message that was displayed by an application if a user typed too large a number into any of its many number fields:

```
Value of field exceeds limit.
```

This message neither identifies the field in question nor does it give users a clue as to what the maximum legal value for that particular field is. Grrr! An error message like this one can result from the use of generic messages (i.e., Variation C), from low-level code that displays error messages directly instead of passing them to the application-level code (i.e., Variation A), or from a combination of the two.

puter. Thus, the user is left wondering what to do to resolve the problem. It seems unlikely that Word cannot distinguish these two quite different problems.

The Mother of all generic, uninformative error messages—the error message that, if there were a Nobel Prize for vagueness, would be the undisputed winner—has to be the error message shown in Figure 4.16, displayed by Eudora Pro 4.0, Qualcomm's email software. Huh? What sort of help? Should I call 911? Should I bring Eudora some chicken soup or warm milk? Should I try to put my arm around Eudora's shoulder and give a reassuring squeeze? Should I tell Lassie to go fetch the sheriff? What the heck is this message asking me to

Figure 4.16

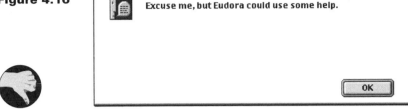

do? Some programmer at Qualcomm (or given the rapid turnover in this industry, probably long gone from there) thought he or she was being really, really clever. Bzzzt. Blooper!

As it turns out, what Eudora was trying to tell me was: "I downloaded your new email for you, as you requested, but when I tried to display a message telling you that you have new mail, I couldn't, for reasons I don't understand. Something is blocking me from displaying that message. So instead, I am displaying this message, and hope you can somehow figure out what is wrong and how to fix it so I can show you the message saying you have new mail." While waiting for Eudora to download my new email, I had begun working in another application, and this somehow was preventing Eudora from displaying its "new mail" message.

But I, of course, did not know that this is what the message was trying to tell me. I clicked on the message's OK button and the message disappeared. I waited to see if anything else would happen. Nothing did. My newly arrived mail was plainly visible in my Inbox. I was about to forget about the strange message and begin reading my new mail, when I noticed a flashing mail icon on the Macintosh application menu (a menu of currently active applications displayed on the right end of the Macintosh menubar). Eudora was still trying to signal me. I opened the menu and selected Eudora, activating it. Suddenly, a dialog box appeared midscreen: "You have new mail." Gee, thanks, but I knew that.

Avoiding Blooper 37: *The design rule*

Software developers who follow these rules can reduce the chances that their software will display error messages that are meaningless to users.

Express the error in the vocabulary of the task domain

A good error message describes the problem in terms that match the application's intended task domain and, as much as possible, the users' goals. If the user has just given the command to paste an image into a document and the software encounters an error, the message should be expressed in terms of pasting images, not in terms of operating system functions, implementation datatypes, program exception codes, or even irrelevant application concepts.

Don't just identify the problem; suggest a solution

A good error message also provides enough information that the user can see how to correct the error. That means providing enough detail that a user can determine what he or she did to cause the problem, or if the problem wasn't the user's fault, what did cause it and why. A programmer friend of mine put it this way:

> Error messages should focus on the *solution*. Geeks love to describe the *problem*.

To counter that tendency, the company she worked for had a policy about error messages: every error message had to conform to the format:

```
Error Symbol  Problem: Solution.
```

Examples of how to improve error messages

Table 4.1 indicates my suggested revisions of each of the example error messages discussed in this blooper.

Pass errors up to code that can translate them for users

Low-level service routines and application software platforms should *never* take it upon themselves to display error messages directly. They should always pass errors back to the application so that it can handle them in the most appropriate way.

When an application receives an error notification from a lower-level procedure, it should pass the error up the call stack to code that can handle the error intelligently. That code should then handle the error in either of the following ways:

- Translate the error into terms that will be meaningful to its users and display the translation along with advice on how to correct the problem
- Assume that the cause of the error was temporary and try the operation again

Parameterize messages and message-bearing components

Error messages and error dialog box components that are intended to cover different situations should be parameterized so that details can be inserted into them at run time. This allows error messages to mention object names (e.g., filenames), constraints (e.g., value limits), data field names, and so on.

Different types of messages have different audiences

Finally, developers should recognize that error messages displayed by software have three possible functions, each having a different audience:

Table 4.1   Examples of how confusing error messages were improved

Original message	Suggested revised message
Cannot delete cached page. Page locked.	*Note: The context of this example was that the user was trying to link to a new page.*
	In this case, the right error message is no message; the browser just leaves the cached file it can't delete and loads the target page.
File.Move() failed.	*Note: The context of this example was that the user was trying to save an email message, but specified the Sent folder as a destination by mistake.*
	Messages cannot be saved in the Sent folder.
Error 500 HTTP Web Server GraphicsNotFoundException	The graphics file < *filename* > on this page was not found.
Login Failed. Please re-enter your login information and try again.	The < *fieldname* > you entered is not valid. Please enter a valid < *fieldname* > and click again on Login.
Name contains invalid characters.	< *Object-type* > names may not contain '-', '/', '@', '#', or '&' characters.
File missing or you don't have access.	Two separate error messages:
	File < *filename* > not found.
	You don't have access to file < *filename* > .
Value of field exceeds limit.	The value of < *fieldname* > cannot exceed < *limit* > .
Order size not multiple of trading unit.	Sorry: < *stockname* > stock must be traded in multiples of < *trading unit* > shares.

- Indicating user errors (for end users)
- Logging activity (for system administrators at users' site)
- Facilitating debugging and tracing (for developers)

By the time software is ready to ship, developers should make sure that each type of message is only seen by its intended audience.

4.2.2 Blooper 38: Misuse (or nonuse) of "…" on command labels

Back in the early 1980s, the designers of Apple Computer's Lisa computer (a predecessor of the Macintosh) decided it would be helpful for commands that execute immediately to be clearly distinguished from ones that first prompt the user for additional information. They decided to mark the latter sort of command by appending "..." (ellipsis) to the end of the command label, for example, "Save As...".

The "..." was intended to indicate that the software will display a dialog box prompting the user for more information. The choice of "..." as a marking was not arbitrary: it suggests that something additional must happen before the command can be fully executed. Commands that executed immediately did not end with "...". This convention was applied consistently to all command labels, whether they appeared in menus or on buttons. Details such as this convention were a part of what gave the Lisa and its more successful descendent the Macintosh reputations as easy-to-use computers.

In the software industry, good ideas spread. This convention was a good idea because it really is helpful for users to know in advance whether a command executes immediately or prompts for additional information. For example, it is safer to click on unfamiliar buttons if users can see that all that will happen is that a dialog box will appear.

Over time, the convention spread beyond the Macintosh to other computer platforms, such as the Commodore Amiga, Microsoft Windows, and Common Desktop Environment Motif standards. Nowadays, it is so pervasive that software not following this convention risks misleading users.

Unfortunately, many developers of GUIs do not follow this convention. In fact, violations of it are becoming more common. Some developers are simply unaware of the convention. Others know there is a convention but misunderstand it. Both sorts of ignorance are due partly to growth and turnover in the population of software developers and a lack of adequate training of new ones. Part of the growth in the number of "software developers" is due to the growth of the Web. As Web sites grow more and more elaborate and move beyond simple static pages, more people are becoming "software developers," often without any training.

Variation A: Omitting "...". The most common variation of this blooper is to omit the "..." on commands that should have it. Designers who commit this variation are usually those who simply don't know about the convention. They don't do anything to distinguish commands that execute immediately from commands that prompt for more information and provide an opportunity to Cancel the command. Users just have to guess or learn from experience how each command operates.

In the dialog box shown in Figure 4.17, which is from Newer Technology's SpellTools software, the Import button is for importing files containing dictionary definitions from other spelling tools. Like most Import buttons, it first displays a file chooser dialog box that allows users to specify a file to import. Therefore, the Import button's label should end with "...", but it does not. The Add Words button also displays a dialog box without indicating that.

Figure 4.17

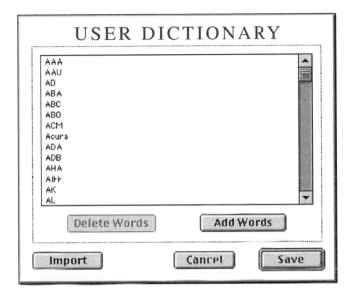

Figure 4.18

Another example from an actual software product is shown in Figure 4.18, a toolbar from the main window of the music accompaniment program Band in a Box Pro 6.0 for Macintosh. The only buttons on this toolbar that do not bring up temporary dialog boxes are Play, Stop, Replay, Hold, Lyrics, and Not'n. The rest all display dialog boxes, and so should have "..." in their labels.

Variation B: Overusing "...". The next most common variation is to append the ellipsis symbol ("...") to command labels that should not include it. Designers who commit this variation of the blooper are those who have overgeneralized the convention. They mistakenly believe they should append "..." to the labels of any command that opens a new window. Therefore, one sometimes sees commands such as Show Graph ..., which displays a graph in a new window. In this case, the command Show Graph executes immediately; it displays the graph. That's what the command does. No additional information is required. The designer included the "..." simply because the command opens a new window.

An example of Variation B can be seen in Figure 4.19 in the Fonts menu of HP's FontSmart font management software. None of the three menu items that end in "..." display a dialog box to collect additional arguments. The Magnify command displays a new window in which the currently selected font is shown magnified. The Info command displays a window providing information about the selected font. The Printer Fonts command displays a window listing the

Figure 4.19

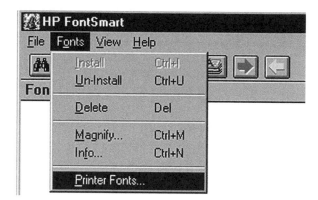

available printer fonts. In all three cases, the window displayed is the result of the command; when the window appears, the command is done. Therefore, none of the menu items for these three commands should end with "…".

Other common examples of this variation of the blooper are "New Browser …", "Debug Program …", "Edit Formula …", "Clone Window …", "Show Clipboard …", and "Help …". Assuming that these commands operate in the usual way (i.e., they open a new window to display the indicated information), these should be simply "New Browser," "Debug Program," "Edit Formula," "Clone Window," "Show Clipboard," and "Help."

Avoiding Blooper 38: *The design rule*

The convention is that "…" (ellipsis) is used to mark commands that display a dialog box to gather additional command arguments. Appending "…" to the label indicates that the application will bring up a temporary dialog box before executing the indicated command and give users a chance to Cancel the command.

Ellipsis is not for any command that opens a window

The "…" should not mark commands that simply open a new window. There are many commands for which opening a new window *is* the function of the command; the resulting window is not a temporary argument-gathering dialog box. For example, "Show Network" might open a window to display the status of a computer network. Such a command does not bring up a temporary argument-collecting dialog box, and so should not include "…" at the end of its label.

True for all GUI platforms

This design rule holds across all current GUI platforms. All the major GUI platform style guides state the same rule. For example:

- *Java Look and Feel Design Guidelines* [Sun Microsystems, 1999], page 134
- *The Windows Interface Guidelines for Software Design* [Microsoft, 1995], pages 136–137
- *Windows Style-Guide Update* [Microsoft, 1998], pages 10–11
- *OSF/Motif Style Guide: Rev 1.2* [OSF, 1993], pages 164–165
- *Macintosh Human Interface Guidelines* [Apple, 1993], pages 67–71

It's not arbitrary

The ellipsis convention may initially seem arbitrary and a hindrance to creativity and innovation. In fact, the convention is not totally arbitrary: "…" on the end of a textual command label actually does suggest to users that something additional will happen after the command is clicked. By convention, the "something additional" is that additional action is required from the user. However, the most important aspect of the convention is not the specific choice of "…" as the marker, but rather the distinction between commands that require additional input before they can execute and those that don't. The exact marking may evolve over time, but the distinction between command types should be maintained.

What about graphical button labels?

One context in which the ellipsis mark does not work is graphically labeled buttons. It is increasingly common for buttons to be labeled graphically rather than textually. Such buttons appear on toolbars and in the application content. Obviously, when a button label is an image, appending "…" to it would seem out of place. Therefore, users can't tell from the labels which commands require more input and which do not. These days, the most common solution for this is to include the ellipsis marking on "tooltip" or "hover help" text, which appears when the mouse pointer is held over the button. While this approach gives users a way to determine which category a graphically labeled command is in, it requires extra work. Perhaps a new convention is called for that works as well for graphically labeled buttons as for textually labeled ones.

4.2.3 Blooper 39: Inconsistent use of colons on setting labels

Controls, settings, and data fields in GUIs typically have textual labels that identify the value that the control or data field represents. This and the next few bloopers describe common errors in how labels are arranged and formatted.

When settings in a GUI have text labels, the issue arises, How should labels be visually separated from their corresponding setting values? The two most common solutions are (1) blank space and (2) a colon and blank space. The use of the colon character (:) rather than other possible separator characters (e.g., a hyphen) probably harkens back to the full-screen forms displayed by many

Figure 4.20

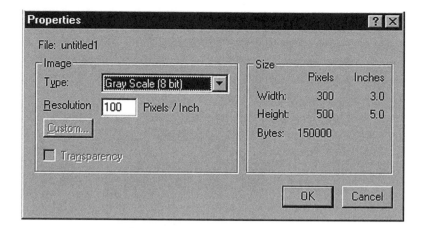

business applications that were designed for character-based terminals and time-shared computers.

A common error in GUI applications is inconsistency in whether property labels end in colons or not. Sometimes no explicit convention exists, so programmers just do whatever they want. If different programmers write different parts of the GUI and don't communicate or coordinate with each other, the result can be anarchy (see Blooper 80: Anarchic development, Section 8.2.2). Sometimes a development team has a convention, but a programmer forgets it and either includes or excludes colons on labels by mistake, perhaps for an entire control panel, or perhaps for just one setting on a panel. An example of a single forgotten colon can be seen in Figure 4.20, in the label of the Resolution setting in a dialog box from Microsoft Photo Editor.

Avoiding Blooper 39: The design rule

Colons or no colons on control labels, that is the question. In fact, it is not so important which of these a development team (or a company) chooses. However, it is important to follow the practice of the product's platform, if there is one, and it is very important to be consistent within an application or family of applications. Otherwise, the software will seem shabby and amateurish to users, even though they may not be able to point to the reason for their negative reaction.

What are the standards?

For most windowed operating systems designed for GUI-based applications, conventions regarding setting labels—such as whether labels should end in colons or not—either were explicitly developed or have developed over time as common practice. The earliest commercially available GUI platform, the Xerox Star, did not end property labels with colons. The same is true of Star's immediate successors, Xerox ViewPoint and GlobalView. The Apple Macintosh did end labels with colons, and its status as the first commercially successful personal computer for GUI-based software made the use of colons on setting labels accepted practice throughout the industry. Most other GUI platforms followed suit. In the Common Desktop Environment (CDE/Motif) window system for Unix workstations (e.g., Sun Solaris and HP/UX), and in Microsoft Windows, colons are the rule.

The World Wide Web has grown so quickly that no clear common practices have had time to emerge. It certainly has had a different history than the personal computer industry, where a few companies (initially Xerox and Apple, now Microsoft) more or less determined the GUI conventions for the rest of the industry. Furthermore, the Web is so huge and is still changing so quickly that it is difficult to get a representative snapshot of it to determine what the trends are. However, I'll venture a prediction that colons on property labels are on their way out because Web designers think they look too stodgy and old-fashioned. It's ironic that "no colons on labels" was the convention in the *first* commercial GUI. What goes around comes around.

Don't include colons on superordinate labels

Whatever a development organization decides regarding the use of colons on setting labels, there is a related design rule that seems to be true for all GUI platforms: a label serving as a superordinate heading for a *group* of settings should not end in a colon. This is true whether or not the superordinate heading is on a group box.

4.2.4 Blooper 40: Tooltips that say the same thing as the visible label

In recent years, it has become common for interactive controls in graphical user interfaces to provide popup text explaining what the control does. The standard term for such popup textual explanations is "tooltips."

A very common and annoying blooper is for software to display the same text in the tooltip as is already shown on the label of the control.

For example, examine the two images in Figure 4.21, from the toolbar on the Web browser Netscape Navigator 3.01. The tooltip provided for the Print button, shown in the image on the left, is "Print," which isn't very helpful. In contrast, the image on the right shows the tooltip provided for the Find button: "Find Text on Page," which provides more information than the button label does.

Redundant, unhelpful tooltips in released products often result from developers allocating insufficient time or resources to devising more helpful ones. Perhaps the developers meant to devise better tooltips, but simply ran out of time. Perhaps the development managers relied on programmers rather than

Figure 4.21

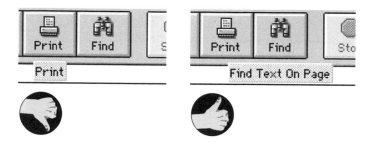

technical writers to write the tooltip messages, but the programmers didn't possess the necessary writing skills.

Avoiding Blooper 40: *The design rule*

The rules for providing useful tooltips are pretty straightforward.

If it's simply redundant, don't bother

Bebop saxophonist Charlie Parker is reputed to have stated the following rule for jazz improvisation: "If what you're playing isn't better than the tune's melody, don't bother." A similar rule can be applied to tooltips: "If a control's tooltip text doesn't explain more than the control's visible label, don't bother." Providing redundant tooltips is a waste of time.

It's an important job, and the tech writers should do it

Instead, software development teams should include time in their schedules for writing helpful tooltips. Furthermore, they should use the right people for the job: technical writers, not programmers. If that isn't feasible, technical writers should review all of the tooltips that the programmers have written.

4.3 Misleading window titles

The last two textual bloopers are cases of window titles in software that hamper the users' ability to tell where they are in the software.

4.3.1 Blooper 41: Same title on different windows

Sometimes one encounters GUI or Web applications in which different windows or Web pages have the exact same title. This design error can mislead users about "where" they are, that is, which function of the application they are using. Such errors have four common causes.

Figure 4.22

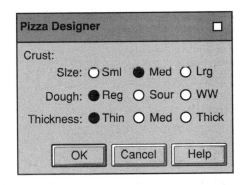

Variation A: Window titlebars don't identify specific windows. All of the windows in the application have the same name—that of the application. Perhaps the programmer thought users would automatically recognize the function of each window. Figure 4.22 shows an example of this variation of the blooper.

Variation B: Programmer copied window code but forgot to change title. GUI programmers often write new code by copying old code and then editing it. For example, new dialog boxes are often added to an application by copying the code from an existing dialog box and editing it appropriately. It is very common for programmers to forget to change the title of the dialog box, so they end up with many dialog boxes in their application with cloned names. Such mistakes are best regarded as bugs.

Variation C: Programmer didn't know title was in use elsewhere. Development teams often assign different windows of a program to different programmers. When this happens but the programmers don't communicate sufficiently, duplicate window titles can result (along with other problems; see Blooper 80: Anarchic development, Section 8.2.2). One can even find duplicate titles on windows developed by a single programmer. Some applications are very large or are developed over a long period of time, so it is possible that the programmer can simply forget that he or she has already used a particular title. Window titles, unlike program variable or procedure names, are not checked by the compiler for uniqueness, so ensuring uniqueness is completely up to the developer(s).

Variation D: Programmer thought title fit both. Sometimes a programmer gives two windows the same title because he or she thinks that the name fits both window's functions and can't (or doesn't want to) think of a better title for either one. Or perhaps the two windows were created by different programmers, who did not realize that they were using the same window titles. In most such cases, the problem is that one or both of the titles aren't as precise as they should be. For example, the following are excerpts from reports I wrote after reviewing two clients' applications:

Figure 4.23

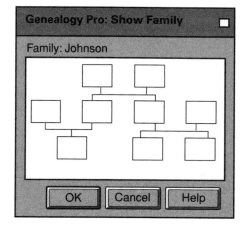
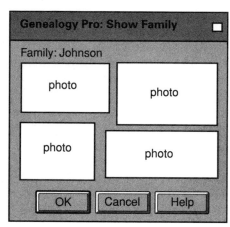

Company 1: The "Network ..." button in the Main Window displays a dialog box named "Control Network," and the "Select ..." button displays a different dialog box also named "Control Network." There shouldn't be two different windows with the same name.

Company 2: The Execution Monitor window that can be displayed from this window is a *different* Execution Monitor window than the one available from the Main Window. Recommendation: These two windows should have different names. Ideally, the program should be designed so that two different windows that are so similar are not needed.

Figure 4.23 shows two windows from a hypothetical genealogy application that contains two different dialog boxes with the same name. While the title "Show Family" is quite reasonable for each of these windows, two different windows with the same title *will* confuse users and so is a definite no-no.

Whatever the reason for duplicate window titles, when they are noticed they are often regarded as a low-priority problem that is tedious to correct. To correct it, the developers must devise a new and unique title for one of the offending windows. Therefore, duplicate window titles in a software product sometimes survive all the way to the marketplace.

Avoiding Blooper 41: *The design rule*

By following these rules, software developers can make it easier for users to navigate with confidence in software products or services.

Every window should have a unique title

Each window or Web page corresponding to a distinct function of an application should have a unique title. The titlebars of the two hypothetical dialog boxes in Figure 4.24 clearly distinguish the two windows.

Figure 4.24

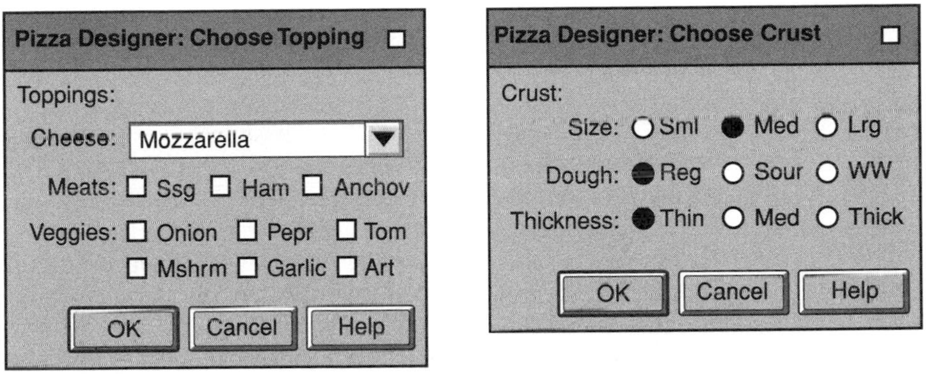

Pizza Designer: Choose Topping ☐
Toppings:
Cheese: [Mozzarella ▼]
Meats: ☐ Ssg ☐ Ham ☐ Anchov
Veggies: ☐ Onion ☐ Pepr ☐ Tom
☐ Mshrm ☐ Garlic ☐ Art
[OK] [Cancel] [Help]

Pizza Designer: Choose Crust ☐
Crust:
Size: ○ Sml ● Med ○ Lrg
Dough: ● Reg ○ Sour ○ WW
Thickness: ● Thin ○ Med ○ Thick
[OK] [Cancel] [Help]

Message files can help

As described in the design rule for Blooper 33: Inconsistent terminology (Section 4.1.1), a practice that can help developers spot and eliminate duplicate window titles is to place all text displayed by the software, including window titles, in a message file, rather than scattering them through the program source code. However, this practice will only *reduce* the likelihood of duplicate window names; it will not eliminate all such errors. If a programmer makes the mistake of pointing the titles of two different windows to the same text string in the message file, the reviewer of the message file will not notice an error unless the message file indicates what parts of the program refer to it (which is extremely rare). This type of mistake would have to be noticed by the programmers, for example, in a code review or user interface review.

Some special cases

Two special cases of duplicate window titles deserve mention:

- *Multiple windows represent same function applied to different data.* For example, text editor windows viewing different files, or stock market monitors showing activity for different stocks. This duplication can and should be prevented by including the data name in the titlebar.
- *Multiple windows represent same function or data with different user options.* Some application programs allow users to bring up several instances of the "same" window to allow users to apply different option settings to the different instances. For example, a factory monitor application might allow users to display multiple windows monitoring the factory's output, each polling the factory telemetry instruments at a different rate. For such cases, the convention is for the window title to end in an integer (separated from the title by a colon) indicating which instance of the window each one is. For example: "Factory Monitor," "Factory Monitor: 2," "Factory Monitor: 3."

4.3.2 Blooper 42: Window title doesn't match invoking command

A very common error I see in GUI-based software is a haphazard relationship between the names or titles on windows (or Web pages) and the labels on the commands (menu item or button) that invoke the windows (see Figure 4.25).

This error may seem minor or even trivial, but it is not. As users invoke the different functions of an application and thereby move around in it, they need constant, unambiguous feedback about what they have done and where they are. They need reassurance that they got what—or where—they were trying to get. Furthermore, computer users are remarkably literal—often astoundingly so—in their interpretations of labels and other navigation aids they see on the screen; if two phrases differ, even if only slightly, users assume they must mean something different. Therefore, when someone chooses a "New Employee" command and a window appears labeled "Add Employee," the person's first impression is that they didn't get what they intended.

Example of mismatched window titles. Figure 4.26 shows several dialog boxes in Microsoft Windows that have titles that do not match the command that displayed them. Double-clicking on the Display icon in the Control Panel window brings up the Display Properties window; that seems close enough. Clicking on "Change Display Type ..." in the Display Properties window brings up a dialog box with a name that exactly matches the button label. However, the remaining windows in the image do not match the commands that invoked them. Clicking the "Change ..." button in the Change Display Type dialog box displays a dialog box titled "Select Device." Clicking on the "Have Disk ..." button in the Select Device dialog box displays a dialog box titled "Install From Disk." Finally, clicking on the "Browse ..." button in the Install From Disk dialog box displays a dialog box titled "Open."

More examples. Table 4.2 shows differences I have seen between command labels and the resulting window titles in software I have reviewed for clients.

Analysis of examples. In some of the examples listed in Table 4.2, the command label and the resulting window title differ in more than one way. Here are some of the ways in which these command labels and window titles differ:

- *Different part of speech.* The command might be a verb phrase while the window title is a noun phrase, or vice versa. A common special case is when a command is labeled with the noun phrase "New X" as shorthand for "Create a New X," and the resulting window is labeled "Create X" or "Edit X." A special problem associated with changing the part of speech is that some words function both as nouns and verbs (e.g., "file," "list," "graph," "query," "record"), so changing the part of speech between the command and the window can increase the perceived ambiguity.

Figure 4.25

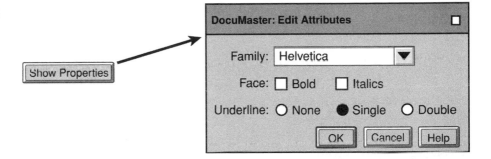

Figure 4.26

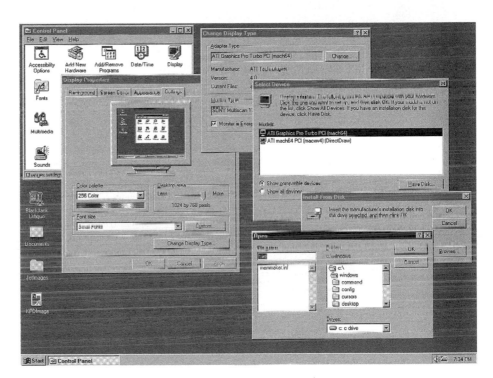

- *Synonymous terms.* The command label and window title use terms that are synonymous in the mind of the developer, for example, "Find" versus "Search," "Query" versus "Inquiry," "Options" versus "Preferences." However, they may not be synonymous to users. In any case, most computer users are well aware that computer programs often assign idiosyncratic and unfamiliar meanings to words, so it is not surprising that users show a clear tendency to assume that there must be a reason for any difference in terms.

- *Different degree of specificity.* The command label is specific (e.g., "Add Employee" or "Delete Table Cell"), but the window title is more general (e.g.,

Table 4.2 Window titles that don't match the corresponding command

Command label	Mismatched title of resulting window
Create Procedure	Edit Procedure
New Employee	Add Record
List Homes	Home List
Show Order Status	Status for Order: < order name >
Account Query	Account Inquiry
Find Message	Search Messages
Add Instrument	New Instrument Dialog
Edit Profile	View Profile
Show Properties	Paragraph Attributes
Delete Table Cell	Edit Table Layout
Save . . .	File Data
Choose Presentation	Presentation Browser
Highlight Exceptions	Exception Highlighting
Chart Options	Edit Chart Preferences

"Add Record" or "Edit Table Layout") or vice versa. One reason for this sort of difference is that the programmer is using the same window for several different related functions and doesn't bother to parameterize the title to allow it to have situation-specific titles. A common special case of this is using an "Edit X" window for the "Create X" and "View X" functions as well as for the "Edit X" function. A second reason for this sort of difference is that a command button, menu item, or keyboard key is nominally generic (e.g., Move), but the exact command and window it invokes depends on the software's state. Examples of software state often used to instantiate generic commands include the type of data object currently selected, the window or page the user is viewing, and the recent history of user actions.

- *Task domain term versus implementation domain term.* The command label uses terms from the task domain while the window title uses terms from the implementation domain. The reverse case is less common. For example, the command may use the task domain term "employee," while the window title uses the computer domain term "data record." Users will be much more familiar with the task domain term and may not recognize the corresponding computer domain term as referring to the same thing. A special case is when the command refers to an action in the task domain, but the window title refers to the window itself in some way, for example, "New Instrument" versus "New Instrument Dialog Box," or "Choose Message" versus "Message Browser."

Any of these types of differences—in fact, any type of difference—can foster confusion in users and hinder learning and productivity.

Avoiding Blooper 42: *The design rule*

The title of a window or Web page should clearly correspond to the command that caused the window or Web page to appear. The point is to make it apparent to users that they got what they wanted. They hit the button or menu item they intended to hit.

The perception of "clear correspondence" must be by *users*, not by developers. The easiest way to achieve it is to make window or Web page titles identical to the names of the commands that invoke them. Furthermore, since command labels should be verb phrases (see Blooper 36: Careless writing, Section 4.1.4), the titles of the windows will, for the most part, also be verb phrases.

Nonexact matches are OK if they work for users

However, a perception by users of clear correspondence can sometimes be achieved between window and command names that are not identical. For example, in Table 4.2, comparing command names and the titles of the resulting windows, the difference between "Show Order Status" and "Status for Order: <n>" would probably be seen by users as minor enough that it wouldn't cause confusion. However, any command and its resulting window that are named differently constitute a potential usability problem, and so should be avoided if possible, and tested on representative users if unavoidable. My experience suggests that most differences—even seemingly minor ones—will cause users to wonder at least temporarily about whether they invoked the command they meant to invoke.

A useful solution: Parameterize window titles

As described earlier, one common reason for a difference between a command's name and the title of the resulting window is that several different commands display the same window. Some typical cases are

1. The Open ..., Save As ..., Import ..., and Export ... commands all bring up a dialog box titled "File Chooser."
2. The Create Account and Edit Account commands both bring up a window titled "Edit Account."
3. The View Graph and Edit Graph commands both bring up a window titled "Graph," although perhaps differing in the editability of the content.

In all three cases, the labeling differences can be eliminated by parameterizing the shared window so that its title—or part of its title—can depend on the context in which it is invoked. In the first of the three cases, that is usually done: file chooser dialog box components usually allow the calling code to specify the dialog box's title, and programmers usually use this to match the file chooser's title to the invoking command. Therefore, that case of the problem actually rarely occurs. However, the other two cases of the problem are fairly common. Obviously, what works for one case would work for the others.

Another reason mentioned above for a mismatch between a command name and the title of the resulting window is that a generic command invokes a different function (and window) depending on the software's state, such as what is selected, what page is being displayed, or what the user has previously done. For example:

- A Show Properties command might display a "Text Properties" dialog box if the selection is a sequence of text characters, but a "Table Properties" dialog box if the selection is a table.

- An Open command might display an "Employee" window if the selected data object is an employee, but an "Organization" window if the selected data object is an organization.

This may be OK because users may make the connection between what they selected and the window, rather than the label on the button and the window. However, differences in wording should always be tested to see if they cause confusion.

Again, user confusion can be avoided or corrected by parameterizing the window title and including the command name in all of the resulting windows or pages, with additional information provided to distinguish the cases. For example, the Show Properties command could bring up a "Show Properties: Text" dialog box if the selection is a sequence of text characters, and a "Show Properties: Table" dialog box if the selection is a table.

Special case: Windows displayed by system events

A developer might wonder how to word the titles of windows that appear based on events or situations the user didn't intend or directly instigate. Prime examples of this are error dialog boxes, calendar reminder windows, or warnings of situations or events. The titles of such windows aren't really relevant to this blooper because they are not cases of a command immediately displaying a window or page. There can't be a mismatch between the window title and the command because there is no corresponding command.

Further reading

Official platform-specific GUI style guides

Apple Computer, Inc. 1993. *Macintosh Human Interface Guidelines*. Reading, MA: Addison-Wesley.

Microsoft. 1995. *The Windows Interface Guidelines for Software Design: An Application Design Guide*. Redmond, WA: Microsoft Press.

Microsoft. 1999. *Microsoft Windows User Experience.* Redmond, WA: Microsoft Press.

Open Software Foundation. 1993. *OSF/Motif Style Guide: Rev 1.2.* Englewood · Cliffs, NJ: Prentice Hall.

Sun Microsystems. 1999. *Java Look and Feel Design Guidelines.* Reading, MA: Addison-Wesley.

Platform-independent GUI guidelines

McFarland, A., and Dayton, T. 1995. *Design Guide for Multiplatform Graphical User Interfaces.* Issue 3, LPR13. Piscataway, NJ: Bellcore.

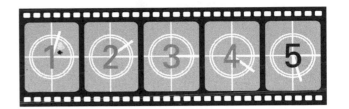

Interaction
Bloopers

Introduction

GUI component, layout and appearance, and textual bloopers are fairly easy to spot when I review software or conduct usability tests. I can usually find enough of them to make client managers feel satisfied that they got their money's worth.

However, it pays to dig a bit deeper because a more important set of bloopers usually lies just below the surface. These are bloopers that are not examples of misusing a specific GUI component, arranging components badly, or displaying incomprehensible labels and messages. Instead, they are violations of well-established general user interface design principles for interactive systems. They concern dynamic aspects of the software: how it *works*, not just how it appears.

I call these "interaction" bloopers. Although they are more abstract than the bloopers described in the previous sections, they nonetheless can make learning to use a product or service—as well as accomplishing one's work once one has learned—difficult, inefficient, and frustrating, thereby hampering productivity. Interaction bloopers are the focus of this chapter of the book.

User interface design principles for interactive systems have emerged from research on human perception, reading, information processing, problem solving, and motivation [Card et al., 1983; Norman and Draper, 1986; Rudisill et al., 1996], as well as from decades of experience with computers, online services, equipment control panels, and electronic appliances. Some important general design principles were presented in Chapter 1.

More comprehensive explanations of user interface design principles are available in any of several books on how to design effective interactive systems [Tufte, 1983; Smith and Mosier, 1986; Shneiderman, 1987; Brown, 1988; Mullet and Sano, 1995; Bickford, 1997; Rosenfeld and Morville, 1998; Weinshenk et al., 1997; Nielsen, 1999d]. These books differ significantly from the various GUI design guides. They are not specific to any particular GUI platform. In fact, they aren't even specific to GUIs. Rather, they present more general design rules that can enhance the learnability, navigability, enjoyability, and efficiency of any computer-based product or service, whatever type of user interface it may have.

Although the GUI component, layout and appearance, and textual bloopers discussed in other chapters of this book outnumber the interaction bloopers discussed in this chapter, I urge you not to focus on the relative numbers of the various types of bloopers. Although interaction bloopers are fewer in number, they are more important than GUI component, layout and appearance, and textual bloopers, for the following reasons:

- *They are larger in scope.* Interaction bloopers are in many cases generalizations of bloopers described in the GUI component, layout and appearance, and textual bloopers chapters. For example, overusing text fields (Blooper 18, Section 2.5.2) is just one of the problems caused by TTY GUIs (Blooper 45, Section 5.1.3). Therefore, recognizing and correcting a single interaction blooper may result in the (eventual) correction of dozens of GUI component, layout and appearance, and textual bloopers scattered throughout a software product or service.

- *They are harder to spot.* Recognizing interaction bloopers requires significant user interface expertise. They aren't directly visible in the software's displays. Put simply, if a person doesn't know what the principles for good user interface design are, he or she won't be able to spot violations of them. Even if a development team looks for usability problems by watching people using the product or service, less experienced observers will tend to focus on more concrete and visible problems users encounter, and fail to extract the deeper and more general problems.

- *They are harder to avoid.* Interaction bloopers are often a result of decisions that were made deep in the implementation of the product, or even in the platform upon which it is built (e.g., GUI toolkit, operating system, communication network). For example, an application programmer may have to go to considerable lengths to avoid committing a blooper that was essentially built into the GUI toolkit upon which the application is built. The programmer may lack the time or the expertise to do that. Even when an interaction blooper is entirely local to the product, it may be the result of a design trade-off the designer had to make, or it may have been the result of an explicit request from a customer.

- *They are harder to correct.* For several reasons, interaction bloopers can be difficult to correct. If an interaction blooper subsumes many more-specific bloopers, correcting it requires finding and fixing all of the related GUI component, layout and appearance, or textual bloopers. If an interaction blooper is the result of deep implementation decisions, fixing it can take significant reimplementation unless it is found very early in the development process.

The only bloopers that are as important as interaction bloopers—that is, that are at least as detrimental to usability and as difficult to correct—are the responsiveness and management bloopers described in Chapters 7 and 8 of this book.

5.1 Allowing implementation to dictate GUI

The first three interaction bloopers concern user interfaces that are too strongly influenced by the software's underlying implementation. Such interfaces distract users from their goals.

5.1.1 Blooper 43: Exposing the implementation to users

An extremely common blooper is for programmers to let the software's implementation "leak out" into the user interface. The textual form of this blooper—exposing terms from the implementation to users, was described in Blooper 35: Speaking Geek (Section 4.1.3). However, it is possible for aspects of the software's implementation to be exposed to users in other ways besides textually.

Products that commit this blooper expose internal details and concepts that may be important for the implementation of the software but have no bearing on what users intend to do with it. Like many of the other bloopers, this one has variations.

Variation A: Forcing users to think like a programmer. In early 1999, a company asked me to critique a prototype of a Web application it was developing. The application had several control panels: one for each of several functions it provided. Each control panel consisted of some text fields and option menus. One particular setting—an option menu—appeared on several different control panels. In reviewing the application, I discovered that changing the value of the menu on one control panel changed its value on all the other panels as well. This seemed counterintuitive to me; I expected the menu on a particular function's control panel to be set as I left it the last time I used that particular function (i.e., panel). However, I realized that my knowledge of the target task domain and experience with the application was limited. The developers might have had a sensible reason for designing it as they had. I wanted to give them the benefit of the doubt. So I asked the lead programmer why the menu worked that way.

I hoped that he would explain to me why users of this particular application expected the menu to change on all panels when they changed it on only one, and how he had found out what users expected. However, his answer was that he had decided it would be inefficient to put copies of the menu on each control panel where it was needed, so he had coded the application such that there was really only one menu, which *appeared* on several different control panels. Needless to say, this was not the sensible, user-centered reason I had hoped for.

The programmer had made a decision based purely on implementation considerations that resulted in nonintuitive program behavior from the point of view of users. Users of this software were going to have to read or figure out that all the menus of the same name scattered across various control panels were really just one menu control that appeared everywhere. The programmer had exposed his implementation to users.

"What do you mean Rumpelstiltskin is too long for a password?!"

Reprinted by permission, Andrew Toos.

Variation B: Imposing arbitrary implementation restrictions on users. Another way in which computer-based products and services can violate users' sense of naturalness and intuitiveness is by imposing arbitrary or seemingly arbitrary restrictions on users. Arbitrary restrictions, like unnatural acts, are hard for users to learn, easy for them to forget, and annoying. For more details, see Principle 3 (Section 1.3).

An example from the early days of personal computing

In the early 1980s, I got a game for my first personal computer. The goal of the game was to steer a vehicle through a maze without hitting any walls. The game could be made more or less challenging by setting the speed of the vehicle. The speed was set by specifying a number between 1 and 10. Unfortunately, the user interface for setting the speed was backwards: giving a higher number made the program run *slower*, so the fastest speed corresponded to the value 1.

I had the source code for the game, so I could examine how it was implemented. As I suspected, the speed value the player typed specified the number of times the program would cycle through a delay loop. The larger the number, the more times the program would cycle through the loop. The more time the program spent in the delay loop, the more slowly the vehicle moved forward.

The programmer had exposed his implementation to users. But users—including me—don't care how the game works internally. Furthermore, they expect higher numbers to indicate higher speeds. As you might expect, players of this game—including me—often set the speed to unintentionally slow or fast values.

Aside from its backwards user interface for setting the speed, the game was fine. I thought it would be useful to have it on my computer to entertain visiting children. But I could not stand that backwards speed control. I revised the program to subtract the number the user entered from 11 and use the difference, rather than the number the user entered, in the delay loop. Making this change took me about two minutes. It would have taken the game's programmer even less time, but it apparently didn't occur to him or her to avoid exposing the implementation to players of the game.

Several years ago, when my stereo amplifier wasn't working properly, I took it to a repair shop. The shop technician had to create an order for the repair job, using a computer terminal. After getting my name, address, phone number, and the make and model of the amplifier, he asked me to describe the problem. As I spoke and he typed, a concerned expression came over his face. He interrupted me, giving rise to the following conversation:

Technician: "Um...can you describe the problem...shorter?"

Me: "Let me guess. You have sixty-four characters in which to explain what's wrong with my stereo."

Technician (eyes widening noticeably): "Thirty-two, but how did you know?"

The programmer who developed the software the technician was using had decided that descriptions of problems had to be limited to 32 characters. The requirement of a size limit on the problem description was probably imposed by the database management system in which the repair order application stored its records. The particular choice of 32—a number that is a power of two—as the length limit of the description was probably an arbitrary decision of the programmer's.

Computer-based software applications, services, and appliances are full of such restrictions: filenames that can't contain spaces; login names that are restricted to 8 characters; personal names that can contain at most 16 characters; documents that can't be longer than 128 kilobytes; passwords that must contain at least one numeral and one alphabetic character; text-formatting software that can't handle text lines longer than 256 characters; data identifiers that must be typed in UPPERCASE to be recognized by the software; graphics terminals that can display any of 4096 colors but only 8 colors at once in any quartile of the screen. None of these examples are made up—I've seen them all.

Obviously, the worst restrictions are the ones that users constantly bump into, like filenames that can't be longer than 8 characters or description fields that can't exceed 32 characters. Such restrictions require users—like the stereo repair technician—to waste time trying to figure out how to express what they need to express without exceeding the limit. Consider the total number of user-hours that have been wasted worldwide since 1975 by millions of computer users trying to devise meaningful filenames that are eight characters or less in length.

Restrictions that users hit only occasionally might at first glance seem less troublesome. In fact, they are almost as bad as restrictions that users hit often, but for a different reason: users who encounter such limits won't have much experience figuring out how to work around them. Of course, if a limit is so large that users never encounter it, it isn't really a problem.

It is common for numerical restrictions imposed by computer software to be powers of two: numbers like 8, 16, 32, 64, 128, 256, 512, 1024, 2048, 4096, and so on. Note that most of the examples of limits I described above are such numbers. The underlying reason for this, of course, is that computers represent and manipulate numbers and memory addresses in binary, that is, in base 2. Computer programmers are therefore used to dealing with powers of two, and regard them as "normal." They often forget that most users aren't used to such numbers.

Most people learned to do arithmetic in base 10 and so prefer powers of 10, like 10, 100, 1000, 10,000, and so on. They consider powers of two to be mysterious, arbitrary, computer-geeky numbers.

A product with many arbitrary restrictions won't have many satisfied users. Many restrictions imposed by software on users are, frankly, due to faulty priorities of the development team. Software developers often fail to realize how many user-hours can be saved by one extra programmer-hour spent overcoming an annoying restriction.

Avoiding Blooper 43: *The design rule*

The best way to avoid exposing a software application's implementation to users is to design its user interface according to a conceptual model that includes only objects and actions that are clearly from the application's target task domain. Designers and developers should be constantly on the lookout for foreign conceptual objects sneaking into the user interface. Creating, maintaining, and enforcing a product lexicon during development helps uncover discrepancies between the user interface and the conceptual model.

Design for the convenience of users, not of developers

Another thing software developers can do to avoid exposing the implementation to users is make a strong commitment to design the user interface for the convenience of users, not the convenience of programmers. All programmers have a tendency to design for their own convenience—even I find myself doing it when I write software. What separates exceptional user interface designers from most designers is a commitment to work to overcome that tendency. Management can of course help with this.

Avoid arbitrary limits

Where possible, I recommend avoiding imposing highly visible numerical limits. One way of doing this is to set limits so high that users won't actually encounter them. Of course, any such solution must be tested thoroughly to make sure it succeeded. Another way is to actually eliminate limits through more sophisticated programming, for example, by allocating memory dynamically at run time, as needed, rather than statically in the source code.

When limits cannot be avoided and users will encounter them, I recommend using powers of ten rather than powers of two. Now that computer-based products and services are mainstream rather than mainly toys for technical elites, most computer users are much more familiar and comfortable with decimal numbers like 10, 100, and 1000 than they are with powers of two like 8, 128, and 1024. Decimal limits seem less arbitrary and "geeky," and are easier for users to remember.

5.1.2 Blooper 44: Asking users for random numbers

A special case of exposing the implementation to users is asking users to supply random numbers that the program needs.

Suppose a software application needs to generate a collection or sequence of novel items, such as unique names for its own internal housekeeping files, indices for sampling elements from a list randomly, or unique data encryption keys. Often this is implemented by having the software invoke a random-number procedure to generate a sequence of unique "random" numbers, then converting the numbers into the required data.

Computers and software are deterministic, so a simple implementation would produce the same "random" numbers—and hence the same names, indices, or keys—each time the program was run. Often, that isn't acceptable; the generated items or program behavior must be different every time the program is run. To make the sequence different, each time the software runs, it needs to get a "seed" value from somewhere that it can feed to the random-number procedure as a starting point—hopefully a different seed value than it got the last time.

Some software products get their seed value by asking users to supply it. They prompt users to enter a number—any number. Some programs supply a text field and ask users to type something into it—anything at all; they just need some random input to use as a seed.

Asking users for random numbers or other random input is a design blooper; it is a form of exposing the implementation to users. Initializing a random-number generator is an internal software matter, not something users should be faced with. Providing a seed value is most certainly foreign to the users' task domain, whatever that task domain may be. Users don't like having to enter meaningless values; it annoys them and takes time and attention away from their work.

Furthermore, asking users for random numbers is ineffective because human beings are very bad at coming up with random numbers. Ask several people (separately) to give you a random number between 1 and 100, and you'll get a collection of numbers that is anything but random. All of the numbers you'll get will probably be *odd* because people don't regard *even* numbers as "random enough." In fact, the number people almost always give in such a situation is 37.

The blooper of asking users for random numbers is both uncommon and common. Overall, it is uncommon because relatively few software applications include functions that require seed values. On the other hand, among software applications that need to make unpredictable choices or generate unique identifiers, this blooper is unfortunately common.

For example, one client of mine was developing software for business statistical analysis. The software included the ability to extract a small sample of data from a large database so that various analyses could be performed on the sample rather than on the entire database. The data had to be sampled randomly from the database so the subsequent analyses could be considered representative of the database as a whole. Usually, users would want the program to extract different random samples from the database each time the sampling function was invoked.

To achieve this, the software asked users to supply a "Sampler Seed" each time the sampling function was invoked. If users supplied the same seed twice in a row, the sampling function would extract the same "random" sample from the database. Different seeds would produce different samples.

Avoiding Blooper 44: *The design rule*

Software should never ask users to supply random values. If your program requires a random seed value, it should get one for itself. There are many ways to do this.

Figure 5.1

 or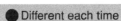

Figure 5.2

Base seeds on variable time intervals

One traditional method has been to obtain the current time or date from the computer's operating system and transform it as necessary to produce a seed. Currently, however, seeds based on the time or date are generally regarded as poor because their values are not really very random. Instead, many modern applications that generate their own seeds base them on highly variable time intervals between user-generated events, such as the timing between the users' keystrokes.

Give users only the control they need

If users will sometimes want the program to use the same seed value on successive runs so the program's behavior will be the same, just give them a way of specifying exactly that rather than asking them to specify the seed value.

For example, provide a button users can click to instruct the software to fetch a new seed for itself, but label it in a way that matches the purpose of the software, rather than implementation details (see Figure 5.1). Alternatively, use radiobuttons to provide the choice shown in Figure 5.2.

Games often need random seeds but don't ask users for them

One type of software in which this blooper is never seen is game software. Computer games often must exhibit random or quasi-random behavior. For example, many games provide built-in opponent characters (e.g., monsters) whose movements must be unpredictable. Similarly, electronic gambling machines have to simulate tossing dice, pulling slot machine levers, and spinning roulette wheels. Therefore, game software makes heavy use of random numbers functions, and so requires changing seed values to ensure that the same "random" behavior does not occur each time the software runs. Nonetheless, one never sees game software or electronic gambling machines that ask users to provide seed values.

The reason, of course, is that game developers are hyperaware that they are developing for a consumer market that would not tolerate this blooper in products. Game software therefore provides an existence proof that this blooper is avoidable. This suggests that requiring users to enter random numbers in *any* software is completely unnecessary and inexcusable.

5.1.3   Blooper 45: TTY GUIs

During the late 1980s and 1990s, GUIs were catching on in the business world. A great deal of business software that had been written for character display terminals connected to time-shared mainframe and minicomputers was converted to run on networked desktop PCs and workstations that had graphical displays and windowed operating systems.

An important aspect of such conversions is redesigning the user interface. The hardware platform for the user interface had formerly been one of two common types of character display terminals: (1) ASCII-based, for example, Digital Equipment VT-100 compatible, or (2) form-based, for example, IBM 3270 compatible. Such terminals were often called "glass teletypes" because they were cathode-ray tube descendants of the paper teletype machines that had been the primary input/output device of the previous generation of time-shared computers. A common software code name for teletypes—both paper and glass—was "TTY."

Updating software user interfaces to the GUI style involved reconstructing them using the components of a graphical user interface toolkit, typically one designed for a particular window-based operating system, such as Microsoft Windows, Apple's MacOS, and various windowed varieties of Unix. Ideally, developers should begin such a conversion by rethinking the user interface carefully and designing a new user interface and software control structure that is appropriate for the GUI design paradigm.

Unfortunately, not all TTY-to-GUI conversions have been carried out carefully. Some have been done very quickly, with little consideration of how the user interface for windows-based desktop computers should differ from the one for character display time-shared terminals. In many cases, these conversion tasks are assigned to relatively junior programmers, who lack the design experience to design an appropriate GUI even if they had enough time, which they usually don't (see Blooper 77: Treating user interface as low priority, Section 8.1.2). On top of all that, these relatively junior conversion programmers are often inadequately supervised.

The result is a blooper that I call a "TTY GUI"—a user interface that essentially recreates the former "glass teletype" user interface using GUI components. They consist of large panels full of labeled text fields into which users must type the indicated data. An example is shown in Figure 5.3. Where the TTY user interface had a data prompt (e.g., "Enter appt. name:") or a form field, the GUI user interface has a labeled text field. In TTY GUIs, the text field reigns supreme; other user interface components—sliders, radiobuttons, and so on—rarely appear. This type of user interface misses the whole point of GUIs.

At a company I once worked for, a newly hired programmer was assigned such a conversion as his first project. He had never written GUI software before; his programming assignments in college had all been C programs using standard text input and output. I was asked to review the "GUI" he had de-

Figure 5.3

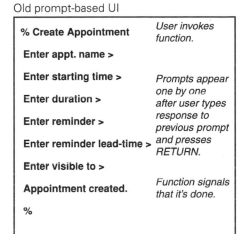

Old prompt-based UI

% Create Appointment	User invokes function.
Enter appt. name >	
Enter starting time >	Prompts appear one by one after user types response to previous prompt and presses RETURN.
Enter duration >	
Enter reminder >	
Enter reminder lead-time >	
Enter visible to >	
Appointment created.	Function signals that it's done.
%	

New TTY GUI

Create Appointment — Displayed when command invoked

Appointment:
Start time:
Duration:
Location:
Reminder:
Reminder Lead-Time:
Visible to:

OK   Cancel

vised. Under the circumstances, I wasn't surprised to find that it was a large panel of text fields corresponding to the previous version's prompts. However, I *was* surprised to find that the text fields in the panel required users to press the RETURN key after entering the data. That is, users couldn't simply type data into a field and then move the insertion point to another field. Even more surprising was that the text fields had to be filled in in the listed order. The "conversion" was just a thin shell that fed data to the old version's command-line prompts. Efforts to redesign the GUI to be more GUI-like and less TTY-like were hampered by the programmer's lack of experience with GUIs.

I should make clear that I didn't—and still don't—consider the programmer primarily responsible for this blooper. Although he had committed the blooper of creating a TTY GUI, that blooper was the result of a blooper committed by his management: regarding user interface as so unimportant that they assigned it to an inexperienced new-hire (see Section 8.1.2). At the very least, they could have assigned a more experienced GUI programmer to supervise his work.

To some extent, the conversion of TTY user interfaces to GUIs continues to this day. A brief review of the computer systems still used by airline, bank, insurance, and telephone company employees reveals that networked desktop PCs with graphical user interfaces have yet to completely replace their time-shared computing systems and character display terminals. Therefore, this blooper cannot yet be relegated to the history books. We can safely assume that more TTY GUIs are being created at this very moment, and will continue to be created in the glorious future.

In addition, the explosive growth of the World Wide Web—and corporate intranet versions of it—in the mid-to-late 1990s started another wave of software conversion. Business applications that had been developed (or converted) for desktop PCs—as well as some that had never been converted from character terminals and time-shared computers—began to be converted to run as Web applications. This new wave of conversion is still building. It didn't replace the

Example of a TTY GUI

Another example of a TTY GUI comes from one of my consulting clients. The company was developing a database query tool. The tool was intended to give users a graphical user interface for specifying the data they wanted to retrieve from a database, freeing them of the need to compose expressions in SQL, a common but cryptic database query language.

However, the "GUI" the engineers built was little more than a keyboard on the screen, with buttons for numbers and for common database terms like "and," "or," and "not." Near the middle of the window was a long text field showing the SQL expression the user was composing.

The main help this "GUI" gave users was in letting them specify databases and database variables by choosing them from menus rather than having to remember and type them. Users still had to remember and type the desired *values* of database variables, and they still bore the burden of producing correct SQL syntax. In other words, this "GUI" had not freed users from composing SQL expressions; it just gave them a more specialized user interface for doing so.

Although I recommended extensive revision of this design, the development team of course did not have time for that before the product was due to be shipped.

earlier conversion wave, but rather was added onto it. It will no doubt employ many programmers well into the 21st century. This suggests that we should be on the lookout for TTY Web sites as well as TTY GUIs.

Avoiding Blooper 45: *The design rule*

Converting a software application's user interface from the character-based teletype style to the graphical user interface style requires more than simply rebuilding the same design using the components of a GUI toolkit instead of text input and output functions. It requires redesigning the control structure of the application to make it fit into the GUI paradigm.

A good GUI design uses controls that best fit each type of setting; it does not use text fields for everything. A good GUI design also allows users to manipulate data directly—for example, by drag-and-drop—where feasible rather than only allowing them to manipulate their data indirectly, through abstracted properties and settings. Finally, a good GUI design allows users to operate its controls in whatever order they choose, rather than forcing them to follow a predetermined sequence. Figure 5.4 shows a good GUI for a Create Appointment function.

GUIs versus TTY UIs: Who is driving?

The most important difference between GUIs and TTY user interfaces is in who is "driving" the interaction. With TTY user interfaces, the software is the main

Figure 5.4

Users should also be able to create appointments by dragging and dropping email messages or attachments that describe appointments into their calendar.

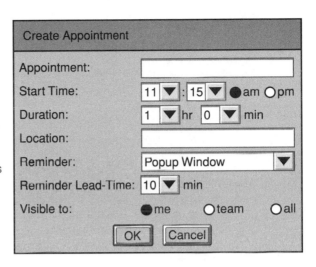

driver; it displays prompts, takes user responses, processes them, displays the results if there are any, and then either indicates that it is done or displays more prompts. With GUIs, the user is the main driver; the user determines what on-screen controls to operate in what order and may switch between several simultaneously displayed control panels at any time. GUIs should be designed and implemented so as to put users in control of what happens when. Otherwise they are examples of this blooper.

Putting users in control of the interaction means, first and foremost, that users should be free to set a control panel's settings or fill in its data fields in whatever order they choose. In this respect, graphical user interfaces are like physical control panels. Imagine what operating your stereo or driving your car would be like if their controls had to be operated in a strict order.

Allowing controls to be set and data fields to be filled in any order does not mean that the order in which they are presented on the display is irrelevant or unimportant. As described in Blooper 21: Layout that doesn't reflect usual or natural order of settings (Section 3.1.2), users expect to be able to work through control panels from top to bottom and either left to right or right to left, depending on the direction in which their primary language is read. Thus, more important controls and settings should be positioned near the top of the window or panel on which they appear. Nonetheless, users should be free to fill out data fields and set controls in whatever order they wish.

GUIs versus TTY UIs: "See and point" versus "remember and type"

A second important difference between TTY user interfaces and GUIs is that, whereas TTY user interfaces require users to *remember and type* commands and data values, GUIs tend to allow users to specify commands and data values by *pointing* at them. Among other things, this means that control panels in GUIs should not rely too heavily on unstructured type-in data fields for user input. Instead, settings should be specialized for the type of values users can specify and should provide guidance to users in specifying or choosing valid values. For example, for a setting that specifies a date, don't just display a text field labeled "Date" and expect users to figure out how to type dates that are acceptable to the software. Instead, provide one of the following:

- Three number fields—day of month, month, and year—that can be changed either by typing into them or by clicking " + " and "-" buttons

- Three option-menus: day (1–31), month (Jan–Dec), year (< some sensible range of years >)

- A noneditable display of the date, with a button for displaying a popup "date chooser": a small monthly calendar from which users can pick a date.

At the very least, a designer should break a "Date" text field into three separate type-in fields so that users don't have to type "/" or "." between the parts. Similar recommendations apply if the data to be specified are dollar amounts, email addresses, Web addresses, and so on. For more on why and how to avoid overusing text fields, see Blooper 18: Overusing text fields (Section 2.5.2).

A final design rule for avoiding TTY GUIs is that text and number fields should not require users to press the RETURN or ENTER key after typing a value in order for the data field to retain the value. Users should be able to type a value into a data field and then simply move the input focus to another control or field using the pointing device (e.g., mouse) or the TAB key. Therefore, when programmers use text and number field components from GUI toolkits, they should write the code such that a newly typed value replaces the data field's previous value when the data field loses the input focus, however that occurs.

5.2 Presenting information poorly

The second group of interaction bloopers concerns the many different ways software developers devise to display information badly.

5.2.1 Blooper 46: Overwhelming users with decisions and detail

Many GUI programs overwhelm users with controls, function, options, and settings. However, what overwhelms users is more subtle than just the sheer number. An application having fewer controls and settings can be harder to learn and use than one having more controls if the controls in the first application are out of place, haphazardly designed, or poorly organized.

There are several common variations of this blooper, each corresponding to a different way of screwing up the selection, design, and organization of an application's controls and settings. Of course, some software products are screwed up in more than one of the following ways.

Variation A: Choices users don't need or care about. Some software products provide choices and settings that users don't need or want. If a software program contains many settings that are foreign to the target task domain, it doesn't matter whether the program has 100 settings or only 20; users will perceive it as difficult to learn and tedious to use.

For example, suppose a genealogy program included a setting for specifying the number of memory bytes the program reserves for information about each person in the family tree. What do people who are compiling family genealogies care—or know—about software memory allocation? Answer: Not much! Although this example may seem far-fetched, there are many software applications in daily use that provide settings that are just as out of place.

Choices that users don't want get into software products for three reasons:

- *Little or no user input.* Engineering teams often develop software without consulting customers or others in the company who talk with customers. Therefore, they really don't know what customers need or want. Instead, they make up requirements based on their own intuitions, which tend to favor power and flexibility over ease of use. See Blooper 80: Anarchic devel opment (Section 8.2.2) for an example of such a situation, as well as further discussion of this all-too-common problem.

- *Focus on implementation.* Engineers focus on the technical aspects of a product, rather than the customer needs that created the demand for the product (if such needs and demand even exist). They therefore include choices that are irrelevant to users' goals.

  For example, cameras and cassette tape recorders used to include film speed and bias settings, respectively, so users could set the device for the type of film or recording tape they were using. Users, who were intent on taking photographs or listening to recordings, often forgot to set these settings. Today, most cameras and cassette recorders set themselves automatically, using indicators on the film and tape cassettes.

  An example from the computer field is Web sites that provide a search facility so that visitors can search the site for information. Some search facilities require users to indicate which of several search engines they prefer to use. Users just want to find something; choosing a search engine is not part of their task goal and is therefore an unwelcome distraction.

- *Inability to make design decisions.* Many software products have far more functionality, flexibility, configurability, controls, settings, or power than any user needs. These excesses are not a problem by themselves, but they usually come at the cost of decreased usability. Often, this problem is the result of developers putting everything they can think of into a software product "in case the user might need it." Of course, the real problem is that the developers don't know what users need. However, it usually doesn't occur to them or their management to solve *that* problem rather than trying to accommodate a wide variety of imagined user needs. The result may be a product that has controls no one ever uses.

A superfluous distinction

I once helped a client company design an email system. One requirement was that users should be able to define email aliases—nicknames—for addresses they used often. Aliases could name a single address or they could name collections of addresses. The programmers wanted the user interface to make an explicit distinction between aliases for individuals and aliases for lists, as the server software did. Having used many email programs in my career, I knew that there was no reason for burdening users with two distinct types of aliases. We could provide one type of email alias, and users could simply create an alias, name it, and decide whether to put only one destination address into it, thereby defining an alias for an individual, or multiple addresses into it, thereby defining an address for a list. The programmers didn't like my idea because it didn't match the way the mail servers worked. Since I was just a consultant, they did it their way. Therefore, users of this email system have to specify, when they create a new email alias, whether that alias is for an individual or a group.

Variation B: Many controls, all equally accessible. Even when every control and setting in a software product or service is relevant to the intended task domain, users may still be overwhelmed by the sheer number of them. One sometimes sees software applications in which everything the user might want to set is equally visible and accessible.

Figure 5.5 shows two dialog boxes from Band in a Box 6.0, a music accompaniment program. The dialog box on the top is for setting overall program preferences. The dialog box on the bottom is for specifying how a piece of music is to be printed. In neither dialog box does either the ordering or position of settings reflect the likelihood that users will want to change them: esoteric, rarely altered settings are placed right next to (and in some cases before) more commonly changed settings.

Variation C: Controls and choices presented in an unnatural order. An excellent way to overwhelm users with detail is to force them to scan through large lists, control panels, or tables of settings, looking for the few that are relevant to a particular situation. How do you force people to scan through large amounts of data? Easy. Scatter the important or frequently used items randomly throughout the display instead of putting the items that are most likely to be needed first.

Figure 5.5

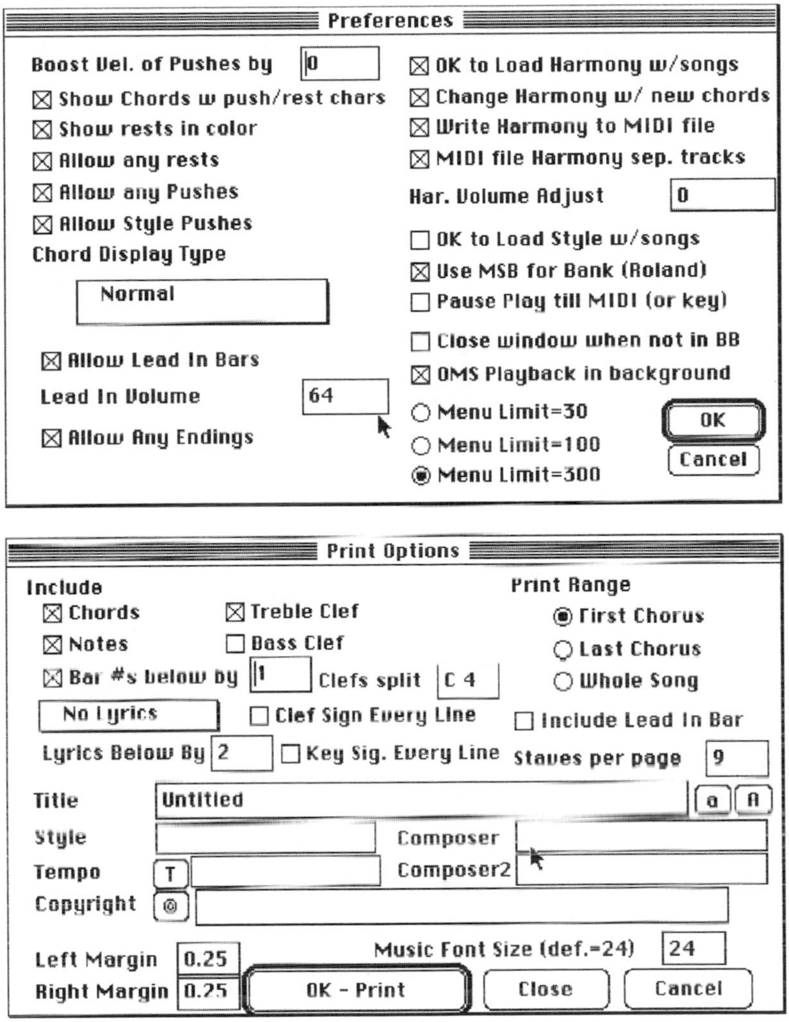

```
╔══════════════════ Preferences ══════════════════╗

  Boost Uel. of Pushes by    [0]      ⊠ OK to Load Harmony w/songs
  ⊠ Show Chords w push/rest chars     ⊠ Change Harmony w/ new chords
  ⊠ Show rests in color               ⊠ Write Harmony to MIDI file
  ⊠ Allow any rests                   ⊠ MIDI file Harmony sep. tracks
  ⊠ Allow any Pushes                  Har. Uolume Adjust      [0]
  ⊠ Allow Style Pushes
  Chord Display Type                  ☐ OK to Load Style w/songs
     ┌──────────────────┐             ⊠ Use MSB for Bank (Roland)
     │     Normal       │             ☐ Pause Play till MIDI (or key)
     └──────────────────┘
                                      ☐ Close window when not in BB
  ⊠ Allow Lead In Bars                ⊠ OMS Playback in background
  Lead In Volume        [64]          ○ Menu Limit=30       ┌────────┐
                                      ○ Menu Limit=100      │   OK   │
  ⊠ Allow Any Endings                 ◉ Menu Limit=300      └────────┘
                                                            ┌────────┐
                                                            │ Cancel │
                                                            └────────┘
╚══════════════════════════════════════════════════╝
```

```
╔══════════════════ Print Options ═════════════════╗

  Include                              Print Range
  ⊠ Chords      ⊠ Treble Clef          ◉ First Chorus
  ⊠ Notes       ☐ Bass Clef            ○ Last Chorus
  ⊠ Bar #s below by [1]  Clefs split [C 4]  ○ Whole Song
  ┌──────────────┐   ☐ Clef Sign Every Line
  │  No Lyrics   │                     ☐ Include Lead In Bar
  └──────────────┘
  Lyrics Below By [2]  ☐ Key Sig. Every Line  Staves per page [9]

  Title    │ Untitled                              │   [a] [A]
  Style    │                    │ Composer  │                  │
  Tempo  [T]│                   │ Composer2 │                  │
  Copyright [©]│                                                │

  Left Margin  [0.25]      Music Font Size (def.=24) [24]
  Right Margin [0.25]  ┌──────────────┐  ┌────────┐  ┌────────┐
                       │  OK - Print  │  │ Close  │  │ Cancel │
                       └──────────────┘  └────────┘  └────────┘
╚══════════════════════════════════════════════════╝
```

Presenting data or settings in an arbitrary, unnatural order has adverse consequences beyond contributing to users' feelings of being overwhelmed. Users may have difficulty finding the settings that must be set in a given situation. In some cases, users may be forced to make choices or provide data before they have the necessary information to do so.

For example, I have seen statistical programs that begin by asking users if they want to save the results of the current analysis in a file, and if so, to specify a filename. But users usually don't know at the beginning of an analysis whether they want to save the results. They won't know if the results are worth saving until *after* they've seen the results. Putting this step near the beginning of the program, when it is initializing its file I/O, may be convenient for the programmer, but it is unnatural and awkward for users.

Blooper 21: Layout that doesn't reflect usual or natural order of settings (Section 3.1.2) discusses this error as it pertains to the layout of information and controls on software panels.

Variation D: No defaults or wrong defaults; users must set everything. One of the most serious design errors one can make is to provide a large number of settings and require users to set them all or even most of them. This prevents users from ignoring settings that they don't care about in a particular situation.

For example, a sales application I once reviewed provided a form for telephone sales operators to use to create new orders in response to customer calls. The form included a "Sales Person" item to identify the employee who took the order. The item was an option menu listing ID numbers for the company's telephone salespeople (of which there were about two dozen) and allowing users to choose one. One would expect this menu to be set by default to the ID number of the salesperson currently logged into the application. However, the menu defaulted to blank, an invalid value for submitting an order, requiring users to set it every time they took an order.

A visual example is provided by the Graphing Calculator, a Macintosh Desktop accessory packaged with MacOS. I recently noticed the Graphing Calculator item on my Mac's Accessories menu. I had never tried it before. When I chose the menu item, the window shown in Figure 5.6 appeared, with the equation appearing exactly as shown, but without the text message at the bottom of the display. The Graph button appeared inactive (i.e., grayed out), as in the image in the figure. I wanted to make the calculator draw a graph—any graph—and the equation already shown seemed reasonable. I wasn't sure what else to do, so I clicked the Graph button even though it looked inactive. The error message shown below appeared in the bottom of the window. It is trying to explain that the equation I had asked it to graph was not valid because it contained the variables a and b. Before I could graph the equation, I would have to edit it to be a simple linear equation such as $y = 3x$. My immediate thought was, If $y = ax + b$ is invalid for graphing, then why is it what appears when I run the program for the first time?

Avoiding Blooper 46: The design rule

Principles 1 and 3 in Chapter 1 describe how software developers can analyze the target task domain of a software product to identify specific actions as "natural" or "unnatural" for that task domain. The basic idea is to consider the task outside of the context of a computer program. What abstract steps are involved in performing the task? The ability of software designers to distinguish task steps that are fundamental to the task from those imposed by tradition, technology, or designer idiosyncrasy is one factor that separates intuitive, easy-to-use software from awkward, frustrating software.

Controls and steps that are required only by the implementation come at a very high cost and should be avoided. An important principle here is "Less is

Figure 5.6

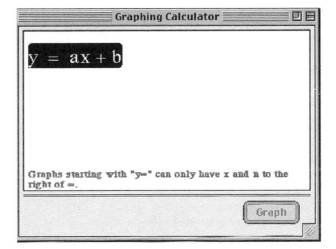

more." Give users the control they need to do the tasks that they need to do. Not more; not less.

Emphasize important controls, and deemphasize less important ones

When an appliance or software application provides a large number of settings or controls, designers should classify the controls into those that users will set frequently and those that only rarely need to be set. Having done this, they can then design the user interface so as to hide rarely used controls until needed.

This approach is exemplified in consumer appliances that hide seldom-used controls behind panels. Many TVs and VCRs do this, leaving only the most commonly used controls out front. In this way, they give users an impression of a much simpler, less threatening product.

In computer software, this approach sometimes takes the form of controls on panels or in menus that remain invisible or inactive (i.e., grayed out) until they are relevant. It can also be achieved by putting less commonly used controls onto separate Details or Advanced dialog boxes that users never see unless they ask to.

Allow users to refer to collections of settings

A related approach is to assign symbols or names to represent combinations of settings. One example of this provided by some computer operating systems is the ability for users to select color schemes for their computer's "desktop" from a list of names like "Rain Forest Hues," "Desert Tones," "Gray Shades," and "Royal Colors." Each color scheme stands for a list of specific color settings for window borders, buttons, and backgrounds.

Another example of named collections of settings is seen in word processors that allow users to format text by assigning a named "style" to it, such as "Body

Text," "Caption," "Heading 2," "Emphasized Text." Most word processors that offer styles allow users to define and name their own styles in addition to providing predefined ones. For more discussion of the merits and variety of document styles facilities, see the article by Johnson and Beach [1988].

Use progressive disclosure

Both emphasizing important controls and allowing users to refer to collections of settings are cases of an important user interface design principle called "progressive disclosure"—keeping detail and complexity hidden until needed. For a more complete explanation of progressive disclosure, see Principle 3 (Section 1.3).

Allow users to rely heavily on defaults

If an application must provide a large number of settings to accommodate the needs of all of its target users, the designers should, in addition to making use of progressive disclosure, provide sensible defaults for as many settings as possible. The goal should be to make it possible for users to safely ignore most of the settings—thereby accepting the defaults—most of the time.

The number of settings users have to specify should depend on how *unusual* the result they want is. If a user wants a result that is very common, he or she should have to specify very little in order to get it; the default values of most settings should suffice. If, on the other hand, a user wants an unusual result, he or she should have to explicitly specify the values of more settings.

In some simple applications, the defaults can be built in and unchangeable because designers can predict which results will be usual and which will be unusual. However, in most applications, designers should allow users to change the defaults to reflect what is usual and unusual for *them*.

Don't make up settings; find out what users really need

This family of interaction bloopers is often the result of Blooper 81: No task domain expertise on the design team (Section 8.2.3). When no one on the design team understands the task domain or has talked with people who do, the developers will not know what settings users need. When no one on the team knows what settings users need, one tendency is to give them every setting the team can think of, just in case they might need it. This is a cop-out solution, not a real solution. The real solution is to find out what users need and give them exactly that.

Test design with a cognitive walkthrough

A different sort of analysis can be used to determine whether a user interface forces users to take steps in an unnatural order or presents them with decisions for which they don't yet have sufficient information: it's called a "cognitive walkthrough." Much has been written about this method of analyzing and evaluating user interfaces [Lewis et al., 1990; Wharton et al., 1994], but the basic idea is simple: get some people who are unfamiliar with the software, give them the software and a list of tasks to do with it, and ask them to perform the tasks as if they were dumb computers or robots rather than intelligent people. Their assignment is to step methodically through each task, interpreting whatever they see on the screen extremely literally, avoiding any deep reasoning, problem solving, or guessing about what is happening, not asking others for help, and generally acting as a simple, stupid robot would act if it were doing the same task. While participants are doing this, they keep notes on what their situation was at each step. Sometimes developers provide forms that guide walkthrough participants in producing thorough, detailed notes. What was their goal at the beginning of the step? What choices did the software display? What information did they have for deciding between the displayed choices? How did they decide?

Acting like a simple automaton may sound...well...simple, but it isn't. It is actually quite difficult and taxing for a normal human being to suppress higher-order reasoning, attempts to guess what the designers *really* meant, and subjective assessments of what is going on. It is also difficult to keep a highly detailed diary of all the minute steps and decisions that are involved in operating most computer software.

Performing a rigorous cognitive walkthrough analysis of a design will uncover any step-order problems in it. Another nice feature of cognitive walkthroughs is that they can be carried out using a design specification, before any code has been implemented. The ability to evaluate a design before much effort and expense has been devoted to it, and at a point when changes are relatively inexpensive, is one reason why this sort of analysis is valuable.

5.2.2 Blooper 47: Easily missed information

Engineers often assume that if a device or software program displays information, users will see it and act accordingly. Or they assume that even if users miss the information initially, they will eventually learn to notice it. For example, developers of GUI-based software for personal computers often assume that all they need to do to ensure that users see a status indicator, warning message, input field, or computed result is put it somewhere on the computer screen. Such assumptions are just plain wrong. They reflect a lack of knowledge about how people perceive and think.

The reality is that people do miss information...constantly. Human perception may well filter out more than it lets in. But that isn't a bug; it's a feature! If people didn't work this way, we couldn't function in this booming, buzzing, rapidly changing world. We'd be overloaded.

Millions of years of prehuman and human evolution "designed" us to overlook most of what is going on around us, and to focus our attention on what is important to us. When our prehistoric ancestors were hunting in the East

African veldt for game, what was important was what was *moving* and what looked *different* from the grassy background. It might be game they regarded as food…or game that regarded them as food.

When an airline pilot is scanning the cockpit panels, what is important is what is *abnormal* and what is *changing* (and the direction of the change). Similarly, when a businesswoman is using software to prepare a presentation at the last minute, what is important are those aspects of the software that either facilitate or hinder progress toward her goal of finishing her presentation on time. Everything else is irrelevant and so is ignored.

A well-designed product or service takes advantage of how human perception works to focus users on the important information. Unfortunately, many computer-based products are not well designed; information that is supposed to be important gets filtered out by users, and unimportant details are noticed.

The history of people using devices, even before computers (B.C.), is full of cases in which poor design caused people to overlook important displayed information and thereby make errors—sometimes serious ones [Norman, 1983]. Such information includes the position of safety switches on guns; the position of gearshifts in vehicles; warning lights on nuclear power plant control panels; teletype printouts from network monitoring systems; fuel gauges and oil lights in cars, trucks, and airplanes; and status lines in computer software.

The types of information that designers of computer-based products and services typically don't want users to overlook, but that often are overlooked because of poor design, are

- *Status indicators:* Displays that show the current status of the system. For example: in a text editor, the position of the cursor; in a fax machine, the phone number being called; in a file transfer utility, the number of files remaining to copy.

- *Mode indicators:* A special type of status indicator that shows which of multiple modes the system is operating in. For example: in a document editor, caps-and-lower versus caps-lock mode; in a sewing machine, forward versus reverse stitching. See Blooper 51: Unnecessary or poorly marked modes (Section 5.3.2) for more discussion of modes and mode indicators.

- *Prompts for input:* Indications from the system that it is waiting for the user to input information. For example:

  ```
  A>
  Password: [_____]
  Delete All? [Yes] [No]
  ```

- *Results:* Data the system has computed or retrieved for the user's benefit. For example:

  ```
  Estimated Monthly Payment: $1530.34
  Current network load: <number displayed as a reading on a dial>
  ```

- *Error and status messages:* Messages displayed by the system to notify the user of errors or other noteworthy situations. For example:

  ```
  Could not import 'godzilla.doc': unknown file format.
  ```

- *Controls:* Interactive components that users manipulate to operate the application, device, or online service. For example: buttons, sliders, menus, and data fields.

Computer-based products and online services exhibit several different ways of making these six types of information hard to notice. Each variation below describes a reason computer users often miss displayed information.

Variation A: Too small or plain. Some electronic appliances and software applications display supposedly important information in such a small size that it might as well not be there. If an indicator is a 16 × 16-pixel image on a 1024 × 1024-pixel display, it will be easy to miss unless it moves (e.g., vibrates) or is extremely bright. This is especially true if the indicator is surrounded by other information or is in the periphery of the user's field of vision.

Similarly, some software applications and Web sites display supposedly important information in the same (small) text font as everything else on the display. For example, in many office applications based on spreadsheets or forms, data input fields and computed-result fields look the same except for their position and perhaps a text label. The result fields are given no special formatting to draw the user's attention to them. Often, this occurs because the programmer had to develop the software in a big hurry and didn't have time to do anything other than put the required text into the program and accept the defaults for font family and size.

Because of the way human (actually, primate) vision works, the size of an indicator and its position in the user's field of vision interact to determine its noticeability, as the next section explains.

Variation B: Not where user is looking. Human visual acuity is good only in a small area in the center of the field of vision, referred to as the "fovea." Our ability to discriminate colors is also mainly limited to the fovea. Outside of the fovea, we have very poor visual acuity and color vision. Because of this, stationary objects that are not right where we are looking are easily overlooked or misrecognized. Most programmers don't know this. That isn't their fault; in-depth study of human perception is not part of the typical software engineer's education. Therefore, programmers often position status indicators and other important information in out-of-the-way locations where users cannot see them.

For example, consider the UCSD Pascal text editor. During the 1970s and 1980s, it was a popular screen-oriented text editor for character-based (i.e., nongraphical) displays. It inspired the design of several other text editors. It and its clones had a "direction" mode that determined whether certain direc-

Figure 5.7

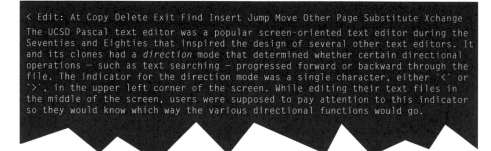

tional operations—such as text searching—progressed forward or backward through the file. The indicator for the direction mode was a single character—either "<" or ">"—in the upper-left corner of the screen. While editing their text files in the middle of the screen, users were supposed to pay attention to this indicator so they would know which way the various directional functions would go when invoked. Needless to say, users of this family of text editors made many mode errors; that is, they invoked directional functions without noticing the direction of the little arrow and found the functions going in the wrong direction. Given the size and position of the arrow, it might as well not have been there. Figure 5.7 shows part of a screen displayed by a text editor called "Screen," which was designed after the UCSD Pascal editor. The arrow that indicates the current direction mode is in the upper-left corner.

In the 1980s, as part of a research project, I developed a computer game called "Money from Heaven," in which players moved a bucket back and forth across the bottom of the screen to catch money falling out of the sky. To study the effect of moded versus modeless user interfaces, I created versions of the game with different controls for moving the bucket, some moded and some modeless (see complete description in Blooper 51: Unnecessary or poorly marked modes, Section 5.3.2).

The moded versions of Money from Heaven had a button that moved the bucket one step in the current direction (left or right) and a button that switched the current direction. I created several variations of the moded version, with mode indicators of differing size and location. One version was similar to the UCSD Pascal editor: the mode indicator was a little arrow at the side of the display, away from the "playing field." As with the UCSD Pascal editor's mode indicator arrow, tests showed that the arrow might as well not have been there; users simply could not see it while they were playing the game. A second moded version of the game had a much larger arrow in the same location. Users said that they could see that arrow, but tests showed that it didn't help them much in playing the game. A third moded version of the game had a small arrow right on the bucket. That helped. The small size wasn't a problem because the mode indicator arrow was exactly where users were looking most of the time; that is, it was in their fovea.

Figure 5.8

```
Enter filename and press RETURN:

Enter command and press RETURN:
```

Variation C: Buried in sameness. Another way to make information easy to overlook is to bury it in a sea of sameness. Computers are great at producing repetition. In some situations this is good, but not when the output of the computer is to be interpreted by human users. For better or worse, human beings are designed such that repetition and sameness essentially put our perceptual systems to sleep. The technical name for this phenomenon is "habituation." Too much sameness can lull us into missing differences when they come along.

For example, consider the two prompts in Figure 5.8. The two prompts differ only in the second word. Furthermore, the capitalized word is what draws the reader's attention, but it is the same in both prompts. It's a safe bet that users of a program that displayed these two messages would sometimes not notice which of the two messages was displayed and therefore type an inappropriate response.

Another situation in which computer software is known for burying information in seas of sameness is the displaying of computed results. This is partly what is meant by the statement, discussed under Principle 6 (Section 1.6), that computers promise a fountain of information, but deliver a glut of data. The data displayed by many software functions is mostly repetitive, uninformative chaff, through which users are forced to sift to find the few grains of wheat.

Consider Figure 5.9, the result of asking a Web search service to find Web sites matching the phrase "acoustic guitar." I won't pick on the particular search service by naming it because the output of all of the popular search services was pretty similar. Notice that in this listing, the first four terms in the category headings convey no information, since they are the same for all of these items. The important information is in the differences between items, but nothing in this display focuses the user's attention on that.

Figure 5.9

- Arts > Music > Instruments > Guitar > Acoustic > Magazines

  Acoustic Guitar Central - The home page of **Acoustic Guitar** magazine

- Arts > Music > Instruments > Guitar > Luthiers

  James Goodall Guitars: Acoustic Guitar Excellence - James Goodall manufactures some of the world's finest accoustic steel string **guitars**. Superb craftsmanship, an exacting finesse for detail and wood choice, combined with robust, three dimensional sound character — these are qualities which embody every James Goodall **guitar**.

- Arts > Music > Instruments > Guitar > Fingerstyle

  Acoustic Guitarists' Annotated Guide to the Internet - A broad overview of the **acoustic guitar** spectrum.

- Arts > Music > Instruments > Guitar > Magazines

  Flatpicking Guitar Magazine Online - specializes in all aspects of flatpicking the **acoustic guitar** - online articles (news & reviews) - info on contributors - US instructors list

Figure 5.10

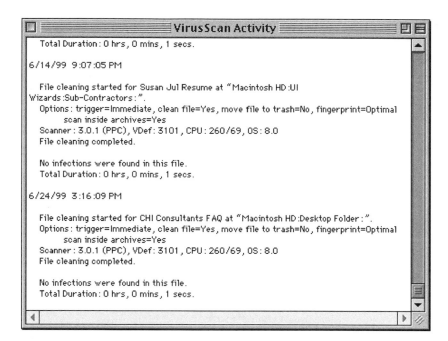

Another way to hide wheat in piles of chaff is shown by the output from VirusScan, a popular utility program that screens files for computer viruses, in Figure 5.10. To check a particular file for viruses, a user drags the file's icon, drops it on the VirusScan desktop icon, and waits for VirusScan to indicate that it is done scanning the file. To see what VirusScan found, the user has to open VirusScan's scanning log, displaying its contents in a window. In the log is a textual description of what VirusScan found, appended to the results of previous file scans. In this case, all the user wants is the answer to the question, Does the file contain a virus? Yes or no? To get one bit of information, the user must look through the log, eventually finding, in the second-to-last line, the answer to the question.

To be fair, VirusScan is not intended mainly for checking individual files. It is mainly designed to allow computer users to scan whole directories or entire disks to find files that are infected with viruses. The approach of writing the scanning results to a log and expecting users to review the log makes a little more sense for that. However, even for that purpose, VirusScan's textual, prose-based output is needlessly wordy and repetitive. It is conducive to having people overlook important information. Imagine scrolling through the log after scanning a directory containing thousands of files, looking to see which ones were found to have viruses. This is, after all, supposed to be the age of GUIs, which stands for *graphical* user interfaces. Can't we do better than glass-teletype output?

Status displays of computer-based systems are another common trouble spot. Consider how the following example buries important information in sameness:

```
Containing tank: normal. Pressure valves: normal.
Fuel rods: abnormal. Discharge pump: normal.
```

This display contains so much repeated, useless data that the important information is effectively buried.

Another common way for software to bury important information in sameness is to post a message in an application window's message line, replacing a similar or identical message that was already there. Unless the new message's arrival is heralded with some sort of fanfare—such as a color change, a font change, blinking, or a sound effect—users will miss it.[1] This problem is made more common by the tendency for message line text to remain after it is no longer needed—or even after it is no longer true. In such cases, if a user does something that causes the same message to be displayed again, the user will see no change, and so will have no way of knowing that whatever he or she is doing is causing a message to be displayed.

 Messages that won't die

Suppose someone is viewing the list of files in a shared folder on a server and tries to delete one of the files, but lacks the necessary access privileges to delete files from this or any shared folder. The software displays a message on the message line at the bottom of the window saying: "Sorry: You don't have permission to delete files from this folder. File not deleted." The user sees the message, understands it, and then opens a different shared folder. After viewing its contents, the user selects one of the files in it and presses Delete. Again the error message is displayed on the message line. If the previous error message is still displayed (which on many systems it would be), the second message would be "replacing" an identical message, resulting in no visible change, providing the user with no apparent feedback. As far as the user is concerned, he pressed Delete in the second folder, and nothing happened.

Variation D: Changes too quickly. Sometimes, developers' attempts to maximize the performance of a software product succeed too well and they end up with displays that change so quickly, users cannot tell that anything changed.

For example, a computer system I once helped design displayed a menu of available functions on its opening screen. There were more functions than would fit on one screen, so the menu was split over two screens. Users switched between screens using NEXT PAGE and PREVIOUS PAGE keys on the keyboard. The programmer wanted changing from one menu screen to the other to be as fast as possible, so instead of writing the code so as to simply display the menu screens using conventional display operations, he had the software preload

---

1. Come to think of it, fanfares for computers might be a good thing. For example: [trumpet call, drum roll, or gong sound] Behold! A message hath arrived!" or, updated slightly: "Yo! Check it OUT!"

both menus into the computer's display memory and, when a user pressed a key, simply instruct the computer to show a different part of the display memory. The menus changed literally instantaneously. Because the two pages of the menu looked very similar (although they listed different functions), users didn't like this; they'd press the NEXT PAGE key and then have to scrutinize the screen to make sure it had changed. We corrected this problem in two ways: (1) we marked each of the menu pages more prominently, and (2) we slowed the change down: when a user pressed the NEXT PAGE or PREVIOUS PAGE key, we blanked the screen for a fraction of a second and sounded a beep before displaying the other screen. Users liked this better.

Similarly, some document viewers prepare the next page for display as the user is viewing the previous page. When the user presses the NEXT PAGE key, the new page is displayed very quickly. Sometimes the new page is displayed so quickly that if the second document page is similar to the first, the user might not notice that the page changed, and so might press NEXT PAGE again, thereby unintentionally viewing the page following the intended page.

This variation of the blooper is noteworthy because it is usually the result of a developer's attempt to avoid another type of blooper: unresponsive software (see Chapter 7). In each of the above examples, the developer tried to make the software more responsive by having it work ahead of the user where possible, but failed to take into account the need for users to be able to notice when the page changed.

Avoiding Blooper 47: *The design rule*

Here are some guidelines for making information stand out.

Bigger is better

You may have noticed that the rear brake lights and turn signals on today's new automobiles are much larger than they were 10 or 20 years ago. This is not purely a design fashion; it is to make the lights more noticeable. Size matters, especially for indicators that must be noticed even though they may not initially be in the center of the viewer's visual field.

The same rule applies to on-screen information, whether it be presented as graphic symbols, text, or color patches. The larger the indicator, the more light receptor cells its image covers in the retina of an observer's eye, and therefore the more difficult it is to miss. Bigger is better, assuming there is sufficient space for everything that must be displayed.

Place important information close to where the user is looking

Regardless of the size of an information display, positioning it so that it is closer to the center of the viewer's visual field—that is, where users look—always improves its visibility and legibility. Putting an indicator on the screen pointer, where there is one, is a good strategy because that is where users are looking most of the time. This is why displaying messages in message lines at the bottom of application windows is problematic. For that to work, other methods should be used to draw the users' attention to the message.

Other techniques to make information stand out

Besides size and position, there are several additional methods that can be used to draw the users' attention to information. They are

- *Boldness, density, saturation:* Text can be made **boldface** to make it stand out. Black-and-white or gray-scale graphics can be drawn with thicker and/or darker lines and fill shades. Color images can be made more saturated. However, heightened boldness, density, and saturation should be used with great restraint. **It does little** or no **good** to make **text bold** if **much or all** of the **text around it is bold**.[2]

- *Sound:* Changes, such as the appearance of messages, or the exceeding of a limit or threshold, can be marked using sounds. Simple beeps are usually enough to announce events if the event details are displayed in one or two standard locations so that users know where to look. If the event details can appear in a wider variety of locations, a set of distinctive sounds may be required to announce the various types of events. As with boldness, audible indicators must be used in moderation or else their value drops precipitously. Of course, using sound to announce changes may not be feasible in certain work environments, such as those in which there is much ambient noise, or in which many people use the same computer systems in close quarters, where the sounds could interfere with each other.

- *Color:* Contrasting colors can be used to draw attention to information displays. For example, in mission-critical systems (such as air traffic control systems, intensive-care medical monitoring systems, and power plant control panels), it is not uncommon for emergency messages to be displayed in red text instead of the usual black. An even more attention-grabbing use of color is to change it on the fly. For example, an error message could briefly blink between red and yellow before settling into the red color. An application I once reviewed displayed error messages on a message line at the bottom of the application's window, which of course hindered their visibility. To compensate, the application displayed messages initially in red, then changed them to black after a few seconds. That not only drew the users' attention to them when they appeared, it also gave the user an indication of whether a message was new or was left over from a previous error.

- *Vibration and animation:* An extremely powerful attention-getting method is to vibrate or animate indicators. The human visual system has evolved over millions of years to be highly sensitive to motion. An interactive TV

---

2. In fact, if the surrounding text is bold, a nonboldface word will stand out, although not as much as a boldface word amidst nonboldfaced text.

prototype I once worked on displayed certain messages in what we called "wiggle font"—the text wiggled slightly. A little motion went a long way. Text displayed in "wiggle font" moved at most one pixel left, right, up, or down from its nominal position, and only moved once or twice a second. Animated graphics can be used for a similar purpose. Of course, a drawback of constantly animating objects (or wiggling text) is that they never stop attracting the users' attention. That is why some Web designers, such as Flanders and Willis [1998], discourage their use. In a commercial product or Web site, it is very important for objects to *stop* wiggling or animating once it is no longer important for the user to notice them.

 ### Using animation discreetly

> A software application I worked on a few years ago started by displaying a Welcome window. Among other things, the Welcome window offered new users a "Quick Guided Tour" of the application. To draw attention to itself, the Quick Guided Tour button was labeled with an image of an airplane on which the propeller spun around every few seconds. The whole airplane image was small—64 × 64 pixels—and the propeller was perhaps 8 pixels long, so it was a tiny, tiny animation, requiring almost no computing resources, but it worked perfectly. ⊕

Don't bury the wheat in chaff

As stated under Principle 6 (Section 1.6), software products and services should deliver information, not just data. To do that, they should avoid displaying data that carries no useful information. This is especially true when the non-information-bearing data will appear repeatedly. Furthermore, they should emphasize important information—by any of the methods listed earlier—so that it stands out.

Instead of displaying computed results as prose text descriptions, GUI-based applications should display results in tables, charts, and graphs. For example, the output of Web search services could be greatly improved by making it more tabular. VirusScan's reporting of results could be improved in two ways:

- When VirusScan is used to check an individual file, it should not require its user to open the log file and read through the most recent scan report to find out whether the file was found to be infected or not. VirusScan should show the answer to this simple question in its main window. It could do so using a graphic (depicting sick versus healthy), a simulated light (ON or OFF), or even text ("Infected" versus "Healthy" or "Yes" versus "No").

- When VirusScan is used to check multiple files, it should display the results using a table or a customized panel. A table would be similar to the current design, but would be much easier for users to scan looking for the important information. The two most prominent columns in the table should be the filename and an indicator of whether or not it was infected. Alternatively, a customized panel would provide summary statistics about the group of files that were scanned, as well as a scrolling list of files that were found to be infected.

If nontabular text is unavoidable for some reason, designers should minimize the amount of verbiage. They should keep in mind that users are searching for the wheat, and non-information-bearing output is useless chaff. Designers should also format the text so as to focus the users' attention on the portions that contain the information the user wants.

Displaying information graphically instead of textually

Several years ago, the developer of a music instruction program called Rhythm-Tutor asked me to review the program's user interface. RhythmTutor's purpose is to help people learn to read music by providing practice in reading rhythm notation—note durations and rests. Users perform exercises by pressing the computer's space bar in time to displayed music and metronome tones. At the end of each exercise, RhythmTutor evaluates the users' performance, indicating how many notes the user missed, how many extra (unwritten) notes the user played, and whether the user started and ended notes late, early, or on time.

The first release of the software presented all of the feedback numerically. To indicate whether the user was starting notes early, late, or on time, RhythmTutor calculated and displayed two pairs of statistics, one pair for note onset, and one pair for note release. The statistics for note onset were:

- *Onset bias:* The average position of the onset of the users' notes relative to when they should have started, expressed in the program's time units. A negative bias indicated that the users' notes tended to start early, a positive bias indicated that they tended to start late, and a zero (or very small) bias indicated that they tended to start at the correct time.

- *Onset error:* A measure of the variability or consistency of the users' note starts and stops. High consistency in when notes were started or ended (relative to where they were supposed to start and end) produced a low error score, and inconsistency raised the error score.

RhythmTutor provided the same two scores for note releases (i.e., ends of notes). The display of the statistics appeared as shown in Figure 5.11.

In my review of RhythmTutor's user interface, I commented that the feedback display was too textual; the note tallies were buried in prose text sentences. More importantly, the bias and error statistics were very difficult to interpret. I advised the developer to redesign the display to make the "missed notes" and "extra notes" scores more prominent. I also suggested that the numerical bias and error scores be replaced by a graphical display using histograms to show how the users' note starts and note ends were distributed around where they should have

Figure 5.11

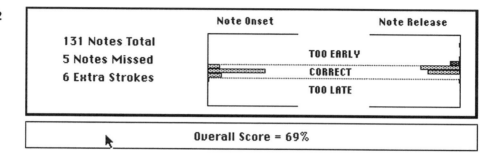

Out of 45 notes: 1 was missed – there were 0 extra strokes

note onset bias = 0	Notes were started without bias
note onset error = 9	Notes were started very consistently
note release bias = -13	Notes were released too early
note release error = 6	Notes were released very consistently

Overall Score = 69%

Figure 5.12

131 Notes Total
5 Notes Missed
6 Extra Strokes

Note Onset   Note Release

TOO EARLY
CORRECT
TOO LATE

Overall Score = 69%

been. The developer took these suggestions and redesigned the feedback display as shown in Figure 5.12.

In my opinion, the developer did a good job of redesigning the feedback display based on my suggestions. I might have made the histograms vertical instead of horizontal so that time would proceed from left to right for both graphs, but that's just a minor detail, and there are some advantages in the histogram design the developer used. Overall, RhythmTutor's feedback display was greatly improved.

5.2.3 Blooper 48: Unexpected rearrangement of display

Suppose you had a word-processing program that, whenever you edited any line of text displayed on the screen, tried to be helpful by automatically scrolling the document so that the line you were editing was in the middle of the screen. Thus, if you put the cursor on a line of text near the bottom of the screen and began typing, the document would shift so that the line where you are typing text was the middle line of the screen. While this might sound convenient at first, if you had a word processor that did this, you would most likely find it annoying and even disorienting. You might even switch to a different word processor.

The user interface blooper that the hypothetical word processor commits is moving the users' data around more than the user asks it to. Imagine how long you would tolerate it if Windows or MacOS frequently rearranged your desktop icons for you. Software that does this sort of thing causes users to lose track of where they are and what they have just done. It also annoys them.

The chances of users becoming disoriented are greater if unrequested automatic rearrangement of the display occurs very quickly. If a big change occurs in the blink of an eye, users won't even be able to figure out what happened. On the other hand, if the display updates too slowly, user frustration at becoming disoriented would be replaced by frustration at having to wait. When designers try to rearrange users' data for them, they are entering a user interface minefield.

Unfortunately, a lot of software designers venture into this minefield and end up committing this blooper. One sees the blooper frequently in software designed for manipulating complex, structured data, such as outlines, tables, highly formatted documents, graphs, trees, and charts. The following are some examples I've seen:

- A Java class browser that displayed a tree graph of the class hierarchy. If a user added or deleted a single class, the entire tree graph would be redisplayed, rearranged so that the tree looked "balanced" (see Figure 5.13). Even just renaming a class could cause a radical rearrangement of the tree: class nodes might be reordered (so they'd be in alphabetical order) or shifted (because the new class name was longer or shorter than the old and so required a different-sized box).

- A network monitoring tool that displayed bar charts, scatter plots, and so on. Users could edit properties of the charts to alter their graphical style, scale, and so on. Charts were always displayed centered in the middle of the program's Chart window. A small change in the properties—such as changing the bars in the chart from 2D to simulated 3D—not only changed the appearance of the chart, but also its position in the window. This made it harder to see what had changed.

- Outline processors or file directory browsers that can expand or contract items to show or hide their subitems. I've seen some that expand and contract items when users executed commands unrelated to expanding or con-

Figure 5.13   *Before*   *After*

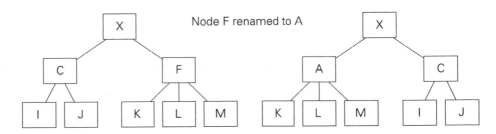

Figure 5.14

Before

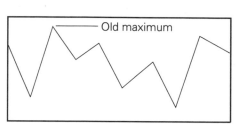

Old maximum

After
Rescaled

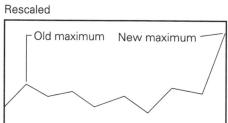

Old maximum   New maximum

New maximum data point appears

tracting. For example, if a user set the text font style for level 3 items in an outline, the outline processor might automatically expand the entire outline down to level 3. Closing them back up again might be tedious. Or if a user drags an item from one file folder into another in a graphical display of the file hierarchy, some file browsers might automatically expand the destination file folder to let the user see what is in it.

- Structured drawing programs that allow graphic objects (e.g., lines, arcs, circles, rectangles) to be layered on top of each other. Users expect to be in total control of the ordering of layers. However, in some drawing programs, simply changing a graphic object's attributes, such as color, line width, or fill pattern, can cause it to be moved to the top layer. This is not usually what users want.

- Data-graphing functions that show how a data value changes over time, such as the price of a stock or the load on a network. Such graphs typically added new data points periodically on one end and scroll the graph slowly towards the other end. Some such graphs automatically scale the vertical axis to fill the height of the window (see Figure 5.14). Although this may initially seem helpful to users, in practice it is very disorienting to users when the graph automatically rescales when a new data point appears that represents a new maximum, or when an existing maximum scrolls off-screen.

- Family tree or organization chart editors. Some of these reorder and shift items—sometimes entire branches of the chart—when a user simply adds or deletes a person, organization, or a relationship.

Overzealous rearranging of displays can occur for two quite different reasons:

1. *Well-meaning but naive developers.* Developers might genuinely want to help users. They might believe that users would want to rearrange the data anyway, and that rearranging it automatically saves them the trouble. Unfortunately, such assumptions are usually wrong.

2. *Overly simple implementation.* The developers don't have time (or don't consider it worth the time) to figure out what exactly the user changed and

how to localize the updating of the display to just that. Therefore, they code the display so that the display is recomputed and reformatted from scratch and redisplayed in full whenever any part or aspect of it changes.

A related annoyance: Place controls differently on different displays. A variation of the blooper is to position controls in a different place on every display in which they appear. For example, some Web sites and Web applications place important navigation links or buttons after variable-length content. Therefore, the position of the navigation links or buttons varies depending on the current page, forcing users to look for the controls and move the mouse before clicking on them.

As a specific example, see Yahoo's message board Web site (*http://messages. yahoo.com*). It displays banner advertisements at the top of each message page. The buttons for navigating to the next and previous message on the current topic are below the ad on each page. Because the ads vary in height, the navigation buttons move up and down from one page to the next. This prevents users from simply placing the mouse over the Next button and clicking through the messages to find an interesting one. Instead, users must look to see where the buttons are on every page. Aaarrgh! Worse, the ads are randomly chosen when a page is displayed, so the Next and Previous buttons won't even be in the same place if a user revisits a particular message. Figure 5.15 shows two successive message pages, in which the Next and Previous buttons are in different vertical positions due to the difference in the height of the banner ads. Bzzzt. Blooper!

Figure 5.15

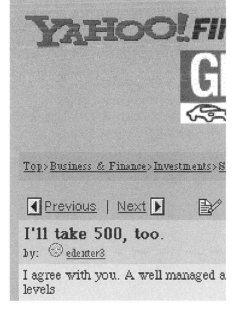

Avoiding Blooper 48: *The design rule*

Cases of this blooper are violations of two graphical user interface subprinciples discussed under Principle 6 (Sections 1.6.2 and 1.6.3): "the screen belongs to the user," and "preserve display inertia."

The screen belongs to the user

Users perceive the computer screen as being under their control. When software changes too much on its own initiative, it disrupts this perception. Users become disoriented, frustrated, and annoyed. This is especially true for activities that involve hand-eye coordination, such as moving the screen pointer or resizing windows. However, it also applies to arranging users' data, such as the layout of icons on a computer desktop, the ordering of files or email messages in folders, the formatting of text or graphs, or the expansion level of an outline.

Therefore, software should not try to be too helpful; it should not rearrange the display *for* users, but rather should let them arrange and manage the display. Software can support users in managing the display without managing the display for them. It can provide explicit "rearrange" commands such as the MacOS Clean-up Desktop command, the Balance or Align functions of some graph editors, or Microsoft Word's AutoFormat command, which users invoke at their own discretion.

Preserve display inertia

Preserving display inertia means that when a user changes something on the screen, as much of the rest of the display as possible should remain unchanged. When software changes a graphical display to show the effect of a user's actions, it should try to minimize what it changes. Small, localized changes to the data should produce only small, localized changes on the display.

When large or nonlocal changes in the display are necessary (such as repaginating a document, or swapping the positions of branches of a family tree diagram), they should not be instantaneous. Rather, they should be announced clearly, and they should be carried out in ways that

- foster the user's recognition and comprehension of the changes that are occurring, and
- minimize disruption to the user's ability to continue working.

One technique for fostering recognition and comprehension of large visual changes is to animate them. This provides visual contiguity—the perception by users that a single object is changing rather than that new objects are replacing old ones. However, animating changes does not mean forcing users to wait for annoyingly slow animations to finish. As can be demonstrated by watching animated cartoons, people can perceive smooth motion even if that motion occurs in a fraction of a second.

Regarding rescaling of data graphs and plots: the default behavior should be that graphs retain the same scale until a user directs the software to rescale them. Users should be able to rescale by a certain factor, and also scale the graph to fit the available space. Automatic rescaling can be an option that users activate if desired, but it should not be the default behavior.

Information displays or controls that appear on multiple displays or pages should be in *exactly* the same place on each page, so that users can predict where they will be. In the case of buttons, it allows users to place the screen pointer once and forget about it. In the case of the Yahoo message board Web pages, it would have been better to either make all the ads the same size or center them inside a fixed-size container so that the navigation buttons wouldn't move from page to page. Alternatively, the navigation buttons could be placed in a fixed location to the left of the ad.

5.2.4 Blooper 49: Instructions that go away too soon

A problem sometimes seen in software designed by people who lack training in user interface design is instructions that appear long before they are relevant but are gone by the time they are needed. This blooper could be nicknamed the "Mission Impossible" blooper, after a TV show about international espionage that was popular in the United States during the 1960s. At the beginning of each episode of the show, Mr. Briggs,[3] the head agent for the elite espionage team, received his mission instructions in the form of a secret tape-recorded message that self-destructed as soon as it was played once.

Check out the dialog box in Figure 5.16, from Microsoft Word 97. It appears after a user has spell-checked a document containing any text marked "do not check" ("no proofing"). The dialog box tells the user that the spell-check operation finished but skipped the marked text. In case the user wants to check the text that was skipped, the dialog box gives a long list of instructions to follow that will do that. The problem is that most users will have to write these instructions down because they disappear along with the dialog box as soon as the user clicks on OK.

Figure 5.16

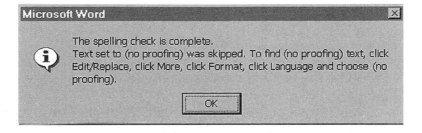

---

3. After the show had been on TV for a few years, Mr. Briggs was replaced by Mr. Phelps.

Common sense suggests that one should not expect computer users to read important instructions before they are needed and then remember them when the instructions are no longer displayed. Expecting this is a form of wishful thinking. Developers of interactive systems are often guilty of wishful thinking.

 A real war story

> A story from the Vietnam War has it that one of the helicopters used in the war had on its main door the instructions for bailing out in a midflight emergency. The problem was that the first step in the instructions was to blow the door off. While frantically trying to bail out of a crashing 'copter, soldiers were supposed to read calmly through *all* of the instructions, blow the door away, and remember enough of the now absent instructions to complete the evacuation procedure. Yeah, sure!

This blooper arises most commonly in computer software when both of the following conditions are true:

- A new application incorporates a function or component that was written long ago or far away (physically or organizationally) and therefore cannot be changed. We will refer to such functionality as "foreign."
- The new application requires people to use the foreign functionality in a particular way that is more constrained than the foreign functionality actually is. Therefore, the new application needs to provide specific instructions for people to follow while they are using the foreign functionality.

Since programmers cannot change the actual foreign software to constrain its behavior or display the new, more-specific instructions, they often have the application display the instructions just before the foreign functionality is invoked. This, by itself, is not a problem. The problem arises when the instructions go away before the user has executed all—or in some cases *any*—of the steps in them.

Avoiding Blooper 49: *The design rule*

The design rule for avoiding this blooper can be stated simply: Detailed instructions should remain displayed while the user is carrying them out. Developers should not assume that users will be able to follow multistep instructions when the instructions are no longer displayed.

When a software development team finds itself needing to incorporate foreign code into an application and determines that the two conditions described above are true, the foreign functionality should be "wrapped" in new code. The new code displays the necessary instructions (in the application's main window or in auxiliary windows) and keeps them displayed while users work their way through the necessary steps using the foreign functionality.

5.3 Setting stumbling blocks for users

Next, we have three interaction bloopers that cover the most common ways to trip users up as they try to accomplish their goals. We wouldn't want those users to get too cocky and self-assured, would we?

5.3.1 Blooper 50: Similar functions with inconsistent user interfaces

A common problem in software I review or test is that the same function or very similar functions encountered in different parts of the application (or in different applications in an integrated collection) have different user interfaces. Two extremely common forms of this blooper are

- Some functions in an application use noun-verb command syntax, while other commands use verb-noun command syntax. Noun-verb command syntax means that users first specify an object or objects that they are going to operate on (e.g., by selecting them), and then specify the operation. Verb-noun command syntax means that users first specify what operation they want, then specify the objects to be acted upon.
- Each type of data object in an application has its own user interface for deleting that type of object. For example, some objects might be deleted by selecting them and pressing the DELETE key on the keyboard; others might require pressing CONTROL-X or COMMAND-X; still others might require clicking on a Delete button that is associated with the type of object.

An example of inconsistent user interfaces can be seen in two dialog boxes displayed by Eudora Pro 4.0, a popular email program (see Figure 5.17). The dialog box on the left is like most of the dialog boxes in Eudora; it prompts the user for some data and provides a Cancel button for canceling the function. The dialog box on the right is the odd one; it offers no Cancel button, but instead directs users to click "elsewhere"—presumably anywhere but on the mailbox menu—to cancel the function. It apparently didn't occur to the programmer who wrote the code for this dialog box to provide a Cancel button like all other Eudora dialog boxes do.

Often, user interface inconsistencies arise between otherwise-similar functions in an application because different programmers designed different parts of the application, and each designed the function her or his own way. Perhaps

Figure 5.17

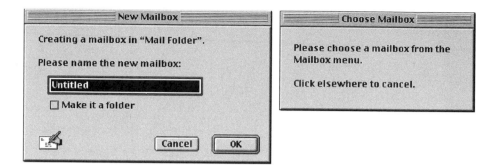

the programmers didn't communicate adequately, or perhaps each considered his or her own design to be best, and management wasn't strong enough to enforce consistency (see Blooper 80: Anarchic development, Section 8.2.2).

Examples of inconsistent user interfaces

The following comments are from reviews I performed of three different client products. The product names have been changed to protect the guilty:

- TestTool allows users to create and manage many different kinds of files, such as scripts, source files, declarations files, compiled files. But TestTool's different functions are inconsistent in how users create and name files. Some functions use a "create and edit data, then specify name of file in which to save" model, but other functions use a "specify filename, then create data" model.

- StockUp has different user interfaces in different windows for functionality that is actually very similar. For example, the program manages several different lists of objects: templates, filters, orders, etc. For each list, an Add function is provided for adding the relevant kind of object to the list. Unfortunately, the user interfaces for the different Add functions vary greatly. In some windows, clicking a list's Add button displays a dialog box that presents a form for describing the object to be added. Users complete this form and then click the dialog box's OK button to add the new object to the list. In other windows, the list always keeps a blank object at the end of the list. When users wish to add an item to the list, they fill out the blank item as desired and then click Add, which enters the newly filled-out object to the database and adds a new blank item to the end of the list. These are only two of many different ways different Add functions operate in StockUp.

- SmartNet presents the exact same ON/OFF setting differently in different windows. In some windows, the setting is presented as a checkbox. In other windows, it is presented as a pair of radiobuttons (On, Off). In still other windows, it is presented as a two-item option menu.

Inconsistencies can also arise even when only one programmer is responsible. If a programmer starts hacking before performing a conceptual design (see

Principle 2, Section 1.2), he or she may fail to notice that two operations in different parts of the application are essentially the same.

However it arises, this blooper has a strong negative impact on the learnability and usability of an application.

Avoiding Blooper 50: *The design rule*

The various reasons given above for this blooper each suggest measures that developers can take to try to avoid it:

- Encourage programmers to communicate effectively with each other, and to communicate with the goal of ensuring user interface consistency across similar functions. Merely admonishing programmers to work together will not suffice. Management must establish performance review and reward structures that support teamwork and a holistic view of the application.

- Provide oversight by project managers, architects, and user interface designers. It is normal for different parts of an application to be assigned to different programmers, but someone needs to be responsible for coordinating different parts of the application. It is of course nice when the programmers who are implementing the various parts coordinate on their own, but ultimately, someone must "own" the combination of the different programmers' efforts.

- Develop a conceptual model before starting to code the user interface (see Principle 2, Section 1.2.3). Perform an object-and-actions analysis encompassing every object that the application will expose to users, and every operation on each object. Doing this provides a clear understanding of the fundamental operations provided by the application. This allows designers to see commonalties between functions that might not otherwise be apparent, and to exploit them in the user interface.

Two highly consistent UIs: Star and Lisa

In any ranking of commercial computer products based on user interface consistency, two historical products stand out as the foremost examples of consistent design: the Xerox Star and the Apple Lisa. Xerox released the Star in 1981, and Apple released the Lisa in 1982. Both products failed in the commercial marketplace for several reasons: they weren't responsive enough (see Chapter 7), they were too expensive, they were closed to applications developed by third parties, and their respective companies weren't sure what their proper market niche was. However, with respect to user interface consistency, these two products were—and still are—without peers.[4]

---

4. However, a few other computer products are worthy of mention for their high degree of user interface consistency: the NeXT workstation, the Metaphor workstation, and Sun's OpenLook user interface toolkit. These systems were designed by some of the same people who designed the Star and the Lisa [Johnson et al., 1989].

Whatever a user learned about how to operate a specific piece of functionality would work throughout most of the rest of the software as well. The same text-editing operations were used to create documents, specify filenames, rename files, compose email messages, and create executable scripts. All types of data objects were moved in the same way. All data was deleted in the same way. As a result, Star and Lisa required users to learn much less than most computer products do in order to operate them productively.

Besides being designed with strong management oversight (see Blooper 80: Anarchic development, Section 8.2.2), the user interfaces of Star and Lisa were largely designed on paper before any code was written. Furthermore, their developers carefully designed all of their functionality at a conceptual level before designing the icons, windows, control panels, and data displays that made up their user interfaces. In short, each was designed according to a *plan*.

Industry pundits have written that Star and Lisa were widely copied, thus giving rise to the modern graphical user interface as seen in today's MacOS, Windows, various windowed varieties of Unix, and, to some extent, the Web. The irony is that what was copied was mostly the superficial aspects of Star and Lisa's design: the windows, buttons, dialog boxes, menus, and so on. The radical level of user interface consistency that Star and Lisa embodied, not to mention the fastidious development processes that produced them, have for the most part been ignored. Designers and developers of modern computer-based products, and budding designers and developers, would be wise to study the Star and Lisa user interfaces and how they were designed.

5.3.2 Blooper 51: Unnecessary or poorly marked modes

When a computer-based product or service does something that its user did not expect and did not want, the problem is often that the software was in a different mode than the user thought it was in. Here are some examples of this:

- Someone is using a drawing program to edit an illustration. She wants to move a previously drawn rectangle to a new location. She tries to select the rectangle and drag it, but sees that she has instead accidentally drawn a second rectangle overlapping the first one. Whoops! The program was in "draw rectangle" mode, not "select" mode.

- Someone instructs a Web browser to print the currently displayed Web page, but is annoyed when the page prints in landscape format, cutting off the bottom of the page. Oops! Forgot to set Page Orientation back to "portrait" after printing that landscape page yesterday.

- Someone opens a document he has been writing, and while paging through it to find where he left off yesterday, notices that the figures he added yesterday seem to be missing. He frantically scrolls back and forth looking for the figures, fearing that he somehow forgot to save the document. A coworker hears his anguished cries, looks at the screen, and tells him what's wrong:

he's looking at the document in the document editor's "Normal" view mode, but figures are only visible in "Page Layout" view mode.

■ Someone using a stock investment Web site creates a stock order and saves it, intending to submit it later when market conditions have improved, but is dismayed when the order is automatically submitted. "Darn! I forgot to turn off Autosubmit mode after showing my brother this morning how it works."

Software has modes if user actions have different effects in different situations. To know what effect a given action will have, users have to know what mode the application is in. For example, the effect of clicking on a button on an application's window might depend on how a particular software option is set. That software option is a mode setting. The following quotations serve both to further define "mode" and to illustrate some of the usability problems modes can cause:

Each...state in which a given operation by the user is interpreted differently by the program is called a command mode. The more modes in a command language, the more likely the user is to make mistakes by forgetting which mode he is in. [Newman and Sproull, 1979]

My observations of secretaries learning to use text editors...convinced me that my beloved computers were, in fact, unfriendly monsters, and that their sharpest fangs were the ever-present modes. [Tesler, 1981]

Text editor users confuse modes, especially when the user spends a long time in a mode other than the "normal" one. [Thimbleby, 1982]

Mode errors occur frequently in systems that do not provide clear feedback of their current state. [Norman, 1983]

The consensus of these comments, and of user interface professionals in general, is that modes detract from a product's or service's usability. Modes force users to try to keep track of what mode the software is in, diverting mental effort from the users' own work. They restrict users' actions to what is permissible in the current mode. Furthermore, they make it possible, sometimes even likely, that users will make mode errors, that is, perform actions they did not intend or attempt actions that are not valid in the current mode. While some mode errors are trivial and easy to correct, others are serious and difficult to correct.

Some software has modes that are unnecessary or inappropriate; a more thoughtful design could eliminate the modes, thereby simplifying the software. Even when software products or services contain modes for good reasons, they often make it difficult for users to cope with those modes by providing poor or nonexistent indicators about what mode the application is in.

Example of badly moded software. As an example of unnecessary modes, I'll describe a database application I reviewed for a client. The application was for browsing and analyzing multidimensional databases of quantitative business data. The data was displayed in tables, in which the rows and columns were data categories defined in the database (e.g., quarters or months of the year, states or cities, types of products). The data in the table cells was a quantity of something that had been measured for that specific intersection of data categories. Users examined the data by choosing which data categories would be shown as table rows and which would be shown as table columns. For example, a user might choose to examine sales totals for each of three product categories for each of the past four quarters, broken down by region, as illustrated in Figure 5.18.

One operation supported by the table display was "drilling down" into a category. Drilling down into a particular column (or row) replaced it with a group of columns (or rows) showing the category's subcategories, if any were defined in the database. For example, drilling down from a region column in Figure 5.18 might replace it with columns for all the states in that region.

The developers wanted it to be easy for users to drill down, so in addition to providing the standard menubar method for drilling down (select a column or row label, then choose Drill Down from the Table menu in the application's menubar), they allowed users to drill down by double-clicking on a column or row label. However, the developers also wanted it to be easy for users to drill *up,* that is, to replace a group of subcategories with their parent category. Their approach was to assign drill up to double-click also, and to have a drill direction mode setting that determined whether double-clicking on a category label drilled down or up. A button on the application's toolbar toggled the drill direction mode between "up" and "down."

	Q1			Q2			Q3			Q4		
	East	*Central*	*West*	*East*	*Central*	*West*	*East*	*Central*	*West*	*East*	*Central*	*West*
fish	12.4	16.3	13.6	24.5	21.6	19.5	10.8	18.9	16.3	25.2	19.8	28.0
poultry	45.3	67.2	54.2	71.7	59.0	33.3	53.8	61.7	35.9	27.9	85.3	26.8
meat	15.3	24.6	18.9	19.8	14.6	20.0	17.8	23.1	22.1	12.5	13.4	18.8

Figure 5.18

Needless to say, I considered the drill direction mode to be a terrible idea. In the short time I spent using the application to familiarize myself with it, I drilled the wrong way *dozens* of times: "Whoops! I wanted to go down, not up." In my review report, I provided the following advice:

Drill-down direction mode is very bad. It is far too easy for users to forget what mode they are in and "drill" the wrong way (I did it several times). Recommendation: Two alternatives:

a) Double-click always drills down. Provide a single button (or a menu listing ancestors) on the toolbar for drilling up. Also, consider that the Output window's Back (left arrow) button already drills up after a drill-down, so maybe a separate drill-up button isn't even needed.

b) Double-click drills down; SHIFT-double-click drills up. This makes the mode control tactile and spring-loaded, greatly reducing the chance of a mode error.

Example of a poorly indicated mode. As an example of poorly marked modes, recall the UCSD Pascal text editor described under Blooper 47: Easily missed information (Section 5.2.2). Its direction mode, which determined whether text searching and other operations progressed forward or backward through the file, was indicated by a single character—either "<" or ">," in the upper-left corner of the screen (Figure 5.7).

Example of moded UI

I once helped a client redesign an application designed for bookstore personnel to use to order books in quantity from publishers. Creating a book order required specifying quite a bit of information: the title, author, publisher, and ISBN number of the book; the quantity desired; whether paperback or hardcover was preferred; the date by which the books were needed; whether the bookstore was entitled to a discount; the ID of the store; the ID of the employee placing the order; any special instructions; and so on.

For various reasons, users might not want to submit an order immediately after entering it. Perhaps they needed to double-check certain information before considering the order complete. Perhaps they wanted to create a batch of orders for different books and submit them all together to qualify for a volume discount. Therefore, the application gave users the option of having orders submitted automatically after they had been entered and saved, or not.

The problem was that the application provided this choice in a very obscure way (see Figure 5.19). At the top of the Create Order dialog box, there was a checkbox labeled "Submit Order." (For present purposes, we will overlook the additional problem that the checkbox label was worded more like a command than an ON/OFF setting, which by itself would confuse users.) In the middle of the dialog box were all of the data fields for specifying an order. At the bottom of the

Figure 5.19

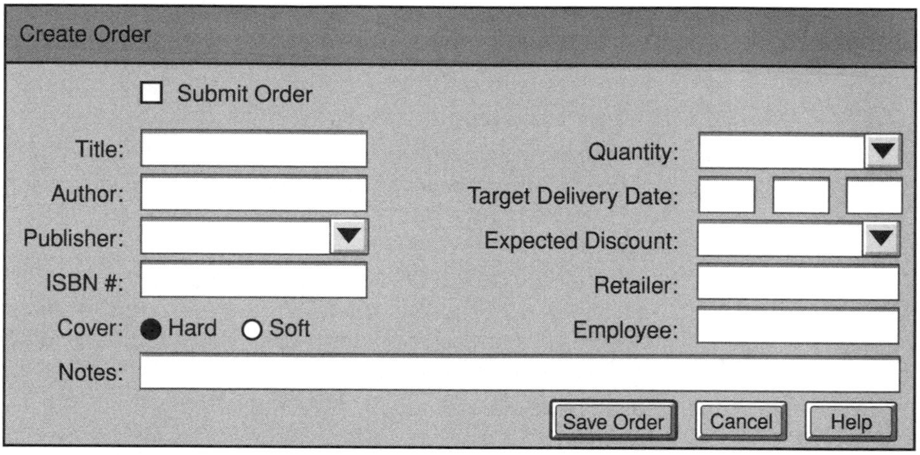

Create Order

Submit Order

Title:

Author:

Publisher:

ISBN #:

Cover: ● Hard ○ Soft

Notes:

Quantity:

Target Delivery Date:

Expected Discount:

Retailer:

Employee:

Save Order | Cancel | Help

Figure 5.20

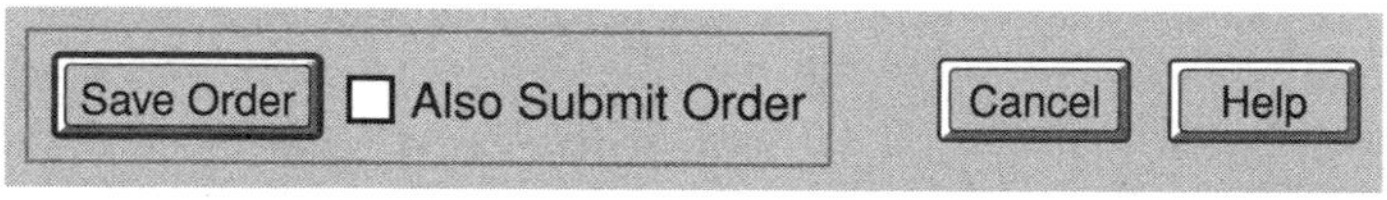

Save Order | ☐ Also Submit Order   Cancel | Help

dialog box were three buttons: Save Order, Cancel, and Help. The "Submit Order" checkbox determined what the Save Order button would do. If "Submit Order" was unchecked (the default), Save Order would simply save the order in the application's database and close the Create Order dialog box. The user could retrieve the order later if desired and continue working with it. If "Submit Order" was checked, Save Order would not only save the order and close the dialog box, it would also submit the order to the publisher.

I considered the "Submit Order" mode setting unnecessary, needlessly obscure, and highly conducive to errors. I advised the developers to eliminate the mode setting by removing the "Submit Order" checkbox. The option of immediately submitting an order when it was saved could be provided by having two buttons at the bottom of the window: "Save Order" and "Save Order and Submit."

The developers didn't like my proposed improvement. They argued that the application had already been in use for a year, and that the users were already used to the mode setting. They said that many users had created default files that preset the "Submit Order" checkbox as they wanted it, so the new version of the application had to provide that setting.

The design we eventually settled on retained the mode setting, but moved the mode checkbox down next to the "Save Order" button, and placed both of them inside a group box to make it clear that they were related (see Figure 5.20). The label on the mode checkbox was changed to "Also Submit Order." ⊕

All modes are not equal. Some are less harmful than others. In moderation (no pun intended), modes can even be helpful.

A common use of modes is for GUI-based software to display so-called modal dialog boxes—dialog boxes that, when displayed, block users from interacting with other windows on the screen. They are called "modal" because they put the computer into a mode in which input to windows other than the modal dialog box is ignored.[5]

Dialog boxes can exhibit different degrees of "modalness":

- *Parent modal:* Block interaction with their own parent window but allow interaction with other windows from the same application or from other applications.
- *Application modal:* Block interaction with all other parts of the same application, but allow users to interact with other applications.
- *Modal* or *system modal:* Block all interaction other than with the modal dialog box.

The purpose of modal dialog boxes is to force users to notice, read, and respond to them before doing anything else on their computer. This is often desirable, such as in the following cases:

- The software detects a serious problem and needs to inform the user. If an error dialog box is not modal, a user can miss it, click on another window, and cause the error dialog box to vanish behind other windows. That, in turn, can lead to later confusion. I've seen this happen in usability tests where the software did not make important error dialog boxes modal.
- The dialog box requires that certain aspects of the application's data not change while the dialog box is displayed. For example, if a dialog box is collecting arguments for a function that the user has invoked in reference to a particular data object, it may be desirable to prevent the user from deleting or altering the object until the function has completed or been aborted.

The only mode errors that modal dialog boxes cause are pretty harmless: the user tries to click on something else but the computer does not respond (or only beeps). It can certainly be frustrating to be blocked from doing anything else while a modal dialog box is displayed, especially if the dialog box says something horrible like

```
Out of memory. All your data will be lost. [OK]
```

---

5. I use the term "moded" rather than "modal" when discussing user interface modes. "Modal" and "modality" have other important meanings in the field of computer technology. For example, "multimodal" systems are those that communicate via a variety of means, and a "modality" is a means of communication. Therefore, calling a user interface "modal" or referring to the "modality" of a user interface (rather than to its "modedness") is highly ambiguous. The one exception is when the subject is dialog boxes that block user input, since "modal" is an industry standard term for them. But even for that subject, "modalness" seems preferable to "modality."

However, modes that mainly restrict users' actions are, in my opinion, not as bad as modes that cause users to make serious mode errors.

As an example of relatively harmless modes, consider Microsoft Word, a popular document-editing program. Word is literally teeming with modes. The following are just some of the mode settings that affect what happens on the screen as a user edits a document's content (with the default values in *italics*):

- View: *Normal*, Outline, Page Layout, Master Document
- Auto Correct: *On*, Off
- Revision Tracking: On, *Off*
- Background Repagination: *On*, Off
- Auto Save: *On*, Off
- Automatic Word Selection: *On*, Off
- Smart Cut-and-Paste: *On*, Off
- Typing Replaces Selection: *On*, Off
- Drag-and-Drop Text Editing: *On*, Off
- Overtype Mode: On, *Off*

Most of these mode settings do not result in users making mode errors. Why? The reason is *not* that the current values of these modes are so prominently indicated that users cannot miss them. In fact, most of them are hardly indicated at all. Rather, the reason is that the vast majority of Word users never change most of these settings from their default values. Many Word users don't even know that these settings are in Word. If a mode setting is never changed, it effectively has only one value. As Larry Tesler [1981] said: "One mode is no modes at all."

The one mode setting in the above list that most Word users do change is the View setting. It is therefore a setting for which one would expect to see mode errors, such as a user trying to edit an outline in the Normal view and wondering why the outline items are not correctly indented.

Notice that in the above list of Word mode settings, only one has the word "mode" in its name: Overtype Mode. A common problem in software that contains mode settings is that the settings tend to be inconsistently named; some are called "modes," and some aren't. Names for mode settings tend to be fairly idiosyncratic as well as inconsistent—whatever a programmer happened to think of at the moment he or she added the setting to the software, often without considering what other settings were or would be named.

I often see mode settings that are named simply "Mode" (see Figure 5.21). This usually happens because the developer of a setting couldn't think of a more descriptive name, and assumed either that the names of the mode setting's values would convey to users the meaning of the setting, or that someone on the development team would think of a better name before the software was released. Both assumptions usually turn out to be wrong.

Figure 5.21

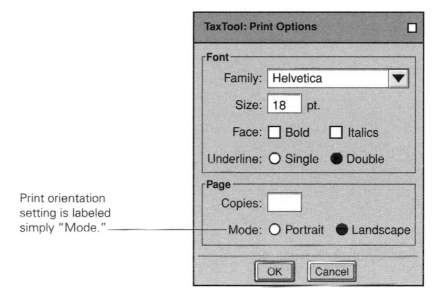

Print orientation
setting is labeled
simply "Mode."

Avoiding Blooper 51: *The design rule*

As described earlier, modes impact software usability in three ways:

1. They require users to expend mental effort to keep track of the modes.
2. They make it possible for users to make mode errors.
3. They constrain users' actions to those permissible in the current mode.

The first two of these are definitely problems. The third can be either a problem or a feature, depending on the intentions of the designer and the needs of users.

Eliminate modes by removing mode settings

The best way to reduce the negative impact of modes is to design the user interface to minimize the presence of mode settings—perhaps even omit them completely. When I find mode settings in software user interfaces, I often try to devise modeless alternatives that preserve the desired functionality. That usually requires the addition of commands, buttons, or menu choices in addition to removing the mode setting.

Recall, for example, the database table application I discussed earlier. One way to eliminate the need for a "drill direction" mode was to assign the "drill up" and "drill down" functions to separate buttons or keys. Similarly, with the book-ordering application in Figures 5.19 and 5.20, the way to eliminate the "Submit Order" mode while retaining the functionality it provided was to add a second button for Saving: "Save Order and Submit."

Minimize the use and impact of modal dialog boxes

A recommendation common to many GUI style guides and design books is to use modal dialog boxes—those that block users from interacting with other parts of the display—only very sparingly. The general consensus is that one should avoid restricting users' actions while a dialog box is displayed unless it is *crucial* that users not interact with other items on the display. Furthermore, the restriction should be as narrow as possible; don't block users' access to data or controls that are irrelevant to the dialog box. Therefore, the relative frequency with which GUI designers should use the various degrees of dialog box modalness is as follows:

- *Modeless:* Most of the time
- *Parent modal:* As necessary
- *Application modal:* Occasionally
- *Modal* or *system modal:* Hardly ever

Avoid forced sequences or temporary restrictions on user actions

Another way to avoid modes when designing interactive software is to avoid (1) requiring user actions to occur in a predetermined order, or (2) temporarily limiting the actions that are valid.

For example, a Move function can be designed in either of two ways: moded and modeless. A moded Move function requires a sequence of actions in which users indicate "Move *this* to *there*," with the software being in one mode while it is waiting for the *this* and another while it is waiting for the *there*. Alternatively, a Move function can be designed as separate Cut and Paste commands, with no intervening modes.

Similarly, a text editor's Find and Replace function can have a user interface that is either moded or modeless. A moded Find and Replace command begins by highlighting the text it found and asking the user whether that text should be replaced. When the user responds, the interaction continues in a loop—during which other text-editing commands are unavailable—until the end of the file is reached or the user escapes out of the command. In contrast, a modeless Find and Replace command has no built-in loop; it highlights the text it found and is done. All of the text editor's commands are now available. If the user wants to replace the text and/or look for the next instance of the text to be replaced, he or she can do so by issuing the appropriate command. With the moded design, the software drives the interaction; with the modeless one, the user drives it.

However, avoiding or eliminating modes is not always practical. Most software applications have modes of one kind or another. It is extremely difficult, if not impossible, to design software that actually does something useful while having a user interface that is entirely free of modes. The reason is that modes usually have advantages as well as disadvantages, so the decision of whether or not to have modes is often a design trade-off. I'll discuss first the advantages and then the disadvantages of modes.

Advantages of modes

An important use of modes is to allow users to prespecify some of the information needed for invoking an application's functions. Invoking a function in any computer application requires (1) identifying the desired function uniquely out of all the available functions, and (2) specifying the function's arguments. With no prespecification of information—that is, without modes—identifying functions and/or arguments can require either excessively verbose input from users, large command vocabularies, or massive arrays of keys or on-screen controls. By allowing (perhaps forcing) users to prespecify information—such as commands, arguments, and key interpretations—moded user interfaces, relative to their modeless counterparts, allow for

- *Terser control:* Information that users would otherwise have to specify repeatedly can be prespecified once in a mode setting, which applies to subsequent actions until the mode is changed.
- *Smaller command vocabularies and arrays of controls:* The same command or control can have different effects in different modes.

In addition to the advantages resulting from prespecification of information, modes also offer the following advantages:

- *More guidance for users.* Software can guide the interaction, taking users through a predetermined sequence of modes in which only certain user actions are possible. Modal dialog boxes are a special case of this; there is only one step, but it is a step the designers really want the user to take.
- *Safety:* Modes can be used to lock certain functions to prevent their accidental use. Trigger locks on guns and on nuclear missile launch panels are examples of safety mode controls for which we should all be thankful.
- *Recognizing exceptional operations:* Modes are sometimes desirable as a way of explicitly recognizing in a user interface that certain operations are exceptional. Software user interfaces are often designed as if all functions they provide are equally important or likely. In contrast, exceptional operations can be supported through modes that temporarily redefine an application's "normal" controls. This makes the exceptional status explicit.

Disadvantages of modes

Although modes have certain advantages, they also have significant costs, which are borne by the users. When a software product or service has modes, its users must

- *Preplan mode settings:* Before they need a mode, they have to think to set it.

- *Set modes:* Setting modes requires extra actions, which are probably foreign to the software's target task domain.

- *Remember the current mode:* They have to keep track of what mode the software is in.

- *Recover from mode errors:* When they fail to do one of the first three items and make an error, they have to clean up afterward.

- *Yield to the software's control:* When software is designed so that it drives the interaction through a sequence of modes, constraining what users can do at each point, users must understand and accept that, even though they may prefer to be less constrained.

Since an important use of modes is to prespecify information to avoid having to supply it on every action, the value of modes is greatly reduced if the users' desired operations do not occur in sequences as supported by the modes, requiring frequent mode shifts. This is why moded software is often accused not only of fostering mode errors, but also of restricting users' options at particular points in the interaction. In other words, users of moded software may make errors because they can't keep track of what mode the program is in, but even if they can keep track, they may find that the mode the software is in is not the one they need at the moment.

Make mode indicators extremely difficult to miss

If an application has modes, it should provide very noticeable indications of the current mode. Two classic and influential user interface design handbooks provide the following recommendations regarding mode indicators:

> 6.4. Mode Designator. DISPLAY MODE INDICATORS—When the system is operating in a special mode for which a different set of commands or syntax rules are in effect, provide users with an indicator that distinguishes this mode from other modes. Provide differences in headings, formats, or prompts, and use labels to remind the user of the mode that is in effect. [Brown, 1988]

> 3.4.4. Display of Operation Mode—When context for sequence control is established in terms of a defined operational mode, remind users of the current mode and other pertinent information. [Smith and Mosier, 1986]

 ### Modes in software products

> *Eudora Pro 4.0 for Macintosh: email send modes.* Qualcomm's popular email software, Eudora Pro 4.0, has many modes. Figure 5.22 shows the top of the email composition window. Most of the items in the toolbar are mode settings for the message being prepared. They play dual roles of allowing users to set the mode and showing the current setting. For example, the third item from the left is a menu for setting the type of encoding to be used for sending attached docu-

Figure 5.22

Figure 5.23

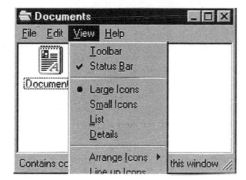

ments with this message. Even though this mode setting seems fairly well indicated, I didn't notice it for years, and wondered why attachments I sent were always binhex-encoded. The item at the left of the middle cluster (labeled "A*b*") is a push-on, push-off togglebutton that controls and indicates whether the Style toolbar is displayed. This is an example of a mode setting that, although it needs a control for setting the mode, doesn't really need an indicator because the Style toolbar is either plainly visible or it isn't. The button positioned second from the right end of the middle cluster is a togglebutton that controls and indicates whether the body of the message will be encrypted. When pushed in, message encryption is ON. Note that all these settings affect what will happen when the message is sent, rather than affecting the message immediately.

Windows: tile view mode. Perhaps the world's most familiar software mode setting is the View mode in Microsoft Windows file folders and in Windows Explorer, shown in Figure 5.23. Depending on the view mode, files are listed as large icons, small icons, by name, or by name with extra details (e.g., size). The only explicit indicator of the current view mode is in the View menu, which is not usually shown. However, that is OK because, like the Style toolbar mode in Eudora, an explicit mode indicator isn't really needed; users can see what the current view mode is by how files are displayed.

Macintosh floppy disk: write-enabled/protected mode. When a Macintosh user opens a floppy diskette, MacOS 8.0 displays the contents of the disk in a window (shown in Figure 5.24) that is similar to a folder window. If the diskette is write-protected, a small lock symbol is included in the upper left of the window. If the

Figure 5.24

Figure 5.25

Figure 5.26

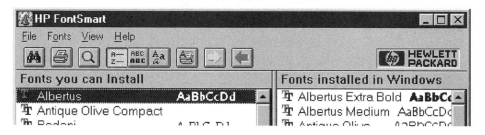

diskette isn't locked, the lock symbol is absent. This mode indicator seems clear enough once a user knows to look for it. However, like the attachment encryption mode in Eudora, it is easily missed. A common mode error among Mac users is to try to copy files onto a locked diskette.

ATI Media Player: display mode. The Media Player software from ATI Technologies, Inc., has an unusual mode setting. The software's main window can be set so that it is "stuck" to the computer screen and so always remains in front of all other windows, or it can be set to behave like any other application window. The setting is controlled and indicated by a togglebutton at the top right of the window—the one labeled with a pushpin in Figure 5.25. If the mode is set to "stuck to screen" (the default mode), the pin is shown sticking into the button; otherwise, the pin is shown lying on the button (as shown above). This mode control/indicator is easily missed, especially since the setting is unusual. My guess is that many Media Player users don't notice this button and don't know what it does.

Hewlett-Packard FontSmart: sort mode. Hewlett-Packard's font management software FontSmart has a sorting mode: the fonts that are available on a user's computer can be listed alphabetically by name or by font similarity. The mode control and indicator is a pair of buttons on the application's toolbar, positioned just below the Help menu (see Figure 5.26). The two buttons at the left of the middle group operate as radiobuttons; only one of them can be pushed in at a time. The left button sorts the fonts alphabetically; the right one sorts them by font appearance. One design flaw that detracts from the effectiveness of this mode indicator is that the rightmost button in the middle group, which is also labeled with letters, is not part of the mode setting/indicator, even though it looks like it is. It is a command button that loads new fonts into the program. This might confuse new users. It's an unfortunate flaw, but users can learn to overlook it. Even though users can see the fonts listed below, it is not always possible to determine solely from the font listing what the current sort mode is, so the mode indicator is often helpful.

The best kind of mode indicator is called "spring-loaded"—users hold the system in an alternative mode (for example, by holding a key down) and as soon as they let go, the software reverts to the "normal" mode. The spring-loaded mode setting most people have encountered is the SHIFT key on typewriter and computer keyboards. Computer keyboards usually require more modes than typewriters do, and so have additional "shift" keys, for example, CONTROL. In contrast, the CAPS LOCK key on keyboards is not a spring-loaded mode control: it stays where it is set until pressed a second time.

When mode indicators are not spring-loaded, they must either be put right where the user is looking (e.g., on the mouse pointer) or be large and attention-grabbing (e.g., flashing red). It doesn't work to put a little mode indicator in a corner of the display because most users will overlook it.

For example, the Xerox Star's Move and Copy commands were moded.[6] They operated as follows: select object to be moved or copied, press Move or Copy button on keyboard (Star enters Move or Copy mode), point to destination (Star moves or copies object to destination). While Star was waiting for the user to point to a destination, it indicated that it was in Move or Copy mode by temporarily changing the mouse pointer to a little Move or Copy symbol. Because users were very likely to be looking at the mouse pointer, it was difficult for users not to notice when Star was in Move or Copy mode rather than in its normal mode.

 ## Modes in noncomputer devices

Condensed from Johnson [1990]:

Modes are not a recent phenomenon. We've lived with them for decades, if not forever. They can be found in many of the non-computer-based devices and appliances we use everyday. The following are some examples of modes in everyday devices, and the problems they cause. Hopefully, an understanding of modes in noncomputer devices, and how people cope with them, will help designers of computer-based products and services create easier-to-learn and less-error-prone software.

Slide projectors. Slide projectors are fairly simple devices; their controls are usually modeless. The controls usually consist of a pair of buttons for advancing to the next and previous slide, and either a dial or a pair of buttons for focusing the image.

However, not all slide projectors are so mode-free. I used to have one that was quite moded. It had one button labeled "Advance," and a switch that controlled whether the "Advance" button changed to the next or previous slide (see Figure 5.27). It thus had a "direction" mode that could be set to either "forward" or "backward."

---

6. Unlike the Apple Lisa and Macintosh Copy, Cut, and Paste commands, which are modeless.

Figure 5.27

One might defend the designers of this projector by arguing that the usual modeless design doesn't take into account that showing the previous slide is less common than is showing the next one. However, if that were the justification for the moded design, one would expect the direction switch to be spring-loaded, with "forward" as the home position. On my projector, it was not, so I frequently made the obvious mode error: backing up when I intended to go forward. Not surprisingly, the manufacturer of this projector has gone out of business.[7]

Automobiles. Automobiles are one of the more complicated interactive devices that people use, even including computers. Driving a car is a skill learned only with difficulty. However, once one has learned, driving becomes second nature; the car seems like an extension of the driver. Software developers would like their products and services to be as successful as automobiles, so it is worthwhile to examine the user interface of automobiles for modes.

One mode setting in automobiles is the gearshift; the effect of pressing the gas pedal depends on what gear mode the car is in. Pressing the gas pedal when the car is in an unexpected or inappropriate gear is a mode error. Some such errors are worse than others: attempting to start moving when the car is in fourth gear simply stalls the car, whereas having the car in reverse when the user thought it was in first, or vice versa, can cause an accident. Note that automatic transmissions remove only the less dangerous of these mode errors.

Another mode setting, found only in manual-shift cars, is the clutch: engaged or not engaged. A mode error consists of accidentally revving the engine when the clutch is disengaged, or trying to start the engine when the clutch is engaged.

---

7.   The most plausible excuse for these awkward slide controls was that Kodak had patented the "correct" design and did not license it to competitors. To avoid infringing on Kodak's patent, competitors were forced to provide poorly designed slide controls.

Fortunately, the clutch control is spring-loaded, providing the driver with continuous tactile feedback about the current clutch mode, as well as explicit support for the fact that "engaged" is the usual mode and "disengaged" is the exceptional one. Imagine what driving a manual-transmission car would be like if the clutch weren't spring-loaded, forcing drivers to remember to switch it back and forth.

Ovens. Some ovens in the United States are moded in that they have an OFF/BAKE/BROIL/SELF-CLEAN mode dial that is separate from the OFF/Temperature dial. What the Temperature dial does is determined by how the mode dial is set. Users make mode errors with such ovens: they turn on the temperature setting, fail to check the mode setting, and discover later that it wasn't set as they wanted.

People rarely self-clean pies. Because that mode is rarely used, the oven is rarely left inadvertently in that mode. It is more common to broil cakes and bake steaks. By far the most common mode error is to discover, just before a meal, that the food in the oven is still raw because even though the Temperature dial was set correctly, the mode dial was set to OFF. It is predictable that this is the most common mode error because when a user sets the Temperature dial and forgets to set the mode dial, OFF is how it usually will be set.

The most common mode error could be removed by removing the OFF setting from the mode control. It serves no useful purpose anyway, since the Temperature dial and thermostat ultimately determine whether the oven is ON or OFF. The "default" setting on the mode dial would then be BAKE, which is much more likely to be what a user wants than is OFF. In other words, oven manufacturers could reduce the likelihood of mode errors by making the most commonly used mode the default one.

Cameras. Most cameras have many mode settings. One is the ASA or film speed setting. It adjusts the camera for different types of film, which, in turn, are best suited for different light conditions. The consequences of a mode error—taking all or part of a roll of film with the camera set to the wrong ASA—can be serious: film is wasted and possibly important photographs are lost.

Of course, the ASA setting is not the only mode dimension on "manual" cameras. It is possible to take a picture at the wrong shutter speed, the wrong aperture, the wrong focus, and, with some cameras, with the lens cap on.

Cameras that force users to set all of these controls are usable by only a small subset of the population. Originally designed only for professional photographers and serious hobbyists who presumably want total control over all possible parameters of their camera's operation, such cameras have over the years become more user friendly through the addition of automatic settings for most of the controls. This renders them relatively modeless in that the automatic settings are determined anew for each photograph, and by the camera instead of by the user. Modern cameras even solve the ASA mode problem by having bar codes on the film cartridge to identify the film's speed to the camera. Of course, serious photographers sometimes *want* to make ASA mode errors: they shoot at the "wrong"

ASA and then "push" the film during development. Thus, cameras intended for serious photographers must include a way to disable the "solution" for the ASA mode problem.

Cameras designed for the masses have a completely different history. Previously, the approach to making them usable was to greatly limit their adjustability. For example, users didn't have to focus the old Brownies, Instamatics, and Polaroids because they were permanently focused at four feet to infinity. Similarly, the shutter interval and aperture were fixed and the view angle was so wide that the camera barely had to be pointed. The ASA mode problem was handled not by limiting the cameras to one type of film, but by putting notches on the film cartridge so that the camera could tell, say, whether the user was using color or black-and-white film. More recently, the evolution of snapshot cameras has been following a path similar to that of more sophisticated cameras. Automatic focus and aperture have largely replaced fixed focus and aperture. Thus, to increase camera flexibility to diverse photographic conditions, device intelligence is replacing lack of functionality as the way of preventing mode errors.

Toasters.   The Darkness setting on toasters is a mode setting. This setting affects what happens when users put bread into the toaster and turn it on. Mode errors consist of burned or "raw" toast.

The nominal purpose of the Darkness setting is to allow users to set the toaster for their preferences. In this nominal role, it would not be moded in practice because users would set the Darkness once and never change it unless they were making toast for someone with different tastes. If this were what the Darkness setting were actually for, mode errors would be very rare.

Of course, that isn't really what it's for. The Darkness setting is misnamed. It controls the duration of toasting or the target temperature inside the toaster rather than the actual shade of the bread. For a given type of bread, both time and temperature are correlated with toast shade, but across different types of bread, the correlation is low; the same setting that turns French bread into smoking carbon barely warms German vollkornbrot. The Darkness setting is actually used mainly to set the toaster for different types of bread, rather than for different users. Most mode errors occur because a user forgets to reset the toaster when putting in a different type of bread from last time.

Another variable when toasting bread is the initial temperature of the bread— for example, whether the bread is frozen or fresh. Someone may buy two loaves of bread, and freeze one and use the other right away. A setting suitable for fresh bread would not be suitable for frozen bread, and vice versa.

One way to eliminate toaster mode errors is to make the toaster modeless by requiring users to set the time or temperature with each use. This sounds unacceptable until one realizes that microwave ovens do exactly that. It seems that toaster designers assume that users tend to stick with one type of bread, while microwave oven designers assume that users heat a wide variety of foods in an unpredictable order.

5.3.3 Blooper 52: Installation nightmares

It doesn't matter how well-designed software is if people who want to use it have to go through Hell to get it installed and working correctly. Unfortunately, many software products are a nightmare to install and set up, even many that are otherwise usable and useful.

My brother, a businessman and father with two kids, sometimes calls on me to help him with computer problems. He says: "Installing software is the *worst*, most time-consuming and frustrating part about owning a computer. It *never* goes as the instructions say it will." And he owns a *Macintosh*.

Currently, setup difficulties are a huge drag on people's acceptance of computer technology and therefore on the success of the industry. To get personal computers and their assorted peripheral devices, people have to master all sorts of things they would prefer to ignore: cables, connectors, "read me" files, drivers, virtual memory, scalable versus nonscalable fonts, software conflicts. Installation procedures often contain confusing and even out-of-date instructions. It is almost as if computer and software companies didn't care about the installation experiences of their customers. Put bluntly, the situation is outrageous, and should be considered the shame of the computer industry.

Some personal installation nightmares. In late 1996, I bought Bill Gates's book, *The Road Ahead* [1996]. It comes with a CD-ROM that lets you read the book online, follow hypertext links, see videos of Bill Gates, and so on. The instructions for installing the CD are very simple...appropriate for a book about how wonderful it will be when we're all online. Unfortunately, they didn't work. When I tried to open the book, a dialog box appeared reading: "Cannot find VBRUN300.DLL." After trying for a few days to find the missing file, I called the customer support number. The fellow said: "Oh, that file is supposed to be installed from the CD. I guess it wasn't for some reason."

Think about those words "for some reason." It's as if my computer were an unpredictable being that follows instructions or not depending on its mood or the phase of the moon. Excuse me, aren't computers supposed to be the ultimate in predictability and slavish adherence to instructions? Is someone not adequately testing their installation scripts, perchance?

A product for which I found the installation especially difficult and frustrating was Eudora Pro 4.0, a popular email program. In Chapter 9, I provide a blow-by-blow account of my experiences in trying to install Eudora.

For someone like me who has a great deal of computer experience, installation nightmares like those described here and in Chapter 9 are just time-wasting, teeth-grinding annoyances, but for many would-be computer users, they are insurmountable barriers.

For example, my brother the businessman tells me his patience for software installation problems lasts about 20 minutes at a time, including time spent on

Other installation nightmares

Here are two nightmarish installation experiences I had. Unfortunately, they were not dreams:

- *Example 1:* A few years ago, I signed up for an online service at home. From the day I first tried to install the software and log on, to the day I actually logged on, took *one month*. A month of calling customer support every few days to try their next theory. I ended up taking my computer to their office and letting someone there find and fix the problem.

- *Example 2:* Two years later, the same Internet service sent me a CD-ROM containing a software upgrade. I hesitated to install it because of the previous installation fiasco, but the service eventually sent me email saying that I had to upgrade because they were phasing out support for the old version, so I crossed my fingers and started the installation procedure. Unfortunately, the installation script aborted in the middle, complaining that the CD contained "disk errors." Repeated attempts yielded the same result. So not only was the new version not installed, the old one had been partially replaced so that it no longer worked. They must not test their disks before they send them to hapless customers. A day later, I had the old version working again well enough to get by temporarily. After another month of phone calls and emails to customer support, I finally had the new version up and running. I would have switched online services, except that friends who used other services had similar stories.

the phone talking with customer support people. If after 20 minutes of struggling to get something installed on his computer, he hasn't managed to get it working, he decides that he has better things to do with his time, and either shelves the effort for later or abandons it entirely. He has a lot of software that has remained partially installed for months—in some cases even years. I believe he is typical of many Americans who own home computers.

Studies of computer use show installation is a serious problem. My foregoing examples are all anecdotal—illustrative, but not necessarily definitive. Two tests of online services in consumer households provide more systematic data. I will summarize them briefly. For details, see the articles in an issue of *Communications of the ACM* guest-edited by Kraut [1996].

In 1995, US West conducted a test of online services in Winona, MN. They had set up a civic net centered around schools to connect schoolkids, teachers, and parents. They provided families with training on setting up and using the system. Their results:

> The biggest obstacle was setup...*Two months* after training, many families had still failed to get set up...Families rated setup tasks more difficult than Internet tasks. [emphasis added]

It took housecalls evenings and weekends by support people to get everyone online.

Also in 1995, Carnegie-Mellon University conducted a test in Pittsburgh. They lent or sold (at reduced price) PCs and modems to 48 families. They supplied a simplified Internet access system: a custom family Web page providing access to email, Web, newsgroups, and MUDs.

Their results: Again, setup was a big problem. Obstacles included bad phone lines, busy signals, poor user interfaces, buggy software, forgotten passwords, erased logon scripts, depressed shift-lock keys, you name it.

Here are some observations common to both studies:

- Families couldn't diagnose problems because they had no basic understanding of the technology.

- Whereas computer professionals faced with a difficult software installation might struggle with the problems for a while, then give up and call customer support, for the people observed in these studies, giving up meant not calling support, but rather just saying "the heck with it."

- Kids are more willing to use trial and error. Parents are timid, afraid of doing the wrong thing.

- Teenagers pick it up fastest, but they often lack understanding. They just learn what works and tolerate arbitrariness.

- Teenagers rarely help other family members, much to the chagrin of the researchers, who hoped teenagers would act as in-house experts. But parents don't like asking their teenagers for help, especially since the teenagers are often impatient: "Dad, like duh! What's so hard?"

- Customer support lines are usually unavailable at times when parents can use the computer.

- Many families have only one phone line, so if they are talking to support, they aren't online, and vice versa, making it rather difficult to diagnose problems by phone.

Reed Hundt, former chair of the Federal Communications Commission, said in a speech at a major computer conference in 1997:

> The number of people who tried the Internet and gave up is equal to the number of Internet users. No other popular technology has that drop-out rate.

Avoiding Blooper 52: *The design rule*

The computer industry has got to get serious about improving installation experiences for the average consumer. Its failure to do so has been, and will continue to be, a heavy drag on the expansion of its market.

The industry must give high priority to improving customers' installation experiences

People have got to be able to bring software home (or download it from the Web), install it, start it up, and have it just work. With electronic information appliances, they need to be able to bring it home, take it out of the box, plug it in, turn it on, and start using it. This is already the case with simple electrical (not electronic) home appliances like toasters and washing machines. It is also true of dedicated game-playing consoles. It is not yet true of personal computers and the application software that runs on them. It also isn't yet true of all electronic information appliances. However, it needs to become true.

User interface professionals must take an interest in installation

Particular responsibility falls on user interface professionals. We often help design and test software products and services, but are rarely involved in designing and testing the installation process. We should take the aforementioned study results and Mr. Hundt's comment as a challenge and get to work on this. The procedure for installing any software should be considered part of the software's user interface. If the installation procedure is confusing or full of glitches, that reflects poorly on the usability of the software as a whole.

Correcting difficult installation: Two case studies

To show the kinds of things that computer and software companies can do to eliminate or minimize installation nightmares, I will briefly describe efforts undertaken by two different software companies. The first story describes an effort to simplify the installation process for a single software application. The second story describes a major effort by a large software company to improve installability across its entire product line.

- *Simplifying installation for a software product.* A colleague who designs user interfaces at a software company told me that customers were complaining that a product he had helped design was a nightmare to install and configure correctly. He realized he had never tried installing it. Soon thereafter, while on temporary assignment in Europe, he had to install it. According to the instructions, installation was supposed to take about 15 minutes. He discovered that that was only one of many false statements in the instructions. The instructions were quite obsolete; they had not been updated to reflect recent changes in the software and the installation procedure. Furthermore, at frequent intervals, the installation script prompted him to make decisions or enter data for which he lacked sufficient information. After several repetitions of the installation procedure, he managed to guess the correct responses based on his knowledge of the software. The total elapsed installation time was four hours. When he returned from Europe, he initiated an effort to simplify the installation process. Today, installing the product requires users to make only one decision: the destination folder on their hard disk where the software is to be installed. After that, they can push a button and go to lunch, confident that the software will be installed when they return.

- *Improving installability across a product line.* The products of a major server software company were being beaten up in the marketplace by competitors that were less functional but easier to install and configure. For example, optional features in the company's products each had their own installation and configuration tools, which besides being separate were often designed inconsistently. In contrast, competitor products tended to have a single, integrated installation and configuration tool that handled all optional features. Although the company had previously enjoyed significant market share, its market share was eroding. One reason was that the market was maturing; ease of installation and use was becoming more important to customers. The company's management realized they had to change how they developed, packaged, and distributed software. To guide this effort, they made "installability," "configurability," and "usability" strategic goals for a specified future major release of the product line. Managers throughout the company were to be evaluated based on their success in achieving this. Management also decided to provide a course for developers and development managers to convey the importance of the strategic goals and methods for achieving them. A colleague and I were hired as consultants to develop that course. As of this writing, the effort is still underway, so I cannot report results, but the fact that management decided to make such steps is itself significant.

5.4 Diabolical dialog boxes

The final category of interaction bloopers is concerned with common errors involving dialog boxes.

5.4.1 Blooper 53: Too many levels of dialog boxes

Sometimes GUI developers are so focused on the design of particular windows in a software application (or pages in a Web site) that they don't step back to look at the larger picture. How many windows (or Web pages) are there, and how easy is it for users to find their way around in them? As a result, many software products and services have far too many windows or pages, or window/page hierarchies in which users get lost easily. "Where am I? How did I get

Figure 5.28 Checkbook window hierarchy

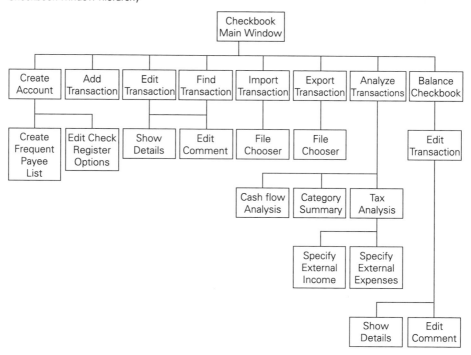

here? How do I get back to where I was? Where the heck is that Line Width set-ting? What was I doing before the phone rang? "

When I review a software product or a Web site for a client, I usually con-struct a representation of the software's entire window or Web page structure. Creating this representation lets me see the "big picture." My preference is to represent the structure as a graph (see Figure 5.28), but some of the software I've reviewed has had so many windows or pages that a graph would have been impractical because it would have covered an entire wall or it would have been such a tangled mess of boxes and lines that it would not have been helpful. In such cases, I use an outline instead of a graph (see Figure 5.29).

Constructing a graph or outline that lays out the entire window or page structure of an application or Web site lets me see places where the structure may be too deep. Imagine an application in which a user can select a data object displayed in the main window and ask to see the object's properties. The properties are displayed in a dialog box. Suppose the object has a lot of proper-ties—so many that the designer elected to hide some under a Details button. Clicking the Details button displays another dialog box containing settings. Thus, the application contains a dialog box on a dialog box. Now suppose that in the Details dialog box, one of the settings is a list of items. To edit the list items, users click on an Edit List... button, displaying yet another dialog box—

Figure 5.29   *Checkbook window hierarchy*

- Checkbook Main Window
    - Create Account
        - Create Frequent Payee List
        - Edit Check Register Options
    - Add Transaction
        - Show Details
        - Edit Comment
    - Edit Transaction
        - Show Details
        - Edit Comment
    - Find Transaction
    - Import Transactions
        - File Chooser
    - Export Transactions
        - File Chooser
    - Analyze Transactions
        - Cash Flow Analysis
        - Category Summary
        - Tax Analysis
            - Specify External Income
            - Specify External Expenses
    - Balance Checkbook
        - Edit Transaction
            - Show Details
            - Edit Comment

the one for editing the list. Thus, the application has a dialog box on a dialog box on a dialog box. Now suppose...well, never mind, you get the idea.

A real-world example of the blooper. Figure 5.30 shows a real-world example: a case in which Microsoft Windows displays five levels of dialog boxes. The user opens the Control Panel window (an application tool window, not a dialog box), opens the settings for the Display, clicks on the Change Display Type... button in the Display Properties dialog box, clicks on the Change... button in the Change Display Type dialog box, clicks on the Have Disk... button in the Select Device dialog box, and clicks on the Browse... button in the Install From Disk dialog box. Now, what were we doing?

Deep hierarchies of dialog boxes are a problem for two reasons: (1) they divert users from their original goals, and (2) users lose track of exactly which OK, Apply, and Cancel buttons are before them. Most computer users don't handle deep hierarchical information structures well; when they have followed a hierarchy down more than a few levels, they tend to lose track of where they are, what they were doing, and how to get back.

Figure 5.30

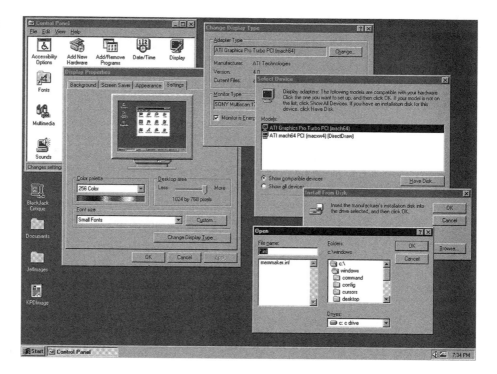

Other examples. The following are examples of feedback I gave to two different clients after reviewing their software, in one case a PC application and in the other a Web application (with details changed so as not to identify the clients or the products):

- The hierarchy outline shows that certain areas of StockUp's window hierarchy are too deep, for example, the hierarchy below the various Monitor windows (five levels) and that below the Analysis window (six levels). Making StockUp easy-to-use will require flattening these deep areas of the hierarchy.

- The graph shows that the designers' concern that the hierarchy of Web pages and dialog boxes is too deep is mostly unwarranted. The only area where the hierarchy seems too deep is in the networking monitoring and maintenance functions, which most users will not use.

Avoiding Blooper 53: *The design rule*

The general rule followed by many user interface designers is this: Avoid more than two levels of dialog boxes. A dialog box can bring up another dialog box, but beyond that, software developers would be making it too easy for users to lose their way.

However, I find this rule to be oversimplified and easy to misinterpret. I believe it should be clarified and qualified in two ways:

Qualification 1: It applies only to dialog boxes

Dialog boxes are relatively transient windows that allow users to specify arguments for a function, set attributes for a data object, or acknowledge having seen a message. As described under Blooper 5: Confusing primary windows with dialog boxes (Section 2.2.1), dialog boxes have window control buttons at the bottom of the window, do not have menubars or toolbars, and are usually (although not always) not resizable.

Many software applications display, in addition to their main window, not only dialog boxes but also other primary windows. Primary windows usually remain displayed for relatively long periods of time. As described under Blooper 5, primary windows include menubars, may include toolbars, and do not have window control buttons at the bottom. Primary windows function like outpost bases of operation and navigation; when they are in use, they serve as a temporary "home away from home." For this reason, they do not count in determining the depth limit of two levels.

On the other hand, primary windows should only come from other primary windows. Dialog boxes should not display primary windows.[8] If they did, it would be very unclear what should happen to a primary window when the user closed the dialog box that displayed it. Therefore, in a graph of an application's window hierarchy, no branch should ever have a primary window below a dialog box. Any single branch of the hierarchy should have some number of primary windows, followed by at most two dialog boxes. In practice, the number of levels of primary windows should also be kept low to avoid disorienting users, but so far, there is no widely used design rule.

The same qualification applies to Web sites and Web applications, but is a bit more complicated because of ambiguity about what qualifies as a dialog box in the Web environment. Obviously, most Web pages are not dialog boxes, and it makes no sense to limit how deeply they can be nested (although I've seen Web sites that could definitely stand improvement in navigability). After all, the whole point of the Web is to provide links to other relevant pages or sites. However, some Web sites and many Web-based applications do contain dialog boxes. The complication is that there are three quite different ways to display a "dialog box" on the Web:

- *True dialog boxes.* Most Web browsers can, when directed to do so by a Web site or Web application, display dialog boxes that are separate from the browser window. They look and behave exactly like dialog boxes in desktop software applications. Most of the popular Web browsers provide several types of dialog boxes, each intended for a specific purpose, such as error, warning, information, and file chooser.

---

8. With the exception of the Help document browser.

- *Separate browser windows.* Some Web applications display certain information or settings by creating a new browser window. This is done so that the page the user had been viewing can remain displayed. Sometimes the content of the new browser window is that of a dialog box: messages or settings with OK and Cancel (or similar) navigation buttons at the bottom.

- *Dialog-box-like pages.* Some Web applications contain normal pages that function as dialog boxes even though they are not displayed in separate windows. Their content is that of a dialog box: messages or settings with navigation buttons at the bottom. They are intended to be transient; users view them briefly, perhaps edit some settings, click OK or Cancel, and return to a previous page.

Web "dialog boxes," regardless of how they are displayed, are subject to the two-level limit. On the other hand, they are also subject to Qualification 2.

Qualification 2: Some types of dialog boxes don't count

Some dialog boxes provide functions that are so simple, idiomatic, and familiar that their presence is highly unlikely to distract or disorient users. Such dialog boxes should be considered exempt from the two-level limit.

For example, many software applications contain functions that require users to specify a filename. In most such software, users can either type the filename or they can invoke a file chooser dialog box to allow them to browse through the file hierarchy for the file, then choose it by clicking on it in a list. File choosers are so common and familiar that most users know what to do when they see them. Like a popup menu, a file chooser is not regarded by users as a "place" in the application, but rather simply as a choice mechanism. Paraphrasing Gertrude Stein, "there is no *there*" in a file chooser. The incremental impact of a file chooser on the perceived complexity of an application is negligible. Therefore, if a file chooser constituted a third dialog box level, I would not consider that to be a violation of the two-level rule. This includes other simple and common "chooser" dialog boxes as well, for example, color choosers and date choosers.

Another type of dialog box that should not be included when counting up dialog box levels is error messages that accept only one response: acknowledgment that the user saw the message.[9] As with choosers, the reason for exempting simple error dialog boxes is that they do not really add navigational "places" to the application, and thus do not noticeably increase the complexity of navigating in it.

Notice that the dialog boxes that are excluded from the two-level limit beget no dialog boxes of their own. In other words, they are all end points in the hier-

---

9.   They can also provide access to Help text, which is not technically a response to the dialog box.

archy. This is very important. Any dialog box that can display another dialog box, regardless of its type, should be counted against the two-level limit.

Graph or outline the window hierarchy

Of course, developers cannot be assured of conforming to the qualified two-level rule unless they keep track of the window structure within their applications. As stated above, many developers don't do this and end up with overly deep structures. I highly recommend creating and maintaining a graph or outline of the window structure as part of the design process. Such a representation can also be used as an illustration in the software's user documentation.

When constructing a representation of the window hierarchy, the only windows I leave out are the various error dialog boxes displayed by the software. It is often difficult for me to discover them all (and I find that the developers seldom can tell me what they are), not to mention that including them would make the graphs or outlines even more unwieldy than they usually are.

Ways to eliminate excess layers

Assuming that a particular application's developers are aware of the application's window hierarchy and feel that there are too many levels in some places, what are their alternatives? The answer is, It depends on why the designers put settings onto separate dialog boxes.

- Sometimes designers use additional dialog boxes as a means of providing progressive disclosure—hiding details until a user asks to see them. In such cases, an alternative is to use a "hidden" panel rather than a separate dialog box.

- Sometimes designers use a dialog box to provide variations on a command the user has given. Consider, for example, Microsoft Word's Change Case command in the Format menu. It displays a dialog box prompting the user to indicate the manner in which the case of the selected text should be changed (see Figure 5.31). This dialog box is not in fact embedded in excessive levels, so there is no need to eliminate it, but imagine for the sake of this discussion that it was. A designer could eliminate the dialog box by putting the choices in cascading menus, as illustrated Figure 5.32.

 Figure 5.31

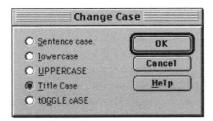

Figure 5.32

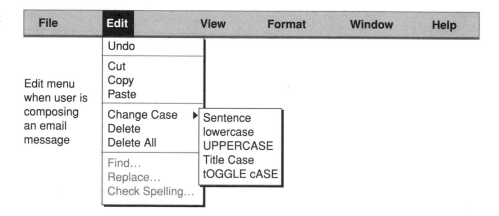

Edit menu when user is composing an email message

5.4.2 Blooper 54: Dialog boxes that trap users

A particularly annoying design error one often sees in GUI software is dialog boxes that provide no way out other than a direction that users don't really want to go in. This blooper comes in two main variations.

Variation A: No choice. First, there are dialog boxes that display a message announcing that something horrible has happened or is about to happen, and asking the user to indicate (at least implicitly) that that's OK (see Figure 5.33). Even if the user understands the cause of the problem, there is nothing he or she can do about it but sigh (or curse), acknowledge the message, and start over. And perhaps consider buying different software. Even when such cases are actually unavoidable, labeling the acknowledgment button "OK" just throws salt on the user's wound. No, not OK.

Variation B: All paths are wrong. A second form of this blooper is dialog boxes that provide more than one way out, but omit one or more choices that users are likely to want. For example, Microsoft Office optionally displays a taskbar along the edge of the screen. If a user clicks the Close button on the Office Shortcut taskbar, the dialog box in Figure 5.34 appears. Besides being overly wordy, this dialog box traps the user: There's no way to Cancel out of the Close operation altogether if it was initiated by mistake. Users are forced to choose between "Yes, close the taskbar now but start it again automatically when I restart Windows" and "No, close the taskbar and don't start it automatically when I restart Windows." Users cannot choose "Oops, I don't want to close the taskbar" even though that will often be what they want.

Sometimes a dialog box exhibits Variation B of the blooper because some of the options it nominally provides are temporarily inactive for some reason. For example, the Microsoft Windows Phone Dialer accessory starts by displaying a wizard—user interface jargon for a multipage dialog box—that gathers the nec-

Figure 5.33

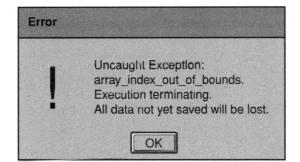

Error

> ! Uncaught Exception:
> array_index_out_of_bounds.
> Execution terminating.
> All data not yet saved will be lost.
>
> OK

Figure 5.34

Microsoft Office Shortcut Bar

> You are closing the Office Shortcut Bar. The Office Shortcut Bar will start again automatically when you start Windows. Do you want the Office Shortcut Bar to start automatically when you start Windows?
>
> Yes   No

essary information from the user. The first page of the wizard (shown in Figure 5.35) asks the user to supply a country, a telephone area code, and, optionally, an outside-line prefix.

The main problem with this wizard is that, when it first appears, the Cancel button is for some reason disabled.[10] The wizard also has the usual Close control on its titlebar, but while the Cancel button is disabled, the Close control also does nothing. This prevents users from quitting the Phone Dialer immediately if they started it by mistake or just to find out what it does. The only available action is clicking on OK, which means "proceed to the next step of the wizard." The user is trapped.

To make matters even worse, clicking OK without filling in an area code is not allowed. If the user does it, the dialog shown in Figure 5.36 is displayed, and the user is not allowed to proceed until he or she has typed an area code. Thus, a user who just wants to get out of the Phone Dialer is not only trapped, but also forced to enter information needlessly, to proceed to a unknown (to the user) next step where hopefully a way out of the program will be available. Major blooper!

Variation C: Poorly described choices. Often dialog boxes only *seem* to trap users; the choices are labeled so unclearly that users aren't sure which one is the one they want. When users encounter such dialog boxes, they are forced to switch from thinking about their task to problem solving about how to operate the software.

---

10. I was not able to determine why the Cancel button is disabled or how to enable it.

Figure 5.35

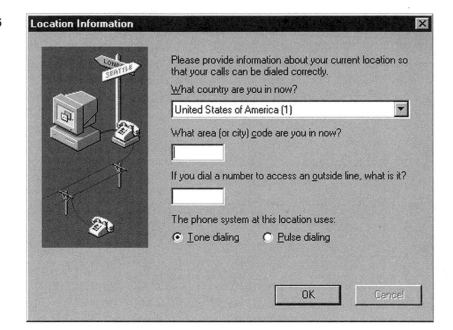

Figure 5.36

For example, if a user opens a Microsoft Word document that is already open, the dialog box in Figure 5.37 is displayed. Let's consider what different options users might want in this situation. Users could have arrived in this situation with any one of three possible intentions:

1. The user didn't realize that the document was already open. Opening it a second time was an accident. In this case, the user would want to simply back out of the second attempt to open the document.

2. The user knew that the document was already open, but wants to replace the version he or she was editing with the last saved version.

3. The user knew that the document was already open, but wants to open the last saved version in a separate window in order to compare the two.

One clear problem with this dialog box is that it provides for only two of the three quite plausible user intentions. As it happens, the intentions provided for

Figure 5.37

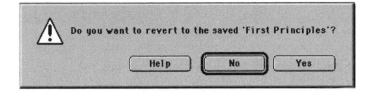

are 1 and 2. Clicking the No button cancels the attempt to open the document. That button is highlighted to indicate that it is the default choice, that is, the one that can be chosen by simply pressing the RETURN key on the keyboard. Apparently, the designer considered No to be the choice users would usually want. Clicking the Yes button replaces the currently opened version of the document with the last saved version. Users with Intention 3 are simply out of luck. Thus, for users with Intention 3, this dialog box commits the interaction blooper of trapping the user: none of the choices is what the user wants.

However, there is another, possibly worse, problem with this dialog box: unclear labeling. Although it is clear from the wording of the displayed question that the Yes button corresponds to Intention 2, it is unclear whether the No button corresponds to Intention 1 or Intention 3. Users may not know that this dialog box supports only Intentions 1 and 2.

The problem with the button labels in this dialog box is similar to Blooper 10: Using a checkbox for a non-ON/OFF setting (Section 2.3.3). Users cannot immediately deduce the meaning of the "negative" response from that of the "positive" one.

If users arrive at this dialog box with Intention 1 or 3, they are likely to stare at the dialog box for many seconds, reading and rereading it until they have convinced themselves that the opposite of "revert to saved" must be what they want, and finally press the No button. If they wanted to cancel the Open operation (Intention 1), they will be in luck because that's what the No button does. They wasted several seconds deducing what button to press, but at least they got what they wanted.

However, if they wanted to open the saved version of the document in a *new* window (Intention 3), most users will be quite perplexed by what happens: nothing. They may assume that the new window opened right over the old one, and so move the window aside to see what is under it. Perhaps they will try again to open the document on the assumption that something went wrong the first time. Maybe they'll even figure out that Intention 3 isn't supported and that what they got was Intention 1. In any case, they will have wasted many seconds—perhaps even minutes—thinking about the software, rather than about the document they are writing. Furthermore, because most users will encounter this dialog box fairly rarely (e.g., every few months), they may not remember from one time to the next what the No button does.

The designer of this dialog box may have assumed that users know (as the designer does) what the two supported actions are, and so would know what the opposite of "revert to saved" is. Perhaps it didn't occur to the designer that some users might arrive at the dialog box with anything but Intentions 1 (accidental Open) or 2 (intentional Revert).

To his or her credit, the designer of this dialog box did provide some extra guidance (in addition to the highlighting of the No button): a Help button. Clicking it displays a fairly clear explanation of which button users should click if they have Intentions 1 or 2. Intention 3 (open saved version in separate window) is not mentioned, so most users could probably figure out that it isn't supported. However, in my experience, it is the rare user who actually presses the Help button. Also, it can be argued that the Help button is only necessary because the labels of the other buttons are unclear.

Microsoft Word also contains a dialog box that traps users not by providing too few options, but rather by being unclear about what Word is going to do. When a user invokes the Print command and sets the resulting Print dialog box to print a specific range of pages rather than the entire document, Word requires the user to specify the numbers of the pages that are to be printed. If the user specifies page numbers that are invalid, Word displays the dialog box in Figure 5.38.

The message in this dialog box is really trying to say: "I'm going to take you back to the Print dialog box, but adjust the page numbers you typed so that they are within range, OK?" However, the message is worded such that most users will interpret it as saying: "I'm going to adjust the page numbers you typed and print the document, OK?" Because most users will want a chance to correct the page numbers before printing, and because the dialog box does not seem to provide that option, most users who get this dialog box will stare at it for a while, trying to figure out what to do, then finally accept the fact that they have no choice but to click OK and get a printout of pages they don't want. When they find themselves back at the Print dialog box and (eventually) realize that nothing is printing, they will realize that they did in fact get what they wanted.

This dialog box is even more troublesome when one considers some of the situations in which it can appear. Suppose a user finishes editing a section of a document and invokes Print. When the Print dialog box appears, the user clicks in one of the page number fields. Word automatically sets the dialog box to print a range of pages rather than all pages. Suppose the user is then distracted by something—the phone rings or someone comes into the office to chat. When the user eventually turns her attention back to the computer, she sees the Print dialog box, but fails to notice that the page number fields are still blank, and clicks OK to start the document printing. Up pops this dialog box. What would be going through the user's mind at that point?

Figure 5.38

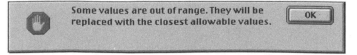

Some values are out of range. They will be
replaced with the closest allowable values.

OK

Figure 5.39

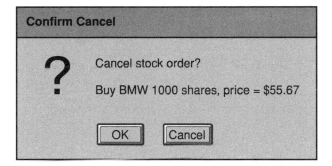

Occasionally, one sees dialog boxes that, while they actually do provide the required choices, are so confusing that users feel trapped anyway. I'm thinking in particular of a dialog box displayed by a prerelease version of an online stock investment service that one of my clients had developed. The service showed users the status of stock orders that they previously placed, and allowed orders not yet fully executed to be canceled. To cancel an order, users selected the order in a list and clicked a Cancel button. If they did this, up would pop a dialog box similar to Figure 5.39.

You guessed it: clicking the OK button canceled the stock order, and clicking the Cancel button didn't cancel it. When I explained that the labeling of the buttons might confuse users, the programmer initially argued that the right way to think about it was that "OK" approves the current operation, which happens to be a Cancel operation, and "Cancel" aborts the operation. Eventually, however, he conceded that some users might be confused about which button to press. In this case, it was very important to eliminate any possible confusion because erroneously canceling or not canceling a stock order can have serious—and expensive—consequences.

Avoiding Blooper 54: The design rule

The rule for avoiding this blooper is, when designing dialog boxes, especially error and warning dialog boxes, provide users with sufficient alternatives (when possible) that they won't feel trapped, and label the choices clearly so that there can be no confusion about what the choices are.

Analyze it! Compare available options against users' likely goals

It helps to perform an analysis like the one I did above for the Word dialog box: list all the intentions users could have had when they did whatever caused the dialog box to be displayed. Taking users' intentions into account helps because perception and comprehension are strongly influenced by what a person's intentions are at that moment. Users may interpret the same message text or button labels differently depending on what they were trying to do.

Then test it!

It is also very important to test the dialog boxes to make sure users understand them and that all the required choices are provided. Dialog boxes can be tested informally long before they are implemented, simply by showing hand-drawn sketches to people, explaining the situation that caused the dialog box to be displayed, and asking test participants to interpret what the message and the buttons mean. When more of the software has been designed, the dialog boxes can be tested in the context of the application using printed screen images. Finally, they can be tested in a working implementation.

Example

An example of an improvement on Word's previously mentioned "document already open" dialog box is provided by another Microsoft product: the spreadsheet Excel. It displays a dialog box for the same situation: attempting to open a file when that file is already open. It provides the same choices as Word's, but with a more tersely worded message, different button labels, different button order, and a different highlighted (default) choice (see Figure 5.40).

Ignoring the fact that the default in this dialog box is probably wrong (for the same reason that the one in Word's corresponding dialog box is probably right), I would argue that this dialog box's buttons are labeled more clearly than those in Word's dialog box. It is clear that the OK button corresponds to the Revert action, and probably clear enough that the Cancel button corresponds to canceling the Open operation, even though it doesn't indicate that explicitly.

If I were designing a dialog box for that situation, I would make it even clearer, so that there could be no uncertainty about what the choices were (see Figure 5.41). Of course, even if these instructions and button labels were perfectly clear—and only usability testing can determine that—this dialog box still has the problem that it omits one quite reasonable choice: opening the saved document in a new window. However, since the software does not provide that capability, the dialog box obviously cannot offer it as a choice. Therefore, the designer's objective should be to make clear what choices *are* offered, so that users who want the missing choice won't be misled into believing that one of the offered choices is it. The corresponding Help text could even explicitly state

Figure 5.40

Figure 5.41

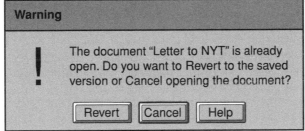

that opening the same document in two different windows is not possible without first copying it.

Bad: "Your work will be lost. [OK?]"

Finally, software developers should try very hard to avoid situations in which only one unpleasant choice is available. Often, this is just a matter of making sure that the application catches all the error conditions that can arise, so that handling them is not delegated to software outside of the application, such as the operating system.

When it is unavoidable that only one unpleasant choice is available, don't pretend that the situation is just like any benign announcement. "You have new mail" and "The program is going to crash and lose all your unsaved work" may both technically be simple announcements of fact for the user to acknowledge, but users regard them very differently. I would label the acknowledgment button "OK" for the former, but something like "Acknowledged," or "Understood," or even "Sigh....I hate computers!" for the latter.

5.4.3 Blooper 55: Cancel button doesn't cancel

Dialog boxes in GUI applications allow users to view and set the properties of data objects, or to view and edit arguments for a command. In both situations, dialog boxes normally provide at least two options for dismissing the dialog box:

- Apply any changed settings back to the corresponding application object or function before closing the dialog box.
- Close the dialog box, discarding any changed settings.

Often the first type of dismissing button is labeled "OK," but sometimes it is labeled with the name of the command that is the reason for the dialog box, for example, "Print." The second type of dismissing button is usually labeled "Cancel," but sometimes it is labeled "Close." Regardless of how the second type of button is labeled, I will refer to it as the Cancel button.

A very common error is for Cancel buttons on dialog boxes to fail to cancel changes a user has made in the dialog box. Users expect to be able to click on Cancel and have the software simply "forget" all the changes they have made in the dialog box since they opened it or clicked the Apply button (if provided). When Cancel doesn't cancel, the OK and Cancel buttons have the same meaning: close the dialog box and retain the settings. This causes users to get confused and annoyed.

In such cases, the problem is not in the code executed when the user clicks Cancel, which typically just closes the dialog box. The problem is in what happens *before* that, that is, when the user manipulates the contents of the dialog box. This blooper comes in four common variations.

Variation A: Dialog box is direct window onto application values. Sometimes this error is due to a simplistic implementation in which the dialog box is a direct window onto the relevant application data, rather than a window onto a *copy* of the application data. Changes to settings in such a dialog box change the application data directly and immediately. Canceling such changes is impossible unless a sophisticated multilevel Undo mechanism has been built-in to the application code, which is rare.

This error is especially common when the application data manipulated in the dialog box is complex, like a table. Programmers in such cases often don't take the trouble to copy the complex data structure so that the dialog box is editing a copy of the application's data. For example, the following is an excerpt from a user interface review I performed of a client's about-to-be-released product:

> In the "Tables Specification" dialog box, Cancel does not cancel changes that have been made. It simply closes the dialog box, leaving in effect any changes that have been made to the table.

This error is also sometimes seen when actions in a dialog box have side effects outside the application, such as creating or deleting disk files. Ideally, no changes to the environment that are specified in a dialog box should take effect until the user clicks OK, so users have an opportunity to cancel.

Variation B: Changing between tabbed panels implicitly applies changes. Cancel buttons that don't cancel are often seen in dialog boxes containing multiple tabbed panels. It is all too common that merely changing from one tabbed panel to another automatically—and without notice—applies any changes the user made in the first panel before switching to the newly chosen one, as if the user clicked the Apply button just before choosing a new tabbed panel. Programmers often implement tabbed panels this way to avoid having to store the data for one panel while displaying another. Whatever the excuse, it is still a mistake.

With dialog boxes containing tabbed panels that behave in this manner, it is a good bet that users who cancel the dialog box will be unpleasantly surprised that some of the changes they made since opening the dialog box were not canceled. As is explained under Blooper 12: Using tabs as radiobuttons (Section 2.3.5), experience shows clearly that users regard tabbed panels purely as a mechanism for navigating between panels. They don't expect that switching from one tabbed panel to another will have consequences for the future behavior of the application. Furthermore, users are unlikely to realize immediately why some setting changes were canceled and some weren't; it will seem mysterious or arbitrary to them. They will probably assume that they encountered a bug in the software.

One can perhaps explain users' expectations that tabs are only for navigation by recognizing that tabbed panels are basically a space-saving way of visually organizing settings into categories. Other visual organization schemes are also available. For example, with a large display screen, all the settings could be placed on one panel, grouped by category using labeled group boxes. In that case, it would clearly be wrong to apply changes made in one group to the application simply when the user moved the mouse and began editing a different group of settings. Why should the behavior be different if the groups of settings happen to be on overlapping tabbed panels?

Variation C: Canceling wizard doesn't cancel side effects of already-completed pages. A situation similar to multiple tabbed panels is seen in so-called wizard dialog boxes—dialog boxes that lead users toward a goal, break the choices and decisions down into a sequence of simple steps, and provide significant explanation and instruction along the way. Wizards contrast with the normal GUI approach of giving users access to all of the necessary controls and settings and letting them figure out which ones to set and the order in which to set them. A wizard therefore is a dialog box that has several pages. Users set the settings on each page (or accept the default values of the settings) and then click a Next button to proceed to the next page of the wizard. Wizards also provide Back buttons to allow users to return to previous steps, change settings there, and then proceed forward again.

Each panel of a wizard normally provides a Cancel button in addition to Next and Back buttons. Clicking on Cancel is supposed to close the wizard and abort the operation for which the wizard was collecting arguments. Unfortunately, some wizards don't actually cancel everything the user did in the wizard before clicking Cancel.

For example, suppose a company provides a wizard that employees can use to create their own Web site. Users proceed through the steps of the wizard providing the requested information, and when the wizard is done, the Web site has been created. Ideally, the wizard's steps just collect information; only on completion does the wizard actually construct the specified Web site. However, a developer might implement the wizard such that it constructs the Web site in a piecemeal fashion, as the user specifies the necessary information. If a wizard is implemented in this way, canceling out of it on, say, Step 4 might not clean up everything that had been created up to that point. Implementing wizards in this way is wrong, but unfortunately not everyone knows that.

As a second example, suppose a user invokes a wizard to design a data table to include in a document. Suppose that Step 1 of the wizard asks the user to select one of several predefined formats for the table. That step may also allow the user to define a custom format if none of the predefined ones are acceptable. If the user defines a custom format, proceeds to Step 2 of the wizard, and then decides to cancel the whole operation, the document editor may retain the new custom table format despite the fact that it was defined as part of an operation that was canceled. The designer may have done this intentionally, on the grounds that it is undesirable to lose the user's work in creating the custom table format, but users may be surprised later to find that the custom format has been retained. Usability testing would be required to resolve this.

Variation D: Multilevel dialog boxes. Another common case of Cancel buttons that don't cancel is seen when an application has multiple levels of dialog boxes. If dialog box A begot dialog box B, and a user makes changes in dialog box B and clicks its OK button, then cancels dialog box A, what happens to changes the user made to the settings in dialog box B?

In a sense, dialog box B acts as an extension of dialog box A. Its settings could, in a slightly different design, have been placed directly in dialog box A instead of in a separate dialog box. In that case, changes canceling dialog box A would definitely cancel changes to those settings. Why should the behavior be different if the settings happen to be in a separate subordinate dialog box? This argues that canceling dialog box A should cancel any changes made in dialog box B. However, in many software products, such changes have already taken effect and cannot be canceled. This is usually a mistake.

Avoiding Blooper 55: *The design rule*

Changes that users make in dialog boxes are not supposed to be applied to the application until the user clicks on OK (or the equivalent button) or Apply (if one is provided). No other action in the dialog box should cause the application data to be updated.

Cancel buttons are supposed to just close the dialog box and not apply any changes. Thus, when a user clicks Cancel, the application data remains as it was when the dialog box was opened or the user last clicked Apply.

Dialog boxes display a copy of application settings

To provide a true Cancel capability, dialog boxes should be initialized with a *copy* of the application settings. The Cancel button should simply discard the copied data and close the dialog box. Clicking OK or Apply should update the application's data with the corresponding data from the dialog box.

This should be true regardless of the complexity of the data manipulated by the dialog box, as illustrated in Figure 5.42. Even when dialog boxes give rise to other dialog boxes, every level of dialog box should be cancelable without affecting the values in the parent dialog box or the application.

Figure 5.42

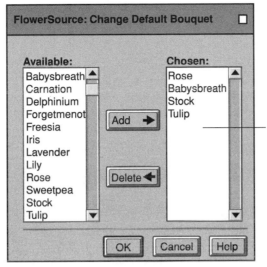

Even after a user has added several items to the Bouquet list or deleted several, canceling the dialog box should leave the Default Bouquet as it was before the Change Default Bouquet dialog box was opened.

Tabbed panels and multilevel dialog boxes are not valid excuses for the blooper

Changing from one tabbed panel to another in a dialog box is not one of the two actions (OK and Apply) that are allowed to update the application data. Switching from one tabbed panel to another should be treated as just an act of navigation. Each panel should retain its state until the dialog box is dismissed, and no settings on any of the panels should be applied to the application until the user explicitly commands it.

When a design has multiple levels of dialog boxes, consistent design suggests that canceling a parent dialog box should cancel changes that were made and applied in any child dialog boxes it displays. As stated earlier, this makes sense because the child dialog boxes are acting as extensions of the parent. I won't go so far as to say that canceling a parent dialog box should *always* cancel changes that were made in its children. But I do regard that as the ideal design—the one that should be implemented unless someone can make a very good case for doing otherwise. Furthermore, if one believes one is faced with a case that warrants an exception, one should (1) consult an experienced user interface designer before making a potentially costly error, and (2) test the design on representative users to see if it matches one's expectations before shipping the product.

Close and Reset

Dialog boxes often contain other buttons that are related to OK and Cancel in their behavior:

- *Close:* The convention for Close buttons is similar to that for Cancel buttons, but differs slightly. The Close button need not cancel changes that were applied from subordinate dialog boxes. It is generally used for dialog boxes that are designed to be kept open for long periods of time. Close buttons are usually paired with Apply buttons, rather than with OK buttons or buttons labeled with a specific command name.

■ *Reset:* The Reset button, where provided, is essentially a shortcut for canceling and reopening the dialog box. It is a way to revert to the settings as they were when the dialog box was last opened (or last applied, if there is an Apply button). Reset is rarely provided.

5.4.4 Blooper 56: OK and Cancel do the same thing

Many GUI applications display dialog boxes in which the OK button and the Cancel button have the exact same effect. In any dialog box, if OK and Cancel have the same effect, a blooper has been committed.

Sometimes the problem is in the OK button, sometimes it is in the Cancel button, and sometimes the programmer simply used the wrong kind of dialog box.

Variation A: OK button doesn't apply. One sometimes sees dialog boxes in which the OK button simply closes the dialog box. Usually this happens because the programmer who created the dialog box did not realize that the OK button is supposed to apply any changes before closing the dialog box. In most such cases, the programmer has provided an Apply button, and expects users to click it to save any changed settings before clicking OK. Of course, this means that OK and Cancel have the same effect.

Variation B: Cancel button doesn't cancel. One way for OK and Cancel to have the same effect is for the programmer to commit Blooper 55: Cancel button doesn't cancel (Section 5.4.3). If changes in dialog box settings take effect immediately in the application, then clicking on Cancel won't abort those changes, and Cancel will have the same result as OK.

Variation C: One-action dialog box with both OK and Cancel buttons. A common form of this blooper results when programmers use generic dialog box components having built-in OK and Cancel buttons in cases in which only one action is really possible. The dialog box pictured in Figure 5.43 is displayed by the West Virginia State Fire Marshal Web site (*www.wvmarshal.org*). For now, we'll ignore the problem that this dialog box is displayed even if the user has the indicated browser. The more pertinent problem is there is only one possible response to this message—"I saw the message"—but two response buttons—OK and Cancel. It isn't just that one of the two buttons is unnecessary; it's that users will be confused about which button to click and will waste time trying to decide.

Figure 5.43

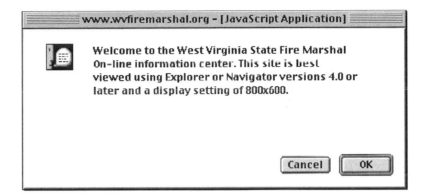

If only one action is possible in a dialog box that has two buttons, many programmers "wire" both buttons to have the same effect. They think the only alternative is to have one of the buttons do nothing, and they don't like that alternative. While that alternative is indeed to be avoided, it isn't really the only alternative. Another alternative is not to use a dialog box component that has two buttons.

Avoiding Blooper 56: *The design rule*

The OK button should mean, "Yes, I want to do this. Use these settings, close this dialog box, and proceed." If the dialog box was showing the properties of a selected application data object, the data object should acquire the new property values specified in the dialog box. If the dialog box was displayed by a command to collect information it needed to execute, the command should be executed with the specified argument values. In the latter case, the "OK" button may have a more specific label corresponding to the function that displayed the dialog box, for example, "Print."

The Cancel button should mean, "No, I don't want to do this. Close this dialog box, ignore any settings I changed, and abort whatever we were doing." If the dialog box was showing the properties of a selected application data item, the data item should retain whatever property values it had when the dialog box was first opened (or the user clicked the dialog box's Apply button if it had one). If the dialog box was displayed by a command to collect information it needed to execute, the command should be aborted. For various reasons, the Cancel button is sometimes labeled "Close."

Sometimes two response buttons is one too many

The OK and Cancel buttons in a dialog box should *never* mean the same thing. If they do, and the problem is not that one of them was misprogrammed, then one of the buttons is superfluous and should be removed. There are two common situations in which only one button is needed:

- The dialog box displays noneditable information. Noneditable information includes computed results and setting-values that the user cannot change (at least not in that context). When a dialog box contains no editable settings, users can make no changes, so there can be nothing to cancel.

- The dialog box displays warning and error messages, for situations in which the problem has already occurred and cannot be reversed. (However, see interaction Blooper 54: Dialog boxes that trap users, Section 5.4.2).

In both these cases, the only action possible is "OK, I saw the information," so only one button is needed. Normally, it is labeled "OK." The programmer should therefore not use a generic dialog box component. Instead, the programmer should use a special "information," "warning," or "error" dialog box. If the GUI toolkit the programmer is using includes no such components, the programmer should either build one or simply create an appropriate dialog box from lower-level components.

Further reading

User interface design principles and guidelines

Bickford, P. 1997. *Interface Design: The Art of Developing Easy-to-Use Software.* Chestnut Hill, MA: Academic Press.

Shneiderman, B. 1987. *Designing the User Interface: Strategies for Effective Human-Computer Interaction.* Reading, MA: Addison-Wesley.

Tufte, E. R. 1983. *The Visual Display of Quantitative Information.* Cheshire, MA: Graphics Press.

Weinshenk, S., Jamar, P., and Yeo, S. 1997. *GUI Design Essentials.* New York: John Wiley and Sons.

Web design

Flanders, V., and Willis, M. 1998. *Web Pages That Suck: Learning Good Design by Looking at Bad Design.* San Francisco: Sybex.

Document styles mechanisms

Johnson, J., and Beach, R. 1988. "Styles in Document Editing Systems." *IEEE Computer* 21(1): 32–43.

Studies of home computer use

Kraut, R., ed. 1996. "The Internet @ Home." Special section of *Communications of the ACM* 39(12): 33–74.

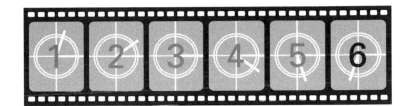

Web Bloopers

Introduction

The emergence and meteoric rise in popularity of the World Wide Web beginning in the mid-1990s has not only immensely broadened access to information (and misinformation), it has also thrust a large number of people into the role of user interface designers...for both better and worse. Furthermore, this trend will continue. To quote Web user interface analyst Jakob Nielsen [1999a, pages 65–66]:

> If the [Web's] growth rate does not slow down, the Web will reach 200 million sites sometime during 2003.... The world has about 20,000 user interface professionals. If all sites were to be professionally designed by a single UI professional, we can conclude that every UI professional in the world would need to design one Web site every working hour from now on to meet demand. This is obviously not going to happen....
> There are three possible solutions to the problem:
>
> ■ Make it possible to design reasonably usable sites without having UI expertise;
>
> ■ Train more people in good Web design; and
>
> ■ Live with poorly designed sites that are hard to use.

Despite the obvious need to provide more design guidance to Web developers, I hadn't originally planned to include a separate chapter in this book for design bloopers that Web developers make. There were two reasons for this.

First, I wasn't convinced that Web bloopers are qualitatively different from the bloopers described elsewhere in this book. Developers of Web sites and Web applications can—and do—make the same mistakes that developers of traditional computer-based applications make. In fact, many of the bloopers described elsewhere in this book are illustrated using examples from the Web (for example, Blooper 31: Tiny fonts, Section 3.4.2). Poor responsiveness, covered in Chapter 7, is a problem for which the Web is infamous. Because of this, it wasn't clear to me that a separate chapter of Web bloopers was warranted.

Second, to the extent that Web bloopers are distinctive enough to be considered separately, they are already well covered elsewhere:

■ Web design consultant Jakob Nielsen has a Web site *(www.UseIt.com)* that lists the top 10 Web design errors [Nielsen, 1996, 1999b, 1999c], provides frequent commentary on many misguided Web design practices, and sometimes offers critical reviews of corporate Web sites. Nielsen has also recently written a book on the subject of Web design: *Designing Web Usablity* [Nielsen, 1999d], which, among other things, describes mistakes that Web designers should avoid.

■ Another excellent resource is the Web site *"Web Pages That Suck" (www. WebPagesThatSuck.com)*, created and maintained by longtime Web site designer Vincent Flanders. A book of the same title, capturing much of the content of the Web site, was coauthored by Flanders and Michael Willis [1998]. The goal of both the Web site and the book is to allow readers to "learn good design by looking at bad design." Flanders and Willis critique a large number of commercial Web sites, pointing out common—and not-so-common—errors, and providing design advice and even implementation tips on how to avoid them.

It wasn't initially clear to me that I had any Web-specific bloopers to add to those described by Nielsen, and by Flanders and Willis.

Despite these concerns, I eventually decided to include a Web bloopers chapter. Why? Three reasons:

1. I became convinced that there are errors that are truly Web-specific, such as those having to do with links.
2. I believe there are common Web bloopers that have not been mentioned (yet) by either Nielsen or Flanders and Willis.
3. Even if a blooper mentioned in this book turns out to have already been covered elsewhere, it can't hurt to include it in this book. The more of us calling attention to common design errors, the better.

However, I *will* avoid covering certain extremely common Web bloopers that have already been well covered by Nielsen or Flanders and Willis. Those include the following:

- Web sites that slow downloading by including large images, lots of images, unnecessary animations, and other time-consuming content
- Web sites that distract users from their goals by displaying gratuitous animations that run continuously
- Web sites that can be viewed only with the most recent browsers and/or esoteric browser plug-ins
- Web pages that require users to scroll down or across the page to see important content, such as the site *www.cybergeography.org/atlas/atlas.html*, which displays its text in a fixed-width format that cannot be read without sideways scrolling or a huge browser window (see Figure 6.1)
- Web sites that format text in fixed-width or proportional-width blocks rather than just letting the width of users' browser windows determine the width of the text[1]

---

1. This practice has several adverse effects. (1) text is clipped when the browser window is too narrow, requiring users to scroll horizontally to see it all; (2) space is wasted when the browser window is too wide because the text does not fill the space; and (3) text formatting can become very weird if the user increases the browser's text font size.

Figure 6.1

One blooper pointed out at *WebPagesThatSuck.com* is especially shocking, both because it shows how careless Web site developers can be and because it is so amazingly common. Go to any Web search service, enter "Lorem ipsum dolor sit amet" (including the quotation marks), and start the search. Depending on which search service you use, the search will return between 1000 and 5000 hits. What does this mean? Many Web site designers initially mock-up their Web sites with fake Latin text so they can determine and evaluate the layout before the actual text is written. Some Web site development tools help designers do this by providing the fake Latin text. The most common fake Latin text begins "Lorem ipsum dolor sit amet, consectetuer adipiscing elit...." When this text appears in an actual Web site, it means that the designer neglected to replace the fake Latin with real text before putting the Web site on the Internet. Even more amazing is that most of the Web sites that exhibit this blooper are not personal Web sites created by individuals, but rather commercial and organizational sites presumably created by professional Web designers.

In contrast to the other blooper chapters of this book, this section focuses on the medium—the Web—instead of on a particular type of design problem. Therefore, it covers problems ranging from management mistakes to incorrect use of graphical elements. It also covers problems having impacts on usability ranging from minor to serious. In a way, this chapter is a microcosm of the entire book.

6.1 Web structure and interaction bloopers

The first three Web bloopers concern design errors that make it difficult for people to find the information they are seeking. They have to do with confusing Web site structure, unpredictable behavior of the browser's Back button, and poor search facilities.

6.1.1 Blooper 57: Web site structure reflects organization structure or history

Many of the Web sites I evaluate for client companies are revealing in ways the developers probably did not intend. A corporate raider or a headhunter could, by examining many corporate Web sites, learn a significant amount about the companies' internal organizational structure. They could also gain insights into how the host companies' organization structure evolved, such as which organizations predated or spawned which others. They might even be able to deduce internal company politics, such as which organizations are currently engaged in turf battles.

The amount of this sort of information revealed by corporate Web sites is significant, even though, as I say, it is probably unintentional. However, I did not bring this issue up because of its ramifications for corporate security. I brought it up because of its ramifications for the Web site's usability. Web sites that are based—even if unintentionally—on a company's organizational structure and history are not user friendly.

Visitors to a Web site have their own goals, and they don't want to waste time in achieving those goals. Perhaps they are looking for information about the company's products and/or services. Perhaps they want to buy something. Perhaps they are trying to use an information service that the site hosts, such as discussion groups, email, or stock investing.

Visitors to a Web site are not interested in how the company is organized or in how responsibility for the Web site's development was divided up among organizations, development teams, and individual developers. They could not care less that some of the Web site was contracted out to Web design firms while some pages were developed in-house. The fact that 7 out of the Web site's 28 pages are leftovers from a previous Web site is of no concern to them. To the extent that matters such as these influence the design of the Web site, they are at best a distraction and at worst a hindrance. They make the site seem arbitrary and ad hoc to users, like a house that has had a lot of cheap add-ons over the years rather than being designed from scratch according to an architect's plan.

For example, a university's Online Education office wanted to improve the facilities that students used to find and enroll in courses. At that time, enrolling in a course required two separate steps: Students had to first use a course catalogue Web site to *find* the classes they wanted, and then login to a non-Web database application to *register* for the classes. The Web site and the database application were entirely separate, so students had to look up every class twice: once in the catalogue, and then again in the registration application. Furthermore, the course listings in the catalogue and the registration database sometimes disagreed due to database and Web site maintenance oversights. The Online Education office wanted to fix these problems by integrating registration into the Web site, while also improving the Web site.

After a few weeks of design meetings, it became clear that the project was becoming mired in interdepartmental politics. One problem was that the Online Education office did not "own" the registration application and so did not have complete control over its development. The application had been developed by the university's MIS department, whose goals and ideas for enhancing the registration application differed from those of the Online Education office. The MIS department developers believed that full integration of the course catalogue and registration would require more time and resources than *they* had, so they opposed that aspect of the Online Education office's plan.

To make a very long story short, the MIS organization largely won: the registration application remained separate and under MIS's control, although it was reimplemented as a Web site. The catalogue Web site was redesigned and improved. The two Web sites were changed to use the same database of classes so they would no longer get out of synch. The only other integration that resulted from the project was that buttons were added to the catalogue Web site to allow students to start the registration Web site once they had found a class they wanted to take. However, students still had to look up the same class in the registration Web site that they had just looked up in the catalogue.

One might think that the losers in this interdepartmental power struggle were the managers in the Online Education department. In fact the losers were the *students* who had to use the system.

I mentioned earlier in this book that I once reviewed a computer company's customer support Web site (see Blooper 36: Careless writing, Section 4.1.4). The site included a Patch page, offering software patches that could be downloaded and installed to correct known bugs in the company's software. The Patch page listed the available patches and described the purpose of each one. One category of patches was "security patches," which were for correcting bugs and loopholes in the software that could compromise the security of the customers' computer systems. However, security patches were not listed on the Patch page. Instead, the Patch page provided a link to an entirely different Web site where security patches were listed.

The reason for this was that although most patches were developed and distributed by the Customer Support organization, security patches were the domain of the Corporate Security organization. Corporate Security distributed security patches through its own Web site. That Web site had been designed and developed long before the Customer Support site was, by different people, using different user interface standards and conventions.

To make matters worse, the "Security Patches" link on the Customer Support Patch page did not link directly to the security patches. It linked to the Corporate Security home page. Thus, a customer who had entered the Customer Support Web site looking for a patch, after eventually finding his way to the actual patch listings, might discover that the patch he wanted was a security patch. (Never mind that the customer might have to figure this out by a process of elimination.) Spotting the link to security patches, the customer would click on it, expecting to be shown the available security patches. But—surprise—the customer would suddenly be staring at the home page for an organization that she didn't even know existed, and then have to find the way from there down to actual patch listings... again.

Web site usability can also be adversely affected by organizational distinctions less weighty than the difference between MIS and Online Education, or between Corporate Security and Customer Support. A Web development organization may assign pages of a Web site, or components used throughout a Web site, to different programmers. As discussed under Blooper 80: Anarchic development (Section 8.2.2), differences between developers in design style, programming style, and writing style, combined with weak oversight, can result in inconsistencies across a Web site that diminish its navigability and usability.

Avoiding Blooper 57: The design rule

Web sites and Web applications should be organized according to the needs of their intended users. In this respect, they are no different from any other software. What do *users* want to accomplish using the site? Developers should take the time to discover the answer to that question and design a system to help users achieve their goals. This means devoting significant resources up-front, before beginning coding, to interviewing prospective users; watching them use predecessors of the planned site, including competitor sites; and getting their reactions to paper or online mock-ups of the site.

Web sites versus Web apps

Does developing a Web site require that one develop a conceptual model first (see Principle 2, Section 1.2.3)? That depends. Designing a Web site that will consist mostly of static pages probably doesn't require the prior development of a conceptual model, since the conceptual model for such a site is pretty much built into the Web: a hierarchy of linked pages. On the other hand, if the site contains dynamic pages, it verges on being an application, and so warrants developing a conceptual model. Of course, if what is being developed is a full-fledged Web-based application, then the design and development process should be no different than for a traditional desktop GUI-based application. In *any* of these cases, including simple Web sites, developing a site lexicon is very important.

Telltale signs of the blooper

As a Web site is being developed, the project management and the site architect should be on the lookout for gratuitous corporate organizational or historical artifacts sneaking into the design. Such artifacts should be eradicated before they have a chance to become entrenched. The following are some questions that project managers and site architects should ask continually:

- Does the organization of the pages make sense to people who haven't seen the company's org chart?
- Have all traces of the company's "dirty laundry"—such as the fact that two different product divisions have developed similar products—been eradicated?
- Can users tell that parts of the site were developed by external Web consultants while others were thrown together by overworked employees in their "spare" time?
- Have pages or components inherited from legacy sites been updated to fit into the new site?
- Can users tell clearly which linked pages are internal or external to the site, and do all internal pages follow the same design conventions and guidelines?

What about links to other sites?

Linking to other sites is a particularly tricky issue. After all, the whole point of the Web is to link to information that might be useful, wherever it might be. Indeed, the distinction between pages that are "in" and "not in" a particular site is fuzzy. Isn't anything a site links to "in" that site? Not exactly.

All pages within a site should have a consistent appearance and layout. Users should be able to tell instantly whether or not they've left a site by whether or not the appearance of the pages has changed. In addition, pages inside a site should provide any information or functionality that users need in order to use the site successfully. Links to pages outside a site should be strictly to provide auxiliary information and functionality. This means that if information necessary to operate a site successfully is provided on another site, the designers of the first site should incorporate the information from the other site into their own site...with permission, of course.

Consider the aforementioned customer support Web site that linked to a different organization's Web site for "security patches." My advice to that client was

Ignore the organizational structure and history. Organize the Security Patches into the Customer Support Patch page. Even though Corporate Security has its own Security Patch pages, you needn't link directly to them. You can devise your own patch lists that take the required information from their pages and integrate it more seamlessly into the Customer Support Patch page.

6.1.2 Blooper 58: Back doesn't go where users expect

A common usability problem in Web sites and Web applications I review or test is the unexpected behavior of the Web browser's Back button. As Jakob Nielsen has pointed out repeatedly on his Web site (*www.UseIt.com*), Web users use the Back button a lot and expect it to do what they want. Therefore, it is important for Web sites and Web applications to manage the Back stack so as to match users' expectations. Unfortunately, many do not.

An example: Back behaving inconsistently. For example, one of my clients developed an intranet search engine for searching for company information. Executing a search returned the usual list of search results. However, the results list did not consist of links to the actual information; it consisted of headings for *categories* of information. Each category could be expanded individually, like folders in a Macintosh or Windows file structure, to show the items underneath it. When a user expanded a results category heading and then clicked on one of the links listed under it, the browser displayed the page of data. Some of the data pages displayed information using expandable topic headings, as the search results page did.

The problem was that the browser's Back button had a different effect in the search results page than it did in the data pages. On the search results page, opening a results category heading was treated as just an action on the same page. Clicking Back after expanding a heading took the user back to the page that had been displayed *before* the search results page—usually the search specification page. In contrast, on data pages, opening a results category heading was treated as going to a new page; clicking Back after opening a heading just redisplayed the search results page with the category closed again. Figure 6.2 shows this inconsistency.

More ways to make Back unpredictable. Other factors that can cause the Back button to behave unexpectedly (from the point of view of users) are

- *Careless use of frames:* When Web pages contain frames, it is less clear what constitutes a page, so it is less clear when a user is changing pages. Some Web pages even use frames without visible borders, so users may not realize that the page is divided into frames. This makes it more likely that the Back button will go to pages that the user does not intend.
- *Forms:* Because forms allow users to enter data into Web pages, they complicate the issue of what the Back button should do. If a user backs up to a form, should the data that the user entered still be there? Should it make a

Figure 6.2

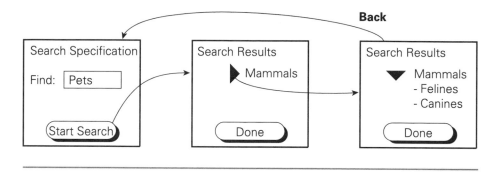

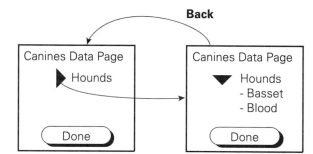

difference whether the user submitted the form or not? What if the form was so far back that it can no longer be reloaded from the browser's cache, but rather must be reloaded from the Web site? These issues increase the chance that Back will behave contrary to users' expectations.

Avoiding Blooper 58: *The design rule*

Because users' expectations regarding the behavior of the Back button are by definition subjective, the design rule for the Back button is more about correct design *processes* than correct designs.

Do what your users expect

The basic rule is that developers must determine what users expect the Back button to do in the important cases within a Web site and, assuming there is substantial agreement among users, try their best to make the Back button match those expectations. It doesn't matter that users' expectations may not be "logically" correct from the developers' point of view. If users' expectations differ systematically from those of the developers, the users' expectations should take precedence.

However, developers of Web sites and Web applications don't have complete control over the function of the Back button. In Web sites that are implemented purely in HTML, the Back stack is managed by the browser; the site developer has no control over what it does. Web sites and Web applications

A second example: Back in the FAQ

A corporate Web site I reviewed a few years ago included a page that provided answers to common questions. Such documents are commonly called FAQs, for "frequently asked questions."

The FAQ was one long Web page with specific questions marked as HTML anchor points. Links to specific questions in the FAQ were scattered throughout the corporate Web site. Clicking on such a link took the user not to the start of the FAQ page, but to the specific question in it. The answers in the FAQ typically contained paragraphs of text and in many cases links to other Web pages or documents that provided more detailed information.

The problem was that if a user linked to a FAQ question, then followed a link from there to another page, then clicked the browser Back button, the browser displayed the *top* of the FAQ, not the question the user came from. Apparently, the browser's Back mechanism was keeping track of only the pages the browser had visited, not the anchor points within those pages. This was very disorienting. I initially did not realize that the FAQ was one long document, and so did not understand what was happening. All I knew was that the Back button was not taking me back to where I had been.

The developers didn't consider this to be a problem because they had "done their best." The popular browsers were at the time, they claimed, incapable of returning to the right anchor point within the FAQ document. I doubted this claim, since the Back mechanisms of the popular browsers do keep track of anchor points within pages. Nonetheless, I skirted the issue by advising the developers simply to break the FAQ into separate documents for each question, which solved the problem.

that are based on Web scripting languages (e.g., Javascript) or Web programming languages (e.g., Java) have more control over what happens when the user presses the Back button, but still lack total control. What's a conscientious Web designer to do?

Avoid the big problems

As with many aspects of software user interface design, the answer is to avoid the *big* problems. In the case of the operation of the Back button, big problems are either those that cause users to become lost and disoriented, or those in which users are faced with inconsistent Back button behavior, which greatly impairs their ability to learn their way around the Web site or Web application.

The FAQ example described earlier is an example of a Back button problem that was causing users to get lost. A bit of effort was required to correct the problem, but it was worth it. The example in Figure 6.2 is a case of the Back button behaving differently in two situations that looked almost the same to users, which would make it hard for them to learn what to expect. In that case, correcting the problem resulted in a simpler implementation overall.

6.1.3 Blooper 59: Complicating searching

Web search facilities are the best thing that has happened to the Internet since the point-and-click Mosaic browser replaced collections of distinct Internet access tools, such as FTP, newsreaders, and Gopher. Search facilities make it possible for people to find needles of information and services in the vast haystack—no, hay*farm*—of the Internet. By making it easier to find information and pull it out of the Internet, they reduce the need for mechanisms that push information at people in case they might be interested, a mode of operation I regard as the "Dark Side" of the Internet [Johnson, 1996a].

However, to be useful, search facilities must be easy to use. Unfortunately, many are not. This Web blooper is about two ways that developers of Web search facilities have devised to make searching user-hostile. The main offenders are search facilities developed by companies or organizations either (1) for their own employees to use to search the company or organization's private intranet, or (2) for external Web visitors to use to find information within the company or organization's public Web site. The popular Web search services on the open Internet do not exhibit these problems. If they did, they probably wouldn't last long.

Variation A: Not including search criteria in search results. A common problem I see in Web search facilities that I use or review is search results pages that do not show the users' search criteria that produced the displayed results. Users see only a list of search hits—links to items that were found to satisfy the search criteria. Users just have to remember how they specified the search, that is, exactly what it was they asked for.

Seeing the search criteria along with the results is helpful for two reasons. First, it can help users interpret and evaluate the results: "What are these things it found? Are they what I am looking for?" Seeing the search criteria can also help users decide whether to try to adjust the criteria in order to refine the search. When search services do not show the users' search criteria on the results page, they are hindering their own effectiveness.[2]

I have also seen search facilities that have the opposite problem: they show the search criteria in each and every listed found item. The real problem in such cases is a naive implementation. Someone assumed—rightly—that users would want to see the search terms that were used to find an item, but didn't think about it enough to realize that a search often finds many items and that all items found by a given search operation would have the same search criteria.

---

2. However, this may be intentional. Search service developers have told me that companies that provide commercial Web search services actually don't want users to find what they are looking for too quickly. Since search services get their revenue from advertising, they prefer to have users flounder around at the search site for a while, increasing the chance that one of the banner ads displayed there will catch the users' eye (and then their mouse pointer).

Figure 6.3

Variation B: Forcing users to distinguish "keywords" from "search terms." Another problem exhibited by search facilities is requiring users to choose between options they don't understand.

Some Web search facilities provide two different ways for users to search: by specifying "keywords" or by specifying "search terms." This distinction, especially worded in this way, assumes that users of the search facility are familiar with the concepts and terminology of information retrieval technology. As some readers of this book may know, keywords are terms that are explicitly attached to a piece of information when it is stored in order to facilitate its retrieval. A keyword search takes the words the user types and looks in its database for pieces of information that have those keywords. In contrast, search terms are words that the search engine will seek in the textual content of the documents it examines.

The search specification forms in Figures 6.3 and 6.4 are examples of Web sites that exhibit this flaw. The form in Figure 6.3 is from the Search page of the Association for Computing Machinery (ACM) Web site *(www.acm.org)*. The ACM can perhaps be excused for asking users to make such a choice, because most visitors to its Web site are probably computer professionals of one sort or another, who might actually understand the choice. However, one might ask why ACM's search facility has to include this choice when most other organizations' search facilities do not. In any case, no such excuse can be given for the search facility in the Institute of Global Communication (IGC) Web site *(www.igc.org)*, which is shown in Figure 6.4.

Of course, most Web users are not familiar with information retrieval technology and terminology. To them, "keywords" and "search terms" seem awfully similar and may even mean exactly the same thing. It's like asking someone who is buying lunch at a hot-dog stand to choose between ordering a hot dog and a frankfurter. Most people would pause, furrow their brow, and then ask the vendor: "What's the difference?" Forced to choose between searching by "keywords" or by "search terms," some users might ask a colleague, "What's the difference?," but most would respond to this apparently meaningless, time-wasting, and annoying decision by simply choosing randomly or leaving the settings however they were set.

Figure 6.4

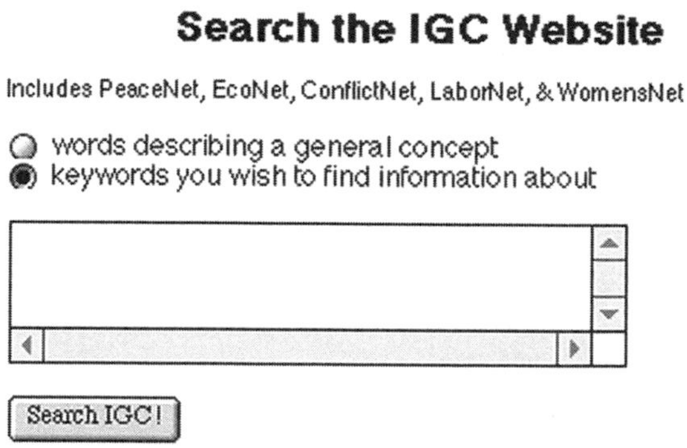

Search the IGC Website

Includes PeaceNet, EcoNet, ConflictNet, LaborNet, & WomensNet

○ words describing a general concept
◉ keywords you wish to find information about

Search IGC!

Figure 6.5

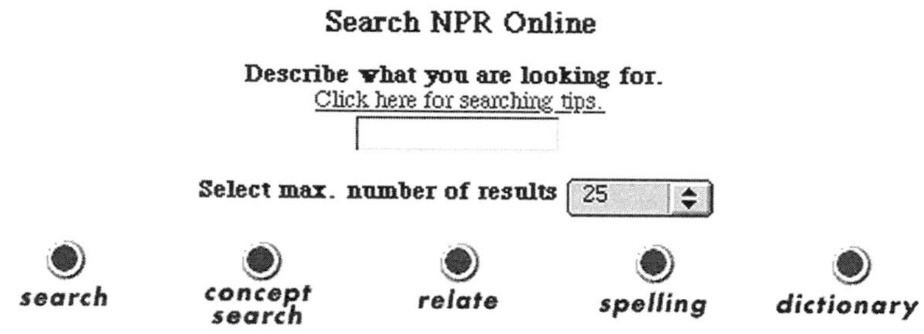

Search NPR Online

Describe what you are looking for.
Click here for searching tips.

Select max. number of results 25

◉ search ◉ concept search ◉ relate ◉ spelling ◉ dictionary

A related but different confusing choice between search options is shown in the search form from the National Public Radio (NPR) Web site *(www.npr.org)*. Users have to choose between "Search," "Concept Search," "Relate," and two other options (see Figure 6.5). Note that although the buttons look a bit like radiobuttons, they are in fact separate command buttons. Thus, there is no default choice; users must make an explicit choice.

The final blooper example is from the Web site *(www.sbc.com)* of SBC Communications, a large telecommunications company that owns several regional Bell operating companies, some cellular telephone companies, and various overseas companies. The problem with the SBC Web site's search function (see Figure 6.6) is that it asks visitors who want to search the site to choose between "Literal Text" search syntax and "Boolean" search syntax. Since SBC's Web site is presumably intended for the general public, wording the choice this way seems questionable; not only would most people not know what "Boolean" means, they might not even know what "search syntax" means. However, at least this choice defaults to "Literal Text" search, so most nontechnical users can simply ignore the setting.

Avoiding Blooper 59: *The design rule*

The general design rule for designing an effective Web search facility is similar to that for designing any software application or service: Determine the user

Figure 6.6

Search SBC Communications Inc.

Search the Entire Site

To search for an article, choose a subject, then enter a single word, several words, or a phrase. For more information about the search process, see the **search tips** page.

Search For: [   ]

Search Syntax: ● Literal Text
○ Boolean

Number of
Files to Return: [100]   [Search]

requirements before you start designing. Develop a conceptual model and a lexicon. Design the services based on the user requirements and on your conceptual model and lexicon. Test the design on representative users both before beginning development and throughout the development process. Revise the design based on the results of the testing.

However, in reference to the specific design mistakes mentioned earlier, here are two specific design rules:

■ Display the search criteria that the user specified somewhere on the search results page, preferably near the top of the page. Ideally, the search criteria should remain visible even when the user scrolls down the results list. Don't overcompensate by dumbly displaying the criteria on each and every item returned by the search.

■ Don't require users to choose between search options that are meaningless to them. Most search facilities on corporate and organization Web sites are very simple: type in some text, click the Search button. No options to set. Simple. Other search facilities provide options, but they are sensible ones that fit the purpose of the site and the expected visitors. The search forms in Figures 6.7 and 6.8 are from the Web sites of the State of California *(www. ca.gov)* and the Sharper Image, Inc. *(www.sharperimage.com)* respectively. Note that each provides search options in its own way, but they are options that would make sense to users of the site.

Figure 6.7

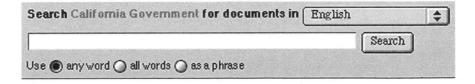

Figure 6.8

6.2 Web component, layout, and appearance bloopers

The remaining Web bloopers are errors in the layout, appearance, and operation of specific Web user interface components.

6.2.1 Blooper 60: Hidden links

A common problem in the Web sites and Web-based applications I have seen is that links to other pages in the same site or to other Web sites are poorly marked, so that users can easily fail to notice them. In my experience, "hidden" links come in three types.

Variation A: Images that aren't clearly links. Web browsers typically mark links through the use of color. Textual links are usually marked by underlining them and rendering the text and the underline in a distinctive color. The color the browser uses to mark links can be specified by the user in the browser's Preferences.

Images can also serve as links. Designers can make an entire image into a link simply by surrounding the IMG tag with the link tags (< A HREF = ... > and < /A >), as shown below:

```
<A HREF=AnotherPage.html>
<IMG SRC=FamilyPhoto.gif ALT="The Johnsons">
</A>
```

When an entire image is made a link in this way, Web browsers, by default, mark it as a link by surrounding it with a border in the same distinctive color used to mark textual links. The Web page designer need not specify that the image has a border; Web browsers automatically show one if the image is a link, as if the IMG tag contained a BORDER = 2 attribute. The width of the border can be adjusted by including an explicit BORDER = n attribute in the IMG tag. If a Web page designer does not want a border around an image link, the designer must include the attribute BORDER = 0 in the IMG tag.[3]

---

3. This contrasts with how Web browsers treat images that are not links. For them, browsers display no border unless the IMG tag explicitly includes a BORDER = n attribute.

Figure 6.9

ACM SIGCHI
Special Interest Group on
Computer-Human Interaction

Shown in Figure 6.9 is the top of the home page for the Association for Computing Machinery's Special Interest Group on Human-Computer Interaction (SIGCHI). On the left is an image that is a link to the Web site for the CHI2000 conference. It has the border that marks it as a link. In contrast, the SIGCHI logo image on the right is not a link and so has no border.

Unfortunately, many Web page designers set BORDER = 0 on linked images, turning the borders off. Usually they do this for aesthetic reasons because they think the colored borders around the linked images clash with the rest of the page. This is usually a mistake—a case of placing aesthetics before usability. It gives users no clue what is a link and what isn't. As a result, users often miss these links entirely. They also waste time clicking on images that are not links.

The image of the camera in the portion of Amazon.com's Web page shown in Figure 6.10 is a link, but users can't see that. There are other images on the same page that are not links. The only way users can determine which ones are links is by moving the screen pointer over each image to see if a Web address appears in the message area at the bottom of the Web browser window.

Another type of image link is called an "image map." It allows a single image to be divided up into several different areas, each linking to a different destination. A very common way to use image maps is to create a single image representing a row of buttons, with each button linked to a different page. As another example: a Web site developer could create a map of the United States, with each state being a link to a page of information about that state.[4]

Web browsers do not mark image map links; each linked part of the image has no surrounding border in the distinctive color that identifies links. It is therefore up to the Web page designers to design the mapped image so as to make clear where each link is. Unfortunately, many image maps on the Web fail

Figure 6.10

Point, Click, and Shoot
So what if you're not Richard Avedon? With an impressive automatic feature set as well as all the manual options, Minolta's Maxxum HTsi Plus is an ideal SLR camera for both the beginning and more advanced photographer. Go to Electronics

---

4. A description of how to create image maps is beyond the scope of this book. For more information, see any book that describes how to use HTML, the Web page description language.

Problems that image links cause users

Example 1. Many companies have Web sites in which the company logo, displayed on every page of the site, serves as the only link back to the site's home page. However, usability tests I conducted for some such companies indicated that few users realize that the logos are links, at least initially. The following are excerpts from my reports to two different clients of the results of usability-testing their site:

> Many test participants didn't know how to return to the Home page. Some participants looked for a link with the term "Home" on it. Because they could not find one, they used the Back button many times to get Home. However, most did eventually learn to click on the company logo at the top of every page to get back to Home.

> Most test participants did not realize that the company logo was a link to the Home page. Only one of twelve test participants clicked the logo to get Home.

Example 2. I once conducted a usability test of a real-estate Web site for a real-estate company. Most of the home listings in the site included photographs of the homes. The photos were not links. The test showed that most users thought the photos might be links (e.g., to a larger version of the photograph or another view of the same room), but weren't sure. Several test participants clicked on photographs several times—waiting each time for the browser to do something—before concluding that the photographs were not links.

at this. For example, users who saw a page containing the aforementioned map of the United States might have no clue that the states were links, and so might never click on them. Even worse are images that have been divided up such that parts of the image are links, but other parts are not. With such images, users have no way of knowing what is a link and what isn't.

The image in Figure 6.11 is from the Web site of the U.S. Olympic Committee *(www.usoc.org)*. This is a single image in which five areas are mapped as links to other pages, as indicated by the labels. Because browsers do not mark image mapped links, the boundaries of the links are unclear.

Figure 6.11

FoxTrot © 1996 Bill Amend. Reprinted by permission of Universal Press Syndicate. All rights reserved.

Variation B: Inconsistent link colors. HTML allows each Web page to specify the color to be used to mark links. The use of this feature is discouraged because it can conflict with the link color settings specified in users' browsers. Nonetheless, some Web site developers use this feature.

Specifying the link color in a Web site causes links on certain sites or pages to be colored differently than elsewhere. There are situations in the world where differences are good. The French saying *"Vive la différence"* is about one good difference. However, gratuitous differences in Web link colors are bad. Users see the color difference and naturally assume that it means something, even if it doesn't. They try to figure out what it means. Thus, they are distracted from their purpose for visiting the Web site.

One example is the customer support Web site I've mentioned elsewhere in this book (see Blooper 57: Web site structure reflects organization structure or history, Section 6.1.1). It included textual links to most of its functions on every page, as any good Web site should. However, on some pages, these links were blue, on others, they were red, and on still others, they were green. Why? Because different functional groups of pages in the Web site used slightly different background images and colors to make it easier for users to see where they were, and the designers felt that the link colors on each functional page group should "go with" the background in that group. As in Variation A, this is a case where graphic design principles were put ahead of user interface design principles, to the detriment of users.

Variation C: Click <u>this</u>! Burying links in text. Many corporate Web sites I review contain elements that make them look more like personal Web pages than like commercial, corporate Web sites. One such element has to do with how textual links are presented.

In personal Web pages, it is common to embed links in paragraphs of text. For example:

> We are happy to announce a new arrival to our <u>family</u>: our new son, <u>Jason</u>. He was born on May 23, 1999 at 12:45 pm. He weighed in at 8 lbs. 6 oz. His <u>grandparents</u> are ecstatic to have a grandchild.

> Our vacation this year was to <u>Yosemite National Park</u> in California. For photos, click <u>here</u>. For photos of our previous vacations, click <u>here</u>.

I often see this same link style in corporate Web sites. For example, the image in Figure 6.12 is from the Web site of the bookstore Barnes and Noble *(www. barnesandnoble.com).* Although Barnes and Noble no doubt wants visitors to the site to visit the page describing the "historical collection" mentioned in the text, the link for it does not stand out very well.

Another example comes from a search service one of my clients was developing for employees to use to find information on a corporate intranet. The Search Web site included a function that displayed the available sources of information, which were called "collections." Each collection in the displayed list included the following text:

> `Click ` <u>`here`</u>` for a description of this collection.`

When I see this type of link in a corporate Web site, I flag it as a design flaw. In my opinion, this style of link is too informal for a commercial, corporate Web site. I think it gives site visitors an impression of an amateurish design. Furthermore, embedding links in body text makes them hard to notice, especially if the same phrase containing an embedded link is repeated many times on the same page, as it was in the previous example (see Blooper 47: Easily missed information, Section 5.2.2).

Figure 6.12

Summer Icebreakers
As we head into the dog days of August, here's a historical <u>collection</u> that will take you to the land of ice and snow.

Examples of "personal Web site" link-style in corporate Web sites

- If the item you want is not listed above, check the <u>next 10</u> or the <u>previous 10</u> items.
- House: 3 BR, 2 BA, near public transit. Asking $123,000. Click <u>here</u> for details.
- Your <u>shopping cart</u> currently contains 3 items, with a total cost of $76.45.
- Click <u>here</u> for information on priority settings and response time.

Avoiding Blooper 60: The design rule

By following a few simple rules, Web designers can ensure that the links in their Web sites are obvious to people who visit the site.

Leave the default border on whole-image links

When an entire image is a link to another page, the Web site designer should let browsers mark it as a link. This is the default, so it is easy to do. Designers should simply accept the default. They should never set BORDER = 0 in the IMG tag on images that are links. Setting the link-marking border to some other width, such as 1 or 3, is perfectly acceptable.

Images that are not links can have borders or not, as the designer prefers. The default color for borders of nonlink images is black, in contrast to the color (usually blue) that marks links. If, for some reason, the designer changes the border color, it should of course never be set to the same color that the browser uses to identify links. Doing that would be perverse.

If no borders will be shown, make sure the image shows where the links are

If for some reason a designer cannot stand to leave the border on an image link, it is the designer's responsibility to convey, either in words or in the image itself, the fact that it does something when clicked on. Images of buttons are a common way to achieve this, although they have other problems (see Blooper 62: Buttons that provide no click feedback, Section 6.2.3).

The Web site of Sears, Roebuck, & Co. *(www.sears.com)* includes an array of images that are all links (see Figure 6.13). Although the link-marking border on the images has been turned off, the instructions above the images makes it clear enough that they are links.

Web site designers who use HTML image maps have a similar responsibility to assure that the links are apparent in images that are divided into multiple links. With image maps, there is no default browser link-marking to fall back on.

Figure 6.13   **Start shopping online by selecting a category.**

Refrigerators   Freezers   Gas Cooking   Dual Fuel Cooking

Electric Cooking/
Microwaves/Hoods   Dishwashers   Washers/Dryers   Compactors

Don't mess with the link colors

The rule Web designers should follow in setting link colors for their pages is very simple: Don't do it. Let the user set the link colors in their own browser. Following that rule avoids gratuitous color differences that only distract users. Following the rule also makes it more likely that users' browsers will be able to indicate whether links have already been traversed (see Blooper 61: Links that don't provide enough information, Section 6.2.2).

Don't embed links in prose text

Corporate Web sites should be less chatty and verbose than personal Web sites. They should also be designed for maximum clarity and usability. Therefore, the "Click here for details" style is inappropriate for corporate Web sites. For example, instead of "Click here for details," present the link as "Details." Furthermore, don't bury links in prose paragraphs (except perhaps in Help text documents). Place them adjacent to—but visually separate from—the data to which they correspond (for examples, see Table 6.1).

Table 6.1   Making textual links stand out

Instead of	*Make links stand out*
Click here for a description of this collection.	Employee Skills Collection Description
If the item you want is not listed above, check the next 10 or the previous 10 items.	Previous 10 items Next 10 items
House: 3 BR, 2 BA, near public transit. Asking $123,000. Click here for details.	House: 3 BR, 2 BA, near public Details transit. Asking $123,000.
Your shopping cart currently contains 3 items, with a total cost of $76.45.	Shopping cart: View Cart Contents 3 items Total cost: $76.45
Click here for information on priority settings and response time.	Priority settings and response time

6.2.2 Blooper 61: Links that don't provide enough information

In many Web sites and Web applications, users can see the links on a page, but can't tell what type of link each one is without actually clicking on it to follow it to its destination. I'm familiar with three variations of this blooper.

Variation A: Links that don't indicate "been there, done that". By convention, Web browsers provide two link colors: one for links to pages that the user (or more precisely, this copy of the browser) has not yet visited, and another for links to pages that the user has already visited. The browser keeps track of the pages it has visited by keeping track of the URLs of the pages. When it needs to display a link, it checks to see if it has a record of having visited the link's destination page and chooses the appropriate link color. This difference in color allows users to see whether or not a link goes somewhere they've already been, which is very helpful when browsing the Web.

Unfortunately, some Web sites and Web-based applications don't provide this useful information—at least not on all of their links. Normally, this happens when a Web site designer turns off link-marking borders on image links, or uses certain types of links that aren't marked at all (see Blooper 60: Hidden links, Section 6.2.1).

For example, in the array of appliances shown on the Sears Web site (Figure 6.13), the text label makes it clear that the images are links, but because the image borders are turned off, visitors to the site won't be able to see which appliance categories they have already visited. They will have to keep track of that themselves.

Links that don't indicate "been there, done that" can also result from a designer setting a page's link-marking colors explicitly rather than simply letting them be set by visitors' Web browsers. Perhaps the designer's two chosen link-marking colors don't differ enough (especially for users who are partially color-blind). Perhaps the link-marking colors are different, but are so unfamiliar to users that they can't tell which color indicates "unseen" and which color indicates "seen."

When links don't indicate whether a user's browser has already visited the page they point to, the navigability of the site suffers; users unintentionally revisit pages they've already seen. This problem is made worse when links to the same destination are labeled differently, such as with different wording or graphics. For example, if links in a Web site—for whatever reason—don't mark whether the user has already visited them, and two different links to the same page are worded "Sign up!" and "Register", users could easily be fooled into visiting the Registration page twice. Since downloading Web pages can take a long time depending on what is on the page, unintended second visits to the same page can be a big time-waster for users.

Because HTML form-submit buttons are not marked at all by browsers, they obviously won't be marked as having been visited. Thus, if form-submit buttons are used in place of regular links, potentially useful information will be missing.

There are also other, more esoteric kinds of links, which may or may not indicate whether the user has visited the linked-to page. Some developers of intranet Web applications use nonstandard Web page components to construct pages and nonstandard browsers to view them; they can do this because they are operating in a closed environment.

For example, one of my clients had a generic online Help facility that was used throughout the company's product line. The Help facility was designed to be Web-like, but was based on proprietary data formats and browsers rather than HTML files and commercial Web browsers. Textual links in the Help files were marked with a distinctive color and underlining, but links whose destinations had already been visited did not appear in a separate color.

Variation B: Not distinguishing links to internal anchor points from external links. A common problem in Web sites I've reviewed—and in many I use—is that users cannot tell whether a link points to an anchor point elsewhere in the same Web page or to a separate page. Users click on a link expecting it to take them to a different page, but instead are taken to a heading further down (or up) in the same document, or vice versa. Either way, they may not even realize that where they have been taken is different from where they expected to go, which means that they will soon become disoriented as they continue to try to maneuver around in the site.

The popular Web browsers do not mark within-page and between-page links differently, so it is not surprising that many Web pages have this problem. Browsers do usually show the destinations of links in a message line at the bottom of the browser window when the mouse pointer is over the links. However, few users pay much attention to that display, largely because the information usually displayed there is too cryptic for them to understand, for example:

```
http://www.musicforce.com/mf/album/1,1289,024350051688,00.html#Summary
```

Furthermore, to determine whether the destination of a link is internal or external, it is not enough to simply look at the Web address displayed in the bottom message line. A user must compare that Web address with the one displayed in the "currently viewing" field at the top of the page. This makes it even less likely that nontechnical users—that is, most users—will check this. Finally, some users turn off the browser's display of the bottom message line in order to leave more screen area for the Web page. For such users, the destination Web address is not available.

Confusion between within-page and between-page links most often arises in Web pages that start with a table of contents at the top of the page. If the table of contents is all that is visible without scrolling, users might easily (but wrongly) assume that they are looking at a table of contents page, containing links to a collection of separate content pages. Confusion can also arise if a link deep in a page points to another section of the same page, but is labeled using

Figure 6.14

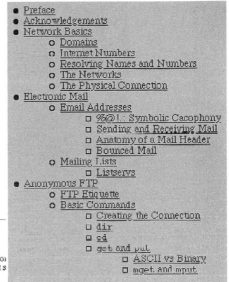

different words than those labeling the referenced section. In such cases, users might easily fail to recognize that the link points to the anchor point.

For example, Figure 6.14 shows tables of contents for two different articles that are available on the Web. The article on the left is at *www.acm.org/sigchi/chi97/proceedings/invited/jj.htm*. The links in its table of contents are all for anchor points further down on the same Web page. The article on the right is at *www.cs.indiana.edu/docproject/zen/zen-1.0_toc.html*. The links in its table of contents are all for separate Web pages. Users cannot tell just by looking at the links whether they are internal or external.

Variation C: Not distinguishing links that bring up a separate browser from those that don't. Another important piece of information about links that is missing from many Web sites is whether or not the link displays its destination in the same browser window or in a fresh one. As with the distinction between links to internal anchor points versus external pages, this distinction is not marked by browsers.

Figure 6.15 is part of the home page of Star Alliance, an international consortium of airlines. The buttons on the right side of this page bring up separate browser windows, whereas the buttons in the middle of the page do not. Nothing indicates which buttons bring up separate browsers and which do not. I would guess that many users of this page fail to notice that a new browser has appeared when they click on one of the airline buttons and would then be at risk for becoming disoriented.

I have watched users in Web site usability tests become completely lost when a new browser window appeared unexpectedly. In many cases, users did

Figure 6.15

not even realize that a new browser appeared because it covered the first one. Once a user misses the fact that a new browser window opened, the subsequent sequence of events becomes very predictable.

- The user does some things in the new browser window and eventually tries to back up to the page that (unbeknownst to the user) is still displayed in the first browser window, hidden by the second one.
- The new browser window can't back up to that page because it was never on that page.
- The user tries to click on the Back button, finds it inactive (i.e., grayed out), and becomes very confused. Browsing is suspended while the user tries to figure out what the heck is going on.
- Eventually, the user discovers that there are now two browser windows, but has no idea how that happened, and simply closes the second browser window.
- The next time the user follows the same link or a similar one, the sequence starts over.

So much for efficient Web site navigation.

Avoiding Blooper 61: *The design rule*

Traversing links is the primary means of navigation on the Web. By designing links so that they provide clear information about where they go, Web developers can make it easy for users to find their way around.

Let users see whether they've "been there, done that"

Web users need to be able to tell whether they have previously visited the destination of a link. Web site designers should try very hard to make sure that links convey that information. The high likelihood of disrupting users' ability to distinguish visited links from unvisited links is one of many reasons why Web site designers should never set link colors.

An inability to indicate "been there, done that" is one reason that the use of form-submit buttons as links is discouraged [Flanders and Willis, 1998].

On the other hand, if buttons are used in dynamic, Web-based *applications*—as opposed to Web sites consisting of static pages—it can be argued that they needn't indicate whether the user has already been to their destination. After all, conventional GUI-based software applications don't indicate whether various windows and dialog boxes have already been displayed. Why should GUI applications that happen to be hosted on Web servers be any different? For example, why should a user need to know whether or not she has previously seen the Print dialog box?

Distinguish within-page and between-page links through careful formatting

The fact that browsers don't distinguish between within-page and between-page links is only a weak excuse, not a valid justification, for creating a Web site in which users can't tell whether links are within- or between-page. It is possible, through careful positioning and labeling, to make it clear to users that the destination of a particular link is inside or outside of the current page. It is just that many Web developers aren't aware of the need for users to know this and so don't do anything to make it clear.

Figure 6.16 shows a table of contents from the Web site for the Internet Engineering Task Force's netiquette guidelines (*http://w3.arl.mil/home/netiquette/rfc18551.html*). The image is a portion of the page that includes the table of contents and the introduction. The other sections of the document are on separate Web pages. The first item in the table of contents could have been a link to the introduction section below, but that would have resulted in one link that was internal while the rest of the links were external, with no way for users to distinguish them. That would have been very confusing. Wisely, the authors chose not to make the first item a link at all, since the Introduction is clearly visible just below the Table of Contents. More Web site designers should be this thoughtful!

Figure 6.16

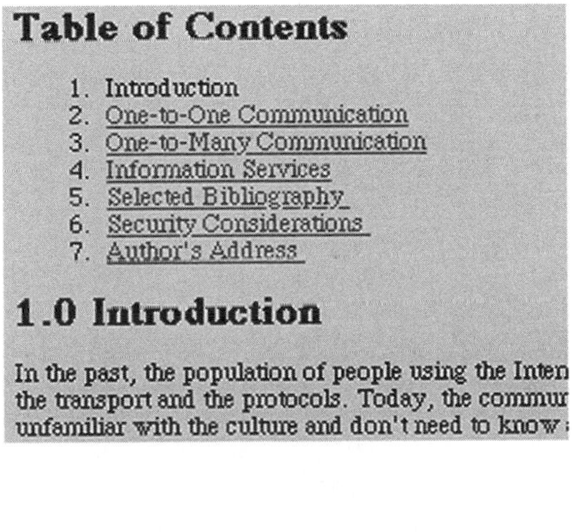

Table of Contents

1. Introduction
2. One-to-One Communication
3. One-to-Many Communication
4. Information Services
5. Selected Bibliography
6. Security Considerations
7. Author's Address

1.0 Introduction

In the past, the population of people using the Inter the transport and the protocols. Today, the commur unfamiliar with the culture and don't need to know

Figure 6.17   <u>Lorem ipsum dolor sit amet...</u> (opens new window)

Label links that display a new browser

Since browsers do not mark links that open new browsers differently from those that simply change the display in the current browser, it is up to Web page designers to indicate this, as Malcolm X said, "by any means necessary." One straightforward way of indicating it is simply to tell users that the link opens a new browser. Since the Web site *www.WebPagesThatSuck.com* criticizes poor Web site design, its author has to be pretty conscientious about making sure the site is well designed. He is, and it is. An example of a link from his Web site that opens a new window is shown in Figure 6.17. It simply tells users what it is going to do.

6.2.3 Blooper 62: Buttons that provide no click feedback

In many ways, the rise of the World Wide Web has caused a great leap backward in GUI design. Many important design principles that were developed and became common practice in the desktop application design have simply been forgotten or rendered moot by the rush onto the Web. As mentioned in the Introduction to this chapter, this is partly because the rise of the Web has vastly expanded the ranks of people who design user interfaces; suddenly, anyone with a copy of Claris HomePage and some family photos or an Amway franchise is a user interface designer.

However, the lack of experience of most Web site developers is only part of the reason for the decline in user interface quality. Four other important contributing factors are

- the weak interaction model embodied in the Web's single-click-to-act paradigm, which derives from the Web's origins as a medium for static hypertext documents
- the limited capabilities of most popular Web browsers, especially in supporting fine-grained interactivity
- the difficulty of developing agreed-upon standards for encoding Web content and control mechanisms
- the immaturity of Web scripting languages, Web programming languages, and Web GUI component libraries

For example, the familiar select-act action paradigm that was embodied by the first GUIs and became standard throughout the computer industry has been nearly eliminated by the Web.

However, the step backward I want to discuss now is much simpler than the loss of the select-act action paradigm. It is simply this: Most buttons on the Web do not provide click feedback.

For two decades, an important design rule for GUIs has been that on-screen buttons should provide nearly instant visual feedback that they have been pressed. The usual way to provide this feedback has been to replace the button's "unpressed" image with a "pressed" image, which looks darker and more inset than the "unpressed" button image. In order for users to perceive the "pressed" button as resulting from their depressing the mouse button, it must occur no later than a tenth of a second after the mouse button goes down (see Chapter 7). In addition, the design rule for buttons in GUIs requires buttons to give feedback on "mouse down," but to delay taking action until "mouse up" (see Blooper 14: Buttons that trigger on "mouse down," Section 2.4.1).

On the Web, there are basically three types of buttons:

- HTML form-submit buttons
- Web GUI toolkit buttons used in applets and applications written in Web scripting or Web programming languages
- Images of buttons that are defined as links

HTML form-submit buttons and Web GUI toolkit buttons are not the problem. HTML form-submit buttons definitely exhibit the correct behavior. Most Web GUI toolkit buttons exhibit the correct behavior, and those that don't tend not to be used. In any case, only a small proportion of the buttons on the Web are of these first two types.

The problem is the third type of button: images of buttons serving as links. Such buttons are the vast, vast majority of all buttons on the Web. Some such buttons are individual button images that are mapped in their entirety as a link to a destination. Other such buttons are contained in images that depict entire arrays of buttons, where the area of the image corresponding to each button is mapped to a different destination. In neither case does HTML provide a way for a Web developer to designate a "pressed" image for the button.

Therefore, when users click on button images, the button does not acknowledge the click. Not within a tenth of a second—not ever. It simply remains as it was. The only feedback users get that the click was received is (1) the browser's busy animation starts, and (2) the cursor changes to a wait cursor. To make matters worse, these two forms of feedback may be delayed well beyond the required 0.1 second after the users' mouse click. This feedback is simply not sufficient for users to feel that they succeeded in clicking the button. Therefore, they will often click it multiple times before they are sure that the system is responding.

For example, the Star Alliance Web site pictured in Figure 6.15, includes two different arrays of button images. Similarly, the Sharper Image Web site *(www.sharperimage.com)* includes the three button images shown in Figure 6.18. None of these "buttons" provide immediate click feedback. The only way a user can tell whether a click on one of these buttons succeeded is by checking to see that the browser's busy animation starts moving, or by listening for a surge in the activity of the computer's hard disk. Such a situation is not user

Figure 6.18

friendly! This of course is not purely the fault of the designers of these Web sites. Any Web site that uses button images—and there are a lot of them—has the same problem.

What an incredible step backward!

Avoiding Blooper 62: *The design rule*

I avoid image buttons in Web sites I design, and I advise others to do likewise. Instead, I recommend using regular textual links, HTML form-submit buttons, or Web GUI toolkit buttons. Regular textual links don't give instant click feedback either, but they aren't supposed to. HTML form-submit buttons and Web GUI toolkit buttons provide the required feedback. Their disadvantage is that they require significantly more setup than image buttons created using client-side image maps. *C'est la guerre.* One does what one must do.

6.2.4   Blooper 63: Displaying long lists as very long pages

Most Web design experts agree that it is a mistake to present long Web pages in which most of the content can be seen only by scrolling down the page. For example, both Nielsen [1996] and Flanders and Willis [1998] criticized Web pages that require users to scroll down to see important content, especially links or other navigation controls. Their observations of Web users convinced them that Web users in fact do not scroll down much and often assume that what is visible without scrolling is all that is there. Recently, Jakob Nielsen [1999b] has moderated his position on scrolling, claiming that Web users are, with experience, becoming more used to scrolling down the page. Nonetheless, Nielsen still discourages designs that require much downward scrolling.[5]

The real culprit: Variable-length pages. In reviewing Web sites for clients, I see many Web pages that are too long. However, they tend to be mostly a certain type of page: lists or tables of data. They are usually not pages in which a designer explicitly laid out every element. Rather, they are mainly pages in which the primary content is some kind of user- or computer-generated listing that can vary in length. Here are some examples of the types of content I am talking about:

---

5.   Web design experts even more strongly criticize Web pages that require users to scroll side to side (e.g., to the right) to see important content. Although users apparently tolerate small to moderate amounts of downward scrolling, they really dislike having to scroll sideways, and often simply will not.

- list of recently received email messages
- contents of a file directory or folder
- table of stocks owned by user, showing number of shares, purchase price, current price, and so on
- schedule of events for a given day, week, or month
- list of items found by a search
- table of airline flights leaving a particular airport on a specified day
- table of servers on a network that are currently up and running
- a long form, containing dozens, perhaps even hundreds, of data fields and settings
- list of products that are on sale this week
- list of postings in an online discussion group, with replies, if any, indented below each posting

One might expect that on pages that display variable-length lists and tables, the need to scroll down would not be a problem for users. However, my observations lend only partial support to that expectation. I have seen many users—in formal usability tests as well as informal situations—simply overlook the browser's scrollbar and assume that what they can see is all there is until they are told otherwise. In such cases, the problem is not that users don't like scrolling down, but rather that they just don't realize that they can or should. The Web pages in question didn't provide enough clues that there was content below the bottom edge of the browser window.

Worse: Buttons below variable-length content. The need for users to scroll a Web page becomes a much more serious usability flaw when a page is designed such that important fixed content is placed below the data list or table. For example, I often see pages in which a long list or table is followed by controls, links, or important instructions. If scrolling down the page is the only way to access those functions or information, the designer has committed a serious blooper.

A customer support Web site I reviewed included many pages that displayed long lists or tables of items, such as available software patches, search results, and the customer's currently open support cases. Below the tables and lists were controls, for example, for downloading patches, initiating new searches, and editing support case status. I advised the client that some site visitors would not find the controls, and those who did find them would be annoyed at having to scroll far down the page to reach them.

A misguided "solution": Multiple copies of buttons. Some Web page designers try to solve this problem by breaking the list or table into parts and placing copies of the controls at intervals along the length of the page. This "solution" is not only ad hoc, it is also misguided. Often, it backfires.

A home-buying Web site developed by a client included a long form that users had to fill out to indicate the features of their ideal home. Because most of the form fields were optional, the designers wisely put all the required data fields first, at the top of the form, thereby making it easy for users to fill them in and ignore the rest. The required fields were followed by Submit and Cancel buttons. The buttons, in turn, were followed by the optional fields, and the form ended with another set of buttons. In a usability test of the Web site, test participants were given a task that required filling in the form, including some of the optional data fields. However, many participants filled in the form down to the first Submit and Cancel buttons, assumed they were at the end of the form, clicked Submit, and then tried to find another page on which to supply the rest of the information.

Avoiding Blooper 63: *The design rule*

I mentioned earlier that the excessively long pages I see rarely consist of fixed content that a designer explicitly placed on the page. Designers of such pages at least appear to be following the recommendations of Web design experts: keeping pages short enough to be viewed without much downward scrolling.

Of course, my observation may be a result of the fact that I visit very few personal Web pages. Almost all of the Web sites I visit were designed by professionals, most of whom have probably heard or read the recommendations of experts like Nielsen, Flanders, and Willis. I would, however, not be surprised to find that amateur designers of personal Web sites are still creating excessively long pages in large numbers.

Some design alternatives

When a Web page displays a list or table that will vary in length and will often be significantly longer than a browser window, four design alternatives are available, each best-suited for particular situations:

1. *Let the page be long:* Place the items or table directly onto the Web page and simply live with the fact that the page will (often) be long. Make it clear to users that there is content below the bottom edge of the browser window by either providing a very noticeable "More Below" indicator or by making sure that data items at the edges of the browser window are only partly displayed (see Figure 6.19). This approach should never be used when the page includes important content below the variable-length list or table, but otherwise is only slightly risky. It is safest when the lists or tables were constructed line by line by users. When users have explicitly constructed a long list, they are more likely to realize that it extends below the bottom edge of the browser window. An example of such a list would be the contents of a file folder created, populated, and managed by a user.

Figure 6.19

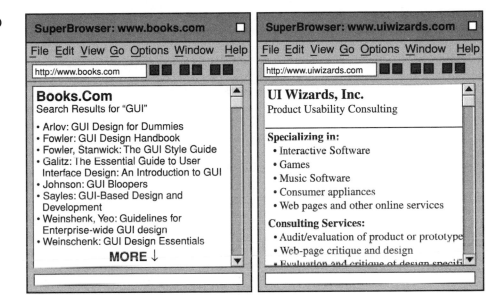

Figure 6.20

2. *Use a scrolling container:* Place the list or table inside a scrolling container (see Figure 6.20), so that the Web page in which it appears is not long and has a fixed length. The scrolling container should be large enough to show a reasonable number of list items or table rows, but small enough to fit entirely within a full-screen browser window. This approach can be used with

Figure 6.21

Page 1
1-12 of 1662 pages matching your query

	Score	**Title**
1)	100	Los Angeles SIGCHI
2)	100	Los Angeles SIGCHI
3)	100	Los Angeles SIGCHI
4)	100	ACM Professional Chapters
5)	100	ACM Professional Chapters
6)	100	FY'95 SIG Annual Report
7)	100	FY'97 SIG Board Annual Report
8)	100	ACM SIGCHI: More About SIGCHI
9)	100	SIGCHI Bulletin Vol.26 No.3, July 1994: From the Chairs: ACM / SIGCHI Program Review
10)	100	SIGCHI Bulletin Vol.26 No.2, April 1994: SIGCHI Email Addresses
11)	100	SIGCHI Bulletin Vol.28 No.1, January 1996: The CHI Conference
12)	100	SIGCHI Bulletin Vol.28 No.1, January 1996: 50 Years ACM, 14 Years SIGCHI

Go to page: 1 . 2 . 3 . 4 . 5 . 6 . 7 . 8 . 9 . 10 . 11 . 12 . 13 . 14 . 15 . 16 . 17

any long list or table, but is especially important if controls, links, or instructions are positioned on the Web page below the list or table.

3. *Show only* N *at a time:* Display only a specified number of list items at a time, with controls to allow users to display the next and previous group of items. This is the approach that most of the popular Web search services use for displaying items found by a search (see Figure 6.21). Ideally, users should be able to adjust the number of list items that will be shown at once.

4. *Use multiple pages:* Break the long list or table up into parts, each on a separate page. This approach works only when the list or table to be segmented consists of meaningful subsections that contain different types of information, such as a list that contains first directories (folders), followed by files. This approach also is well suited for long data entry forms; users fill out and submit each part of the form separately. Not only can most forms be broken easily into meaningful parts, but doing so is good because it lessens the

chance of significant data loss if a user's net connection fails or the browser crashes while the user is filling out a form.

As stated earlier, placing controls at intervals in the list (instead of only at the beginning or end) is not a good solution, largely because it sometimes backfires: users assume that the controls signal the end of the data and don't scroll further down.

Whatever you do, be consistent, and test it!

Whatever design alternative is chosen should be used consistently. This does not mean that all variable length lists, tables, and forms in a Web site must use the same one of the four alternatives. The four alternatives differ in the situations for which they are best suited, so a designer might decide to use Alternative 4 for long forms, and Alternative 2 for long lists. Thus, being consistent simply means sticking to the same approach for all similar types of data displays.

Finally, whatever solution is adopted should be usability-tested to determine whether it makes sense to users. If testing shows that an approach isn't working for users, then it isn't a solution.

Further reading

Web Design Guidelines

Nielsen, J. 1999d. *Designing Web Usability: The Practice of Simplicity.* Indianapolis, IN: New Riders Publishing.

Web Bloopers

Flanders, V., and Willis, M. 1998. *Web Pages That Suck: Learning Good Design by Looking at Bad Design.* San Francisco: Sybex. (See also *www.WebPagesThatSuck.com*)

Nielsen, J. 1996. "The Top-Ten Mistakes of Web Design." *www.UseIt.com/Alertbox*. May.

Nielsen, J. 1999b. "'Top Ten Mistakes' Revisited Three Years Later." *www.UseIt.com/Alertbox*. May 2.

Nielsen, J. 1999c. "The Top Ten *New* Mistakes of Web Design." *www.UseIt.com/Alertbox*. May 30.

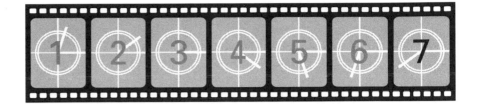

Responsiveness Bloopers

Introduction

© 1998 Randy Glasbergen. www.glasbergen.com

"Since we can't afford faster computers, we're going to hire slower workers because that will make our computers *seem* faster."

As I stated in Section 1.7 of Chapter 1, First Principles, a very important factor in determining the usability of software products or services is their responsiveness. Notice that I said "responsiveness," not "performance" or "speed." There is a difference. Explaining that difference and how to achieve responsiveness when performance is limited—as it almost always is—is largely what this chapter is about.

For the benefit of readers who skipped Chapter 1, I'll provide a brief definition of responsiveness, and distinguish it from performance.

Highly responsive software lets you know instantly that your actions were received (e.g., button presses, mouse movements), lets you estimate how long lengthy computations will take, frees you to do other things while waiting for a function to complete, manages queued events intelligently, performs housekeeping and low-priority tasks in the background, and makes use of idle time to anticipate (and precompute) your likely future requests.

Performance, on the other hand, has to do with how quickly the software computes and displays the desired *results*. High-performance software gives users their desired results quickly; low-performance software makes users wait.

The good news is that software can be responsive even when its performance is low. The bad news is that much of the software in today's market has both low performance and low responsiveness. Bad combination.

This chapter describes the most common responsiveness bloopers and explains why developers commit them. It is organized differently from the other bloopers chapters of this book because responsiveness bloopers are all closely related to each other; they are all really variations on the same underlying blooper, with the same underlying reasons and solutions. Therefore, instead of describing each blooper separately, accompanied by the reasons for it and the design rule for avoiding it, the responsiveness bloopers are described together, along with some examples. Section 7.2 presents the reasons why developers commit responsiveness bloopers. Following that, in Section 7.3, I present principles for designing responsive software—several insights about human-computer

The 5th Wave
By Rich Tennant

"He must be a Macintosh user—there's a wristwatch icon etched on his retina."

© The 5th Wave by Rich Tennant, Rockport, MA. Email: the5wave@tiac.net.

interaction that suggest ways to improve user interface responsiveness. Finally, in Section 7.4, I provide techniques for making software responsive.

Because most responsiveness bloopers cannot be illustrated with software screen images, they are mainly illustrated instead by brief scenarios in which human-computer interaction is portrayed as if it were human-human communication. I also describe cases of poor responsiveness in computer products I have seen or used.

7.1 Common responsiveness bloopers (Bloopers 64–75)

Anyone who has used a computer has encountered some—if not most—of the most common responsiveness bloopers. The most bothersome ones I frequently encounter are the following:

- **Blooper 64:** Windowed operating systems in which the pointer on the screen doesn't keep up with the users' movements of the pointing device, jumps around erratically as the system gets around to processing mouse movements, and continues to move after the user has ceased moving

- **Blooper 65:** Word processors and text editors that can't keep up with users' keystrokes, forcing users to stop and wait to see if they typed what they intended to type, and sometimes even missing some of the text users type

- **Blooper 66:** On-screen buttons that don't acknowledge mouse clicks, or that acknowledge clicks after such a long delay that users think they missed and so click again

- **Blooper 67:** Menus, sliders, and scrollbars that lag behind the users' actions, thereby destroying the hand-eye coordination that is required for their successful operation

- **Blooper 68:** Moving and sizing operations that don't keep up with user actions, but also don't provide temporary "rubber-band" feedback

- **Blooper 69:** Applications that periodically—and unpredictably—become unresponsive while they automatically save the current document, swap a needed program segment from disk into the computer's memory, or purge no-longer-needed temporary files

- **Blooper 70:** Software that ignores all user input—including Cancel and Abort—until it is finished with whatever it is doing, forcing users to wait for lengthy unwanted operations to finish

- **Blooper 71:** Applications that don't display busy indicators when they are busy, that don't display progress bars for lengthy operations, or that display phony progress bars

- **Blooper 72:** Window management systems and windowed applications that ignore user input while they repaint irrelevant areas of the screen, sometimes multiple times for no apparent reason

- **Blooper 73:** "Killer" Web sites that are so loaded with images and animations that they are unviewable without a super-high-speed Internet connection such as cable modem
- **Blooper 74:** Printers and fax machines that cease *all* operations—not only printing—when they run out of paper or ink
- **Blooper 75:** Software that sits idle waiting for the user to issue a command and, when the user finally issues a predictable command, takes a long time to execute it

7.1.1 Examples of responsiveness bloopers

A particularly annoying sort of responsiveness blooper is mentioned in Blooper 71 above: the phony progress bar. Phony progress bars look deceptively like real progress bars—a bar is filled in over time from one end. However, in a phony progress bar, the degree of fullness of the bar does not indicate the degree of completion of the operation. Some phony progress bars show the "progress" of the software in processing each item in a long list of items; they fill up once for each item, starting over for the next item. Other phony progress bars simply fill up cyclically in correspondence to nothing in particular, or display animating bands in the "bar" area.

CoOOol but useless

Microsoft Windows (98 and NT) displays a phony progress dialog box when it copies files from one place to another, for example, from a hard disk to a floppy disk. As is shown in the screen image in Figure 7.1, the display consists of two animations: (1) a sheet of paper that flies between two folders, and (2) a "progress" bar. The flying-paper animation doesn't correspond to any meaningful file transfer event, such as the transfer of a certain number of kilobytes or of a complete file, so it is useless as a progress indicator. The progress "bar" fills up once for each file transferred, so it is unhelpful unless only one file is being copied. Thus, what looks superficially like a progress display is actually just a busy animation. Although a programmer had fun creating the "coOOol" flying-paper animation, this dialog box provides almost no useful information.

Figure 7.1

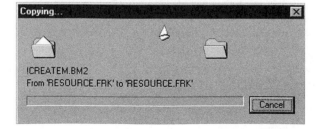

Figure 7.2

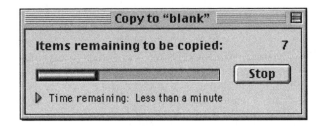

A well-designed progress bar

Compare it to the progress dialog box displayed by the Apple Macintosh for file transfers, shown in Figure 7.2. In sharp contrast to the Windows "progress" display, the Mac progress display shows how many files remain to be copied, graphs the cumulative progress in a progress bar, and provides a rough estimate of the remaining time. Of course, it has no snazzy animation, so it isn't as "coOOol" as the Windows file transfer dialog box. But it is *much* more useful.

Another phony progress bar

Phony progress bars are unfortunately fairly common. Another example of one is shown in Figure 7.3. It is displayed by the installer software for the shareware CAD program Drawing Board LT. Instead of showing users the progress of the entire installation, it shows them the "progress" of installing each file. Since Drawing Board LT consists of hundreds of files, most of them very small, users get to watch the bar flash rapidly as it fills up several hundred times in rapid succession.

This is not very useful to users, who simply want an estimate of how long they have to wait. I think it is safe to say that the developers of this display did not understand the purpose of progress bars.

The lack of responsiveness seen in many computer-based products would be considered dysfunctional, perhaps even intolerable, if it occurred in communication between people. Figure 7.4 gives examples of poor computer responsiveness presented as if they were person-to-person communication. Do any remind you of computer software you use?

Figure 7.3

Figure 7.4   *Example 1.* Both participants are locked in a single foreground process.

> "Hello. I'd like to fly from San Francisco to New York next Thursday, returning Sunday evening, as cheaply as possible."
>
> "OK, I'll check flights and fares. I don't know how long it will take, but you must stay on the line, not doing anything else, until I find the answer. If you hang up, I'll forget about your request."

Example 2. Participants fail to communicate time requirements and time estimates.

> "I'd like to have this camera repaired." [Doesn't say that he needs it in two weeks for a wedding.]
>
> "Sure. Once I get your information and a $25 deposit, I can put the job on our repair technician's queue." [Doesn't say that the technician is on vacation in Botswana and won't be back for six weeks.]

Example 3. When the system is busy, the user gets no response at all, not even feedback that input has been received.

> "Fred, what are our plans for this weekend?"
>
> [Busy writing; no reply.]
>
> "Hey! Do you know if we have any plans for this weekend?"
>
> [Still no reply.]
>
> "Earth to Fred! Earth to Fred! Do you read me?"
>
> [Finishes writing.] "OK, that's done." [Looks up.] "Did you say something?"

7.2 Reasons for poor responsiveness

Computer-based products exhibit poor responsiveness for seven reasons. The most fundamental reason is a lack of understanding in the computer and software marketplace of what responsiveness is and how important it is. The other reasons are more specific to the various professions that are involved in software development. One reason is attributable to negligence on the part of user interface designers. Three reasons are attributable to mistakes by programmers. One reason is a lack of adequate software tools, components, and platforms. One reason is a common mistake of software development managers.

7.2.1 Reason 1: The facts about responsiveness are not widely known

As I said in Section 1.7 of Chapter 1, responsiveness has been repeatedly shown to be one of the most—if not the most—important factor in determining user

Real examples of poor responsiveness

As an indication of how common severe responsiveness problems are, the following are excerpts from user interface reviews I performed of several clients' software. The first two were released products; the third was being prepared for beta release.

- *Product 1:* When a user invokes Generate Declarations, it can take up to five seconds for the window to appear, during which absolutely no feedback is provided that anything is happening. Many users will invoke the function again, and (eventually) get two Generate Declarations windows. *Recommendation*: When the function is invoked, the cursor should change immediately to an hourglass, and the button should be disabled.

- *Product 2:* After users login, the Main Window appears and the program connects over the intranet to its various databases and downloads certain data. This can take 10–20 seconds. During this time, the program displays "connecting to ..." and "loading ..." messages in the message area at the bottom of the window, but the messages are so unobtrusive and appear and disappear so quickly that most users won't notice them. The function buttons on the Main Window appear active and ready immediately, even though they ignore all clicks until the initialization has completed. Many users will begin clicking on the buttons and wonder why they don't respond. *Recommendation. Best:* Don't display the Main Window until the initialization has finished; display a temporary "Loading data. Please wait." dialog box that shows a progress bar, so users can estimate how long loading will take. *Alternative:* Display the Main Window immediately (as you do now), but deactivate its functions and display a wait cursor until loading is complete.

- *Product 3:* When the user clicks on Create Graph, it can take 10–60 seconds for the Create Graph dialog box to appear. Meanwhile, there is no feedback (e.g., no wait cursor) that anything is happening. The button doesn't even register a press. Therefore, users will click on the button multiple times, and then get (and have to wait for) several Create Graph windows. *Recommendation*: In addition to providing a wait cursor, the button should go inactive if a Create Graph window is already up (or in the process of coming up).

satisfaction with computer technology. Unfortunately, this fact seems virtually unknown in the industry.

If few developers and development managers know how important responsiveness is, it is not surprising that they continue to churn out unresponsive software. Similarly, if software customers don't fully understand the impact of responsiveness on their preferences, they can't very well demand it from software vendors.

7.2.2 Reason 2: UI designers rarely consider responsiveness during design

Many responsiveness bloopers are the fault of user interface designers, not of GUI programmers. User interface designers rarely consider performance and

Figure 7.5

responsiveness issues when designing software. They usually don't specify in their design documents what response times are desirable, acceptable, and unacceptable, but just assume that the specified functions will be fast enough. Most importantly, they fail to consider how the best design might *depend* on what response times are achievable. If the response times tend to be very long, a different design would be called for than in the case where response times tend to be short or highly variable.

Consider the operation of scrollbars. Scrollbars typically display an "elevator" to show users what part of the entire document is currently being viewed. Figure 7.5 shows scrollbars from the Apple Macintosh (left) and Microsoft Windows (right). Despite their superficial differences, both have an "elevator."

A responsiveness issue with scrollbars is how updating the scrollbar itself—the position of the elevator—is linked to updating (i.e., scrolling) the displayed content. The issue is whether the scrollbar updates its appearance before or after the content scrolls. There are two common designs:

- In some scrollbars, the position of the elevator is absolutely tied to the position of the window content, so the elevator does not move until the window content has scrolled.

- In other scrollbars, the elevator first follows the mouse to where the user drags it, then, when the user releases the elevator, the window content scrolls to its new position.

Which design one should use depends on whether it is computationally expensive or cheap to scroll the document content to a new position. If scrolling the window content is easy and quick, the first method is preferred because it keeps the window content synchronized with the elevator and thus provides more accurate feedback. However, if scrolling the window content is expensive and slow, the second method of operation is better because otherwise the elevator would lag behind the user's pointer.

If a user interface designer has not specified what scrolling response times are acceptable or unacceptable, the GUI implementors cannot be faulted for choosing the form of scrollbar operation that is easiest for them to program.

The bottom line is that poor responsiveness can render an otherwise well-designed feature useless. Unfortunately, the software marketplace is full of fancy features that are useless because of poor responsiveness. Examples of such features were given in the list of common responsiveness bloopers in Section 7.1.

7.2.3 Reason 3: Programmers equate responsiveness with performance

When a software product is not responsive enough, programmers tend to blame poor algorithms and inefficient implementation. This leads them to try to improve their algorithms and tune the performance of the application's functions. Their ideal is that all functions should execute as close to instantaneously as possible. A common result of this view of the problem is unplanned delays in release dates while programmers try to improve performance of unacceptably "slow" products. In such cases, the software is often eventually released even though it is still "slower" than developers and management (and customers) had hoped.

Programmers also often blame poor responsiveness on slow computer hardware. According to this view, poor responsiveness is a trivial problem because higher-performance computers will soon be available, and upgrading to those will solve the problem. This view ignores history: in the past 25 years, computer power and speed have increased by a factor of several hundred (maybe even more), yet software responsiveness is still as much of a problem as it ever was.

 Poor responsiveness in a commercial product

I am writing this book partly on my Apple Macintosh PowerBook 170 laptop computer, using the Microsoft Word 6.0 word-processing software. When I am typing text into Word, I often hear the PowerBook's hard disk come to life. I keep Word's Automatic Periodic Save option turned off, so this disk activity must be something else, such as Word having to swap program segments or parts of the data file from the hard disk into the computer's memory. Whatever the reason, at such times, Word temporarily turns the mouse pointer into a watch (the Mac's busy indicator) and suspends all updates to the text display. When this happens, I've learned that I should stop typing and wait (3–5 seconds) for the busy cursor to return to normal. If I continue to type while display updates are suspended, I can't see what I'm typing and so sometimes lose track of what I've typed. Even if I don't lose track, when Word finally finishes its disk activity and updates the display to show what it thinks I've typed, it is often missing text I typed. In other words, not only does Word sometimes fail to keep up with typing, it sometimes even drops characters that users type while it is lagging. That is bad, very bad.

Granted, both the PowerBook 170 and Word 6.0 are several years old now (1999). However, as is explained later in this chapter, the old word processor WordStar had no problem keeping up with typists. If software that was released in 1995 running on a computer with a 68020 processor and eight megabytes of memory can't keep up with typists while software released in 1979 running on a computer with an 8080 processor and 64 kilobytes of memory could, it is obvious that the difference isn't simple performance.

Viewing poor responsiveness simply as a need to upgrade to faster hardware also ignores the real world. Customers typically run software products on less powerful computers—and with slower net connections—than the software's developers use (see Blooper 82: Giving programmers the fastest computers, Section 8.2.4). Computer companies have been releasing new, more powerful models at least once a year, but customers can't afford to replace their computer equipment that often. The faster computers and Internet connections that programmers use may therefore take years to appear in significant numbers in the marketplace. Furthermore, customers often run software under higher load than the developers anticipated (Section 7.3.2, Processing resources are always limited).

7.2.4 Reason 4: Programmers treat user input like machine input

A fourth reason for poor responsiveness in computer-based products is that programmers—and hence the software they write—tend to regard input from users as being the same as input from other computers or software. In fact, some software user interfaces, such as early versions of Unix, are explicitly designed not to distinguish between being operated by a person and being driven by another program.

Figure 7.6 presents an example of a design that treats human input like machine input, presented as if it occurred in person-to-person communication. Do you recognize any software you've used?

Equating human user input with machine input leads to mistaken design rules. One commonly believed but mistaken rule is that all user input is sacrosanct, and that user interfaces that discard, lose, or overlook any user input are seriously flawed. In fact, with human users, simply discarding certain user-generated events is precisely the right thing to do.

For example, since moving the cursor using a mouse or cursor keys is a hand-eye coordination task, throwing away queued mouse movements or cursor keystrokes is a reasonable action when the system is lagging behind in its processing. Users don't miss the discarded input because they are paying attention to the pointer on the screen, not to how much they have moved the mouse or how many times they have pressed the LEFT key. Ignoring backlogged mouse

---

Figure 7.6   *Example 4.* Event queue is a straight FIFO (first-in, first-out queue). No recognition that human operators, unlike computers, pay attention to external feedback, not the number of commands they've issued.

"OK, back 'er up juuust a tad. A little more ... more ... more ... more ... more ... more ... more ... a little more ... OK, stop. Stop! STOP!"

[CRRRRUNNNNCH!!!]

"Aw, man! Why didn't you stop when I said 'stop'?"

"Because I got behind on the 'mores' and still had a couple more to deal with before I could process your instruction to stop."

movements and cursor keystrokes avoids frustrating overshooting of targets common in systems that don't do this.

On the other hand, discarding input is not appropriate when the controlling events are generated by another computer program. The software generating the input is not using the hand-eye feedback loop that people use. It has no basis for control other than keeping track of the events it has generated. Since the requirements of human and programmatic control of applications differ so greatly, it is wrong to believe that the same user interface can serve both.

Why do programmers often treat interaction with human users as if it were interaction with another software program? The tendency of developers to rely on simple, easy-to-code implementations (see Reason 5, next) is one factor. Another is that programmers understand the behavioral characteristics of computers and software much better than they understand the perceptual, motor, and cognitive characteristics of human users. Therefore, in their designs, the requirements of programmatic control often prevail over those of human users.

7.2.5 Reason 5: Developers use simple, naive implementations

Software developers often use simple algorithms, data structures, architectures, and communications protocols in order to minimize schedule risk and maintenance costs. They prefer implementations that are easy to program: for example, single-threaded, synchronous. Their managers usually support them in this. While this usually makes sense, it often hinders the goal of making software highly responsive.

Figures 7.7 and 7.9 present, in the guise of person-to-person communication, examples of overly simple implementations that harm responsiveness. Do any remind you of software you use?

Though the examples in Figures 7.7 and 7.9 may seem exaggerated, in fact they correspond to the behavior of many computer-based products. Consider the following computer-based examples:

- Many Web browsers and Web-based applications waste time repainting areas of the display that don't need to be repainted. Sometimes areas of the display are repainted several times in rapid succession. Meanwhile, the software is unresponsive, or perhaps the user is waiting for the screen to settle down before proceeding. In either case, valuable time is wasted, all because the implementation is too simple-minded to determine (1) what parts of the display actually need repainting, and (2) the right order in which to repaint the display's various components.

- Some Web browsers display phony progress bars while they download pages. As explained earlier, phony progress bars look superficially like they indicate progress, but in fact do not. In some cases, when the bar fills up, it

Figure 7.7 *Example 5.* Synchronous dialog; requests completely independent of each other; no anticipation of likely future requests.

> "Hello, I'm shopping for shock absorbers for my '99 Toyota Camry. Do you carry Acme shocks?"
>
> "Dunno. I'll check the warehouse. Please wait."
>
> [Caller drums fingers on table for two minutes.]
>
> [Salesman returns to phone.] "Yes."
>
> "How much do they cost?"
>
> "Hang on. I'll check."
>
> [Caller drums fingers for another minute.]
>
> "They're $50 each installed."
>
> "What about Excelsior shocks?"
>
> "Dunno. I'll check the warehouse. Please wait ..."

Example 6. User interface does not take into account that (1) from the user's point of view, the operation requires feedback, iterative refinement, and hence repeated invocation of what the system regards as the semantic operation, and (2) the semantic operation is "heavyweight."

> "Let's try putting the piano here."
>
> [Mover moves piano to indicated location.]
>
> "No, that doesn't work. How about over by the window?"
>
> [Mover moves piano.]
>
> "That's even worse. Let's try here ..."

Example 7. Event queue is a simple FIFO. No recognition that reordering queued events can save time and work.

> [An apartment building custodian starts his day.]
>
> "Let's see. What's first on my list for today? Sweep hallway floors. OK, let's do it!"
>
> [Sweeps floors.]
>
> "OK, that's done. What's next? Sand baseboards in hallway. OK...."

just empties and starts filling again. In Netscape Communicator 4.5, the bar simply displays moving bands that indicate activity but not progress, as Figure 7.8 shows.

- Even the percent-loaded status messages that many browsers display aren't very useful because they show only the status of loading a single file. Most Web pages these days consist of multiple files, for example, frame sets, text files, and graphics files. Therefore, it isn't very useful to see the percent loaded for each individual file; users would prefer to see the percent of the *total* file volume that remains to be loaded. But that is more difficult to provide, so the simpler, naive implementation often wins.

Figure 7.9   *Example 8.* Tackling a large, difficult task based upon prior instructions, without rechecking their validity before starting.

> "Here it is! I postponed my family's vacation and worked overtime all week to make sure I got the Smith proposal done on time."
>
> "Oh? Didn't someone tell you? We've decided not to go after the Smith contract."

Example 9. Tackling a large, difficult task based upon default assumptions, not knowing until too late that the task is moot.

> "Well, if it isn't the new owners! Come on in!"
>
> "We just stopped by to take some measurements."
>
> "Really? You're in luck. We just finished measuring the whole place. As you can see, we're putting in the new carpeting that we promised in the sale agreement. We'd intended to replace it before we put the house on the market, but didn't get around to it."
>
> "Oh? Well, don't bother. We like hardwood floors, so we're planning to rip out the carpet."

- Modern computer printers have to render document pages as images to print them. Rendering pages for printing can take significant time. Unfortunately, many printers stop rendering queued pages if they run out of paper or ink. Therefore, it is a common experience for users to send a document to the printer, wait a while for it to finish, then go to the printer to pick up the document, only to find that the document was not printed or only partly printed because the printer ran out of paper. The user puts more paper into the printer and expects the next page to begin printing immediately, but there is a delay because the printer first has to render the next page. It was not able to do that while it was waiting for more paper because of a simplistic, single-threaded implementation that stops everything when any part of the process is blocked.

- Many office fax machines quickly scan document pages into their memory and then transmit them. This is useful because it lets users return to other activities. It makes a fax machine more responsive even though its transmission rate is fixed. Unfortunately, some implementations of this feature are frustratingly naive. I recently fed a multipage document into a fax machine and waited for its display to tell me the document was being transmitted. Instead, the display said that the machine was out of toner. I didn't know how to add toner to this machine. I assumed it didn't need toner to send my documents anyway, so I continued waiting for it to dial the recipi-

Figure 7.8

ent's phone number and begin transmitting. It didn't. After a minute or two, I asked an administrative assistant for help. She looked at the machine and explained that it wouldn't transmit documents when it was out of paper or toner because it needed to know it was going to be able to print a confirmation page when it finished transmitting. My fax was held up because the machine didn't have toner to print an acknowledgment I didn't want.

In all of these examples, developers chose a simple, straightforward implementation to minimize development risk. The cost of that decision was reduced responsiveness, which may have reduced customer acceptance and therefore sales revenue.

7.2.6   Reason 6: GUI software tools, components, and platforms are inadequate

Given the importance of responsiveness in determining user satisfaction with interactive software, it may seem odd that software developers often opt for overly simple implementations that hinder responsiveness. Don't they—or at least their managers—know that by doing so they are limiting demand for their products?

Often, the answer is yes, they know, but they are working in an environment that does not provide the support they need to do better. Modern GUI platforms (such as Windows, MacOS, CDE/Motif, and Java) do not provide adequate support for writing software that has to meet real-time deadlines or prioritize tasks at run time.

Furthermore, given the complexity of modern GUI platforms, even responsiveness enhancements that should be easy are in fact difficult. Blooper 16: Not showing busy cursor (Section 2.4.3) describes some of the problems GUI programmers have when they try to display busy cursors. It turns out that displaying a busy cursor in Java or Windows requires writing multithreaded code, even if nothing else in the application requires multiple threads. This increases the level of programming complexity immensely compared to single-threaded code. It is therefore not really surprising that some developers simply choose not to bother displaying busy cursors.

7.2.7   Reason 7: Managers hire GUI programmers who lack the required skill

Contributing to a lack of responsiveness in GUI-based software is a lack of skill and experience among GUI programmers. Variation E of Blooper 77: Assigning the GUI to less-experienced programmers (Section 8.1.2) describes the relatively low status of GUI programmers in the software development industry, and how development managers often assign GUI development to their more junior programmers. This almost guarantees that subtle aspects of GUI design and implementation—such as those that enhance responsiveness—will be short-changed.

This problem is exacerbated by the fact that writing highly responsive software often requires using real-time and multithreaded programming techniques. As described in Reason 6 above, GUI software tools, components, and platforms provide poor support for real-time and multithreaded programming, thereby placing the burden on programmers. A colleague who is a software development manager and programmer told me:

> Multithreaded applications are hard. They require hiring expensive senior developers, and often take a long time to debug and maintain. Correctly writing object-oriented multithreaded applications is even more difficult.

Of course, some software developers do manage to write real-time software. For example, the software inside jet fighters, cruise missiles, factory robots, nuclear power plants, and NASA space probes is heavily oriented toward satisfying real-time constraints.

The issue, therefore, is not that no one knows how to write such software. Rather, the issue is that the economics of the desktop and Web software industry, together with a lack of understanding among software developers of the importance of software responsiveness, discourage development managers from hiring programmers who have the required level of skill to write highly responsive GUIs.

7.3 Avoiding responsiveness bloopers: Design principles

In Chapter 1, I summarized seven important responsiveness design principles of interactive systems, which define what it means for software to be responsive and suggest how to achieve that (see Section 1.7). I will now fully describe those responsiveness design principles with examples to help clarify them. Following the principles, I describe design and implementation techniques that can improve responsiveness.

7.3.1 Responsiveness is not the same thing as performance

Software can be highly responsive even if its functions take time. If you call a friend on the phone to ask a question, he can be responsive to you even if he can't answer your question immediately; he can acknowledge the question and promise to call you back.

For example, the Xerox Star's document editor included a sophisticated structured drawing program. Drawings were contained in frames embedded in documents [Johnson et al., 1989]. Graphics frames, like most objects in Star, had properties that controlled details of their appearance and location. The implementation of graphics frames had a performance problem: repainting a frame could take many seconds if the drawing was complex. However, that wasn't the real problem. The real problem was that a simplistic implementation turned the performance problem into two annoying responsiveness problems:

- Once a graphics frame began displaying its content, it could not be interrupted. All subsequent user input was ignored until the graphics frame finished displaying.

- Changing *any* property of a graphics frame caused the frame and its content to be completely redisplayed, even if all that had changed was the frame's border. This implementation naiveté resulted in much unneeded redisplaying of graphics frames.

Without these two additional problems, the slow painting speed wouldn't have been so much of a problem for users. The two responsiveness problems were eventually fixed in ViewPoint, Star's successor, greatly reducing the impact of the performance problem, which remained. Thus, the product's responsiveness was improved even though its performance was not.

 Responsiveness versus performance in elevators

An urban legend has it that the occupants of a large office building were complaining about how long the building's elevators took to respond to the elevator call buttons. The building's management called the elevator company and asked them to improve the elevator response time. The elevator company sent an analyst to review the problem and recommend a solution. The analyst spent a couple of days in the building watching people wait for the elevators, then recommended a solution, which was implemented.

Instead of altering the response algorithms used by the elevators' controlling computer, the elevator company installed mirrors on the walls next to the elevators. The complaints about waiting ceased. Problem solved. ⊕

7.3.2 Processing resources are always limited

The faster computers get, the more software people will load onto them: for example, inits, desk accessories, multiple applications. Also, the faster computers get, the more users will try to have their computers do at once: for example, playing music from an MP3 file while editing a document, downloading data or software from the Web while browsing other Web pages, running various autonomous agents while doing other work. Peter Bickford, a former user interface designer at Apple, put it this way in his book *Interface Design* [1997]:

> Macintosh II users rejoiced at a computer that effectively ran at four times the speed of the Macintosh Plus, and then willingly gave up much of the potential speed increase to run in color. As machines continued to get more powerful, users added 24-bit video, file-sharing, sound input and output, desktop movies, and so on. There's no real end to this trend in sight.

Also, as described above in Reason 3 (Section 7.2.3) and in Blooper 82: Giving programmers the fastest computers (Section 8.2.4), it is likely that customers have slower computers than the developers have. Even having the latest-model computer doesn't necessarily mean that more computing resources will be available to a particular application.

7.3.3 The user interface is a real-time interface

Like software that collects data from scientific or medical instruments, software that interacts with people should be designed to meet real-time constraints. Three time constants in human behavior set goals that computer systems must meet in order to be perceived as responsive [Nielsen, 1993; Robertson et al., 1989, 1993]:

- The first time constant, 0.1 second, is the limit for perception of cause-and-effect between events. If software waits longer than 0.1 second to register a reaction to a user action, perception of cause-and-effect is "broken": the user will not associate the displayed reaction with his or her action. This 0.1 second time constant is what Xerox PARC researcher Stuart Card and his colleagues call the perceptual "moment." It is also the approximate limit for perception of smooth animation.

- The second time constant, 1 second, is the maximum comfortable gap in a conversation—the point at which one of the participants will say something to keep the conversation going, even if only "uh" or "uh-huh." It's the comedian's "beat"—the time to wait after setting up a joke before delivering the punch line. In human-computer interaction, it is the limit for displaying busy indicators or progress bars, for opening or closing a display, or for returning the answer to a simple computation. One second is also the approximate minimum response time for reacting to unanticipated events, as when a child unexpectedly runs in front of a driver's car. This also holds in human-computer interaction: when information appears on the screen, it is very unlikely that the user can react to it in less than a second.

- The third time constant, 10 seconds, is the unit of time into which people usually break down their planning and execution of larger tasks. Card and his colleagues call this the "unit task" time constant. It is the approximate amount of time people can concentrate exclusively on one task. Every 10 seconds or so, people have to look up from their task, reassess their task status and their surroundings, relax, and so on. After 10 seconds, users want to mark a unit task complete and move onto the next one. This time-constant has been observed across a wide range of tasks, for example, completing a single edit in a text editor, entering a check into a checking account program, making a move in chess, executing a combat maneuver in an airplane dogfight. In the case of "heavyweight" computer operations like copying files or conducting searches, 10 seconds is roughly the amount of time people are willing to spend setting up the operation and starting it before they begin to lose patience. The operation itself can then take longer (assuming that sufficient progress feedback is provided).

These three time constants are rough approximations of a variety of more precise time constants observed in a variety of research situations,[1] but they are accurate enough to guide user interface design. They are summarized in Table 7.1. Notice that they increase by factors of 10: 0.1 second, 1 second, 10 seconds, making them easy to remember.

For example, if an on-screen button does not "depress" within 0.1 second after a user has clicked on it, users will assume they missed the button and click it again, even if the button has "depressed" in the meantime. Similarly, if an on-screen object the user is "dragging" to a new location—or a "rubber-band" outline of it—lags more than 0.1 second behind the mouse pointer, users will have difficulty positioning the object in its new location and will complain about the software's responsiveness. If a function delays more than 1 second before displaying a busy or progress indicator, users will wonder what is happening and will consider the software to be unresponsive.

7.3.4 All delays are not equal; the software need not do everything immediately

Some events require immediate feedback; some don't. Software can therefore prioritize its handling of user events in order to give timely feedback where it is needed and delay other tasks.

For example, feedback for hand-eye coordination tasks such as mouse movement, selection, button presses, and typing should be immediate, that is, within 0.1 second. Internal bookkeeping, updating of areas of the screen where users

---

1. For example, the accepted maximum interframe interval for perception of smooth animation is less than 0.1 second: it is 0.065 seconds (or 16 frames/second). Similarly, the official unprepared reaction time in driving is less than 1 second: it is 0.7 second. Finally, the 10-second time constant is an approximation of several psychological time constants ranging from 5 to 30 seconds.

Table 7.1 The three time constants for human-computer interaction [Robertson et al., 1989, 1993]

Time constant	Aspect of human behavior it applies to	Situations where relevant
0.1 second	▪ Perception of successive events ▪ Perception of causation ▪ Perceptual fusion, for example, perception of smooth animation	▪ Feedback for successful hand-eye coordination, for example, pointer movement, window movement and sizing, drawing operations ▪ Feedback that a button has been clicked ▪ Displaying "busy" indicators ▪ Interval between animation frames
1 second	▪ Turn-taking in conversation, for example, maximum pause before someone says something, even if only "uh" or "uh huh" ▪ Minimum response-time for unexpected events, for example, time to react to a child running in front of a moving car	▪ Displaying progress indicators ▪ Finishing most user-requested operations, for example, opening a dialog box ▪ Finishing unrequested operations, for example, reformatting a paragraph, autosaving
10 seconds	▪ Unbroken concentration on a task ▪ Unit task: completing one "unit" task in a larger task, for example, make a move in chess, execute a combat pilot action	▪ Completing one step of a multi-step task, for example, a single edit in a text editor, entering a check into a checking account program ▪ Completing user input to an operation ▪ Completing one step in a wizard (a multipage dialog box)

aren't working, results of explicitly requested calculations or searches need not be immediate.

The classic user interface design handbook *Human-Computer Interface Design Guidelines* [Brown, 1988] uses the concept of task "closure" to determine when software response delays are acceptable and unacceptable:

> A key factor determining acceptable response delays is level of closure. Delays that occur after the user has completed a planned sequence of actions are less disruptive than those that occur in the middle of a sequence. A delay after completing a major unit of work may not bother a user or adversely affect performance. Delays between minor steps in a larger unit of work, however, may cause the user to forget the next planned steps. In general, actions with high levels of closure, such as saving a completed document to a file, are less sensitive to response time delays. Actions at the lowest levels of closure, such as typing a character and seeing it echoed on the display, are most sensitive to response time delays.

Trying to complete all operations instantly is a naive strategy that cannot succeed. It can actually degrade responsiveness when important tasks get stuck behind less important ones that were supposed to execute quickly but didn't.

Furthermore, instant responses to certain user actions can be undesirable even when they aren't delaying more important feedback. Faster is not always better. Users don't trust complex searches or computations that finish too quickly. A slight delay, blink, animation, or other feedback may be required when a display changes in order for users to notice the change. Many old computer games can't be played on newer computers because they run too fast. Thus, the time deadlines given previously for different sorts of feedback are not just maximums.

7.3.5 The software need not do tasks in the order in which they were requested

As Example 7 in Figure 7.7 (about the janitor sweeping and then sanding) suggests, performing tasks in a naive, first-in, first-out order can cost extra work, thereby hurting responsiveness.

Intelligently reordering tasks in one's queue can save work and therefore time, thus enhancing responsiveness. Tasks can also be reordered so that higher-priority tasks are attended to before lower-priority ones.

7.3.6 The software need not do everything it was asked to do

Sometimes an operation the user requested is unnecessary. For example, suppose a user is editing a document and directs the software to save it. If the user has not changed anything since the last time the document was saved, there is no reason for the software to waste time resaving it (assuming that the file into which the document is to be saved is the same as before). Instead, the document-editing software can display a message indicating that the file is already saved or it can pretend to do the task very quickly. Many document-editing applications do this, but some do not. Microsoft Word saves a document every time the user directs it to do so, whether or not there are any changes to save. So does Sybase PowerBuilder. For users such as myself who have developed the habit of invoking Save reflexively every few minutes to guard against software crashes, this is often an annoyance, especially when the document is large and takes a long time to save.

Sometimes queued tasks become moot before they are executed. Perhaps the deadline for completing them expired. Maybe the conditions that motivated them changed. If a queued task becomes moot before the software has started on it, there is no reason to do it; it can simply be dropped. If a task becomes

Figure 7.10   *Example 10.* Some requests are frivolous and evaporate completely when it is revealed that fulfilling them is not free.

> "Can you reformat this document in two columns?"
>
> "Yes, but it will take an hour (or cost $100)."
>
> "Ack! Forget it! I don't want it that much."

moot *while* it is being executed, it can be aborted. If it can be predicted before a task is started that it cannot be done on time, maybe there is no reason to do it. Finally, some requests are frivolous and evaporate completely when it is revealed that fulfilling them is not free. In a sense, fulfilling such requests at all is a waste of time and resources.

Example 2 (see Figure 7.4) presents a case in which two parties to a transaction initiate a task without communicating time requirements and estimates, and so doom themselves to missing an important deadline. Figure 7.9 presents examples of people starting a queued task without first checking whether the task is still necessary. Figure 7.10 presents an example of how adequate communication can save unnecessary work. Computer-based examples, which are all too common, include software that gives users no clue as to how long an operation might take, or that does not provide easy ways for a user to stop a lengthy operation the user no longer wants.

7.3.7 Human users are not computer programs

Human users operate software very differently than computer programs operate other programs. They cannot sustain high rates of input indefinitely. They may be able to keep the system busy for several seconds (about 10, maximum), but eventually, they pause to think or rest.

People, unlike most computers, are also not single-channel sources and sinks for serial data. Human perception and cognition are of course not fully understood, but what is known is that people can do several things in parallel. For example:

- Type text or play music while reading ahead to the next text or music
- Read a book while humming a tune
- Tune to a station on a radio with one hand while steering a car with the other
- Play a melody on an organ keyboard with their hands while playing a bass line on the organ's pedals with their feet
- Walk and chew gum at the same time (well, some people, anyway)
- Dial a telephone while planning dinner

The 5ᵗʰ Wave   By Rich Tennant

"I'M WAITING FOR MY AUTOEXEC FILE TO RUN, SO I'M GONNA GRAB A CUP OF COFFEE, MAYBE MAKE A SANDWICH, CHECK THE SPORTS PAGE, REGRIND THE BRAKEDRUMS ON MY TRUCK, BALANCE MY CHECKBOOK FOR THE PAST 12 YEARS, LEARN SWAHILI, …"

© The 5th Wave by Rich Tennant, Rockport, MA. Email: the5wave@tiac.net.

Most importantly for human-computer interaction, people perceive the results of their actions with their eyes and ears while they operate the computer with their hands.

This gives rise to another important difference: people are unlike computers because they pay attention mainly to the feedback they receive from the software, rather than keeping close track of the actions they have performed, as Example 4 (about the vehicle backing up) suggests. Thus, human users don't know or care how many times they've pressed the DOWN arrow or NEXT key or the scrollbar arrow, or how many mouse movements they've made; they watch the *display* and base their decision about whether to continue on what they see there.

If the scrollbar or the screen pointer lags behind user actions, users will overshoot their targets. If a button doesn't acknowledge a press immediately, users will press it again, just as in a conversation with another person, if a listener doesn't respond quickly, the speaker will rephrase what he or she said or ask a tag question, such as "OK?" or "Understand?"

The bottom line is that people are not computers. Software designed so that its user interface is the same as its interface with other computer software is doing its human users a great disservice.

7.4 Avoiding responsiveness bloopers: Techniques

Of course, just understanding principles is not enough. In order to produce software that is highly responsive to its users, developers need implementation techniques and methods that support that design goal. This chapter describes several such techniques.

The techniques described here range from simple and static to complex and dynamic. They are grouped into four categories: timely feedback, parallel problem solution, queue optimization, and dynamic time management. Most of these techniques are methods of managing time, which can be applicable in many domains besides implementing computer software. I've even found some of them helpful in managing my own time and interacting with the people around me.

7.4.1 Timely feedback

The first group of responsiveness techniques all pertain to providing timely feedback to users.

Acknowledge user input immediately

Acknowledge user input immediately, even if you can't act on it immediately. Design the user interface to distinguish between acknowledging user actions and acting on them. Feedback for hand-eye coordination must be nearly instantaneous, that is, within 0.1 second; otherwise users' perceptions of cause-and-effect break down and they assume their action wasn't received (so they may try it again). Delayed acknowledgment of user actions is almost as bad as no acknowledgment.

Figure 7.11 provides an example of this approach, expressed as if it were human-to-human communication. Wouldn't it be nice if more computer software worked this way!

The most familiar computer software example would be a button component that always immediately acknowledges being pressed by changing appearance or color. It should not matter whether the function the button invokes takes a long time to execute. When a button is notified or detects that it has been pressed, its highest priority should be to acknowledge that fact. All other responsibilities of the button are secondary and can be delayed.

Yet another software example is a scrollbar that keeps up with mouse actions (such as dragging the scrollbar "elevator" using the mouse) by not bothering to scroll the actual window content until the user has released the scrollbar in its new position. This is in contrast with scrollbars that first scroll the window content and don't update the "elevator" position until the content has been repainted in its new position. The latter type of scrollbar is fine if the content can scroll in 0.1 second, but if it can't—that is, if scrolling or repainting the window content is for some reason a time-consuming operation—the former design is preferable. GUI toolkits should let programmers specify which protocol will be used.

Given the speed of today's computers, there really is no excuse for GUI components that can't acknowledge user input within 0.1 second. Today's comput-

---

Figure 7.11 *Example 11.* Providing immediate acknowledgment of input is helpful even if the system can't provide the desired answer right away.

"Fred, what are our plans for this weekend?"

"Just a minute. I'm trying to get this idea down on paper."

"OK."

[Eventually finishes writing.] "OK ... done. Our plans for this weekend? Let's see...."

ers execute tens of millions of instructions in that amount of time. If a GUI component cannot acknowledge a user action within 0.1 second, that means that the GUI component—or the window system that dispatches the action to the component—is wasting time executing millions of nonessential instructions at a highly inappropriate time. This in turn suggests serious architectural flaws, either in the component or in the window system. What is needed is a strong commitment to responsiveness at the time these systems are architected. For example, processing of events could be ordered so that acknowledging user input is always the software's highest priority.

Provide busy indicators and progress indicators

Provide busy indicators and progress indicators for functions that take longer. This includes busy cursors, busy animations, progress bars, and the like. The real-time deadline for such feedback is 1 second. If no feedback has been provided by then, users begin wondering what is happening, and the perceived responsiveness of the software suffers greatly. If software can display a busy or progress indicator within 0.1 second—the hand-eye coordination feedback deadline described above—the busy indicator can double as the action acknowledgment. If not, the software's response should be split into two parts: a quick acknowledgment within 0.1 second, followed by a busy or progress indicator within 1 second.

Sometimes software developers don't bother displaying a busy cursor or progress bar because the function is always supposed to execute quickly (see Blooper 16: Not showing busy cursor, Section 2.4.3). It may in fact always execute quickly on the programmer's computer. Users, however, may have different experiences for a variety of reasons: their computers may be slower, they have more software running on their computers, their computers may not be optimally configured, their network configurations may differ from those of the developer (see Blooper 82: Giving programmers the fastest computers, Section 8.2.4).

I recommend that functions display busy indicators even if they will normally execute quickly (e.g., in under 1 second). This can be very helpful if for some unanticipated reason the function gets bogged down or hung. Furthermore, it doesn't harm anything; when the function executes at the expected speed, the busy indicator will appear and disappear so quickly that users will barely see it.

Unfortunately, as is pointed out in Blooper 16 (Section 2.4.3), modern window-based operating systems, which are user-driven, multitasking, and multithreaded, make it difficult for application programmers to assure that busy cursors are displayed at the appropriate times and screen locations. Thus, the responsibility for poor responsiveness in applications lies not only with application developers, but also with operating system and GUI platform developers. Stated more positively, operating system and GUI platform developers have at least as much of an opportunity to improve software responsiveness as application developers do. They need to develop tools and building blocks that allow application developers to do the right thing with less effort than is required today.

Some busy indicators are more helpful than others

Busy indicators range in sophistication. At the low end, we have simple, static wait cursors (e.g., the familiar hourglass). They provide very little information—only that the system is temporarily occupied and unavailable to the user for other operations.

Next, we have wait animations. Some of these are animated wait cursors, such as the MacOS watch, with its moving hands. Other animated wait cursors I've seen are a hand that counts with its fingers, a swinging pendulum, and an hourglass with falling sand. Some wait animations are not cursors, but rather larger graphics positioned elsewhere on the screen, such as the "downloading data" animations of the various Web browsers. Wait animations are more "friendly" to users than static wait cursors because they show users that the system is working, not crashed or hung up waiting for a network connection or a data lock.

Even better than wait animations are progress indicators, which not only show that the system is working, but provide an estimate of how much work or time remains. Progress indicators can be graphical, like a progress bar; they can be textual, like a count of files remaining to be copied; or they can be a combination of both, like MacOS 8's file transfer progress indicator. Whether textual or graphical, progress indicators greatly increase the perceived responsiveness of a product, even though they don't shorten the actual time to complete operations.

Progress indicators are more important the more time-consuming the operation. So many noncomputer devices provide progress indicators that we take them for granted. Elevators that give no indication of the elevator car's progress toward one's floor are pretty annoying. Imagine how people would feel about a microwave oven that provided no indication of the remaining cooking time. When someone rewinds an audio cassette or videotape, the tape itself provides a visual indication of the amount of time remaining. If the little window onto the tape were covered up, people wouldn't like it. Many tape recorders and players also provide a tape counter, augmenting users' view of the tape itself.

Progress indicators can be approximate

Software engineers often hesitate to provide progress indicators because they don't feel they can estimate the remaining time accurately. This is an unwarranted concern. Users aren't computers; they don't require absolute accuracy. A progress indicator can be off by a factor of 10 or more and still be helpful. For example, a multiple file transfer operation can provide a useful progress indicator by simply showing how many files (or what percentage of files) remain to be transferred, even though some of the files may be 1 kilobyte in size while

Figure 7.12

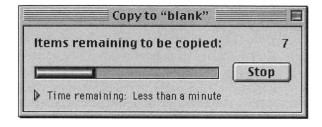

others are 12 megabytes. Any information is better than none. Users just want to know if they should wait, check their voice mail, or go to lunch.

As an example of this, Apple Computer's MacOS 8.0 displays progress bars for multifile transfer operations, including an initial estimate of the total expected time (see Figure 7.12). The time estimate is very rough. It is also often greatly overestimated at first, but is adjusted to a more realistic value as the transfer proceeds. Despite the approximation, Apple's progress display tells users what they want to know, and so is an example of good design.

Display important information first

Display important information first, details and auxiliary information later. Don't wait until the display has been rendered in its full glory before letting users see it. Give users something to think about, or even act upon, as soon as possible.

This has several benefits. It is a "sleight of hand" technique, not unlike a magician who makes a flamboyant gesture with one hand to distract observers from what he is doing with his other hand. It distracts users from the fact that the rest of the information isn't there yet, and fools them into thinking that the computer did what they asked quickly. It also lets users start planning what they are going to do next, that is, their next unit task (see Section 7.3.3). Finally, because of the minimum response time for users to respond to what they see (see Table 7.1), it buys at least 1 more second for the software to catch up before the user tries to do anything. A second is a lot of time to a computer.

This technique can be applied in two different ways. If software would take too much time to display everything the user asks to see, it can be designed to display certain information first. An example of this approach would be a stock investment Web site designed so that as the user's "current investments" page is downloaded to the Web browser, the names of the stocks the user owns and their current market prices are displayed before anything else, with other information and formatting niceties filled in later. A second example is document-editing software or a Web browser that, when the user asks it to open a document or Web site, shows the first screenful of information as soon as it has it, rather than waiting until it has loaded the entire document before displaying anything. A third example is a database or Web search facility that lists some found items as soon as they are known, while continuing to search for other items that match the user's query.

Alternatively, if information is displayed in a complex, time-consuming format, the software can be designed to display the same information in a simplified, quick-to-display form first, replacing or elaborating it later, as time permits. Web browsers that render graphic images in gross form first and then refine them are a good example of this.

Example of an early software program designed for responsiveness

In the early 1970s, when I was an undergraduate in college, many time-shared computer systems had a "time-of-day" utility program that displayed the current time, for example, "10:50 a.m." I once saw a fancy time-of-day program that displayed a graphical image of a clock. The clock displayed the time with clock hands, rather than digits, and was very elaborate and decorated. Computers and graphics displays were much slower then than they are now, and the program took several minutes to draw the clock in full detail.

Whoever had written the program realized that the clock displayed slowly, and also that people wouldn't want to wait all that time just to find out what time it was. The program was therefore designed so that the first thing it drew was two simple lines representing the clock's two hands. Drawing these lines took only a fraction of a second. This let users see immediately approximately what time it was. Next drawn were the numbers 3, 6, 9, and 12, giving viewers a better idea of the time. The remaining numbers were filled in after that. Next, the program drew the clock's outline. After that, the program began elaborating the clock's hands and numbers, and drawing in decorations. At any point along the way, a user could stop the program by hitting a key (see Figure 7.13).

If users just wanted to know what time it was, they stopped the program as soon as it drew the hands. Perhaps they waited until the numbers appeared to be more sure they were reading the time correctly. If, however, users were showing the "cool graphic clock program" to a friend, they let it run longer, perhaps to completion. This clock program was an outstanding example of how software can be designed to be responsive even though its performance is limited.

Figure 7.13

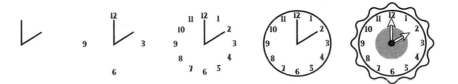

Fake heavyweight computations

Programmers should fake heavyweight computations until they are finalized. Highly interactive computer applications and electronic appliances often provide operations that users must invoke repeatedly in order to get the precise solution they want. If such operations are time-consuming, allowing users to invoke them repeatedly in rapid succession often results in feedback that lags badly behind user actions. In such cases, a better approach is simply to provide the required feedback, but not actually execute the operation until the user knows what he or she wants.

For example, I described in Section 7.2.2 how a scrollbar can be designed to detach its user feedback, which must be very fast, from scrolling the window's content if that is slow. In a way, such scrollbars are an example of this method: doing the minimum required to give users the feedback they need. However, no faking of the feedback is required in the case of a scrollbar; the moving scrollbar "elevator" would be the feedback even if the window content could be scrolled in a fraction of a second.

Examples where real fakery is required to provide responsive feedback are, however, not hard to find. Window managers and graphics editors are faking the feedback when they provide rubber-band outlines of objects that a user is trying to move or resize. The software could not meet the required real-time deadlines if it tried to move or resize the actual screen objects, so it doesn't try.

Other software examples involve making quick-and-dirty changes to internal data structures in order to represent the effect of user actions, and straightening out the data later. Most modern text editors, for example, maintain what is called a "piece table"—a temporary, pointer-based representation of changes that is very wasteful of memory space but quick to update. When a user inserts a paragraph into the middle of a document in such an editor, the editor does not bother to spread the surrounding text apart to make room for the new paragraph, even though the editor's display "pretends" that that's what it does. Instead, it just inserts a pointer at the insertion point to a free segment of the computer's memory, puts the new paragraph there with a pointer back to the continuation of the document. Similarly, deleting a paragraph does not really close up the space in the internal representation of the document. Rather, the editor simply inserts a pointer connecting the text before the deletion to the text following it. The "deleted" text is still where it was, but is "invisible" to the editor because the pointers now point around it. Text editors that use piece tables must eventually untangle the table to produce a compact representation of the revised document, but they can do that when they aren't under pressure to be responsive to the user.

Another example is operating systems that respond to a user's command to delete a file from a directory by merely removing the file's listing from the directory. Delisting the file takes practically no time and provides the feedback that the user needs. Actually deleting the data from the disk so that the space can be

Figure 7.14   *Example 12.* When there will be repeated invocation of a "heavyweight" function, provide feedback via a "lightweight" simulation until the adjustments have ceased.

> "Let's try putting the piano here."
>
> "OK, but to save strain on my back, I brought a cardboard piano that we can move around until you know where you want it, then I'll bring the real piano in and put it there."

Example 13. Interaction need not be synchronous. Delegating longish tasks to agents who operate in parallel with you can be useful.

> "I'd like to fly from San Francisco to New York next Thursday, returning Sunday evening, as inexpensively as possible."
>
> "OK, I'll check the flights and fares and call you back."

---

reused takes longer and so is delayed until the operating system has some extra time on its hands or the user specifically requests it.

Example 12 in Figure 7.14 illustrates this approach, presenting it as if it were human-to-human communication.

7.4.2 Parallel problem solution

A step upward in sophistication is to use parallel processing methods. This second group of responsiveness techniques consists of two different ways to use parallel processing: *offloading non-time-critical work* and *working ahead*.

Offload non-time-critical work

Offloading non-time-critical work consists of delegating longish tasks to background processes, to leave the main process free to respond to users. The tasks to offload are longish ones for which users don't require immediate feedback, such as the software's own internal housekeeping, or requests that users expect will take a long time.

Example 13 in Figure 7.14 illustrates this approach, presented as if it were human-to-human communication.

In the common case where a delegated task isn't actually executed by a separate computer, this technique amounts to giving the computer several tasks to juggle at once. It therefore runs the risk of bogging the entire computer down, thereby failing to do what it is intended to do, namely, free the main process to be responsive to users. If done badly, it can hurt responsiveness more than it helps it. However, if the main process is assigned a very high priority relative to the background process (at least while the main process is handling user input), the background process will simply be put on hold until there is time.

What if there isn't time? As stated above under Design Principles (Section 7.3.7), human users are not computers; they can't sustain high rates of input for very long. That is good because it ensures that the background task will eventually—in fact, soon—get done.

A software example of this technique is provided by Microsoft Word, a popular document-editing program. Before version 6.0, repaginating a document—adjusting the page boundaries, renumbering pages, and so on—was an explicit task that executed in the foreground. Users had to intentionally invoke repagination, and then wait many seconds—for long documents, minutes—for it to complete before they could return to editing the document. Since version 6.0, repagination in Word has been a background task, executed automatically on an as-needed basis, usually in such a way that users can continue editing the document. Spell-checking in Word has a similar history, although it remained an explicit foreground task until a more recent version.

Work ahead

Working ahead of users when possible is a valuable technique that can enhance responsiveness. Software can use periods of low load to precompute responses to high-probability requests. Furthermore, it is almost guaranteed that there will be periods of low load because the users are human. For example, interactive software typically spends a lot of time waiting for input from the user. Why waste that time? Why not use it to prepare something the user will probably want? And if the user never wants it, so what? The software did it in "free" time; it didn't take time away from anything else.

Figure 7.15 provides examples of this approach, expressed as if they were human-to-human communication.

Of course, working ahead should be done as a very low-priority background process, so it doesn't interfere with anything the user might be doing. Furthermore, processes that are working ahead need to monitor constantly whether the task they are working on is still relevant, and abort if it is not.

One example of software using background processing to work ahead of users is a spell-checker that looks for the next misspelled word while the user is deciding what to do about the current one. When the user directs the spell-checker to move on to the next misspelled word, it already has it and so appears to be very fast.

Another software example is a document viewer that renders the next page while the user is viewing the current page. When the user presses the button to display the next page, it is already ready. Even if the user never looks at the next page, the time spent rendering it wasn't wasted because it was done while the software would otherwise have been idle.

Figure 7.15   *Example 14.* It is often possible to anticipate what users will want and take advantage of their pauses and a low processing load to work ahead of them.

> "Here are the overheads for your talk. Also, I figured you'd want paper copies to hand out to the audience, so I made twenty."
>
> "Thanks, Fred, you're a godsend!"

Example 15. Though the previous example required some intelligence, it is often possible to work ahead of the user without any educated guesswork. (Notice that in the scenario below, it is difficult to decide who is the main process and who is the offloaded one.)

> "And what would you like for the main course?"
>
> "Hmmm. We haven't decided yet. There's so much to choose from!"
>
> "Well, while you decide, I'll go get your appetizer started and fetch your wine. When I return, you can tell me what you want."

7.4.3 Queue optimization

The third group of implementation techniques for improving software responsiveness falls under the general category of queue optimization. The basic idea is to review the to-do list periodically to decide what tasks to do and in what order. Two different ways to optimize a task queue are reordering it, also known as "nonsequential input processing," and flushing tasks from it that have be come moot.

Nonsequential input processing

The order in which tasks are done often matters. Blindly doing tasks in the order in which they were requested may waste time and resources or even create extra work. Software should look for opportunities to reorder tasks in its queue. Sometimes reordering a set of tasks can make completing the entire set more efficient, as is illustrated by Example 16 in Figure 7.16. Airline personnel are using such a technique when they walk up and down long check-in lines looking for people whose flights are leaving very soon so they can pull those people out of line and get them checked in.

This technique was even used in the days before GUIs: typing CTRL-C to a command-line-oriented application usually sent an immediate signal to the program to terminate, even though the program might still be working on user actions that were submitted earlier.

Perhaps the most familiar modern examples of this technique are seen in Web browsers: clicking the Back or Stop buttons or on a displayed link *immedi-*

Figure 7.16   *Example 16.* Reordering queued events can save time and work. Prescan the queue and optimize its order.

> [An apartment building custodian starts his day.]
>
> "Let's see. What's first on my list for today? Sweep hallway floors. Sand baseboards in hallway. Repaint stairway banisters."
>
> "Well, let's see.... I won't bother sweeping until after I've sanded because sanding will leave dust and grit everywhere. If I paint the banisters first, I'll have to wait a day or two for the paint to dry before I can sand the baseboards. So I'd better sand, then sweep, then paint."
>
> *Example 17.* Before starting a task that's been on your queue for a while, check to see if it is still needed. You might not have to do it.
>
> "Well, if it isn't the new owners! Come on in!"
>
> "We just stopped by to take some measurements."
>
> "Really? We tried to call you but you must have been on your way over here. We promised in the sale agreement to replace the old carpet. We ripped out the old carpet, but we wanted to double-check with you to make sure you want the new carpet."
>
> "Well, you're in luck. We've decided to expose the hardwood floors, so we won't need the new carpet. But thanks for ripping out the old stuff!"

ately aborts any ongoing activity to load and display the current page. Given how long it can take to load and display a Web page, the ability to abort an ongoing task is crucial to user acceptance of a browser. As we saw from the earlier example of the Xerox Star's noninterruptable, slow painting of graphics frames, not all software has had that capability.

Flush tasks that have become moot

Sometimes tasks on a to-do list become moot. New decisions may change requirements, deadlines for tasks may expire, recent requests may supersede earlier ones. Software can scan the queue so that moot tasks can be recognized and flushed from the queue or, if they have already been started, aborted. Doing this can save a lot of wasted time and effort. This technique therefore can be described as "faking speed by doing less than requested." Example 17 in Figure 7.16 gives an example of the technique, presented as human-to-human communication. The software examples given under "Nonsequential input processing" are also examples of flushing moot input.

Another example can be found in the EMACS text editor. EMACS provides both absolute-move commands (e.g., move cursor to line 10) and relative-move commands (e.g., move cursor 6 lines ahead). When EMACS is behind in processing the user's commands, it prescans its input queue and if it finds an absolute-move command late in the queue, it ignores all earlier move commands and just does the absolute move. A related technique used by some text editors is to compress 8 UP arrow keypresses and 3 DOWN arrow keypresses found in the queue into 5 UP arrow keypresses.

As described earlier, an important technique used to maximize the responsiveness of the mouse is to delete or ignore queued mouse movements. Mouse users pay attention to the position of the mouse pointer, not to the distance they've moved the mouse. Moving the mouse is a hand-eye coordination task and so requires immediate feedback. Hopefully, handling mouse events is such a high-priority task that the software processes events as fast as the user gener ates them, but if not, the software should simply skip the queued mouse events. In other words, queued mouse movements are moot by definition. Processing queued mouse events is *always* wrong. The same is true for trackballs, joysticks, relative touchpads, and other relative-movement pointing devices.

7.4.4 Dynamic time management

The most complex of the four categories of responsiveness techniques is dynamic time management. Unlike the aforementioned techniques, which reflect particular static strategies for prioritizing and handling user input, dynamic time management involves changing strategies at run time, depending on what is happening at the moment. Dynamic time management techniques are sometimes referred to as "real-time" programming techniques, although that term traditionally refers to interfaces between computers and instruments, rather than between computers and human users.

I will describe four variations of dynamic time management that can be useful in implementing responsive user interfaces.

Monitor event queue; adjust strategy if not keeping up with user

Software can monitor its event queue and adjust its strategy if it isn't managing to keep up with the user. In other words, it can keep track of how many events are backlogged on the queue, and switch to a faster strategy if the queue contains more than N items. Banks, supermarkets, and highway toll plazas are using exactly this strategy when they add tellers, checkout clerks, or toll takers when the lines are long. In my opinion, they don't do this often enough.

The following is an example of a software product that used dynamic queue-processing.

The original WordStar word-processing software monitored its event queue and used dynamic time management to enhance its responsiveness. When a user is typing text into a document, a word processor has a lot of work to do: display the text the user typed, reformat the paragraph, and update the cursor position indicators. Given the limited performance of personal computers in the late 1970s and early 1980s, a fast typist could easily cause the program to lag behind in processing keystrokes. However, WordStar's way of handling being behind was superior to that of its competitors.[2] When lagging behind the typist, most word processors of that day would queue up keystrokes and process them in the order received, so that the display at any given time would reflect not what the user had typed but where the program was in processing the input queue. In contrast, WordStar made sure that characters the user typed were visible immediately. When the user got ahead of the software, WordStar changed its display strategy: it concentrated on getting typed characters up onto the screen, and stopped wrapping words, updating cursor position indicators, and tending to other niceties until the user slowed down.

Now fast-forward to 1999. In Section 7.2.3, I described Microsoft Word 6.0's tendency to fall behind typists and drop typed text. In these two examples, we have the odd situation in which WordStar running on late 1970s and early 1980s PCs was in many ways *more* responsive to users than Word running on 1990s PCs. This is progress?

Example of dynamic real-time programming

In the mid-1970s, I worked as a student-intern programmer at the Jet Propulsion Laboratory (JPL) in Pasadena, California. JPL is run by the California Institute of Technology for the U.S. National Aeronautics and Space Administration (NASA). It is the command center for the United States' unmanned space program.

At JPL, I was assigned to a team that developed software for processing image data transmitted by Mars orbiter and lander spacecraft. This was classic real-time programming. The data arriving from the space probes was only going to be transmitted once because the space probes did not store data for later retransmission. The data was therefore regarded as priceless; we weren't supposed to miss *any* of it.

Our computers, although large, were very slow by today's standards. The software was supposed to receive the data, decode it, store it on disks, and, as time permitted, begin processing it to produce pictures that people could look at and scientists could analyze. However, if the software got behind in handling the data transmissions—and it often did—it had to suspend all of its other tasks and focus on saving the data. The software had to adapt its processing strategy based on how well it was keeping up. The rule was "Do whatever you have to do to keep from losing any of that data!"

Monitor time compliance; decrease quality or quantity of work to keep up

Monitoring the size of the input queue is a fairly gross way for software to monitor how well it is keeping up with users. Often that is good enough, but some-

2.   Which may be one of the reasons it remained the market leader until GUIs and WYSIWYG document editors took over in the mid-1980s.

times it isn't. A more precise way for software to measure how well it is keeping up with users is to time itself, that is, monitor its compliance with real-time deadlines. If the software isn't meeting its deadlines, it can decrease the quality or quantity of its work in order to catch up.

In this approach, the designer specifies—explicitly, in the code—maximum acceptable completion times for various operations, and the software continuously times itself in order to evaluate how well it is meeting its deadlines. If the software is missing its deadlines, or if it determines that it is at risk of missing a pending deadline, it adopts simpler, faster methods of doing its work, usually resulting in a temporary reduction in the quality or quantity of its output. This approach must be based on real time, not on computer processor cycles, so that it yields the same responsiveness on different computers.

Some interactive animation software uses this technique. As described under the seven responsiveness design principles (Section 7.3), a frame rate of at least 10 per second (preferably 16 per second) is required for a succession of superimposed images to be perceived as smooth animation. Stuart Card and his associates at Xerox PARC have developed a software "engine" for presenting interactive animations that treats the frame rate as the most important aspect of the animation [Robertson et al., 1989, 1993]. If the engine is having trouble maintaining the minimum frame rate because the images are complex or the user is moving them around a lot, it begins sacrificing other aspects of the images: three-dimensional effects, highlighting and shading, color, and so on. The idea is that it is better to reduce an animated 3D image of an airplane temporarily to a simple line drawing than it is to let the frame rate drop below 10 per second.

One relatively straightforward way to implement a software function in a deadline-driven manner is to start with a gross approximation of the desired result and keep generating better approximations until time runs out. For example, a clock-drawing function operating under a real-time deadline could use the strategy illustrated in Figure 7.13 of rendering successively fancier clocks into a hidden display buffer, and simply displaying the last clock it has completed when the deadline arrives.

Predict completion time; decide how to perform task

Even better than having software measure how well it *has been* doing is to have it predict how well it *will* do and decide based on those predictions how to proceed. This type of dynamic time management requires that software services and functions be able to provide estimates of how long they will take.

For example, when a user buttons down on the elevator of a scrollbar and begins dragging, the scrollbar could ask the window that contains the to-be-scrolled content how long it would take to scroll the content a few pixels. If the window responds that it would take 0.1 second or less, the scrollbar would then invoke the scroll operation; otherwise, the scrollbar would simply move the elevator along with the user's pointer, and wait to invoke the scroll operation until the user releases the elevator in its new position.

One use of time predictions is to avoid problems of simpler dynamic time management schemes. For example, simply tracking past compliance to real-time deadlines and adjusting the quality of work as necessary can sometimes result in undesirable oscillations. Consider an animation program that adjusts its rendering quality based on the average frame rate it has achieved over the last 10 frames. If the software detects that the last 10 frames were rendered too slowly (i.e., at under 16 frames per second), it might decrease the image quality to a level that can be easily rendered in the required time. Soon, it detects that it is rendering frames too quickly or that it has free time available, so it increases the rendering quality, causing the frame rate to drop again, and so on, back and forth. Basing rendering quality on predicted time compliance as well as on past time compliance can eliminate such oscillations.

Software can also use time predictions to decide whether to do a task in the foreground or background. Software that is preparing to invoke a function first asks the function for a time estimate. It then uses the estimate to decide whether to execute the function in the foreground (meaning that it will wait for the function to complete) or in a background process (which frees the calling process to do other work). Figure 7.17 gives an example of this method, expressed as person-to-person communication.

The important point about this technique is that the decision about whether to execute the function as a foreground versus a background task is made at run time, not at design time. Obviously, if a function always takes approximately the same amount of time, the decision about whether to run it in the foreground or background can be made statically, when the software is written. Postponing the decision until run time is only necessary if the time required by the to-be-invoked function can vary widely from one invocation to the next. However, this might well be true if, for example, the execution time depends on the current system load or availability of network resources.

For example, suppose a user directs an email program to fetch newly arrived email. If the program discovers that there isn't much mail to fetch, the software

---

Figure 7.17   *Example 18.* Estimates of how much time a request will take to fulfill allow negotiation about what communications protocol to use.

"Are you ready to order?"

"Almost. N more minutes. Everything looks so good!"

"OK, I'll ..." SWITCH N: {

N < 1 minute: "... wait here."

1 <= N < 3 minutes: "... take these other folks' orders and
                                  be right back."

N >= 3 minutes: "... go away, and come back when I see
                                  that you're ready."

}

might download it as a foreground task, tying up the user interface for the few seconds it takes to do so. However, if the program discovers that there is a lot of email to fetch, it might spawn a background task to do that, letting the user get back to composing or reading email (and informing the user of what it is doing).

Predict time compliance; negotiate quality or whether to do the task at all

Finally, software can predict whether it will complete an assigned task on time and, based on that prediction, negotiate the quality of its work or whether to do the task at all. This is the most sophisticated type of dynamic time management. The basic idea is that when a program is preparing to invoke a function, it negotiates with the function about the quality and completion time. If the negotiating parties arrive at an agreed-upon trade-off between quality and completion time, the computation proceeds; otherwise, it doesn't. To be able to carry out this negotiation, the following must be true:

■ The controlling software must be able to state its time requirements. As above, these can be coded into it when it is implemented.

■ The controlling software must be able to communicate its job requirements to the subordinate function without actually invoking the function.

■ The subordinate function must at least be able to predict its completion time and give some indication of the quality of its work. Ideally, it should offer a range of completion times corresponding to a range of quality levels.

■ A protocol must exist for negotiating, that is, finding the highest-quality result that can be completed within the time requirements.

As an example, imagine a slide presentation program that provides several types of fancy transitions between slides in addition to a simple instant slide switch: fade, wipe, zoom, morph, and page flip. Users specify the desired transitions when they create the presentation. The fancy transitions are supposed to be smooth and quick. However, once a presentation is created, it must work on computers of varying speeds. When a user who is giving a presentation signals a slide change, the slide program negotiates with the relevant transition procedure to find the best-quality transition (image quality and number of frames) that can be accomplished in the required time on this particular computer. If the negotiation fails to find any acceptable version of the desired transition, the slide program simply switches the slides instantly.

Recall Example 2 of Figure 7.4, in which the two parties in a transaction fail to negotiate or even communicate their time requirements, and so unintentionally blunder into a scheduling disaster. In contrast, Figure 7.18 presents situations in which the parties *do* communicate and negotiate their requirements, with more satisfactory outcomes.

Figure 7.18   *Example 19.* Some requests are time-dependent.

> "Can you type this memo for me?"
>
> "I'm pretty busy. How soon do you need it? I can perhaps get to it tomorrow afternoon."
>
> "I need it in two hours. Never mind. I'll find someone else to do it or do it myself."

Example 20. There is a trade-off between quality and cost. People will often accept something of lesser quality if more quality costs more.

> "Can we get the documents for tomorrow's presentation copied in color?"
>
> "Yes, but I'll have to send it to Reprographics. They usually have a two-day turnaround, so I'll have to submit it as a rush order, which raises the cost to 50 cents a page. Given the amount of stuff to copy, I figure it would cost us about $500."
>
> "Sigh. Just copy them on our own black-and-white copier."

Techniques involving run-time negotiation between software components may seem overly complicated. However, in fact they are no more complicated than widely used protocols by which software components negotiate at run time to find their best common format for a pending data transfer operation (for example, CORBA, OpenDoc, ActiveX).

7.4.5 Summary of responsiveness techniques

By using these four categories of implementation techniques, developers can create software products and services that are responsive to users despite having performance limitations. As described earlier, being responsive to users means

- letting users know instantly that their actions were received (e.g., button presses, mouse movements)

- letting users estimate how long lengthy computations will take

- freeing users to do other things while waiting for a function to complete

- managing queued events intelligently and efficiently

- performing housekeeping and low-priority tasks in the background

- making use of idle time to anticipate (and precompute) users' likely future requests

For the convenience of readers, I will here summarize the four above-described categories of implementation techniques.

- ■ Timely feedback
  - Acknowledge user input immediately (within 0.1 second)
  - Provide busy indicators or progress indicators for operations that take > 1 second
  - Display important information first
  - Fake heavyweight computations until final
- ■ Parallel problem solution
  - Delay work until there is time to do it
  - Work ahead where possible
- ■ Queue optimization
  - Reorder input queue for efficiency
  - Flush tasks that have become moot
- ■ Dynamic time management
  - Monitor event queue; adjust strategy or resources if too far behind
  - Monitor time compliance; decrease quality or quantity to keep up
  - Predict response time; decide how to perform task
  - Predict time compliance; negotiate quality, whether to do task at all

7.4.6 Overcoming the obstacles to adoption of responsiveness techniques

Having reviewed the principles and techniques for making software responsive, we can ask what the obstacles are that impede their adoption, and seek ways to overcome those obstacles. The obstacles are pretty much the same as the reasons I gave in Section 7.2 for a lack of responsiveness in GUI based software. I will take those reasons one by one and examine possible remedies.

The importance of responsiveness is not widely known

The obvious remedy for this problem is to educate software developers and development managers about the impact of responsiveness on the usability and market acceptance of software products and services. It would also be beneficial to make software customers and users more aware of how software responsiveness affects them because it would help create demand for improved responsiveness.

Educating these constituencies means publicizing the issue and summarizing the research findings in ways that are understandable and accessible to nonresearchers. Few software developers, managers, and consumers read human-computer interaction research journals or conference proceedings.

To some extent, that is my reason for including responsiveness bloopers in this book. However, the importance of responsiveness will have to be publicized more widely than the readership of this book if it is to become a more mainstream concern of the software industry.

UI designers rarely consider responsiveness during design

User interface designers, like software developers and consumers, need to be made more aware of the impact of software responsiveness on user acceptance and usability. However, they also need more specialized information; they need to be shown that software responsiveness is, as Bickford [1997] put it, "...not just an engineering issue, it's one of interface design as well." Performance is an implementation issue, but responsiveness is a user interface design issue.

In other words, user interface designers need to learn to include *target* response times when specifying user interfaces, and to recognize that it is important to consider the *achievable* response times when choosing among design alternatives. If a function will take many seconds to execute, its user interface should be qualitatively—perhaps radically—different than if the function will execute in a fraction of a second.

Unfortunately, most books about GUI design don't mention responsiveness, performance, or anything related to the real-time behavior of software. Of the few that do mention real-time issues, most talk only about "performance" or "response time" [Brown, 1988] or focus on providing guidelines for displaying busy cursors and progress bars [Fowler, 1998]. Such guidelines are useful, but they are only a small part of what GUI designers need to know in order to design responsive applications.

One of the few GUI design books that gives significant attention to responsiveness is one I have cited several times in this book: *Interface Design* [Bickford, 1997]. It includes a chapter that explains: (1) the difference between "real and perceived speed," and (2) the greater importance of perceived speed.

On the other hand, most guidelines for Web site design do at least touch on responsiveness issues, probably because responsiveness and performance are so noticeable on the Web. At least two recent books on Web site design (and their corresponding Web sites) urge designers to avoid unnecessary graphics and animations in order to reduce downloading times [Flanders and Willis, 1998; Nielsen, 1999d]. They also provide tips on how to include images and other graphic elements in Web sites without delaying users' access to textual information and navigation links.

The bottom line is that although some books aimed at user interface designers discuss responsiveness and how it is related to user interface design, more such books need to. That is exactly why I included this section on responsiveness bloopers in this book. Ideally, issues of responsiveness should be included in the formal education and training of budding user interface designers.

Programmers equate responsiveness with performance; programmers treat user input like machine input

I lumped these two obstacles together because the solutions for them are the same. Both require a combination of

- educating programmers about the relevant differences, and
- training them to defer to user interface professionals on matters of user interface design.

Developers use simple, naive implementations

Another obstacle to widespread adoption of responsiveness techniques is that developers tend to use proven, straightforward methods until a better method is convincingly demonstrated and simply explained. This conservatism is not restricted to responsiveness techniques. For example, consider the issue of sorting algorithm performance. Most programmers develop the bubblesort algorithm on their own because it is so intuitive and straightforward. As a result, the bubblesort algorithm is used in many software products, even though it has severe performance limitations for most sorting applications.

We should augment the education and training of programmers to include the aforementioned responsiveness techniques. Real-time and multithreaded programming, as well as other techniques for ensuring software responsiveness, should become an integral part of the education of computer programmers. The goal of this tactic would be to wean programmers from "obvious," straightforward implementation techniques that may be easy to invent and code but limit or prevent responsiveness in the user interface. This is not unlike how programmers are weaned from bubblesort in preference to more complex but higher-performance sorting algorithms, such as quicksort.

GUI software tools, components, and platforms are inadequate

As I said earlier, few tools and components exist to support programmers in using responsiveness techniques. Furthermore, the operating systems on which most GUI-based software runs are getting more—not less—complex. Modern computer languages and operating systems support multiple threads and remote procedure calls, but many programmers still don't know how to use them; few programmers are skilled at writing multithreaded or real-time code. The situation is worse for nonsequential input processing and dynamic time management; hardly any programmers are familiar with such techniques.

Without high-level software support, incorporating responsiveness techniques adds complexity—and therefore risk—to development schedules that are often already at risk. Development managers don't like risk, and encourage their teams to do everything they can to reduce it. For example, using threads is still too risky for most development teams.

Even if the required techniques become a common part of the typical programmer's education, it will be years before those skills appear in industry. Meanwhile, a lot of unresponsive software will be developed.

Therefore, another goal in a campaign to improve software responsiveness should be to provide designers and developers with tools, design templates, and reusable components that encapsulate the above-described responsiveness techniques, such as multithreaded processing. For example, if a programmer who is writing a simple GUI application needs to display a busy cursor, she shouldn't have to master multithreaded programming to do it; multithreaded programming should simply be built into whatever software components the programmer uses to display the busy cursor.

In addition to providing programmers with higher-level software components, we should offer them programming tools that explicitly support the development of responsive software. For example, programming tools could help programmers decide where opportunities for threaded implementations exist and supply examples for them to draw upon.

Some small steps toward providing better tools and components have been taken, such as the intelligent scheduling monitors described by Duis [1990] and the animation engine described by Robertson et al. [1993]. These prototypes are still mainly restricted to research labs. The ideas they embody need to be rolled out into the industry as quickly as possible.

Managers hire GUI programmers who lack the required skill

Although most of the responsiveness techniques described above have rarely been applied to the interface between computers and human users, most of them are well known to programmers who are familiar with real-time software engineering. In the very short term, software development managers may have to change their assessment of who is qualified to write GUI software.

Stated more bluntly, software development organizations should not rely on neophyte programmers to develop GUIs. To ensure that their products are high quality—which as we have seen means highly responsive—managers should hire programmers who have the skills to develop real-time, multithreaded software. Such programmers of course cost more, but then again, the software they develop will be worth more to customers. At the very least, every development team should include at least one highly skilled real-time programmer to oversee the work of less-experienced programmers.

Conclusion

As long as the software industry considers responsiveness to be of relatively low importance in determining user satisfaction, the same as performance, purely an implementation issue, and solvable merely by performance tuning or faster hardware, software consumers will find themselves grinding their teeth wondering what their computer is doing or whether it has crashed.

History shows that faster processors will not solve the problem. Even when desktop computers and electronic appliances attain the power of today's most powerful supercomputers (i.e., teraflop computation rates), responsiveness will still be an issue because the software of that day will demand so much more from the machines and the networks that connect them. For example, future software applications will probably be based on

- deductive reasoning
- image recognition
- real-time speech generation
- data encryption, authentication, and compression techniques
- downloading gigabyte files
- communication between dozens of household appliances
- collation of data from thousands of remote databases
- full-text searches through the entire World Wide Web

Stated in more pragmatic terms: What good will your cable modem Internet connection and Pentium IX or Macintosh G9 be when your sister-in-law sends you email telling you to check out her Web site because she replaced the family vacation photos with high-resolution narrated movies? Answer: Not much. But, hey, it will all be wonderful again if you would just upgrade your Internet connection to a T1 line and your computer to a Pentium X or a Macintosh G10.

It is time to start treating responsiveness as a usability issue, and more specifically, as a user interface *design* issue. An important one.

Further reading

Design guidelines books that discuss responsiveness

Bickford, P. 1997. *Interface Design: The Art of Developing Easy-to-Use Software.* Chestnut Hill, MA: Academic Press.

Flanders, V., and Willis, M. 1998. *Web Pages That Suck: Learning Good Design by Looking at Bad Design.* San Francisco: Sybex. (See also the authors' Web site: *www.WebPagesThatSuck.com.*)

Nielsen, J. 1999d. *Designing Web Usability: The Practice of Simplicity.* Indianapolis, IN: New Riders Publishing. (See also Nielsen's Web site: *www.UseIt.com.*)

Research basis for user interface real-time time constants

Robertson, G., Card, S., and Mackinlay, J. 1989. "The Cognitive Co-Processor Architecture for Interactive User Interfaces." *Proceedings of the ACM Conference on User Interface Software and Technology (UIST'89)*, pp. 10–18. New York: ACM Press.

Robertson, G., Card, S., and Mackinlay, J. 1993. "Information Visualization Using 3D Interactive Animation." *Communications of the ACM* 36(4): 56–71.

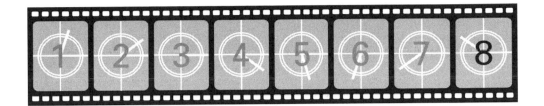

Management
Bloopers

Introduction

As a user interface consultant, I am often called in by companies to review, critique, and redesign a product's shoddy user interface shortly before the product is to be released into the marketplace. In this role, I often feel like a participant in a dysfunctional relationship with a self-destructive person. I do my best to smooth over the problem of the moment—the client's flawed product—but have no mandate or resources to address the flawed processes and attitudes that produced it. I find this unsatisfactory for two reasons.

First, "smoothing over" is a good way to describe what can be done late in development: improvements are limited to superficial changes. Deeper improvements are ruled out because of insufficient time or because the organization is incapable of making them. A colleague called these last-minute attempts to rescue a bad user interface "putting lipstick on a bulldog."

Second, my limited role makes it difficult to leave my clients better off than they were when I started. Clients hire me to solve an immediate problem: identify their product's usability flaws and indicate how to fix them quickly and cheaply. They do not hire me to advise them on how to correct the more fundamental problem: the development processes, management practices and structure, or company culture that allowed a product to be developed with so many usability "howlers"—or even worse, that doesn't match any customer need—in the first place. I find that the more clients I "help," the greater my concern grows that I'm helping many of them to continue to ignore, and therefore perpetuate, their real problem. I'm like a codependent wife smoothing over problems caused by an alcoholic husband.

When I started as a consultant, this didn't bother me so much. "Oh, well. They're paying me good money, so what do I care?" was one rationalization. Another was "Their dysfunction is my gain. It means they'll be a perpetual source of consulting work, at least as long as they stay in business." But as the years have gone by and I've seen client after client who seem to be structured or behaving contrary to their own interests (assuming that their interest is to have high and broad demand for their products), I've become less and less satisfied with my codependent relationships.

In particularly serious cases, I sometimes go beyond my assignment and offer advice about the management problems I see that are getting in the way of designing good, usable products. Alas, such advice is usually ignored. If they wanted a management consultant, they would have hired one instead of a (cheaper) usability consultant. And besides, management change is difficult and takes a long time, but the product has to be shipped next month. In many cases, the systemic problems I point out are beyond the purview of the particular manager who hired me anyway. Therefore, after my consulting work for the client is complete and I am gone, the company goes right back to developing unusable, unuseful products.

In the long run, this is bad for the clients, bad for the industry, and bad for the public. It is bad for the clients because focusing on quick fixes and ignoring the more fundamental problems costs companies far more in customer support expenses and lost sales than it saves them. It is bad for the industry because companies that churn out "bulldog" products—with or without lipstick—drag down expectations for, and interest in, entire product categories and computer-based products in general. It is bad for the public because consumers can't easily detect poor usability or lack of usefulness in a product until after they've bought it and are trying to use it. It is also bad for the public because entire markets consisting of barely usable and marginally useful products deny the public the benefits of the technology's true potential.

I would like to break the cycle of codependency—escape from the dysfunctional relationships! Toward that goal, this chapter describes management mistakes and misconceptions that are outside of the normal purview of user interface consultants, but that nonetheless lead to poor product user interfaces. I have collected them in my many years of working in the computer industry as a user interface designer, developer, evaluator, and manager at various companies, and in my years of working in these roles as a user interface consultant for a variety of clients.

Most multistep programs for breaking out of dysfunctional behavior patterns in the personal realm claim that the first step is recognizing and admitting the problem. That would seem applicable here also. My hope is that by reading about these bloopers, my clients and others developing computer-based products will recognize them, admit that they have a problem, and take the additional steps necessary to design an organization that produces usable and useful products. This, in turn, would allow me and my fellow user interface professionals to spend less time trying to "put lipstick on bulldogs."

Before turning to the management bloopers, I want to make clear that these are difficult problems with nontrivial solutions. In this relatively brief section, I discuss only a few bloopers with which I have direct experience. Other authors have devoted entire books to management-level problems that hinder software ease of use and usefulness. I encourage readers to read one or more of the following noteworthy books on this subject:

- *The Trouble with Computers*, by Tom Landauer [1995]

- *The Invisible Computer*, by Don Norman [1999]

- *The Inmates Are Running the Asylum*, by Alan Cooper [1999]

8.1 Counterproductive attitude

Management bloopers that hinder an organization's ability to develop easy-to-use, useful products and services fall into two categories (1) counterproductive attitudes about usability, and (2) counterproductive development processes. I will start with counterproductive attitudes.

8.1.1 Blooper 76: Misunderstanding what user interface professionals do

Those of us who design or evaluate user interfaces of computer-based products, either as consultants or as employees of a company, have a problem: few people in the computer industry understand what we do. I wish I had $25 for each time I've had the following conversation:

> Other: "You're a user interface consultant? Are you a Windows toolkit hacker or a Java toolkit hacker?"
>
> Me: "Neither, although I can write Java code when necessary."
>
> Other: "Oh. Then you must be a DHTML hacker, or a Mac Toolkit hacker...or a CDE/Motif hacker."
>
> Me: "No. I design user interfaces. If I need a programmer to implement or prototype my designs, I hire one."
>
> Other: "Hmmm...a designer. You draw the icons and make the Web links and open/close buttons look cool."
>
> Me: "Um, no. I'm not a graphic designer. I'm a user interface designer. My artistic skills are pretty rudimentary. If I need a graphics designer to draw art for a design, I hire one."
>
> Other: "You're not a GUI programmer, and you're not a graphic designer...so what *do* you do?"

It is surprising how many people in the computer field are unclear on the distinction between user interface *designers* and user interface *programmers.* Likewise, many are unclear on the distinction between *graphic* designers and *user interface* designers. Some are unclear on both distinctions. Perhaps the confusion is due to the shared words in each pair of job titles. The distinction between user interface programmers and graphic designers doesn't seem to be as difficult to understand, but then, those two job titles share no words. Let's tackle the two misconceptions in turn.

Variation A: Assuming GUI programmer = GUI designer. Many software development managers mistakenly believe that all it takes to develop easy-to-use software is to hire skilled GUI programmers—people who have experience using development tools and component toolkits designed for building graphical user interfaces. According to this misconception, once you have "hot" GUI programmers on board, you just have to tell them what software is needed and give them the time and resources to write it. Such managers often consider it wasteful to hire people who design GUIs or conduct usability testing but write little or no code.

This is a very serious blooper. It reflects a profound misunderstanding of what user interface programmers versus user interface designers contribute to a development effort. It can also reflect a willful disregard for the value of good user interfaces (see Blooper 77: Treating user interface as low priority, Section 8.1.2).

Most development managers already know that novice programmers who are inexperienced in using a particular user interface toolkit often produce substandard user interfaces. Their limited knowledge and skills mean that they can't always make the toolkit do what they want it to do. They understand how to program 17 of the 208 controls in the toolkit, so they use those 17 controls for everything, whether the controls fit the situation or not. Or perhaps they know how to call up most of the controls, but not how to set their detailed attributes or subclass them to produce the desired variations.[1]

What fewer development managers appear to realize is that even top-notch programmers who know a toolkit inside and out can produce poor user interfaces, even when given plenty of time and resources. There are several reasons for this.

A lack of experience designing user interfaces is one obvious reason. Just because a programmer has a great deal of programming experience doesn't mean he or she has much experience with user interfaces. Furthermore, experience programming user interfaces is not necessarily experience *designing* user interfaces. For example, consider the following excerpt from an imaginary telephone conversation between two software development managers:

> "Bill. Fred here. I've figured out how to solve our resource problem on the Titanic project: You know Lara the hot programmer who optimized our compiler back end so it beat all our competitors on the performance benchmarks? Well, she's idle for a few months. I'll ask Sam to loan her to you and you can put her on the Titanic GUI.... Yeah, I know she doesn't know your GUI toolkit, but give her three weeks and she'll know it inside and out."

If Bill is worth his salary as a development manager, he'll tell Fred that Lara might well be able to learn the toolkit in a few weeks, but she still won't know what to do with it.

---

1. It can be argued that there is value in having user interface designers and development managers who understand the development tools; this makes it possible to detect when a programmer's failure to follow the design specification is due to a limitation of the toolkit or of the programmer.

A second reason good GUI toolkit programmers often produce bad GUIs is not widely acknowledged: Deep familiarity with a particular user interface toolkit can easily influence a programmer to design software based more on the toolkit's capabilities than on user needs. If a programmer knows the toolkit very well but lacks insight into—or empathy for—how people think and work, programmer expedience and convenience can easily win out.

A third reason good GUI programmers can produce bad user interfaces is that top-notch programmers are often strong-willed people who don't compromise or negotiate easily with others. When a development team contains several such members and when their management does not assert sufficient authority, the result can be important inconsistencies between portions of the application or Web site developed by different programmers; each one did things his or her own way. This problem is covered in more detail in Blooper 80: Anarchic development (Section 8.2.2).

Other bloopers in this chapter and throughout this book provide other important reasons why good programmers produce bad user interfaces. Additional discussion of this topic can be found in an insightful article by Gentner and Grudin [1990]. The bottom line for present purposes is that having good GUI programmers on a design team does not satisfy the need for a GUI designer.

Variation B: Assuming graphic designer = GUI designer. Some development managers understand that a development team needs more than just good GUI programmers in order to develop easy-to-use interactive software, but still are unclear on exactly what additional skills are needed. Many don't understand the distinction between user interface design and graphic design. They consider the user interface to be just the surface of an application and that *beautiful* or *coOOool* is the same thing as *usable,* so they hire graphic artists to design it. The result of such a decision can easily be a product that looks great in demos but isn't usable or useful for real work.

Unfortunately, this misconception is becoming more common as so-called multimedia software grows in popularity and as Web sites and Web-based applications grow ever fancier, bringing issues of aesthetic appeal and entertainment value more to the forefront. With increasing frequency, prospective clients are asking interview questions that suggest to me that they are interviewing me and graphic design consultants for the same job. I take this as a warning that the hiring manager may not understand what user interface design is.

The main result of a user interface designer's work is not what the software looks like when it's finished, but rather how it changed from one version to the next, how easy it is to learn, and whether it helps users accomplish their goals. For example, an application's buttons might be snazzy and metallic-looking, but its users still might not know what buttons to press to get their work done.

Here are some examples of the kinds of work user interface designers are trained to do:

- Reduce the number of commands in an application from several hundred to 48

- Flatten its menu hierarchy from four levels to two

- Decrease the total number of windows from 23 to 11

- Eliminate half of the mouse actions formerly required to complete a common task

- Revise the menu commands so that all are now consistently verb phrases where previously they were an inconsistent mishmash of different grammatical forms

- Rewrite error messages that were formerly expressed in terms of operating system codes so that they are in plain, task-relevant English and provide solutions rather than just describing problems

 Fancy graphics is not what's lacking

At one client company, the hiring manager, a company vice-president, explained that he wanted me to make his company's software look "really fancy, like those online news services." Since his company develops tools for programmers rather than online news services for the general public, I was concerned about his stated goal. Within a few days of starting my review of the software, my concern intensified because it was clear that the appearance of the software's screens was the least of its problems. The main usability problems were much deeper, for example, inconsistent operation of similar functions in different parts of the program, overly tedious and error-prone operation, and the need for users to master concepts that were foreign to the task domain. Over time, I managed to convince this client to forget about making the product look like a TV production, and to pay more attention to whether it helped users perform the intended tasks.

A common area of overlap between the responsibility of graphic designers and those of user interface designers is the layout of controls and information in software displays. The detailed appearance of each control is clearly the responsibility of a graphic designer. Exactly what controls are provided and how they are labeled is clearly the responsibility of the user interface designer. But both sorts of designers will have ideas about how the controls are laid out on the display. This overlap in roles is one reason people sometimes confuse the two kinds of designers.

Avoiding Blooper 76

To avoid both variations of this blooper, software development managers need to understand the relevant differences: the difference between user interface programmers and user interface designers, and the difference between user interface design and graphic design. Then, managers need to act on that understanding, which means making sure that all the necessary skills are present on—or at least available to—the development teams for which they are responsible.

Don't confuse GUI programmers with GUI designers

Knowing how to operate woodworking tools doesn't make someone a designer of sought-after furniture. Possessing carpentry skills doesn't make someone a skilled home designer. Learning how to read and write music notation doesn't turn someone into a composer of enduring melodies. The ability to paint whatever one can imagine doesn't guarantee that person can imagine a masterpiece. Similarly, knowing how to use GUI programming tools and components doesn't mean that someone will know what to do with them to create usable and useful software.

As explained above, the problem is not just that most programmers lack user interface design skills. When a programmer designs a user interface, he or she will have a tendency to design based more on the capabilities of the tools than on the requirements of the users. I've seen this tendency even in myself in situations when I have worked as both designer and programmer.

The remedy is for management to make sure that the design specification is prepared by someone who understands human-computer interaction and the user requirements, and that the user interface implementation follows the specification faithfully. If the tools and building blocks aren't capable of implementing the specified design, it is they that should be questioned, not the design.

Don't confuse graphic designers with GUI designers

Designing software user interfaces and designing the graphics used in software user interfaces are two very different activities. The skills required to do them well also differ.

Graphic designers are skilled at creating aesthetically appealing controls and displays, conveying function graphically, devising consistent graphic styles for use throughout an application or application suite, matching the graphics to the display technology, and presenting data in such a way that users can extract information easily.

User interface designers are skilled at analyzing and understanding user task requirements, at presenting controls and information to make sense in the work context, at simplifying complexity, at recognizing where users will have trouble learning or using an application. Some user interface designers are also skilled at devising, conducting, and analyzing informative usability tests, although there is a growing trend for those who design user interfaces and those who test them on target users to be different people.

Regardless of who designs it, a user interface that is eye-catching, sexy, glossy, and exciting is not the same thing as one that is easy to learn and use.

Table 8.1   Comparing the skills of UI designers, graphic designers, and GUI programmers

Role	Skills
UI designer	▪ Task analysis, conceptual design ▪ UI design with task flow and context ▪ Specifying real-time responsiveness criteria ▪ Usability evaluation, usability testing ▪ Assessing conformance to usability standards ▪ Layout
Graphic designer	▪ Creating recognizable images, intuitive symbols ▪ Aesthetic appeal ▪ Making best use of the available display medium ▪ Conveying function graphically ▪ Visual consistency ▪ Layout
GUI programmer	▪ Programming, implementation, internal architecture ▪ Knowledge of GUI toolkit ▪ Maximizing performance ▪ Understanding technical constraints on implementation

The user interface of an application is not just how it looks; it is how easy it is to learn, how well it recedes into the subconscious of experienced users, and how well it supports users' tasks.

Table 8.1 summarizes the skills of the three roles discussed above.

8.1.2 Blooper 77: Treating user interface as low priority

I have met quite a few software developers and managers who consider user interface issues to have low priority compared to other issues involved in software development. Assigning low priority to the user interface takes several forms, described below as variations of the blooper.

Variation A: Assuming that usability has low impact on market success. Some software managers and developers just don't believe that user interface has much of an impact on software's market success. But they are wrong. Studies have shown that considering usability issues early in development may initially appear to be raising expenses but easily repays that investment by increasing revenue and reducing costs downstream.

Specifically, having a more usable product speeds market acceptance and hence increases the slope of the revenue curve. The slope of the revenue curve at product introduction has a much greater impact on the total revenue over the life of the product than does the exact date of product introduction, especially since rushing the product to market without attending to its usability usually decreases the initial slope of the revenue curve. Paying attention to usability before releasing software also lowers the cost of providing customer support services. For a well-written summary of the impact of usability work on the profitability of software products, I recommend an article by Conklin [1996]. More comprehensive analyses of the same subject can be found in the book *Cost-Justifying Usability* [Bias and Mayhew, 1994].

Variation B: Assuming that the user interface is only "fonts and colors." Some software managers and developers have an overly narrow view of what "user interface" encompasses: a mistaken belief that it is only about the most superficial aspects of software and can therefore be put off until just before shipping or ignored altogether. For example, an employee at one of my client companies told me that "User interface design is sometimes referred to by managers here as 'fonts and colors.' "

However, as discussed in Blooper 76: Misunderstanding what user interface professionals do (Section 8.1.1), user interface is not only about "fonts and colors." It isn't even mainly about fonts and colors. It is more about *interaction:* how the software behaves, rather than what it looks like. It encompasses "deep" issues such as the ease with which users can learn the software, the fit of the software's functionality to users' goals, the degree to which users must translate concepts from the task domain to those in the software, and the efficiency with which common operations can be carried out. Such issues—unlike labeling, layout, and color choices—cannot be put off until the end of the development process. If they aren't given adequate consideration early in development and tested along the way, they won't be adequate in the released version.

Variation C: Assuming that users can adapt to anything. Some software managers and developers have a sincere belief that people can learn to use anything if the software provides the required functionality.

It is true that people are amazingly adaptable and can learn astounding things if sufficiently motivated, but it is a faulty leap of logic to assume that prospective customers will overlook a shoddy user interface and buy a product for its feature list. Why should they? Maybe they don't have time to learn how to use it. Maybe they aren't motivated to learn it. Maybe a competitor's product is easier to use while providing similar functionality. Whatever the reason, if potential customers think your software "sucks" and don't buy or use it, they aren't the losers, you are.

Variation D: Rationalizing. For some software managers and developers, considering user interface to be low priority is just a rationalization: one way to perform triage in response to tight budgets, tight resources, and tight schedules.

However, it is a mistake to treat user interface as just another product feature that can be cut to meet a budget goal. The user interface is not a product

DILBERT reprinted by permission of United Feature Syndicate, Inc.

feature; it cuts across all of the product's features, determining each one's value as well as the value of the overall product. A product without an effective user interface is like a warehouse with no doors or windows: the goods are in there, but they might as well not be because no one can get at them.

Variation E: Assigning the GUI to less experienced programmers. Many software development managers hold the user interface in such low regard that they assign it to younger, less experienced programmers. I've even seen projects in which the job of developing the GUI for a product was assigned to a new-hire or a summer intern.

The following is an exchange I had at a client company with the programmer in charge of the GUI for one of the company's products. We were finishing up a discussion of the product's many usability problems:

Me: "Hey, look at the time. It's nearly 1:00. Shall we break for lunch? What does one do for lunch around here?"

Programmer: "Well, some people go out to lunch, but my parents make my lunch so I usually just eat here."

Of course, youth per se is not the problem. Age is, however, correlated with the amount of experience people have. It is the rare 20-year-old programmer who will have gained enough user interface experience to be entrusted to design a company's product without significant supervision.

The flip side of assigning GUI development to inexperienced programmers is that engineers who design and develop user interfaces tend to have lower status than those who develop system software. Not only have I experienced this myself, many of my programmer friends have mentioned it. One friend who develops GUIs told me, "GUI programmers are the peons of programming." This phenomenon was described more fully by Ellen Ullman in an insightful essay about working as a programmer [1995]:

In regular life, "low" usually signifies something bad. In programming, "low" is good. Low is better.

If the code creates programs that do useful work for regular human beings, it is called "higher". Higher-level programs are called "applications". Applications are things that people use. Although it would seem that usefulness by people would be a good thing, from a programmer's point of view, direct people-use is bad. If regular people, called "users", can understand the task accomplished by your program, you will be paid less and held in lower esteem. In the regular world, the term "higher" may be better, but, in programming, higher is worse. High is bad.

If you want money and prestige, you need to write code that only machines or other programmers understand. Such code is "low".

The practice of assigning GUI development to less-experienced programmers is due in part to a desire to keep labor costs down. Younger, less-experienced programmers are paid less. Experienced user interface designers or programmers demand high salaries (or consulting fees). Thus, hiring lots of relatively junior programmers, but few highly experienced programmers, software architects, managers, or designers, "saves" money.

However, you get what you pay for. I put "saves" in quotes because I believe that staffing in this manner costs more than it saves. Whether it is due to perceived unimportance of the user interface or from unwillingness of experienced developers to work on user interfaces, the effect on the software industry is the same: poor usability, high customer support and training costs, unsatisfied customers, lackluster sales, and small, stagnant markets.

Low priority of user interface in the music software industry

Underestimating the importance of the user interface is a common problem in the music software industry. One might expect companies in this market to have high respect for usability because their customers are mostly not technically oriented, but alas, it is not so. Companies in the music software industry tend to hire programmers who are also musicians and assume that they will design usable and useful software. According to this view, it is sufficient to understand the required functionality and to possess the programming skills. People who have expertise in user interface design or usability evaluation are seldom found in music software companies.

A development manager at a music software company told me that a lot of little companies are fighting for a share of a small market and cannot afford to hire user interface designers or conduct usability tests. They use programmer-musicians as designers and do their usability testing in the marketplace.

This strategy has some advantages, of course: it is definitely an improvement over the all-too-common situation in which software developers lack *both* experience with designing user interfaces and an understanding of the tasks that the software is supposed to support (see Blooper 81: No task domain expertise on the design team, Section 8.2.3). However, it also has disadvantages:

- Programmers who happen to be musicians are not representative of most musicians. They are more representative of other programmers than they are of other musicians. They have learned the most arcane and complex aspects of interacting with computers, so their perception of difficulty and of how people think is fundamentally skewed.

- As discussed in Blooper 76: Misunderstanding what user interface professionals do (Section 8.1.1), good programmers seldom possess sufficient UI design or evaluation skills.

- As discussed in Blooper 80: Anarchic development (Section 8.2.2), having user interface amateurs design a company's products can have serious business implications.

Once, at a party, my sister excitedly led me across the room to introduce me to someone she knew who was a chief software architect for a music software company. She thought he would be interested in meeting her brother the user interface consultant, and vice versa. I had used some of his company's software and found it to have some usability problems. However, when she introduced me and told him what I do, he said: "User interface! Eeewww!" and put his finger in his throat as if to gag himself. Given this clear expression of his low regard for user interface matters, my interest in continuing the conversation vanished. I decided it would be a good time to visit the punch table.

Given the music software industry's low regard for user interface expertise, it is not surprising that its market remains small. Those who buy such software despite its amateurish user interfaces tend to learn just enough about it to accomplish their limited goals, ignoring fancy features that in theory open up new possibilities for users, but in practice only open up Pandora's boxes for them. Users of music software also spend a lot of time fighting the software instead of playing or composing music. A lot of music software sits on hard disks unused because buyers found it not worth the trouble. While music software companies may not care whether the software actually gets used because the users did already purchase it, that is short-sighted because unused software does not generate upgrade sales or word-of-mouth recommendations.

Avoiding Blooper 77

I believe that my discussion of this blooper pretty much explained how to avoid it. To summarize: Management should make it a high priority to develop products that have high-quality user interfaces, because

- Usability has a powerful impact on the success of products, especially on the initial market acceptance.

- User interface is about "deep" issues, not just "fonts and colors." The most important usability issues, if discovered late in development, will be difficult to correct because they will require changes in the software's architecture. It's better to discover and fix such problems early, and best to design in ways that avoid making them in the first place.

- Human users can adapt to poor user interfaces, but banking on that is foolhardy because, in an open, competitive marketplace, customers have no need to adapt. They can simply buy someone else's software or no software at all.

- The user interface is not a feature that can be dropped to meet a schedule or budget constraint. It pervades and affects the entire product. If a product's user interface is shoddy, the product is shoddy, because the user interface is the part of the product that customers experience.

- Experience matters. Designing highly usable software requires previous experience doing that, including receiving feedback on the effectiveness of the user interfaces one has designed (see Blooper 78: Discounting the value of testing and iterative design, Section 8.1.3). Developing user interfaces not only requires sensitivity to users and their problems, it also requires an ability to make a GUI toolkit do everything short of backflips. Furthermore, as explained in Chapter 7, developing user-friendly GUIs requires significant skill in real-time programming techniques, including multithreaded programming. Designing and developing user interfaces should have high status. Those assigned to program user interfaces should be among the organization's most skilled programmers. Student interns and new-hires should be assigned string comparison functions and device drivers, not GUIs.

My admonition to software development managers to give higher priority to user interface and usability may seem self-serving. I am, after all, in the business of helping companies improve the usability of their products. But development managers can elevate the priority given to usability without using me as a consultant. In fact, as is explained in Blooper 80: Anarchic development (Section 8.2.2), managers would in most cases do better to hire usability experts onto their permanent staff rather than hiring consultants as needed.

8.1.3   Blooper 78: Discounting the value of testing and iterative design

Development managers who don't know much about user interface design often consider it unimportant to include usability testing or time for significant user interface revisions in the development plan. The reasons for this vary.

Variation A: Good designers don't need iteration. I've already explained that many development managers don't understand what user interface designers contribute to a software development effort (see Blooper 76: Misunderstanding what user interface professionals do, Section 8.1.1). Unfortunately, that isn't the only misunderstanding. Even development managers who know the difference between user interface designers, user interface developers, and graphic designers may still misunderstand how user interface design is best done.

Many development managers regard user interface design as a "black art"— a mysterious creative talent some people have. In such a manager's view, the user interface designer simply conjures up a user interface from a description of the software's intended functionality. The better the designer, the better the design and the sooner it will be ready.

There are of course advantages to being treated as a practitioner of a black art. I can charge clients higher rates if they need what I do but have no clue how I do it. Managers are less likely to try to micromanage me if they think of me as a creative "artiste" (with an *e* on the end) whom they've hired to do my magic to their product. So perhaps I shouldn't kvetch about this misperception of my profession.

But kvetch I will, for the disadvantages of being regarded as a magician outweigh the advantages. One big disadvantage of the perception of user interface design as black art is that it produces a "superstar" mentality—a marketplace for consultants in which everyone wants their product designed by one of a few well-known design consultants who charge high rates and are booked long into the future, while hundreds of quite competent designers have trouble finding either permanent jobs or consulting clients. Such a situation is not healthy for the industry because many software products and services don't receive the user interface attention they require.

Another important disadvantage of being viewed primarily as a creative artist is that the expectations of clients are wrong. User interface design is in fact much more an engineering discipline than a creative art. Done properly, it has many of the characteristics seen in other types of engineering: a scientific basis (the sciences of human perception, learning, action, information processing, and motivation), a need for clear requirements, generation and consideration of alternatives, working with constraints and trade-offs, and a need to test, evaluate, and revise. We don't just conjure up user interfaces out of thin air.

Treating user interface design as a creative art rather than as an engineering discipline leads one to overlook the above-listed normal characteristics of engineering efforts. In particular, it leads one to discount or ignore a designer's need to generate and consider alternative designs and to test, evaluate, and revise a design. Considering multiple alternative designs is, according to this view, wasteful and a sign of indecisiveness and inexperience. Revising a design is considered an admission of failure: if the new design is good, the old one must have been bad and therefore is a demerit for the designer. The more extensive the revision, the bigger the demerit. In the view of development managers who have this mind-set, a designer who called for usability testing of his or her own design would be admitting incompetence.

The foregoing may seem an exaggeration, but I have actually had clients tell me the following (paraphrased):

> "Why are we wasting time considering design alternatives we won't use? Don't you know which design is better?"

> "Why do we need to test it? We hired you because you are supposed to be a good designer. Aren't you?"

> "We don't have time for testing and revising. We need you to really make an effort to design it right the first time."

When development managers at client companies say these sorts of things to me, I take it as a strong sign that they don't understand what I do or how I work. They would never consider saying such things to a software engineer about the program code. However, they consider me to be an artiste (again with the *e*) who can engage my right brain, invoke my muse, and visualize an excellent user interface in a blinding flash of inspiration. I'm not. I'm an engineer—a user interface design engineer. I'll even be immodest and claim that I'm a good one. But I am good precisely *because* I consider design alternatives and check my designs by arranging for feedback from representative users and from other usability professionals. Those steps aren't superfluous or wasteful; they are a crucial part of the process.

I will go out on a limb and make one claim that may get me into trouble with some of my colleagues in the user interface profession. With an experienced user interface designer on your development team, you can have more confidence that the first design will be closer to the "right" design than you can if the designer is inexperienced. Experienced designers commit fewer and less serious design mistakes than inexperienced ones do. There is no doubt about this.

However, using an experienced designer does not eliminate the need for usability testing and iterative design. Presumably, a software development team wants to produce the best product that it can given the available time and resources. Let's assume for the sake of argument that user interfaces range in quality from 1 to 10. A neophyte user interface designer might initially propose a design that is of quality 3–5. Usability testing and redesign might improve it to a quality of 6–8. In contrast, an experienced designer's initial design might have a quality of 5–7. Even though it would be better than an inexperienced designer's first try, testing and revision would still raise the quality, perhaps to 8–10. Regardless of which user interface designer a manager had hired, testing and revision would be beneficial.

Furthermore, by "experienced," I mean not only design experience, but also evaluation and testing experience. A designer may have previously designed a hundred software products, but if he or she hasn't received feedback on those designs from other user interface professionals and from observing representative users, the hundred designs count for very little in gauging her or his experience level. Simple success or failure of one's products in the marketplace is insufficient feedback because many factors other than usability contribute to that. The relevant experience is built up by receiving explicit feedback about usability problems in one's designs, and using that feedback to revise the designs. Thus, usability testing and revision not only produces better designs, it also produces better *designers.* Not surprisingly, entry-level jobs in the software usability profession tend to be usability-testing jobs rather than user interface design jobs.

Another way to view the value of testing and revision is in terms of business risk. It is in a business's interest to reduce its risk to a "reasonable" level. Of course, reducing risk below a certain level is impractical because of the high cost, and reducing risk to zero is impossible. The main risk with a new software product is that potential customers don't like it so it fails in the marketplace. Conducting usability testing, and revising the user interface based on the feedback thus obtained, is an excellent and relatively cheap way of reducing risk. This is obviously true when the user interface designer is inexperienced (or the project has no bona fide designer), but it is even true when the designer is highly experienced. In fact, even if a usability test were to show that a software product's user interface was perfect and no changes were called for (as unlikely as that is), just *learning that* would constitute a valuable reduction in the risk of launching the product.

The most succinct argument for testing and iterative design comes from Fred Brooks's book *The Mythical Man-Month* [1975], even though Brooks wasn't referring only to user interface design:

> Plan to throw one away. You *will* do that, anyway. Your only choice is whether to try to sell the throwaway to customers.

Brooks's quote should not be interpreted as giving license to create a shoddy, incoherent initial design and hope it can be revised into shape. Designers should use principled methods and standard guidelines to produce the best possible initial designs.

What the quote means (at least in the context of GUI design) is that designers should not fool themselves into believing that they can get a design exactly "right" on the first attempt.

Variation B: "We don't have the luxury of usability testing." A common variation of this blooper is for software development managers to try to shorten the development schedule by skipping usability testing. Some omit usability testing when planning the schedule; others include it initially but later squeeze it out when the schedule slips.

It is a mistake to treat usability testing as an expendable development step that can be dropped to reconcile a schedule with a looming deadline. User testing is how you tell whether your design is on course and what midcourse adjustments are needed. Without it, you are flying blind and so may actually take longer to finish. Remember the old saying: "There is never time to do it right, but always time to do it over."

Development managers are also making a mistake if they omit or drop usability testing as a cost-cutting measure, for two reasons:

1. *Testing needn't be expensive.* Many people think of usability testing as taking place in elaborate testing facilities with large banks of video equipment and rooms of observers behind half-silvered mirrors making notes as paid subjects in the test chamber use alpha-release versions of the software to conduct realistic tasks. Some usability testing is done that way, certainly. However, there is also a place for low-cost, quick-and-dirty tests devised on short notice to answer specific design questions and carried out using non-engineering staff recruited from the hallways (or relatives of employees) and paid in chocolate, perhaps even using a paper prototype of the software. Such tests can yield crucial information about, for example, which of two design alternatives for a part of the product is best, or whether users can find commands in menus, or whether icon images convey their intended meanings. (See Section 10.1 for a case study of a development effort where very low-cost tests were used to resolve design issues despite a nonexistent usability-testing budget.)

2. *Skipping testing doesn't really save money.* By avoiding usability testing, a development organization may save some money (which, unfortunately, may be all the development manager cares about), but the company as a whole will not. The money the developers save by not doing a test-and-revise cycle before shipping will be spent on increased customer support costs, perhaps many times over. And that is the *optimistic* scenario; the pessimistic one is that lost revenues due to a lack of customers further offsets what the company saved by skipping usability testing.

Whatever the excuse for skipping usability testing, managers who make that decision are deluding themselves. They *will* perform usability testing—it cannot be avoided. By deciding not to conduct usability tests before releasing the product, they are implicitly deciding to conduct their tests in the marketplace, with paying customers as unwilling subjects. When a company does this to its customers, it may end up with fewer customers than it would have liked.

However, a more serious problem with conducting usability testing in the marketplace is that the data thus obtained—otherwise known as complaints from unsatisfied customers—is not very useful. It is unsystematic, subjective, anecdotal, sketchy, poorly timed, self-selected, and mixed up with bug reports and complaints about missing functionality. Relying on one's customers to volunteer sufficient data to indicate how to improve the product's usability is overly optimistic. That isn't their job; it's the development team's. Imagine trying to decide how to improve a product based on emailed comments such as "It SUCKS!" or "The commands make no sense to me" or "i use your software only

DILBERT reprinted by permission of United Feature Syndicate.

because everyone else here docs but i hate it because it's so different from my old software and it also crashes a lot :-(." Imagine basing the user interface changes for release 2.0 exclusively on second- and third-hand comments relayed through the sales staff.

Finally, relying solely on marketplace feedback makes you vulnerable to the "squeaky wheel" phenomenon. You have no way of knowing whether the feedback you receive is representative of the problems users are having, so you will be biased toward addressing the complaints of your more vocal customers. There is simply no substitute for data obtained from explicit, closely monitored usability testing.

Of the many excuses I have heard for a company's failure to conduct usability tests, the only one that I believe has some validity is that a particular product's target users are difficult or expensive to get as test participants. If the intended users of a software product are scarce, perpetually busy, or highly paid—for example, corporate executives, doctors, stockbrokers, airline pilots, members of Congress, astronauts—conducting tests on representative users will be difficult. But that doesn't mean testing is impossible. For some suggestions on how to overcome this obstacle, see "Avoiding Blooper 78," later in this section.

Variation C: Allowing no time to fix usability problems. The most perplexing variation of Blooper 78 is when development managers conduct a review or test of a pending product's usability, but then allow no time to correct the problems that the review or test uncovers. I wish I could say that this hardly ever happens, but unfortunately, it happens all too often.

Some managers hire me as a consultant to review or conduct a usability test of their team's software, but when I hand them the evaluation report, including my recommendations for improving the user interface, they say: "We don't have time to change most of these things. Thank you very much for your report. Good-bye." Amazing! Perhaps I shouldn't complain because they paid me for my work, but I can't help wondering: why did they spend all that money?

Here are four answers to that question:

1. The first is related to Blooper 76: Misunderstanding what user interface professionals do (Section 8.1.1). Under the common management misconception of user interface as pertaining only to graphic design issues and surface-level aspects of the software, a user interface review or usability test can only discover surface-level problems because that's all user interface is. Surface-level problems, such as those related to labeling, dialog box layout, and button labels, are usually easy to correct. It often comes as a surprise to managers who labor under this misconception that usability reviews and usability tests often uncover deep problems requiring significant redesign or rearchitecting of the software. It is not surprising that such managers don't plan for much revision after a usability evaluation and resist correcting major problems that are uncovered.

2. The second answer is related to Blooper 77: Treating user interface as low priority (Section 8.1.2). Developing a software product involves deciding which subset of all the desirable features will "make the cut." All too often, "user-friendly front end" is considered just another feature to rank-order against other features, such as "the ability to import Lotus 1-2-3 files." I've seen development teams refuse important usability improvements on the grounds that there wasn't time to make them, while simultaneously wasting time adding noncritical bells and whistles that the programmers considered "cool." An even more frustrating situation is when the release date slips continuously for several months because of implementation problems or new functional requirements, yet the development manager resists making usability improvements because at any given point it seems that there isn't enough time!

3. The third answer could be labeled "wishful thinking": conducting the test to "prove" that the user interface is wonderful. Some developers, managers, and even some user interface designers don't really understand the concept of usability testing. They have so much of their ego invested in the software's design that they can't imagine a test finding anything wrong. If they can't imagine the test finding anything wrong, they won't plan time to correct problems. If, contrary to expectations, the test *does* find problems in the software's usability, it must be that the test was badly designed, or that the wrong test participants were used.

4. The fourth answer may seem cynical but is, unfortunately, real-world truth. The development manager may have ordered a review or usability test only because doing so was a mandatory step in the company's development process. In such a case, the manager doesn't really care what the evaluation finds, he or she just wants to be able to check off the required step as done. Conducting a test is on the checklist, but fixing usability problems found by the test is not. Bzzzzt! Major blooper by the manager's management!

Table 8.2   Two-dimensional categorization of usability testing, categorizing examples given in this section

Formality of testing method	Development stage		
	Before	During	After
Informal	1	5	9
Quasi-formal	2, 3	6, 7	10
Formal	4	8	11

Avoiding Blooper 78

I hope I have made it clear that user interface design is not a black art based on innate talent and blinding flashes of creativity, but rather a learned engineering discipline with a scientific basis, accepted practices, and industry standards. User interface design involves design alternatives, trade-offs, iteration, and, above all, requires systematic feedback obtained by observing and collaborating with users. That should be sufficient to motivate development managers to *want* to include usability testing and design iteration in their development processes. What remains is to provide some practical advice on how to include usability testing with various levels of resources or time, and at various stages in development.

There are tests for every stage and purpose

As described in Principle 8 (Section 1.8) as well as earlier in this chapter, usability testing is not just something that is done when a software or service is nearly ready to ship. Furthermore, testing needn't involve elaborate testing facilities and equipment. During a development effort, many situations arise in which some kind of testing would provide useful feedback. There are also many different ways to conduct usability tests, each having its benefits and drawbacks.

In Principle 8, I categorized usability testing along two independent dimensions: (1) the point in the development process when testing occurs, and (2) the formality of the testing method. Developers can conduct usability tests before any software is implemented, when only early prototypes have been implemented, and after much of the actual software has been largely implemented. Tests can also be conducted informally, quasi-formally, or formally. Any combination of formality and implementation stage is possible (see Table 8.2).

Predevelopment tests provide great value

I've conducted usability tests at all three stages of development and all three levels of formality. However, I want to highlight the value of testing before development (at any level of formality). It's low tech, it's cheap, it's not hard to do, it provides valuable feedback, and it can be done early enough for the results to have a major impact on the design. I use preimplementation testing a lot because it allows me to test ideas before the development team goes to the expense of putting them into the design.

For example, to test whether the graphical labels on toolbar buttons convey their intended meanings to users, I might print them in color or put them on a Web page and ask people to match them with a list of function names. To find out if the location and naming of items in the menubar menus makes sense to users, I might print out the menubar and the menus (or even hand-write them!) and ask people to find specified items. Preimplementation testing is good for testing issues of comprehension and navigation, but of course bad for testing issues related to the responsiveness and timing of the software.

Listed below are examples of usability tests that I or colleagues of mine have conducted. The list illustrates the wide variety of tests designers can perform to get valuable feedback on their designs. The examples listed here are tabulated in Table 8.2.

1. *Before implementation, informal:* Conducted interview and focus groups with teachers to learn how they use videos in the classroom and what they like and dislike about the current (noncomputerized) system for finding, choosing, and showing videos. This was done in preparation for designing an online video locator and viewing service for classroom use. For more details, see Section 8.2.3.

2. *Before implementation, quasi-formal:* Tested graphical symbols that were to be used in a computer game to see whether they conveyed their intended meanings. The symbols were printed on paper. Test participants wrote their interpretations on paper answer sheets. A detailed description of these tests is provided elsewhere in this book (see Section 10.1).

3. *Before implementation, quasi-formal:* Tested the design of the windows in business decision-support software. Screen images of the tool's windows were created using graphics software and then printed on paper. Test participants performed prescribed tasks by "clicking" on controls shown on the printed screens while the tester flipped the paper images in response. The test sessions were videotaped.

4. *Before implementation, formal:* Tested desktop icons for an office workstation. Test participants were asked both to guess the meaning of icons and to match icons with function names. The responses were statistically analyzed to yield "confusability" matrices indicating which icons tended to be confused for one another, and which icons were easy to recognize. For details, see the article by Miller and Johnson [1996].

5. *During implementation, informal:* Tested a user interface for finding movies to see if it made sense to people. It was only implemented in pieces and wasn't far enough along that we could let people operate it themselves, so

we showed it to people and asked them questions to check their comprehension and appreciation of it.

6. *During implementation, quasi-formal:* A preliminary implementation of a home-buying Web site was tested on eight people to find design problems. The test was conducted in an unused conference room. Faces of participants and the computer screen were videotaped. The paid test participants performed brief tasks requested by the testers. After the test, the Web site was redesigned substantially.

7. *During implementation, quasi-formal:* Play-testing of a computer game. As successive versions of a game were built, they were handed over to another organization that conducted play-test sessions in which young game enthusiasts were observed while they played specified segments of the game.

8. *During implementation, formal:* In order to evaluate a new remote control for operating on-screen controls for interactive television services, a test was conducted comparing a prototype of the remote control with several other, more traditional pointing devices. Test participants used the pointing devices to try to hit randomly selected buttons that were displayed in an array on the screen. The measure was the time required for participants to hit the designated target button. Test sessions took place in a formal usability lab and were videotaped. For details, see Johnson and Keavney [1995].

9. *After implementation, informal:* Interviewed users of a beta release version of a C++ development environment, asking them what they liked and didn't like about it. Interviews took place in the participants' offices, at their computers, so they could show the testers what they meant. The interviews were audiotaped.

10. *After implementation, quasi-formal:* A released version of a hand-held Internet appliance was tested on 10 people to find usability problems and suggest improvements for the next release. Test participants performed brief tasks dictated by the tester. Test sessions were conducted in vacant offices. Observers took notes, but the sessions were not taped.

11. *After implementation, formal:* Several text editors were compared for efficiency of operation by testing them on users. The purpose was to help guide the design of future text editors. Participants performed editing tasks given them by the testers. The testers timed participants' performance and noted problems they had. For details, see the paper by Roberts and Moran [1983].

   The point of the examples is to show the variety of ways one can conduct usability testing, and that usability testing can be done at any point in the development process. It can be done to check raw ideas or finished products. Test participants can be paid hundreds of dollars or they can be "paid" in t-shirts or chocolate. Some tests can consume many months, but other tests can provide useful information in a few hours. As far as I am concerned, it is just plain stupid to develop and ship a computer-based product without conducting some kind of usability testing at some point along the way.

When test participants are hard to get

Above, under Variation B ("We don't have the luxury of usability testing"), I noted that there are situations in which developers would like to conduct usability testing, but their ability to get representative users to participate in the test is limited by the fact that the intended users of the product are scarce, busy, or prohibitively expensive. While this is indeed a difficult situation to be in, it does not mean that usability testing is ruled out. Consider the following ways of overcoming this obstacle:

- Some aspects of a software product won't depend on the user having expertise in the software's target task domain. For example, if an air traffic control system includes a mouse as a pointing device, one doesn't need air traffic controllers to check whether buttons on the screen are large enough to be easy to hit. If a Web-based medical reference for doctors uses a table widget that is designed to be operated just like tables in Windows applications, one doesn't need doctors to check whether that design goal was achieved.

- For tests in which task domain expertise *is* required, one can use less expensive, easier to recruit approximations of the target users, for example, nurses or medical students instead of doctors, private pilots instead of airline pilots, middle managers instead of top executives, computer science students instead of professional programmers, congressional staffers instead of congressional representatives. Though questions may remain about how the real target users would perform, many important design questions will be answered and important design flaws will be found.

- Finally, if actual representative users are needed, it may be difficult or expensive to get them, but it isn't impossible. Put simply: It has been done. It simply depends on whether the development manager thinks the benefits of testing are worth the expense of paying experts what they charge (or devising some other, creative way of attracting them) and the hassle of trying to schedule them. Unfortunately, development managers tend to underestimate both the benefits of usability testing and the costs of not doing it. Furthermore, if the product is seen by experts as being a significant advance for them, it may be surprisingly easy to enlist their participation. For example, a team designing a system for neurosurgeons to use to preplan brain operations managed to test their design on 50(!) neurosurgeons and an assortment of other surgeons. The neurosurgeons volunteered their time because (1) the work was cosponsored by a medical school neurosurgery department, (2) they saw the tool as a potential great advance for them, and

(3) some of their colleagues had contributed ideas to the design. Fifty neurosurgeons, free! For details, see Hinckley et al. [1998].

Why test if you're going to ignore the results?

Finally, if usability tests are to have value, managers need to schedule sufficient time after the test to the correct the usability problems it uncovers.

8.2 Counterproductive process

The second category of management bloopers focuses on development processes that negatively affect software usability and usefulness.

8.2.1 Blooper 79: Using poor tools and building blocks

Most people realize that it is difficult to build high-quality products using poor-quality tools or shoddy materials. This is as true for software as it is for furniture, houses, pottery, and automobiles. It is particularly true for graphical user interfaces.

The tools for designing and building graphical user interfaces for interactive software include user interface toolkits, user interface management systems, interactive GUI builders, Web page editors, graphics libraries, query languages, scripting languages, and declarative specification languages.[2] Developers of computer-based products and services obviously want to choose the best and most appropriate tools for their particular development effort.

However, there is an important problem that limits a development organization's ability to evaluate and choose the best GUI tools and building blocks to use in building a product or product line: those who decide what GUI tools to use do not have all of the skills required to evaluate the quality of those tools. In particular, neither development managers, who usually make the decisions about which GUI tools to buy, nor GUI programmers, who use GUI tools to build user interfaces and advise their managers about what tools to buy, are user interface experts. Thus, the decision of what GUI tools to use is often made based upon criteria other than the usability of the user interfaces that can be built with them. Such other criteria include

1. how easy the tool is for programmers to learn
2. how quickly programmers can develop user interfaces using the tool

---

2. In some sense, programming languages, text editors, compilers, syntax checkers, debuggers, performance analyzers, logic analyzers, and memory analyzers are also tools for building user interfaces, since they are tools for building software, and user interfaces are software. However, such tools are not specific to graphical user interfaces and will not be discussed here.

3. how easy the resulting user interfaces are to maintain

4. how well the tool fits into the organization's development processes and practices

5. how compatible the tool is with other development tools the team uses

6. whether the tool runs on the operating system the developers use

7. how compatible the resulting user interfaces are to back-end software (e.g., databases) and existing components

8. whether the tool is already owned by the company

9. whether the tool has been previously used in the company by this or other organizations

10. how much code or computer memory the resulting user interfaces require

11. whether the programmer used the tool at a prior job[3]

12. how much the tool costs

13. whether the toolmaker charges royalties on products made with the tool

14. whether the tool is currently in fashion or considered "cool" in the computer industry

Most of these are important criteria. In fact, criteria 1–5 are traditional usability considerations, albeit applied to the tool itself rather than to the user interfaces produced using it. My purpose is not to denigrate or discount the value of the above criteria (except perhaps criterion 14). Rather, it is to point out that, because of who usually makes decisions about development tools, criteria 1–14 are typically given much more weight than are criteria related to the usability and usefulness of the applications that will be built using the tools. The latter sort of criteria include

15. how compliant user interfaces developed with the tool are with GUI standards and conventions for the target application platform, such as Windows, Macintosh, CDE/Motif, Web

16. how compliant user interfaces developed with the tool are with general standards and conventions for user interface design

17. whether the tool provides any guidance to help programmers create user interfaces that conform to GUI standards and design guidelines and avoid mistakes such as those described in other chapters of this book

18. whether the tool provides all the GUI components that are required for the intended application or allows programmers to easily create them

19. whether the tool provides enough adjustments in details of user interfaces and their components to allow the resulting user interfaces to conform to a desired company or application suite look-and-feel

---

3. This can influence the decision in either direction, depending on whether the previous experience was positive or negative, and whether the programmer wants to stay with a familiar tool or expand his or her experience.

20. whether the tool provides rich-enough communication between user interface components and semantic or back-end components that users can get accurate and timely feedback for their actions

21. how easy user interfaces developed with the tool are to internationalize and localize

22. whether user interfaces developed using the tool are sufficiently responsive (see Chapter 7, and also an article by Duis and Johnson [1990])

23. how well user interfaces developed with the tool support individual user differences in operation, for example, by people who prefer using a keyboard to a mouse, or are disabled or elderly (e.g., sight-, hearing-, or motor-impaired)

Few managers and programmers know enough about human cognition and performance, user interface design, and usability evaluation and testing to be able to evaluate tools based on criteria 15–23. However, the usability, and hence perceived quality, of the resulting products depends at least as much on these criteria as on criteria 1–14.

As pointed out by Grudin [1991], developers, including development managers, tend to focus much more on their own development costs and benefits—time, money, prestige—than on the costs and benefits that the resulting product will generate for others. "Others" includes both people who support the product (both in the developers' company and outside of it) and those who use it. Because a product's lifetime is (hopefully) many times longer than its development time, and because the number of product support people and users far exceeds the number of developers, focusing on development costs and benefits when selecting development tools is a serious misweighting of criteria.

The experts who are in a position to evaluate tools based on the second set of criteria are user interface designers and evaluators. However, they rarely are the ones who decide what tools to use. This is especially true for the many companies that have no user interface professionals in-house and instead bring in outside consultants when they need a user interface designed, reviewed, or tested. By the time the consultant is brought in, the tools have long ago been chosen.

The result is that many design recommendations made by user interface designers and usability testers are rebuffed by the developers because "the development tool won't let us do that," or because "that would be too hard to do with this tool."

The following are five cases from my consulting experience where usability was hampered by the development tools.

Example 1: Menus that violate users' muscle memory. One of my client companies had developed and was already marketing a software application that made heavy use of Option menus, that is, menus that display a current value and allow users to select a new value. Users should be able to operate such menus by either of two methods:

A. place pointer over menu, press mouse button down to display all choices, drag pointer to desired choice (i.e., move pointer while holding button down), release mouse button, or

B. place pointer over menu, click (i.e., press and release mouse button) to display all choices, move pointer to desired new value, click to choose value and close menu.

I noticed while reviewing the application's user interface that its Option menus could be operated by method B but not by method A. The problem was made even more serious by the fact that menubar menus in the application allowed both methods of operation. When I told the developers about this problem, they said that there was nothing they could do about it because the dropdown menus provided by the user interface toolkit they were using did not allow method A operation. The menubar menus came from the same toolkit, but did not have the same problem.

Because method A is by far the more common method of operating menus, and because menu operation is a muscle memory action that people don't consciously think about after they've learned it, this was a serious usability flaw in the development tool they had committed to using long before I got there. I urged the developers to contact the toolkit developer to ask that this problem be corrected, but they said they were too busy and didn't have the required support channels, and it wasn't that important anyway because there was at least one method of operating the dropdown menus. We can safely assume that users of this application will be stumbling over this problem for years to come.

Example 2: Unresponsive components.   Another client was developing an application using GUI components that were extremely unresponsive to user actions. Buttons would take many seconds to even acknowledge being pressed, scrollbars would not respond to mouse movements until after the scrolled window content was repainted in its new position, window sizing and moving actions would take up to a minute to take effect, and so forth. Again, I mentioned this as being a serious problem because these are hand-eye coordination tasks requiring tight visual feedback, but the developers told me that the GUI toolkit they were using was just slow and would remain so until its next release. Never mind that the developers had to release their application based on the *current* release of the toolkit.

Example 3: Inadequate navigation feedback.   A usability test I conducted of a client's product showed that users were getting lost in the product's online Help documentation. One reason they were getting lost was that the links between topics in the documentation did not indicate whether the user had already visited the linked-to section or not (unlike most Web links, which do show this). Several test participants realized that this was why they were getting lost and explicitly suggested that the links should change color or appearance once they had been followed. However, when my test report suggested this improvement, the developers declined. Their reason: The toolkit used to build all Help documentation in the company did not support that.

Example 4: Missing important visual distinctions. One of my clients was developing an application in Java, using a popular Java GUI toolkit. I noticed a problem in the application's menubar menus: independent checkbox menu items looked the same as mutually exclusive sets of radiobutton menu items; both types of menu items had a circular dot to the left of the item that was either filled in or not, indicating whether that setting was ON or OFF. Users of this application therefore could not tell simply by looking at such menu items whether they are independent or part of a mutually exclusive set; they had to learn this by clicking on items to see what they did. I assumed that the programmers had simply made the common error of using the same type of component for the two types of menu items, and urged them to correct the error. However, they replied that they could not because they had made no error. They had used the right controls, but the GUI toolkit they were using gives the two different types of controls the exact same appearance when they are in menus. This contrasts with most popular GUI toolkits, which distinguish visually between radiobutton items and checkbox items whether or not they are in menus, as they should.

Example 5: Focus on appearance and layout, rather than semantics, of controls. A problem common to many of the tools my clients and other software developers use is that they require developers to begin by deciding what the user interface is going to look like. For example, developers have to decide upfront how a particular choice setting is going to be presented (e.g., as a menu or a set of radiobuttons). Most GUI tools force developers to work this way because they classify components based on appearance (e.g., menu, text field, radiobuttons), rather than semantics (e.g., one-from-many choice, ON/OFF setting, number in range). They usually also have to decide where it should be placed, because most GUI tools require that each component in the user interface be explicitly positioned. This distracts programmers and designers from more important design work: deciding what users need to be able to set and control in order to do their work [Johnson, 1992].

Although these five examples may seem minor, the fact is that usability flaws mandated by the choice of a particular GUI tool can add up. If using a particular tool results in user interfaces that have too many problems, the developers should reconsider their decision to use that tool. However, in my experience, developers are never receptive to suggestions of that sort.

Avoiding Blooper 79

It is difficult to give good advice on how to avoid this blooper because so many GUI development tools and building blocks are so bad. I have used a great many GUI builders and toolkits, and I can't say that I recommend any of them highly. For example, all commercially available GUI tools I have seen focus on appearance instead of user interface semantics [Johnson, 1992]; the only ones that don't are research prototypes. In any case, I won't endorse specific tools here. My main purpose in this section is simply to explain how a development organization should evaluate the tools and building blocks it will use to develop user interfaces for its products.

Most important criterion for choosing a GUI tool: How usable are the resulting GUIs?

When evaluating and comparing tools, place significant weight on criteria 15–23 above. The bottom line is that your customers don't care how you built your product or what pieces it is built from; they care only about your product as a whole: is it good enough for them, or isn't it? If your product's usability is poor because of the GUI tools you used, the loser isn't the tool developer; after all, you already bought their tool. They won. The loser is you.

For example, when developing a software application, set responsiveness criteria for each of the application's functions. Parts of the application that don't meet their responsiveness goals should be regarded as showstoppers, whether the problem is in your own team's software or in the GUI components you are using. Don't just say, "Those problems are in the components, not in our software, so there's nothing we can do about them." You can do something about them: demand improvements from the component developer, get different components, or build your own components. If you ship with unresponsive GUI components, it is your sales that will suffer, not those of the component developer.

Since the best-qualified people to judge how well a particular GUI tool or toolkit meets criteria 15–23 are your user interface people (you do have some of those, don't you?), make sure they are heavily involved in the decision. I'm not saying that criteria 1–14 should not be considered by management and the programmers (although I do believe that criterion 14 has no merit whatsoever). Rather, I am saying that criteria 15–23 are at least as important for the success of your product and that management and the programmers are not qualified to judge how well the tools meet those.

If the user interface designers can't use the tools directly (e.g., they consist of component libraries), this means that the programmers will have to try implementing some of the GUI using the tools, and then let the user interface people evaluate the results. Thus, when shopping for the GUI tools your team will use to build its applications, it's a good idea to have some ideas about your design already and actually try to implement crucial parts of the GUI using the various candidate tools. This of course takes significant time, but then again, choosing GUI development tools is a big decision because once your programmers become familiar with the tool you choose, you have a significant investment in it and so are unlikely to change tools for a while. Therefore, take the time and effort to choose your GUI development tools very carefully.

Tools can't design software; only designers can do that

Some people in the software industry claim that increasing the use of interactive GUI development tools such as PowerBuilder, UIM/X, and XDesigner, or interactive Web development tools such as PageMill, Home Page, and Front Page, will make it possible for less-skilled employees to design professional-quality user interfaces. That is just marketing hype or wishful thinking, or both.

In fact, interactive GUI and Web development tools simply allow less-skilled employees to create user interfaces, most of which will be of amateur quality. Knowing how to use tools does not imply knowing what to do with them. Simply allowing developers to build GUIs by dragging and dropping components instead of programming does not ensure that the resulting GUIs will be good ones. One reason for this is that the tools, like GUI platform standards, are too unconstrained. Another reason is that, as Cooper [1999] points out, the fact that a GUI was constructed does not mean that it was *designed*.

Drag-and-drop GUI construction tools are not and will never be the solution to the problem of difficult-to-use software. Indeed, it is more likely that increased use of interactive GUI and Web development software will bring about an overall *decrease* in the quality of software user interfaces, as more people who don't know what they are doing develop software.

8.2.2 Blooper 80: Anarchic development

A rampant problem in the software industry is development processes that are anarchic. By "anarchic," I mean uncontrolled, nonrepeatable, and driven by individual whim and the crisis-of-the-moment, rather than by proven, repeatable practices, company goals, and customer and user requirements.

This problem has been discussed extensively by others. For example, Alan Cooper devotes much of his book, *The Inmates Are Running the Asylum* [1999], to explaining why it is that management has so little control (and programmers have so much) over the computer-based products and services that their companies develop, even though this situation is detrimental to product usability and hence company success.

One impact of anarchic development on software user interfaces is easy to see: products that are fraught with inconsistencies, both major and minor. Every development team—sometimes every programmer—has done things differently. To master the software, users have to learn separately how to operate each program or each function within a program. For example:

- A document editor requires users to specify a name when they start a new document, but a graphics editor from the same company doesn't ask for a filename until the work is to be saved.

- In one dialog box, pressing the TAB key moves the insertion point to the next data field, but in another dialog box, it doesn't.

- In one function, new data objects are created by invoking a New... command and filling out the dialog box that appears, but in another function, they are created by filling out an always-visible form and clicking an Add button.

- In a file hierarchy displayed in one window of an application, files can be moved by dragging them to the desired new location, but in a file hierarchy displayed in a different window, files are moved by selecting them, invoking a Move function, and clicking on the desired new location.

- One program preserves the previous version of a graph in a backup file, but a companion program does not.

- A command in the menubar menus is labeled "Database Search," but the same command on the toolbar button is labeled "Query Repository."

Unfortunately, the examples are endless. As is explained in Principle 5 (Section 1.5), users want to fall into unconscious habits as quickly as possible. They want to be able to focus on their own work. Consistent design allows users to do that. Software that is riddled with inconsistencies forces users to keep thinking about the software itself, thereby distracting them from their true task. The bottom line is that inconsistent, incoherent user interfaces hinder learning and productivity—and ultimately, sales revenue.

I've seen products in which similar functions had very different user interfaces because the programmers who designed them didn't talk to each other, or because each one thought his design was better. I've seen corporate Web sites cobbled together from pages produced and maintained by separate organizations within a company, in which each organization's pages looked and worked differently from those of other organizations. I've even seen programmers design one dialog box one way one day and a similar one quite differently the next day simply because they weren't motivated to check how they did it the day before. Such discrepancies are a problem in and of themselves, but a much more serious problem is that many development organizations are not set up to discover, resolve, and prevent them.

Another impact of anarchic development is products and services that are so full of programmerisms and design bloopers that customers reject them, resulting in market failure. Even if customers don't reject a product outright, they may just barely tolerate it. As Cooper [1999] points out, when customers use a product despite cursing it daily, they have no loyalty to it and will switch to a competitor with no hesitation.

A colleague once commented that organizing and managing software engineers "is like herding cats." We can assume that he speaks from experience, and we should give him credit for at least trying. When it comes to organizing teams to produce coherent user interface designs and products that are aligned with company goals, it is apparent that many software development organizations don't try very hard.

Poor software usability results from three main varieties of anarchic development. Many development organizations manage to commit more than one variation simultaneously, and in some cases, all three!

Variation A: No design. When I am called by a client company to evaluate the user interface of a product or Web site, I always ask to see the user interface design specification from which the developers have been working. More often than not, there is no design specification. The programmers are just hacking, based on a vague list of features that someone—probably in Sales or Marketing—devised.

Some clients are slightly embarrassed to admit to me that this is how they operate, but some are decidedly unapologetic about it: "We don't do that here. In our market, we don't have time for specifications." Furthermore, as development schedules across the software industry accelerate to so-called Internet time, the tendency to skip an explicit design phase and jump straight into coding is *increasing*.

Landauer discusses this problem in depth in his book *The Trouble with Computers* [1995]. Cooper also covers it in his book *The Inmates Are Running the Asylum* [1999]. Therefore, I'll simply refer readers to their books and say only that unguided hackery is almost guaranteed to produce software that

- reflects engineering considerations more than it reflects user requirements
- is laden with user interface inconsistencies and design bloopers
- is not congruent with company goals

On top of all that, skipping design may actually cost extra time rather than saving it, as ad hoc user interfaces and software architectures are built, found to be inadequate, torn apart, and rebuilt multiple times during development. In other words, hacking without a spec results in a lot of aimless *commotion,* rather than purposeful *motion* toward a goal.

Variation B: No standards or guidelines. Many companies that produce software have no standards or guidelines that specify how products of the company should look and operate. They apparently don't realize that they are in the publishing business, like companies that create magazines, newspapers, books, TV shows, and movies.

Traditional publishers and broadcasters have strict standards for how information will be presented (e.g., "ten" versus "10"; in graphs versus tables), how words will be spelled (e.g., "color" versus "colour"; "Khadafy" versus "Gadhafi"), what fonts will be used (e.g., serif versus sans serif; Times Roman versus Bookman), how text will be formatted (e.g., bullets versus numbered items), whether articles begin with brief summaries or not, which direction people in photographs will face (e.g., in magazines and newspapers, usually away from the outer edge of the page), how long sound bites or video clips will last, whether people in a movie scene maintain their left-right relationship over time, and so on. Publishers who fail to establish standards and guidelines produce products that seem amateurish and cheap, even to people who cannot articulate exactly what it is about the products that looks bad. The design flaws may be minor annoyances that just leave people with an unfavorable impression, or they may be major flaws that hinder understanding of the content.

Software companies, as publishers, should develop and adhere to standards and guidelines that are appropriate for their products and intended customers. Unfortunately, few do. Programmers often consider it anal-compulsive overkill to worry about inconsistencies in details such as the wording of commands and messages, the capitalization of setting labels, the spacing of controls, and the like. Management doesn't press the issue because doing so would add time to the schedule and would have to be assigned to the programmers themselves because no one else is authorized to change the source code.

Some managers assume that the standards of their target platform(s)—Windows, Mac, CDE/Motif, the Web—are sufficient. That assumption is false because the standards for those platforms are insufficiently constrained. An application can conform to the Macintosh user interface standards and still be full of design bloopers. Two software products can both be Windows compliant, and yet look and feel so different that users would have difficulty switching between them. Software development organizations that want to develop easy-to-use products need design guidelines that go well beyond the minimal conformance requirements for a given GUI platform. They also need a development *process* that ensures compliance with those guidelines.

Variation C: No oversight. It amazes me how common it is for companies to hire programmers to develop interactive applications, give them little or no guidance, and hope for the best. One software manager I knew characterized this practice as

> Hire nerds, tell 'em what you want, lock 'em in their offices, and throw in pizza and t-shirts every few weeks.

The mistaken assumption that good programmers can, by themselves, produce usable and useful software is due in part to Variation A of Blooper 76: Assuming GUI programmer = GUI designer (Section 8.1.1). Also, as described in Variation E of Blooper 77: Assigning the GUI to less experienced programmers (Section 8.1.2), this assumption is partly due to management's desire to save on labor costs. In fact, to do this is to be "penny wise but pound foolish."

One aspect of software development for which managers frequently fail to provide sufficient oversight is the writing of text displayed by the software. It is often left completely to each programmer to devise the command labels, button labels, setting names, and error messages that his or her code will display. However, programmers are not hired for the breadth of their vocabularies and clarity of their writing. In fact, they typically are somewhat limited in that regard. Therefore, management failure to arrange for review of the program text by skilled technical writers and editors can result in software that ships with inconsistent terminology, programmer jargon, obscure error messages, spelling errors, grammatical mistakes, and general poor writing. Chapter 4 describes in detail the sorts of problems that can arise and provides some examples from my experience.

A lack of oversight can be due to weak management as well as to management misconceptions about what programmers are and are not good at. Development managers in software development organizations are often former engineers who have climbed a rung or two up the company's management ladder. Those who were unskilled (or even downright inept) at managing other people before their promotions, generally still are afterwards. Some companies send new and prospective managers to management training classes, also known as "charm school." Such training, which typically lasts all of three days, is limited in effectiveness, especially since many attendees don't really want to be there and so spend much of the class time doodling or checking their email and voice mail. Many companies don't even pay lip service to training people to be effective managers. The result is that a high proportion of managers in software development organizations have very weak people management skills.

Combine weak managers with programmers who lack user interface design training and who often don't cooperate or communicate well with each other, and you get anarchic development. The following is a scenario that is unfortunately not atypical:

> The design and coding is divided up among several programmers by program function, based on their interests and skills. The programmers either disagree about how the software should present controls and information or don't talk to each other about it. Each programmer designs the user interface differently in the part of the software for which he or she is responsible. Their manager or team leader is aware of the design inconsistencies and would like to correct them, but can't convince the programmers to confer and reach agreement among themselves, and is too weak or indecisive to force his own decision on the team.

In situations such as this, some development managers have had a hidden agenda when they brought me in as a consultant. I was supposedly hired to find user interface problems and recommend solutions, but soon discovered that I had actually been hired to solve a personnel problem. The manager needed an outside "authority" to recommend what the manager already knew the programmers should do.

Whether the reason for a lack of oversight is unwarranted optimism or weakness on the part of management, this laissez-faire approach can have serious negative consequences for a business. Regardless of how highly trained

GLASBERGEN

"My team has created a very innovative solution, but we're still looking for a problem to go with it."

and professional the programmers may be *as programmers,* most are amateurs at designing user interfaces. Therefore, following this strategy amounts to letting amateurs design some of the most important parts of one's products—the parts that users experience.

Years ago, a programmer and I were arguing about improvements I had suggested for the user interface of a text editor he had written. My position was that certain aspects of the text editor were extremely arbitrary and would therefore be difficult for users to learn. He was resisting any changes. He said of the users: "If they want to use computers, they're gonna have to learn like I learned." What this programmer didn't understand is that the intended users are not like him. They don't "want to use computers"; they want to get their work done—in this case, create or edit text documents. In an open, competitive software marketplace, they aren't "gonna have to" do anything because they can buy someone else's software or even avoid using computers altogether.

Although managers may believe that the programmers are making only technical decisions, in fact the programmers are making important *business* decisions. They are deciding

- who the product's customers will be and how much they will value the product
- which functions of the software will be heavily used and which will be so rarely used they might as well not be there
- what the company's reputation as a software developer will be for years to come
- how fast the company's revenue from the product will rise, when it will peak, and how long it will last
- what the demand for customer support services will be

Unfortunately, it is usually not until the product has been shipped to beta customers—or even later—that all the business consequences of the programmers' decisions become apparent.

It is at such points that I am often called in as a consultant to "fix" product user interfaces. Unfortunately, unless the client is willing to commit to a comprehensive redesign process (which few are; see Blooper 78: Discounting the value of testing and iterative design, Section 8.1.3), all that can be done is smooth over some of the product's more superficial usability problems. What a shame that management didn't exert some oversight earlier. What a shame that customers were not consulted sooner. What a shame that someone who knew how to clarify user requirements and create and evaluate designs based on those requirements wasn't involved from the start.

Example of programmers making business decisions by default

Recently, I was called as a consultant to redesign the user interface of a software product. The product manager told me that the product had been under development for over a year with no user interface designer on the team (see Blooper 81: No task domain expertise on the design team, Section 8.2.3), and—surprise!—prospective customers were telling her that the product was unusable. During our conversation, I used the metaphor of their software product as a camera, in an attempt to check my understanding:

> Me: "Let me see if I understand. Your customers want an Instamatic, but your programmers built a Leica." [Note: Comparing a popular point-and-shoot camera with a camera for professional photographers that has dozens of manual controls.]

> She: "No, it's worse than that. I wish they'd built a camera. They built a kit for building cameras. You can build any camera you want with it. But our customers don't want to *build* a camera. They just want a camera."

In short, the programmers designed and developed the software that *they* would want if they had the job of managing a network. But they don't have that job. Other people have that job, and the software *they* want is not what the programmers designed.

By developing a product that could not be sold directly to the intended customers, but rather would have to be sold through third-party system integrators and value-added resellers, the programmers had made an important business decision for the company—a decision that management had not intended. It amazes me that management at this company—a major computer and software vendor—allowed development to proceed for over a year when what the programmers were developing was such a gross mismatch with what customers wanted. Was no one paying attention? ⊕

Avoiding Blooper 80

If you want your software products and services to succeed in today's marketplace, you need a professional development process. Having a professional development process requires following certain rules. Following these rules is *not* easy, but it is very, very important.

Don't hack; design

Before a software development team begins writing code, it should have a user interface design to work from. That design should be developed by someone who has experience designing user interfaces, and who understands the user requirements. Without a design, a development team is just asking for trouble, both during development and when the software is released.

This is the main point made by Cooper in *The Inmates Are Running the Asylum* [1999]. He argues that if you carefully design what you're going to build before you start building it, the building will go faster and you're more likely to build a product that customers like. He considers it a big mistake to simply start coding and assume that a product can be iterated into shape using customer feedback and usability tests. While I don't agree with everything in Cooper's book, I agree with him completely about this.

An important first step in producing a design is to perform an analysis of the task domain and develop a system conceptual model before designing the user interface. This development step is described more fully in Principle 2: Consider function first, presentation later (Section 1.2). For present purposes it is enough to say that explicitly enumerating all the user-visible objects and actions that the software will provide greatly facilitates the development of a clean, simple, consistent user interface.

Developers are publishers, and should act like it

As suggested earlier, developers of software products need to realize that they are in the publishing and media businesses and so must, like all others in those businesses, establish design standards, conventions, guidelines, and above all, development processes that yield consistent interaction style, layout, formatting, fonts, terminology, writing style, use of color, and so on.

Regarding themselves as being in the publishing or media business would also help development managers understand the difference between "it works" and "it's ready to ship." The gap between these two states may be almost as large as the gap between "here's an idea" and "it works." Imagine if *The New York Times* or *National Geographic* were sent to subscribers as soon as all the contributing journalists turned in their stories and photographs. Suppose the first cut of Alfred Hitchcock's *The Birds,* Stanley Kubrick's *2001,* or Steven Spielberg's *Schindler's List* had been released. Software is a media product, and developers need to realize that it pays to "sweat the details," just as it does with movies, newspapers, and magazines.

Quality user interfaces require an investment

Many software development companies would be wise to invest in

- training programmers on principles of user-centered design
- hiring full-time user interface designers and usability testers
- providing programmers with GUI guideline books for their reference; for example:
  - Industry standard platform style guides: Windows, Mac, CDE/Motif, Java

 – McFarland and Dayton, *Design Guide for Multiplatform Graphical User Interfaces* [1995]
 – Weinshenk et al., *GUI Design Essentials* [1997]
 – Mullet and Sano, *Designing Visual Interfaces* [1995]
 – Bickford, *Interface Design: The Art of Developing Easy-to-Use Software* [1997]
 – Nielsen, *Designing Excellent Websites: Secrets of an Information Architect* [1999d]

- developing departmental or company user interface guidelines and standards

- using a development process that ensures conformance to design guidelines, for example, the Bridge methodology, which was designed to bridge the large gap between GUI style guides and true usability [Dayton et al., 1998]

- including explicit design and testing phases in development schedules

- having a project architect responsible for ensuring consistency between different parts of the software (especially when different programmers develop different parts)

- having technical writers and editors review all text messages and labels used in the software

- developing a software infrastructure in which all program text resides in message files to facilitate review and translation, and to allow a single text string to be referenced by any part of the program that needs to display that text

- using GUI components and templates that embody and support user interface standards

- conducting empirical tests of usability

- revising designs based on usability test results

 Layers of GUI standards

> User interface standards and guidelines can be treated as multilayered, with inner layers having ever more specific scope. There are industry-wide guidelines for user interface design. There are platform-specific ones, for example, for Windows, Macintosh, and CDE/Motif. Some companies develop their own corporate standards and guidelines so that their products exhibit a distinctive look-and-feel. It might make sense for all the products in a particular product line produced by a company to look and work more like each other than do the company's products in general. Finally, standards and guidelines can be developed for a specific product, to foster consistency between different parts of it. The inner layers augment, rather than contradict, the outer ones. ⊕

Give UI experts more clout

Yet another remedy is to structure the development organization so as to give user interface designers and usability test engineers more authority to declare usability problems to be showstoppers. One way to achieve this is for more user interface designers to become managers of development teams; this would give them the clout they need. User interface experts could also function as advisors to managers, to help the managers foresee the business implications of user interface design flaws (see Variation C of this blooper).

Additionally, Cooper [1999] suggests—and I agree—that once a development team has gone to the trouble and expense of producing a user interface design, the project's GUI programmers should commit to implementing it exactly. They should not treat it—as programmers sometimes do—as a collection of suggestions that can be interpreted loosely. If a programmer doesn't like something in the team's design specification, he or she should lobby to change the specification rather than unilaterally coding the GUI however he or she sees fit.

Take responsibility

Finally, management can help overcome anarchic development simply by being more assertive. Who, after all, is ultimately responsible for the success of the products?

8.2.3   Blooper 81: No task domain expertise on the design team

You might think that it would be difficult to design an effective user interface for a software product without a deep and detailed understanding of the work the intended users do, the work environment in which the software will be used, and what users would do with the software. You might think that, but if you did, you would be out of step with the thinking of many development managers in the software industry. Many apparently believe that a brief introduc-

SALLY FORTH • Greg Howard and Craig MacIntosh

© 1996 Greg Howard, distributed by King Features Syndicate.

tion to the software's target task is all a designer or programmer should need in order to design a suitable user interface. Development teams often include no one who understands the task domain, and many make no effort, as the product is being developed, to acquire such understanding.

One reason for this is historical. As Grudin [1991] and Norman [1998] point out, it wasn't so long ago that computer-based products were intended and designed only for technically trained users: engineers, scientists, and other programmers. Product developers designed essentially for themselves and people like them, and assumed that would be good enough. When the intended users were other software engineers, it *was* good enough. Even when the intended users were not software engineers, the designs sort of worked because the users (physicists, chemists, computer enthusiasts, and other kinds of engineers) were technically savvy enough to be able to adapt to the technocentric designs that software engineers produced. Software developers got used to being able to assume that they already knew what they needed to know in order to design successful products.

However, the market for software products intended for technogeeks is now only a tiny, tiny part of the entire software market. Computer-based products have gone mainstream. The Internet, originally the exclusive domain of a few thousand elite computer researchers, is now a household concept. The intended users are now workers in every type of business and consumers in homes across the developed world, and even in parts of the "Third World." The assumption that software developers can design usable and useful products without much special effort to import task domain expertise is now completely invalid, even if it ever was valid, which is doubtful.

A second reason for a lack of task domain expertise on development teams is, frankly, a certain amount of arrogance and contempt for users by developers. Engineers know about technology, and technology is what they are developing. So what else is there to know? Knowledge about the task domain is discounted: users don't know about technology, so they don't know anything.

One can see this attitude in the terms that software developers usually use to talk about the level of expertise of users for whom the software is being designed. It's a linear scale, starting with "novice" or "naive" users, who don't know much about computers, and ending with "expert" users, who are hardcore engineers like the developers. The scale focuses on users' general knowledge of computer technology. Expertise or skill in a non-computer-related task domain, whether high or low, plays no role in placing a person on the scale. Even knowledge of a particular software product is not factored in.

Such a scale of course ignores the obvious. Three fairly independent sorts of knowledge can affect a person's performance using a particular software product: knowledge of computer technology in general, knowledge of the particular software product, and knowledge of the product's target task domain. A particular person can have high, medium, or low levels of each sort of knowledge independent of the other two. For example:

- A longtime C programmer may not have figured out how to program his VCR or even set its clock.
- An experienced Unix hacker may struggle with Microsoft Word, while an office secretary who has never even heard of Unix handles Word with ease.
- A Macarthur Fellow in physics who is the idol of many of her colleagues may find herself stymied by the "physicists workstation" many of her colleagues use.
- Computer novices and experts alike may get lost in an online travel agency's Web site.
- A novice accountant who has programming experience may have trouble learning how to use an accounting program, while an experienced accountant with no programming background learns it right away, or vice versa.
- A businessman who is a hotshot with Lotus 1-2-3 and Microsoft Excel takes a Java course and finds himself dumbfounded by the concepts of object-oriented programming, while his brother the hotshot Java programmer wastes an hour trying to make Excel add up a column of numbers and finally gives up and writes a Java program to do it.
- A computer science professor may be too clueless about PCs to help his brother-in-law buy one and set it up.
- A telemarketer's workstation and a C++ programming environment both share a badly designed file chooser dialog box, and user testing reveals that their respective users—minimum wage temporary workers in one case and highly paid experienced programmers in the other—make the same "errors" when trying to find data files.

The three-dimensional nature of the knowledge that affects people's use of a software product suggests that different kinds of expertise are also required to *design* a usable and useful product. Software product developers typically possess only technical expertise. They lack expertise in the task domain, limiting their ability to produce successful products. Developers' tendency to disregard the task domain expertise of users is therefore misguided and counterproductive. Nonetheless, it is a fact.

A third reason for a lack of task domain knowledge on software design teams is that importing such knowledge into a development team, whether by bringing representative users onto the team or by sending developers out to talk to them, is not easy. Grudin [1991] catalogues obstacles that even well-meaning development teams can encounter. For example:

- Working with task domain experts requires lots of revisions in the design, a.k.a. iteration. Design iteration requires the cooperation of the entire team because it affects implementation, documentation, schedules, and budgets. Getting buy-in from the entire team, including management, is difficult.
- It is sometimes not entirely clear who the users of a product will be. The Apple Macintosh was supposed to be for "everyone," but its core market is

in the graphic design industry. Identifying the appropriate task domain experts may not be straightforward.

- Business realities can sometimes stymie developers' efforts to seek input from potential users of a software product (see Variation B, following). Obstacles to user involvement can be found both in software development organizations and in customer organizations.

- Getting useful feedback or suggestions from task domain experts before one has a product to show them is not straightforward; it requires concerted effort and creativity. Developers are tempted to wait until the product is far enough along to be "showable." However, by then, it's usually too late for suggestions from users to have much of an impact on the design.

Finally, one mustn't overlook the fact that all development teams are not equal: some simply don't do their homework as well as others. A development team's persistent lack of expertise about the target task domain may be due to simple carelessness or lack of due diligence.

Whether the reason is history, arrogance, carelessness, or legitimate obstacles, ignorance about the intended users of software products and their tasks is rampant in the software development industry. In addition to the general form of this blooper—no one on the development team really understands what intended users do—two special variations are worth mentioning.

Variation A: No in-house UI designer for high-semantics applications. Most organizations that develop computer-based applications specialize in a particular application area, for example, home finance, medical database, education, military, business decision support, document processing, personnel record keeping, games. One way for such organizations to assure that the design of their products is informed by at least some knowledge of the target task domain and work context is to use user interface designers who have experience developing products for that target market and task domain. Over time, by talking with customers, attending focus groups, meeting with marketing and sales staff, and conducting usability tests, most designers acquire some understanding—sometimes a deep understanding—of the users' tasks, goals, problems, and work context. The more time spent developing products for the task domain, the better a designer's understanding of it, and the better the designs he or she will produce.

This is more important when the application domain is highly specialized or very complex. Designing an effective user interface for an air traffic control system, a hospital intensive-care monitoring system, or a hotel registration system requires knowing more than does designing a desktop arithmetic calculator or an email reader. Applications for complex or specialized task domains are sometimes called "high-semantics" applications.

One example of a high-semantics application area is tools for professional programmers. Both before I became a consultant and after becoming one, I have worked for organizations that developed programming tools. Two such organizations were part of the same company, which developed computers and software. The company had a central user interface group whose charter was to supply user interface design and testing expertise on an as-needed basis throughout much of the company—an internal consulting group, if you will. The internal user interface group was staffed with very smart, highly skilled people who could produce an excellent design or evaluation in just about any application area they were called upon to work on. However, both programming tools organizations in this company had learned from experience that "renting" user interface designers from the central user interface group was not effective for them. They had learned that designing tools for programmers required designers who knew more about programming and the development organization's own approach to it than the designers in the central user interface group knew or could be expected to learn in a reasonable time. Both programming tools organizations found it most effective to hire their own user interface designers—preferably ones with significant programming experience—and keep them around for as long as possible. This policy shows a recognition that using user interface designers who have task domain expertise is especially important in high-semantics application areas.

Surprisingly, however, many companies or organizations within companies design and develop high-semantics applications with no dedicated user interface designer on staff. Instead, they hire consultants—internal or external—and expect them to somehow turn out effective user interfaces in a short time. Many of the companies that hire user interface consultants do so because they have no user interface designers *at all* on staff as permanent employees.

When consulting for clients who are developing high-semantics applications about which I know little or nothing, I usually find it necessary to lower their expectations to a reasonable level. I tell them that I am happy to do what I can for them, but that my lack of experience in their target task domain places limits on what they should expect, at least in the short term. If a company hires me to critique the user interface of its software product, I tell the client that I can usually evaluate superficial aspects of the user interface right away, without knowing much about the application domain, but that a deeper evaluation requires a deeper understanding, which will take time. For example, it is relatively easy to evaluate a design's compliance with the standards and guidelines of the developer's target platform, such as Windows, MacOS, Java, or CDE/Motif. It is also relatively easy to spot usability bloopers such as those listed in Chapters 2, 4, and 5 of this book.

However, it is impossible—repeat: *impossible*—for someone who lacks a deep understanding of an application's high-semantics task domain to judge how *useful* the application will be to its intended users. A thorough understanding of the target task domain is crucial if the assignment is to design or radically redesign a user interface rather than just to critique one. It doesn't matter how good a user interface designer or evaluator one is.

**Examples of high-semantics applications
developed with no UI designers on staff**

Here is a sampling of some of the high-semantics applications that clients or would-be clients of mine developed without any permanent user interface designers on staff (company names withheld to protect the guilty).

- *Equities trading.* Workstation for professional stockbrokers, stock traders, and their support staff. The developer had received feedback from current and prospective customers that the software was overly complicated and "amateurishly designed." They initially wanted me to simplify the user interface radically, within a few months. We soon settled on the lesser goal of bringing the application's windows and dialog boxes into compliance with design guidelines. Only after eight months of working with them did I feel competent to suggest more radical improvements.

- *Telephone call routing.* Tools for administering and configuring automatic call-routing software, which directs incoming calls to voice menus ("To check your account balance, press 1. To transfer funds, press 2 ...") or to banks of telephone operators, sales agents, customer service agents, and so on. In a week, I was supposed to critique the user interface and suggest improvements. I made sure the client understood that my comments and suggestions would be mostly about relatively superficial aspects of the design. I also convinced the client to invest in user interface design training for the development team, so that those who already had some understanding of the application domain's business logic would also know something about user interface design.

- *Health insurance.* A distributed information system for insurance companies to use in processing and tracking applications for health insurance. The developer—a startup company—hired me occasionally to conduct half-day reviews of its designs and give suggestions for improvement. Since I had had to obtain my own health insurance when I became a consultant and had been denied coverage by one company, I wanted to learn more about how insurance companies process applications. Even though the client expressed appreciation for the input I gave them during our brief review sessions, I sometimes had the feeling that I was learning more about the insurance business than the client was learning about user interface design.

- *Wide-area computer network administration.* A prospective client wanted me to help improve the user interface of their wide-area network administration software. The product had been two years in development with no user interface expertise on the team. Not surprisingly, they were getting feedback from prospective customers that the software was impossible to use. The irony is that the client company was at the time running ads to convince customers that they were serious about usability. This product's intended task domain was so far beyond my understanding that I decided I couldn't help them and turned down the job.

Clearly, many managers in companies that are developing highly complex, specialized products believe that they can be successful without having user interface designers in-house who are well-versed in the business logic of the company's target application domain. To me, it is quite obvious that they are mistaken. Why do they believe it? Perhaps it is related to Bloopers 76 and 77: a lack of understanding and/or low regard for what user interface designers do.

I invariably tell clients who are developing high-semantics applications that they really ought to hire a user interface designer as a full-time employee. I feel obligated to give them this advice, even though I realize that if they follow it, they probably won't need me as a consultant anymore. But I have plenty of work and it's the right advice to give them, so I do it. So far, not one of dozens of clients I have given this advice to has followed it.

Variation B: UI designers have no contact with task domain experts. In many companies I've worked or consulted for, those in charge of designing a product's user interface would have welcomed design advice from existing or potential users, but found arranging to get such advice to be frustratingly difficult. In some cases, the task domain experts were constantly busy and/or prohibitively expensive (e.g., doctors, stockbrokers, or airline pilots; see Blooper 78: Discounting the value of testing and iterative design, Section 8.1.3). In other cases, the development team wasn't allowed to contact potential users for organizational or legal reasons. As Grudin [1991] points out, technology companies are rarely set up to facilitate direct contact between developers and users. In fact, most are set up explicitly to prevent such contact.

Several years ago, before I became a consultant, I worked for a company that was participating in a multicompany effort to develop a video-on-demand system for elementary schools. The project's goal was to develop special classroom video equipment and a supporting network and server infrastructure to allow teachers in the participating school district to locate and show educational videos for their classrooms online. Teachers would no longer have to order physical video cassettes months in advance from the school district's central video library. They would no longer have to worry about whether the video they needed for their lesson plan was already checked out by another teacher. They would no longer have to dig through a canvas bag that arrived in the teacher's lounge each Monday with that week's videos from the school district. The group I was working in was assigned to design the user interface that teachers would use to locate, select, and show videos.

One big problem was that we were supposed to design the user interface without talking to any teachers. The project was, as explained earlier, a joint effort between several companies. The company I worked for was only a subordinate partner in the project. The primary partner, a telephone company, wanted to be the only one to have direct contact with the school district or any of its employees. They wanted the customer, the school district, to identify the project with their company and their company alone. They didn't want to "confuse the school district by presenting them with representatives from several participating companies." Because of this policy, the user interface designers were forbidden from contacting any of the school district's teachers.

The managers and lead engineers at the project's primary-partner company didn't see this as a problem because they expected us to quickly devise a simple menu-based topic hierarchy for finding and selecting videos, add some buttons for starting the selected video, and be done with it. We felt that such a naive design would be neither usable nor useful for schoolteachers, and wanted to do better than that. However, we felt that it would be impossible to design a better user interface when none of us knew anything about how teachers in the target school district select, order, or use videos for their classes.

We decided to do an end run around the restriction. We contacted a different school district and arranged to interview and conduct focus groups with teachers from that district. In these interviews and focus groups, we asked teachers to describe how they planned and selected videos to show in their classes, how they ordered videos, how they showed them, and what they liked and didn't like about the process. We also described possible capabilities and designs for an online video system and asked the teachers to comment on them. We learned many things that influenced our thinking. For example:

- An arbitrary hierarchical classification scheme for organizing video titles would not be useful to teachers. First, teachers use a specialized jargon when discussing how classroom materials should be categorized. Whereas we engineers thought in terms of "topics," "subtopics," and "sub-subtopics," teachers refer to educational "units," "subjects," and "lessons." Furthermore, teachers told us that they pick videos based on what is *in* them, not on what they are nominally about. For example, a video might be about sea animals, but if it includes a segment of a fishing boat, they might show that segment in a lesson on transportation. This indicated that some sort of keyword indexing of videos would be important, perhaps even with user-supplied keywords.

- Teachers show videos in their classrooms for two fundamentally different reasons: (1) to support what they are teaching, and (2) as indoor entertainment for rainy days or rewards for good performance. Videos that support the teacher's lesson plan are planned weeks or months in advance—sometimes before the school year even begins. Videos that are shown for entertainment are selected on the spur of the moment.

- Teachers almost always preview a video before showing it to their students unless they are very familiar with what is in it. This is partly to find out whether—or what parts of—the video fits their lesson or their students' age level. It is also to screen it for content that might be objectionable for the age level of the children. One teacher told us that she once neglected to preview a school-district-approved video on mammals before showing it to her third-grade class and was surprised to see that it was a bit more comprehensive than she expected in showing mammalian mothers nursing their young: "It showed, you know, *all* mammals!" With videocassettes, most teachers can preview videos at home. The new online system, which had to be used at the school, would require teachers to stay after class or come in early to preview videos, which would be a strong strike against it.

- Teachers often cut or edit educational videos to match their class's attention span and to present only the segments most relevant to their lesson. They also might start, pause, and stop a given video several times during a class in order to leave time to talk about it. A system that didn't allow teachers to easily start, stop, and pause videos at arbitrary locations would be ignored in favor of videotapes and VCRs.

- Teachers share information about—and reviews of—videos with each other. In most schools, a few teachers who are "video buffs" serve as resources for their colleagues, as much for their knowledge of the content of a large number of videos and their personal tape libraries as for their understanding of how to operate video equipment.

- Many of the teachers we talked to had already given up using their school district's video library out of frustration with its bureaucracy, slowness, and meager selection. Instead, they developed their own video collections, either buying videos with their own money or recording TV shows.[4] Thus, assuming that the situation in the target school district was similar to that in the one for which the teachers we interviewed worked, the new video-on-demand system would be competing with teachers' private video collections as well as replacing the district's central videocassette library.

The point of this example is that, without access to task domain experts—in this case teachers—we would have had to design our user interface "in the dark." Probably the best we could have done would have been the simplistic subject hierarchy the prime contractor initially recommended. As our interviews and focus groups showed, that would have been a mistake. Unfortunately, many software development organizations make such mistakes.

While pointing out that product development organizations often limit contact between developers and users, Grudin [1991] also notes that obstacles to user involvement in software design can be encountered in *customer* organizations as well. Managers at a customer company may not be enthusiastic about diverting personnel and time away from normal company work to contribute task domain expertise to a software development effort. At the very least, most will need to hear a strong argument about what is in it for them before they will warm up to the idea. This can be seen even when software is being developed for a specific customer, so of course it is a *big* concern when software is being developed as a product to be sold on the open marketplace:

---

4. Many public TV stations permit teachers to copy broadcast shows for classroom use. In fact, some public stations broadcast educational videos in the middle of the night for the explicit purpose of allowing teachers to tape them. This of course assumes that enough teachers know how to program their VCRs to record shows at 3 A.M.!

"You want me to loan you one of my employees two days a week for six months to help you develop software that you will then sell not only to us but also to our competitors? I...don't...think...so!"

The pushback from customer companies on allowing developers to talk to potential users isn't always from managers concerned about resources, either. Customers and users, like developers, may not fully understand the importance of task domain expertise for designing usable and useful software. In their case, this is at least partly because they aren't software developers and therefore know very little about what is involved in software development. Alternatively, customers and users may wrongly assume that the developers must understand the task domain because, after all, they are developing software for it!

Case where a user didn't want to talk to developers

A manager at one of my client companies told me that there was a user at a customer company in Japan who had been a fairly vocal critic of the software. However, when the manager and members of her development team flew to Tokyo to interview him to get his suggestions on improving the design, he rebutted them, reportedly saying, more or less:

"I just don't like it the way it is. I don't have time to tell you how to improve it. You're developing the software. You should know!"

Even when the barriers keeping developers and users apart are in the customer's organization, I regard it as a failing of the development organization. Without design input or at least feedback from task domain experts, a computer-based product is likely to fail. In an open marketplace of computer-based products, when a customer refuses to grant a developer access to users, the main loser is the developer, not the customer. Therefore, the burden is on the development organization to try to figure out a way around the barrier. For example, development managers can try to find customers who *are* willing to participate. They can try to change the recalcitrant manager's mind. They can escalate the request to higher management in the customer organization. The bottom line is that failure to circumvent the barrier means that you've committed a major blooper.

Avoiding Blooper 81

Countering this blooper requires reorienting the design and development process to be more centered on expertise about the target task domain than on expertise about computers and technology. It means making it a high priority to determine and meet user requirements. It means using designers who understand the activity that the product is supposed to support. It means involving prospective users in the design process, as advisors, consultants, test participants, and even co-designers.

User-centered design process

The buzz term is "user-centered design." It must be stressed, however, that the term is about *process,* not products per se (although the reason for doing it is that it results in better products). One does not look at products and pronounce whether they are or are not user-centered. Rather, one examines the process by which a developer produces products, and gauges the extent to which that process is or is not user-centered.

Plenty of good books have been written about why it is beneficial to focus the design and development process on users, and how to do it:

- Norman and Draper [1986] produced a collection of essays and articles that defined the concept of "user-centered design" and presented the case for using it in computer system development.

- Nielsen [1993] provides detailed instructions on cost-effective ways to incorporate tests and evaluations of usability into every stage of a product's development.

- Landauer [1995] documents the failure of computer technology to improve the productivity of office workers, lays the blame for that failure on a lack of user-centered design, and outlines what it would mean to develop computer technology in a user-centered manner.

- Norman [1998] argues that the personal computer industry's failure to adopt user-centered design is causing stagnation of their market, and describes the major philosophical, organizational, and product changes that will be required to bring computer technology up to the same level of popularity as, say, televisions and telephones.

- Greenbaum and Kyng [1991] and Schuler and Namioka [1993] provide a wealth of advice on how to go beyond merely observing and testing users to actually making them members of the design team in order to tap into their task domain expertise. Muller et al. [1997] provide a more recent catalogue of participatory design methods.

All of the above books are recommended reading for managers who want to know how to improve their development processes by making them more user-centered, and why they should. For the complete references, see the Further reading section at the end of the chapter. For those who are too impatient to read those books, my own advice is as follows.

Users' task domain expertise is a crucial ingredient

First and foremost, developers—managers as well as programmers—need to change their attitudes about task domain versus technical expertise. Users are

"No, I don't want to play chess. I just want you to reheat the lasagna."

not ignorant; they are experts in the task domain. Conversely, software engineers aren't omniscient; they are novices in the task domain and they are novices in understanding the requirements of human users in general. Software engineers need to acquire some humility. They need to admit their ignorance of most task domains and of human-computer interaction, and either work to overcome it by learning from the experts, or work around it by asking the experts to join them on the design team, or both. This is crucial in order to design successful software products in today's marketplace.

Before designing anything, developers should spend lots of time talking to representative users. Do this in one-on-one interviews, where each participant's comments are uninfluenced by the comments of others. Also do it in focus groups, where participants' ideas, thoughts, and reactions contradict and complement each other. Find out how those who might eventually use the planned product do their work now, what they like and don't like about it, and how they could imagine it being better.

Learn about the users' work

At some point early in the process, send some developers to become immersed in the task domain: observing users, hanging out with them, and, if it can be arranged, actually doing some of their work. At the very least, the team's user interface designer should be well exposed to the work users do.

Even better—but usually harder to arrange—go get some target users and bring them onto the design team. Warning: It is not trivial figuring out how to involve users effectively once you have some of their time. Just letting them sit in on project meetings with programmers and development managers won't work. Most will hesitate to participate because they feel out of place. Even if they muster the courage to speak up, they don't think or talk like developers, so there will be miscommunication and mistrust. On the other hand, treating users as second-class team members also won't work. It must be made clear to them that they are needed because of their task domain expertise, which the developers lack. Structured sessions—probably led by a facilitator who also serves as interpreter—are required. For example:

- Meetings focused on understanding the current workplace, yielding an analysis of the tasks users perform (e.g., an outline of the main tasks and each of their subtasks, ranked by frequency or importance) and a list of problems people currently have that the planned product should overcome

- Meetings devoted to developing a project vocabulary or lexicon: what are the concepts of the task domain and what should they be called?

- Meetings focused on developing imaginary scenarios of people using the planned product, expressed at a conceptual level, not the level of a specific user interface

- Sessions in which task domain experts envision possible designs for the product, yielding initial sketches

- Sessions in which users are shown fleshed-out designs or prototypes and asked for feedback and suggestions

- Sessions in which users and developers enact roles in a simulated work-place, using initial prototypes (perhaps jury-rigged ones)

The aforementioned books by Greenbaum and Kyng [1991] and Muller et al. [1997] are good sources of ideas on how to enlist and engage prospective users successfully as co-designers.

Use testing to guide design, not to grade designers

Create a development culture in which usability testing is regarded as an indispensable tool for guiding design development in the right direction, rather than as a way to evaluate the performance of designers. Testing should also not be regarded as a big, expensive step that can be carried out only near the end of development. A quick little empirical test can do wonders to resolve sticky design issues as they arise. Therefore, designers should be empowered to make creative use of quick-and-dirty tests whenever they feel the need. And yes, at important points in development, subject the software to comprehensive usability testing. In short, take the phrase "test early and often" to heart; build it into your organizational culture. Examples of tests that are informal, formal, early, and late are described above under Blooper 78: Discounting the value of testing and iterative design (Section 8.1.3).

When all else fails

If other approaches are infeasible, hire software engineers who are task domain experts. As described above in Blooper 77: Treating user interface as low priority (Section 8.1.2), the music software industry does this by hiring programmers who are also musicians. As explained earlier, this approach has limitations because programming skill + task domain skill does not = user interface design skill, but it is better than having *no* task domain expertise on the team. Sometimes it can work extremely well. For example, a company where I once worked that developed medical equipment and medical information systems had on its staff an engineer who was also a medical doctor. In fact, that fellow was the lead designer on the project. The products that this team developed were very successful. Of course, people with the required dual expertise are difficult to find.

8.2.4 Blooper 82: Giving programmers the fastest computers

This may be the most controversial blooper in this chapter. Nonetheless, I feel strongly that the common practice of giving developers the fastest computers and highest-speed Internet connections is one important cause of the responsiveness bloopers described in Chapter 7.

Some justifications. Management often goes to considerable expense to make sure software engineers have the latest, fastest computers and fastest available connections to the Internet. This is done for several reasons:

- Engineers like speed. They like having the fastest computers that are available. They like being able to download stuff from the Web instantly. Some even demand these things as a condition of working.
- Other things being equal, faster computers and network connections improve programmer productivity, especially when development involves much compiling or script-driven construction of new versions.
- Computer companies like to have their own programmer-employees using their latest hardware as one way of shaking out flaws
- Computer companies like to build software for their newest models because it encourages customers to upgrade their older models.

Some costs. However, one cost of always giving programmers the fastest computers and network connections is that their computers will be faster than those of the majority of the company's customers. Just because a computer company announces a new, faster model doesn't mean that all their customers will instantly buy it (in some cases replacing their old computers). Just because a large computer or software company can afford T1 lines to the Internet doesn't mean that the company's customers can. Customer adoption of new technology typically follows a bell-curve distribution (see Figure 8.1): a few companies take the plunge right away, then adoption of the new technology by old and new customers begins to accelerate, then market saturation sets in and the sales curve begins to flatten out and drop, and finally the last few holdouts bite the bullet and catch up with everyone else. The important part of the bell curve is the middle—that's where most of the customers are.

Another disadvantage of making sure programmers have the latest hardware and net connections is that they become accustomed to frequent upgrades

Figure 8.1

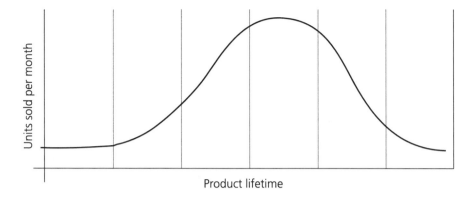

Units sold per month

Product lifetime

and so view performance and responsiveness problems as only temporary, "until the next upgrade." Never mind that customers don't upgrade nearly as often because computers and Internet connections cost them real money; they have to wait to upgrade until their accountants have amortized the cost of the last upgrades down to the level where upgrading again can be justified. In contrast, upgrading the programmers' computers costs *them* nothing. Therefore, they tend to be unsympathetic to customer complaints about performance and/or responsiveness: "Look, just upgrade your computers and the problem will be solved."

Net connections: the masses are way behind the technology elite. Internet connection speed is another area where the general public lags significantly behind people who work in the computer and software industries. A survey conducted in 1998 by Georgia Tech's College of Computing (*www.gvu.gatech.edu/gvu/user-surveys*) found that 34.9 percent of the surveyed Internet users had modems that connect at 33.2 kbaud or less—over one third! Another 31.4 percent had 56 kbaud modems. This means that two thirds of the surveyed Internet users were connected at 56 kbaud or less.

A similar survey conducted in March 1999 by Intercommerce Corporation (*www.survey.net*) found an even higher percentage of Internet users to have slow connections: 53.5 percent at 33 kbaud or slower, and 74.1 percent—almost three quarters of their respondents—at 56 kbaud or slower.

My point is that most customers will not have today's most powerful computers or highest-speed Internet connections for many months—even many years. By then, many of the programmers in the computer company will have already upgraded to the *next* new models and net connections. As a result,

© 1998 Randy Glasbergen. www.glasbergen.com

"You need to slow down, Bob. I'm prescribing a 386 computer with a 9600 baud modem."

software that is acceptably responsive on the programmers' computers will often not be so on the customers'.

Avoiding Blooper 82

Without question, programmers need access to fast machines for compiling and building software. But compiling and building can be done on servers. The computers on which programmers *run* the software they develop should be like those that most customers are using. Otherwise, the programmers will produce software that customers will find sluggish and unresponsive. At the very least, engineering teams should have slower machines to test on. Furthermore, development teams should have a development process that makes such testing mandatory, with firm criteria for deciding whether a product is responsive enough to release.

Former Apple user interface designer Peter Bickford shares my opinion. In his book *Interface Design* [1997], he wrote:

> There's a school of thought that says that programmers should be forced to work on the least-powerful systems in their target market, instead of the high-end workstations they tend to use. While this seems a bit like cruel and unusual punishment to me, I've seen programmers...rewrite routines to work 20 times faster when they were forced to run their applications on the department secretary's machine.

Try it out with slow net connections

Although I do not advocate forcing software developers—especially Web developers—to use slow Internet connections, I do advocate requiring developers to test Web applications and Web sites using connection speeds that are typical of their customers. That of course requires finding out what sort of network connections customers have.

Further reading

Business impact of usability and user-centered design

Bias, R. G., and Mayhew, D. J. 1994. *Cost-Justifying Usability*. San Diego, CA: Academic Press.

Conklin, P. F. 1996. "Bringing Usability Effectively into Product Development." In M. Rudisill, C. Lewis, P. Polson, and T. McKay, eds., *Human-Computer Interface Design: Success Stories, Emerging Methods, Real-World Context*. San Francisco: Morgan Kaufmann Publishers.

Cooper, A. 1999. *The Inmates Are Running the Asylum*. Indianapolis, IN: SAMS.

Landauer, T. K. 1995. *The Trouble with Computers: Usefulness, Usability, and Productivity*. Cambridge, MA: MIT Press.

Norman, D. A. 1999. *The Invisible Computer: Why Good Products Can Fail, the Personal Computer Is So Complex and Information Appliances Are the Solution*. Cambridge, MA: MIT Press.

Management-level sources of poor usability

Gentner, D., and Grudin, J. 1990. "Why Good Engineers (Sometimes) Create Bad Interfaces." *Proceedings of ACM Conference on Computer-Human Interaction (CHI'90)*, pp. 277–282.
Grudin, J. 1991. "Systematic Sources of Suboptimal Interface Design in Large Product Development Organizations." *Human Computer Interaction* 6: 147–196.

Usability engineering methodologies

Dayton, T., McFarland, A., and Kramer, J. 1998. "Bridging User Needs to Object Oriented GUI Prototype via Task Object Design." In L. Wood, ed., *User Interface Design: Bridging the Gap from Requirements to Design*, pp. 15–56. Boca Raton: FL: CRC Press.
Nielsen, J. 1993. *Usability Engineering*. San Diego, CA: Academic Press.

Directly involving users in software design

Greenbaum, J., and Kyng, M. 1991. *Design at Work: Cooperative Design of Computer Systems*. Hillsdale, NJ: Lawrence Erlbaum Associates.
Muller, M. J., Haslwanter, J. H., and Dayton, T. 1997. "Participatory Practices in the Software Lifecycle." In H. Helander, T. K. Landauer, and P. Prabhu, eds., *Handbook of Human-Computer Interaction*, second edition. Amsterdam: Elsevier Science B.V.
Schuler, D., and Namioka, A. 1993. *Participatory Design: Principles and Practices*. Hillsdale, NJ: Lawrence Erlbaum Associates.

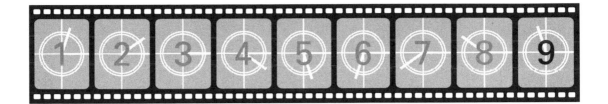

Software
Reviews

Introduction

The bloopers chapters of this book focus on specific common design-mistakes. Examples from real software are used to illustrate many of the bloopers. But most real software applications commit *many* design bloopers. Though presenting real-world examples of each blooper is useful (the bloopers are, after all, the main subject of this book), it is also useful to examine some software products in detail, discussing the bloopers they exhibit, as well as aspects of their design that are well done. That is the purpose of this chapter.

I begin by reviewing the installation process for Eudora Pro 4.0 for Macintosh, a popular email program. I then review the user interface of Kodak Picture Disk 1.2 for Windows, an application intended for viewing, editing, and organizing images that have been digitized from photographic film.

9.1 Eudora Pro 4.0 installation

I have a love/hate relationship with Eudora. I use Eudora to read and send email. It is my current favorite email program. But Eudora often tests my faithfulness. As the blues musician would sing if he knew Eudora: "Eudora, oh Eudora, why do you treat me so mean?"

Eudora is the software that provides more examples of user interface bloopers than almost any other software I use (with the possible exception of Microsoft Word). In the other chapters of this book, many of the bloopers are illustrated with examples from Eudora. You may recall my example of the dialog box that says "Excuse me, but Eudora could use some help" (see Blooper 37: Clueless error messages, Section 4.2.1).

Rather than reviewing all of Eudora here, which would require rehashing many of its flaws already mentioned elsewhere in this book, I have chosen to focus this review exclusively on the Eudora installation process. This review therefore serves as an additional, highly detailed example for Blooper 52: Installation nightmares (Section 5.3.3). The specific version of Eudora that this review covers is Eudora Pro 4.0.

Eudora was originally developed by students at the University of Illinois, but was later taken over, commercialized, improved, and marketed by Qualcomm Incorporated. Despite many annoying flaws, it is relatively easy to use. One reason for this may be that it has had over a decade of use, user feedback, and revision. However, it is not easy to install, as I can attest from personal experience.

9.1.1 The ordeal

In early 1999, I decided that my version of Eudora was too old and that I should upgrade to a more recent version. I visited Qualcomm's Web site, found the product-ordering page, and ordered a copy, choosing the low-tech option of having them ship me the software in a box. I chose that option because I wanted the instruction manual in my hands rather than on a disk that my computer might not be able to read. The box arrived two days later. So far, so good.

The installation instructions in the *Eudora Pro User Manual* were very specific. They began by reassuring me that I could install Eudora 4.0 over an existing Eudora version with no problems:

> Just follow the instructions below, and when you open Eudora Pro 4.0, your Settings, mailboxes, etc. are updated for this version. Also, all of your messages, folders, filters, and options are maintained.

Reassuring words, indeed. I wish they had been true.

Getting started

The instructions began:

> To install Eudora, do the following:
> 1. Restart your Macintosh while holding down the shift key. This turns off your Macintosh extensions. You must hold down the shift key until you see the message "Extensions off."

Since my Macintosh was already running with the extensions enabled, I restarted it as instructed. When the computer was again ready, I proceeded to Step 2:

> 2. If you are installing Eudora from CD-ROM, insert the Eudora Pro CD into your Macintosh CD-ROM drive. If you are installing from a software archive, double-click on it. Remember, do not restart with extensions off.

Wait a second. Didn't they just say in Step 1 to restart with extensions off? Now they're reminding me *not* to do that? My initial confidence began to evaporate. What now? Do I install with extensions on or off? I'm installing Eudora from a CD-ROM. Is the last sentence of Step 2 perhaps just for the case of installing from a software archive? If so, why does it say "Remember ..."? Or maybe either "do not" or "extensions off" in that sentence is a typographical error. Maybe the typographical error is in Step 1 instead, although on second thought, that seems unlikely, since most installation instructions require that extensions be off. My mind is racing, trying to make sense of these contradictory instructions before I execute Step 2.

I soon figured out that the CD-ROM driver is an extension, so extensions must be on if software is to be installed from a CD-ROM. Step 2 of the instructions was therefore correct, although it was still a mystery what "remember" was referring back to. Step 1 was simply wrong, at least for the case of installing from a CD-ROM, which is a common case. The authors of these marvelous instructions apparently expected readers to read Step 2 before executing Step 1, even though Step 1 is a common step when installing software onto a Macintosh.

It goes downhill from here

I restarted the computer again, this time with extensions on. I inserted the CD-ROM into the drive as instructed. At this point, my confidence in the instructions was gone. I've experienced enough aggravating software installations to know that the contradictory instructions were a bad sign. This installation was not going to be easy. Sigh, please, not another time-consuming installation nightmare!

Steps 3 and 4 read:

3. Double-click the Eudora Pro 4.0 Installer icon. The Eudora Pro Installer window is displayed.

4. In the box to the left of each software application, check the software you want to install with Eudora. Uncheck the software you do not want to install. Click Start. Installation begins, and the Eudora Pro Welcome window is displayed.

   Note: Each software application you checked installs automatically after Eudora is completely installed.

I double-clicked the Eudora Pro 4.0 Installer icon, but the window that appeared was not the Installer window shown in the manual. Instead, it was a Eudora Pro Installer splash screen. On it was a single button: Continue. I clicked the button and then the Installer window appeared (see Figure 9.1).

Figure 9.1

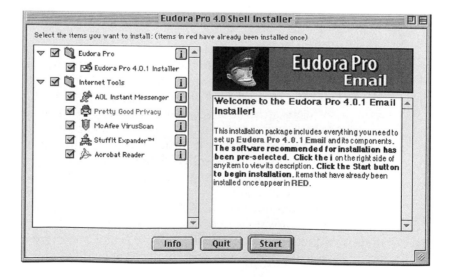

The Installer window did not match the illustration in the manual. The Installer window in the manual listed Eudora Pro 4.0 and two folders of supplemental applications: Internet Tools and CommCenter Software. My Installer window (see Figure 9.1) did not include the CommCenter Software folder, and the Internet Tools folder included software not mentioned in the manual. Apparently, the contents of the installation disk can vary. The manual should have made that clear so users wouldn't be concerned when what they see doesn't match the manual.

A more serious problem was that the Installer window did not show the version numbers of the supplemental applications it listed. This was a problem because I already had some of those programs, and didn't want to install older versions over newer versions. Clicking on the **i** button next to each listed application displayed information about it in the box on the right side of the Installer window. I tried that in the hope that that would give me the version numbers of the listed programs. Acrobat Reader supplied its version number, but the other applications did not. After some hesitation, I decided to install all the applications I wanted, including ones I already had, and hope that I would be able to preserve my current versions.

All of the supplemental applications were checked, so I just unchecked the ones I didn't want. As instructed in Step 4, I clicked the Installer window's Start button. The dialog box shown in Figure 9.2 appeared.

Now what? I'm supposed to install Eudora before PGP? That's what I thought I was doing, since the note on Step 4 of the instructions said Eudora would be installed *before* the others. It seemed that they wanted me to uncheck PGP, install Eudora, and then come back to the Installer later to install PGP. Why else would I be getting this warning? But if so, why did the Installer start with PGP checked? It seemed odd that an item they didn't want me to choose would be checked by default, forcing me to uncheck it before I clicked Start.

After poring through the instructions trying to get a clue of what I was supposed to do, I canceled the warning dialog box, unchecked PGP, and clicked Start again.

OK, let's try again

Step 5 of the instructions read:

> 5. Read the Welcome window, click Next. The Software License Agreement is displayed.

Figure 9.2

It is strongly recommended that you install Eudora Pro 4.0 before installing Pretty Good Privacy. To go back and select a different install setting, click Cancel. If you wish to install Pretty Good Privacy anyway, then click

[Install Anyway] [Cancel]

After I clicked Start on the Installer window, a Eudora splash screen appeared. I assumed this was what the instructions meant by "Welcome window." However, the only button on it was labeled "Continue," not "Next." I clicked it, expecting the licensing agreement to appear. Instead, a window appeared displaying a ReadMe file. I clicked the window's Print button to print the file to read later, and then clicked its Continue button. Now, the license agreement appeared.

Steps 6 and 7 of the instructions read:

6. Read the Software License Agreement. If you agree to the terms, click Yes. The User Code dialog is displayed.

7. Enter your user code. Your user code number is printed on the technical support information sheet found inside the Eudora Pro retail product box. Click Continue.

I skimmed the license agreement, then looked for a Yes button. There wasn't one; the buttons were labeled "Save...," "Print," "Agree," "Disagree." I decided that "Agree" was close enough to "Yes" and clicked that, although I was annoyed that Qualcomm apparently didn't care enough about its users or its installation instructions to reconcile the wording used in the manual with that used in the software.

User code? What user code?

As promised, the User Code dialog appeared (see Figure 9.3). I wasn't sure why they referred to this window with the GUI jargon term "dialog" (see Blooper 35: Speaking Geek, Section 4.1.3) when they had used the word "window" for the other windows displayed so far. I also noted that the dialog box had only the Continue button. It did not provide a way for users to stop the installation process at this particular step. It therefore committed Blooper 54: Dialog boxes that trap users (Section 5.4.2).

However, these concerns were quickly replaced by a more urgent one: I wasn't sure what to enter as a "User Code," or even where to find it. The dialog box suggested looking for the code on the inside cover of my user manual, but

Figure 9.3

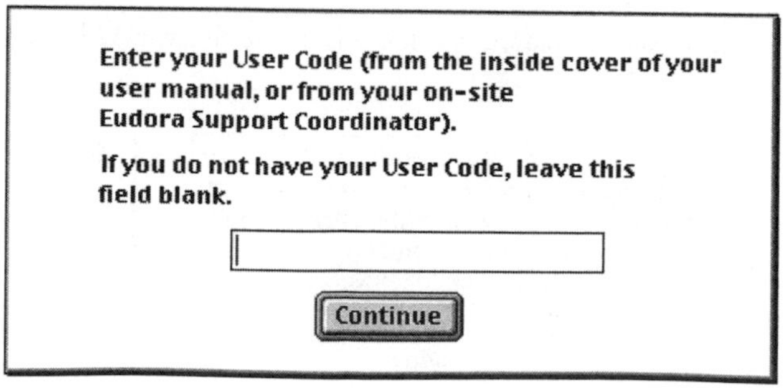

Enter your User Code (from the inside cover of your user manual, or from your on-site Eudora Support Coordinator).

If you do not have your User Code, leave this field blank.

[Continue]

Step 7 of the instructions said it would be on a sheet inside the product box. I looked in the manual and found nothing. I looked in the box and found a sticker (not a sheet) with two numbers on it: a "Registration Number" and an "Installer Code." There was nothing labeled "User Code." Was one of these two numbers the "User Code"? If so, why did neither label match the label in the manual? Which of these numbers should I enter?

The registration number seemed promising, so I typed that into the text field and clicked Continue. An error dialog box appeared informing me that the User Code I had entered was invalid. I then tried the Installer Code, and that apparently worked. Qualcomm had committed Blooper 33: Inconsistent terminology (Section 4.1.1). As with the button labels mentioned above, they didn't care enough to reconcile their terminology.

Even if we allow them their inconsistent terminology, some kind of indication on the dialog box showing the approximate form of a valid "User Code" would have helped because the two numbers I had to choose from were quite different: one was a seven-digit number; the other was two letters and three digits. For example, the text field label could have shown a sample User Code. Alternatively, the text field could have been sized to show that it was intended to fit a maximum of five characters; instead, it was misleadingly sized to fit about 30. Therefore, I was forced to guess, and then correct my guess when I guessed wrong.

The ordeal continues

I was looking forward to being done with this installation, but I was *not* looking forward to the rest of it. The rest of Step 7 read:

> The Eudora Install dialog is displayed, allowing you to select which items you want to install. To see a description of an item, click on the item (the description is displayed just below the selection area).

Again they used the term "dialog," a GUI toolkit jargon term that users don't care about, and even then, an abbreviation of "dialog box." The content of the dialog box (see Figure 9.4) was also confusing, in two respects:

- It showed how much disk space it needed, but not how much was available.
- It referred to "Full Eudora Pro Installation," "Eudora Pro Only," and "Documentation." Three dialog boxes earlier, I had selected an item labeled "Eudora Pro" as well as several other software items. And before that, to start the whole installation, I had double-clicked on an icon labeled "Eudora Pro 4.0 Installer." Qualcomm was using the term "Eudora Pro" in at least three different ways: the entire installation, the Eudora program and its documentation, and the Eudora program by itself (see Blooper 33: Inconsistent terminology, Section 4.1.1).

Figure 9.4

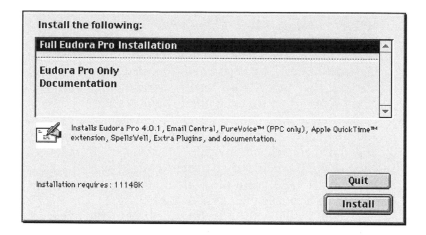

Step 8 of the instructions read:

8. To install Eudora Pro and all of the items listed, select Full Eudora Pro installation and click Install. Full Eudora Pro installation is the default. Eudora
installs all elements of version 4.0.

< *explanation of other choices omitted for brevity* >

The Eudora Version Selection dialog is displayed, allowing you to select
which version you want to install.

Step 8 also explained the other two installation choices. Step 8 was a welcome
relief from previous steps because it actually made sense. It also had a sensible
default, allowing most users to simply click Install. Why Step 4 didn't also have
sensible defaults was unclear. I decided to take the default (full) installation,
and so clicked the Install button.

The Version Selection dialog appeared (see Figure 9.5). I noted that the instructions misused the term "selection," a reserved term in GUIs that should be
used only for clicking on an item to highlight it (see Blooper 33: Inconsistent
terminology, Section 4.1.1).

The Version Selection dialog box had a button for each of the three available
versions. Like the User Code dialog box, it lacked a Cancel or Quit button for

Figure 9.5

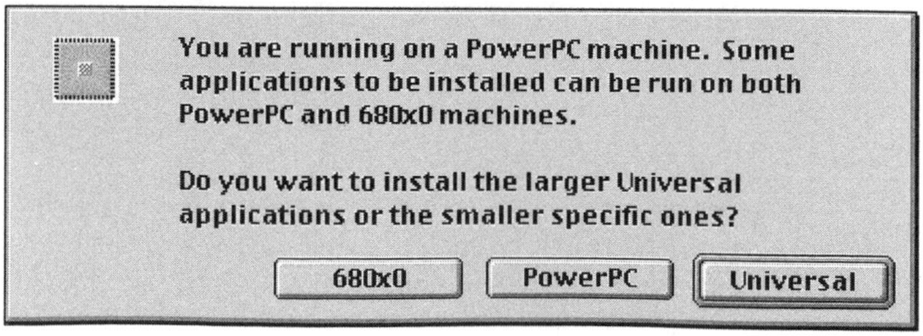

You are running on a PowerPC machine. Some
applications to be installed can be run on both
PowerPC and 680x0 machines.

Do you want to install the larger Universal
applications or the smaller specific ones?

680x0   PowerPC   Universal

Figure 9.6

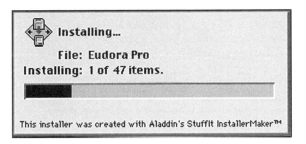

aborting the installation (Blooper 54: Dialog boxes that trap users, Section 5.4.2).

Step 8 of the instructions in the manual went on to explain the three choices; they seemed clear. I knew which one I wanted.

It gets worse

Steps 9–11 read:

> 9. Select the version you want. A dialog is displayed asking you where you want to install the Eudora Pro folder.
>
> 10. Select the destination folder and click Install. The install program begins installing the items you selected onto the appropriate locations on your disk.
>
> 11. Once the installation is complete, you are prompted to restart your Macintosh. Click Restart.

Again we have that unnecessary jargon abbreviation, "dialog." Aside from that, it was clear what to do. I clicked the button corresponding to the version I wanted. As promised, a file chooser dialog box appeared. I set the location of the folder as I wanted it and clicked Install.

The installation of the Eudora software began. My hard disk began whirring. As good design would require, the cursor immediately changed to an animating busy cursor and a dialog box containing a progress bar appeared (see Figure 9.6) (see Chapter 7). Nice.

When the progress bar filled up, a dialog box appeared announcing that the installation was successful. However, it did not match the dialog box shown in the manual or the instructions in Step 11. I was not prompted to restart my Macintosh. Instead, the dialog box appeared as shown in Figure 9.7. I was again annoyed that the instructions didn't match what was happening. Didn't Qualcomm care?

Where are we?

However, I was more concerned that I didn't understand what this dialog box was telling me. I had instructed the installer to install several supplementary

Figure 9.7

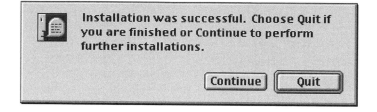

applications in addition to Eudora: VirusScan, StuffIt Expander, and Acrobat Reader. As far as I could tell, it hadn't installed those yet. The dialog box didn't say *which* installation was successful: Eudora, or the whole collection of applications. I wasn't sure whether Quit meant "quit installing Eudora" or "Quit the whole sequence." The developers must have been thinking "inside-out" instead of "outside-in" (see Principle 5, Section 1.5.1); they assumed users would know what they know about how the software works and therefore interpret the various messages correctly. That's a bad assumption.

I didn't want to abort out of the entire sequence and have to start over from the beginning, so I clicked Continue. It took me back to Step 8: the Eudora Install dialog box, where one chooses the components of Eudora itself that one wants installed. That isn't what I wanted. I didn't want to install any more components of Eudora itself. I clicked the Quit button on the Eudora Install dialog box.

The light at the end of the tunnel: An oncoming train?

The next thing that appeared was a splash screen for Acrobat Reader. Ahh! Finally I was beginning to understand. We had finished installing Eudora, and now we were moving on to the next application to be installed. There was a master installation script, which invoked several subordinate installation scripts: one for each application to be installed. Quitting one of the subordinate installations did not quit the top-level installation; it just proceeded to the next application to be installed. I proceeded to install Acrobat Reader, VirusScan, and StuffIt Expander. When each one finished installing, it displayed the "Installation was successful" dialog, but now I knew to choose Quit. When I had installed the last one, the dialog box shown Figure 9.8 appeared.

Even though this dialog box didn't identify which installation it was talking about any better than the subordinate "installation complete" dialog boxes had, I assumed that this one was from the master script. I still needed to install PGP because the master script, for reasons I still didn't understand, apparently wanted me not to install it on the first pass. Therefore, instead of clicking Restart to restart my Macintosh, I clicked Continue. It took me back to the master Installer window, where I unchecked everything except PGP and clicked Start. Astoundingly, it still displayed the same dialog box, warning me to install PGP only after installing Eudora. "I'm not installing Eudora now, you stupid @#$^&* $@#%!" I screamed at my computer. I decided the warning was

Figure 9.8

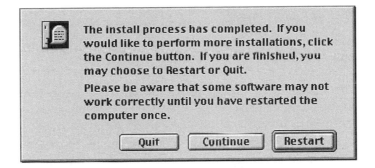

> The install process has completed. If you would like to perform more installations, click the Continue button. If you are finished, you may choose to Restart or Quit.
>
> Please be aware that some software may not work correctly until you have restarted the computer once.
>
> [Quit] [Continue] [Restart]

meaningless and that I could have left PGP checked for installation on the first pass. At this point, I simply clicked "Install Anyway" and went ahead with the PGP installation. It seemed to work.

The ordeal was over.

9.1.2 Conclusions

So what were the results of this installation? Did I get what I had wanted?

Outcome: Only partly successful

In the end, the difficult installation was only partly successful. Here is a summary:

- The programs I had wanted installed were in fact installed. In that sense, I got what I wanted.
- Only Eudora itself asked me to specify a destination folder. The other programs were installed in various fixed locations, and I had to find them and move them to where I wanted them.
- Eudora Pro 4.0 was installed, but when started, it did not find all my folders of archived mail from my previous version of Eudora. I tried moving my mail folders around and, through a time-consuming process of trial and error, eventually got Eudora 4.0 to recognize and display my mail folders.
- Somehow, I ended up with VirusScan 68K, even though I had indicated that I wanted the PowerPC-specific versions. I only discovered this when I ran VirusScan and it displayed the message: "There are two VirusScan extensions on this system. Please delete one." I found VirusScan 68K in the extensions folder and deleted it.

The total elapsed time for the installation process was well over an hour. It took an additional several hours (interlaced with other activities) to get Eudora working properly. I believe I also gained a few gray hairs in the process.

Advice for Qualcomm

I'll end this review with some post-mortem comments about this installation process.

- The extremely confusing conflicting instructions in Steps 1 and 2 about starting with extensions on versus off really must be reconciled. As it is now, the entire installation starts off on a bad foot.

- I eventually realized that there was a hierarchy of installation scripts, and so began to be able to predict the behavior of the installation process reasonably well. But I'm a trained computer scientist. The concept of embedded installation scripts might be difficult for nonengineers to grasp. It doesn't help matters that the master script has a very similar name to the Eudora-specific script: both are called "Eudora Pro 4.0 installation." In the short run, clarifying the script hierarchy through distinctive labeling would help somewhat. It would also help if (1) subordinate scripts ran in the order indicated in the master list, and (2) users could abort the master script from any point. In the long run, it might be better to make the conceptual model be one of *chained* sibling scripts rather than a master script that runs subordinate scripts.

- The terminology and images in the software and the manual really need to be reconciled. They not only confuse and mislead users, they also destroy users' confidence in the accuracy of all of the instructions, so users are never sure whether they are doing the right thing.

- Overall, the developers of Eudora should commit themselves more thoroughly to testing the installation process, first on themselves and then on representative users. By doing that, they will greatly increase the popularity of Eudora.

9.2 Kodak Picture Disk 1.2

Many photographic film-processing services these days offer their customers the option of receiving the photographs in digital form. The pictures are delivered on diskette, on CD-ROM, or over the Internet.

In 1997, I had some 35-millimeter color slides converted to digital images, so I could include them in an article that was going to be put onto the Web. The camera shop to which I took the slides sent them to Kodak for digitizing. I received the pictures back on a floppy disk. With the pictures on the disk was some software for viewing, organizing, and performing minor editing on the pictures: Kodak Picture Disk 1.2.

Kodak Picture Disk 1.2 is a small, simple, and useful program that nonetheless exhibits many user interface flaws. Some of the flaws are common and thus are examples of some of the bloopers discussed in this book; other flaws seem unique to Kodak Picture Disk.

I thought it would be instructive to include a user interface review in this book of the sort that I prepare for clients, but nondisclosure agreements prevent me from including actual reviews of client software. Furthermore, most of the reviews I prepare for clients are quite long—longer than there is room for in this book. Because Kodak Picture Disk is a small program that exhibits a variety of user interface flaws, it serves nicely as a subject of a software review.

In contrast with the preceding review of Eudora Pro installation, this review concerns the Kodak Picture Disk software *after* it has been installed successfully. Thankfully, installing Kodak Picture Disk was pretty easy, as one would expect for software that (1) was provided mainly as a way of viewing the pictures the customers ordered, and (2) most people will use in a nonwork situation without instruction.

This review differs from my usual user interface review report in one respect: it refers, where relevant, to other sections of this book, especially to specific bloopers. Otherwise, the remainder of this review follows the format I usually use when reviewing software user interfaces for my clients.

9.2.1 Executive summary

Kodak Picture Disk 1.2 is a useful program, especially considering that it is distributed at no charge (or at least its cost is included in the price of developing and digitizing pictures). It is fairly easy to learn to use without reading any documentation, as one would expect for a program that is provided mainly as a utility for viewing the pictures a customer had digitized.

However, it has a large number of usability problems, especially for such a small program. Most of them could have been easily avoided with the help of an experienced user interface designer, and with a development process that included usability testing at several points during development. (Because of the state of the program, I am assuming that neither of these occurred.) Fortunately, these problems can still be corrected. Many improvements are suggested in this report. Some of these suggested improvements will be easy; others will be more difficult.

Hopefully, in the process of trying to improve the usability of the Picture Disk software, Kodak will also improve its ability to create better software in the future.

9.2.2 Organization

This review begins with a section devoted to usability problems that are general to the entire application. This is followed by sections that review, in turn, each of the functions (windows) in the application. Within each section, I have ordered the problems from more important to less important. All problems are numbered to facilitate referring to them.

9.2.3 Limitations

This review is based on several sessions spent using Kodak Picture Disk over a period of two years. This review report was written in a few hours. Although it proved possible to provide a lot of feedback, there are limitations to what this review can provide.

The first limitation is that although I made an effort to review all parts of the application and believe that I have come close to this goal, there may be some parts that I missed. In such cases, it is hoped that the comments I have made on parts I did review will provide feedback that can be generalized to any parts I missed.

A second limitation is that the recommendations in this report do not constitute a coordinated redesign of Kodak Picture Disk. Rather, this review was a time-limited effort to locate and recommend corrections for most of the software's usability problems. The result is a loosely connected set of suggestions, each of which pertains to a specific aspect of the software. As a result, some recommendations made in this report interact with each other. For example, I may have pointed out how to improve the presentation of information in a specific display, and elsewhere have proposed that that display be merged with another one or eliminated altogether. Though such recommendations may seem contradictory, they are both provided to allow the developers to pick and choose which recommendations to incorporate.

Third, although recommendations are provided for correcting most of the usability problems pointed out in this report, I did not take the time to devise recommendations for all of the problems. In some cases, I merely point out the problem and urge the developers to consider ways of fixing it.

Fourth and finally, usability reviews such as this should not be considered a substitute for usability testing. Kodak Picture Disk should be usability-tested—both before and after any design changes—to check the design, identify additional problems, and suggest improvements. The development schedule should allocate time for changes based on the test results—potentially major changes.

9.2.4 General

1. Many of the windows displayed by Kodak Picture Disk are confusing the distinction between tool windows and dialog boxes; they contain elements of both, such as a menubar and control buttons at the bottom. Specific examples are given in the relevant sections below. Recommendation: See Blooper 5: Confusing primary windows with dialog boxes (Section 2.2.1).

Redesign every window to be clearly either a primary window or a dialog box.

2. Several of the function windows displayed by Kodak Picture Disk are not actually separate windows from the Main Window, but rather are displayed in the same window, temporarily replacing its normal content. *All* of the window's content is replaced, from the menubar down to the bottom of the window. All that remains constant is the titlebar. This is confusing: many users won't realize that this is what is happening and will wonder where the Main Window has disappeared to while these other windows are displayed. Recommendation: The windows that currently "reuse" the Main Window should be separate windows. The Main Window should remain displayed while these windows are up.

3. Commands in the menubar menus are activated and deactivated as they become relevant and irrelevant. This is good. However, this is done inconsistently. Some user actions that render commands irrelevant do not cause those commands to deactivate. Instead, the commands remain active and display errors when users attempt to use them. Specific examples are provided below. Recommendation: All actions that render commands moot should deactivate those commands.

4. The software uses certain terms inconsistently. See Blooper 33: Inconsistent terminology (Section 4.1.1). Recommendation: Be extremely consistent in the use of terms throughout the software and its documentation. Develop a lexicon for the product, and assign a technical writer to maintain and enforce the lexicon.

5. Most of Kodak Picture Disk's windows and dialog boxes do not include the name of the application. A user running multiple applications at once might not be able to determine immediately that a displayed window came from Kodak Picture Disk. Recommendation: Every window's title should begin with the name of the application, followed by the name of the function. For example: Kodak Picture Disk: Rotate Picture.

6. In all windows that have a menubar, the menubar does not appear to be a distinct bar because it lacks a bottom border separating it from the window's content. Recommendation: Menubars should be a visible bar; they should have a visible bottom border. Ideally, the GUI toolkit should provide a menubar component that has the correct appearance. Otherwise, it is necessary to add a separator between the menubar and the remaining content.

7. In all windows that have a toolbar, the toolbar does not appear to be a distinct bar because it lacks a bottom border separating it from the window's content. Recommendation: Toolbars should be a visible bar; they should have a visible bottom border. Ideally, the GUI toolkit should provide a toolbar component that has the correct appearance. Otherwise, it is necessary to add a separator between the toolbar and the remaining content.

8. Kodak Picture Disk's approach to displaying messages is to display them in a message area at the bottom of the window. There are two problems with this approach:

   a. The messages are easily missed, especially since they are displayed without any "fanfare" (such as an error sound).

   b. The error messages remain displayed until the next message is displayed. Thus, if users don't notice a message immediately, they won't be able to tell what action caused it. Also, if a user makes a mistake, sees the error message, and commits the same error again, the user will see no change in the error message, and so won't know whether the displayed message is from the first attempt or the second one.

   Recommendation: Error messages should be displayed in error dialog boxes, or at least the software should provide some sort of fanfare (sound, flash) that they have been posted. Less important messages, such as command documentation or completion confirmation messages, can remain in the message area.

9.2.5 Startup

9. Kodak Picture Disk is listed in the Windows Startup menu under a menu item titled "Photos." The "Photos" item is a pull-right menu that has only one item: "Kodak Picture Disk," which invokes the program. The "Photos" item seems unnecessary. It is also vague: many users will overlook it and have trouble finding Kodak Picture Disk on the Start menu. Recommendation: Place an item on the Start menu named Kodak Picture Disk, which is a pull-right menu that contains the program, the documentation, and an uninstaller for the program.

10. When Kodak Picture Disk is started, it always displays a warning dialog box (see Figure 9.9), saying that the software requires the display to be using at least 256 colors. This warning is displayed *regardless* of the display setting; it is displayed even if the display is set to 256 colors or more. Recommendation: No warning should be shown if the display is set as the software requires.

Figure 9.9

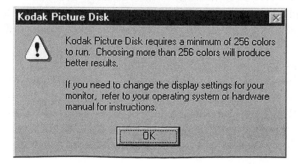

Kodak Picture Disk requires a minimum of 256 colors to run. Choosing more than 256 colors will produce better results.

If you need to change the display settings for your monitor, refer to your operating system or hardware manual for instructions.

OK

9.2.6 Main window

11. In the File menubar menu, the Print Preview and Print Picture commands are inactive unless the user has first selected one or more pictures. To print or preview all of the pictures in the collection, a user must first select them all. In contrast, the Print Thumbnails command in the same menu remains active when no pictures are selected, presumably because it always prints all the thumbnail images, even though users would probably expect to be able to print only certain ones (see Figure 9.10). Recommendation: Improve consistency. Allow users to print or preview all of the pictures by invoking those functions when no pictures are selected. Also, selecting pictures should constrain the Print Thumbnails command to printing only the selected thumbnails.

12. The Print Picture toolbar button is not deactivated when no pictures are selected, even though the same command in the File menubar menu is deactivated in that case. Clicking on the Print Picture toolbar button when no picture is selected displays the message "Please select one or more pictures" in the message line at the bottom of the window (see Figure 9.11). Recommendation: Deactivate the toolbar button whenever no pictures are selected, just as the corresponding menu command is deactivated. Don't tell users they made an error; prevent them from making the error.

Figure 9.10

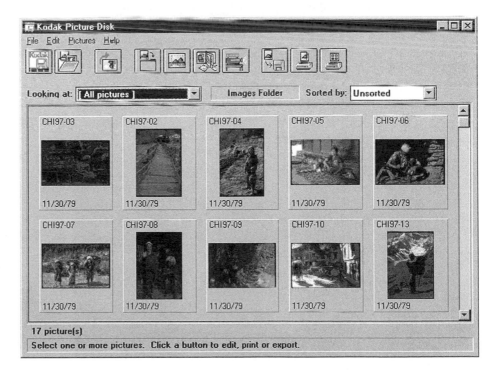

Figure 9.11

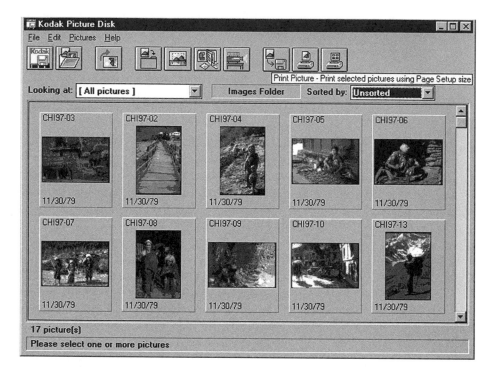

13. Invoking File:Export or Edit:Edit Picture when two or more pictures are selected displays the error message in the message area at the bottom of the window: "Please select one picture." In contrast, when no pictures are selected, these menu commands are deactivated, so they cannot be invoked. In other words, in one situation where these commands are invalid, they are inactive, but in another situation where they are invalid, they are active but display an error message (that is easily missed, but that's a separate problem). This is inconsistent. Recommendation: Whenever a command is invalid, it should be inactive.

14. In the Pictures menu, the "Sort in descending order" toggle is unclear. Many users will not understand what the OFF state means: sort in ascending order, or don't sort at all? See Blooper 10: Using a checkbox for a non-ON/OFF setting (Section 2.3.3). Recommendation: Change this from a checkbox menu item to a pair of radiobutton menu items, or perhaps three radiobutton menu items, if "unsorted" is to be an option here as it is elsewhere in the program.

15. Invoking File:Open Picture Disk displays an information dialog box (see Figure 9.12) prompting the user to put a Picture Disk into drive A, even if the disk is already in the drive and ready to go. Also, I don't think that an information dialog box is the right kind for this prompt. Recommendation: Only display this dialog box if no Picture Disk is in the drive, and make it an error dialog box.

Figure 9.12

16. The sorting options in the Pictures menubar menu are named inconsistently with the same options in the "Sort by" option menu on the upper-right side of the Main Window. The menubar menu uses "Name" but the option menu uses "Title." Also, the menubar uses "No Sorting" but the option menu uses "Unsorted." Recommendation: Use the same terms everywhere. Have technical writers check and enforce this.

17. The thumbnail images displayed on this page are best shaped for vertical (portrait) format pictures. Horizontal (landscape) format pictures are shown smaller because their width is limited by the width of the area available to each thumbnail. This is inconsistent with the format of the Slideshow screen, which favors horizontal (landscape) format pictures. Recommendation: At least reconcile the inconsistency between the thumbnail view and the Slideshow view. Even better, devise a thumbnail view that shows horizontal and vertical pictures at the same size.

18. The Pictures menu seems misnamed. It contains functions for organizing pictures, not for editing pictures. The Edit menu contains several Picture commands. It seems odd to have Picture commands not in the Picture menu, and commands in the Picture menu that don't operate on pictures. Recommendation: Rename the Pictures menu "Slideshow" or "Organization."

19. The menubar does not look like a menubar because it has no border separating it from the window content. Recommendation: It should be a visible bar. Use a real menubar component from the GUI toolkit, or add a separator.

20. The toolbar does not look like a toolbar because it has no border separating it from the window content. Recommendation: It should be a visible bar. Use a real toolbar component from the GUI toolkit, or add a separator.

9.2.7 Slideshow dialog box

21. The window is titled Slideshow (see Figure 9.13). But it isn't the window for displaying a slideshow; it's the dialog box for starting a slideshow. Hence, the window title is misleading. Recommendation: Call it "Start Slideshow."

Figure 9.13

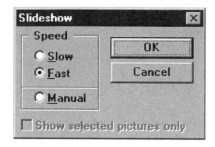

22. The window does not include the name of the application. Recommendation: Change the window title to "Kodak Picture Disk: Start Slideshow."

9.2.8 Slideshow window

23. Users cannot change the display mode between Fast (automatic), Slow (automatic), and Manual while viewing a slideshow. They have to close the Slideshow window (Figure 9.14), start the function again, and choose the display mode in the Slideshow dialog box. This is tedious, and results in a dialog box that isn't really necessary. Recommendation: Make it possible for users to set the display mode from this window. Add a pair of radio-

Figure 9.14

Figure 9.15

Advance slides: ● Manually   ○ Automatically

buttons as shown in Figure 9.15. The default setting should be Manually. Just right of the radiobuttons, place a slider that ranges from Slow to Fast. The slider should be active only when the radiobutton is set to Automatically. Eliminate the Slideshow dialog box.

24. When in Automatic Slideshow mode, the manual control buttons and the Pause button are active during the interdisplay timeout. However, they are inactive while the next picture is loading, which takes a couple of seconds. When the slideshow speed is slow, this is OK because there is plenty of time for users to click Pause or the manual control buttons. But when the show speed is fast, the buttons are inactive most of the time. Users have only a very brief time window in which the keys are active: between 0.5 and 1 second. Hitting the keys outside this time window has no effect. Thus, it is very difficult to pause or affect a fast automatic slide show, and the software feels frustratingly unresponsive. See Chapter 7. Recommendation: Leave the buttons active while slides are loading, even though they might not take effect until the slide loads.

25. This "window" isn't separate from the Main Window. When the Slideshow function is invoked, the Main Window's content, from the menubar to the bottom of the window, changes to the Slideshow screen and controls. Many users will wonder where the Main Window went. Furthermore, the Close button and the [×] control on the titlebar don't close the window; they revert back to the Main Window display. Recommendation: Make this a separate window.

26. The Slideshow "screen" is more suited for displaying horizontal (landscape) format pictures than it is for showing vertical (portrait) format pictures (see Figure 9.16). Vertical format pictures are displayed in a much smaller size by the height of the "screen." Recommendation: Make the "screen" square, so that vertical format pictures are shown at the same size, as is true of real slide shows.

27. This window is a combination of a primary window and a dialog box. It contains both a menubar (with only one menu on it: Help) and a window control button at the bottom: Close. See Blooper 5: Confusing primary windows with dialog boxes (Section 2.2.1). Recommendation: Make it one or the other. I'd suggest making it a dialog box, eliminating the menubar. If it becomes a primary window, it needs at least a File menu with a Close command.

28. The menubar does not look like a menubar because it has no border separating it from the window content. Recommendation: If the menubar is retained (but see item 25, above), it should be a visible bar. Use a real menubar component from the GUI toolkit, or add a separator.

Figure 9.16

9.2.9 Edit Picture window

29. This "window" (Figure 9.17) isn't separate from the Main Window. When the Slideshow function is invoked, the Main Window's content, from the menubar to the bottom of the window, changes to the Slideshow screen and controls. Many users will wonder where the Main Window went. Furthermore, the File:Close command, the Close button, and the [×] control on the titlebar don't close the window; they revert back to the Main Window display. Recommendation: Make this a separate window.

30. This window is a combination of a primary window and a dialog box; it contains both a menubar and a window control button at the bottom: Close. See Blooper 5: Confusing primary windows with dialog boxes (Section 2.2.1). Recommendation: Make it one or the other. I'd suggest making it a dialog box, eliminating the menubar.

31. When the Edit Picture window is "closed," the picture that was selected is no longer selected. Recommended: The picture that was selected (and edited) should still be selected when the Edit Picture window is closed.

32. The menubar does not look like a menubar because it has no border separating it from the window content. Recommendation: If the menubar is retained (but see item 30, above), it should be a visible bar. Use a real menubar component from the GUI toolkit, or add a separator.

Figure 9.17

9.2.10 Print Preview window

33. This "window" (Figure 9.18) isn't separate from the Main Window. When the Slideshow function is invoked, the Main Window's content, from the menubar to the bottom of the window, changes to the Slideshow screen and controls. Many users will wonder where the Main Window went. Furthermore, the Close button and the [×] control on the titlebar don't close the window; they revert back to the Main Window display. Recommendation: Make this a separate window.

34. The "One Page" versus "Two Page" button is a command button being misused as a toggle. See Blooper 11: Using command buttons as toggles (Section 2.3.4). Recommendation: Change this either to an option menu with two values, or to two radiobuttons.

35. The Next Page and Prev Page buttons are in the opposite order from what one would expect in a society in which pages are ordered left to right. Recommendation: The order of the two buttons should be switched, except when the program is localized for countries, such as Japan, where the normal page order is right to left.

36. The Close button (a window control button) is not separated from the content control buttons: Zoom in, Zoom out, and so on. (See Blooper 20: Mixing dialog box control buttons with context control buttons, Section 3.1.1).

Figure 9.18

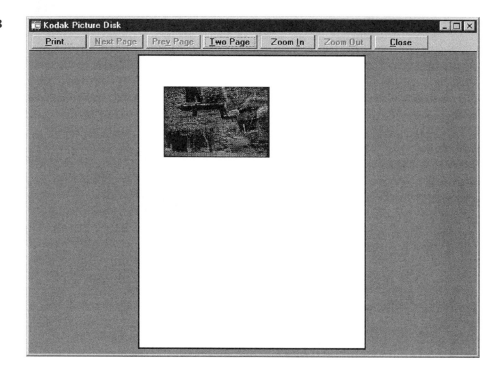

Recommendation: Move the Close button to the bottom right of the window.

9.2.11 Print Setup dialog box

37. The window (Figure 9.19) does not include the name of the application. Recommendation: Change the window title to "Kodak Picture Disk: Print Setup."

Figure 9.19

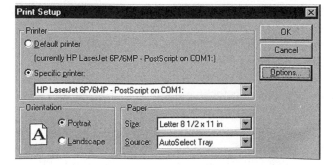

Figure 9.20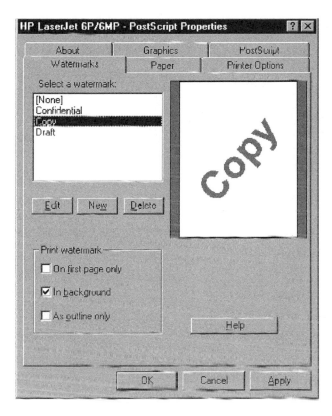

9.2.12 Print Setup Options dialog box

38. The window (Figure 9.20) has two rows of tabs, which in addition to being too many for the window size, exhibits the disorienting "dancing tabs" behavior where tabs change positions. See Blooper 13: Too many tabs (Section 2.3.6). Recommendation: Redesign this dialog box so one row of tabs suffices. Widen the window, reorganize the content of the tabs, or both.

39. The window title, which names the printer driver, identifies neither the application nor the function. Users could be in a situation where they don't know what application displayed this window. Recommendation: Change the window title to "Kodak Picture Disk: Print Setup Options–< printer driver identifier > ."

9.2.13 Rotate Picture dialog box

40. The window (Figure 9.21) does not include the name of the application. Recommendation: Change the window title to "Kodak Picture Disk: Rotate Picture."

Figure 9.21

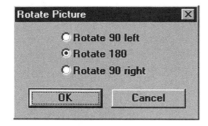

Figure 9.22

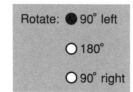

41. The radiobutton values "Rotate 90 left," "Rotate 180," and "Rotate 90 right" contain the redundant word "Rotate" and don't provide the units (degrees). They also don't include any graphic images depicting rotations, unlike the picture rotation buttons in the Edit Picture window. Recommendation: Factor the word "Rotate" out of the values, and make it a label for the setting. Include the degree symbol in each value. Thus the control would appear as in Figure 9.22. Perhaps also include graphics depicting the rotations—the same graphics as are used in the Edit Picture window.

9.2.14   Organize Pictures dialog box

42. The checkbox labeled "Move selected picture(s) to this album" (see Figure 9.23) is confusing, for several reasons:

   a. It is referring to the pictures in the Main Window, but many users will interpret "selected" to be referring to the list in this window.

Figure 9.23

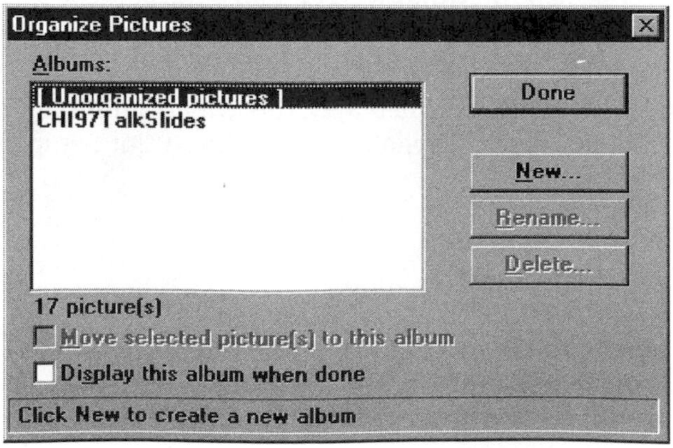

Organize Pictures	☒

Albums:

[Unorganized pictures]	Done
CHI97TalkSlides	
	New...
	Rename...
	Delete...

17 picture(s)

☐ Move selected picture(s) to this album

☐ Display this album when done

Click New to create a new album

b. The label sounds like a command for an action, but this is a checkbox. It is unclear when this move will take place. Presumably, the pictures are moved when the user clicks Done.

Recommendation: Rethink this panel. Perhaps add a scrolling list on the left that lists the pictures that are available to move to the selected album, and include buttons for Move Selected, and Move All. Possibly also support moving of pictures into albums via drag-and-drop. Consider ways to allow pictures to be included in multiple albums.

43. This is the only dialog box in the application that refers to the concept of an album. The concept, which seems useful, is effectively buried in this one dialog box. It would seem that the concept of albums would also be useful for displaying pictures. Recommendation: Make the concept of albums more prominent in the application.

44. The window does not include the name of the application. Recommendation: Change the window title to "Kodak Picture Disk: Organize Pictures."

45. The button for closing the dialog box is labeled "Done" instead of "Close," unlike elsewhere in the application. See Blooper 33: Inconsistent terminology (Section 4.1.1). Recommendation: Change it to "Close." If possible, all Close buttons throughout the application should reference the same text string in a message file.

46. The button for closing the dialog box is in an unusual location. Recommendation: Move it to the bottom right of the window.

9.2.15 Export dialog box

47. This function does not actually support all the image formats it appears to support (see Figure 9.24). More precisely, it does not support certain conversions. Pictures that were digitized by Kodak are in JPEG format, although the Picture Disk does not reveal this (which is fine). Pictures can

Figure 9.24

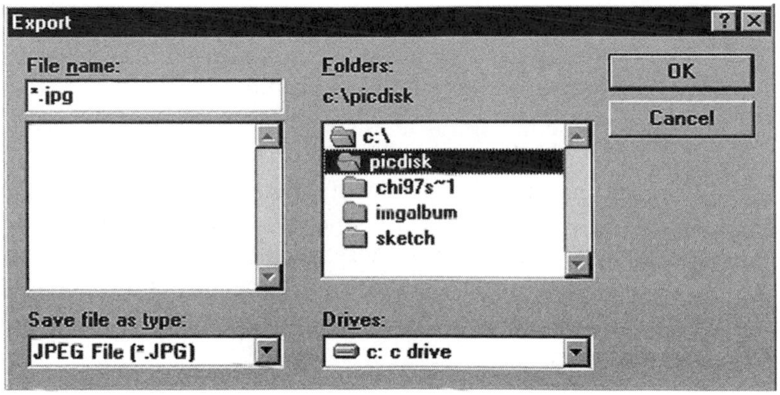

Figure 9.25

supposedly be exported in the following formats: JPEG, TIFF, PICT, PCX, Photoshop, TARGA, and BMP. However, if an image was imported as a TIFF file, it is apparently still stored internally as TIFF. Attempts to export it as JPEG initially starts the export operation (i.e., the computer's disk begins clicking) and then displays a confusing error dialog box (see Figure 9.25) that says that JPEG is an "unknown or incompatible format" and also an error message in the Main Window's bottom message area saying that it could not export the picture. But *other* images can be exported as JPEG. Recommendation: If this is just a bug, fix it. Otherwise, convert all imported pictures to an internal format that can be exported to all of the program's supported formats.

48. Bug: If several pictures are exported in the same session, later ones are likely to be exported as incomplete or garbled images. When the program begins doing this, it is necessary to quit the program, restart it, and then try again to export the desired picture. It must be some sort of memory corruption problem. Recommendation: Fix this!

49. The folders list uses indentation to depict the path down to the current folder. It therefore looks like a tree control, but isn't because only one branch of the hierarchy is shown. Many users will scroll the list looking for the other branches of the tree, and won't find them. The way to "back" up the hierarchy, to show the parent folder of the current top-level folder, is to click on the top-level folder. This is very unusual and confusing. Recommendation: Either just list the folders in the current directory with a special "go up to parent folder" item first in the list, or display a real tree control.

50. The dialog box for exporting is the same as the one for importing. It has certain aspects that seem less appropriate for specifying an output file than it does for specifying input files.

    a. The file list on the left lists the names of files in the current destination directory. It seems more suited for picking an external image to be imported than for specifying the name of a picture to be exported.

    b. When the Export command is invoked, the default filename for exporting is "*.jpg," which causes the file list to list all files ending with "*.jpg." This is a useful default for importing, but it is wrong for exporting.

    Recommendation: Design a directory browser specifically for the Export command.

51. If any files are listed in the file list, they are grayed out, suggesting that they are inactive, but selecting one still changes the content of the filename field. Recommendation: Grayed out means inactive. These filenames aren't inactive, and so should not be grayed out.

52. If the user specifies an illegal filename (e.g., "*.jpg"), the Export operation fails, but the user receives no indication that the command failed. No error dialog, no error message at the bottom of the Main Window, nothing. To make matters worse, when the Export command is invoked, the default filename for exporting is "*.jpg." Recommendation: When Export is invoked, the filename should default to something sensible, like the name of the picture (if it has a name). Even "Picture1" would be better than "*.jpg." Also, if the user specifies an illegal filename, some sort of error message should be displayed.

53. It is unclear whether users need to include a filename extension (e.g., ".jpg") when they specify a filename. The default filename "*.jpg" includes a filename extension. If the user changes the export format to another format (by changing the "Save file as type" option menu), the extension on the export filename changes to match. But the various values of the "Save file as type" option menu indicate what extension they will use, and in fact, the picture will be exported with the correct extension whether or not the user includes the extension in the filename. Some users will wonder: "Should I include the extension or not? If I do, will the resulting file have *two* extensions?" Users shouldn't have to wonder about questions like this. Recommendation: Either remove the extension indicator from the option menu values, or make it clear that the filename need not include an extension.

54. The window does not include the name of the application. Recommendation: Change the window title to "Kodak Picture Disk: Export Picture."

War Stories of a User Interface Consultant

Introduction

Many of the bloopers described in this book are illustrated using brief anecdotes from my professional experience. One might call these "war stories." In addition to those brief war stories, which mainly pertain to specific design or management issues, I thought it would be useful to describe a few of the consulting experiences I have had in greater detail, that is, tell some war stories in their full glory. That is the purpose of this chapter. Each war story in this chapter touches on many different issues discussed elsewhere in this book.

The fact that an engineer, organization, or company commits some of the bloopers described in this book does not mean that the engineer, organization, or company is bad. As Gentner and Grudin [1990] and Grudin [1991] point out, software product development involves balancing competing interests and goals, and making trade-offs on many issues. In fact, in some of the situations described below, I committed bloopers. I admit it. Sometimes designers are forced into corners. Sometimes one must choose between the lesser of two bloopers.

The first war story, about my experience redesigning the user interface of a computer game, is adapted from a previously published article [Johnson, 1998]. Since that article was written with the approval of the client and identifies the client, there is no reason not to identify the client in this adaptation of the article. In the second war story, about designing the user interface for a television set-top box, the name of the client company is altered.

10.1 *A Fork in the Tale*: Simplifying the controls of an interactive movie game

In July 1996, Advance Reality, a game software developer, hired me as a consultant to solve a user interface design problem in a game they were developing. I was referred to them by AnyRiver Entertainment, the game's "producer."[1] AnyRiver was responsible for testing the game on computer game enthusiasts (referred to as "play-testing"), and their tests indicated that players were having difficulty operating the game's controls.

10.1.1 Background

The game is called *A Fork in the Tale*, abbreviated *Fork*. The developers had shot a full-length feature film viewed through the eyes of the protagonist. In contrast to a normal movie, each scene was filmed with many outcomes. The developers were editing the footage together to create an interactive game.

---

1. It is common for three companies to be involved in the preparation and marketing of a computer game: the designer/developer, the producer/funder, and the distributor. In this case, the distributor was Electronic Arts.

Such games are known in the game software industry as "full motion video" (FMV) games.

Every few seconds while the movie is playing on an individual's computer screen, mouse-sensitive control symbols appear over the movie action, providing opportunities for the player to affect what the protagonist does or says, for example, leave, enter door, ask question, make comment, don magic cloak, dodge punch. The software selects the sequence of clips to show based on the player's choices and various state variables.

The high frequency of choices provided in *Fork* represents an advance over previous interactive movies, which offer players a choice only every several minutes. The frequency of choices also makes the game much more complex (i.e., branchy) than most FMV games: five CD-ROMs are required to hold all of the footage a player might encounter. To keep the game's complexity manageable, at most three control symbols are presented at a time.

Another difference between *Fork* and most other FMV games is that it is real time: the movie does not stop while a player considers which action to choose. If a player fails to make a choice within a few seconds, the opportunity passes and a choice is made by default.

The game's premise is that you, the player and movie protagonist, innocently walk into the midst of a shoot out, get wounded, black out, and wake up washed ashore on an island. The goal is to figure out where you are, who the other people on the island are, and how to get back home. Your character (the protagonist) is an average guy who has an active sense of humor (his voice is that of comedian Rob Schneider). He is basically nonviolent, but will defend himself if attacked. Others on the island range from friendly and helpful to hostile and dangerous.

The design problem

The problem facing the developers was that the symbols for controlling the movie action were much too complicated for players to master. They were nonintuitive, unsystematic, and too numerous. Players could not make meaningful choices between control symbols quickly enough.

Simplifying the controls was regarded as critical to the success of the game. The game developers of course wanted the game's mysteries and puzzles to be challenging, but they didn't want operating the game to be difficult.

The developers had tried three times to design action controls for the game, but none of the resulting control schemes had proved satisfactory. They were therefore open to the game producer's suggestion to hire a consultant.

The assignment

My task was to devise a new control scheme—a way of organizing and representing protagonist actions that was easier to understand than the previous schemes had been.

The game developers first wanted to be sure that they could work with me and that I would design a control scheme that they liked, so they structured my assignment such that they could decide quickly if they wanted me to continue. In three days, I was to produce a document describing a new control scheme. It didn't have to have the final action categories or control art, but it did have to explain, abstractly, how actions would be categorized and approximately how many categories would be needed.

10.1.2 The analysis

I started by playing *Fork* and asking questions about it. I played it not as a normal player would, but rather using special production software that allowed me to jump around, replay clips, and so on. I focused on a few game scenes that the designers said contained intensive action or conversation. My goal was to understand the expressive requirements of the game.

Previous action controls

I also examined the most recent control scheme. Though it had been designed with care and thought, rather than in an ad hoc fashion as many game designers do, it had several flaws that contributed to its poor usability:

1. *Too many symbols.* Action symbols were organized in a three-dimensional set, with color, shape, and bitmap image as independent axes of meaning. With five colors, about 10 shapes, and dozens of images, the old scheme used hundreds of symbols. Furthermore, the meanings assigned to shapes and colors were arbitrary, for example, *color:* yellow = helpful, green = curious; *shape:* spiked = aggressive, rounded = passive. It was nearly impossible for players to learn all of the symbols.

2. *More semantic resolution than necessary.* The old control scheme distinguished each action situation in the game from every other. This would make sense if players were in control of the time, subject, object, and mood of their actions, but in this case the *game* is in full control of the timing and effect of actions, only a few of which are available at a time. Therefore, the action resolution required is much lower.

3. *Similar representation of very different actions.* In the old control scheme, most symbols were stationary opaque plates that appeared at the bottom of the screen. Whether a displayed symbol depicted, for example, a physical movement or a speech act was indicated only by the shape of the plate. This hindered recognition of even what general *type* of action a symbol represented.

4. *Flawed implementation.* The game editors (who, along with their other editing duties, added action symbols to movie clips) didn't understand the old

scheme, so they implemented it haphazardly. Each editor tended to use a subset of symbols that he or she understood or liked the appearance of. Furthermore, editors made up new symbols occasionally, not all of which fit the scheme. The result was an ad hoc implementation of a principled (albeit flawed as described in points 1–3) design.

Expressive requirements

Although the old control scheme was to be replaced, it was clear that an important feature of it should be retained: clickable action symbols that appear at choice points in the movie. The real-time (i.e., non-stop) nature of the game required that all available protagonist actions at choice points be simultaneously visible, ruling out a control scheme such as that used in slower-paced games, where the cursor changes shape as it is moved around the screen to indicate what action is available there.

The main redesign task was therefore to design a simpler but sufficient categorization of actions, and symbols to represent the categories. Initial analysis of the game suggested that protagonist actions fell into six categories: *navigate* in a direction, *look* in a direction, *interact* physically with objects or people, *speak*, *think* silently, and *memorize* events or faces.

Experience with iconic user interfaces [Johnson et al., 1989] suggested to me that choosing among available actions would be easier if these six classes were grouped into two superordinate action classes—physical movements (navigate, look, and interact) versus speech acts and thoughts—with gross differences in how the two classes would be presented.

Opportunities for physical actions would be represented by black-and-white, semitransparent, animated "hotspots." They would usually float over the action and pan with it (e.g., enter door, block punch), but might appear at the edges of the screen if they had no clear direct object (e.g., turn right, jump). A few such "hotspots" had already been introduced into the game by editors dissatisfied with the existing controls and seemed successful.

In contrast, opportunities for speech and thought would be represented by cartoon speech balloons containing a symbol representing the specific speech or thought action. They would appear at the bottom edge of the screen (to appear to come from the protagonist's own mouth) in one of three fixed positions.

Memorizing events and faces posed a dilemma: which main symbol class should it be in? Memorizing is a mental act, but has a definite target in the movie action, like looking closely at something. The game editors had already used hotspots to represent opportunities to memorize things, and play-testing indicated that it worked well. Following the principle "if it ain't broke, don't fix it," I left this aspect of the game as it was.

An important goal was to reduce the number of actions and symbols representing them. The recognizability and discriminability of graphical symbols in a set does not depend *exclusively* on set size; people can discriminate fairly large sets if the symbols in the set are different enough from each other and if the mappings from symbols to meaning are intuitive [Mullet and Sano, 1995]. Nevertheless, other things being equal, smaller symbol sets are preferable. Whatever the optimal number might be, hundreds of actions was clearly too many. It was also clear, however, that the game's expressive requirements ruled out having 10 or fewer actions per main action-class. Somewhat arbitrarily, I set myself the goal of having at most 30 symbols in each of the two main classes.

After playing critical game scenes, I devised preliminary categorizations of movement and speech actions that seemed to cover the expressive requirements while not exceeding this limit (details later). Although the final control symbols would be drawn by graphic artists (one artist per set to assure consistent appearance within each set and clear differences between the two sets), I made rough sketches for each of the speech and movement actions.

Having satisfied myself that a simplified control scheme that met the game's expressive needs was feasible, I presented it to the developers. They liked the simplified control scheme and asked me to continue refining it and to work with the graphic artists, game editors, and programmers to get it implemented.

Additional requirements

Over time, I learned that, in addition to the game's expressive requirements, there were requirements and constraints arising from Advance Reality's schedule and resources, and from the wishes of the game designer.

An important constraint on the redesign effort was that the only funded usability testing was the play-testing being conducted by AnyRiver. Their support for *Fork* was based, in part, on positive results from testing early prototypes of the game on computer game enthusiasts. They continued play-testing throughout the development period, reporting player enjoyment, usability problems, and bugs to Advance Reality. Any other usability testing had to be done very quickly and at essentially no cost. However, we sometimes needed to test specific design ideas before adding them to the game. In such cases, we had to devise quick, cheap tests.

A final set of requirements was based on the game designer's wishes and goals. Before describing them, it is important to clarify my role in the project.

In the computer game industry, the game designer is usually also the user interface designer (supported by art directors and graphic artists). Because the roles were separate in this case, it was possible to observe how our concerns overlapped and interacted. The game designer was concerned mainly with how entertaining and aesthetically pleasing the game was and how well it embodied his overall vision. I was concerned mainly with usability. Our different concerns often led us to differences of opinion. As a consultant, I had to accept the game designer's judgment if he insisted. He respected my judgment and yielded to it more often than he overruled it, but, naturally, he was difficult to convince if a proposal ran counter to his vision of the game. His ideas about the game that affected the redesign included the following:

- Although he realized that the new control scheme had to have far fewer actions than the old scheme, the game designer tended to favor having more actions than I did. To him, each protagonist action had a meaning, and he preferred to represent actions in terms of the intended meaning, rather than in terms of just what was necessary to distinguish them at choice points. This issue arose repeatedly during the redesign effort.

- The game designer had strong feelings about the appearance of the control symbols. He wanted them to have three-dimensional depth, that is, not appear flat in the plane of the screen. They had to "lead players' eyes into the movie action." The controls also had to fit with the game's woodsy, old-world fantasy theme; they had to look "antique and classy." While these graphic style requirements did enhance the aesthetic appeal of the game, they also biased the symbol art toward more detailed styles, rather than toward the abstract, minimalist styles that graphic designers agree are easier to recognize [Mullet and Sano, 1995].

- The game designer wanted to minimize the use of text throughout the game. The game software can display a text label under any action symbol, but the game designer felt that labeling every control symbol would slow players down and divert their attention from the movie action, as well as hinder translating the game into other languages. I agreed, so my initial design used text labels (1) only on speech symbols, not on physical action symbols, (2) mainly in early game scenes to help players learn the symbols, and (3) thereafter, only where necessary to distinguish choices (e.g., when multiple speech acts of the same type were offered). However, as is described later, the game producer disagreed with the game designer and me on this issue.

10.1.3 Redesign: Physical actions

As described earlier, my initial analysis of the requirements for controlling the protagonist's physical actions yielded four action categories that were to be represented by hotspots: navigating in a direction, looking in a direction, interacting physically with objects or people, and memorizing events or faces. From playing the game, it seemed that the following actions in the four categories were required:

- *Navigate*: Forward, 45° Right, 45° Left, Right, Left, Backward, Turn Around Right, Turn Around Left, Turn Right, Turn Left, Turn 45° Right, Turn 45° Left, Stop/Stand Still
- *Look*: Up, Down, Left, Right, Here
- *Interact*: Hit/Knock, Kick, Push, Block, Grab/Catch, Duck, Dodge Left, Dodge Right, Spin Left, Spin Right, Break Free
- *Memorize*: This

Each action would be represented by its own symbol.

The total number of actions (and therefore symbols) in this initial version of the physical action controls was 30. This was worrisome because it seemed likely that additional experience with the game would expose the need for additional actions. For example, I soon realized that we needed an action and symbol for Jump.

Fortunately, further analysis also indicated that some of the initial actions were not needed. For example, it became clear that many Look opportunities in the game could be represented by navigate symbols such as Turn Left, and the rest could be represented by a single Look Here symbol placed in the relevant screen location. It also became clear that because users were choosing between available actions, not generating actions, it was not necessary to distinguish Hit from Kick. Both could be represented by a single Strike symbol. Similarly, it was not necessary to distinguish Push from Block, or Dodge Right and Left from Navigate Right and Left. Finally, the need for some actions disappeared as the game evolved: Break Free and Turn 45° Right and Left. Figure 10.1 shows early sketches of some of these symbols.

The final set of actions to be represented by hotspots numbered 21. It contained the following:

- *Navigate*: Forward, Right, Left, 45° Right, 45° Left, Back Up, Turn Around Right, Turn Around Left, Turn Right, Turn Left, Stop/Stand Still
- *Look*: Here
- *Interact*: Strike, Push/Block Left, Push/Block Right, Grab/Catch, Duck, Jump, Spin Left, Spin Right
- *Memorize*: This

Figure 10.1

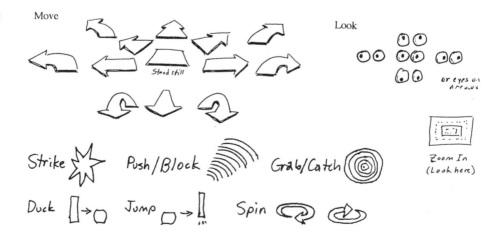

Once these actions had been finalized, we instructed the game editors to use them throughout the game. It didn't matter that the symbols for the actions did not yet exist because each use of an action symbol in the game is just an index into a table of symbol bitmaps. We filled the table with placeholder images initially, and replaced them one by one as the symbols were finalized.

Even as the physical actions were being refined, symbols to represent them were designed. My sketches served as input for a graphic artist, who produced successive iterations of the symbol set with feedback from me and the game designer.

Some of the actions were easy to represent graphically. It was obvious that symbols for navigation actions should be arrows such as those painted on roads and road signs. The only difficulty in designing the symbols for these was in achieving the animated three-dimensional perspective appearance that the game designer wanted. Other physical actions that proved easy to design symbols for were Strike (a jagged starburst borrowed from comic books), Grab/Catch (a target), Spin (an animated arrow chasing its tail), and Memorize (a small pulsating cloud). Once these symbols were in the game, AnyRiver's play-testing indicated that game players easily understood them.

Figure 10.2

In contrast, some physical actions were hard to represent graphically. I initially sketched Stop/Stand Still as a stop sign, but it proved impossible to create a recognizable black-and-white stop sign bitmap within the size and perspective constraints. We eventually settled on a perspective *X*—a cartoon pirate's "X marks the buried treasure" (see Figure 10.2).

To represent Look Here, I initially sketched a pair of eyes, but the game designer was rightly concerned that symbolic eyes would not be recognizable, and that realistic eyes would look like something peering out of the movie rather than a symbol. We chose a zooming rectangle. Other actions that were difficult to find suitable symbols for were Jump, Duck, and Block.

With each of the hard-to-depict actions, the game designer and I worked with the graphic artist until we had a hotspot we considered worth trying in the game, then put it into the image table and judged its effectiveness for ourselves as well as awaiting feedback from AnyRiver's play-testing. If it didn't work, we sent the artist back to the drawing board (or more precisely, the paint program).

Play-testing yielded many complaints about early versions of the hotspots, but with revisions, the complaints ceased. In fact, it eventually seemed that players were using the physical-action symbols without being fully conscious of them. Figure 10.3 shows some of them. When AnyRiver was preparing the game's instruction manual, they asked for a list of the hotspots. When we sent them the list, they were surprised that there were so many distinct images. We pointed out that, with the exception of the Stop/Stand Still symbol, people don't perceive the navigation symbols as distinct symbols, but rather as the same arrow pointing in different directions. AnyRiver made use of this in the manual to simplify the explanation of the hotspots.

Figure 10.3

Move right.   Turn around.

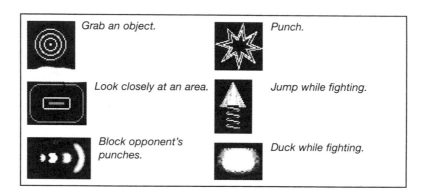

Grab an object.   Punch.

Look closely at an area.   Jump while fighting.

Block opponent's punches.   Duck while fighting.

10.1.4 Redesign: Speech and thought

The speech/thought controls were designed in parallel with the physical-action controls. Opportunities to speak were to be depicted by a cartoon speech balloon enclosing a symbol representing the type of speech act. Opportunities to think internal thoughts would be represented by a thought balloon enclosing a subset of the speech act symbols. As with the physical-action controls, we had to develop both the actions and symbols for them.

My initial analysis of conversation-intensive game scenes suggested a need for 12 speech actions: statement, question, accept, refuse, offer help, aggressive/insult, sarcastic, humorous, need help/frustrated, flatter/praise/thank, grovel/beg/plead, and recall memory. An additional "speech" type was to represent keeping silent (although see the discussion later). The actions for thought were to be a subset of those for speech.

After defining the initial speech actions, I began sketching symbols for them. I suggested using text characters for some speech types (e.g., "?" for Question), faces for some (e.g., a comedy mask for Humorous), and hand gestures for others (e.g., a shaking fist for Aggressive). The game designer preferred a scheme having a common visual theme for all speech symbols (in addition to their being inside the speech balloon), and decided that we would use human figures making mime gestures.

Based on my initial sketches (see Figure 10.4) and input from the game designer, an artist (not the one who created the hotspots) drew human figures miming the current set of speech actions. Each mime figure consisted of two frames, which would alternate rapidly on the display to produce a simple animation (see Figure 10.5). Initially, the game designer and I met with the artist

Figure 10.4

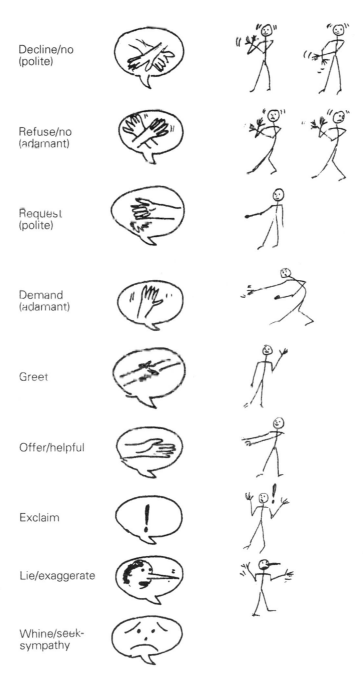

Decline/no (polite)

Refuse/no (adamant)

Request (polite)

Demand (adamant)

Greet

Offer/helpful

Exclaim

Lie/exaggerate

Whine/seek-sympathy

almost weekly over a two-month period to critique the latest mime figures and inform the artist of changes in the speech actions.

Figure 10.5

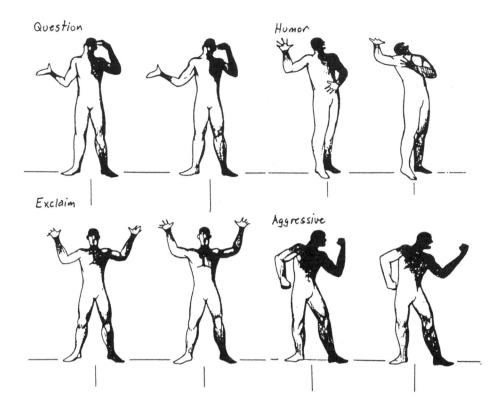

By this time, based on further experience with the game and pressure from the game designer (who tended to favor more specific speech actions), the number of speech actions had expanded to 27. They were statement, question, accept/yes, decline/no (polite), refuse/no (adamant), request (polite), demand (adamant), greet, offer/helpful, exclaim, lie/exaggerate, whine/seek sympathy, accuse, gratitude/thank, flatter, humorous/witty, sarcastic/snide, aggressive/insult/defiant, grovel/beg/plead, flirt, manipulate, reason/persuade/explain, care/empathy, deal/negotiate, get real/get a grip, and recall memory.

Unlike the hotspots, which had been drawn using painting software, the new speech symbols and the speech balloon were drawn on paper. Digitizing them and combining the mime figures with the speech balloon would be very expensive and time-consuming, so we wanted to wait until we were more confident that the speech actions were stable and the symbols were adequate. But this meant that the speech controls weren't being play-tested.

To get empirical data on how well the mime gestures conveyed their intended meanings, I conducted informal paper tests. I recruited 10 volunteers who were not associated with Advance Reality or AnyRiver and knew nothing about the game, showed them the figure pairs, told them that each pair was an

Figure 10.6

Speech Symbol	Participant Responses
Lie/Exaggerate 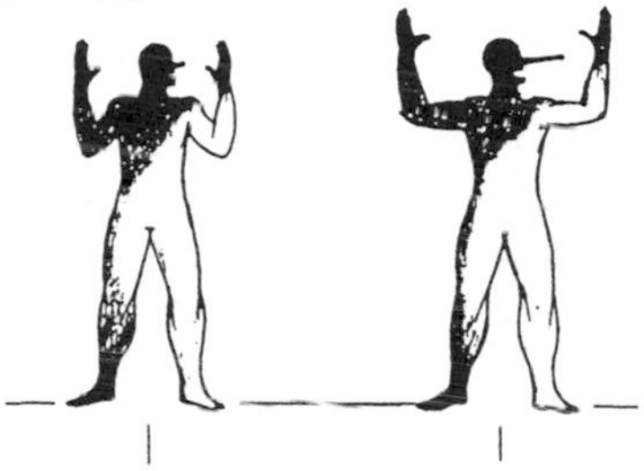	1. Exaggerating or lying. 2. Lie. Telling a tall tale. 3. Telling a lie. 4. Bigger. 5. He told a big lie. 6. Telling a fish story. 7. Lie. 8. The Pinocchio syndrome. 9. Telling a big lie. 10. Lying—Exaggerate.
Sarcastic/Snide 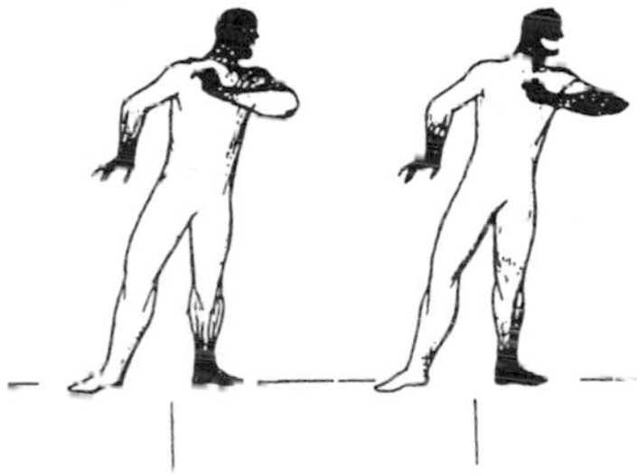	1. Nudging. Getting their attention. 2. Bravado, brag. 3. Let me tell you. 4. Hey, big guy. 5. Don't you get it? Heh, heh. 6. D'ya get it? Huh? 7. ??? 8. Anger. 9. I'm the man. 10. Coughing.

animation of a man trying to express something silently, and asked them to write on an answer sheet, in a few words, what the man was trying to say. I then assigned each response a subjective score between 1 (missed intended meaning) and 10 (got it).

The results of the first such test were discouraging: a few symbols were conveying their intended meaning to most subjects, but most were not (see Figure 10.6). I reported the poor test results to the artist and game designer, and we changed the basic miming figure, revised some of the symbols (see Figure 10.7), and repeated the test with different participants. Some symbols did better in the second round of testing; others didn't. Based on the results of the second test, we revised some of the figures again.

We briefly considered adding color to the mime figures as a *redundant* indicator of mood (in contrast to the old scheme's use of color as an *independent* dimension). To be helpful, the color scheme had to be obvious to players, rather than something additional to learn. Further analysis revealed that such a plan required finding not only a universal mapping of emotion level to color, but also a universal mapping of our speech actions to emotion level. To check the latter, I conducted a quick informal test: I asked eight employees of Advance Reality who weren't involved in developing the speech symbols to rate each speech action for "amount of emotion" on a 0–5 scale (0 = low; 5 = high). Some actions received uniformly high emotion ratings (e.g., accuse, exclaim,

Figure 10.7

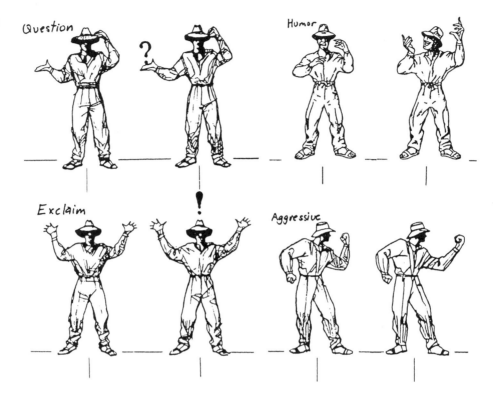

refuse), while others received uniformly low ones (e.g., statement, keep silent), but most received a wide range of ratings (e.g., accept, fear, manipulate, humorous). Comments from test participants suggested that variability for certain items was due to some people separating *amount* of emotion from *type* of emotion, while others did not. Since finding the required two universal mappings seemed unachievable, we abandoned the idea of augmenting speech symbols with color.

The speech symbols still weren't satisfactory, and time was getting short. We decided to put some of them into selected game scenes and use our own reactions and play-testing to guide further design. This exposed two new issues:

1. On-screen, the mime figures were too small to be easily recognized. Enlarging both the figures and the enclosing speech balloon would obscure too much movie action. Our solution was twofold. First, we enlarged the figures but repositioned them in the speech balloons so that their legs were clipped off. All the information was in the upper bodies anyway. Second, we exaggerated whichever features carried the meaning (e.g., hands, mouth). This is a common practice of cartoonists and graphic artists [Mullet and Sano, 1995].

2. Although the two-frame animation of the mime figures worked well, it proved distracting and disorienting to have several speech symbols displayed at once, all animating in synchrony over the movie action. Simply assigning different animation rates to different speech symbols broke up this effect, reducing the visual impact of multiple speech symbols to acceptable levels.

Once these graphic design issues were resolved, the main issues returned to the fore: determining the final speech actions and symbols to convey them. The deadline was looming and we had to allow time for the editors to add the new speech actions throughout the game. We were worried that we had too many speech actions for players to remember: 27, not including the thought actions. We were also concerned that many of the mime figures didn't convey their intended speech category well.

To finalize the speech actions and symbols, we had to resolve several issues about which the game designer and I had different opinions:

- *Did we need speech actions that were proving very difficult to depict?* These were sarcastic/snide, reason/persuade/explain, care/empathy, deal/negotiate, whine/seek sympathy, and flatter. I had concluded that the problem was not simply that we hadn't yet found the right mime figure to depict these concepts, but rather that they were too abstract to represent graphically. I convinced the game designer that we should drop them and "bend" other actions to cover those situations.

- *Did we really need multiple symbols for thoughts?* The game designer preferred having a variety of thought symbols to depict the different types of "silent" remarks the protagonist could make. I argued that thoughts can't be heard by other characters and don't affect the outcome of the game (most are just opportunities to hear one of Rob Schneider's funny wisecracks), so there was no need to distinguish one from another. We ended up with only one thought symbol (an empty thought balloon).

- *Did we really need a symbol for* not *speaking?* I favored eliminating the symbol and having players keep silent by not selecting any speech symbol. The game designer wanted keeping silent to be an explicit choice because there are situations in the game where remaining silent is a strategic move. We compromised: eliminate Keep Silent, use no symbol wherever keeping silent isn't strategic, and use the Thought symbol wherever keeping silent is strategic (although this meant finding and adding a suitable recorded protagonist "thought" line).

- *Did we really need symbols that were hardly used?* Two speech symbols were needed only once or twice in the entire game: manipulate, get real/get a grip. They seemed to me to be good candidates for elimination, but the game designer wanted to keep them because he felt that the attitudes they represented were critical for the scenes in which they appeared. We kept them. We also added a symbol for "Shhh!" (i.e., telling someone else to be quiet), even though it was only used once.

With these decisions behind us, the set of speech/thought actions numbered 22. We felt comfortable with this number and with how the remaining mime symbols were working, so we began instructing the game editors on how to install the new speech actions throughout the game. Assigning speech actions required much more care and judgment than did adding physical actions. I developed guidelines for editors to follow.

Unfortunately, installing the new speech controls was as difficult for the game editors to do correctly as installing the old speech controls had been. After the editors had made one pass through the game assigning speech symbols, I did some checking and estimated that about half of the thousands of assignments were incorrect. I revised my guidelines to be more explicit, and explained them verbally to most of the editors, to no avail. The game designer asked the editors to be more careful, to no avail.

The game editors had a complex job, which included editing together video sequences, voice tracks, and sound effects as well as placing the control symbols in space and time. Furthermore, they were working under intense time pressure. One finally told me that she didn't have time to determine the correct speech actions; she simply made everything a Statement, and assumed that someone else would fix it later. In response to this, I learned to use the editing software well enough to allow me to go through the entire game, listen to all the protagonist's lines, and assign speech actions.

Once the speech controls were in the game, feedback from AnyRiver (based in part on their play-testing) was swift in coming. They wanted two further changes:

1. They wanted all speech symbols to be supplemented by text labels. Although the game designer and I had decided to use text very sparingly, Any-River convinced us that the advantages of text labels outweighed the disadvantages. I went back through the game, listening to all the protagonist's lines, composing and adding one- and two-word labels summarizing each line. For example, a question about another person's father was labeled "Father?" and a demand for another person to leave was labeled "Go away!"

2. They wanted the set of speech symbols reduced further. They were preparing the user manual and were worried that the list of speech symbols would seem daunting. The game designer and I felt that the set was as small as it could be. A compromise was reached, based on the recognition that in most of the game, only a few speech actions were needed (seven), but some scenes were "conversation games" requiring more expressiveness and hence a greater variety of speech actions. AnyRiver wrote the manual so as to list the seven frequently used speech symbols separately from the rest (Figure 10.8).

Figure 10.8

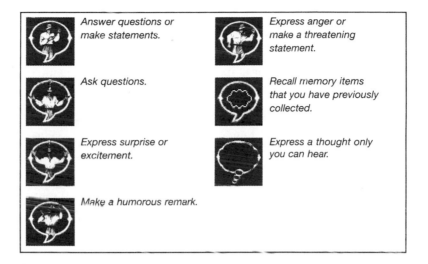

10.1.5 Redesign: Evaluation and discussion

One goal of the redesign effort was to reduce drastically the number of control symbols game players had to distinguish and choose between without compromising the expressive choice that was needed to make the game entertaining and rewarding. We ended with 21 physical-action symbols and 22 speech/thought symbols, a total of 43. Obviously, this was a drastic reduction from the several hundred symbols of the old control scheme. The game designer also felt that we had done so without compromising expressive choice.

In critiquing the old control scheme, I treated the lack of compliance by game editors with it as an indictment of it. However, the editors also had trouble assigning the *new* speech actions. It is tempting to conclude that this has more to do with their heavy workload than with the control scheme, but that conclusion won't withstand the observation that editors did not have much trouble installing the new physical-action controls. Perhaps workload contributes to the problem, perhaps deciding the appropriate speech action for a specific protagonist line is as hard as is devising a good categorization of speech actions, and perhaps our speech categorization was still not intuitive enough.

We can also ask how well the final control symbols depicted their intended meanings. Based on informal feedback from play-testing, I feel confident that the symbols for physical actions and memorizing were highly successful— so good that players hardly notice them even while using them heavily.

Whether the speech/thought controls were successful is debatable. In the end, we had to augment them with text labels. Play-testing indicated that, thus augmented, they were usable. With more time, I might have suggested revising the mime figures yet again or trying other ways to represent speech actions.

10.1.6   Other aspects of the user interface

Although I had been hired to redesign the action controls, the game developers expanded my charter to include other aspects of the game's user interface that needed refinement or redesign. These included

- the cursor's various shapes, which indicate whether or not the movie is at a choice point and how much time remains to choose
- the visual feedback when control symbols are hit or missed
- the score counters that appear in certain scenes
- the user interface for making use of saved magical objects
- the control panel for starting, saving, and loading games and setting game options

Play-testing indicated that these aspects of the user interface were successful, but the processes by which they were designed are beyond the scope of this chapter.

10.1.7   Lessons and concluding thoughts

Working on *Fork* taught me the following lessons:

- A picture may be worth a thousand words, but finding the right picture to convey a verbal concept can be very hard. The best way to convey some verbal concepts is verbally.
- If symbols in a set depict their meanings well, people can discriminate and recognize them even if the set is large. Users may not even realize that the set is large.
- Universally recognized mappings between color and emotion depend on a universal emotion scale, which may not exist. Designs that map color to emotion are risky.
- Game developers understand the need to test on real users (better than do most software developers), but they could use help from user interface specialists in understanding the distinction between play-testing and more focused usability testing, and the importance of the latter. In particular, testing need not wait until a game is playable. As the user interface for *Fork* was redesigned, tests of various types were used throughout the process, from ideas to implementation. For more discussion of the value and variety of usability testing, see Principle 8 (Section 1.8).
- User interface designers have different concerns and skills than game designers and graphic designers (see Blooper 76: Misunderstanding what user

interface professionals do, Section 8.1.1). User interface skills are as important for designing games as for productivity software, but the reverse is also true: the skills of game designers could be useful in making productivity software more engaging and fun.

Earlier, I stated that the game designer often yielded to my judgment on user interface issues. But what is a user interface issue, especially in contrast to a game design issue? The game's plot and dialogue and the challenge of solving its mysteries and puzzles clearly fall under game design. Users' ability to navigate successfully in the game world and keep track of how they are doing clearly falls under user interface design.

But consider the issue of deciding who the intended users are and designing a suitable product for them. That is often cited as an important, though neglected, concern of user interface designers [Landauer, 1995]. After I had played *Fork*, I had concerns about who it was for and whether it would appeal to them.

As someone who rarely plays computer games, I felt that the interactive-movie aspects of *Fork* were great; that is, it was easy to become engrossed in the mystery and want to solve it. However, I was put off by some embedded puzzles that were not integral to the story—points at which the movie disappears and the player (not the protagonist) negotiates a maze or manipulates objects to find a combination. These were included to make *Fork* appealing to "hard-core gamers." I worried that they might make it unappealing to light gamers and nongamers, and that we ought to think more about the question of who *Fork* was for rather than glibly answering "everyone!" but even I didn't consider this a user interface issue at the time.

Similarly, AnyRiver, *Fork*'s producer, prepared cover art for the package and manual that included sophomoric drawings of near-naked women, even though there is nothing so racy in the game. Again, this was done to appeal to gamers, but I felt that it would turn off nongamers, light gamers, parents (who often control purchases), and female gamers.

As it turns out, the game is selling rather poorly. I frankly don't think that this is due to poor controls; play-testing indicated that they were adequate. I think it is due to insufficient consideration of the target market. Maybe that should be treated as part of the user interface after all.

10.2 The Flintstones may be in your TV: Designing controls for a set-top box

Over a one-year period from summer 1996 through summer 1997, a consumer appliance company hired me as a user interface consultant for a series of four related short-term jobs. The four jobs were

1. A user interface review job that unexpectedly turned into a fast-paced user interface design job

2. A user interface review job to check the implementation of the product designed in the first job

3. An eleventh-hour emergency job to redesign the physical front panel of the product designed in the first job

4. A user interface design job, for a second, sibling product

This war story describes these four jobs. I describe the first one in considerable detail because it sets the stage for the others. The remaining three jobs are described more briefly. Like the previous war story, this one ends with some lessons I learned from the experience, for user interface consultants as well as for companies that hire them.

10.2.1 Job 1: UI review that unexpectedly turned into a UI design

In the summer of 1996, when I was just starting out as a UI consultant, a friend called to ask if I had time to review the user interface of a product his company was developing. The company, which I will call Acme (not its real name), was an American R&D subsidiary of a Taiwanese consumer electronics development company. Acme's role was to design and prototype products for its parent company. The Taiwanese parent company, in turn, developed products for appliance manufacturers and service providers, mainly in Asia.

The product

In this case, the product was a television set-top box for controlling reception of digital satellite TV broadcasts. The industry name for such boxes is "integrated receiver and decoder" (IRD). IRDs are intended for households and institutions that have satellite dishes and subscribe to a broadcaster's services. Sometimes consumers buy such boxes on their own, but in many cases, digital broadcasters provide the set-top IRD boxes to their subscribers.

The user interface of an IRD consists of a handheld remote control, software controls that appear on the television screen, and some buttons on the front panel of the set-top box.

Acme had a small team of hardware and software engineers designing and developing the IRD, but no user interface designer. Responsibility for the user interface had been assigned to a programmer who had no formal user interface expertise. He had developed GUIs before but never a consumer product.

The design problem

One team member—who happened to be a friend of mine—had become concerned that the user interface would not be usable by consumers. He presented his case to the vice-president who headed Acme. He recommended that they hire a user interface designer consultant. The VP hadn't known there was such a thing. He was willing, but didn't want to spend much time or money.

My friend called me to see if I could review their user interface and suggest improvements. I said I was busy with other work, but had some time. My friend said he estimated that the review shouldn't take more than five person-days: three to review the user interface and two to write a report including suggested improvements.

That seemed reasonable to me, so I agreed to do it, as long as the five person-days of work could be spread over a couple of weeks so I could tend to other commitments. I prepared and faxed Acme a proposed contract for a five-day user interface review. (Acme had never worked with a consultant before and didn't have a contract of their own.) Surprisingly, the VP signed the contract without changes and faxed it back to me, so I signed it and sent a copy back to Acme.

Up to this point, the entire arrangement had been made by phone and fax. I had never visited Acme, seen the user interface I was to review, or met anyone on the team other than my friend. In retrospect, this was a mistake. I should not have signed a contract without having first had a closer look at the situation. Live and learn.

A few days after signing the contract, I visited Acme to begin the review. My friend introduced me to the VP and the programmer in charge of the user interface. Both seemed supportive and receptive to my having been called in. That isn't always true. Managers are sometimes skeptical that a consultant will provide value worth the cost. Programmers are sometimes hostile when management brings in a user interface consultant to improve their designs. Happily, in this case it was clear that there would be no need to win over the people with whom I would be working.

The programmer showed me the "IRD Man Machine Interface Software Design Specification" he had written. It consisted of a total of seven pages. It began with a half-page list of functional requirements. Less than a half page was devoted to a verbal description of the planned on-screen user interface's most frequently used screens: the Program Viewing screen and the Program Guide screen. No illustrations were provided for these two screens.

Most of the specification (five pages) was devoted to describing the utility menu hierarchy, which users would use only occasionally for setting the IRD's various options, such as favorite channels, program blocking options, and so on. This section of the specification included illustrations of some of the menus and displays. It also included many inconsistencies and programmerisms. One programmerism was that the menus were all numbered starting at zero. Another programmerism was that user interface customization settings were provided under the menu choice "User Settings," even though that is a developer term, not one that users use to refer to themselves.

The specification ended with a few paragraphs describing the remote control. It included no illustrations of the remote control.

I asked to see the prototype IRD user interface. The programmer said he hadn't implemented any on-screen controls yet; all he had was the specification and a prototype remote control.

I went back to my friend's cubicle. I told him that there didn't seem to be much of a user interface for me to review. He said they were hoping I would design them one. That is, they wanted a document saying: "Here is how the current design is inadequate (including that it is largely nonexistent) and here is what you should do." He said the new design should be "like our competitors' designs, only better."

I was so shocked I didn't know what to say. I didn't want to offend the client or my friend by expressing my rapidly growing concerns. I just said, "I need to think about this" and left.

That same day, I called the VP and told him there was a problem: we had signed a contract for a five-day user interface review, but there was almost no user interface to review. He hadn't been aware of how little had been done. He asked if I could design a user interface. He stressed that they still needed it by the contracted deadline. They had promised their parent company that they would deliver a design shortly after that date.

I agreed to try. Why? I wanted the job. I was just starting out as a consultant and needed to build a client base. I had a few other clients, but I especially wanted consumer-appliance clients, and this was one.

However, I first took pains to set the VP's expectations to reasonable levels. I told him that if I was going to design a user interface in the contracted five days, he needed to understand what I was and was not going to do:

- All illustrations would be hand-sketches, drawn on paper. I didn't want to waste time fighting graphics software.

- The design wouldn't cover every detail. Some details would be left for the developers (in the United States or in Taiwan) to decide. For example, I would not have time to cover all possible error conditions and the corresponding error messages. I would also leave the screen colors largely unspecified.

- IRD functions intended mainly for service personnel would be left unspecified: Setup, Maintenance.

- I would probably have to redesign the prototype remote control once I had designed the on-screen controls, so they would be compatible.

I also told the VP that with a five-day contract, I couldn't do usability testing, but the design would definitely need to be tested. The VP wasn't sure who would test it, but was sure that testing wasn't his organization's responsibility. This was a red flag for me, but I went ahead.

I returned to Acme and asked for all information they had that might be relevant to the IRD user interface. They showed me a competitor IRD they had there (DiSH), so I could see how it functioned. I spent a few hours trying it. This was helpful because I hardly watch TV at all, don't own a satellite dish, and had never previously used an IRD or even a cable set-top box.

They also gave me user manuals from three competitor IRDs. Lastly, they gave me the documentation for the user interface toolkit the implementors in Taiwan would be using. This was so I'd understand the constraints for the user interface implementation. I was surprised to see that the toolkit was not a real GUI toolkit, but rather just a graphics library. It provided no predefined controls, such as buttons, but rather only line- and shape-drawing functions. From my point of view, this was both good and bad. It was bad because the programmers would have to build everything from scratch, so implementation time would be an issue. On the other hand, it was good because with such primitive components, there were few design constraints other than time and programmer skill.

I took the documents and the notes I had made while trying the competitor IRD, went home, and started work.

The analysis

The first step was to analyze the known competition and Acme's partial design.

Evaluation and comparison of competitor IRDs

Acme's engineers had supplied me with instruction manuals for three competitor IRDs: Pace, Panasat, and DiSH. As described earlier, they had also allowed me to spend a few hours trying out the DiSH IRD. The user interfaces of these products consisted of three parts: the on-screen controls, the remote control, and the instruction manuals.

To provide a basis for design issues that arose in the design of the Acme IRD, here are some highlights of the findings of my competitive analysis.

- Two of the three competitor IRDs—Pace and Panasat—had very similar on-screen controls. They had the same menu structure, function names, setting options, even logos. I assumed that either one had licensed the other's design, or they had both bought their software from the same vendor. Therefore, in the rest of my analysis, I treated them as one design. Oddly, their remote controls differed (see below).

- In all three competitor IRDs, the default function screen—the one that appears when a user simply turns on the IRD—is Viewing Program Content. This makes sense because viewing program content is clearly the most common activity.

- One difference between designs was the relationship between the various function screens. On this issue, I felt that the Pace/Panasat design was superior to the DiSH design. In the Pace/Panasat IRD, the Program Guide and the

Main (Utility) Menu were treated as separate peer functions, both directly accessible from the Viewing Program Content screen. Neither was subordinate to the other. In the DiSH IRD, the Program Guide was an item in the Main (Utility) Menu, and was thus subordinate. It could also be invoked directly using the Guide button on the remote control, but its presence in the Main Menu seemed potentially confusing and unnecessary.

- On the issue of operational efficiency, I felt that the Pace/Panasat design beat the DiSH design. The designers of the DiSH IRD had basically transplanted a PC-like GUI to the TV; the software's screens looked like dialog boxes. Each screen contained different types of selectable items. Operating the DiSH IRD required moving the selection around the screen from menu choices to data fields to control buttons. Perhaps the designers' intent was to leverage upscale consumers' presumed familiarity with GUIs on PCs. In my opinion, this attempt did not succeed. With a mouse or a trackball as a pointing device, it might have worked, but there was no mouse, only a remote control with arrow and number buttons. Therefore moving the selection around on the screens was quite tedious. A subsequent review of the DiSH IRD in *Consumer Reports* supported this finding.

  In contrast, the Pace/Panasat design was better suited to a TV display and a remote control having buttons. Menu screens contained only menu items, and there was at most one menu on each screen. Settings screens contained only settings, and there was at most one text entry field on each screen. There were no on-screen buttons. There was no concept of selection other than choosing menu items. Common actions—OK, Cancel, Help—were invoked by pressing dedicated buttons on the remote control. The only navigation was from screen to screen.

- Several functions on most IRDs require users to create and manage lists, for example, lists of favorite channels. I found DiSH's user interface for creating and managing lists to be much more natural than Pace/Panasat's. Pace/Panasat's user interface for defining and managing lists seemed "backward" and tedious: users specify what items on a main list should be "skipped." Furthermore, the list order was specified separately from the list content. With the DiSH IRD, users specify what items are *on* each list, not which ones are not on it, and the list order and content are unified.

- Some information displays on IRDs are temporary: they appear over another display for a certain amount of time, then disappear. One design issue is whether the display duration of temporary displays should be adjustable. In the Pace/Panasat IRD it was; in the DiSH IRD it was not. I felt that the temporary displays on the DiSH IRD would vanish too quickly for some users, frustrating them and leaving them no remedy other than buying a different IRD.

- In the brave new world of digital television, the familiar concept of TV channels may be changing. Several digital broadcasts can occupy the spectrum bandwidth that in analog TV is called a "channel." One design issue is how—or whether—to expose this to IRD users. The Pace/Panasat IRD and its manuals used the term "service" for a broadcast, and the term "channel" for a frequency range. Users had to be aware of both concepts. In my opinion, this was a poor decision; the fact that multiple digital broadcasts can fit in each old analog "channel" is an implementation detail users don't care about. I felt that the DiSH IRD and manuals handled this better. They simply redefined "channel" to mean a digital broadcast and did not expose anything analogous to the old concept of a channel.

- Functionally, I felt that the DiSH IRD was superior to the Pace/Panasat IRDs. Whereas the Pace/Panasat IRDs allowed only one customized channel list per box, the DiSH IRD allowed up to four, which would allow most families to create separate ones for parents, children, and so on. Another important aspect of functionality is the Program Guide. The Pace/Panasat Program Guide was fairly primitive: a simple grid showing the *order* of upcoming shows on each "service," but not their broadcast times. In contrast, the DiSH Program Guide looks similar to most printed program guide charts and includes show times.

- All three competitor IRDs had different remote controls. Even the Pace and Panasat remote controls differed, although their on-screen controls did not. All three remote controls arranged the arrow buttons in a diamond pattern (north, south, east, west). On the Pace and DiSH remote controls, the Select/OK button was positioned in the middle of the diamond, making it easy — too easy, I felt—to press it by mistake. The DiSH remote control provided a Recall button to make it easier to bounce back and forth between two channels; the Pace and Panasat remote controls did not.

As described earlier, Acme didn't have much of a design for me to evaluate. I did examine their seven-page "IRD Man Machine Interface Software Design Specification" and had some detailed criticisms, some of which I already mentioned earlier. However, as my friend had suggested, my main feedback was "There isn't nearly enough here to indicate how the software will work; we need to flesh this out in much more detail." Fleshing out the design was the next step.

Functional requirements and user interface goals

The first step in designing anything should be understanding and clarifying the goals of the design. What are users supposed to be able to do with this thing? What, if any, design goals are there for the user interface itself? This section summarizes my answers to these questions.

Functional requirements

As described earlier, Acme's brief specification provided a half-page of functional requirements. I augmented that by taking ideas for functionality from the instruction manuals of the three competitor IRDs. The idea was to construct a comprehensive list of desired functions: an abstract list of things users should be able to do with the IRD.

Acme IRD functional requirements (sample)

View content of currently broadcast program
- Choose new currently broadcast program
  - By program
  - By channel number
- View program summary
  - For currently viewed program
  - For not currently viewed, currently broadcast program
  - For future program
- View/set current time and date
- View program schedule/guide
- Set access
  - Ratings-based blocking
  - Content-based blocking
  - Pay-per-view blocking
  - Block all use of IRD
  - Set or change ID code
- Set viewing preferences
- Set UI preferences

It is important to realize that the functional requirements outlined in the list I created was not a description of the planned user interface. It was just a list of the planned functionality—tasks users can accomplish with the IRD. The point of such lists is to enumerate all functions, treating each as separate, even though some of them might end up being combined in the actual user interface. For example, viewing the program schedule and the time/date were listed as separate functions even though the time and date information might be displayed on the same program schedule display.

User interface goals

As with the functional requirements, the goals for the user interface came from Acme's brief specification, augmented by my own design experience and what I had learned from my analysis of the competitor IRDs. The following is a sampling of the goals I devised for the ACME IRD's user interface.

- Intuitive design to minimize learning obstacles and need for users to refer to manual.

- Consistency of design and layout across different functional areas to facilitate learning.

- Controllable using Acme's handheld remote control (probably modified).

- Minimize keystrokes, especially in frequently used functions.

- Recognize that the Viewing Program Content and Program Guide screens are used much more than the Utility Menu hierarchy, even though the latter accounts for most of the software's screens.

- Minimize need to maneuver around on screen; avoid designs more suited for mouse-controlled PCs than for button-controlled TVs.

- Graphics must be large: the information must be comprehensible from across a room, unlike a computer display.

UI Design

The user interface design began with conventions that I devised for the Acme IRD user interface (or borrowed from its competitors). The following are some examples of conventions.

- The **i** key always invokes additional information about the current context. For example, in the Viewing Program Content screen, it shows the banner for the current program. In the Program Guide, it shows the long description of the currently highlighted show. In the menus, it displays Help information.

- In menus, as the user moves between menu items, the highlighted item is explained in the information area at the bottom of the menu screen.

- The CANCEL key always exits the current context without changing anything.

- The SELECT key always selects the currently highlighted or displayed item.

- Menu format: All menus have (from top to bottom) a title at the top, a horizontal separator, an area for the menu items, a line listing other options that are available, a horizontal separator, and an area for item explanations. The "Other Options" line lists keys on the remote control, usually DONE, CANCEL, and **i**.

- Each context (screen) contains only one choice space. Users never have to maneuver within any given screen between distinct choice spaces (e.g., two different lists) or between semantic items (e.g., viewable programs, submenu names, values of settings) and purely user interface items (e.g., interface control buttons).

The design conventions were followed by a brief overview of the Utility Menu hierarchy, presented in outline form. The purpose was to give the implementors a quick overview of the menu hierarchy and the items on each menu.

Figure 10.9

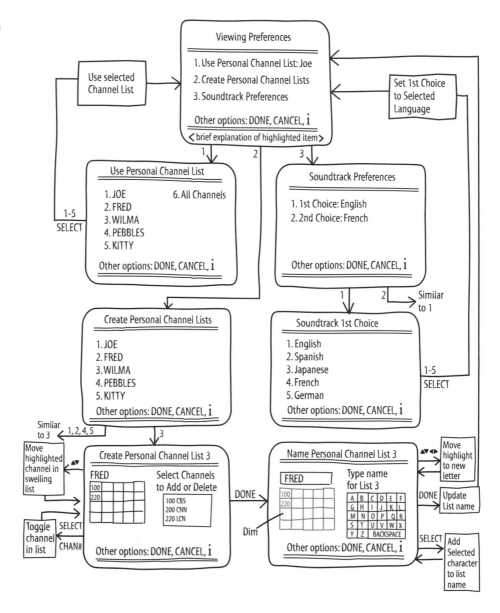

The bulk of the user interface specification consisted of detailed descriptions of most of the IRD's control screens: Viewing Program Content, Program Guide, and the Utility Menu hierarchy. The description of each screen included its purpose and listed the effect on that screen of all relevant remote-control buttons. Hand-drawn sketches were provided for most screens, with transition graphs showing the effect of various user actions (see Figures 10.9 and 10.10).

Figure 10.10

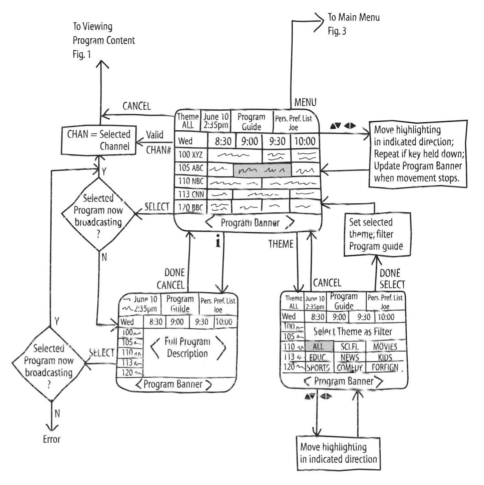

The descriptions of the IRD's control screens included sample data where relevant. For example, the Personal Channel List screens needed an example family. I used the Flintstones (a family in a television cartoon show I watched in my childhood): Wilma, Fred, Pebbles, and Kitty. Another part of the design that needed sample data was the list of available languages for program soundtracks. I simply made up a brief list of plausible languages and assumed the developers would do the right thing.

A very important part of any set-top box user interface design is its remote control. I had already warned the Acme VP and engineers that I would probably have to make changes to their prototype remote control in order to reduce its geekyness and match it with the new software controls. They were amenable to that. Accordingly, my specification document proposed the following improvements to the remote control:

- Larger labels (so elderly users can read them)
- Redundant buttons eliminated (for simplicity)
- Some buttons colored to stand out
  - POWER and CANCEL: red
  - DONE/OK: green

I wanted to make additional improvements beyond these, but I wasn't sure how much freedom Acme had to change the remote control. Therefore, I proposed two sets of alternative designs: one set of alternatives based on the assumption that only button labels could be changed from the prototype, and a second set of alternatives based on the assumption that button labels, shape, and placement could be changed.

All of the alternative designs were more like the Pace and Panasat remote controls than like the DiSH remote control. They had more buttons, to provide access to functions without the need to navigate to them on-screen.

The specification ended with a list of open design issues—issues that I lacked the time, knowledge, or authority to resolve.

Result

The resulting specification document was 40 pages long, providing significantly more detail than the previous 7-page document. More importantly, the Acme vice-president and engineers liked the design. They quickly sent it to Taiwan to be implemented.

Unfortunately, I saw no sign that either Acme or its parent company planned to conduct any usability tests of the IRD before shipping it. My warnings that this was unwise fell on deaf ears.

10.2.2 Job 2: UI review to check implementation of design

In October 1996 (a few months after Job 1), I wrote the vice-president of Acme and suggested that he have me review the implementation the programmers in Taiwan had done. I suggested this for four reasons:

- To check for deviations from the specification that should be brought into compliance.
- To review the design of functionality that the engineers in Taiwan had had to devise on their own because it had not been covered by the specification.
- Determine whether the specification itself had faults that needed to be adjusted. Maybe the implementors had deviated from the specification for good reason. Maybe the specification needed to be extended or fleshed out in certain areas. Maybe the developers had specific user interface design questions.

- My client load was temporarily low and I wanted the work.

The VP agreed with my suggestion and asked me to conduct the review. I went to Acme and looked briefly at the software. We estimated the job at two days: one day to review the design and one day to write the report. I went home and faxed a contract to Acme. The VP signed it and faxed it back.

Summary of review findings

For the purposes of this war story, it isn't necessary to describe the review findings in detail. I will simply summarize three main points that pertain to issues discussed elsewhere in this book.

Accuracy of implementation

The developers in Taiwan implemented the specified design very accurately. I had considered it a problem that they wouldn't be in touch with me while implementing the design (partly because of sheer distance, partly because of language, and partly because my first contract with Acme ended when I handed over the design specification document). However, the separation turned out not to be a problem, perhaps even somewhat of an advantage. Since the implementors couldn't talk with me, they couldn't argue with me about the design. Their management told them to follow the specification As it turns out, they followed the specification religiously.

There were of course some deviations that needed correcting. For example:

- Some text fonts were too small. The programmers had apparently viewed the screen mainly from close up, not from a normal TV-viewing distance (see Blooper 31: Tiny fonts, Section 3.4.2).
- Scrolling was too jumpy in most displayed lists, such as the list of available channels. Clicking on a scrollbar arrow moved items that were just out of view to the *middle* of the list control, rather than just to the top or bottom line. The programmers had done this because they thought it would help users scroll faster. I consider it an example of Blooper 48: Unexpected rearrangement of display (Section 5.2.3).
- The menu navigation buttons on the remote control were not debounced, making it far too easy to traverse two levels in the menu hierarchy unintentionally.

But other than these and a few other errors, I was amazed at how true to the specification the implementation was. I've rarely seen such an accurate implementation even when I've worked with the implementors daily. In fact, there were a few aspects of the implementation that were *too* true to the specification. How, you may ask, could a software implementation be too true to the design?

Remember that in my UI design specification (see Job 1), I included sample data in screens that needed it, such as names of family members and available sound track languages. In reviewing the implementation, I found that the programmers had built most of the sample data into the actual software. I had wrongly assumed that they would be able to distinguish sample (variable) data from the actual (fixed) user interface.

The result was somewhat amusing in the case of the sample family. There in the IRD were the Flintstones. The implementors in Taiwan weren't familiar with the Flintstones; perhaps the show was purely an American phenomenon. They didn't realize that I had used the Flintstones only as an example family in my specification. Therefore, they dutifully included the Flintstones in their implementation of the software. The software was actually *firmware;* it was burned into read-only memory in the IRD box. As part of my review report, I had to tell Acme to take the Flintstones out of the implementation.

Similarly, my sample list of program sound track languages had to be deleted from the firmware. The actual languages would be downloaded to each subscriber's IRD at run time by their satellite TV services.

Required extensions to the design

The implementors also did a good job applying the general design approach embodied in the specification to functionality I had left unspecified, such as the IRD installation and maintenance controls. This was encouraging because it meant that one of my design goals had been achieved: a design that had an underlying consistent logic that could be learned and applied to new situations.

Problems in my design

Some aspects of my original design turned out to be problematic and needed to be corrected. I was not surprised or bothered by this. The Acme IRD was the first product of this type that I had ever designed. Even had it not been, I would have expected to have to make revisions at various points along the way. That's just how engineering works (see Blooper 78: Discounting the value of testing and iterative design, Section 8.1.3). It is one of the reasons I suggested the review (see above) and is also the reason for my repeated—but unheeded—calls for usability testing.

Here are some aspects of the design I had to rethink and revise once I saw the implementation:

- The specified Program Guide screen had tried to display too much information. It wasn't possible to fit it all with text fonts that could be seen from across a room. I reduced the amount of information and rearranged the display.

- The specified operation of the remote control's SELECT, DONE, and CANCEL buttons was flawed, causing situations in which buttons conflicted and important capabilities were inaccessible. The programmers had noticed these flaws and tried to fix them, but their "corrections" had caused other problems. I redesigned the operation of these buttons.

- The specification had said little about what colors to use other than black and white, but some of the colors the programmers chose made it difficult to read displayed information. I suggested better colors for the problem cases and was more explicit about colors throughout the design.

When I sent the review report to Acme, they seemed satisfied. Again, they sent the document off to Taiwan. As my two-day contract was at an end, I moved my attention to other client work and forgot about Acme and IRDs for several months.

10.2.3 Job 3: Emergency redesign of a front panel

In March 1997, the VP at Acme called me again. He said that the IRD software had been implemented, but there was a problem: they didn't see how users could control the IRD's functions from the IRD's front panel.

I said: "Um...We didn't design a front panel."

He said that the engineers had developed a front panel for the IRD. It was intended mainly for cases in which a user loses or breaks the remote control.

We arranged a short consulting job for me to look at the problem and suggest solutions. I visited Acme and the VP showed me the front panel. It turns out that Acme's engineers had designed (and implemented) a front panel for their IRD that was very similar to the DiSH IRD front panel. As the reader may recall, that is the competitor IRD Acme had in-house for examination purposes while designing their own.

It apparently had not occurred to the Acme engineers that the DiSH front panel was designed for the DiSH user interface, and that the Acme user interface, which was quite different, might require a different front panel.

The VP explained the situation. As usual, time was tight. Deadlines were looming. The physical makeup and layout of the front panel would be very difficult to change at that point, but the function of the buttons was defined in software and so could be changed. He wanted me to devise a way that all of the IRD's functionality could be accessed using the existing front panel buttons, perhaps reassigned and relabeled.

I tried to explain that this was probably impossible. I said (more or less):

You should have called me before committing to a design for the front panel.

Your engineers designed the Acme IRD's front panel after the DiSH front panel. The DiSH user interface is modeled on a Windows-like GUI. Many of its buttons are on-screen. Fewer physical buttons are needed to control it, but this comes at the expense of requiring users to navigate around much more on-screen. I believe operating the DiSH IRD is overly tedious, and the recent review of it in *Consumer Reports* supports this.

I designed the Acme IRD's user interface with the goal of avoiding the problems of the DiSH design, that is, minimizing the need to navigate around on the screen.

The problem we face now is that the Acme user interface was designed in conjunction with the Acme remote control. The remote control has the minimum number of buttons required to operate the user interface efficiently. This new front panel has many fewer buttons than the remote control has. If we could provide access to all of the IRD's functions with just the buttons that are on this front panel, then we wouldn't need so many buttons on the remote control either.

The VP saw the logic of my argument, but said adding buttons to the front panel would be nearly impossible. I told him I'd give some thought to the problem and would try to come up with a list of possible solutions. I drove home, grinding my teeth most of the way.

At home, I pulled out my copies of the Acme IRD user interface specification and the instruction manuals for the competitor IRDs. I started by analyzing the front panels of the competitor IRDs.

Like the Acme IRD front panel, the DiSH front panel had eight buttons on its front panel. Because its user interface had more on-screen controls, those eight buttons provided access to most of its functionality. Nonetheless, several functions of the DiSH IRD were not available through its front panel, such as Cancel, View, Volume Control, Mute, Recall Channel.

In contrast, the Pace IRD had only four buttons on its front panel, and the Panasat IRD had five. This was many, many fewer buttons than were on the remote controls of these two products. It became clear that these two front panels provided access to only a small subset of their respective IRD's functionality.

Since it was now clear to me that Acme's request that "all the functions of the IRD be available through the front panel" was not justified by its competition, I made a list of Acme IRD functions for which front-panel access might be expendable. I discussed the list with the Acme VP and engineers to get their feedback. They agreed that some functions need not be provided via the front panel.

I wrote a report outlining three possible solutions to the front-panel problem:

- No additional buttons: Operation would be very clumsy, and severely restricted.
- One additional button: Operation would be less clumsy, less restricted.
- Two additional buttons: Operation would be almost as good as the remote control, with a few low-priority missing capabilities.

I also wrote that regardless of the solution that was chosen, I recommended moving the Power button on the front panel further away from the other buttons, because it was too easy to hit it by mistake. I myself had done so twice in only a couple of hours of interacting with the front panel.

I sent the report to the VP. He thanked me and said he would push for two additional buttons, but might only be able to get one. He wasn't sure what they would do about the Power button. I sent him my bill with a note: "Next time, check with me first!" I later learned that Acme elected not to add any buttons to the front panel, even though controlling the IRD that way would be very restricted, awkward, and error-prone. That's life in Silicon Valley!

10.2.4 Job 4: Second UI design

In June 1997, Acme contacted me a fourth time. They had to design another IRD, one that their parent company in Taiwan would develop for a different customer company. They needed a design that was functionally similar to the first IRD design, but with a noticeably different user interface. As before, they wanted it done in five days of consulting time, with no budget, resources, or time for usability testing. However, they did want the new design to include a better front panel for the new IRD.

I wrote a proposal suggesting a basic redesign of the previous IRD, as well as some optional supplemental changes. The basic redesign would improve the layout of the Viewing Program Content and Program Guide screens and simplify the Utility Menu structure and labeling, while using more or less the same remote control as did the previous design. It would also add a button to the front panel and improve the front panel's layout.

The optional additional changes I proposed were (1) use graphical symbols on menu items to supplement the textual labels and give the menus a different appearance than the previous design, and (2) make the Utility Menu hierarchy one of the program channels instead of a distinct functional area requiring a dedicated MENU button on the remote control.

I also proposed a radically different design alternative: a Web-like design, to make browsing the IRD's controls more like browsing the Web. I noted that such a design would require an entirely new remote control, with a built-in pointing device, such as a touchpad or trackball.

Acme opted for the basic redesign, supplemented by graphical symbols on menu items. They commented that they considered the Web-link design to be a long-term goal. We wrote and signed a contract for the job, and I began work.

For present purposes, it will suffice to summarize how the user interface I designed differed from that of the previous IRD.

First, I changed the new IRD's conceptual model (see Principle 2, Section 1.2.3) from that of the previous one in two ways:

1. The model for blocking specified program content was simpler. The previous design, following the design of competitor IRDs, separated the specification of the *type* and *degree* of blocking from actual activation or deactivation of blocking. Users could set up blocking as desired, and then turn it ON or OFF at will. I considered it likely that many users would not understand this dis-

tinction and would expect blocking to take effect when they simply specified what type and degree they wanted. Therefore, in the new design, I made the blocking settings immediate and eliminated the separate ON/OFF control.

2. I eliminated blocking based on content tags such as "violence," leaving blocking based on age appropriateness ratings such as PG-13. Content-based ratings were, it turns out, not provided by most digital broadcast services.

Second, I changed the new IRD's user interface from that of the previous one in several ways. Some examples are the following:

1. I reorganized and simplified the Utility Menu hierarchy. For example, I combined the Viewing Preferences and Operation Preferences menus into a single Preferences menu. I also reduced the number of places where the IRD would prompt for a "parental" access code by having it request the code when users entered the Blocking or Maintenance menus rather than in each function that required parental privileges.

2. I provided default names for channel lists: "Dad," "Mom," "Child1," "Child2." In the previous IRD, these were blank text fields that users had to fill in (at least after the developers removed the names of the Flintstone family that they had copied from my first specification). Providing default names allowed users to just use them if they didn't want to bother creating their own list names, reducing the amount of learning and setup required to use the device (see Blooper 46: Overwhelming users with decisions and detail, Section 5.2.1).

3. I changed the text explanations at the bottom of each menu to be static instructions for the entire menu. In the previous design, the explanations were for each menu item: they changed depending on which item was highlighted. I had decided that item-specific explanations just increased the complexity of the implementation without providing much additional benefit relative to well-written static instructions. They also required users to highlight a menu item in order to see its instructions. I provided suggested instructions for each menu.

4. As proposed, I added graphical symbols to the items in the Main utility menu so the menu would look substantially different than that of the previous IRD. Because I am not a graphic artist, I hired one to create the symbols, and directed his work until I was satisfied with the symbols. The Acme VP was initially surprised at how much four custom 48 × 48 symbols cost, but decided that the cost was acceptable.

5. Since I had a chance to design a better front panel for this IRD, I did so. Nonetheless, Acme wanted to keep the number of buttons on the front panel to a minimum to keep manufacturing costs low. I decided that nine front-panel buttons (as compared with eight previously) would provide access to

the IRD's important functions. The functions that would be unavailable from the front panel were Cancel, Mute, Information, Theme. I changed the button layout to make it very unlikely that users would hit buttons, especially the Power button, by mistake. As you may recall, this was a problem in the previous IRD's front panel.

As before, when I sent the completed design document to Acme, they enthusiastically accepted it and forwarded copies to the developers in Taiwan. I sent them my bill and they paid me.

That was the last I heard from Acme. About a year after the last job, my friend told me that Acme had been dissolved by its Taiwanese parent company. The parent company still exists. My friend was not sure what had happened to the two IRD projects, but told me that he suspects that both projects were eventually canceled. Could it be that Acme's steadfast avoidance of usability testing had doomed them? Who knows?

10.2.5 Lessons learned

I believe I learned the following lessons from this series of jobs regarding working as a user interface consultant:

- Never commit to any contract without a first-hand, close look at the status of the client's project. In the case of Job 1, I plead ignorance; it was one of my first consulting jobs. But now I know, and so do you.
- Don't accept design jobs when the client is not committed to usability testing, unless you want a lot of anxiety. If you do decide to accept a design job under such circumstances, be sure to require payment in cash, not stock.
- Don't assume clients know anything about usability. Don't assume they will do the right thing, such as (1) plan to test their product, or (2) ensure compatibility between different aspects of a user interface or between different user interfaces.
- Be careful what you put in your design specifications. The programmers may implement it! Distinguish example content from the actual design.
- Do the best job you can, but don't get too personally invested in your work. The client company may drop it before it reaches the market, due to reorganizations or other reasons.

Developers and development managers who read this war story will no doubt draw their own conclusions, but here are a few I recommend that they draw:

- Don't expect miracles from user interface consultants. They are just engineers, like your own engineer employees, albeit ones with a specific type of expertise.

- Marketing products without usability testing is foolhardy. For a more complete explanation and some suggestions on how to test without busting your budget or schedule, see Principle 8: Try it out on users, then fix it! (Section 1.8) and also Blooper 78: Discounting the value of testing and iterative design (Section 8.1.3).

- Good graphic design work is not cheap. You get what you pay for. Graphic artists are like musicians: you're not really paying them for the time they are working for you; you're paying them for all the time they spent developing their skills, prorated to the time they are working for you.

Appendix

How This Book Was Usability Tested

Why test the book?

This book places great importance on testing the usability of products as early as possible in the development process and as often as is feasible along the way. Indeed, the book lambastes developers who don't usability-test their products before releasing them into the marketplace. It would therefore have been hypocritical of me to write and publish this book without making an effort to test its usability on people who are representative of the intended (hoped for) readership.

Reviewing is not usability testing

When this book was initially proposed to the publisher and while it was being written, outlines and drafts of it were of course sent to designated reviewers to evaluate and comment upon. The reviewers were, in general, experienced user-interface professionals. Some were professors and industrial researchers; others were user-interface designers or usability testers working either for companies or as consultants. All of the reviewers were well familiar with the process of reviewing book drafts from years of experience reviewing other books and articles, and having their own books and articles reviewed. Getting input from people who are peers—or even superiors—of a book's author is standard practice for technical books. However, this sort of reviewing does not constitute a valid usability test of this book, for two reasons:

1. The reviewers normally solicited by the publisher are not really the intended readers of this book. The primary intended readers are software developers who often work without professional user-interface support. A

second group of intended readers are managers of software developers. Third on the list of intended readers are professional user-interface designers, especially those who are just starting out. Therefore, getting feedback from people representing the upper echelons of the Human-Computer Interaction field is very different from testing the book on its intended audience.

2. Asking someone to read a book and comment on it is not the same as asking someone to use it—or consider how they would use it—in their work.

Getting developers to test the book

Because I felt it important to have this book usability-tested, not just reviewed, the publisher and I asked several professional programmers (some of whom were also development managers) to read versions of the manuscript, and either use it in their work or consider how they would use it. Some actually did begin using the book—unfinished though it was—to help find and clean up bloopers in their organization's software. Others just read the book and tried to imagine how they would use it. In addition to accepting whatever feedback they wanted to give us, we asked them to address specific questions about the book's content and organization. Although this testing was quite informal, it was extremely valuable in guiding the "design" of the book as we advanced from the first draft to the published version.

What we learned from testing

Here is what we learned from usability testing early versions of this book.

Make it more random access

For example, the programmers expressed a clear desire not to have to read the entire book from front to back. They wanted to be able to look up bloopers and the corresponding design rules pertaining to their specific design questions. They also wanted each blooper and its corresponding design rule to either be totally self-contained, or to point to a specific section (not just a chapter) where additional information could be found. In other words, they wanted the book to be more—in one programmer's words—"random access." No such recommendations came from the academics and researchers who reviewed the book.

As a result of this feedback, the bloopers were revised in an attempt to make each one self-contained. Where that wasn't possible, we followed the example of the highly successful cookbook *Joy of Cooking* [Rombauer and Becker, 1967]. It often refers readers to other sections of the book. For example, in the recipe for making a pie, it refers to a separate recipe for making a pie crust. The cross reference is designed to make it very easy for a reader to find the pie crust recipe. It also has an extremely comprehensive index.

Following this model, we worked to make it easy for readers of this book to follow cross-references. The result is a comprehensive table of contents and a comprehensive index.

Make important points stand out

Related to the programmer-testers' request that the book be more "random access" was a clear desire for important information to be presented in ways that make it *stand out*, for example, through extensive use of headings, bullet points, tables, callouts, and highlighting of various sorts. Stated bluntly:

> *Programmers did not like it when important points*
> *were buried in the middle of paragraphs.*

They wanted to be able to browse or flip through the book and still get useful information out of it. As a result of this feedback, I revised many passages to make more use of headings, emphasis, tables, and bullet points, and worked with the publisher to format and lay out the book so as to make it easy for readers to pick out information.

Explain why the bloopers are bloopers

A third request from the programmer-testers was that the book provide more rationale for why the bloopers are considered bloopers, as well as more of the principles underlying the design rules. Furthermore, the programmers wanted these explanations up front, *before* the descriptions of the bloopers. Early drafts of the book jumped straight into the bloopers, on the assumption that GUI programmers would want to focus on concrete design mistakes and avoid abstract principles and theory. Bits and pieces of design principles were scattered as needed around the design rules for avoiding the bloopers. Testing showed that that assumption was wrong. As a result of this feedback, Chapter 1 was added.

Provide more examples

A not-so-surprising request from several programmer-testers was "more examples, more screen-images." The same request came from some of the regular reviewers. Early versions of the manuscript had a distinct lack of illustrative screen images and anecdotal stories. Partly as a result of this feedback and partly based on preexisting plan, many more examples have been added, and some bloopers for which good examples could not be found or devised were deleted.

In addition to wanting more examples, programmer-testers wanted the visual examples of bloopers and correct design to be clearly marked as "good" or "bad." They didn't want to have to read the text to find out whether a figure was intended as an example of a blooper to avoid or of a design they should emulate. In short, they wanted us to provide "good" and "bad" symbols. We conducted paper tests of various symbols for "good" and "bad," and settled on hands with thumbs up and down for "good" and "bad," respectively.

Don't "dis" programmers

Finally, several programmer-testers (as well as some reviewers) criticized early drafts of the book for being too critical of programmers for committing bloopers. Sometimes, they said, bloopers aren't the programmer's fault, but rather are the fault of the tools or building blocks that the programmer is required to use or of the development process the programmer must follow.

I agree. Many of my best friends are GUI programmers. They work very hard and do good work. Furthermore, this book is intended mainly for GUI programmers. It certainly would be unwise for me to insult my main audience. My purpose is not to bad-mouth GUI programmers. I am using the bloopers format purely as an instructional device: to get developers to see the kinds of mistakes they make and learn to avoid them. Nonetheless, as a result of the suggestions not to offend my audience, I have tried to make the book less critical of the *people* and more critical of the development *process*.

As I explain in Chaper 8, the root cause of many GUI bloopers is that the job of designing the GUI was assigned to the wrong kind of expert: programming experts rather than user-interface design experts and task-domain experts. Unfortunately, that statement by itself may annoy some programmers. Earlier, I quoted a friend who is a programmer as saying "Most programmers believe they are UI experts." Another programmer I know put it this way:

> "I don't entirely understand it but it is true: Highly skilled carpenters don't get insulted when told they are not architects, but highly skilled programmers do get insulted when told they are not UI designers."

I don't want to insult any programmers, but I will say this: we can't all be experts at everything. I urge programmers to understand the limits of their expertise, considerable though it may be. I urge development managers to try to get the right sort of experts involved in each part of the development process. Your customers will thank you for it.

Bibliography

Apple Computer, Inc. 1993. *Macintosh Human Interface Guidelines*. Reading, MA: Addison-Wesley.

Barber, R., and Lucas, H. 1983. "System Response Time, Operator Productivity, and Job Satisfaction." *Communications of the ACM* 11: 972–986.

Beyer, H., and Holtzblatt, K. 1998. *Contextual Design: Defining Customer-Centered Systems*. San Francisco: Morgan Kaufmann Publishers.

Bias, R. G., and Mayhew, D. J. 1994. *Cost-Justifying Usability* San Diego, CA: Academic Press.

Bickford, P. 1997. *Interface Design: The Art of Developing Easy-to-Use Software*. Chestnut Hill, MA: Academic Press.

Brady, James T. 1986. "A Theory of Productivity in the Creative Process." *IEEE Computer Graphics and Applications* 6(5): 25–34.

Brooks, F. P. 1975. *The Mythical Man-Month*. Reading, MA: Addison-Wesley.

Brown, C. M. 1988. *Human-Computer Interface Design Guidelines*. Norwood, NJ: Ablex Publishing Corporation.

Card, S., Moran, T., and Newell, A. 1983. *The Psychology of Human-Computer Interaction*. Hillsdale, NJ: Lawrence Erlbaum Associates.

Carroll, J., and Rosson, M. 1984. "Beyond MIPS: Performance Is Not Quality." *BYTE* 9(2): 168–172.

Conklin, P. F. 1996. "Bringing Usability Effectively into Product Development." In M. Rudisill, C. Lewis, P. Polson, and T. McKay, eds., *Human-Computer Interface Design: Success Stories, Emerging Methods, Real-World Context*. San Francisco: Morgan Kaufmann Publishers.

Cooper, A. 1999. *The Inmates Are Running the Asylum*. Indianapolis, IN: SAMS.

Dayton, T., McFarland, A., and Kramer, J. 1998. "Bridging User Needs to Object Oriented GUI Prototypes via Task Object Design." In L. Wood, ed., *User Interface Design: Bridging the Gap from Requirements to Design*, pp. 15–56. Boca Raton, FL: CRC Press.

Dix, A. 1987. "The Myth of the Infinitely Fast Machine." *People and Computers III: Proceedings of HCI'87*, pp. 215–228. Cambridge, MA: Cambridge University Press. *www.soc.staffs.ac.uk/7Ecmtajd/papers/hci87*.

Duis, D. 1990. "Creating Highly Responsive Interactive Software Despite Performance Limitations." Masters thesis, MIT, May.

Duis, D., and Johnson, J. 1990. "Improving User-Interface Responsiveness Despite Performance Limitations." *Proceedings of IEEE CompCon'90*, pp. 380–386.

Flanders, V., and Willis, M. 1998. *Web Pages That Suck: Learning Good Design by Looking at Bad Design*. San Francisco: Sybex. (See also the authors' Web site: *www.WebPagesThatSuck.com.*)

Fowler, S. 1998. *GUI Design Handbook*. New York: McGraw-Hill.

Gates, B. 1996. *The Road Ahead*. New York: Penguin Books.

Gentner, D., and Grudin, J. 1990. "Why Good Engineers (Sometimes) Create Bad Interfaces." *Proceedings of ACM Conference on Computer-Human Interaction (CHI'90)*, pp. 277–282.

Greenbaum, J., and Kyng, M. 1991. *Design at Work: Cooperative Design of Computer Systems*. Hillsdale, NJ: Lawrence Erlbaum Associates.

Grudin, J. 1989. "The Case Against User Interface Consistency." *Communications of the ACM* 32(10): 1164–1173.

Grudin, J. 1991. "Systematic Sources of Suboptimal Interface Design in Large Product Development Organizations." *Human Computer Interaction* 6: 147–196.

Hinckley, K., Pausch, R., Proffitt, D., and Kassell, N. F. 1998. "Two-Handed Virtual Manipulation." *ACM Transactions on Computer-Human Interaction* 5(3): 260–302.

Johnson, J. 1990. "Modes in Non-Computer Devices." *International Journal of Man-Machine Studies* 32: 423–438.

Johnson, J. 1992. "Selectors: Going Beyond User-Interface Widgets." *Proceedings of ACM Conference on Computer-Human Interaction (CHI'92)*, pp. 273–279.

Johnson, J. 1996a. "The Information Highway: A Worst-Case Scenario." *Communications of the ACM* 39(2): 15–17. (Also available at *www.uiwizards.com,* under Publications.)

Johnson, J. 1996b. "R < — > D, Not R&D." *Communications of the ACM* 39(9): 32–34.

Johnson, J. 1998. "Simplifying the User Interface of an Interactive Movie Game." *Proceedings of the ACM Conference on Computer-Human Interaction (CHI'98)*, pp. 65–72.

Johnson, J., and Beach, R., 1988. "Styles in Document Editing Systems." *IEEE Computer* 21(1): 32–43.

Johnson, J., and Keavney, M. 1995. "A Comparsion of Remote Pointing Devices for Interactive TV Applications." In *A Collection of Papers from FirstPerson, Inc.* Technical Report SMLI TR-95-41. Mountain View, CA: Sun Microsystems Laboratories.

Johnson, J., and Nardi, B. 1996. "Creating Presentation Slides: A Study of User Preferences for Task-Specific versus Generic Application Software." *ACM Transactions on Computer-Human Interaction* 3(1): 38–65.

Johnson, J., Roberts, T., Verplank, W., Smith, D. C., Irby, C., Beard, M., and Mackey, K. 1989. "The Xerox Star: A Retrospective." *IEEE Computer* 22(9): 11–29.

Kraut, R., ed. 1996. "The Internet @ Home." Special section of *Communications of the ACM* 39(12): 33–74.

Lambert, G. 1989. "A Comparative Study of System Response Time on Program Developer Productivity." *IBM Systems Journal* 23(1): 407–423.

Landauer, T. K. 1995. *The Trouble with Computers: Usefulness, Usability, and Productivity.* Cambridge, MA: MIT Press.

Lewis, C., Polson, P., Wharton, C., and Rieman, J. 1990. "Testing a Walkthrough Methodology for Theory-Based Design of Walk-Up-and-Use Interfaces." *Proceedings of the 1990 ACM Conference on Human Factors in Computing Systems (CHI'90)*, Seattle, WA, pp. 235–247.

Mandel, T. 1997. *The Elements of User Interface Design.* New York: John Wiley and Sons.

McFarland, A., and Dayton, T. 1995. *Design Guide for Multiplatform Graphical User Interfaces.* Issue 3, LPR13. Piscataway, NJ: Bellcore.

Microsoft. 1995. *The Windows Interface Guidelines for Software Design: An Application Design Guide.* Redmond, WA: Microsoft Press.

Microsoft. 1998. *Windows Style-Guide Update.* Redmond, WA: Microsoft Press.

Microsoft. 1999. *Microsoft Windows User Experience.* Redmond, WA: Microsoft Press.

Miller, L., and Johnson, J. 1996. "The Xerox Star: An Influential User-Interface Design." In M. Rudisill, C. Lewis, P. Polson, and T. McKay, eds., *Human-Computer Interface Design: Success Stories, Emerging Methods, Real-World Context*, San Francisco: Morgan Kaufmann Publishers.

Miller, R. 1968. "Response Time in Man-Computer Conversational Transactions." *Proceedings AFIPS Fall Joint Computer Conference.*

Muller, M. J., Haslwanter, J. H., and Dayton, T. 1997. "Participatory Practices in the Software Lifecycle." In H. Helander, T. K. Landauer, and P. Prabhu, eds., *Handbook of Human-Computer Interaction*, second edition. Amsterdam: Elsevier Science B.V.

Mullet, K., and Sano, D. 1995. *Designing Visual Interfaces: Communications Oriented Techniques.* Mountain View, CA: SunSoft Press.

Nardi, B., and Johnson, J. 1994. "User Preference for Task-Specific vs. Generic Application Software." *Proceedings of the 1994 ACM Conference on Human Factors in Computing Systems (CHI'94)*, pp. 392–398.

Newman, W. M., and Sproull, R. F. 1979. *Principles of Interactive Computer Graphics.* New York: McGraw-Hill.

Nielsen, J. 1993. *Usability Engineering.* San Diego, CA: Academic Press.

Nielsen, J. 1996. "The Top-Ten Mistakes of Web-Design." *www.UseIt.com/Alertbox.* May.

Nielsen, J. 1999a. "User Interface Directions for the Web." *Communications of the ACM* 42(1): 65-71.

Nielsen, J. 1999b. "'Top Ten Mistakes' Revisited Three Years Later." *www.UseIt.com/Alertbox,* May 2.

Nielsen, J. 1999c. "The Top Ten *New* Mistakes of Web Design." *www.UseIt.com/Alertbox,* May 30.

Nielsen, J. 1999d. *Designing Web Usability: The Practice of Simplicity.* Indianapolis, IN: New Riders Publishing.

Norman, D. 1983. "Design Rules Based on Analysis of Human Error." *Communications of the ACM* 26(4): 254–258.

Norman, D. A. 1988. *The Design of Everyday Things*. New York: Basic Books.

Norman, D. A. 1999. *The Invisible Computer: Why Good Products Can Fail, the Personal Computer Is So Complex and Information Appliances Are the Solution*. Cambridge, MA: MIT Press.

Norman, D. A., and Draper, S. W. 1986. *User Centered System Design: New Perspectives on Human-Computer Interaction*. Hillsdale, NJ: Lawrence Erlbaum Associates.

Open Software Foundation. 1993. *OSF/Motif Style Guide: Rev 1.2*. Englewood Cliffs, NJ: Prentice Hall.

Roberts, T. L., and Moran, T. P. 1983. "The Evaluation of Text Editors: Methodology and Empirical Results." *Communications of the ACM* 26: 265–283.

Robertson, G., Card, S., and Mackinlay, J. 1989. "The Cognitive Co-Processor Architecture for Interactive User Interfaces." *Proceedings of the ACM Conference on User Interface Software and Technology (UIST'89)*, pp. 10–18. New York: ACM Press.

Robertson, G., Card, S., and Mackinlay, J. 1993. "Information Visualization Using 3D Interactive Animation." *Communications of the ACM* 36(4): 56–71.

Rombauer, I., and Becker, M. R. 1967. *Joy of Cooking*. Indianapolis, IN: The Bobs-Merrill Company.

Rosenfeld, L., and Morville, P. 1998. *Information Architecture for the World Wide Web*. Sebastopol, CA: O'Reilly and Associates.

Rudisill, M., Lewis, C., Polson, P., and McKay, T. 1996. *Human-Computer Interface Design: Success Stories, Emerging Methods, Real-World Context*. San Francisco: Morgan Kaufmann Publishers.

Rushinek, A., and Rushinek, S. 1986. "What Makes Users Happy?" *Communications of the ACM* 29: 584–598.

Schuler, D., and Namioka, A. 1993. *Participatory Design: Principles and Practices*. Hillsdale, NJ: Lawrence Erlbaum Associates.

Shneiderman, B. 1984. "Response Time and Display Rate in Human Performance with Computers." *ACM Computing Surveys* 16(4): 265–285.

Shneiderman, B. 1987. *Designing the User Interface: Strategies for Effective Human-Computer Interaction*. Reading, MA: Addison-Wesley.

Smith, S. L., and Mosier, J. N. 1986. "Guidelines for Designing User Interface Software." Technical Report ESD-TR-86-278. Springfield, VA: National Technical Information Service.

Sun Microsystems. 1999. *Java Look and Feel Design Guidelines*. Reading, MA: Addison-Wesley.

Tesler, L. 1981. "The Smalltalk Environment." *Byte Magazine* 6(8): 90–147.

Thadhani, A. 1981. "Interactive User Productivity." *IBM Systems Journal* 20(4): 407–423.

Thimbleby, H. 1982. "Character-Level Ambiguity: Consequences for User-Interface Design." *International Journal of Man-Machine Studies* 16: 211–225.

Tufte, E. R. 1983. *The Visual Display of Quantitative Information*. Cheshire, MA: Graphics Press.

Ullman, E. 1995. "Out of Time: Reflections on the Programming Life." In J. Brook and I. A. Boal, eds., *Resisting the Virtual Life: The Culture and Politics of Information*, pp. 131–144. San Francisco: City Lights Books.

Weinshenk, S., Jamar, P., and Yeo, S. 1997. *GUI Design Essentials*. New York: John Wiley and Sons.

Wharton, C., Rieman, J., Lewis, C., and Polson, P. 1994. "The Cognitive Walkthrough: A Practitioner's Guide." In J. Nielsen and R. L. Mack, eds., *Usability Inspection Methods*. New York: John Wiley and Sons.

Zarmer, C., and Johnson, J. 1990. "User Interface Tools: Past, Present, and Future Trends." HP Laboratories Technical Report HPL-90-20.

Index

About the Author

Jeff Johnson is president and principal consultant for UI Wizards, Inc., a product usability consulting firm founded in 1996 and based in San Francisco. Client companies of UI Wizards include Advance Reality, Aspect Technologies, AT&T, Informix, InfoSpace, InXight, Oracle, Optical Microwave Networks, Inc., RightPoint Software, Silicon Graphics, Studio Archetype, Sun Microsystems, Tibco Financial Technologies, and Vitria. Prior to founding UI Wizards, Jeff worked as a user interface designer and implementor, manager, usability tester, and researcher at Cromemco, Xerox, US West, Hewlett-Packard, and Sun Microsystems. He has authored and contributed to numerous articles and books on a variety of topics in Human-Computer Interaction and technology policy (for details see his Web site at *www.uiwizards.com*). He cochaired the first U.S. Conference on Participatory Design of Computer Systems (PDC'90). He holds a B.A. from Yale University and a Ph.D. from Stanford University, both in experimental psychology, with additional studies in computer science.